Images
of Otherness
in Russia,
1547-1917

Other Titles in this Series

For more information on this series, please visit:
academicstudiespress.com/imperialencounters

Images
of Otherness
in Russia,
1547-1917

Edited by Kati Parppei
and Bulat Rakhimzianov

BOSTON
2023

Library of Congress Cataloging-in-Publication Data

Names: Parppei, Kati, editor, author. | Rakhimzianov, Bulat, 1976-
editor, author.
Title: Images of otherness in Russia, 1547-1917 / edited by Kati Parppei
and Bulat Rakhimzianov.
Description: Boston : Academic Studies Press, 2023. | Series: Imperial
encounters in Russian history | Includes bibliographical references.
Identifiers: LCCN 2022059976 (print) | LCCN 2022059977 (ebook) | ISBN
9798887191461 (hardback) | ISBN 9798887191478 (adobe pdf) | ISBN
9798887191485 (epub)
Subjects: LCSH: Ethnology--Russia. | Group identity--Russia. | Other
(Philosophy) | Russia--History--Philosophy.
Classification: LCC DK33 .I486 2023 (print) | LCC DK33 (ebook) | DDC
305.800947--dc23/eng/20230106
LC record available at https://lccn.loc.gov/2022059976
LC ebook record available at https://lccn.loc.gov/2022059977

ISBN 9798887191461 (hardback)
ISBN 9798887191478 (adobe pdf)
ISBN 9798887191485 (epub)

Book design by Lapiz Digital Services
Cover design by Ivan Grave
On the cover: Anon., *K voine Rossii s Iaponiei* (On the war of Russia with Japan),
Popular war Lubok poster, ca. 1904.

Published by Academic Studies Press
Academic Studies Press
1577 Beacon street
Brookline, MA 02446, USA

Contents

Preface

The present volume is a product—or rather, an offshoot—of a five-year research project funded by the Academy of Finland and entitled *Images and Attributes of Enemies in Pre-Revolutionary Russia*. The idea of compiling a collection of articles was generated by the editors' wish to further explore and bring together contemporary research on perceptions, representations, and images of ethnic, religious, and social "others" in Muscovy and the Russian Empire. The human tendency to create and maintain categories is as topical as ever and examining the formation and maintenance of historical images allows us to understand some of the modern challenges in international and interethnic relations and their collective mental premises. As of Russia, its war in Ukraine can be seen as a consequence of not confronting and critically assessing the country's imperial and colonial legacies, a part of which are the ways it positions itself to its historical and contemporary "others".

Our international call for articles produced an interesting array of scholarly undertakings on the theme, from which we tried to choose a thematically and temporally coherent selection to be published as a volume. From the beginning, we were fully aware that producing any comprehensive presentation of such a multifaceted and complicated phenomenon was out of the question—especially as we wanted to cover a relatively long period. Many interesting and important topics were, therefore, left untouched, but we hope that the case studies in this volume will inspire researchers to probe more deeply into the theme of historical "otherness" in Russia and examine the missing subjects in the future.

Like any edited volume, this is a result of relentless collective labors. We wish to express our warmest gratitude to all the authors for their contributions and patience, and especially to David Goldfrank, Michael Khodarkovsky, and Stephen M. Norris for kindly providing the thoughtful summaries that bring together the diverse topics of each section. Moreover, we want to thank Rupert Moreton and Ian Mac Eochagáin for their efforts in translating and editing the chapters, all the other devoted experts for their involvement in the editing work, and our colleagues for their explicit and implicit support for our project. Finally, we would like to express our gratitude to the Academy of Finland for making the preparation of the volume financially possible.

—Kati Parppei and Bulat Rakhimzianov

Introduction: Images, Otherness, and Images of the Others

Kati Parppei and Bulat Rakhimzianov

What Is an Image?

The Circassians hate us. We have forced them out of their free and spacious pasturelands, their auls are in ruins, whole tribes have been annihilated.—Friendship with the peaceful Circassians is unreliable: they are always ready to aid their rebellious fellow tribesmen. The spirit of their wild chivalry has declined noticeably.— The dagger and the sword are parts of their body, and an infant begins to master them before he can prattle. For them killing is simple bodily motion.—What can one do with such a people?[1]

In 1829, the Russian poet Alexander Pushkin (1799–1837) ventured to Arzrum (Erzurum) in eastern Turkey, as the war between Russia and the Ottoman Empire raged on. Without official permission to go abroad, he traveled through the Caucasus and made notes of what he saw and experienced, and the people(s) he encountered. His travel diary *A Journey to Arzrum* was published in 1836, along with the contemporary wave of travel stories and literature in Russia as well as elsewhere in Europe. However, already in 1822, Pushkin had published a poem *The Prisoner of the Caucasus*, presenting a romantic story of a

---

1 Alexander Pushkin, *A Journey to Arzrum*, trans. Birgitta Ingemanson (Ann Arbor: Ardis, 1974), 23–24.

Russian officer who is captured by Circassian tribesmen and saved by a beautiful Circassian woman. This poem has been said to have brought the Caucasus to the cultural horizon of Russian readers for the first time.[2]

Both of these works and their multilayered meanings have been studied and analyzed from many viewpoints.[3] For us, they offer a convenient starting point to shortly introduce the central concept of our book—the *image*. Pushkin's published texts on Caucasus were widely distributed and their influence on the general perceptions—that is, images—of the disputed frontier area and its peoples was significant. For example, the Circassians were represented as free, exotic, and enchanting people, as well as dangerous enemies needed to be controlled. This twofold imagery gave readers a chance to reflect on their own "Russianness" and the expansive Russian Empire (for further pondering on these themes, see the section "Images of the 'Others'").[4] On the other hand, compared to *The Prisoner of the Caucasus*, the travel diary offers a more cynical and even gritty imagery, presenting the Caucasus as a combat zone instead of a romantic Alpine resort and emphasizing the negative attributes of the Circassians and other Caucasian inhabitants at the expense of the idea of their "wild chivalry."[5] Thus, we can say that in *A Journey to Arzrum*, Pushkin challenged the already established collective images of Caucasus and Caucasians with new and at least partially contradictory ones.

It is said that "the image" is an ambiguous concept which describes a phenomenon that is equally ambiguous.[6] As is the case with all such concepts—for example, concepts of identity, tradition, and myth, just to mention a few—using them as methodological tools, let alone forming a theoretical framework for a study, requires these concepts to be defined in each context on each occasion.

This book's broad context is that of image studies, an interdisciplinary approach that is utilized, for example, in cognitive psychology, sociology,

---

2   Susan Layton, *Russian Literature and Empire: Conquest of the Caucasus from Pushkin to Tolstoy* (Cambridge: Cambridge University Press, 1995), 5.

3   See, for example, Layton, *Russian Literature and Empire: Conquest of the Caucasus from Pushkin to Tolstoy* (Cambridge: Cambridge University Press, 2009); Susan Layton, "Nineteenth-Century Russian Mythologies of Caucasian Savagery," in *Russia's Orient. Imperial Borderlands and Peoples, 1700–1917*, ed. Daniel R. Brower and Edward J. Lazzerini (Bloomington: Indiana University Press, 2001), 80–99. Monika Frenkel Greenleaf, "Pushkin's 'Journey to Arzrum': The Poet at the Border," *Slavic Review* 50, no. 4 (1991): 940–53; John Lyles, "Bloody Verses: Rereading 'Pushkin's Prisoner of the Caucasus," *Pushkin Review* 16 (2014): 233–54.

4   Layton, "Nineteenth-Century Russian Mythologies of Caucasian Savagery"; Hubertus F. Jahn, "'Us': Russians on Russianness," in *National Identity in Russian Culture: An Introduction*, ed. Simon Franklin and Emma Widdis (Cambridge: Cambridge University Press, 2006), 53–73.

5   Layton, *Russian Literature and Empire: Conquest of the Caucasus from Pushkin to Tolstoy*, 61–65.

6   David Ratz, "The Study of Historical Images," *Faravid* 31 (2007): 191.

international relations, literary studies, geography, and historical studies. In image studies, the image is understood less as a visual representation of a certain object and more as an abstract concept that refers to a perception formed of an object by the human mind encountering said object. Together, these "mental images"—or *schemas* to use the vocabulary of cognitive psychology—operating in the subconscious can be said to form the world view of a person.[7]

Images have crucial tasks in the human mind: they help to arrange new information and assist the person in navigating reality and making decisions. For example, certain preestablished categories of people help us make initial sense of the multitude of strangers we meet.[8] However, images formed in our mind never truly reflect the complexity of reality quite as it is. Images tend to be simplified models, lacking details and exact features; they can be said to represent reality almost as a map represents actual terrain, and they are similarly biased, with the viewpoint depending on the producer of the map or the owner of the image. Moreover, in the mental image formation process, new information can be said to be filtered through the person's previous images, emotions, experiences, and beliefs, which altogether create subjective and unique perceptions.[9]

Moreover, mental images once formed tend to be difficult to change, which is partly due to their subconscious nature; we are only rarely aware of our set of images, their function in our minds, or the influence they have on our everyday decisions. Generally, a person is more prone to receive and accept information that supports previously held images and to reject any information that contradicts established imagery. This phenomenon is close to the idea of confirmation bias in the field of media studies: the tendency to selectively think and notice what confirms one's beliefs and ignoring any information and details that challenge might challenge these beliefs.[10]

Despite their initial subjectivity, mental images also have a collective dimension, which, for example, interests cultural historians and literary researchers keen to utilize the approach of image studies. As members of a society or another group, people share certain perceptions, conceptions, and traditions. The existence of this immaterial cultural heritage also means there is

---

7 Ibid., 191–95.

8 Marja Vuorinen, Noora Kotilainen, and Aki-Mauri Huhtinen, eds., *Binaries in Battle—Representations of Division and Conflict* (Newcastle-upon-Tyne: Cambridge Scholars Publishing, 2014), ix.

9 Ratz, "The Study of Historical Images": 200–202, 208; Olavi K. Fält, "Introduction," in *Looking at the Other. Historical Study of Images in Theory and Practice*, ed. Kari Alenius et al. (Oulu: Oulu University Press, 2002), 8.

10 Kenneth Boulding, *The Image* (Ann Arbor: The University of Michigan Press, 1975), 8–9; Ratz, "The Study of Historical Images": 202–3, 215.

a sphere of shared images that overlaps or intertwines with our subjective ones. Furthermore, these collective or shared images do not appear from nowhere; rather, they are often intentionally formed and distributed by certain institutions that prioritize societal cohesion, such as the media or schooling system. For example, school textbooks have effectively distributed powerful and durable images of the shared national past in each country. It has been noted that the most persistent images are those formed in childhood, which emphasizes the role of schooling and other kinds of indoctrination aimed at children and young people in the formation of shared images.[11]

Creating, consolidating, and maintaining collective images often serves the interests of contemporary power structures. An examination of the most prominent shared images distributed by "official" institutions thus opens opportunities to study those structures and their motives at each given time (whilst the perceptions of the more marginal or subtle actors of society are apparently left aside).[12] This notion brings us to the main idea of image studies: instead of the images themselves, or the objects of which the images have been formed, the actual subject of research is the image's *producer*, and the processes of an image's production, consolidation, and maintenance.[13] According to Olavi K. Fält, the researcher may ask, "what an image is like, how we have formed a particular image of a certain thing, why we have this image, what purpose it serves, what changes have taken place in it, and what all this tells us of the creators of the image."[14]

Paradigmatically, historical image studies can be placed under the broad umbrella of cultural history with strong interdisciplinary connections; for example, the image as a concept is very close to the equally ambiguous concept of *representation* often discussed in cultural and media studies.[15] It can be seen as belonging to the study of the history of mentalities, or at least, overlapping

---

11 Boulding, *The Image*, 56, 68; Olavi K. Fält, "The Historical Study of Mental Images as a Form of Research into Cultural Confrontation," *Comparative Civilizations Review* 32, no. 32 (1995): 101.

12 Jan Nederveen Pieterse, "Image and Power," in *Alterity, Identity, Image. Selves and Others in Society and Scholarship*, ed. R. Corbey and J. Th. Leerssen (Amsterdam: Rodopi, 2011), 198. Fält, "Introduction," 11.

13 Nederveen Pieterse, "Image and Power," 200.

14 Fält, "Introduction," 9.

15 According to Stuart Hall, representation is the process by which meaning is produced and exchanged between members of a culture through the use of language, signs, and images which stand for or represent things (Stuart Hall, *Representation: Cultural Representations and Signifying Practices* [London: Sage Publishing, 2003], 17–19). As such, it describes the basic idea of a shared image from a slightly different angle, emphasizing the audience and reception which—for obvious reasons—are mostly beyond the reach of historians.

seamlessly with it; both are occupied with the cultural models of the past. Also, the idea of mental images is very close to the concept of mental mapping which has been used, for example, in geography and behavioral science. Mental maps refer to socio-cultural constructions of spatiality formed in the human mind, and the idea has been found to be a useful theoretical and methodological tool for historians as well to analyze issues such as, for example, world views, colonial encounters, and the formation and dissolution of historical regions and realms.[16]

The sources used for applying an imagological approach can be very versatile. Essentially, any material that can be considered to have contributed to the formation and consolidation of a shared image of a certain issue in a certain society can be used for research. It may include diverse texts from medieval chronicles to newspapers, from textbooks and travel guides to plays, poetry, and folktales, as well as pictorial representations from icons to photographs, cartoons, caricatures, and animations. In tracing and analyzing the long-term development of a certain image, heterogenic source material may be used. Of course, this versatility of sources may bring with it certain problems when sorting the "layers" of image formation: for example, it may be impossible to determine whether an oral folktale has preceded a written version of a story, or vice versa.[17]

Despite the intriguing possibilities of the approach, a historian utilizing the imagological tool to study shared images must be aware of certain issues to avoid anachronistic pitfalls. For instance, we cannot examine truly *shared* images before the emergence of general literacy and mass media. In medieval cultures the producers and consumers of the images largely consisted of the same groups, mostly those with an ecclesiastical background in education and seamless connections with the contemporary power structures.[18] Of course, to some extent these "elite images"—and the messages they conveyed to support the contemporary politico-religious structures—were also distributed to larger

---

16 See, for example, Norbert Götz and Janne Holmén, "Introduction to the Theme Issue: 'Mental Maps: Geographical and Historical Perspectives,'" *Journal of Cultural Geography* 35, no. 2 (2018): 157–61.

17 Fält, "The Historical Study of Mental Images as a Form of Research into Cultural Confrontation": 101. For examples of the examination of long-term image formation, see Kati Parppei, *"The Oldest One in Russia": The Formation of the Historiographical Image of Valaam Monastery* (Leiden: Brill Publishing, 2011) and Kati Parppei, *The Battle of Kulikovo Refought—"The First National Feat"* (Leiden: Brill Publishing, 2017).

18 For a deeper understanding of the connections between the medieval power authorities, the ecclesiastical circles serving these authorities, and therefore the focus of texts produced by them, see, for example (concerning Muscovy): Edward Keenan, "Muscovy and Kazan, 1445–1552: A Study in Steppe Politics," PhD diss., (Harvard University, 1965).

groups of people in pictorial form such as frescoes and icons in churches. Furthermore, as the primary object of the imagological study is the producer of the image rather than its recipients, this restriction is neither crucial to nor does it compromise a successful research project; it only sets certain preconditions for it. Similarly, it is of secondary importance for an image researcher whether an image examined is "true" to the reality (as we have noted, they rarely are, or at least they only reflect one side of it).[19]

Another issue to keep in mind is the researcher's unavoidable subjectivity—something every historian acknowledges nowadays, no matter what their chosen theoretical and methodological approach may be. Yet operating with an unquestionably vague concept such as the image introduces further epistemological problems for consideration. As David Ratz argues, examining the mind and mentality of the people of the past inevitably produces subjective information: it can be said to be one more step removed from the objective reality when compared, for example, with "factual information" or "raw data" collected from historical documents. As researchers, we are products of our own time and we also represent another contemporary filter between the past and present, bringing to the research process our own personal images, perceptions, choices, and interpretations.[20] Being aware of these issues and taking them into account when planning and conducting research is essential for successful historical image research.

Images of "the Others"

One of the popular applications of the imagological approach has been studying images of *the Others*, "Otherness" being the other central concept in the title of this volume alongside the concept of the "image." Defining "them" in relation to one's own reference group, "us," has been an essential phase in the formation of so-called collective identities and societal cohesion in any given country or region, and as mentioned above, it is closely connected to the idea of mental maps and constructions of spatiality in the human mind. Perceptions of "the Others" (hetero-images) have often been pejorative in nature, equipping the representatives of "them" with negative and stereotypical features to emphasize

19 For the application of the imagological approach to medieval sources, see, for example, Mari Mäki-Petäys, "On the Applicability of Image Research to the Study of Medieval Hagiographies," in *Looking at the Other: Historical Study of Images in Theory and Practice*, ed. Kari Alenius et al. (Oulu: Oulu University Press, 2002), 89–103.

20 Ratz, "The Study of Historical Images": 197–98.

the positive attributes connected with the ideas of "us" (auto-images).[21] Typically, stereotyping is easily detected when "we" are defined by others, while we tend to consider our own perceptions of other groups as neutral and well founded.[22]

In times of conflict, perceptions and stereotypes of the other, as well as attempts to influence certain identification processes, tend to become more prominent and the dualistic approach to the qualities of "us" and "them" are more blatant and uncovered. The result is extremely negative and threatening images of the enemy—either external or internal—that are often deliberately produced and distributed for propaganda purposes. In the process, historical imagery is often combined with contemporary perceptions to lend authority and persuasion to a certain message. Ultimately, the process of enmification (the process of making someone into an enemy) can lead to the dehumanizing of the Other, sometimes concretized in comparing them to animals or even pests. This, in turn, allows for the elimination of that nonhuman Other, perceived as an ultimate threat to "Us."[23]

On the other hand, romanticizing and exoticizing the Other has contributed to further isolating them from "Us." It thus serves the purpose of self-definition for its part; being exotic and different is seen as a function of the Others.[24] Stereotypical images of the Others can also consist of seemingly contradictory qualities and attributes. For instance, an ethnic group or a nationality can be seen as poetic, romantic, or exotic in one context, and violent and threatening in

---

21 "Goodness, honesty, righteousness, purity, proper manners, hard work, right religion, high but not over–ripe culture and decency are the hallmarks of the Self, while the Other is accused of being evil, untruthful, crooked, impure, ill-mannered, lazy, superstitious, barbaric or decadent, and immoral. What is natural and normal, genuine and legitimate, are always 'our' qualities" (Marja Vuorinen, *Enemy Images in War Propaganda* [Newcastle-upon-Tyne: Cambridge Scholars Publishing, 2012], 3). See also Joep Leerssen, "Imagology: History and Method," in *Imagology—the Cultural Construction and Literary Representation of National Characters: A Critical Survey*, ed. Manfred Beller and Joep Leerssen (Amsterdam: Rodopi, 2007), 27; Manfred Beller, "Perception, Image, Imagology," in *Imagology—the Cultural Construction and Literary Representation of National Characters: A Critical Survey*, ed. Manfred Beller and Joep Leerssen (Amsterdam: Rodopi, 2007), 4–7; Hercules Millas, "History Writing among the Greeks and Turks: Imagining the Self and the Other," in *The Contested Nation: Ethnicity, Class, Religion, and Gender in National Histories*, ed. Stephen Berger and Chris Lorenz (Basingstoke: Palgrave Macmillan, 2008), 494.

22 Vuorinen, *Enemy Images in War Propaganda*, ix.

23 Ibid., 3–5. See also Kati Parppei, "'This Battle Started Long Before Our Days. . .' The Historical and Political Context of the Russo-Turkish War in Russian Popular Publications, 1877–78," *Nationalities Papers* 49, no. 1 (2021): 162–79.

24 Dorothy M. Figueira, *The Exotic: A Decadent Quest* (Albany: State University of New York Press, 1994), 2.

another, as in the case of Pushkin's imagery of the Circassians described above.[25] This holds true, for example, also in the case of Finnish national stereotypes of Russians: on the one hand, Russians have been represented as the primary "hostile Other" in Finland's national narrative; on the other hand, Russian music, literature, and art have been culturally admired and revered, and certain "Slavic melancholy"—as expressed, for example, in Russian traditional songs much favored by Finns—is even eagerly embraced as a feature shared by both Finns and Russians.

Critical examination of "othering" and stereotyping as a psychological and cultural phenomenon was possible only after the idea of national characters as explanatory categories or models had been abandoned in scholarly discourse, which took place after the Second World War.[26] One of the pioneers and classics of the field is Edward Said's *Orientalism* (1978), which examines the images and conceptions of the "East" by the "West." According to Said, the "Orient" has helped to "define Europe (or the West) as its contrasting image, idea, personality, experience."[27] Robert Young has noted that Said was the first scholar to approach colonialism as a discourse of domination rather than as policies and practices of military rule, thus creating a starting point for a new paradigm for analyzing the colonial and imperial ideologies and their manifestations.[28] The immense legacy of *Orientalism* has indeed inspired a multitude of scholarly commentaries, critiques, and interpretations in the field of postcolonial studies.[29]

Said has been accused of over-simplification for delivering his persuasive message: for example, he did not clearly pinpoint the "Orient," and represented the equally vague "West" as an entity producing the Eurocentric view on the East (leaving "Orient" undefined was, according to Said himself, a deliberate choice).[30] This brings us to a central feature of image formation in relation to concepts. From a "European" point of view, the adjectives "Oriental" and "Eastern" are good examples of concepts which may evoke strong and meaningful (but equally vague) images in a European's mind, the vagueness feeding on the lack of firsthand experiences of actual cultures perceived as "Eastern." In the same way, the equally vague concepts such as "Western," or

25 Leerssen, "Imagology: History and Method," 29.
26 Ibid., 21.
27 Edward W. Said, *Orientalism* (London: Penguin, 1995), 1–2.
28 Robert Young, *Postcolonialism: An Historical Introduction* (Chichester: Wiley-Blackwell, 2016), 383–84.
29 For a good overview on that legacy, see Daniel Martin Varisco, *Reading Orientalism: Said and the Unsaid* (Seattle: University of Washington Press, 2007).
30 See, for example, Figueira, *The Exotic: A Decadent Quest*, 3; Said, *Orientalism*, 331.

"European," or "African" quite likely call forth stereotypical images in the recipients' minds, as do other demonyms referring to people living in a certain area, country, or place. The places and regions themselves may evoke intriguing images, or "geographical visions," which historically have often been connected to colonialist enterprises.[31]

It is indeed typical of image formation in general that physical or mental distance and a lack of familiarity produce blurred, coarse perceptions. Members of a distant group—or rather, people more or less arbitrarily perceived as members of the same group—may appear homogenic and their qualities stereotypical.[32] As Joep Leerssen argues, in reminding his readers of the intertextual nature of images that "whenever we encounter an individual instead of a national characterization, the primary sounding board is *not* to empirical reality but to an intertext, a sounding-board, of other related textual instances."[33] However, the more one meets members of a certain group in person, the more effectively the previous simplified and stereotypical image begins to disintegrate and is gradually replaced by more detailed, heterogenic perceptions.[34]

Notably, distance here does not necessarily refer to actual geographical remoteness, but any unfamiliarity resulting from lack of personal experiences and interaction with a certain group. Generally, it is this vagueness, coarseness, and initial "foreignness" that gives stereotypical shared images the potential to be developed into "enemy images" as described above. However, as could be seen in ethnic conflicts such as, for example, the Wars of Yugoslavia, historical enemy images can also be deliberately used by political actors to turn relatively peacefully coexisting ethnic and religious groups against each other and to launch a self-feeding circle of hatred and destruction.[35]

Recognizing blatant enemy images is straightforward—especially if one is aware of their existence in general—and it may also be relatively easy to detect and examine certain hetero-images in national narratives, such as those formed of the inhabitants of neighboring countries with whom there may be a long-shared history of conflict and violence (and also, sometimes, cooperation). However, national narratives as such have tended to exclude minorities and

---

31 Mark Bassin, *Imperial Visions: Nationalist Imagination and Geographical Expansion in the Russian Far East, 1840–1865* (Cambridge: Cambridge University Press, 1999), 5–6.
32 See, for example, Nederveen Pieterse, "Image and Power," 196–202.
33 Leerssen, "Imagology: History and Method," 26.
34 Ratz, "The Study of Historical Images": 215
35 Duško Sekulić, Garth Massey, and Randy Hodson, "Ethnic Intolerance and Ethnic Conflict in the Dissolution of Yugoslavia," *Ethnic and Racial Studies* 29, no. 5 (September 2006): 797–827.

marginal groups. Those ethnic, religious, cultural, or social minorities are— either explicitly or implicitly—labelled as "the Other" in relation to the majority, and they indeed may be as unfamiliar to the representatives of the latter as members of some geographically distant group. The concept of master-narrative is useful here; Thijs defines it as "an ideal typical 'narrative frame' whose pattern is repeated, reproduced and confirmed by highly diverse historical practices" and which dominates the representations of the national past.[36] This dominance of a coherent, established national historical narrative, which more often than not emphasizes the alleged unity of the nation based on shared language and descent, either gives the diverse ethnic and religious minorities of the area only a subordinate role or completely fails to notice them.[37]

Further, it is obvious that positions in relation to auto and hetero-images, as well as the majority-minority setting, fluctuate and oversimplification must always be avoided: every group represents "the Others" to another group, and even minorities have internal minorities of their own, to which their relationship is that of a majority. All the diverse and shifting perceptions have potentially contributed to a group's or individuals' self-positioning to the social reality of their time.[38] Nevertheless, a researcher must bear in mind that images do not reflect identities as such; instead, images constitute possible identifications either explicitly via auto images ("this is what we are like") or implicitly via hetero-images and negations ("that is what they are like [and we are not]"), or both.[39]

Fluctuating Images of the Others in the Russian Context

In post-Soviet Russia, the concept of multiethnicity has been addressed alongside the concept of "unity," for example, in presidential addresses. Both

---

36 Krijn Thijs, "The Metaphor of the Master: 'Narrative Hierarchy,' in National Historical Cultures of Europe," in *The Contested Nation: Ethnicity, Class, Religion and Gender in National Histories*, ed. Stephen Berger and Chris Lorenz (Basingstoke: Palgrave Macmillan, 2008), 68–72.

37 Ibid., 69–74.

38 See, for example, Ernst van Alphen, "The Other Within," in *Alterity, Identity, Image. Selves and Others in Society and Scholarship*, ed. R. Corbey and J. Th. Leerssen (Amsterdam: Rodopi, 2011), 1–16; Kari Alenius, "The Images of Neighbours: Estonians and their Neighbours," in *Looking at the Other. Historical Study of Images in Theory and Practice*, ed. Kari Alenius et al. (Oulu: Oulu University Press, 2002), 53.

39 Leerssen, "Imagology: History and Method," 27.

are represented as unique historical features of Russia and premises of its contemporary and future success.[40] Behind these simplified idea(l)s, a certain complexity can be detected, namely concerning the heritage of the Soviet Union and the challenges of contemporary administration in maintaining cohesion and negotiating the relations between diverse groups (also reflected at the conceptual level, as in the meanings of the concepts *russkii* and *rossiiskii/rossianin*, both translated as "Russian," but the first referring to ethnic Russianness, the second to "civic" belonging).[41] These ideas also vaguely refer to the historical spectrum of the Soviet Union's multiethnic and multireligious relations, in the context of which reciprocal collective images of the external and internal others have been formed, established, changed, and utilized over centuries.

The medieval texts produced in the area of Rus' created and distributed quite exclusively "elite images," as noted above. Religion represented the most important dividing line: Orthodox Christians were contrasted to non-Christians or Christians of other denominations. Notably, this simplistic and dualistic imagery was transferred to national histories of Russia, in which the period from the thirteenth to the sixteenth centuries was depicted as a time of Russian survival under the "Tatar yoke" when Muscovites struggled to gain and later maintain their independence under ceaseless Tatar pressure. Such depictions are accurate to a certain extent but generally incomplete. In reality, the relations between ethnic and religious groups were much more complex,

---

40 See, for example, Vladimir Putin, "Poslanie federal'nomu sobraniiu Rossiiskoi federatsii," April 25, 2005, accessed June 2, 2022, http://kremlin.ru/events/president/transcripts/22931; Vladimir Putin, "Poslanie federal'nomu sobraniiu Rossiiskoi federatsii," April 26, 2007, accessed June 2, 2022, http://kremlin.ru/events/president/transcripts/24203; Dmitrii Medvedev, "Poslanie federal'nomu sobraniiu Rossiiskoi federatsii," November 5, 2008, accessed June 2, 2022, http://kremlin.ru/events/president/transcripts/1968; Vladimir Putin, "Poslanie federal'nomu sobraniiu Rossiiskoi federatsii," December 23, 2012, accessed June 2, 2022, http://kremlin.ru/events/president/transcripts/17118.

41 See, for example, Pål Kolstø, "The Ethnification of Russian Nationalism," in *The New Russian Nationalism: Imperialism, Ethnicity and Authoritarianism 2000–2015*, ed. Pål Kolstø and Helge Blakkisrud (Edinburgh: Edinburgh University Press, 2016), 18–45. Helge Blakkisrud, "Blurring the Boundary Between Civic and Ethnic: The Kremlin's New Approach to National Identity Under Putin's Third Term," in *The New Russian Nationalism: Imperialism, Ethnicity, and Authoritarianism 2000–2015*, ed. Pål Kolstø and Helge Blakkisrud (Edinburgh: Edinburgh University Press, 2016), 249–74. Despite of the eloquent political statements of alleged multiethnic harmony in contemporary Russia, in reality discrimination and "othering" take place in various strata of the society, such as labor market. Moreover, certain hierarchies exist in categorizing diverse groups; for example, people of Southern origin—from Central Asia and Caucasus—are treated with more suspicion than ethnic Russians or groups of European origin, such as Germans, Jews, or Ukrainians (see, for example, Alexey Bessudnov and Andrey Shcherbak, "Ethnic Discrimination in Multi-Ethnic Societies: Evidence from Russia," *European Sociological Review* 36, no. 1 [2020]: 104–20).

and the complexity increased with the ongoing expansion of the empire.[42] These relations tended more often towards realpolitik and pragmatic "partnerships of necessity," in which religious and national antagonism played no significant role.[43]

Moscow assuming the dominating position amongst the principalities of Rus' during the fifteenth and sixteenth centuries was a prerequisite for Russia's expansionistic activities. The conquests of the multireligious and multiethnic khanate of Kazan (1552) and the city of Astrakhan (1556) were followed by the conquest of the khanate of Sibir in the 1580s, and during the following centuries, the expansive movement continued eastward across Siberia to the Far East, into the steppe, the northern Caucasus, and also westward to challenge Poland, Sweden, and the Ottoman Empire.[44] The motives for Russia's expansion, too, were largely pragmatic rather than ideological, and were related to the desire to access material resources and trade routes.[45]

This colonizing expansion brought numerous ethnic and religious groups under the administration of the Russian Empire, turning "external others" into internal minorities. The colonization of Russia was administered by the state rather than being a result of private initiative and interest. As part of its colonization project, the Russian empire established certain administrative tools, such as diverse institutions and agencies in order to bring the newly acquired frontier areas and their inhabitants under imperial control.[46] In addition to and overlapping with administrative practices, the representatives of the Russian Empire had to deal with mental and ideological issues relating to facing "otherness" and adapting their thinking to accommodate the ethnic and cultural diversity. Concerning Europe, Jan Nederveen Pieterse asserts that

---

42 For examples of the complexity of practical *Realpoltik* relations between ethnic and religious groups in the case of Muscovy, see, for example, Bulat Rakhimzianov, *Moskva i tatarskii mir: Sotrudnichestvo i protivostoianie v epokhu peremen, XV–XVI veka* (St Petersburg: Evraziia, 2016).

43 Edward Keenan, "Muscovy and Kazan: Some Introductory Remarks on the Patterns of Steppe Diplomacy," *Slavic Review* 24 (1967): 549, 557–58.

44 For general overview of the expansion in the context of the other developments of the Russian empire, see Nancy Shields Kollmann, *The Russian Empire 1450–1801* (Oxford: Oxford University Press, 2017) and Valerie A. Kivelson and Ronald Grigor Suny, *Russia's Empires* (Oxford: Oxford University Press, 2016).

45 Bassin, *Imperial Visions: Nationalist Imagination and Geographical Expansion in the Russian Far East, 1840–1865.*

46 Dittmar Schorkowitz, "Was Russia a Colonial Empire?" in *Shifting Forms of Continental Colonialism*, ed. Dittmar Schorkowitz et al. (Singapore: Palgrave Macmillan Publishers 2019), 117–47.

> All the attributes assigned to non-European peoples have also
> and first been attributed to European peoples, in a gradually
> expanding circle from neighboring to further removed peoples.
> This applies to the entire complex of savagery, bestiality,
> promiscuity, incest, heathenism, cannibalism, and so forth.[47]

This holds true for Russia too and reveals the relativity of attributes linked to "Otherness"; the images of Russians in Western Europe from the fifteenth century specifically emphasized the qualities described in the quotation, and which were in turn variably applied to Russia's "Others."[48] Following the ongoing process of expansion, the attributes and degrees of belonging to certain diverse groups had to be renegotiated accordingly in the context of their assimilation and integration into the empire. One way to deal with the situation in the eighteenth century were the administrative attempts to classify and categorize the non-Russians according to partly overlapping political, economic and religious criteria.[49]

However, only with the formation of national identities during the nineteenth century did the negotiations of Russia's geopolitical position and "Russianness" begin in earnest, taking place primarily in relation to vague metonymies such as Europe and Asia, or West and East. The complexity and controversy related to the issue—which culminated in the formation of the two groups called Slavophiles and Westernizers in the nineteenth century—reflected the profound intricacy and relativity of the issue of "Otherness." This intricacy was manifested also, and perhaps primarily, on the grassroot level due to processes of acculturation and assimilation having taken place throughout the expansion. For instance, many Russians had Asian background themselves.[50]

Nevertheless, despite the shifting and blurred issues of belonging inside the Empire, in the case of external "Others" it was—and indeed, still is— sometimes useful to create and maintain the ideas of sharp division between "us" and "them." During the nineteenth century, increasing literacy and the

---

47 Nederveen Pieterse, "Image and Power," 198.
48 See, for example, David Schimmelpennick van der Oye, *Russian Orientalism in the Russian Mind from Peter the Great to the Emigration* (New Haven: Yale University Press, 2018), 2–3; Michael Khodarkovsky, "Ignoble Savages and Unfaithful Subjects," in *Russia's Orient. Imperial Borderlands and Peoples, 1700–1917*, ed. Daniel R. Brower and Edward J. Lazzerini (Bloomington: Indiana University Press, 2007), 10.
49 Khodarkovsky, "Ignoble Savages and Unfaithful Subjects," 21–22.
50 Schimmelpennick van der Oye, *Russian Orientalism in the Russian Mind from Peter the Great to the Emigration*, 9. See also Michael Khodarkovsky, "The Indigenous Elites and the Construction of Ethnic Identities in the North Caucasus," *Russian History* 35, no. 2: 129–38.

emergence of popular printed material such as newspapers, textbooks and *lubok*[51] pictures, and booklets allowed for the more effective distribution of ideas and perceptions, and ultimately led to the emergence of shared images and stereotypes. These were effectively used in war propaganda, for example, and reproduced and further consolidated in expressive pictorial forms such as caricatures.[52] The publishing activities were regulated by censorship, which sought to ensure that the printed material accorded with official views and promoted societal cohesion.

However, this imagined cohesion was challenged throughout the nineteenth century, culminating in the severe tensions between the autocratic administration and its subjects at the turn of the twentieth century, and ultimately contributed to the fall of the empire during the revolution in 1917. Once again, new internal and external enemy images had to be created and distributed for the consolidation of the inner cohesion of a society based on new policies, ideas, and doctrines.

This book combines the theoretical and methodological tools and premises briefly introduced in the previous sections with an array of case studies— diverse in scope and style—that together cover the timespan from the sixteenth to the beginning of the twentieth centuries; from the beginning of Ivan IV's coronation in 1547 to the revolution of 1917. This ambitious timespan allows for an examination of not only the formation of early stereotypical images but also their influence on the formation of new imagery. Moreover, this timespan also brings out the development from "elite images" to the shared images of the nineteenth and early twentieth centuries.

The first section, "Creating Prototypes," examines how fundamental ideas of otherness—as a counterpart to Russian Orthodox Christianity—found their textual and pictorial form in medieval and premodern Russia. This section contains chapters dealing with the results and consequences of the rule of certain epochal rulers like Ivan the Terrible and Peter the Great.

The chapters of the second section, "Classifying the Internal Others," address themes related to the expanding empire and the perceptions of the ethnic and

---

51 *Lubok* covers the production of cheap, popular prints, the production of which increased during the nineteenth century. They were either illustrations with short texts or booklets. The subjects ranged from folktales to contemporary events such as ongoing wars.

52 See, for example, Jeffrey Brooks, *When Russia Learned to Read* (Princeton: Princeton University Press, 1985); Stephen Norris, *A War of Images* (Cornell: Cornell University Press, 2006); Elena Vishlenkova, "Strategies of the Visual Construction of Russianness and Non-Russianness, 1800–1830," in *Defining Self: Essays on Emergent Identities in Russia Seventeenth to Nineteenth Century*, ed. M. Branch (Helsinki: Finnish Literature Society, 2009).

religious groups in the context of the integration processes. We see that, in many cases, the emerging Russian Empire was simply unprepared for the vast groups of various "newcomers" and as a result, used various tactics to maintain at least some impression of uniform imperial rule.

The final section, "The Other in Times of Conflict and Crisis," deals with the external and internal enemy images emerging at the turn of the twentieth century along with the culmination of multiple military, political, and social problems in the Russian Empire. Despite the contributing authors' wide problematical scope and various styles, most of the texts convey the feelings of mutual hostility, anger, and general unacceptance of "the Others" between the competing sides of Russian society, tensions that eventually led to the downfall of the empire.

The chapters of each section are preceded by section summaries written by David M. Goldfrank, Michael Khodarkovsky, and Stephen M. Norris respectively.

Works Cited

Alenius, Kari. "The Images of Neighbours: Estonians and their Neighbours." In *Looking at the Other. Historical of Images in Theory and Practice.* Edited by Kari Alenius, Olavi K. Fält and Seija Jalagin, 53–72. Oulu: Oulu University Press, 2002.

van Alphen, Ernst. "The Other Within." In *Alterity, Identity, Image. Selves and Others in Society and Scholarship.* Edited by R. Corbey and J. Th. Leerssen, 1–16. Amsterdam: Rodopi, 2011.

Bassin, Mark. *Imperial Visions: Nationalist Imagination and Geographical Expansion in the Russian Far East, 1840–1865.* Cambridge: Cambridge University Press, 1999.

Beller, Manfred. "Perception, Image, Imagology." In *Imagology–The Cultural Construction and Literary Representation of National Characters: A Critical Survey.* Edited by Manfred Beller and Joep Leerssen, 3–16. Amsterdam: Rodopi, 2007.

Bessudnov, Alexey, and Andrey Shcherbak. "Ethnic Discrimination in Multi-ethnic Societies: Evidence from Russia." *European Sociological Review* 36, no. 1 (2020): 104–20.

Blakkisrud, Helge. "Blurring the Boundary Between Civic and Ethnic: The Kremlin's New Approach to National Identity under Putin's Third Term." In

The New Russian Nationalism: Imperialism, Ethnicity, and Authoritarianism 2000–2015. Edited by Pål Kolstø and Helge Blakkisrud, 249–74. Edinburgh: Edinburgh University Press, 2016.

Boulding, Kenneth. *The Image*. Ann Arbor: The University of Michigan Press, 1975.

Brooks, Jeffrey. *When Russia Learned to Read. Literacy and Popular Culture 1861–1917*. Evanston: Northwestern University Press, 2003.

Figueira, Dorothy M. *The Exotic: A Decadent Quest*. Albany: State University of New York Press, 1994.

Fält, Olavi K. "The Historical Study of Mental Images as a Form of Research into Cultural Confrontation." *Comparative Civilizations Review* 32, no. 32 (1995): 99–108.

———. Introduction to *Looking at the Other: Historical of Images in Theory and Practice*. Edited by Kari Alenius, Olavi K. Fält, and Seija Jalagin, 7–11. Oulu: Oulu University Press, 2002.

Greenleaf, Monika Frenkel. "Pushkin's 'Journey to Arzrum': The Poet at the Border." *Slavic Review* 50, no. 4 (1991): 940–53.

Götz, Norbert, and Janne Holmén. "Introduction to the Theme Issue: 'Mental Maps: Geographical and Historical Perspectives." *Journal of Cultural Geography* 35, no. 2 (2018): 157–61.

Hall, Stuart. *Representation: Cultural Representations and Signifying Practices*. London: Sage Publishing, 2003.

Jahn, Hubertus F. "'Us': Russians on Russianness." In *National Identity in Russian Culture. An Introduction*. Edited by Simon Franklin and Emma Widdis, 53–73. Cambridge: Cambridge University Press, 2006.

Keenan, Edward. *Muscovy and Kazan, 1445–1552: A Study in Steppe Politics*. PhD diss., Harvard University, 1965.

———. "Muscovy and Kazan: Some Introductory Remarks on the Patterns of Steppe Diplomacy." *Slavic Review* 24 (1967): 548–58.

Khodarkovsky, Michael. "Ignoble Savages and Unfaithful Subjects." In *Russia's Orient. Imperial Borderlands and Peoples, 1700–1917*. Edited by Daniel R. Brower and Edward J. Lazzerini, 9–26. Bloomington: Indiana University Press, 2007.

———. "The Indigenous Elites and the Construction of Ethnic Identities in the North Caucasus." *Russian History/Histoire Russe* 35, nos. 1–2 (Spring–Summer 2008): 129–38.

Kivelson, Valerie A., and Ronald Grigor Suny. *Russia's Empires*. Oxford: Oxford University Press, 2017.

Kollmann, Nancy Shields. *The Russian Empire 1450–1801*. Oxford: Oxford University Press, 2017.

Kolstø, Pål. "The Ethnification of Russian Nationalism." In *The New Russian Nationalism: Imperialism, Ethnicity and Authoritarianism 2000–2015*. Edited by Pål Kolstø and Helge Blakkisrud, 18–45. Edinburgh: Edinburgh University Press, 2016.

Layton, Susan. *Russian Literature and Empire: Conquest of the Caucasus from Pushkin to Tolstoy*. Cambridge: Cambridge University Press, 1995.

———. "Nineteenth-Century Russian Mythologies of Caucasian Savagery." In *Russia's Orient. Imperial Borderlands and Peoples, 1700–1917*. Edited by Daniel R. Brower and Edward J. Lazzerini, 80–99. Bloomington: Indiana University Press, 2001.

Leerssen, Joep. "Imagology: History and Method." In *Imagology—The Cultural Construction and Literary Representation of National Characters: A Critical Survey*. Edited by Manfred Beller and Joep Leerssen, 17–32. Amsterdam: Rodopi, 2007.

Lyles, John. "Bloody Verses: Rereading 'Pushkin's Prisoner of the Caucasus." *Pushkin Review* 16 (2014): 233–54.

Medvedev, Dmitrii. "Poslanie federal'nomu sobraniiu Rossiiskoi federatsii." November 5, 2008. Accessed June 2, 2022. http://kremlin.ru/events/president/transcripts/1968.

Millas, Hercules. "History Writing Among the Greeks and Turks: Imagining the Self and the Other." In *The Contested Nation. Ethnicity, Class, Religion and Gender in National Histories*. Edited by Stephen Berger and Chris Lorenz, 490–510. Basingstoke: Palgrave Macmillan, 2008.

Mäki-Petäys, Mari. "On the Applicability of Image Research to the Study of Medieval Hagiographies." In *Looking at the Other. Historical of Images in Theory and Practice*. Edited by Kari Alenius, Olavi K. Fält, and Seija Jalagin, 89–103. Oulu: Oulu University Press, 2002.

Nederveen Pieterse, Jan. "Image and Power." In *Alterity, Identity, Image. Selves and Others in Society and Scholarship*. Edited by R. Corbey and J. Th. Leerssen, 191–203. Amsterdam: Rodopi, 2011.

Norris, Stephen M. *A War of Images. Russian Popular Prints, Wartime Culture, and National Identity*. DeKalb: Northern Illinois University Press, 2006.

Parppei, Kati. *"The Oldest One in Russia": The Formation of the Historiographical Image of Valaam Monastery.* Leiden: Brill Academic Publishers, 2011.

———. *The Battle of Kulikovo Refought: "The First National Feat."* Leiden: Brill Academic Publishers, 2017.

———. "'This Battle Started Long Before Our Days . . .' The Historical and Political Context of the Russo-Turkish War in Russian Popular Publications, 1877–78." *Nationalities Papers* 49, no. 1 (January 2021): 162–79.

Pushkin, Alexander. *A Journey to Arzrum.* Translated by Birgitta Ingemanson. Ann Arbor: Ardis, 1974.

Putin, Vladimir. "Poslanie federal'nomu sobraniiu Rossiiskoi federatsii." April 25, 2005. Accessed June 2, 2022. http://kremlin.ru/events/president/transcripts/22931.

———. "Poslanie federal'nomu sobraniiu Rossiiskoi federatsii." April 26, 2007. Accessed June 2, 2022. http://kremlin.ru/events/president/transcripts/24203.

———. "Poslanie federal'nomu sobraniiu Rossiiskoi federatsii." December 12, 2012. Accessed June 2, 2022. http://kremlin.ru/events/president/transcripts/17118.

Rakhimzianov, Bulat. *Moskva i tatarskii mir: sotrudnichestvo i protivostoianie v epokhu peremen, XV – XVI veka.* St. Petersburg: Evraziia, 2016.

Ratz, David. "The Study of Historical Images." *Faravid* 31 (2007): 189–220.

Said, Edward W. *Orientalism.* London: Penguin, 1995.

Schimmelpennick van der Oye, David. *Russian Orientalism in the Russian Mind from Peter the Great to the Emigration.* New Haven: Yale University Press, 2018.

Schorkowitz, Dittmar. "Was Russia a Colonial Empire?" In *Shifting Forms of Continental Colonialism: Unfinished Struggles and Tensions.* Edited by Dittmar Schorkowitz, John Chavez, and Ingo Schröder, 117–47. Singapore: Palgrave Macmillan, 2019.

Sekulić, Duško, Garth Massey, and Randy Hodson. "Ethnic Intolerance and Ethnic Conflict in the Dissolution of Yugoslavia." *Ethnic and Racial Studies* 29, no. 5 (September 2006): 797–827.

Thijs, Krijn. "The Metaphor of the Master: 'Narrative Hierarchy' in National Historical Cultures of Europe." In *The Contested Nation. Ethnicity, Class, Religion and Gender in National Histories.* Edited by Stephen Berger and Chris Lorenz, 60–74. Basingstoke: Palgrave Macmillan, 2008.

Varisco, Daniel Martin. *Reading Orientalism: Said and the Unsaid.* Seattle: University of Washington Press, 2017.

Vishlenkova, Elena. "Strategies of the Visual Construction of Russianness and Non-Russianness, 1800–1830." In *Defining Self. Essays on Emergent Identities in Russia Seventeenth to Nineteenth Centuries*, edited by Michael Branch, 173–192. Helsinki: Finnish Literature Society, 2009.

Vuorinen, Marja. *Enemy Images in War Propaganda*. Newcastle-upon-Tyne: Cambridge Scholars Publishing, 2012.

———. Introduction to *Binaries in Battle—Representations of Division and Conflict*. Edited by Marja Vuorinen, Noora Kotilainen, and Aki-Mauri Huhtinen, vii–xxiv. Newcastle-upon-Tyne: Cambridge Scholars Publishing, 2014.

Young, Robert. *Postcolonialism: An Historical Introduction*. Chichester: Wiley-Blackwell, 2016.

Part One

CREATING PROTOTYPES

Section Summary

David M. Goldfrank

By the fifteenth century, the elites of the future Russia—then just comprising the combination of Novgorod-Pskov and Northeastern Rus', that is, the Grand Principality of Vladimir (cum Moscow)—possessed, as adumbrated in the early twelfth-century *Primary Chronicle*, a developed sense of identity and alterities. These reflected a) the eighth to tenth century, advanced iron age, conquest-colonial origin of Rus'[1]; b) regional geography[2]; c) the predominance of proto-Russian East Slavic dialects,[3] which were connected with the extension of agriculture as the primary, though in no way exclusive, plebeian occupation in Russia's forest-rich territory[4]; and d) starting in the late tenth century, the

---

1 Simon Franklin and Jonathan Shepard, *The Emergence of Rus 750–1200* (London: Longman Publishing, 1996), 3–138. The chronicle authors also understood the role of allied elites, subject peoples, and the Khazar competition (Donald Ostrowski, Daniel J. Birnbaum, Horace G. Lunt, ed., *The Povest' vremmenykh let: An Interlinear Collation and Paradosis*, 3 vols. [Cambridge, MA: Harvard University Press/Harvard Ukrainian Research Institute] 1:86–91, 99–106; *The Russian Primary Chronicle* (hereafter cited as RPC). *The Laurentian Text*, trans. and ed. Samuel Hazzard Cross and Olgerd T. Sherbowitz–Wetzor [Cambridge, MA: The Medieval Academy of America, 1953], 58, 59–60) (hereafter cited as RPC).
2 PVL, 1:29–34; RPC, 53.
3 PVL, 1:24–29; RPC, 52–53.
4 Paul M. Barford, *The Early Slavs* (Ithaca: Cornell University Press, 2001), 98, 153, 180, 236–42.

acquisition and spread of a liturgically Slavic Eastern Orthodox Christianity as the realm's official religion.[5]

Let us explore these matters at bit further. Conditioned necessarily by geography and the production techniques of the time and bolstered by the temporary overlay of the second and rather rapid overrunning of the land by the Mongols, the conquest origin of Rus' determined that a combination of tribute gathering, slavery, and eventual peonage or serfdom of some genre would characterize most elite-plebeian relations. Such social interaction, in turn, created the elite's need to justify their "othering" of millions of fellow Russians—an issue which this historian regrets as lying outside the main subject matter of any of the current volume's chapters.[6] Geography also determined that both coastal-sea peoples to the west and steppe folk to the east and south were occupationally different from Rus' in fundamental ways and, hence, decidedly "other," though not ipso facto in a negative way on these grounds, while agrarian neighbors to the west were less different—simply ethnically and religiously distinct to some degree. In fact, the coastal-sea peoples hardly ever posed a physical threat for Rus' border zones,[7] but proved useful trading partners and carriers of commerce. They differed from Hungarians, Poles, and Lithuanians, who, starting around the year 1200, aimed at various times to occupy Western Rus' territories. On account of a shared Christianity (except for the Lithuanians until the late-fourteenth century), these East-Central and East European agrarians were also less mentally different to these proto-Russians than were the neighboring pagans in the forest regions to the north and east. All the same, because the most useful, secular content of the late medieval and early modern high culture of its Western neighbors was much greater than Russia's, attitudes towards them had to be a mixture of curiosity, acquisitive envy, and defensive fears. Due to threats of devastating raids and even conquest, it was different with respect to the warring and pillaging steppe peoples, with whom

---

5   PVL, 1:141–61, 2:832–952; RPC, 62–63, 111–19.

6   For the context of linking of the unfree and semi–free labor to alterity, see Yasmin Y. DeGout, "Emancipation in the Danish West Indies: Reading Representations in History and Historical Fiction," *Otherness: Essays and Studies* 2, nos. 1–3 (2015); also Peter Kolchin, *Unfree Labour: American Slavery and Russian Serfdom* (Cambridge, MA: Harvard University Press, 1987), 173: "Russians, then, developed an essentially racial argument in defense of serfdom, even though no racial distinction divided lord and peasant."

7   The exception before 1400 was the period of crisis on the tail of the 1237–1240 Mongol conquests, when Swedes invaded Novgorod's Neva River estuary, and a German Livonian force temporarily seized Pskov, but the Rus' drove the invaders back and out. It was different for the Western Rus' lands which, starting around 1200, Hungary claimed and Lithuania and/ or Poland took over.

Rus' nonetheless also had complex symbiotic relationships based on their complementary physical environments and material utilities for each other—crystallized in the words of one specialist concerning the Rus' and Polovtsians as: "a complex, joint two-century history of the two peoples full of marriages and battles, raids and military alliances."[8]

A central theme in the *Primary Chronicle* is the establishment of Eastern Orthodox Christianity, so the alterity of the casting of paganism, Judaism, Islam, and Western or Roman Christianity in negative colors is a given. The first part of the *Primary Chronicle* depicts with disgust most pagan Slavic customs,[9] while the conversion narrative rages against Judaism, Islam, and Catholicism.[10] In subsequent narratives, pagan shamans, as either competitors of Christian clergy or effectors of murderous violence, are singled out,[11] but the greatest invective in the Chronicle is reserved for the Polovtsians (Qipčaq, Cumans), specifically the 1096 raid on Kiev, including the Pecherskii Monastery, where this chronicle originated. There, the author(s) were influenced by the anti-Saracen, seventh-century *Apocalypse of Pseudo-Methodius of Olympus/Patara*,[12] and thus the Polovtsians now number among the Eastern barbarians from the "Desert of Yathrib (Medina)."[13] Interestingly, this same attribution, more tropic than geographic—the Arabian Desert and Medina are due south of Kiev—is applied in the *First Novgorod Chronicle* (around 1224) to the Mongols for their 1223 destructive invasion of Polovtsian territory in the North Caucasus and then defeat of the combined central and southern Rus' at Kalka, north of the Black Sea.[14]

---

8 S. A. Pletneva, "Polovetskaia zemlia," in *Drevnerusskie kniazhestva X–XIII vv.*, ed. A. Beskrovnyi, V. A. Kuchkin, and V. T. Pashuto (Moscow: Nauka, 1975), 160.

9 PVL, 1:62–74; RPC, 56–57.

10 PVL, 1:615–38; 2:884–901; RPC, 96–98, 115–16.

11 PVL, 2: 1399–462; RPC, 150–54.

12 As in the Syriac text, St. Jerome identified the original Methodius, an erudite Platonist theologian, who polemized against Origen, and was martyred in 311 or 312 in the Roman Empire's last pagan persecution, as bishop of Olympus, while Greek tradition places his cathedra in Patara, both of these towns being located in Lycia (Katharina Bracht, "Methodius of Olympus: State of the Art and New Perspectives: Introduction," in *Methodius of Olympus*, ed. Katharina Bracht [Berlin: de Gruyter, 2018]: 1; differently: Andrew Louth, "Byzantium transforming (600–700)," in *Cambridge History of the Byzantine Empire c. 500–1492*, ed. Jonathan Shepherd [Cambridge: Cambridge University Press, 2009], 247).

13 PVL, 3:1835–862; RPC, 183–85.

14 *Novgorodskaia pervaia letopis' starshego i mladshego izvodov* (Moscow–Leningrad: Izdatel'stvo Akademii nauk SSSR, 1950), 264; *The Chronicle of Novgorod, 1016–1417*, trans. Robert Michell (London: Offices of the [Royal Historical] Society, 2010), 64; and for contextualization, Leonid S. Chekin, "The Godless Ishmaelites: The Image of the Steppe in Eleventh–Thirteenth Century Rus'," *Russian History* 19, nos. 1–4 (1992): 9–28.

This section's chapters commence with Charles Halperin's "Varieties of Otherness in Ivan IV's Muscovy: Relativity, Multiplicity, and Ambiguity," which addresses squarely the fundamental issues connected with alterity and the contingency of a society's own inner differentiation relative to status, ethnicity, religion, and language. Hence, for example, a high-ranking aristocrat was nearly the same as (for example, hardly "other" than) a fellow high-ranking aristocrat, except that each belonged to a different and competing boyar clan. Specifically, under Ivan IV, though only for a limited time, the *oprichniki* were by tsarist decree "other" than the non-*oprichniki*—this phenomenon standing as a unique case for Russia, when a ruler created a distinct status for his privy domain (*oprichnina*) servitors, cutting across social strata. Of course, all Muscovites, except for one, were "other" than the divinely ordained tsar, whose personal diplomacy in Ivan's case, actually played with his legendary non-Russian ancestry. Overall, regarding ethnicity, religion, and language, Halperin extracts from the sources and gives us a creatively useful diagram of the hierarchy of degrees of otherness, which I would emphasize indicates a great deal of continuity from pre-Mongol Rus'. And who were the most "other" under Ivan IV? Jews, of course.

Jaakko Lehtovirta's "The Depiction of 'Us' and 'Them' in the Illuminated Codex of the 1560s and 1570s"—a gigantic chronograph and chronicle undertaking covering Russia and its relevant world from Biblical beginnings, with more than sixteen thousand extant completed, unfinished, or revised illustrations—addresses graphic sources of ethnic "others," who appear differently relative to Russians from what the textual sources might indicate. For in the written sources, as noted above, non-Russian, non-Orthodox Christians are less "other" than the steppe people, but in the graphics presented here, namely from the Illuminated Codex (*Litsevoi svod*), the opposite is true. The average Mongol/Tatar, like his Polovtsian predecessors in the fifteenth-century illustrated *Radzivil Chronicle*, which likely has twelfth-century precedents, appears very much as does his Rus' or Russian counterpart.[15] On the other hand, the gradations of "otherness" of non-Russian Christians found in the texts hold in a literally most broad-brush manner, in that all Westerners, distinguished by rounded headdress, appear the same, as do all Orthodox, whereas Lithuanians, envisioned not as today's Roman Catholic ethnic Lithuanians but as kindred, Orthodox Rus', constitute a "gray zone," their rulers alone depicted as Westerners. Insofar as the Russians were heirs to the Rus' appropriation of Byzantine (East Roman) sacred history for themselves, so the ancient "in people," Hebrews, Greeks, and then Romans in succession, are depicted as contemporary Russians, while others,

---

15 *Radzivilovskaia letopis'* (St. Petersburg: "Glagol", Moscow: "Iskusstvo", 1994), 196.

such as the Phoenicians of ancient Tyre, bear different headgear. One possible inconsistency here, indicating an identification with later Roman secular history, is the different headwear of fourth-century BCE Jews, whose Law, from the standpoint of Christian sacred history, was still valid at a time that they were being politically marginalized by the succession of Empires controlling Judaea.

Nuances of "otherness" permeate M. V. Moiseev's "The Image of the Other: The Perception of Tatars by Russian Intellectuals and Clerks in the Fifteenth to Seventeenth Centuries (Chroniclers, Diplomats, Governors, and Writers)." This chapter brings us back to texts whose detailed investigation reveals to us the ambiguity posed by the discrepancy between Halperin's analysis of hostile, distancing attitudes towards Tatars and the kindred images Lehtovirta brings into play. Moiseev commences with the most hostile *Primary Chronicle* depiction of the Polovtsians, which he sees in a uniquely ambiguous way when applied to the Tatars.[16] He also notes how the late mid-fifteenth-century Tver merchant Afanasii Nikitin, who could be envisioned as an early Russian "Orientalist," promoted the trope of Muslims as inherently aggressive, while the Russian efforts to vassalize and eventually capture Kazan seems to have required the characterization of Tatars as treacherous. The diverse discourses related to Kazan in Moiseev's opinion indicate that certain figures such as Metropolitan Makarii were more interested in promoting a Holy Rus' than in conquest as such,[17] with *Kazanskaia istoriia* asserting that the conquest saved Kazan from "Satanic" Islam, with others like the influential high official Aleksei Adashev allegedly claiming that Tatar treachery justified annihilation, and, finally, the Ivan IV of the first extant epistle issued in his name to Prince Andrei Kurbskii lauding the loyalty of Tatar soldiers in Russian service.[18] Of a different genre altogether is the productivity of Muscovy's chanceries. The *stateiinii spisok* (factual report) of the diplomat Daniil/Danila Gubin from 1534–1535 is typically full of fascinating details of his complex mission to the loosely organized

---

16 I may disagree here but competing conclusions from literary analysis deserve examination and respect.

17 I see the holiness, insofar as the Church was concerned, as a necessary precondition for a successful campaign, as with Patriarch Nikon (David Goldfrank, "Probing the Collapse of Nikon's Patriarchate," in *Russia's Early Modern Patriarchate: Apogee and Finale*, ed. Kevin M. Kain and David Goldfrank [Washington: Academica, 2021], 118–23; or Patriarch Ioakim, *Dukhovnoe zaveshchenie, 1690 g*, accessed June 2, 2022, https://sedmitza.ru/lib/text/443583/).

18 A critical if small contingent of US specialists follow the late Edward Keenan (1971) in doubting at least that the alleged Andrei Kurbskii-Ivan IV correspondence and Kurbskii *History*, as extant, are authentic. The latest US work treats these works as authentically Ivan's and Kurbskii's, but not at all necessarily reliable as truthful (Charles Halperin, *Ivan the Terrible: Free to Reward and Punish* [Pittsburgh: University of Pittsburgh Press, 2020], 8).

Nogai polity and of the local society, though it ignores some local customs, such as holidays, which in Moiseev's opinion the envoy chose to exclude as "beyond the threshold of understanding" and hence completely "other." Furthermore, the reports (*otpiski*) of frontier governors, such as that from 1614 by the *voevoda* of Samara, Prince Dmitrii Petrovich Lopata Pozharskii,[19] indicate solid Russian knowledge of the statuses of the various groups of regional Astrakhan Tatars. Indeed, Moiseev considers such reports to be the forerunners of Russia's genuine ethnographic studies.

Russia's piece-meal, technology-driven Westernization, seen clearly in the Kremlin renovation of the 1470s–1510s, accelerating in the seventeenth century, especially dramatic in many sectors under Peter the Great's rule (1695–1725), and then continuing in zigzags down to our times, could not but catalyze the ambiguities of alterity relative to domestic life and other societies. The ultimately victorious coalition during the early seventeenth-century Time of Troubles exploited the otherness of the Catholic Poles and mobilized Orthodoxy as a unifying factor.[20] Afterwards, as Georg Michels has recently shown, Patriarch Filaret Nikitich (r. 1619–33), fearing Western influence on Orthodoxy, was far more concerned with debriefing and sanitizing even Orthodox "Belarutsy" (that is, Belarusians and Ukrainians) and also Russians returning from time spent voluntarily or involuntarily among "Belarutsy" in Poland-Lithuania, than he was worried about Muslims or the occasional Jew.[21] The state-backed move by Patriarch Nikon (authoritatively in office 1652–1658) to eliminate via ritual reforms Russia's subjective otherness from the rest of the Orthodox Christian world backfired at home due not only to their resolute rejection by some of the faithful, but also the Western-influenced, blanket labelling of such "Old Believers" as heretics and the initiation of state-supported persecution of them. Indeed, in the seventeenth century the real issue regarding Europe for Russia was not whether to allow Western influences, but which ones and to what extent, as leading Churchmen railed against use of the razor and other imported fashions. Peter the Great's insistence that his elite secular subjects dress like Europeans

---

19 This personage is not to be confused with his celebrated contemporary and hero of Russia's 1612–13 liberation campaign, Prince Dmitrii Mikhailovich Pozharskii.

20 V. G. Anan'ev shows the normal continuity of Duma boyars through the political changes of the Troubles (V. G. Anan'ev, "Sostav Semiboiarshchina: Popytka semeingo portreta v inter'ere," in *Rusistika Ruslana Skrynnikova. Knigi po Russistike/Ruszisztikai Könyvek*, 30 [Budapest–Volgograd: Russica Pannonnica, 2011], 176–86).

21 Georg Michels, "Policing the Boundaries of Russian Orthodoxy: Catholics, Belorustsy, and Polish Spies during the Patriarchate of Filaret Romanov," in *Russia's Early Modern Patriarchate: Foundations and Mitred Royalty*, ed. Kevin M. Kain and David Goldfrank (Washington: Academica, 2021), 150–55.

and shave created the potential for the essential domestic othering of loyal Orthodox who resisted such marked, rapid personal Westernization, but such marked alterity in fact did not really occur, even if a goodly number of Orthodox othered Peter himself.[22] Rather, with Orthodoxy as essential glue for most Russians in this expanding and ever more multi-ethnic and multi-confessional society, the state and culture allowed for a spectrum of fully, partially, and barely or not at all Europeanized imperial subjects.

Ricarda Vulpius's "From *Inozemtsy* to *Inovertsy* and *Novokreshchenye*: Images of Otherness in Eighteenth-Century Russia" concludes this section with a rigorous and sophisticated analysis, which grasps well the contingency and flexibility of the "otherness" of the official designations of non-Russians and the dependence of such terms upon the needs or whims of state policy. Considering the official legal and administrative sources the best for understanding how Russia's elites defined alterity, she notes that such designations perforce affect to some degree the subject and clearly subordinate domestic "others" themselves. Vulpius envisions Peter I as key here for identifying Christianization with the spread of European cultural values. Additionally, she sees him as crucial in restricting *inozemtsy* (people from [ethnically] other lands) to immigrants and applying instead *inovertsy* (people of other faiths) to subject non-Orthodox "others." Employing such terms as "intersectionality," she likewise underscores that the successive favorite terms inozemtsy, inovertsy, and *novokreshchennye* (newly baptized) influenced and reinforced each other. Indeed, as in early modern Spain, Russia's *converso* equivalents, except at the very top level of society and the bottom (due to even more potent socially degrading stigma, such as full slaves' lack of any rights whatsoever?), passed such a designation on to their offspring. And if Peter the Great truly wished novokreshchennye to become genuine Russians, actual state policy in the eighteenth century evinced a great deal of resistance to full integration, such obstacles' being consistent with the normal operational mixture of "incorporation and differentiation" typical of empires.[23]

Together, aided hopefully by this summary, the chapters by Halperin, Lehtovirta, Moiseev, and Vulpius provide a sound introduction to the problem of ethnic and religious alterity in medieval and early modern Russia. The first

---

22 Lindsey Hughes' magnum opus on Peter's reign is as good as any place to acquire a sense of cultural life under Peter in a very broad sense (Lindsey Hughes, *Russia in the Age of Peter the Great* [New Haven: Yale University Press, 1998]).

23 The reference here is to a recent general study of empires (Jane Burbank and Frederick Cooper, *Empires in World History: Power and the Politics of Difference* [Princeton: Princeton University Press, 2010], 13).

cultural transformation, after an earlier conquest formation, of Rus' polity into an Orthodox East Slavic realm created the overall alterity framework lasting even beyond Russia's Westernizing and modernizing cultural transformation—a development which was greatly accelerated against some serious opposition by Peter the Great,[24] but had been in the works well before his reign due to the unavoidability of useful close contacts with Roman Catholic and Protestant "others" from the start. Together as well, these chapters reveal the inevitable contingencies, ambiguities and even contradictions among such attitudes of Russian individuals and statesmen as they dealt with both internal and external "others" in a variety of situations and manners.

Works Cited

Primary Sources

Ioakim, Patriarch. *Dukhovnoe zaveshchanie.* 1690. https://sedmitza.ru/lib/text/443583/

Novgorodskaia pervaia letopis' starshego i mladshego izvodov. Moscow-Leningrad: Izdatel'stvo Akademii nauk SSSR, 1950.

Radzivilovskaia letopis'. St. Petersburg: "Glagol", Moscow: "Iskusstvo", 1994.

The Chronicle of Novgorod, 1016–1417. Translated by Robert Michell. London: Offices of the [Royal Historical] Society, 2010.

The Povest' vremennykh let. An Interlinear Collation and Paradosis (PVL). 3 vols. Compiled and edited by Donald Ostrowski, Daniel J. Birnbaum and Horace G. Lunt. Cambridge, MA: Harvard University Press/Harvard Ukrainian Research Institute, 2003.

The Russian Primary Chronicle: The Laurentian Text (RPC). Translated and edited by Samuel Hazzard Cross and Olgerd T. Sherbowitz-Wetzor. Cambridge, MA: The Medieval Academy of America, 1953.

---

24 The Testament of Patriarch Ioakim (1674–1690), for example, railed against non-Orthodox officers commanding Orthodox troops in battle (Ioakim, *Dukhovnoe zaveshchanie*).

Literature

Anan'ev, V. G. "Sostav Semiboiarshchina: Popytka semeinogo portreta v inter'ere." In *Rusistika Ruslana Skrynnikova: Knigi po Russistike/Ruszisztikai Könyvek*. Vol. 30, 176–186. Budapest–Volgograd: Russica Pannonnica, 2011.

Barford, Paul M. *The Early Slavs*. Ithaca: Cornell University Press, 2001.

Bracht, Katharina. "Methodius of Olympus: State of the Art and New Perspectives. Introduction." In *Methodius of Olympus: State of the Art and New Perspectives*. Edited by Katharina Bracht. 1–17. Berlin: de Gruyter, 2017.

Burbank, Jane, and Frederick Cooper. *Empires in World History: Power and the Politics of Difference*. Princeton: Princeton University Press, 2010.

Chekin, Leonid S. "The Godless Ishmaelites: The Image of the Steppe in Eleventh–Thirteenth-Century Rus'." *Russian History* 19, nos. 1–4 (1992): 9–28.

DeGout, Yasmin Y. "Emancipation in the Danish West Indies: Reading Representations in History and Historical Fiction." *Otherness: Essays and Studies* 2, nos. 1–3 (2015).

Franklin, Simon, and Jonathan Shepard. *The Emergence of Rus 750–1200*. London: Longman Publishing, 1996.

Goldfrank, David. "Probing the Collapse of Nikon's Patriarchate." In *Russia's Early Modern Patriarchate: Apogee and Finale*. Edited by Kevin M. Kain and David Goldfrank, 97–127. Washington: Academica, 2021.

Halperin, Charles. *Ivan the Terrible: Free to Reward and Punish*. Pittsburgh: University of Pittsburgh Press, 2020.

Hughes, Lindsey. *Russia in the Age of Peter the Great*. New Haven: Yale University Press, 1998.

Kolchin, Peter. *Unfree Labour: American Slavery and Russian Serfdom*. Cambridge, MA: Harvard University Press, 1987.

Louth, Andrew. "Byzantium Transforming (600–700)." In *Cambridge History of the Byzantine Empire c. 500–1492*. Edited by Jonathan Shepherd, 221–48. Cambridge: Cambridge University Press: 2009.

Michels, Georg. "Policing the Boundaries of Russian Orthodoxy: Catholics, Belorustsy, and Polish Spies during the Patriarchate of Filaret Romanov." In *Russia's Early Modern Patriarchate: Foundations and Mitred Royalty*. Edited by Kevin M. Kain and David Goldfrank, 145–78. Washington: Academica, 2021.

Pletneva, S. A. "Polovetskaia zemlia." In *Drevnerusskie kniazhestva X–XIII vv*, Edited by A. Beskrovnyi, V. A. Kuchkin, and V. T. Pashuto. Moscow: Nauka, 1975.

1

Varieties of Otherness in Ivan IV's Muscovy: Relativity, Multiplicity, and Ambiguity

Charles J. Halperin

Abstract

During the reign of Ivan IV, Muscovites had multiple identities. Consequently, they also formulated multiple concepts of otherness. Religious identity as Russian Orthodox Christians was primary, but "other" religious confessions exhibited degrees of otherness depending upon their distance from Russian Orthodox Christianity. Jews were so "other" that they could not be permitted even to step on Russian soil, unlike Muslims and animists who, although not Christians, could reside in Russia. "Russian" was more a political than an ethnic category; "others" were people, even those who spoke another East Slavic language and prayed in Slavonic, living under an "other" ruler, like the grand duke of Lithuania and king of Poland. Still, newly baptized Tatars in Russia did not become "Russians." Socially, there were multiple distinctions among classes, but Ivan imposed a political "us-them" dichotomy on his subjects when he created the *oprichnina*, his state within-a-state. To *oprichniki*, anyone living outside the *oprichnina* became the "other." Relativity, multiplicity, and ambiguity governed concepts of "Otherness" in Ivan IV's Muscovy.

Introduction

Concepts of the Other derive from concepts of the Self. Who is "them" depends upon who is "us." Consequently, multiple self-identities produce multiple concepts of the Other. Concepts of the Other may also be relative in degree. Any analysis of the Other in Muscovy during the reign of Ivan IV[1] should take into account the social and cultural complexities of the period. As Sergei Bogatyrev notes, "In the sixteenth century, to be an Other meant largely to profess another religion or confession for both Europeans and Muscovites."[2] The religious and ethnic[3] Other have received the most attention in scholarship, but other Others also existed between Muscovite society and other societies, and within Muscovite society.

Multiple identities began at the apex of the social pyramid, with Ivan IV himself, who ascribed different identities to himself. Each social class could define itself as "us" versus "them" of members of other social classes through the legal medium of dishonor legislation, but these social boundaries could be porous. The nobility was "us" as collectively entitled to the benefits of the Precedence (*mestnichestvo*) system,[4] but each clan was "us" in precedence disputes versus the "them" of every competing clan. Historians have projected identities on to segments of the Russian aristocracy depending upon their ethnic or geographic origin. Additionally, there were social hierarchies within each social class, defining sub-sets of its members as "us" and "them." Apart from that, when Ivan established the *oprichnina*,[5] he created a nonclass social group of *oprichniki* (members of the oprichnina) who became "us" as opposed to everyone else in Muscovy as "them."

---

1 Ivan Vasil'evich, Ivan *Groznyi* (Ivan the Terrible), born 1530, reigned 1533–1584. On Ivan's personality and reign now see Charles Halperin, *Ivan the Terrible: Free to Reward and Free to Punish* (Pittsburgh: University of Pittsburgh Press, 2019), which does not contain the material presented in this chapter.

2 Sergei Bogatyrev, "Diplomats and Believers: Herberstein and Cross-Confessional Contacts in the Sixteenth Century," in *450 Jahre Sigismund von Herberstein Rerum Muscovitiarum Commentarii 1549–1599*, ed. Frank Kämpfer and Reinhard Frötschner (Wiesbaden: Harrassowitz Verlag, 2002), 215.

3 Of course, the modern conception of "ethnicity" did not exist in the sixteenth century, but I use the term, without quotation marks, as the lesser evil compared to referring to "nation" at the time because ethnicity carries less ideological baggage than nationalism.

4 The precedence system ranked relative noble status based upon biological place within a clan and the relative service records of all previous members of all clans.

5 The *oprichnina* was Ivan's state-within-a-state, formally an appanage, established in 1565 and abolished in 1572, by which he imposed mass terror upon Muscovite society.

Definitions of the religious Other were more fluid than one would expect. There were degrees of religious Otherness; adherents of one religion in particular, Jews, were the most Other. Ethnic identity did exist, sometimes in a straightforward manner, sometimes not. Finally, linguistic identity, for example, what is "our" language in contrast to "their" language, overlapped ethnic and religious identities. In early modern Europe, multiple identities differed from the kinds of monolithic identities found, or foisted upon, people in the modern period,[6] but they did not lack their own complexities.

Ivan IV's Identity

Ivan IV was a complicated man whose personality was a congeries of contradictory traits. It should occasion no surprise that he articulated multiple identities, although one might not expect those identities to be ethnic. Of course, he was Russian (*russkii*); sixteenth-century Russians did not call themselves "Muscovites," a term found only in foreign sources.[7] But Ivan was not just a Russian. He claimed ancestors—real and legendary—who were not Russian.

At different times, Ivan variously proclaimed himself to be of Varangian, Scandinavian, German, or Roman origin. The Kievan "Tale of Bygone Years" ("Povest' vremennykh let") traced the Rus' dynasty to a Varangian Rus' named Riurik. The Rus' were Varangians, Vikings and Scandinavian (the term was not used), but generically the word "German" (*nemets*) applied to all but especially northern Europeans. However, in the sixteenth century in official diplomatic documents, Russians traced Riurik's origin back to Prus, the brother of Augustus Caesar, which made Ivan a Roman.[8] Ivan never tired of invoking his "ancestors" (*praroditeli*) from the Kievan dynasty, including St. Vladimir, baptizer of Rus', and Vladimir Monomakh, who had supposedly received an imperial crown from the Byzantine emperor Constantine Monomachus (which was no more than a legendary fiction; the two men were not contemporaries).

---

6   On the differences between early modern and modern "national" identity see Istvän Zimonyi, "The Concept of Nation as Interpreted by Jenö Szüces," in *Medieval Nomads in Eastern Europe: Collected Studies*, ed. Victor Spinei (Bucharest: Editoru Romane, 2014), 355–61.
7   This chapter addresses only Russian conceptions of the Other, not foreigners' conceptions of Russians as the Other.
8   *Sbornik russkogo istoricheskogo obshchestva* (St. Petersburg: Tipografiia V. S. Balasheva, 1892), 71:231 (hereafter cited as SRIO).

Gyles Fletcher, an English diplomat who visited Muscovy during the reign of Ivan IV's son Fedor, wrote that Ivan IV boasted many times to an English goldsmith that all Russians were thieves. The goldsmith objected that Ivan was describing himself as a thief, but Ivan replied that he was not Russian, his ancestors were "Germans."[9] According to the Livonian chronicler Balthazar Russow, Ivan told Livonians that he was of German descent, of Bavarian extraction. He wished the Germans to be free from the Poles, Lithuanians, and Swedes.[10] Ivan's conception of how to "free" the Livonian Germans was to take them under Muscovite rule. Nikolai Karamzin recorded a comparable assertion from a letter in the Königsberg archive according to which Ivan also claimed to be a German of Bavarian extraction. Here he supposedly played philologist and etymologist, claiming (quite erroneously) that the word *boiar* meant "Bavarian."[11] Why Ivan would single out Bavaria is mysterious, but not significant. According to a document in the Copenhagen archives by the Danzig (Gdansk) citizen Hans Schulze, who accompanied Duke Magnus to Moscow, Ivan told Magnus that he was of "German origin and Swabian blood."[12] In the seventeenth century, the Croatian priest Iurii Krizhanich wrote that Ivan wanted "to become a Varyia and a German and a Roman or anyone else but Russian and Slav."[13] These multiple ancestries implied that to Ivan the Russians were both "us" and "them." It is no surprise that he emphasized his foreign origin in communication with foreigners, but he certainly did not hide his Roman and Scandinavian forefathers from the court elite. The Prus connection was part of official Muscovite ideology.

---

9 Lloyd E. Berry and Robert O. Crummey, eds., *Rude and Barbaous Kingdom. Russia in the Accounts of Sixteenth-Century English Voyages* (Madison: University of Wisconsin Press, 1968), 126–27.

10 Balthasar Russow, *The Chronicle of Balthasar Russow and A Forthright Rebuttal by Elert Kruse and Errors and Mistakes of Balthasar Russow by Henrich Tisenhausen*, trans. Jerry C. Smith with the collaboration of Juergen Eichhoff and William L. Urban (Madison: Baltic Studies Center, 1988), 18; on the Livonian chronicles, see Charles J. Halperin, "The Double Standard: Livonian Chronicles and Muscovite Barbarity during the Livonian War (1558–1582)," *Studia Slavica et Balcanica Petropolitana* 1 (2018): 126–47.

11 Nikolai Karamzin, *Istoriia gosudarstva rossiiskago* (St. Petersburg: Izdanie Evgeniia Evdokimova, 1892), 9:166, 30.

12 Magnus, brother of the king of Denmark, became Ivan's puppet king of Livonia; see Andres Adamson, "Magnus in Moscow," *Acta Historica Tallinensia* 16 (2011): 82; Iu. N. Shcherbatov, ed., "'Akty Kopengagenskago arkhiva, otnosiashchiesia k russkoi istorii,' Part 2: 1570–1576," *Chteniia v Imperatorskom Obshchestve istorii i drevnostei rossiiskikh pri Moskovskom universitete* 257, no. 2 (1916): 34.

13 John M. Letiche and Basil Dmytryshyn, eds., *Russian Statecraft: The Politika of Iurii Krizhanich*, (New York: Basil Blackwell, 1985), 133.

Princes and Otherness

Ivan's foreign origin did not distinguish him from all Russians. Neither Ivan nor modern historians noted that if Ivan descended from a Roman emperor's brother or a "German" chief, then so did all descendants, in practical terms, of St. Vladimir, categorized in traditional scholarship as Riurikovichi, more recently as Volodimerovichi. In Ivan's Muscovy, some of these princes belonged to the boyar aristocracy, but overwhelmingly most belonged to the gentry (*deti boiarstva*, literally "sons of the boyars").[14] Thus a major segment of the nobility (boyars and gentry) could consider "us" to be different ethnically from "them," the "lower-class" population of Muscovy, 90% of whom were peasants. However, boyar and gentry genealogies did not intrude on Ivan's claims. They discretely began with a later "Rus'" prince, not with Prus or even Riurik.

It should be added that not all "princes" in sixteenth-century Muscovy were descendants of St. Vladimir. One group of princes descended from the Lithuanian dynasty of Gedimin. Tatar princes were not Chinggisids, who bore imperial (tsar, tsarevich), not princely, titles, but aristocrats who held the rank of *beg* or *bii* in Turkic.

Despite these differences in ethnic origin, some historians have treated all princely boyars as a social and political faction (given the prominence of kinship in Muscovy, what was "social" and what was "political" cannot always be disentangled), which made non-princely boyars the Other.[15] In practice princely and non-princely boyars intermarried and collaborated politically, and princely boyars did not show any greater affection for princely gentry than non-princely boyars.

Aristocrats and Otherness

Some historians have treated sub-sets of boyars of different ethnic origins as coherent political factions. Mikhail Krom notes that the dying Grand Prince

---

14 The word *dvorianstvo* did not acquire its modern meaning in Russian of "gentry" until the seventeenth century, when it translated the Polish *szlachta*. In Ivan's time, dvorianstvo meant members of the Royal Court or Household (*dvor*).

15 Dividing the court elite into princely and non–princely factions was widespread among Soviet historians of Ivan's reign, including Ruslan Skrynnikov (see Charles J. Halperin, "Ruslan Skrynnikov on Ivan IV," in *Dubitando. Essays in Culture and History in Honor of Donald Ostrowski*, ed. Brian J. Boeck, Russell E. Martin, and Daniel Rowland [Bloomington: Slavica Publishers, 2012], 193–207).

Vasilii III, Ivan IV's father, had to justify the presence of his wife's uncle, Prince Mikhail Glinskii, of Gediminid ancestry, among the executors of his testament. Evidently, Krom infers, Lithuanian[16] princes[17] inspired opposition from the old Muscovite elite as "foreigners" (*chuzhaki*), the word in the narrative that means "of foreign origin," the Other. The flight across the border to Lithuania of two chuzhaki of Lithuanian origin, Princes Bel'skii and Liatskii, Krom concludes, was used as an excuse for a major assault on Lithuanian immigrants, including their arrest and disgrace. Vasilii III's widow, Grand Princess Elena Glinskaia, took power by sacrificing her relatives to her allies among the "native" Muscovite elite.[18] Certainly Glinskii was labeled a "foreigner" and his relatives suffered from his political defeat, but that would have happened and did happen to relatives of "old Muscovite boyars" in comparable circumstances. There is no evidence that all Gediminid princes were repressed, let alone that they were targeted for their ethnic origin.

Donald Ostrowski ascribes great importance to the high percentage of elite families of Tatar origin, or who at least claimed Tatar origin in their family genealogies, which he treats as reliable.[19] These clans transmitted the "Tatar principle" to Muscovy embodied in the oprichnina, which Ivan used to fight the growing influence of the Russian Orthodox Church in Muscovite politics. One of the leaders of the *oprichnina* was Prince Mikhail Cherkasskii, of Tatar origin. Ivan invited Germans to join the *oprichnina* because they owed no allegiance to the Russian Orthodox Church. Ivan's seventh wife was Mariia Nagaia, of Tatar descent, chosen by Ivan for his uncanonical marriage to disrespect the Russian Orthodox Church.[20]

As was the case with boyars of Gediminid origin, it cannot be shown that Russian boyars and gentry of actual or fictitious Tatar origin acted as a coherent social group of "us" who defined themselves against an Other of boyars and gentry of different ethnic origins. The "Tatar" nature of the *oprichnina* is a

---

16 Here as below "Lithuanian" denotes subjects of the Grand Duchy of Lithuania, not necessarily ethnic Lithuanians. However, Gediminids were of course ethnic Lithuanians.

17 Krom uses the word *kniazhata*, whose meaning is less clear than its translation. No Muscovite source from Ivan's reign ever identifies a specific prince as a member of the kniazhata, so whether Glinskii or any other Gediminid belonged to the kniazhata can only be inferred.

18 Mikhail Krom, *"Vdovstvuiushchee tsarstvo": Politicheskii krizis v Rossii 30–40-kh godov XVI veka* (Moscow: Novoe literaturnoe obozrenie, 2010), 47, 103, 256–68.

19 Vásáry also evaluates the reliability of the legends of the Tatar origins of elite clans favorably (see Istvän Vásáry, "Claims of Tatar Descent in the Muscovite Elite of the 14th–16th Centuries," in *Mesto Rossii v Evzrasii* [Budapest: Magyar ruszisztika Interzet, 2001], 101–13.

20 Donald Ostrowski, *Muscovy and the Mongols: Cross-Cultural Influences on the Steppe Frontier* (Cambridge: Cambridge University Press, 1998), 21, 56–58, 193, 197.

topic for a different discussion, but for now it should be mentioned that Ivan let several monasteries join the *oprichnina*, that only four Germans (out of at least one thousand, or perhaps as many as six thousand *oprichniki*) joined the *oprichnina*, that Prince Mikhail Cherkasskii was a Tatar only on his mother's side and his primary identity, discussed below, was as a Kabarda Circassian, and that Mariia Nagaia's Tatar origin is not clearly established.

Prince Mikhail Cherkasskii was Ivan IV's brother-in-law, brother of Ivan's second wife, Tsaritsa Mariia Cherkasskaia. He and several relatives from the North Caucasus entered Muscovite service. Unlike the case with elite members from the Gediminids and "Tatars," the continued ties of the Cherkasskiis to their "old country" can be documented. Whether the Muscovite elite treated the Cherkasskiis as the Other, on the other hand, is less obvious, but the Muscovite court does seem to have been more than willing to exploit their Caucasus connections. The Cherkasskiis were both "us" and "them," Russian princes and Circassian murzas.[21]

It was common in sixteenth-century Europe for aristocracies to claim foreign origin. Many Russian and gentry clans claimed a foreign, often generic "German," immigrant as their ancestor in genealogical books. How many of these claims were no more than legendary is beside the point, because foreignness—if you will, Otherness—was a sought-after social marker.[22]

There was a hierarchy within the aristocratic boyar class too. Boyars who served the grand prince and later tsar of Moscow occupied the top rung. Beneath them stood boyars of his wife and blood relatives, including collateral appanage uncles and nephews. Boyars of the metropolitan, bishops, and monasteries all stood lower in society than boyars of the ruling family.[23] Gentry were divided between members of the royal household (*dvor*) and nonmembers, as well as between all gentry of the royal family and gentry who served ecclesiastical lords. Little evidence survives to trace these intra-class concepts of "us" and "them."

---

21 Paul Bushkovitch, "Princes Cherkasskii or Circassian Murzas. The Kabardians in the Russian boyar elite 1560–1700," *Cahiers du monde russe* 45 (2004): 9–29.

22 "Rodoslovnaia kniga po trem spiskam," *Vremennik Obshchestva istori i drevnostei rossiiskikh* 19 (1851), 1–266; M. E. Bychkova, *Rodoslovnye knigi XVI–XVII vv kak istoricheskii istochnik* (Moscow: Nauka, 1975).

23 Charles J. Halperin, "Hierarchy of Hierarchies: Muscovite Society during the Reign of Ivan IV," *Russian History* 44 (2017): 570–84. Such graded social distinctions also existed among the clerks and bureaucrats, merchants, and peasants.

The Elite and Otherness

All members of Muscovite society belonged to a social class defined by the fine for dishonoring a member of that class. However, the boyars and members of the upper gentry were distinguished from the crowd by belonging to the Precedence system. No one could serve as a subordinate to or sit at a lower seat in a ceremony than a member of another clan of lesser "honor." Thus, each clan treated members of all other clans as Other, but all clans included in the Precedence system also considered all servitors outside it as the Other. Precedence was both exclusive and inclusive.[24]

Finally, oprichniki—mostly gentry but also boyars—were socially distinct from and outranked members of their "original" social classes and everyone else. Oprichniki served Ivan's separate appanage, wore black clothes, and road black horses with dogs' heads and brooms on their necks to symbolize that they were the dogs of the tsar and would sweep treason from the land. They took an oath not to socialize with nonmembers of the oprichnina, people who belonged to the "land" (*zemlia* or *zemshchina*), even if those people were their own parents. Some oprichniki belonged to a pseudo-monastic brotherhood at the sometime capital of the oprichnina, Aleksandrovskaia sloboda. To the oprichniki, "us" were the oprichniki, and "them" were everyone else in Muscovy. To be sure, this concept of Otherness lasted only as long as the oprichnina did, from 1565 to 1572. Arguably the oprichniki "us" was the most politicized social identity in Muscovy during Ivan's reign.[25]

Religion and Otherness

Religious identity was paramount in sixteenth-century Muscovy, but "us-them" religious distinction went far beyond a simple dichotomy. Bogatyrev explains that Muscovite diplomatic correspondence "condemned other Christian

---

24 Nancy Shields Kollmann, *By Honor Bound. State and Society in Early Modern Russia* (Ithaca: Cornell University Press, 1999).

25 Charles J. Halperin, "Did Ivan IV's *Oprichniki* Carry Dogs' Heads on Their Horses?" *Canadian-American Slavic Studies* 46 (2012): 40–67; Valerie A. Kivelson, "How Bad Was Ivan the Terrible? The Oprichnik Oath and Satanic Spells in Foreigners' Accounts," in *Seeing Muscovy Anew: Politics—Institutions—Culture: Essays in Honor of Nancy Shields Kollmann*, ed. Valerie A. Kivelson, Michael Flier, Daniel Rowland, and Erika Monahan Downs (Bloomington: Slavica Publishers, 2017), 67–84.

confessions as heresies."[26] In the middle of the sixteenth century Muslim diplomatic personnel lost the right to enter the Kremlin through the parvis of the Dormition Cathedral (*Uspenskii sobor*), which became the exclusive privilege of non-Russian Orthodox Christians. "Excessive use of Christian rhetoric" in diplomatic exchanges created a "virtual common religious identity" that legitimized proposed alliances with Poland-Lithuania, the Holy Roman Empire, or even the Papacy against Muslims, either Tatars[27] or Ottoman Turks. Like Europeans, Russians consented to the practices and rites of other Christian confessions that were common to their own practice, thus mitigating, but not removing religious differences.[28]

Bogatyrev considers such blurring of the religious divide among competing Christian confessions as pragmatic, which it certainly was, but I would consider it more than expediency. Ivan's declaration to the Holy Roman Emperor that feuds among Christian rulers permitted Muslims to shed Christian blood was not totally insincere.[29] The religious Other was defined relatively as well as absolutely. Of course, only Russian Orthodox Christians, living in Russia under (after Ivan's coronation in 1547) the rule of a Russian Orthodox Tsar, were "true" Christians, and adherents of other confessions or faiths were the religious Other. But some were more Other than others. We can illustrate the Russian conception of religious Otherness as a series of nine concentric circles (see fig. 1).[30]

Russian Orthodox Christianity occupied the innermost circle, the only totally "true" Christians. The nearer another circle to the core, the more it resembled Russian Orthodox Christianity, and the less Other it was. The outermost circle was religiously without any redeeming traits. The Ruthenian (East Slavs living in Poland-Lithuania, emerging Ukrainians and Belarusians) Orthodox Christians of the second circle were suspect religiously because they were under non-Orthodox, Catholic rule, but Russians carefully distinguished

---

26 Bogatyrev, "Diplomats and Believers. Herberstein and Cross-Confessional Contacts in the Sixteenth Century," 227–30, quotes 227, 228.

27 For further discussion of the interplay of Tatar and Muslim identities, see Maksim Moiseev, "The Image of the Other: The Perception of Tatars by Russian Intellectuals and Clerks in the Fifteenth to Seventeenth Centuries" in this volume.

28 Bogatyrev, "Diplomats and Believers. Herberstein and Cross-Confessional Contacts in the Sixteenth Century," 227–30, quotes 227, 228.

29 *Pamiatniki diplomaticheskikh snoshenii drevnei Rossii s derzhavami inostrannymi*, (St. Petersburg: Izdanie II otdelenia EIV kantselarii, 1851), 768.

30 I wish to express my sincerest appreciation to Richard Hamlin for preparing this illustration. Note that in terms of relative population size, Illustration 1 is totally reversed. The largest Muscovite religious population segment was Russian Orthodox, which occupies the smallest circle in the Illustration, and the smallest (at zero, it could not be any smaller) religious population segment, Jews, occupies the largest circle.

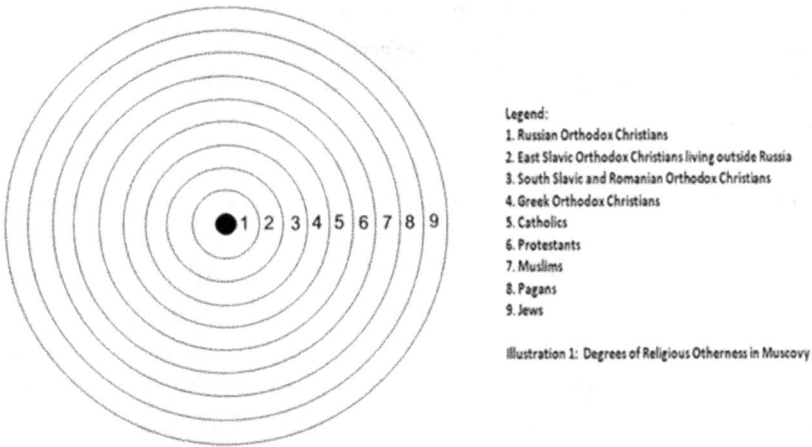

Legend:
1. Russian Orthodox Christians
2. East Slavic Orthodox Christians living outside Russia
3. South Slavic and Romanian Orthodox Christians
4. Greek Orthodox Christians
5. Catholics
6. Protestants
7. Muslims
8. Pagans
9. Jews

Illustration 1: Degrees of Religious Otherness in Muscovy

FIGURE 1.

between diplomatic personnel from Poland-Lithuania who followed the "Latin" or "Polish" "law" (*zakon*), meaning the Catholic confession, or Protestants, from those who were Orthodox. The head of the Russian Orthodox Church—the metropolitan—could shake the hand of a Catholic or Protestant "Lithuanian" but could not bless him if he followed the Roman Law.[31] Metropolitan Makarii entertained a private petition from an Orthodox envoy from Poland-Lithuania, although he could, as circumstances dictated, also communicate with members of the Lithuanian Royal Council (*Rada*), including the Catholic bishop of Vilnius.[32] Orthodox Ruthenians (and other Orthodox Christians, see below) were permitted to enter Russian Orthodox churches and listen to the liturgy. Catholics could not be allowed to do so, but also might not want to do so. There was a diplomatic dance when Muscovite diplomats wanted to curry favor with Antonio Possevino, the Jesuit Papal envoy sent to Eastern Europe to negotiate an end to hostilities between Russia and Poland-Lithuania over Livonia, by letting him attend an Orthodox liturgy, but Possevino was too bigoted to do so.[33] Protestants were in principle similarly barred from Russian Orthodox churches. When Danish Duke Magnus, Ivan IV's puppet "king" of Livonia, was married to Ivan's first cousin once removed, the daughter of Ivan's cousin Prince Vladimir

---

31 SRIO (1887), 59:64, 560.
32 Charles J. Halperin, "Metropolitan Makarii and Muscovite Court Politics during the Reign of Ivan IV," *Russian Review* 73 (2014): 462.
33 Antonio Possevino, *The Moscovia of Antonio Possevino*, trans. Hugh F. Graham (Pittsburgh: University of Pittsburgh Center for International Studies, 1977), 15, 77–78, 179.

Andreevich Staritskii, Magnus's Lutheran representative had to stand outside the Russian Orthodox church during the ceremony.

Other Orthodox Christians from the Balkans, Serbs, Bulgarians, and Romanians (Wallachians, Moldavians) occupied the third circle. These peoples shared the Slavonic ritual and Muslim Ottoman rule or subordination. Ivan IV was in regular contact with the Serbian Hilandar Monastery on Mt. Athos. He permitted Hilandar monks to make fund-raising tours of Russia and he sent alms to Athos.[34] Ivan granted a refugee Moldavian (called "Wallachian") *voevode* an appanage in Russia.[35] Obviously these Orthodox Christians were perceived as very close to Ruthenian Orthodox, but I have separated them in part because of their greater geographic distance from Russia and their Muslim rather than Catholic overlord, and in part because they spoke languages that the Moscow court did not label "Rus'" (discussed below).

Greeks filled the fourth circle. Of course, Rus' and Russian Orthodox Christianity derived from Greek/Byzantine Orthodox Christianity, but Ivan took extreme umbrage when Possevino, trying to persuade Ivan to accept the 1438 Union of Florence between the Byzantine and Catholic Churches, called his faith "Greek." "I believe in the Christian faith, not the Greek faith" he declared vehemently.[36] The Greeks were respected but not always trusted. They did, after all, live under Muslim rule. The Greek translator Maksim, a monk on Mount Athos, who was sent to Muscovy under Vasilii III, knew too much Renaissance philology for his own good and was convicted of heresy when he "corrected" the ecclesiastical works he was editing. Again, Greek Orthodox prelates were welcome in Muscovy and received alms. Ivan did turn to the Patriarch of Constantinople for recognition of his coronation as tsar, which did not turn out exactly as he planned.[37]

The fifth circle contained Catholics. When he wanted to, Ivan could seek common ground with Catholics by fulminating against Protestant heresy and "Lutheran" iconoclasm.[38] Ivan in effect seduced the pope to send Possevino to him by feigning interest in an anti-Ottoman crusade. As a rule, Catholics were

---

34 M. Dmitrijevich, "Dokumenti koji se tichu odnosa izmeću srpske tsrkve i Rusije v XVI veku," *Spomenik, Srpska kralevska akademija* 39 (1903): 16–42.

35 K. V. Baranov and T. B. Solov'eva, "Novye dokumenty o prebyvanii v Rossii valashskogo voevoda Bogdana Aleksandrovicha," *Russkii diplomatarii* 4 (1998): 159–65.

36 Possevino, *The Moscovia of Antonio Possevino*, 173; Peter Nitsche, 'Nicht an die Griechen glaube ich, sondern an Christus'. Russen und Griechen in Selbstverständnis des Moskauer Staates an der Schwelle der Neuzeit (Dusseldorf: Droste, 1991).

37 The "Greek" issue became much more prominent in Muscovy during the seventeenth century in connection with the Nikonian reform and the schism in the Russian Orthodox Church, to the Nikonians Greek Orthodox became less Other, to the *raskolniki*, more Other.

38 SRIO (1892), 71:239, 743–44.

not permitted in Russian Orthodox churches. Indeed, they were not permitted to build a church in Moscow or hold public services.

Inconsistently, the Protestants of the sixth circle were permitted to build churches in Moscow, or at least in its outskirts. Although Russians called all Protestants "Lutherans," Russian actions might reflect some appreciation of differences among them. The Livonian Lutherans were the enemy (along with Livonian Catholics), but Anglicans from the English Muscovy Company were valued trading partners and Ivan never slandered their faith. In theory Ivan's opposition to all Protestants, evinced in his debate with Jan Rokyta of the Polish and Czech Brethren, knew no limits,[39] but practice was not as consistent.[40]

For Ivan's reign the relative religious otherness of Catholics and Protestants remained ambiguous.[41] In the seventeenth century, some inconsistency remained, but the level of anti-Catholic animosity escalated monumentally as a result of the Time of Troubles.[42]

Muslims in the seventh circle are the first non-Christians in the illustration. Rus' and Russians had no great interest in Muslim theology,[43] but even the most rabid Russian Orthodox anti-Muslim clerics knew a great deal about the Muslim religious establishment in neighboring states such as the Kazan Khanate before its conquest in 1552[44] and were willing to overlook the Muslim faith of

---

39 Valerie Tumins, *Tsar Ivan IV's Reply to Jan Rokyta* (Berlin: de Gruyter, 1971); Nikoletta Marchalis, *Liutor' izhe liut'. Prenie o vere tsaria Ivana Groznogo s pastorom Rokytoi* (Moscow: Iazyki slavianskoi kultury, 2009).

40 I suspect that Russians would have equated Armenians with Protestants as heretics and schismatics, but there isn't enough evidence from Ivan's reign to make a case. In 1558 Ivan's emissary lied to the Patriarch of Alexandria that Ivan did not permit Muslims and Armenians to have dwellings in Muscovy, which Muslims certainly did, and Armenians probably did, at least temporary dwellings, in Astrakhan' or even Moscow when they came to Russia for commerce on their own or as representatives of the Sultan ("Poslanie tsaria Ivana Vasil'evicha k Aleksandriiskomu patriarkhu Ioakim s kuptsom Vasil'em Pozniakovym i Khozhdenie kuptsa Pozniakova v Ierusalim i po inym sviatym mestam 1558 goda," *Chteniia v Imperatorskom obshchestve istorii i drevnostei rossisskikh pri Moskovskom universitete*, v. 128, book I, I–XII, 1–32).

41 When convenient, as in tales about the campaign of Stephen Batory against Pskov, Catholics and Protestants could be treated collectively as heretics, e.g. non-Orthodox Christians (Endre Sashalmi, "The Image of the Enemy: Poles and Lithuanians in Russian Literary and Chancery Sources of the Late Sixteenth and Early Seventeenth Centuries," *Specimina nova. Pars prima. Section Mediaevalis* 1, no. 4 [2007]: 42–45).

42 Serhii Plokhy, *The Origins of the Slavic Nations: Premodern Identities in Russia, Ukraine and Belarus* (Cambridge: Cambridge University Press, 2006), 148–49, 152, 158, 223.

43 Paul Bushkovitch, "Orthodoxy and Islam in Russia 988–1725," *Forschungen zur osteuropäischen Geschichte* 76 (2010): 117–43.

44 Charles J. Halperin, "The Muscovite Attitude Toward the Outside World During the Reign of Ivan IV," in *Aktual'nye problem istorii i kul'tury tatarskogo naroda. Materialy k uchebnym v chest' iubileiia akademica AN RT M. A. Usmanova*, ed. D. A. Mustafina and M. S. Gatlin (Kazan: Izdatel'stvo MOiN RT, 2010), 188–201.

loyal servitors of Moscow.[45] Ivan insisted to the Ottoman Sultan that Muslims were free to practice their faith in his realm,[46] but boasted to the king of Poland, Holy Roman Emperor, and pope that he had replaced mosques in Kazan with churches. His professions of agnosticism to a Nogay leader on whether Islam or Christianity was superior, that different faiths can be friends, that Christianity forbids the use of coercion to achieve conversion, that God would decide whose faith was correct "in the future" (hereafter? or the future on earth?) might have been no more than diplomatic spin but prove Ivan's familiarity with such arguments for (sometimes relative) tolerance.[47]

I have assigned "pagans," that is, animists, practitioners of native religions in contrast to the three Mediterranean "world" religions, to the eighth circle. They were objects of conquest and conversion but no threat to Russian Orthodox Christianity. I have deliberately rated paganism less Other than Judaism, the ninth and outermost "other" circle, to make a point. In terms of religion Jews were more Other and any other "Other." Ivan IV ruled animists, in the middle Volga River region or in Siberia, without compunction, but he would not let Jewish merchants from Poland-Lithuania, despite prior practice, befoul his realm, and when his armies conquered Polatsk in 1563 he offered its Jews the choice of conversion or death. The Jewish community chose death, so instead of baptism they were drowned.[48] No Jew could step on Russian soil and continue breathing, as long as he was a Jew. The extreme Otherness of Judaism, in Ivan's eyes, forbade even their temporary presence in his realm.[49] Ivan could not

45 Janet Martin, "Religious Ideology and Chronicle Depictions of Muslims in 16th Century Muscovy," in *The New Muscovite Cultural History: A Collection in Honor of Daniel B. Rowland*, ed. Valerie Kivelson et al. (Bloomington: Slavica Publishers, 2009), 285–99; Janet Martin, "The Mongol Elite in Muscovy, Rhetoric and Reality: The Portrayal of Tsar Shah Ali in *Degrees of the Royal Genealogy*," in *The Book of Degrees of the Royal Genealogy and the Genesis of Russian Historical Consciousness*, ed. Gail Lenhoff and Ann M. Kleimola (Bloomington: Slavica Publishers, 2011), 217–29.

46 George Vernadsky, *The Tsardom of Moscow, 1547–1689* (New Haven: Yale University Press, 1969), 5.

47 *Pamiatniki diplomaticheskikh snoshenii drevnei Rossii s derzhavami inostrannymi*, 317–19; Gary Hamburg, "Religious Toleration in Russian Thought, 1520–1825," *Kritika: Explorations in Russian and Eurasian History* 13, no. 3 (2012): 515–19.

48 SRIO (1895), 59:341–42; N. N. Pokrovskii and G. D. Lenkhoff, eds., *Stepennaia kniga tsarskogo rodosloviia po drevneishim spiskam. Teksty i kommentarii* (Moscow: Iazyki slavianskoi kultury, 2008), 2:388.

49 Isaiah Gruber, "Russia, Jews and Hebrews: The Makings of Ambivalence," *Australian Journal of Jewish Studies* 25 (2011): 119–52. Because of geographic expansion, in the seventeenth century Russia had much more difficulty excluding all Jews from entering, let alone residing in, its territory (see David A. Frick, *Kith, Kin and Neighbors: Communities and Confessions in Seventeenth-Century Wilno* (Ithaca: Cornell University Press, 2013), 290–321; Isaiah Gruber, "Jewish History in Patriarchal Muscovy: Toward an Understanding of Old and New

have barred Jews from Muscovy if he had no conception of them as a religious category.

Bogatyrev may have underestimated the extent to which an "all-Christian" identity in Russia was artificially inflated in diplomatic correspondence. Descriptions by Russian diplomats of society and government in Poland-Lithuania, Sweden, England, and the Ottoman Empire suggest a sub-text that Russia was more like non-Orthodox Christian countries than the Muslim Ottoman Empire.[50] Of course this "soft" attitude toward non-Orthodox Christians was manipulated, but it had some genuine roots. The concept of relative religious Otherness expresses this phenomenon in a more nuanced way than dismissing it as sheer opportunism. Its expression was opportunistic, but not entirely forced.

Ethnicity and Otherness

Ethnically, as Paul Bushkovitch emphatically declares, sixteenth-century Russians did not confuse themselves with other East Slavs. Muscovy was Rus', the Russian Land (*russkaia zemlia*), or Rossiia. The East Slavs who lived in Poland-Lithuania were "Lithuanians" (*Litva*) or Cossacks (*Cherkassy*).[51] When Ivan took Polatsk he thought he was conquering the people and land of Litva, his patrimony like Kazan and Livonia, but not Rus'. Of course, Ivan was aware of the common past in Kievan Rus' shared by Polatsk and Moscow, that the people of Polatsk were closer to Russians than Poles, Germans, or Tatars, but "Russians" meant subjects of the ruler of Moscow. "Russians" carried a simple ethnographic meaning.[52]

Bushkovitch's conclusions illustrate very well that the ethnic concept of "Russians" was hardly "simple." Litva was definitely not an ethnic term but a

---

Jerusalem," in *Russia's Early Modern Orthodox Patriarchate: Foundations and Mitred Loyalty 1589–1647*, ed. Kevin M. Kain and David Goldfrank (Washington, DC: Academica Press, 2020), 71–90. I wish to express my appreciation to Isaiah Gruber for providing me with a copy of his 2011 article.

50 Charles J. Halperin, "Russia Between East and West: Diplomatic Reports During the Reign of Ivan IV," in *Saluting Aron Gurevich*, ed. Y. Mazour-Matusevich and A. Korros (Leiden: Brill, 2010), 81–103.

51 Confusingly, this is also the term for "Circassians."

52 Paul Bushkovitch, "The Formation of National Consciousness in Early Modern Russia," *Harvard Ukrainian Studies* 10 (1986): 355–56. For an argument based upon visual evidence that Lithuanians were "us" to the Russians see in this volume Jaakko Lehtovirta, "The Depiction of 'Us' and 'Them' in the Illuminated Codex of 1560s–1570s."

political term for residents of the Grand Duchy of Lithuania. "Rus'" was and was not an ethnic term. Not everyone who lived in "Russia" was ethnically Rus'. Narrative sources of course refer constantly to *russkie liudi*, Russian people. For example, a Muscovite envoy to Poland-Lithuania announced that "Russians" (*russkie liudi*) now lived in Kazan, Astrakhan, and Polatsk since their Russian conquest. Diplomatic personnel were instructed to prevent Polish-Lithuanian representatives in Moscow from carrying on conversations with Russians (*russkie*) or Germans.[53] But Tatars and various Finno-Ugric subject peoples of the middle Volga River like Cheremis' and of Siberia like Ostiaks were described by their own ethnic names; they were conspicuously not "Russians." Even Tatars who converted to Russian Orthodox Christianity did not "become" Russians but "Newly Baptized People" (*Novokshcheny*).[54] Foreign enslaved prisoners of war living in Russia were always described according to the native ethnic or political identity, including German, Pole, "Lithuanian," and Swede. Ros/ Rossiia was used more-or-less interchangeably with Rus', but with an additional imperial or ecclesiastical tint.[55] Moreover, some Litva actually resided in the or rather "a" "Rus' Land." Epistles to King Sigismund Augustus of Poland in the names of Princes I. D. Bel'skii and I. F. Mstislavskii, whose authorship is usually attributed to Ivan IV, responding to an invitation to defect, included in Sigismund's titles that he ruled the "Rus' Land" (*russkaia zemlia*). This was a translation of "terra Russiae" meaning Galicia, the term used in Latin by thirteenth-century Galician Rus' princes which was acquired by the Polish crown when it annexed Galicia.[56] Therefore in these epistles Russians implicitly acknowledged Poland's claim to have inherited the most potent political myth of Kievan Rus', the Rus' Land.[57]

Some Litva, therefore, shared Orthodox Christianity with the Russians, and the Russians were sensitive to identifying them and then accommodating that common religious heritage. In addition, there was a linguistic affinity.

53 SRIO (1892), 71:116, 154.

54 Janet Martin, "The Novokshcheny of Novgorod: Assimilation in the 16th Century," *Central Asian Survey* 9, no. 2 (1990): 13–38.

55 Charles J. Halperin, "*Rus'* versus *Ros* in Ivan IV's Muscovy," *Slavica*, no. 4 (2017): 367–75.

56 Dmitrii S. Likhachev and Ia. S. Lur'e, eds., *Poslaniia Ivana Groznogo* (Moscow–Leningrad: AN SSSR, 1951), 245, 253.

57 Charles J. Halperin, "The Concept of the Russian Land from the Ninth to the Fourteenth Century," *Russian History* 2 (1975): 29–38; Charles J. Halperin, "The Concept of the *ruskaia zemlia* and Medieval National Consciousness from the Tenth to the Fifteenth Centuries," *Nationalities Papers* 8 (1980): 75–86.

Language and Otherness

The chancellery language of the Grand Duchy of Lithuania was called the "Rus' language" (*russkii iazyk*) there. Linguists call it Belarusian. Ivan allowed prisoners from Poland-Lithuania to meet some Polish-Lithuanian envoys if they agreed to speak "the Rus' language, not Polish" (*russkim iazykom, ne polskim*). Ivan assured envoy Lithuanian Jan Chodkiewicz that he could understand Chodkiewicz's "Rus' language" (*russkii iazyk*) even with its admixture of "Polish phrases" (*polskie poslovitsy*).[58] In these instances "the Rus' language" may be translated as "Ruthenian." Of course, the liturgical language of the Orthodox East Slavs of Poland-Lithuania was Slavonic, comprehensible enough for Russians to import Slavonic books from Lithuania, like the Ostrih Bible, and Ruthenians to import Slavonic books from Russia. The lack of an impenetrable linguistic barrier between chancery Russian and Slavonic further facilitated this linguistic communication across the Lithuanian-Russian border.[59]

The distinction between Ruthenians and Russians, while very real, was also very qualified, ethnically and religiously. One wonders if the Ruthenians living in Polatsk when it was under Russian occupation from 1563 to 1579 were not called "russkie." The East Slavs living in Poland-Lithuania were the least Other of any of the foreign Others in Ivan IV's time.

Conclusion

The tendency in discussions of Otherness is to think in dualistic terms, "us" versus "them," and to minimize any qualifications that impugn contrastive simplicity. In a confessional age such as the sixteenth century, this proclivity toward Manichean concepts of "us" versus "them" manifested itself most strongly in religion, including in Russia. However, the universe was more complicated than that. Otherness could be genealogical, ethnic, religious, social, or linguistic. Overlapping and relative degrees of Otherness permitted graduated and flexible articulations of "us" versus "them."

Ivan IV claimed to be both Russian and non-Russian genealogically, but even his non-Russian personae did not distinguish him from the entire population of Russia, because all other Volodimerovich princes shared his Roman,

---

58 SRIO (1892), 71:281–82, 289.
59 Charles J. Halperin, "The 'Russian' and 'Slavonic' Languages in Sixteenth–Century Muscovy," *Slavonic and East European Review* 85 (2007): 1–24.

Varangian, or German origin. Among the nobility claims of foreign origin were valued. What they meant concretely in terms of identity is not easy to establish. Precedence compelled each aristocratic clan to treat all other aristocratic clans as Others, but also to treat all clans within the Precedence system as "us," versus the Other of all clans devoid of noble birth. Ethnically not everyone living in Russia was Russian, and Orthodox East Slavs living in Poland-Lithuania, by religious and linguistic criteria, were the least "other" of any "Others." Most importantly, the concept of religious Otherness was deceptively simple. Russian Orthodox Christianity was the only pure and true faith, but other Orthodox, Catholic, and Protestant Christians could be more-or-less Other depending upon circumstances, and allowances could be made even for Muslims. "Pagans" were the Other but nonthreatening. The only unqualified religious Other, by the middle of the sixteenth century, was Judaism. No allowance was made whatsoever for ameliorating or qualifying Jewish Otherness. Ruthenians, Serbs, Bulgarians, Romanians, and Greeks were still Orthodox, even if subject to non-Orthodox rulers. Catholics and Protestants were still Christians, even if schismatics or heretics, who might be tolerated as allies or even as foreign residents if they served a necessary function in Russia. Even Muslims might be succored abroad for national security reasons, like the Ottoman Turks, or at home, for Tatars who served the Russian Orthodox Tsar faithfully. But Russians cut no slack whatsoever for Jews. Ivan the Terrible forbade Jewish merchants and doctors, who had previously been allowed to transit to Russia, to enter the country. He would not allow any Jew to live under his sovereignty. The alternative to conversion to Christianity was death. In the case of Judaism, there were no degrees of Otherness and no mitigating circumstances. The Russians had difficulty maintaining such an absolute ban on Jewish Others in the seventeenth century, which only foreshadowed what happened after the partitions of Poland made it impossible to avoid Jews residing in the Russian Empire, but that is another story.

Works Cited

Adamson, Andres. "Magnus in Moscow." *Acta Historica Tallinensia* 16 (2011): 31–61.

Baranov, K. V., and T. B. Solov'eva. "Novye dokumenty o prebyvanii v Rossii valashskogo voevody Bogdana Aleksandrovicha." *Russkii diplomatarii* 4 (1998): 159–65.

Berry, Lloyd E., and Robert O. Crummey, ed. *Rude and Barbarous Kingdom: Russia in the Accounts of Sixteenth-Century English Voyages.* Madison: University of Wisconsin Press, 1968.

Bogatyrev, Sergei. "Diplomats and Believers. Herberstein and Cross-Confessional Contacts in the Sixteenth Century." In *450 Jahre Sigismund von Herbersteins Rerum Moscovitiarum Commentarii 149–1599.* Edited by Frank Kämpfer and Reinhard Frötschner, 215–34. Wiesbaden: Harrassowitz Verlag, 2002.

Bushkovitch, Paul. "The Formation of National Consciousness in Early Modern Russia." *Harvard Ukrainian Studies* 10 (1986): 355–76.

———. "Princes Cherkasskii or Circassian Murzas: The Kabardians in the Russian boyar elite 1560–1700." *Cahiers du monde russe* 45 (2004): 9–29.

———. "Orthodoxy and Islam in Russia 988–1725." *Forschungen zur osteuropäischen Geschichte* 76 (2010): 117–43.

Bychkova, M. E. *Rodoslovnye knigi XVI–XVII vv kak istoricheskii istochnik.* Moscow: Nauka, 1975.

Dmitrijevich, M., "Dokumenti koji se tichu odnosa izmeću srpske tsrkve i Rusije v XVI veku." *Spomenik, Srpska kralevska akademija* 39 (1903): 16–42.

Frick, David A. *Kith, Kin and Neighbors: Communities and Confessions in Seventeenth-Century Wilno.* Ithaca: Cornell University Press, 2013.

Gruber, Isaiah. "Russia, Jews and Hebrews: The Makings of Ambivalence." *Australian Journal of Jewish Studies* 25 (2011): 119–52.

———. "Jewish History in Patriarchal Muscovy: Toward an Understanding of Old and New Jerusalem." In *Moscow's Early Modern Orthodox Patriarchate: Foundations and Mitred Royalty, 1589–1647.* Edited by Kevin M. Kain and David Goldfrank, 71–116. Washington: Academica, 2020.

Halperin, Charles J. "The Concept of the Russian Land from the Ninth to the Fourteenth Century." *Russian History* 2 (1975): 29–38.

———. "The Concept of the *ruskaia zemlia* and Medieval National Consciousness from the Tenth to the Fifteenth Centuries." *Nationalities Papers* 8 (1980): 75–86.

———. "The 'Russian' and 'Slavonic' Languages in Sixteenth-Century Muscovy." *Slavonic and East European Review* 85 (2007): 1–24.

———. "The Muscovite Attitude Toward the Outside World During the Reign of Ivan IV." In *Stepennaia kniga: Aktual'nye problemy istorii i kul'tury tatarskogo naroda. Materialy k uchebnym: v chest' iubileiia akademika AN RT M. A.*

Usmanova. Edited by D. A. Mustafina and M. S. Gatin, compiled by I. A. Giliazov, 188–201. Kazan: Izdatel'stvo MOiN RT, 2010.

———. "Russia Between East and West: Diplomatic Reports During the Reign of Ivan IV." In *Saluting Aaron Gurevich: Essays in History, Literature and Other Subjects.* Edited by Yelena Mazour-Matusevich and Alexandra S. Korros, 81–103. Leiden: Brill, 2010.

———. "Ruslan Skrynnikov on Ivan IV." In *Dubitando: Essays in Culture and History in Honor of Donald Ostrowski.* Edited by Brian J. Boeck, Russell E. Martin, and Daniel B. Rowland, 193–207. Bloomington: Slavica Publishers, 2012.

———. "Did Ivan IV's *Oprichniki* Carry Dogs' Heads on Their Horses?" *Canadian-American Slavic Studies* 46 (2012): 40–67.

———. "Metropolitan Makarii and Muscovite Court Politics during the Reign of Ivan IV." *Russian Review* 73 (2014): 447–64.

———. "Hierarchy of Hierarchies: Muscovite Society during the Reign of Ivan IV." *Russian History* 44 (2017): 570–84.

———. "*Rus'* versus *Ros* in Ivan IV's Muscovy." *Slavia* 86 (2017): 367–75.

———. "The Double Standard: Livonian Chronicles and Muscovite Barbarity During the Livonian War (1558–1582)." *Studia Slavica et Balcanica Petropolitana* 1, no. 23 (2018): 126–47.

———. *Ivan the Terrible: Free to Reward and Free to Punish.* Pittsburgh: University of Pittsburgh Press, 2019.

Hamburg, Gary M. "Religious Toleration in Russian Thought, 1520–1825." *Kritika: Explorations in Russian and Eurasian History* 13 (2012): 515–59.

Karamzin, N. M. *Istoriia gosudarstva rossiiskago.* Vol. 9. St. Petersburg: Izdanie Evg. Evdokimova, 1892.

Kivelson, Valerie A. "How Bad Was Ivan the Terrible? The Oprichnik Oath and Satanic Spells in Foreigners' Accounts." In *Seeing Muscovy Anew: Politics— Institutions—Culture, In Honor of Nancy Shields Kollmann.* Edited by Valerie A. Kivelson, Michael Flier, Daniel Rowland, and Erika Monahan Downs, 67–84. Bloomington: Slavica Publishers, 2017.

Kollmann, Nancy Shields. *By Honor Bound. State and Society in Early Modern Russia.* Ithaca: Cornell University Press, 1999.

Krom, Mikhail. *"Vdovstvuiushchee tsarstvo": Politicheskii krizis v Rossii 30–40 godov XVI veka.* Moscow: Novoe literaturnoe obozrenie, 2010.

Letiche, John M., and Basil Dmytryshyn, eds. *Russian Statecraft: The Politika of Iurii Krizhanich; An Analysis and Translation of Iurii Krizhanich's Politika.* New York: Basil Blackwell, 1985.

Likhachev, D. S. and Ia. S. Lur'e, editors. *Poslaniia Ivana Groznogo.* Moscow–Leningrad: Izdatel'stvo AN SSSR, 1951.

Marchalis, Nikoletta. *Liutor "izhe liut". Prenie o vere tsaria Ivana Groznogo s pastorom Rokytoi.* Moscow: Iazyki slavianskoi kul'tury, 2009.

Martin, Janet. "The Novokshcheny of Novgorod: Assimilation in the 16th Century." *Central Asian Studies* 9 (1990): 13–38.

——. "Religious Ideology and Chronicle Depictions of Muslims in 16th-Century Muscovy." In *The New Muscovite Cultural History. A Collection in Honor of Daniel B. Rowland.* Edited by Valerie Kivelson, Karen Petrone, Nancy Kollmann, and Michael Flier, 285–99. Bloomington: Slavica Publishers, 2009.

——. "The Mongol Elite in Muscovy, Rhetoric and Reality: The Portrayal of Tsar Shah Ali in *the Book of Degrees of the Royal Genealogy*." In *The Book of Royal Degrees and the Genesis of Russian Historical Consciousness.* Edited by Gail Lenhoff and Ann Kleimola, 217–29. Bloomington: Slavica Publishers, 2011.

Nitsche, Peter. *"Nicht an die Griechen glaube ich, sondern an Christus." Russen und Griechen in Selbstverständnis des Moskauer Staates an der Schwelle der Neuzeit.* Düsseldorf: Droste Verlag, 1991.

Ostrowskii, Donald. *Muscovy and the Mongols. Cross-cultural influences on the steppe frontier.* Cambridge: Cambridge University Press, 1998.

Pamiatniki diplomaticheskikh snoshenii drevnei Rossii s derzhavami inostrannymi, Part 1: Snosheniia s gosudarstvami evropeiskimi, v. 1: *Pamiatniki diplomaticheskikh snoshenii s Imperieiu Rimskoiu.* Vol. 1: *s 1498 po 1594 god.* St. Petersburg: Izdanie. II otdelenie EIV kantseliarii, 1851.

Plokhy, Serhii. *The Origins of the Slavic Nations: Premodern Identities in Russia, Ukraine, and Belarus.* Cambridge: Cambridge University Press, 2006.

Pokrovskii, N. N., and G. D. Lenkhoff, ed. *Stepennaia kniga tsarskogo rodosloviia po drevneishim spiskam. Teksty i kommentarii.* Vol. 2. Moscow: Yazyki slavianskikh kul'tur, 2008.

"Poslanie tsaria Ivana Vasil'evicha k Aleksandriiskomu patriarkhu Ioakim s kuptsom Vasil'em Pozniakovym i Khozhdenie kuptsa Pozniakova v Ierusalim i po inym sviatym mestam 1558 goda." *Chteniia v Imperatorskom Obshchestve istorii i drevnostei rossiiskikh pri Moskovskom universitete.* Vol. 128, book 1, i–xii, 1–32.

Possevino, Antonio. *The Moscovia of Antonio Possevino, S. J.* Translated by Hugh F. Graham. Pittsburgh: University of Pittsburgh University Center for International Studies, 1977.

"Rodoslovnaia kniga po trem spiskam." *Vremennik Obshchestvo istorii i drevnostei rossiisskikh* 10 (1851): 1–266.

Russow, Balthasar. *The Chronicle of Balthasar Russow and A Forthright Rebuttal by Elert Kruse and Errors and Mistakes of Balthasar Russow by Henrich Tisenhausen.* Translated by Jerry C. Smith with the collaboration of Juergen Eichhoff and William L. Urban. Madison: Baltic Studies Center, 1988.

Sashalmi, Endre. "The Image of the Enemy: Poles and Lithuanians in Russian Literary and Chancery Sources of the Late Sixteenth and Early Seventeenth Centuries." *Specimina nova. Pars prima. Sectio Mediaevalis* 4 (2007): 137–50.

Shcherbatov, Iu. N., ed. "'Akty Kopengagenskago arkhiva, otnosiashchiesia k russkoi istorii,' Part 2: 1570–1576." *Chteniia v Imperatorskom Obshchestve istorii i drevnostei rossiiskikh pri Moskovskom universitete* 257, no. 2 (1916): 1–224.

Sbornik russkogo istoricheskogo obshchestva. Vol. 59. St. Petersburg: Tipografiia V S Balasheva 1887.

Sbornik russkogo istoricheskogo obshchestva. Vol. 71. St. Petersburg: Tipografiia V.S. Balasheva, 1892.

Tumins, Valerie A. *Tsar Ivan IV's Reply to Jan Rokyta.* The Hague: Mouton Publishing, 1971.

Vásáry, István "Claims of Tatar Descent in the Muscovite Elite of the 14th–16th Centuries." In *Mesto Rossii v Evrazii,* 101–13. Budapest: Magyar Ruszisztikai Interzet, 2001.

Vernadsky, George. *The Tsardom of Moscow, 1547–1682, Part 1.* New Haven: Yale University Press, 1969.

Zimonyi, István. "The Concept of Nation as Interpreted by Jenö Szüces." In *Medieval Nomads in Eastern Europe: Collected Studies.* Edited by Victor Spinei, 355–61. Bucharest: Editoru Academiei Române; Brăila: Editura Istros a Muzueului Brăile, 2014.

2

The Depiction of "Us" and "Them" in the *Illuminated Codex* of the 1560s–1570s

Jaakko Lehtovirta

Abstract

This chapter seeks to analyze sixteenth-century Muscovites' self-identity through visual depictions of various groups presumed as "us" and "them" in chronicle illustrations. The main source, the *Illuminated Codex*, is a chronicle compiled during the 1560s and 1570s. While the Codex text is a variation of the Nikon Chronicle with unique material about Ivan IV's reign, the most striking elements are its approximately sixteen thousand miniatures. Created by a small studio of illustrators under strict supervision, the miniatures provide large and systematic source material that often extends the scope of the text. While the Chronicle text repeats the clerical narrative of an Orthodox Russia in constant struggle against the infidel Tatars and Catholics, underlining continuity with Kievan Rus', the miniatures depict only some of the presumed archenemies as "others," and some as just like the Muscovites. There is no automatic visual separation between Christians and non-Christians, or between Russians and foreigners. The clearest group of "them" is that of Catholic and Protestant westerners. Lithuanians seem to form a category between "us" and "them." Tatars are practically indistinguishable from Muscovites. In conclusion, the miniatures suggest a familiarity with neighbors that the more religious text hides.

Illuminated Codex Miniatures as a Historical Source

The current chapter seeks new perspectives on sixteenth-century Muscovites' self-perception as expressed in chronicle illustration. The main source will be the massive *Illuminated Codex* of the last decades of Ivan the Terrible's rule (1533–1584), a key transformation period of the Muscovite or Russian realm.[1] The illustration of the official story of how the realm came about is likely to provide valuable insights through its depiction of the familiar and exotic, ours and theirs, friends and foes, in both ancient history and the more contemporary reality.

The Illuminated or "Facial" Codex (*Litsevoi svod*) is a manuscript compilation that has been preserved until our time in ten massive volumes. The name stems from its unusual form: the volumes are lavishly decorated with colorful miniatures, which mostly occupy more space than the text. The illustrations are often almost full page in size and have deservedly long fascinated scholars. The bulk of the Codex text is a development of the Nikon Chronicle of the 1520s.[2] The last two volumes, the Synod Volume and the unfinished Book of Tsardom, contain unique text about Ivan's reign. Yet the most striking element of the Codex is its approximately sixteen thousand miniatures. Although other books with miniatures have survived from the era, and a much larger number appears to have been lost, the sheer volume and dominant role of the illustration, the overarching world-historical nature of the narrative, and the tight supervision of production make the Codex miniatures a highly interesting and informative source group.

As far as we know, the magnificent Codex was only produced as a solitary example for the tsar's court, where it seems to have remained until different volumes ended up in various locations around 1700. Their later life explains the current status and various names of the actual volumes: scattered between different archives and museums in St. Petersburg and Moscow, with pages and sections bound in chronologically incorrect places and in completely incorrect volumes, and some parts missing altogether. We cannot be certain how much has been lost. As it is, the Chronicle jumps from tenth-century Byzantine to twelfth-century Russian history. I can see no credible explanation of why a comprehensive narrative of the known history from Creation through Biblical,

---

1   I use *Muscovy* and *Muscovites* for the realm and its inhabitants for clarity. Muscovites called themselves Russians, and their realm Russia, and their neighbors contested this usage. This occasionally creates confusion with the wider use of "Russia" in various forms, i.e. as the historical *Rus'*, and the Muscovite claim over its lands.

2   See, among others, B. M. Kloss, *Nikonovskii svod i russkie letopisi XVI–XVII vekov* (Moscow: Nauka, 1980), 206–14.

Greek, Roman, Byzantine, and Russian history, culminating in the Muscovite Tsardom, would omit the birth of Rus', including the invitation legend of Riurik, St. Vladimir, and the baptism of Rus'. These were core parts of Ivan's view of history and his claim to ancestral inheritance of Rus'.[3]

Soviet and Russian scholars have undertaken painstaking work in reassembling the misplaced lists so that we at least know the chronological order of the remaining Codex. The task has been further complicated by the fact that the last volumes of the Codex were never quite finished. There are some overlapping parts, editorial markings, and unfinished (mainly uncolored) illustrations in the Book of Tsardom. According to B.M. Kloss, the Synod Volume was heavily re-edited, and parts of it were attached to the new Book of Tsardom, which was intended to be the final volume but was left unfinished for unknown reasons.[4]

Another jungle through which the scholar needs to cut is the timing of the Chronicle. While most scholars now agree that the compilation was made during the latter part of Ivan's reign (1533–1584), questions remain about the decade: the 1560s to the 1570s or the 1570s to the 1580s. I do not feel these questions are crucial to the current study. It remains safe to say that the *Illuminated Codex* reflects the Muscovite worldview during the last decades of Ivan's rule.[5]

The text of the Codex is available in key publications of Russian chronicles as a variation of the Nikon Chronicle.[6] The miniatures, as a whole, were difficult to access in full until recent decades. Hundreds of miniatures have been replicated or reproduced as black and white drawings in Soviet and Russian books, mainly

---

3　Shmidt agrees that the first part of "domestic history" is missing, and possibly also a late "world history," for example, Byzantine history from the tenth century (see S. O. Shmidt, "K faksimil'nomu izdaniiu litsevogo letopisnogo svoda," in *Litsevoi letopisnyi svod XVI veka. Russkaia letopisnaia istoriia* [Moscow: Akteon, 2010], 24:5). It is possible that for some reason the early Rus' history part was unfinished when the work on the Codex was abandoned. It is more likely that a volume or volumes have been destroyed.

4　Kloss, *Nikonovskii svod i russkie letopisi XVI–XVII vekov*, 264–65. For a good compact description of the volumes, see, for example, A. A. Amosov, *Litsevoi letopisnyi svod Ivana Groznogo* (Moscow: Editorial URSS, 1998), 11–16. Concerning the Synod volume and Book of Tsardom, see also V. V. Morozov, "Ivan Groznyi na miniatiurakh Tsarstvennoi knigi," in *Drevnerussko iskusstvo. Rukopisnaia kniga. Sbornik tertii* (Moscow: Nauka, 1983), 234–35.

5　Kloss's observations on the source texts of the Codex confirm that the missing early Rus' history volume was at least planned. There are also frustrating references to lost pages describing Fedor Ivanovich's coronation in 1584, obviously after Ivan's death, that seem to have existed into the eighteenth century. Watermarks give a *terminus post quem* at best, and it is possible that there were some efforts to continue writing after Ivan's death. See Shmidt, "K faksimil'nomu izdaniiu litsevogo letopisnogo svoda," 5–10; Kloss, *Nikonovskii svod i russkie letopisi XVI–XVII vekov*, 207–14.

6　*Polnoe sobranie russkikh letopisei*, vols. 9–14.

as illustrations of particular events. For Soviet historiography they provided much-sought material depicting ordinary people, workmen, and peasants. Things began to improve when two facsimile selections from the Codex appeared. In 1984, the "Tale of the Battle on the Kulikovo Field" was published in the aftermath of the six hundredth anniversary of Dmitrii Donskoi's epic victory over the Tatars in 1380.[7] This was followed by the "Life of Aleksandr Nevskii" in 1990, to celebrate the seven hundred and fiftieth anniversary of the battle on the ice against the Livonian knights.[8] Both publications were patriotically motivated, and their miniatures are somewhat monotonic battle scene depictions, but they gave a much better idea of what the Codex was like. Yet at the end of the 1990s, A. A. Amosov estimated that only about five to eight per cent of the Codex miniatures had been published.[9]

Fortunately, the current century and modern technology have rapidly improved the situation. A scholarly facsimile version by "Akteon" with good indexes and editorial remarks covers the Russian history parts of the Codex, that is, from 1114.[10] The entire Codex, including the pre-Russian volumes, is now readily available as a facsimile internet publication from Runivers.[11] Both published versions show the text in the presumed chronological order, but unfortunately, the two versions do not quite communicate.[12] In this chapter, I refer to the Akteon version for the parts that it covers and the Runivers internet publication for the early parts.

Before delving into the question of "us" and "them" in the Codex, we must consider the value of the Codex miniatures as a source. The images were hardly widespread. The beautiful volumes remained in the Kremlin, and their influence was limited to the ruling family and people working at the heart of the central administration. The compilation may have been a source of pride and pleasure, but to very few. Consequently, the key role of the miniatures is not in their influence, such as a printed and widely circulated book or even a widely copied

7   *Povest' o Kulikovskoi bitve. Tekst i miniatiury litsevogo svoda XVI veka* (Leningrad: Avrora, 1984).

8   "Zhitie Aleksandra Nevskogo," *Tekst i miniatiury Litsevogo letopisnogo svoda XVI veka.* vol. 2. (St. Petersburg: Avrora, 1992).

9   Amosov, *Litsevoi letopisnyi svod Ivana Groznogo*, 23.

10 *Litsevoi letopisnyi svod XVI veka. Russkaia letopisnaia istoriia*, Moscow: Akteon. 2010) (hereafter cited as RLI with volume number).

11 *Litsevoi letopisnyi svod Ivana Groznogo. God izdaniia: 1568–1576*, Biblioteka "Runivers." Book 6958 (2020). Accessed October 12, 2021, https://runivers.ru/ (hereafter cited as LLS, with volume number).

12 Cross-references between the archive volumes used in all previous studies and the two publications remain unduly complicated. The *Runivers* version also sometimes incorrectly lists the years covered by individual volumes.

manuscript could have, but rather in the mental world they reflect. Whose world do the miniatures depict? We do not know the names of the individuals who created them, but quite a lot is known and can be concluded about the circumstances of the writing and illustration process. We are not dealing with the artistic whims of one or two persons. We have a carefully controlled product that reflects the views of the state's central apparatus. Created by a studio of illustrators working with the clerks and editors under strict supervision, the miniatures provide an abundant and systematic source material that visualizes the narrative and extends the scope of the written text. Always loyal to the text, the illustrators simply had to fill in where the narrative fell short. They clearly had a rich tradition of icon painting and earlier manuscript illustration for norms and models—they were not creating *ex nihilo*. As G. P. Georgievskii put it, "not every sixteenth-century icon painter was a miniaturist, but every miniaturist was an excellent icon painter."[13] However, the miniaturists were less bound by rules than icon painters, and their topics varied much more. We know quite a bit about miniatures being copied from earlier manuscripts in some hagiographies that survive in multiple versions. Copying would explain some of the archaisms in the Codex images, like weapons that would be obsolete by the sixteenth century.[14]

Few of the possible models for the Russian history illustrations of the Codex survive, whereas the biblical parts have more links to icons and sacred texts. The chronographic volumes depicting the Hellenic and Roman era clearly have a lineage based on foreign manuscripts as their models. The most obvious source for Russian history illustration known to us is the Radziwiłł (or Königsberg) Chronicle from the late fifteenth century. We cannot be certain if a version of it was at the disposal of the miniaturists of the *Illuminated Codex*.[15] If it was, its influence was minor. The miniatures of the overlapping sections (1114–1206) show some resemblance only in places where there would have been limited options to depict the scene. In several miniatures depicting the same event, there is no similarity at all. Certain elements from the Radziwiłł Chronicle are systematically missing: the allegorical figures and the use of the sword as a

13 G. P. Georgievskii, "Russkaia miniatiura XVI veka," in *Drevnerusskaia miniatiura. 100 listov miniatiur s opisaniem i stat'iami M. Vladimirova i G. P. Georgievskogo* (Moscow: Akademiia, 1933), 44.
14 A. V. Artsikhovskii, *Drevneruskie miniatiury kak istoricheskii istochnik* (Moscow: Izdanie MGU, 1944), 54–55, 157–59.
15 It has been suggested that the surviving version of the Radziwiłł Chronicle was not final. There is some evidence that the piece was written in Belozersk, part of Muscovy at the time (M. V. Kukushkina, "Predislovie k izdaniiu," in *Radzivilovskaia letopis'* [St. Peterburg: Glagol/ Moscow: Iskusstvo, 1994], 5–6, 9–10).

symbol of investiture. Either the Radziwiłł Chronicle was not available to the Codex team, or it did not impress them.

In any case, the Codex text was unique in many parts, and the miniatures so numerous that the illustrators could not resort to merely copying existing depictions. There are also certain uniform features throughout the Codex that make systematic comparisons possible. There were also rules: both the scribes and miniaturists worked under close supervision. Although the main scholarly interest has been directed at the famous editorial remarks in the Synod Volume, sometimes previously attributed to Ivan himself, there are also editorial changes in the miniatures themselves.[16] Let us examine one case more closely to get an idea. The longish entry describing the construction of the new Uspenskii cathedral in 1479 underwent a detailed inspection. First, in a number of cases, princely figures visiting churches or in prayer have had their princely caps removed from the original sketch.[17] Two intentions obviously conflict: the need to identify the person and his rank, and the need to observe church protocol. In the *Illuminated Codex*, the latter has won.[18] In any case, an unknown editor of the Codex miniatures found this detail sufficiently important to call for redrawing. Second, the same story describes in detail how the remains of the key patron saints, Metropolitans Peter and Iona and others, are brought into the new cathedral. The remains of the ruling grand prince's early predecessor, Prince Iurii Danilovich, were ceremoniously carried in and laid down next to the saintly clergymen. The illuminator first depicted Iurii with a princely cap to show his rank. Someone must then have noted that Iurii took monastic vows on his deathbed, so the princely attribute was replaced by a shroud.[19] To complete the picture, the same miniaturist bundled the deceased prince with the saints and accidentally gave him a halo, which was also then removed as a mistake. The correction is clearly visible.[20]

---

16 The written editorial remarks, *pripiski*, are printed separately in RLI, 24:404–89.
17 RLI, 16:373, 375, 388, 397.
18 In the earlier Radziwiłł Chronicle, the princes pray in their princely caps. Artsikhovskii, *Drevneruskie miniatiury kak istoricheskii istochnik*, 29, and *Radzivilovskaia letopis'*, 91, 200v, 205v.
19 Redrawing is clearly visible in RLI, 16:387.
20 RLI, 16:387–88, 396, 401. The prince's halo may have been the result of more than confusion with the saintly bodies lying next to the dead prince. Fedotov counted Daniil, the founder of the Muscovite branch of the Riurikid dynasty, as a recognized saint (Georgii Fedotov, *Sviatye drevnei Rusi* [Moscow: Moskovskii rabochii, 1990], 103). There may have been attempts to portray him as a saint, and the illuminator may have known this. For more on the princely sainthood and their monastic vows see Jaakko Lehtovirta, *Ivan IV as Emperor: The Imperial Theme in the Establishment of Muscovite Tsardom* (University of Turku: Painosalama, 1999), 162–68.

Finally, the sheer number of miniatures makes the Codex stand out as an ideal source for systematic study. For perspective, an illuminated Chronicle of Georgios Hamartolos executed in Tver and surviving from the late thirteenth or early fourteenth century, has 127 miniatures.[21] The closest Muscovite predecessor to the *Illuminated Codex*, the fifteenth-century Radziwiłł (or Königsberg) Chronicle, where the proportion of images in relation to the text approaches that of the Codex, has more than six hundred miniatures, several with multiple episodes, which in turn number more than twelve hundred.[22] These works pale in comparison with the *Illuminated Codex* with its more than sixteen thousand miniatures, many or most containing several episodes.[23] We can safely assume that if—and when—the illustrators systematically depicted something in the same way many thousands of times, this verifies a fixed convention.

Defining "Us" in the Codex Miniatures

The previously linear narrative of "Russian" history—extending as an unbroken chain from St. Vladimir of Kiev to the modern Russian Empire and jumping to Moscow during Tatar rule—is being rewritten or has been dismantled, not least because of the appearance and better visibility of Ukrainian and, more recently, Belarusian perspectives. The old story was very much based on how the Russian church wanted history to be depicted. History texts were mainly produced by hierarchs and monks, and it was the relocation of the Kievan Metropolitans to Moscow in the fourteenth century that seemed to shift the emphasis to that part of the Russian lands. Many now ask what happened to the imagined identity of Rus'. Was it simply transferred to a new location, or did it evolve into something different in the Polish-Lithuanian Commonwealth, and did a new and distinct Muscovite identity emerge? If so, how did it position itself *vis-à-vis* its immediate neighbors? Who was familiar? Who was alien? Who was one of us? The Chronicle illustration suggests an addition to what the plain text tells us.

Since we are dealing with a source that covers a very long period and extends far into the past of the time of its actual writing, there are obviously two elements, the contemporary and the past. Imagine a T shape, where the horizontal bar depicts contemporary events, and the vertical bar the past. One way to approach

---

21 O. I. Podobedova, *Miniatiury russkikh istoricheskikh rukopisei russkogo litsevogo letopisania* (Moscow: Izdatel'stvo Nauka, 1967), 11–12.

22 Amosov, *Litsevoi letopisnyi svod Ivana Groznogo*, 229.

23 Sometimes the number given is more than seventeen thousand. See Shmidt, "K faksimil'nomu izdaniiu litsevogo letopisnogo svoda," 5.

our topic is to enquire whether the presumed "us" and "them" differ in the past, or indeed if any "us" is to be found in the distant past. As a starting point, earlier studies have shown we can presume that at least Rus' would be depicted as "us" in the illustrations, because this is the approach of the chronicles of the period.

We must also ask if the miniatures depict otherness at all. Although it may not be obvious to a casual browser, the illustrators had ways of identifying different groups of people through clothing and identifying attributes. An expert can navigate the miniatures with tools to identify the actors. We rely greatly on the systematic groundwork of Artsikhovskii during the Second World War. However, he did not directly address the question of otherness in the Codex—it was not a fashionable topic at the time and may even have proved sensitive in the Soviet Union. Second, like most Soviet and Russian scholars, Artsikhovskii only covered the "Russian" part of the Codex. There is room to expand.

The simplest starting point is to identify "us" in the Codex. It may be assumed that the contemporary Muscovites in the last volumes of the Codex (the Synod Volume and Book of Tsardom) are people with whom the reader was intended to identify. This very quickly opens the archetypal characters, who are so widespread throughout the Codex that they dominate the illustration. The attention turns to the "others," or exceptions.

The basic dress and form of peasants, soldiers, and princes remain the same throughout the almost five centuries of Russian history covered. There are no identifying features of the inhabitants of the various Russian principalities, nor any development with time.[24] The miniatures are in this sense ahistorical. The reader therefore automatically connects contemporary Muscovites with all the people of Rus', centuries before Moscow even appears in the narrative. To anyone who knows how the chronicles connected Muscovy in a direct line with and as a logical continuation of early Rus', this inner circle of "us" comes as no surprise. The illumination accompanies the overall thrust of the Chronicle and is also in line with the other narratives circulated at the time—most importantly, the Tale of the Grand Princes of Vladimir, widely used as legitimation for Ivan the Terrible's claim to All-Russian rulership and the title of tsar, which he adopted in 1547.[25]

---

24 Artsikhovskii, *Drevneruskie miniatiury kak istoricheskii istochnik*, 59–63, 101–4, 111–18.

25 The tale is published in English in Jack V. Haney, "Moscow: Second Constantinople, Third Rome or Second Kiev?" *Canadian Slavic Studies* 3, no. 2, (Fall 1968): 359–67. Full Russian texts of the whole cycle can be found in R. P. Dmitrieva, *Skazanie o kniaziakh vladimirskikh* (Moscow–Leningrad: Izdatelstvo Akademii nauk SSSR, 1955), 159–213. See also Lehtovirta, *Ivan IV as Emperor*, 100–107.

Consequently, for both the scribes and illuminators, the Muscovite realm was unsurprisingly part of the historical continuation of Rus', and the people of Rus' were "us," just like contemporary Muscovites.

Were there "others" among the Russians? One group that might easily be imagined as outsiders is people who break rules and norms, betray the ruler, and worst of all, endanger the whole society. The Codex has several illustrations of such outcasts, often being punished for their trespasses. Some have joined small-scale unrest or outright mutinies; some have conspired against the ruler. Then there are heretics, to whom the text devotes much attention from the times of the early church all the way to the sixteenth century. Were they highlighted as not belonging to "us" in the miniatures?

One example helps us understand both how the Codex was edited, and how it depicted outcasts. In 1537, Ivan's uncle Andrei Ivanovich was arrested— allegedly after failing to join a campaign against Kazan at the grand prince's command. Andrei was a senior male relative of Ivan, who was still a minor. The incident provided a good case for the regency to oust him. This tended to happen to uncles and brothers who were potential pretenders. Andrei suffered harsh imprisonment, which soon led to his death. All this is described in detail in the Chronicle's text and illustrations—twice. First, there is the Synod Volume version, with numerous editorial comments (*pripiski*) in the margin.[26] Second, there is the later version of the same story in the Book of Tsardom, which follows those editorial instructions. Here there are changes not only to the text but to the miniatures.[27] The main observation for us is that despite the editing and the seemingly obvious benefits of underlining the evilness of the prince and the righteousness of his punishment, the image of Prince Andrei and his servants, who also suffered painful deaths, remains completely neutral. There is nothing to suggest he is evil or an outcast of any sort. The betrayers are normal Muscovites, pictured according to their rank, not their evil deeds.

This is not an exception. Codex illustrations remain neutral about those who trespass in one way or another. As the crimes were considered severe, the punishments were harsh and often graphically depicted. First, tongues and noses are torn off, and feet and hands severed; then the poor people are thrown into rivers to drown or put to death by hanging, burning, or decapitation by axe or sword. Yet the illustrators do not suggest these people were somehow

---

26 RLI, 19:511.
27 Young Ivan is given a tsar's crown in the later version; in the earlier version he wears the grand princely cap: he was not crowned tsar until 1547. It seems the editors felt he had to be pre-emptively depicted with the more prestigious headgear. RLI 19:529–32.

anything but "us." Their faces and gestures sometimes show suffering, although many remain laconic. Criminals of western origin are depicted accordingly, but this is the normal convention, as we will soon see.[28] There is no visual contrast between evil and good people. The only way to underline evil in the Codex is the occasional devil in the background of religious events—a convention from iconography.[29]

Evildoing Muscovites were still "us." Muscovites and Russians in general were depicted very systematically as members of their rank but otherwise neutrally, even when they deserved the narrative's condemnation. This creates an image of unity and harmony extending beyond the individual's deeds.

Depicting Non-Russians

Another possible borderline could be assumed between Russians and non-Russians. Here we come to the key nuances. We can quickly identify dividing lines in the Codex illustrations between something we could call "us" and "them." The miniaturists did not lack ways to make a distinction when required, but the visual division was not simply Russians versus foreigners.

The most strikingly different figures are to be found in times well before the existence of a Russian state in any form. As has been observed, this period has been omitted from many studies. The early volumes depict the exotic races Alexander the Great encountered in India, for example. It is difficult to tell if some were human at all. There are people with dogs' heads, giants, headless fishermen, and so on.[30] These are the basic stuff of medieval teratology, and these illustrations undoubtedly had foreign sources as inspiration. Indian wonders had been depicted for Muscovites in the 1539 version of "Christian Topography" by Cosmas Indicopleustes.[31] In the *Illuminated Codex*, these characters are an extreme example. Against this colorful variation, Alexander and his party and troops are perfectly "normal" throughout—so much so, they could easily be sixteenth-century Russians. So, the Codex clearly sees an "us" very early in world history. The reader automatically identifies with Alexander's Greeks. Besides the oddities described above, Alexander encounters others who

---

28 Some examples: heretics in Novgorod, RLI, 9:94; heretics in Moscow, RLI, 18:43–45; small-town traitors, RLI, 11:390–92; a local prince and a foreign interpreter, RLI, 17:229; boyars fallen into disfavor, RLI, 17:385.

29 See, for example, LLS, 8:410; LLS, 10:128–130; LLS, 11:405.

30 LLS, 6:353, 366, 371.

31 A. N. Svirin, *Iskusstvo knigi drevnei Rusi, XI–XVII v.v.* (Moscow: Iskusstvo, 1964), 118–21.

are normal people yet identifiably different. For example, the people of Tyre are pictured with turbans, which clearly distinguishes them from the Greeks. There are also Jews in the story, who are identifiable by their headgear.[32]

The "otherness" of the Jews also applies to the volume covering Flavius Josephus's History of the Judean War. The Romans are depicted like contemporary sixteenth-century Russians, while Jews are distinguished by their headscarves (or special cap for the rabbis) whether they are in full armor or civilian dress. There is no question concerning "who is who," and the perspective is Roman in both the miniatures and the text.[33] However, this distinguishing of the Jews does not apply to the selection from the Old Testament that starts the whole Codex. One could speculate that the "otherness" of the Jews stems from their not recognizing Christ, which diverts them from "our" history. Ordinary Israelites in the first Codex volumes appear much like the Russians of the later volumes, although the style of the early part differs somewhat. I am unaware of contemporary (not biblical) Jews depicted in the Russian parts of the Codex. Ivan the Terrible did not tolerate Jews in his realm.[34]

A large and important group that stands out in the latter parts of the Codex is those we might call "westerners." The Italians, Germans of various kinds, Swedes, English, French, and occasional Spaniards who appear in the Russian history volumes of the Codex are depicted in elaborate renaissance garments. Notably, this may mean breeches, in stark contrast with the higher-echelon Muscovites, who wore long robes. The western military figures also differ from Russians: they wear hemispherical helmets, while Russians always wear pointed ones. The distinction is not merely between westerners and Muscovites. The people of all the principalities of Rus' are inseparable in the Codex, and westerners are indistinguishable from each other. This Rus'-West division runs through the six Russian history volumes of the Codex, which Artsikhovskii studied meticulously. Again, there is no different fashion for the earlier centuries—the miniatures are timeless. Headgear, in particular, distinguishes the westerners from the tens of thousands of personalities in the Codex.[35] It is quite clear that

---

32 LLS, 6:237 (Tyre), 218, 808 (Jews).

33 LLS, vol. 7 throughout. A classic battle scene LLS, 7:378; a typical priest LLS, 7:561. Less self-evidently, the Arab and Syrian auxiliary forces also look like "us." LLS, 7:308.

34 That at least is what he wrote to the king of Poland. *Pamiatniki diplomaticheskikh snoshenii*, 341–42. See Halperin, "Varieties of Otherness in Ivan IV's Muscovy: Relativity, Multiplicity, and Ambiguity" in this volume for more on Jews as the ultimate "others."

35 Artsikhovskii, *Drevnerusskie miniatiury kak istoricheskii istochnik*, 59–62, 100–101. For a very good example of the exotic westerners see RLI, 5:485–91.

here we find the "normal" and the "exceptional," the "us" versus "them." The reader identifies with Rus'.

Why did the westerners stand out? They were, of course, representatives of an outside realm. However, not all foreigners looked exotic. You did not have to be from the Russian principalities to look "normal." A more nuanced explanation might be that the Chronicle reflects the religious divide of the sixteenth century. Muscovites were not concerned with who was on the papal side, and who was on the Protestant side in the bitter division of the western church. For them, there was the Orthodox world and the schismatic world, and this seems to be reflected in the miniatures of the *Illuminated Codex*. Is "us" synonymous with Orthodoxy, and "them" with non-Orthodox people?

The religious interpretation is encouraged by the treatment of other Orthodox nations, which receive quite a lot of attention in the Codex. A chapter on the fourteenth century "Serbian Tsardom" depicts Serbs as similar to Russians. The only dissimilarity is that the Serbian rulers are given an exotic crown when called "kings."[36] The people in the entries on Bulgarian history also look quite familiar.[37] This is not an ethnic or linguistic "Slavic" connection. East Romans are also depicted like Russians throughout the various parts of the Codex.[38] Even "Latins" can be depicted like the Orthodox Byzantines until their heresy.[39] Clearly, Orthodox history was "our history."

A Lithuanian Gray Zone

In his recent study of identities and visual narratives in the *Illuminated Codex*, A.V. Martyniouk has carefully combed the Codex scenes depicting Lithuanians, making valuable observations. Although Lithuania was a western power for Muscovites and in a deepening relationship with Poland, the Lithuanians constitute a gray zone in the Codex illustrations. Their rulers were usually depicted as western rulers, but ordinary citizens and soldiers are often indistinguishable from Muscovites. Opposing forces can sometimes be

---

36 RLI, 7:305–38.
37 See, for example, RLI, 4:22, where Latins stand out from the Greeks and Bulgarians; or the entry on Nikephoros I's (802–811) Bulgarian wars in LLS, 10:79–84.
38 See, for example, the whole publication volume covering Roman/Byzantine history between 87 and 460, LLS, vol. 8; or on the Turkish-Byzantine war, RLI, 14:236–470.
39 LLS, 10:8–33.

recognized only through their leaders.[40] When there are prisoners of war from a joint Polish-Lithuanian army, western and nonwestern prisoners are depicted.[41] Even the Lithuanian Gedyminas dynasty is somewhere in between. Martyniouk points out that when they appear as rulers of formerly Russian cities, Lithuanian princes are occasionally depicted in the round, fur-lined princely cap that invariably identifies a Russian prince.[42]

There was therefore a pictorial message concerning Lithuania, and here I agree with Martyniouk: the Lithuanians as a people were part of "us," the Russian, domestic, or "our" historical narrative of the whole Codex but ruled by an alien ruler and dynasty. There were, of course, Orthodox Ruthenians in Lithuania, but it seems the Codex stresses the historical connection with Rus', which was used as the argument when Muscovite rulers claimed their ancestral lands.[43]

Martyniouk concludes that the overarching visual narrative of the Chronicle can be seen as an illustration of *translatio imperii*, culminating in the Muscovite realm, best known as the Third Rome theory, formulated by the Pskovian monk Filofei in the early sixteenth century.[44] I have elsewhere disputed the idea that Third Rome might have been a key narrative of Ivan the Terrible's Muscovy. It played no role at all before Fedor's reign, when the patriarchate was established in 1589. Yet there were other versions of *translatio*, the key one being the Tale of the Princes of Vladimir and its parts such as the Tale of the Monomakh Regalia. This invented official narrative anchored Muscovy firmly within the ancient Russian heritage of lands controlled by Lithuania and later Poland.[45] We do not need Third Rome to explain the resemblance between Muscovites and Lithuanians in the *Illuminated Codex*—the connection was there through other means. Finally, the cultural and linguistic border between the two states was, naturally, porous, and noblemen frequently crossed it to seek protection or a better position in the service of the neighboring ruler.

40 A. V. Martyniouk, "Formi i urovni identichnostei v vizual'nykh narrativakh Litsevogo letopisnogo svoda," in *Narrativy rusi kontsa XV—serediny XVIII v.: v poiskakh svoei istorii*, ed. A. V. Doronin (Moscow: Rosspen, 2018), 198–200.
41 RLI, 6:33–34; RLI, 13:70.
42 Martyniouk, "Formi i urovni identichnostei v vizual'nykh narrativakh Litsevogo letopisnogo svoda," 196–97.
43 Ibid., 202.
44 Ibid., 203.
45 Third Rome was not mentioned in contemporary official documents. It was not used to explain Ivan the Great's coronation as tsar, nor to defend the title against foreign repudiation. Lehtovirta, *Ivan IV as Emperor*, 302–20, 347–55.

FIGURE 1. Aleksandr Nevskii's army escorts captured Lithuanians. The latter are identifiable by their rounded, "Western" helmets and some, but notably not all, by "Western" civilian garments. (Under the year 1245.) *Litsevoi letopisnyi svod. Faksimil'noe izdanie rukopisi. Kn. 5 Ch. 2. S. 1886 (Laptevskii tom)*. By courtesy of Aleksei Martyniouk.

FIGURE 2. Livonian envoys to Novgorod. In the foreground, Livonians (on the right) are identifiable by their headgear and partly fancy Renaissance dress, as opposed to typical Russians (on the front left). (Under the year 1268.) *Litsevoi letopisnyi svod. Faksimil'noe izdanie rukopisi. Kn. 6. Ch. 1. S. 94 (Ostermanovskii pervyi tom).* By courtesy of Aleksei Martyniouk.

Depicting Non-Christians

The idea that the illustrations depict religious borderlines and identities does not withstand detailed study. The visual connection between Russians, Serbs, and Byzantines or Orthodox Lithuanians is not exclusive. We have already seen that familiarity extends much further into history. Besides Alexander's Greeks, pre-Christian Romans look just like Christian Romans—or contemporary Muscovites.[46] Yet certain signs indicate that the miniaturists understood they were not looking at Christians. Temples bear no crosses, and occasional idols here and there represent non-Christian worship.[47] Obviously, Christianity did not limit whom the miniaturists made look like "us" in the long narrative.

Finally, the Tatars, who are so eminent in the Chronicle from their first appearance, do not stand out in any way. First, ordinary Tatars—usually warriors—are indistinguishable from Russians. Tatar-Russian battle scenes may as well be depictions of internecine Russian wars. A classic example is the depiction of Ivan III's "victory" against Khan Ahmed at the Ugra River in 1480. Only the rulers indicate the opposing armies.[48] This is the norm. Meanwhile, the Turks form a more mixed picture. Their military equipment is mostly "our" style, but the Turks sometimes wear turbans, a clearly exotic flavor.[49]

Consequently, the miniatures may be seen to suggest that the Tatars were "us," at least no less than Bulgarians, Serbs, or Byzantines. The same concerns some smaller eastern nations like the Mordvins. While the Chronicle writers, usually clerics, attempted to depict the Tatars as heathen enemies of Russia in the text and the battle against them as an existential struggle to defend Christianity and save Rus', the miniatures create a very different image.

The Tatars and Tatar empires were part of the legacy of the Muscovite rulers, although official texts do not mention this—one could not build a Christian legitimation entirely on infidel rulers, and the Chronicle texts are religious in nature. Yet there was a layman's need to underline the strength and glory of the empires Muscovy had conquered. In some concrete ways Ivan the Terrible was a successor of the khans, especially after the conquest of Kazan. When the Codex was compiled and illustrated, the once impressive and awe-inspiring Tatar rule was effectively over. Muscovy had turned the tide, albeit not without

---

46 See volumes on the Judean War, LLS, vol. 7, and Early Roman and Byzantine history, LLS, vol. 8.

47 For example: sacred buildings and idols in Rome, LLS, 7:917, 935, 937, 943.

48 RLI, 16:443–48.

49 Artsikhovskii, *Drevnerusskie miniatiury kak istoricheskii istochnik*, 63. For turbans see RLI, 14:264; RLI, 14:275; and RLI, 16:1.

setbacks. They had for some time had a Tatar client state in Kasimov, and the conquests of Kazan and Astrakhan in 1552 and 1557 greatly changed the nature and demographics of the realm. The new regions were in direct contact with the rest of the country. Despite the efforts to Christianize the populations, the Tatars did not become Russians overnight, if they ever did. Despite some hindrances in assimilation and the obvious need to convert to achieve a proper status, interaction increased rather than decreased with the end of Tatar rule over Russia.[50]

The notion that the Tatars were far from simply enemies of the Muscovites is not new. When the Codex was compiled, the Tatars had been part of Russian life in one way or another for more than three centuries. The famous Eurasianist historian George Vernadsky wrote of a multinational "Russian Commonwealth."[51] Michael Cherniavsky famously suggested that Russians more or less blurred Byzantine and Tatar "tsars" into a combined image of a single supreme ruler.[52] Folk songs did not hesitate to connect the tsar's new title with the conquest of the Tatar khanates.[53] Russians had for centuries recognized the Mongol Chinggisid dynasty, and the numerous members of that clan who came into Muscovite service were held in high respect. Ivan the Terrible even appointed Simeon Bekbulatovich, a Tatar convert, as substitute grand prince of Muscovy for a short time. His name was mentioned as a possible next tsar after the extinction of the Riurikid dynasty.[54] Charles J. Halperin has pointed out that it was fashionable to claim even a fabricated Tatar ancestry in the sixteenth century.[55] A recent thorough analysis by Bulat Rakhimzianov of diplomatic material and the *iurt* territories granted to the Tatar nobility further deepens our understanding of the dynamic contact between Russia and the steppe. Despite the religious and dynastic divide, Muscovy was an insider in

---

50 See Michael Khodarkovsky, "Four Degrees of Separation: Constructing Non-Christian Identities in Muscovy," in *Culture and Identities in Muscovy: 1359–1584*, ed. A. Kleimola and G. Lenhoff (Moscow: ITZ Garant, 1997), 248–266.

51 George Vernadsky, *The Tsardom of Moscow 1547–1682: A History of Russia.* (New Haven: Yale University Press, 1969), 1:2–8.

52 Michael Cherniavsky, "Khan or Basileus: An Aspect of Russian Mediaeval Political Theory" (1959), reprinted in *The Structure of Russian History: Interpretive Essays*, ed. Michael Cherniavsky (New York: Random House, 1970), 65–73.

53 Maureen Perrie, *The Image of Ivan the Terrible in Russian Folklore* (New York: Cambridge University Press, 1987), 66–67, 186.

54 A. A. Zimin, *V kanun groznykh potriazhenii. Predposylki pervoi krestianskoi voiny v Rossii* (Moscow: Mysl', 1986), 35–42, 224–25.

55 Charles J. Halperin, *Russia and the Golden Horde: The Mongol Impact on Medieval Russian History* (Bloomington: Indiana University Press, 1987), 111–13.

the post-Golden Horde rivalry and knew the Tatar world intimately.[56] It was probably this familiarity that was reflected in the Codex miniatures. In this sense, they break what Halperin described as the Russian chronicles' "ideology of silence" concerning the intimate relationship with the Tatars.[57] Depicting Tatars in various text genres was a much more complex matter, and its evolution is described well by Maksim Moiseev in another chapter of the present book.[58]

Rulers Separating "Us" from "Them"

Finally, we will examine whether ruler illustrations in the Codex actually can reflect identity. At first glance, the Codex seems to provide a very clear division between "our rulers" and "their rulers." The attribute of the familiar domestic princes is a round princely cap, usually lined with fur. This runs as a symbol of the Russian princely figure throughout the Codex—whether in Kiev, Muscovy, or other principalities, and making little distinction between princes and grand princes. Colors and forms vary, and the fur lining is sometimes absent, but Russian princes are always recognizable. Non-Russian rulers are in turn given different headgear, sometimes quite fantastic, and easily recognizable as crowns of some sort. This differentiation works well throughout the Russian history part of the Codex, though it is obviously not applicable to the pre-Rus' world. This was a convention inherited from the earlier miniaturists, including those of the Radziwiłł Chronicle, and known in other art forms, such as icons.[59]

However, things become complicated when we move to the contemporary bar of the chronological T shape. The Codex illuminators were among the first to depict the new situation of having a Russian tsar. Ivan the Terrible had been solemnly crowned tsar in 1547, a change with significant symbolism, but also one that seems to have posed problems for the miniaturists. All the "tsars" in the

---

56 Rakhimzianov describes the successful policy of attracting Tatar nobility with their retinues to settle in Muscovite lands from the fifteenth century, the various cities and territories granted to the Tatars, and the evolution of the Muscovite rulers' relationship with the Chinggisid dynasty. See Bulat Rakhimzianov, *Moskva i tatarskii mir: sotrudnichestvo i protivostoianie v epokhu peremen, XV–XVI vv.* (St. Petersburg: Izdatel'stvo Evraziia, 2016), 53–56, 158–76, 195–232 et passim.

57 Halperin, *Russia and the Golden Horde*, 4–6.

58 Moiseev, "The Image of the Other: The Perception of Tatars by Russian Intellectuals and Clerks in the Fifteenth to Seventeenth Centuries (Chroniclers, Diplomats, Warlords and Writers)" in this volume.

59 Artsikhovskii, *Drevnerusskie miniatiury kak istoricheskii istochnik*, 28–29, 111–18. A second identifying feature is a decorated cloak with sleeves hanging loose, given only to Russian princes, but interestingly also to Ivan the Terrible as tsar.

text had been systematically depicted with very distinctive headgear: a yellow five-pointed radial crown. "Tsars" came from a variety of backgrounds: there were Biblical, Roman, Byzantine, and Serbian tsars. All the Tatar khans were called tsars and depicted as such.[60] Throughout the Codex the illuminators were meticulously loyal to the text in this respect. The Tatar Prince Mamai's usurpation is a good example: as soon as he begins to be called tsar in the text, he is depicted as one, though his position was unrecognized.[61]

A brief comparison with the fifteenth-century Radziwiłł Chronicle is in order here, not least because it covers the "invitation legend" that is missing from the surviving *Illuminated Codex*. Although the Radziwiłł miniatures differ somewhat in style, Russian princes are recognizable by their fur-lined caps, just as in the later Codex. The "tsars," in turn, have a golden crown, though it lacks the distinctive five points. In the invitation legend the Varangians Riurik, Sineus, and Truvor are depicted with Russian-style princely caps—they are "us."[62] Unfortunately, the Radziwiłł Chronicle does not cover the arrival of the Tatars, so we lack a comparison here.

How, then, should we depict the transformation of Ivan the Terrible, a Russian grand prince, into a tsar? The Codex miniaturists first thought of the obvious choice: he would receive a new headgear at his coronation. In the Synod Volume the infant Ivan is almost invariably depicted wearing the familiar princely cap.[63] However, one of the editorial changes to the Shumilovskii volume and the Book of Tsardom is that Ivan is occasionally shown in the tsar's radial crown from his infancy, as if predestined for tsardom.[64]

Either way, the depiction of a Russian ruler with the radial crown changes the identity framework quite dramatically. Ivan comes to resemble the earlier Orthodox Byzantine emperors, which was obviously the idea in the clerical minds behind the coronation and the new title. However, incidental or not, he comes to resemble the Tatar khans, whom the clerics sought to depict as

---

60 Ibid., 115–18.
61 RLI, 9:354.
62 *Radzivilovskaia letopis'*, 8–8v.
63 RLI, 20:34–202.
64 RLI, 19:28–39; 47 in contrast with his father wearing a princely cap. In the long narrative of Vasilii III's death, there is little logic (RLI, 19:227–371), but then Ivan ascends the throne in 1533 depicted as a tsar RLI, 19:372. He mostly remains such, but not invariably, until the coronation in 1547 (RLI, 20:300–19). A few pages appear later with the princely cap—pages and drafts must have been seriously mixed (RLI, 21:498–500). Concerning the 1547 coronation depictions, see Lehtovirta, *Ivan IV as Emperor*, 147–51.

enemies. Now, nothing at all distinguished the Tatars and Russians in the miniatures, not even the ruler figure.[65]

Conclusion

Ultimately, we have a very complex picture of how the *Illuminated Codex* reflected assumed otherness. A very large and varied inner group of "us" emerges, identifiable only by the existence of rare exceptions, groups of clearly exotic people. Returning to the T shape's historical dimension, we find Muscovite and Russian history linking smoothly with Byzantine and Ancient Rome, as well as with Alexander the Great and his folk. This matches the ideological setup of Ivan's reign well. Jews and some other exotic nations of the distant past are clearly "them." Lithuanians are often, but not invariably, depicted as an inner group of "us." Considering the territorial claim and shared religion, this is logical. We also know that the cultural barrier was very low. The familiarity of the Tatars, who do not stand out as alien at all, may have been more difficult to digest for some.

Considering the second level of otherness, that of the horizontal, contemporary level, we find a clear border only between "western people" and all the others, whom we would call eastern or oriental.[66] Religion is not essential, except when separating Catholics and Protestants from all others, Orthodox and Muslims alike. It is difficult to see this as religious identity. It is also clear that the illustration makes no attempt to distinguish between good and evil.

It would be too far-fetched to conclude that sixteenth-century Russians did not have an identity separate from the Tatars. There is also no reason to see the miniatures as a super source that reveals a truth the texts seek to hide. Yet the notions are not irrelevant. What the Codex miniatures suggest is a general familiarity with the Tatars in particular, as well as Lithuanians. If we generalize the main division in the Codex as between East and West, the Muscovites clearly depicted themselves as part of the East. The Renaissance westerners looked genuinely much more exotic to the Muscovite eye than their eastern neighbors. Perhaps we should recognize that when western travelers compared the Muscovite—usually maliciously—with oriental people, they actually saw something with which the Muscovites would have subconsciously agreed.

---

65 See, for example, the conquest of Kazan in 1552 (RLI, 21:398–461), or Devlet–Giray's expedition (RLI, 23:396–429).

66 Artsikhovskii, who did not study the pre-Rusian volumes, notes this as an overall division in civilian clothing. Artsikhovskii, *Drevnerusskie miniatiury kak istoricheskii istochnik*, 100–104.

Works Cited

Amosov, A. A. *Litsevoi letopisnyi svod Ivana Groznogo. Kompleksnoe kodikologicheskoe issledovanie*. Moscow: Editorial URSS, 1998.

Artsikhovskii, A. V. *Drevneruskie miniatiury kak istoricheskii istochnik*. Moscow: Izdanie MGU, 1944.

Cherniavsky, Michael. "Khan or Basileus: An Aspect of Russian Mediaeval Political Theory." Reprinted in *The Structure of Russian History: Interpretive Essays*. Edited by Michael Cherniavsky, 65–79. New York: Random House, 1970.

Dmitrieva, R. P. *Skazanie o kniaziakh vladimirskikh*. Moscow–Leningrad: Izdatelstvo Akademii nauk SSSR, 1955.

Fedotov, Georgii. *Sviatye drevnei Rusi*. Moscow: Moskovskii rabochii, 1990.

Georgievskii, G. P. "Russkaia miniatiura XVI veka." In *Drevnerusskaia miniatiura. 100 listov miniatiur s opisaniem i stat'iami M. Vladimirova i G. P. Georgievskogo*. Moscow: Akademiia, 1933.

Halperin, Charles J. *Russia and the Golden Horde: The Mongol Impact on Medieval Russian History*. Bloomington: Indiana University Press, 1987.

Haney, Jack V. "Moscow: Second Constantinople, Third Rome or Second Kiev?" *Canadian Slavic Studies* 3, no. 2, (Fall 1968): 359–67.

Khodarkovsky, Michael. "Four Degrees of Separation: Constructing Non-Christian Identities in Muscovy." In *Culture and Identities in Muscovy: 1359–1584*. Edited by A. Kleimola and G. Lenhoff, 248–66. Moscow: ITZ Garant, 1997.

Kloss, B. M. *Nikonovskii svod i russkie letopisi XVI–XVII vekov*. Moscow: Nauka, 1980.

Kukushkina, M. V. ed., "Predislovie k izdaniiu." In *Radzivilovskaia letopis'*, St. Peterburg: Glagol/Moscow: Iskusstvo, 1994.

Radzivilovskaia letopis'. St. Petersburg: Glagol/Moscow: Iskusstvo, 1994.

Lehtovirta, Jaakko. *Ivan IV as Emperor: The Imperial Theme in the Establishment of Muscovite Tsardom*. University of Turku: Painosalama, 1999.

Litsevoi letopisnyi svod XVI veka. Russkaia letopisnaia istoriia (RLI), 1–24. Moscow: Akteon, 2010.

Litsevoi letopisnyi svod Ivana Groznogo. God izdaniia: 1568–1576 (LLS), 1–27. Biblioteka "Runivers." Book 6958, 2020. Accessed October 12, 2021. https://runivers.ru/

Martyniouk, A. V. "Formi i urovni identichnostei v vizual'nykh narrativakh Litsevogo letopisnogo svoda." In *Narrativy rusi kontsa XV—serediny XVIII v.: v poiskakh svoei istorii.* Edited by A. V. Doronin, 190–207. Moscow: Rosspen, 2018.

Morozov, V. V. "Ivan Groznyi na miniatiurakh Tsarstvennoi knigi." In *Drevnerussko iskusstvo. Rukopisnaia kniga. Sbornik tretii,* 232–40, Moscow: "Nauka," 1983.

Pamiatniki diplomaticheskikh snoshenii moskovskogo gosudarstva s pol'sko-litovskim. Tom II (1533–1560). Edited by G. F. Karpova. St. Petersburg: Sbornik Imperatorkogo Russkogo Istoricheskogo Obshchestva 59, 1887.

"Patriarshaia ili Nikonovskaia letopis'." In *Polnoe sobranie russkikh letopisei IX–XIV.* St. Petersburg: Tipografiia Eduarda Pratsa, 1862–1910.

Perrie, Maureen. *The Image of Ivan the Terrible in Russian Folklore.* New York: Cambridge University Press, 1987.

Podobedova, O. I. *Miniatiury russkikh istoricheskikh rukopisei russkogo litsevogo letopisania.* Moscow: Izdatel'stvo Nauka, 1967.

Povest' o Kulikovskoi bitve. Tekst i miniatiury litsevogo svoda XVI veka. Leningrad: Avrora, 1984.

Rakhimzianov, Bulat. *Moskva i tatarskii mir: sotrudnichestvo i protivostoianie v epokhu peremen, XV–XVI vv.* St. Petersburg: Izdatel'stvo Evraziia, 2016.

Shmidt, S. O. "K faksimil'nomu izdaniiu litsevogo letopisnogo svoda." *Litsevoi letopisnyi svod XVI veka. Russkaia letopisnaia istoriia.* Vol. 24. 1–24. Moscow: Akteon, 2010.

Svirin, A. N. *Iskusstvo knigi drevnei Rusi, XI–XVII v.v.* Moscow: Iskusstvo, 1964.

Vernadsky, George. *The Tsardom of Moscow 1547–1682: A History of Russia.* Vol. 1. New Haven: Yale University Press, 1969.

"Zhitie Aleksandra Nevskogo." Tekst i miniatiury Litsevogo letopisnogo svoda XVI veka. Vol. 2. St. Petersburg: Avrora, 1992.

Zimin, A. A. *V kanun groznykh potriazhenii. Predposylki pervoi krestianskoi voiny v Rossii.* Moscow: Mysl', 1986.

3

The Image of the Other: The Perception of Tatars by Russian Intellectuals and Officials in the Fifteenth to Seventeenth Centuries (Chroniclers, Diplomats, Voivodes, and Writers)

Maksim Moiseev

Abstract

In their textual products, Russians had to describe the Tatars according to the categories of equality and conquest after the Russian state had been released from dependence on the Horde—thus entering the struggle with the Tatar States for hegemony in the European steppes—and before the period when the "Tatar threat" ceased to be perceived as an existential danger. In this chapter, the following questions are examined in the light of versatile textual material consisting of embassy documents, chronicles, correspondence, and historical tales. How were the Tatars described, how did the strategy for describing the Tatars coincide with descriptions of Muslims in general, and was there a difference in the description of "service" Tatars and Tatars living in independent Tatar states? The chapter will reveal different techniques and strategies applied by Moscow administrators and diplomats to describe what was initially alien.

Introduction

The long experience by Russians and Tatars of living side by side created a surprising phenomenon: their cultures, initially foreign to each other, became quite close and influenced each other on various levels, from the everyday to the elevated. However, this process was neither painless nor fast. On the contrary, historians have recorded times of intense rejection and cultural self-isolation alternating with processes of assimilation and periods of alienation. The present study focuses on the stage at which Russians were forced to describe Tatars in terms of equality and conquest—that is, when the Russian lands were freed from the rule of the Golden Horde, and the Muscovite state entered a struggle with the Tatar states for hegemony on the European steppes, extending also to the period when the Tatar threat ceased to be perceived as an existential danger.

The main sources for this study are texts written in grand ducal and monastic scriptoria, chancelleries, offices of voivodes (*voevoda*, at various times warlords or governors), and pavilions of diplomats. These consist not only of chronicles and compositions but also of orders to and reports by envoys and voivodes' letters missive and their messages to foreign travelers. I will try to identify the descriptive devices that Muscovite administrators and diplomats used to describe what was inherently foreign, as well as the strategies that Russians used to limit the sphere of the Other and thus make it accessible to understanding. Defining the Muslim identity of Tatars was important in these practices, and we will therefore need to keep this always in mind when analyzing how the Tatars were perceived.

The East and the Image of the Tatars in Russian Narrative Texts

Researchers justifiably note that the boundary between "ours" and "other" in Russian culture had a natural origin and followed the division between forest and steppe. David Schimmelpenninck van der Oye holds that this demarcation arose even earlier than other differentiating markers.[1] But did this mean that Russians also automatically formed a concept of "the East"? And what did they understand by "the East"? If we turn to the texts, it becomes obvious that Old Russian scribes used the term "East" only as a direction and did not imbue it

---

1 David Schimmelpenninck van der Oye, *Russkii orientalizm. Aziia v rossiiskom soznanii ot epokhi Petra Velikogo do Beloi emigratsii* (Moscow: Politicheskaia entsiklopediia, 2019), 21.

with any additional meanings. The ethnogenealogies constructed in the *Primary Chronicle* placed Turkmen, Pechenegs, Torkils, and Polovtsians (Qıpčaqs) among the peoples living "from the desert of Yathrib, between the east and the north . . ." and connected them to the descendants of Ishmael. Nomads were combined within this conceptual framework and perceived as the enemies of Christianity and heralds of the end of the world.[2] Incidentally, chroniclers did not link the Polovtsians and the Islamic world, although they had adopted the strategy of Byzantine anti-Islamic rhetoric.[3] Outside that tradition, religious restraint is noticeable, and some epithets, such as "filthy," bear an ethnic rather than religious connotation.[4] This is particularly noticeable if we turn to the perceptions of Islam and Muslims of the author of the *Primary Chronicle*, recently analyzed by Marianna Andreicheva. The story of Prince Vladimir Sviatoslavich's choice of a religion contains a description of Muslim worship and characterizes Islam itself. The chronicler connected Islam and Judaism, particularly stressing circumcision and the prohibition of eating pork. He goes on to interpret the act of anointing in a way that presents it as a deviant practice typical of homosexuals. He also writes that Muslims ingest semen, thus classifying their religion not only as a depraved faith but a pagan one. In describing the Muslims' appearance, he particularly notes that they do not wear belts; accordingly, their faith is untrue, and their very worship revealed them as possessed. The bad odor they exude was evidence of their sinfulness and connection with the Antichrist. Such a descriptive model was strongly anti-Muslim and was formed under the very strong influence of the Byzantine anti-Islamic tradition, although the chronicler did add his own touches to this repulsive description. In summary, the *Primary Chronicle* identifies Islam as a deeply sinful and perverted religion strongly linked with Judaism and paganism.[5]

The pre-Mongol Old Russian intellectual tradition, therefore, saw not "the East" but two large communities: Muslims and nomads. Somewhat similar rhetorical models were used to describe both groups, but, while Muslims were perceived as adherents of a harmful and sinful cult, nomads were primarily understood as harbingers of the impending Apocalypse.

As the Mongols were classified as nomads, whom Old Russian intellectuals saw as heralds of the end of the world, it is unsurprising that the Mongol conquest was perceived as nothing other than an apocalyptic catastrophe. This

---

2 M. Iu. Andreicheva, *Obrazy inovertsev v Povesti vremennykh let* (St. Petersburg: Nestor-Istoriia, 2019), 133, 140, 145, 150, 152.
3 Schimmelpenninck van der Oye, *Russkii orientalizm*, 24.
4 Ibid., 24–25.
5 Andreicheva, *Obrazy inovertsev v Povesti vremennykh let*, 96–112.

was even more the case because the overly proud Russian princes were unable to oppose them and themselves became victims. In other words, the relatively victorious story of confrontation with the Polovtsians was over, and the Russian land perished! Serapion, the bishop of Vladimir, formulated this viewpoint quite distinctly. The main point was that defeat was God's punishment for sins and that the only path to salvation was through repentance and purification.[6] A similar understanding of events became relatively widespread,[7] though it was not the only one. Thus, in *The Tale of the Life and Courage of the Noble Prince Alexander*, such a perspective is barely discernible, but in it we do meet the image of a prince sacrificing himself for his subjects' sake.[8] The author of the *Novgorod First Chronicle*, writing in the 1220s and 1230s,[9] asks who exactly the Tatars are and cannot immediately answer. In discussing the events preceding an ill-fated battle, as well as the battle itself and its outcome, he draws a seemingly paradoxical conclusion. The Tatars, like the Polovtsians, are "Ishmaelites," but they are the "Scourge of God" for the Polovtsians, not the Russians. Precisely for this reason, the Tatars try to avoid confrontation with the Russians, sending two embassies to the princes, but the princes, blinded, reject the peace treaty offered, for which they are punished by God. By this logic, the Tatars are not godless, and their arrival does not necessarily lead to the Last Judgment. Furthermore, the Tatars could be taken as an instrument of God, sent to punish the godless Ishmaelites: the Polovtsians and the Russian princes tempted by them.[10] However, it must be acknowledged that the way the scribes reflected on the invasion and subsequent dependency at the time was significantly softer than at the end of the dependency and immediately after liberation. Some scholars link this to the "ideology of silence" first identified by Charles Halperin.[11] The radicalization of the relationship toward the yoke and the conquerors takes place later, from

---

6 A. O. Amel'kin, "Natsional'naia katastrofa v obshchestvennom soznanii pravoslavnogo naseleniia v epokhu srednevekoviia," in *Nashestvie Batyia i ustanovlenie ordynskogo iga v obshchestvennom soznanii Rusi XIII–XVII vekov*, ed. A. O. Amel'kin and Iu. A. Seleznev (Voronezh: Tipografiia IP Aleinikova, 2004), 9.

7 Ibid., 10.

8 Iu. V. Seleznev, "Ideino-religioznaia otsenka sovremennikami russko-ordynskikh otnoshenii 1240–1270 gg," in *Nashestvie Batyia i ustanovlenie ordynskogo iga v obshchestvennom soznanii Rusi XIII–XVII vekov*, ed. A. O. Amel'kin and Iu. A. Seleznev (Voronezh: Tipografiia IP Aleinikova, 2994), 40.

9 V. N. Rudakov, *Mongolo-tatary glazami drevnerusskikh knizhnikov serediny XIII–XIV vv.* (Moscow: Kvadriga, 2009), 26.

10 Ibid., 26–34.

11 Charles Halperin, *Tatarskoe igo. Obraz mongolov v srednevekovoi Rossii*, trans. M. E. Kopylova (Voronezh: Izdatel'stvo Voronezhkogo gosudarstvennogo universiteta, 2012), 78–111; Schimmelpenninck van der Oye, *Russkii orientalizm*, 28.

the late fifteenth century, but it is important that the period of the yoke led neither to a textual base describing the Asiatic invaders nor to the formation of a particular attitude toward the East. Furthermore, contemporary sources were more likely to record the integration of the elites of the Russian principalities into the power elite of the Horde. Iurii Seleznev notes that the titles of Russian princes had equivalents in the Horde's power hierarchy, the Horde's law applied to the princes, and with time the Russian and Tatar aristocracy built personal connections.[12]

The following may thus be noted. If the invasion itself and the early years of dependence led to the formation of ideas about punishment for sins and a concept of the imprisonment of Russians analogous to the Babylonian exile of the Jews, these ideas were later significantly attenuated, particularly in the context of realpolitik, and the tsar (*khan*) of the Horde gained the features of a legitimate supreme ruler. Alongside that, descriptions of nomads and Muslims employed the same old rhetorical practices but did not develop any new ones. This means that there is no cause for speaking about any new perceptions of the "East" in the thirteenth to fifteenth centuries. For the time being, the "East" and "easternness" for the Russians was limited to the Golden Horde, and on an abstract level we can assume that the "East" as an idea was understood in the framework of the same idea of a large area "from the desert of Eritrea, between the east and the north" inherited from the Old Russian scribes.

In these conditions, liberation from dependence on the Horde should have been accompanied by the appearance of texts that should have pushed the Horde and everything to do with it into the zone of the "other." Such a revision of the recent past and established practices began around the second half of the fifteenth century.

An intensive attempt to grasp the range of questions we now customarily generalize as the "East" led in the fifteenth and sixteenth centuries to the appearance of a collection of texts that examined this problem from several angles. First, for Russians at that time, the "Orient" meant first and foremost the Horde and its heirs—that is, the Tatars. Second, it meant the world of Islam, and only third did it mean the world of the geographic East in all its religious and ethnic diversity. One of the most influential texts about Russian orientalism was evidently compiled by Afanasii Nikitin, a merchant from Tver. I deliberately place the question of how frequently and widely his work was read in the fifteenth and sixteenth centuries beyond the scope of the present study for the

---

12 Iu. V. Seleznev, *Russkie kniaz'ia v sostave praviashchei elity Dzhuchieva ulusa v XIII–XV vv.* (Voronezh: Tsentral'no-Chernozemnoe knizhnoe izdatel'stvo, 2013), 303–10.

sake of identifying a range of rhetorical devices used to describe Eastern peoples. Afanasii provides a description of several Eastern "peoples" in his work: Tatars, the state of Aq Qoyunlu, the subjects of the Delhi Sultanate, and the Hindus. If we are to generalize on religious grounds, we see a division into Muslims and Hindus. It is precisely these generalizations that show us Afanasii's perspective. In his descriptions of Muslims, he resorts to the topoi of "aggression" and "violence," while the non-Muslim peoples, to the contrary, appear as meek, even though their customs cannot be accepted as normative practices. I hasten to note, however, that this was far from a peculiarity of the author's reflection. It is interesting that the author of the *Kazanskaia istoriia*, who also distinguished between Russians and Tatars, noted that for the latter aggression and a tendency to violence were inherent by nature because the Tatars "were given the blessing of their forefathers—Esau and the proud Ishmael—to earn their living through their weapons," while Russians descend "from our meek and humble forefather Jacob, and therefore we cannot resist them with strength and often humble ourselves before them."[13] It must be noted that, according to all Russian texts of the period, aggression is inherent by nature in Muslims in general. This is precisely how the majority of texts describe Muslims.

For example, in the tale of Timofei of Vladimir, a Russian priest, who had committed a crime and found cover in the Kazan Khanate, enjoys a dizzying career after converting to Islam, going from ordinary priest to Tatar military commander. He becomes an extremely aggressive and imperious person but lacks inner calm. He finds peace only upon returning to the bosom of the Orthodox Christian faith.[14]

Thus, we must recognize that intellectuals conduct a thought operation from the fifteenth century onward that defines Muslims somewhere in the East who are distinguished from all other inhabitants of that geographic region by their originally inherent aggressive behavior and domineering nature. From our point of view, this event is of special significance. Russian thought during the period of dependence was not prepared to perceive "the East" outside the framework of a concrete political formation, the Golden Horde. However, as liberation progressed, the picture of "the East" became more complex. Russians now distinguished between "Tatars," "Muslims," and all the others, who could not be defined by these aggregates. Thereafter, Russian demographic description encountered a serious problem: Tatars could be described either

---

13 T. F. Volkova, ed., *Kazanskaia istoriia*, vol. 10 (St. Petersburg: Nauka, 2000), 312.

14 "Povest' o Timofee Vladimirskom," text prepared, translated and annotated by N. S. Demkova (St. Petersburg: Nauka, 2000), 9:106–13.

as "Ishmaelites" or "Muslims." In such a framework, they had to acquire all the negative traits that old Russian thought had developed for them. It was precisely for this reason that Tatars were traitors, perjurers, godless, and aggressive. At the same time, other Muslim peoples were not necessarily treasonous by nature, but they were always aggressive. The other Eastern peoples could not be perceived in the framework of the existing discursive practices, and so a certain latitude was therefore retained for understanding them, albeit limited by their religious adherence.

The topos of "treason" applied to the Tatars by Russian scribes in the fifteenth to sixteenth centuries was based on the history of political relationships between the Muscovite and the Turkic-Tatar states. It was particularly fully expressed in the corpus of texts devoted to relations with the Khanate of Kazan. Let us examine this matter in more detail.

Russian soldiers captured Kazan on October 2, 1552. A long war and a diplomatic confrontation preceded this event. No less important was the ideological justification for the war itself and the necessity of subjugating the Khanate of Kazan, which is often seen through the prism of the war's crusading nature. "The roots of the conquest plans against Kazan lay in the sphere of religious fanaticism," M. G. Khudiakov wrote in the 1920s.[15] A. A. Zimin linked the development of the theory of legitimizing the conquest of the khanate with the "Josephite" (followers of Iosif Volotskii) scribes of Metropolitan Makarii's circle.[16] To a greater or lesser degree, this perspective is retained in modern historiography.

To establish how justified this reconstruction is, it is logical to analyze texts written by a prelate to see if they contain "crusader ideas" and a struggle with Islam. Among the missives of Makarii about the "Kazan war," the one to Sviiazhsk stands out. Interestingly, this missive contains 1,670 words, but Kazan (including words derived from it) is only mentioned five times! The number of mentions alone is clearly not highly significant. Let us therefore examine the contexts in which Kazan figures:

1. The Lord God gave our devout tsar [. . .] a glorious bloodless victory over all his opponents, and the Kazan kingdom submitted;
2. The tsar and tsaritsa of Kazan put themselves into his hands [. . .];

---

15 M. G. Khudiakov, *Ocherki po istorii Kazanskogo khanstva* (Moscow: INSAN, 1991 [1923]), 124.
16 A. A. Zimin, *I. S. Peresvetov i ego sovremenniki. Ocherki po istorii russkoi obshchestvenno-politicheskoi mysli serediny XVI veka* (Moscow: Izdatel'stvo AN CCCR, 1958), 71, 75–76, 78.

3. Our tsar and ruler gave the city of Kazan to its tsar Shahghali with all the *uluses* [encampments] of Kazan;

4. The native Kazan princes and nobles [. . .] came of their own volition and showed their desire to serve our devout tsar.[17]

All the mentions of Kazan in this epistle are aimed at underscoring the bloodless and willing nature of the taking of Kazan in 1551. There are no negative connotations. However, perhaps an analysis of religiously inflected words will yield such connotations. Here, again, the researcher is disappointed: "heathen" (*poganye*) appears twice, in the context of the release of prisoners "from heathen hands";[18] and "Hagarites" (*agariane*) just once, in the conclusion of the missive to the garrison of Sviiazhsk:

> And you, O beloved children of Christ, noble princes, boyars, voivodes, noblemen, and all Christ-loving soldiers of the devout Tsar Ivan, from now on with God's help will try to do all you can with all your strength, if your strength suffices, bravely and manfully, to work together for the holy churches and our holy Orthodox faith *against the godless Hagarites* in everything, by the order of the devout and Christ-loving Tsar Ivan [emphasis added].[19]

An analysis of this missive makes it completely clear that its purpose was an appeal to the soldiers of the garrison to maintain religious and moral purity. It is a typical "teacher's missive" and nothing more! It is important that the metropolitan's next missive, sent to the tsar during the Kazan campaign of 1552, also does not go beyond the church tradition of spiritual fortification for battle.[20] In this work, Makarii intensifies his anti-Kazan rhetoric slightly. The people of Kazan are now "godless" and "traitors and apostates."[21] However, here Kazan, its inhabitants, "filthy pagans" are also rare statements, serving to concretize the admonition. Moreover, not all the epithets used by the prelate are of a religious nature; more on this below.

---

17 *Polnoe sobranie russkikh letopisei*, vol. 13 (Moscow: Iazyki russkoi kul'tury, 2000), 180–81 (hereafter cited as PSRL).

18 Ibid., 182.

19 Ibid., 183.

20 Makarii arkh. (Veretennikov), *Iz istorii russkoi ierarkhii XVI veka* (Moscow: Podvor'e Sviato-Troitskoi Sergievoi Lavry, 2006), 69.

21 PSRL, 13:193.

Upon consideration, we see that Makarii, the ideologue of the "Kazan war," is justifying it ex post facto. He sends a "didactic missive" to Sviiazhsk in 1551 after the capitulation of Kazan and instructs the tsar during the march against the capital of the rebellious khanate in 1552. Yet more questions arise when we examine the "Kazan correspondence" of the tsar and metropolitan in the light of the *Extract from the Russian Chronicle*. V. V. Shaposhnik came to the following conclusions after studying this subject. The data from this source about the correspondence is more reliable than the *Chronicle of the Start of the Reign of the Tsar and Grand Prince Ivan Vasil'evich*. When news was received of the campaign of the Crimean khan (defeated near Tula), the metropolitan called on the tsar to return to Moscow.[22] This fact is quite interesting, no matter how we interpret it.[23] In this case, the metropolitan's behavior was exactly the opposite of that of Vassian Rylo. Whereas Rylo required consistency and firmness on the part of the grand prince in his struggle against the Tatars, Makarii was prepared to pause the Kazan campaign, if not curtail it, when danger struck.

On the whole, it seems that the role of Metropolitan Makarii in the justification for the taking of Kazan and imparting upon it the nature of a crusade is highly exaggerated. However, is it possible that another member of the church hierarchy expressed himself more openly about it? In this context the most attractive source is Nifont (Kormilitsyn), who, G. Z. Kuntsevich proposes, wrote two accounts of the Kazan campaigns. Let us examine the first, dedicated to the campaign of 1550. The text has 855 words, and Kazan (and words derived from it) is found six times.

1. The Grand Prince Ivan Vasil'evich was greatly insulted by the violence of the Hagarite offspring and of the Kazan Tatars;
2. Himself attacked Kazan with a great number of men;
3. Were the tsar, the grand prince, to do battle near Kazan, and were he [the Crimean khan–M. M.] to do battle against the Russian land;
4. If you come to Kazan yourself [...];
5. All the soldiers attacked Kazan;
6. The Orthodox Tsar, Grand Prince Ivan Vasil'evich, came upon Kazan.[24]

---

22 V. V. Shaposhnik, *Tserkovno-gosudarstvennye otnosheniia v Rossii v 30–80-e gody XVI veka* (St. Petersburg: Izdatel'stvo S.-Peterburskogo universiteta, 2006), 214–23.

23 V. V. Shaposhnik writes that Makarii did not propose halting the campaign (Shaposhnik, *Tserkovno-gosudarstvennye otnosheniia v Rossii v 30–80-e gody XVI veka*, 221, 223).

24 G. Z. Kuntsevich, "Dva rasskaza o pokhodakh tsaria Ivana Vasil'evicha Groznogo na Kazan' v 1550 i 1552 godakh," *Pamiatniki drevnei pis'mennosti i iskusstva*. Vyp. CXXX. Otchety o zasedaniiakh Imperatorskogo obshchestva liubitelei drevnei pis'mennosti v 1897–1898 gody s prilozheniiami (St. Petersburg: Tipografiia V. S. Balashov i Ko, 1898), 26–29.

It is obvious that Kazan is merely an identifying politonym in this text as well. All the definitions of the Kazan inhabitants as "Hagarite offspring," "godless," and "heathen" are definitions of their Muslimism, as contemporary Orthodox scribes perceived it; it does not have an emotional connotation. The only sharp terms of invective are when the Kazan Tatars are labeled as "traitors" and "bloodthirsty." The latter is connected with the tragic course of relations between the Russians and Kazan in the 1530s and 1540s, and "traitors" is a very interesting word choice. It must be said that for Russian scribes the most outrageous aspect of the people of Kazan was not their religion but a certain "traitorousness," which all but constituted the entire essence of the Kazan Tatars as a people (to the mind of Russians). Let us examine this in more detail, considering that this view is strongly connected with the practical justifications for the conquest of the Kazan khanate.

From the 1520s onward, the Russian political narrative commonly speaks of the Middle Volga region as having originally belonged to Russian rulers. This view is also presented in official chronicles. An essential element of the narrative of the chronicles of Russo-Kazan relations is the selection primarily of cases in which the people of Kazan asked for a "tsar" or requested forgiveness for a "transgression." As a result of this editing, the full spectrum of diplomatic contacts between Russia and the Kazan khanate are reduced to questions of succession.

We may assume that the idea of the Kazan khanate belonging to Russia originated with diplomats. This idea was most likely derived from the outcome of the Russo-Kazan agreements of June 1516. At that time, the fatally ill Khan Möxämmädämin wanted to vow "that they would not, without the knowledge of the grand prince, take any tsar or tsarevich for Kazan."[25] The outlines of this theory had already formed by the 1520s, but to become a full-fledged concept, it had to rely on international precedent (the fact of the Kazan vow of 1516 was considered insufficient). Such a precedent was found in the context of Crimean-Turkish relations. In 1522, following the taking of Astrakhan by the armies of Mehmed I Giray, the Nogais conducted a raid on the Crimeans. The Crimean khan and his son died, and the Crimean troops were crushed. Some sultans managed to escape to Crimea, where, amidst anarchy, Ğazı I Giray proclaimed himself khan. His rule was short. The Turkish sultan Suleiman, who had placed his henchman Saadet I Giray on the throne, intervened in matters. The kaleidoscopic changes demanded an explanation, and the new khan sent an envoy to Moscow, who gave the following explanation: "And the Sultan Suleiman, having heard me [Saadet I Giray–M. M] said, 'The Nogais killed your brother Mehmed I Giray and his son the Prince Bagatyr, and now your younger brother *Ğazı* Giray has become tsar in Crimea, making Tsarevich Bibey kalga *without our knowledge*'" [emphasis added].[26] Thus, the basis for the Turkish intervention in the Crimean khanate was the independent proclamation of a khan and *kalga*. Russian diplomats accorded utmost importance to this circumstance, as there were obvious parallels with Russo-Kazan relations. Moscow proceeded from this newly found international precedent and decided to put the theory of its claim to the Kazan khanate into broad practice.

Soon after the visit of the Crimean envoy, the Russian envoys in Crimea were required to explain to the Crimean khan Saadet the essence of the disputes with the Kazan khan Sahib I Giray as follows:

> I think, lord, that you know that from the times of our ancient lords and of our present lord, the father Grand Prince Ivan and our lord the Grand Prince Vasilii have placed tsars on [the throne of] Kazan with their own hands. And the Kazan princes Seit betrayed our lord in their own minds and took a tsar for Kazan *without the knowledge of our lord*. And our lord does not want to set this matter of his aside [emphasis added].[27]

The Russian envoys were required to deflect any Crimean attempts to claim Kazan as their territory (*yurt*) with similar words, noting, "We, lord, do not know that that territory is yours. But we do know, lord, that from the beginning our lords have placed tsars in Kazan with their own hands," and that Sahib's guilt consisted in his coming to the throne "without the knowledge of our lord."[28]

In this manner, the Russian ruling classes refused to recognize Sahib I Giray as the Kazan khan because of the illegality of his enthronement; moreover, this illegality was defined precisely as in the case of Ğazı I Giray's ascent to the Crimean throne. The rights of Russia to the Kazan khanate and of Turkey to the Crimean khanate thus exhibit clear parallels. Such parallel reasoning allowed the Russian diplomats to use their singular concept of the Russian grand princes' ancient entitlement to Kazan more actively when negotiating, not only with their western but also with their eastern counterparts.

---

26 Rossiiskii gosudarstvennyi arkhiv drevnikh aktov, f. 123, op. 1, kn. 6, l. 10ob. (hereafter cited as RGADA).

27 RGADA, f. 123, op. 1, kn. 6, l. 32.

28 RGADA, f. 123, op. 1, kn. 6, l. 34.

When Sahib I Giray was replaced on the throne by another Crimean sultan, Safa Giray, this offered the Russians, the Crimeans, and the Kazan Tatars a way out of the looming diplomatic impasse. As is commonly known, Safa Giray assumed the throne of Kazan in exceptional circumstances. In the spring of 1524, Russian troops began their march on Kazan; under these circumstances, Sahib I Giray fled the city, and Safa Giray was chosen as khan. The Kazan troops were defeated on the Sviyaga River, after which the grand ducal troops "started to approach the city." The Kazan Tatars decided to end their resistance and "swore an oath to the entire will of the lord grand prince."[29] In the autumn of 1524, a delegation of Kazan envoys arrived in Moscow and supplicated "for their guilt and on behalf of tsar Safa Giray." Vasilii III "looked upon their supplication with favor" and sent his envoys, Prince V. D. Penkov and clerk A. F. Kuritsyn to Kazan.[30] As a result, the Crimean khanate was informed that "our lord looked upon the princes and all the people of Kazan with favor and gave Safa Giray to them as tsar."[31] This incident is evidence that Moscow was basically uninterested in the origin of a claimant to the throne of Kazan. Of most importance was that his investiture with power came from Moscow. We therefore have reason to state that, from the perspective of Russian political ideologists, the grand prince alone was considered the source of power for the Kazan khanate. All alternative sources were accordingly deemed unlawful, and any attempts to use them were logically deemed as *treason*. Intervention in Kazan's affairs in such a case was thus not only legal but imperative.

This doctrine also required the writing of an "ideal history" of Russian-Kazan relations, which was done. The text of the "ideal history" initially included "traitorous" tsars, albeit placed on the throne "with our own hands,"[32] but later these cases began to be expunged. Whereas I. Iu. Shigona-Podzhogin,[33] a trustee of Grand Prince Vasilii III Ivanovich, told Sigismund von Herberstein that Abd al-Latif was dethroned for "evil deeds," the subject is absent from the political

---

29 PSRL, 13:44.

30 Ibid.

31 RGADA, f. 123, op. 1, kn. 6, l. 156ob.

32 *Pamiatniki diplomaticheskikh snoshenii drevnei Rossii s derzhavami inostrannymi*, vol. 1., part 1 (St. Petersburg: pechatano v tipografii II Otdeleniia Sobstvennoi Ego Imperatorskogo kantseliarii, 1851), 288.

33 Ivan Yur'evich Shigona-Podzhogin (died before June 15, 1542). A member of an estate-owning family of Tver and Staritsa, a member of Grand Prince Vasilii III's trusted circle, active diplomat, primarily in the west. Became a boyar scion in 1517, one who "was a member of the grand prince's duma." From 1526 to 1527, in contempt of the tsar; this was revoked in 1530. Around 1532, awarded rank of steward [*dvoretskii*] of Tver. See Zimin, *Formirovanie boiarskoi aristokratii v Rossii vo vtoroi polovine XV – pervoi treti XVI v.*, 221–23.

biography of the khan in Ostania Andreev's speech in Crimea.[34] The "ideal history" assumed its final form later. Furthermore, its authors returned to the principles of the early version: the khans mentioned in it were enthroned "with our own hands," but some of them, and in particular Abd al-Latif, did not "toe the line," which became the reason for their dethronement. This version was reflected in the missive to the Turkish sultan Selim in 1569,[35] and, considering the recipient's high status, it may be considered a benchmark.

The following may therefore be noted. Calling the Kazan Tatars "traitors" was not connected with their faith but was a statement of their relations with Moscow in the framework of the idea of the vassalage of Kazan as created by Russian intellectuals. In the bigger picture, the "Kazan war" was for Russia not a crusade and not a war for the title of tsar but a struggle with rebels for the restoration of a disrupted order.

This does not, however, explain the "ecclesiasticism" of the narrative texts dedicated to the "taking of Kazan." However, if we examine "Makarii's doctrine" as a form of ideology and not as foreign policy, the ecclesiasticism of his "Kazan" texts becomes clear. It is evident that the metropolitan and the scribes of his circle were not very interested in Kazan or the war against it. The marginal number of mentions of the city's name in their writings vividly demonstrates this. Central to their reasoning are the rightness of the behavior of the Russian troops, conformity with religious and moral norms, the tsar's actions in the church's dispensation, and his faith. The lion's share of their texts is therefore devoted to precisely these themes. For example, most of Nifont's composition is not about the Kazan campaign of 1550 but about the establishment and restoration of churches in Vladimir. According to the chronicles, in 1552 the tsar spent more time at prayer than commanding his troops. All this is aimed at creating an image of a truly Orthodox tsar. In essence, the texts of "Makarii's circle" are the history of the construction of a territory of an ideal Orthodox Muscovite tsardom, the idea of a "Holy Russian tsardom," "Holy Rus'."

An analysis of the corpus of ideas of a "Holy Russian tsardom" lies beyond the scope of the present work, but it is important to note that this direction of ideas in nascent Russian political and philosophical thought also had supporters among laymen close to power, such as A. F. Adashev and Prince A. M. Kurbskii, the latter of whom paid attention to it and continued its development in the Grand Duchy of Lithuania. The tsar himself also thought in this context, though

---

34 *Pamiatniki diplomaticheskikh snoshenii drevnei Rossii s derzhavami inostrannymi*, 288; RGADA, f. 123, op. 1, kn. 6, l. 34.
35 RGADA, f. 89, op. 1, kn. 2, ll. 18–21.

in a way that differed from the so-called "Chosen Council." This complex of ideas also had a certain influence on relations with non-Russian peoples, as they clearly did not constitute a unity with the main "body" of the Orthodox monarchy. A clearly distinguished "otherness" of the Muslim Tatars should have led to the development of perceptions of them in the frameworks of theory and policy, in the framework of practice. The previously assimilated concept of "treason" gave politicians a broad range of measures and actions, the extreme form of which would have been physical annihilation. This project existed but was never executed.

Tsar Ivan Vasil'evich, responding to the first missive from the fugitive Prince Kurbskii, wrote the following: "When Aleksei's and your canine power abates, that is when those kingdoms will submit to us completely, and more than thirty thousand captives will come forth to help Orthodoxy."[36] The crowned author indicates a certain conflict within the ruling Russian elite in relation to the subjugated Muslims. The subject of that conflict becomes apparent from the writing of Prince A. M. Kurbskii. In describing his advice regarding the policy in the conquered region, the author notes that there were several points of view on this matter. Certain "wise and sensible" men advised the tsar to "totally eradicate the whole Muslim host."[37] The prince does not specify who these wise and sensible men were, but Ivan the Terrible names Aleksei Adashev, among others. Kurbskii, in turn, names the tsar's brothers-in-law, Danila and Nikita Romanovich Zakharin, as opponents of such "wise" policy. A. G. Bakhtin wrote that "some more voivodes and priests" were among the supporters of the tsar's relatives.[38]

As we see, the theoretical constructions of the "holy Russian tsardom" came into conflict with real politics. And the position of the opponents of such a radical interpretation of this idea is the more interesting one. If for Adashev and his supporters the Tatars—or, more precisely, the ruling and military strata in the khanate—were immanently "traitorous" and devoted to "Bakhmet" and accordingly could not be turned, and thus their physical annihilation was a fully reasonable and logical measure, his opponents, without any doubt, should have been able to develop some concept of their own that would enable them to get out of the intellectual impasse that had emerged. This concept was unlikely to

36 *Perepiska Ivana Groznogo s Andreem Kurbskim*, text prepared by Ia. S. Lur'e and Iu. D. Rykov (Moscow: Nauka, 1993), 37.

37 K. Iu. Erusalimskii, *Sbornik Kurbskogo*. vol. 2: Issledovanie knizhnoi kultury (Moscow: Znak, 2009), 68.

38 A. G. Bakhtin, *XV–XVI veka v istorii Mariiskogo kraia* (Ioshkar-Ola: Mariiskii poligrafichesko-izdatel'skii kombinat, 1998), 135.

have presupposed a radical denial of the idea of the "holy Russian tsardom," but it is obvious that the person of the tsar was moved to the forefront instead of the church and relations with it. In this regard, the attitudes of allegiance to the tsar were the decisive factor, not the people's adherence to the Orthodox faith and church or its "genetic predisposition." In a certain sense, this allegiance was thought of as a personal subordination, and precisely for this reason it was interpreted in the framework of "serfdom." Simply put, the subjugated Kazan Tatars expunged their treason through faithful service. This treason, in turn, ceased to be their inherent quality, and their "Hagarite" aggression now strengthened the Orthodox troops.

This shift of the center of gravity in the concept of the "holy Russian tsardom" from church and faith to the tsar had a deep impact on all subsequent policy and, among other things, enabled the rather painless inclusion of Muslim lands and the incorporation of the Tatar elite into the Muscovite state. However, the internal intellectual tension remained, as it was necessary to make sense of this process of absorbing non-Christian territories into the "holy Russian monarchy." The celebrated *Kazanskaia istoriia* (History of Kazan) may be an example of the resolution of this problem. Its author characteristically strove to attribute a global meaning to the taking of Kazan. He took it beyond the boundaries of a narrow local conflict; for him, this was a battle between Christianity and Islam and, more broadly, between Good and Evil. In his view, the fair Kazan land was from the outset conquered by evil forces. The expulsion of the snakes by wizardry gave this land up to demons irrevocably. Worship of the "foul Bakhmet," who for the author of the *Kazanskaia istoriia* is indistinguishable from demons, was an element of this insidious occupation. Therefore, the Russians' battle was not a battle with the Tatars as such but a battle for their salvation. The tsar and his soldiers set off not to conquer but to liberate the Kazan land. In such an understanding, the tsar's main task was less to lead the military operation directly than to ensure an "accompaniment of prayer." Tsar Ivan thus prayed and tearfully beseeched, but he is consequently barely mentioned as a warrior in the *Kazanskaia istoriia*. And it is the tsar's prayers that attract the assistance of higher forces. This union of humans and saints ensured the liberation of Kazan from evil and returned it to the bright, harmonious world.[39]

---

39 M. V. Moiseev, "Sviatye protiv Kazanskogo khanstva: 'chudesnaia' istoriia kazanskoi voiny," in *Evropa sviatykh. Sotsial'nye, politicheskie i kul'turnye aspekty sviatosti v Srednie veka*, ed. S. Iatsyk (St. Petersburg: Aleteia, 2018), 273–84.

Theoretical thought thus developed a durable descriptive stereotype of the eastern peoples as early as the old Russian period.[40] The "East" at that time did not yet exist as a descriptive category beyond geographical connotations. An understanding developed, however, of nomads as a people of the "last days" and of Muslims as Judaizing pagans whose religious practices and behavior were unacceptable and condemnable. The invasion of and subsequent dependence on the Horde did not effect a cardinal change in this descriptive model, although the images of the nomadic Ishmaelites and the Muslims gradually merged. The result was the emergence of an image of Tatars as an aggressive and treasonous people. The topos of treason came to be defining in descriptions of the Tatars and was replicated from text to text. The Russian mind did not develop other descriptive strategies, neither under the Golden Horde nor later, following liberation from it. However, it is obvious that more complex models that would perforce facilitate the process of assimilation and, finally, appropriation of this "Other" were bound to be produced within the framework of intensive military, diplomatic, and trade contacts. To clarify this question, we must turn to another group of sources—namely, diplomatic materials.

Strategies for Describing the Tatars in Diplomatic Documentation

Between the late fifteenth and the seventeenth centuries, Russian diplomacy developed a corpus of documents that reflected the means of international communication and the method of organizing foreign relations. These documents include an interesting group of reports by diplomats on their stay in their destination country and the conditions of fulfilling their mission, known as digests (*otpiski*) and summary reports (*stateinye spiski*). These reports were first oral but gradually became written. Scholars generally note a clerical connection between the digests and itemized notes and the envoy's instruction, known as a commission (*nakaz*) or warrant (*nakaznaia pamiat'*). However, even though this connection existed, it was not rigidly definitive.

The report was similar in form to a journal: the envoys recorded where possible their arrival dates, main ceremonies and negotiations, and the time of their departure. Often, the chronology in these texts was relative and anchored

---

40 For more information about the Otherness problem, see Halperin, "Varieties of Otherness in Ivan IV's Muscovy: Relativity, Multiplicity, and Ambiguity" and Lehtovirta, "The Depiction of 'Us' and 'Them' in the Illuminated Codex of 1560s–1570s" in this volume.

by church holidays but sometimes also Muslim ones. The earliest type of document to appear in clerical practice was the digest. Digests were progress reports written during a journey and stay in the country of destination. The final report, or itemized note, composed after the conclusion of the mission and the return to the homeland, appeared later, around the middle of the sixteenth century. The itemized note was written based on the digests and other materials from the mission, with the texts of the digests being condensed and edited. The utilitarian nature of these documents meant they were for a long time used solely as diplomatic sources, while all the other rich information—on the host country, on noted behavioral practices, on rituals, and so on—was ignored.

Aleksandr Brikner, in a series of works on diplomat-tourists, suggested a step toward reinterpreting the content of itemized notes as their own form of travelogue.[41] He described his working method with this type of source as follows:

> In the stories of Russian travelers, what attracts us is not the very facts mentioned but the storyteller's relationship to the fact. From the impressions made on a Russian by various objects in western Europe in the seventeenth century, say, we can draw a conclusion on the Russian traveler's horizons, his taste and preferences, his manner of thinking, his opinions in various respects.[42]

The venerable professor at the University of Dorpat (Tartu) used ambassadorial itemized notes as a source in studying the cultural level of Russian diplomats and later as a source for the history of western cultural influence on Russia's culture, noting the paths of Europeanization of the Muscovite state under Peter I. In doing so, Brikner ignored the corpus of information on the internal structure of the countries to which the Muscovite ambassadors were posted and did not try to analyze the descriptive strategies they employed. This approach in and of itself still contained serious research potential, but alas, it has not been tapped by scholarship.

---

41 A. G. Brikner, "Russkie diplomaty-turisty v Italii v XVII stoletii," *Russkii vestnik* (Moscow: v universitetskoi tipografii [M. Katkov] na Strastnom bul'vare, 1877), 5–62; A. G. Brikner, "Russkii turist v Zapadnoi Evrope v nachale XVIII v.," *Russkoe obozrenie* (Moscow: v universitetskoi tipografii [M. Katkov] na Strastnom bul'vare, 1892), 5–38.

42 Brikner, "Russkie diplomaty-turisty v Italii v XVII stoletii," 5–62; Brikner, "Russkii turist v Zapadnoi Evrope v nachale XVIII v.," 5–6.

Yet another attempt to read the itemized notes as travel notes was made later. In 1954, in the *Literaturnye pamiatniki* (Literary Monuments) series under the supervision of D. S. Likhachev, Ia. S. Lur'e and R. B. Miuller published several itemized notes under the common title of *Puteshestiviia russkikh poslov XVI–XVII vv.* (Travels of Russian ambassadors in the sixteenth to seventeenth centuries). However, in the final article, D. S. Likhachev defined the itemized notes as stories (*povesti*) and characterized them as sui generis literary monuments.[43] Concluding his survey, the scholar wrote:

> The itemized notes played a large role in the development of Russian prose. They incorporated traits of living reality and fresh impressions, they mixed official and colloquial language, and they developed the art of dialogue and the art of storytelling. The itemized notes paved the way for the emergence of complex travel literature: travel notes and storytelling given a literary treatment.[44]

Overall, the reports of Russian diplomats are a complex source that is genetically tied to recordkeeping but also has the traits of literary works close to travelogues. These texts allow us to reconstruct the frame of mind of Russian people of the sixteenth and seventeenth centuries, as well as the strategies Russians used to describe the image of the "Other." Let us examine these sources in more detail.

The earliest form of the itemized note, a final report, was a list sent by the envoy Vladimir Plemiannikov, who was with the legation in the Holy Roman Empire of the German Nation in 1518. Letters missive (*gramoty*) "with news" or digests remained the primary reporting document until the 1560s.[45] The message of Daniil Gubin, son of Ivan, the Russian envoy to the Nogai Horde in 1534, was a document of precisely this kind.

He sent all of three digests to Moscow during his mission; they were all copied into the ambassadorial book (*posol'skaia kniga*).[46] Gubin was sent to the Nogai bey (title of the ruler of the Nogai Horde) Said-Ahmed in the autumn

---

43 D. S. Likhachev, "Povesti russkikh poslov kak pamiatniki literatury," in *Puteshestiviia russkikh poslov XVI–XVII vv.*, ed. D. S. Likhachev, Ia. S. Lur'e, and R. B. Miuller (St. Petersburg: Nauka, 2008 [1954]), 319–46.

44 Ibid., 346.

45 Likhachev, "Povesti russkikh poslov kak pamiatniki literatury," 326–27, section written by Ia. S. Lur'e.

46 N. M. Rogozhin, ed., *Posol'skie knigi po sviaziam Rossii s Nogaiskoi Ordoi. 1489–1549* (Makhachkala: Dagestanskoe knizhnoe izdatel'stvo, 1995), 124–30, 145–55, 158–63.

of 1534 during a worsening in Russian-Nogai relations. The first digest was delivered to Moscow on May 2, 1535.[47] Daniil Gubin reached the Nogai uluses on November 19, 1534, where he received a more than cool reception.

The bey's ambassador left the Russian embassy, and the ambassadors from the Nogai mirzas fell upon the Russian ambassador and his entourage of Tatar servicemen, demanding they immediately arrange a "wake" for their lords. When this demand was refused, the Nogai attacked, beat the commander of the Tatar servicemen, confiscated the Russian legation's horses, and stole some of the ambassadorial gifts.[48] They then managed to reach Said–Ahmed's dominion, where they started to demand they be paid duties. "Give us three times nine, and nine for each horse–load."[49]

In this description, apart from the practice of extracting duties from the legation, what is notable is the fact that the Russian envoy separated the concepts of "Nogai uluses" and "Shyidiakov's princely uluses." This allows for the suggestion that, from Gubin's perspective, the Nogai Horde was not fully a state, as the borders of the Horde were not the same as the borders held directly by the bey. In other words, from the diplomat's perspective, not all the Horde was subject to the power of its supreme ruler. It may be suggested that he perceived the Horde as a collection of various nomadic domains or alliances.

After reaching the "prince's uluses," the diplomat describes the standard situation in which he was met and allotted provender ("a barren cow and carts"), but he refuses to perceive the extraction of duties as normal practice and calls it robbery.[50] Significantly, the practice of providing maintenance of the legation was still observed. Gubin himself, describing his own altercations very emotionally, stressed that he had been completely robbed; however, he also wrote that "The prince, sire, gave me food in the amount of a calf three or four weeks of this month."[51]

He then goes on to describe a ceremony that he defines as *kornysh* (the ritual of the meeting). This meeting took place on 3 February 1535. Gubin delivered speeches from the Russian tsar, and the bey Said-Ahmed listened to them. After that, he described a drinking ritual (this was apparently an element of the table ceremony). Said-Ahmed ordered that the Russian diplomat be served drink with the words: "I do not serve you with my own hands, as I am angry with your

---

47 Ibid., 123–24.
48 Ibid., 124.
49 Ibid., 125.
50 Ibid., 126.
51 Ibid.

ruler."[52] Such a caveat shows that here we are encountering a deviation from normal practice when the bey should have served a drink to the ambassador personally. In Gubin's description, the kornysh is not just a ritual but a real power institution of the Nogai Horde at which foreign policy matters are decided.

The next digest arrived in Moscow on September 26, 1535. Gubin writes in this document about a conference of the Nogai mirzas then goes on to write again about a kornysh, one to which he was not admitted, reasoning that Said-Ahmed was waiting for a general conference of mirzas "for their holiday, June 12."[53] The final digest was delivered on October 7, 1535. Here, the envoy again laid out all the twists and turns of accomplishing his mission.

The text of the digests itself is quite densely written and contains information about a wide sphere of questions of international affairs beyond the scope of Russian-Nogai relations. At the same time, they contain very few observations of everyday life in the Horde, and those that are present are as a rule linked with political and military matters. This rare lack of the curiosity we are entitled to expect from a traveler has long stumped researchers of Russian diplomatic reports. Various explanatory models are proposed to explain it, but we can assume that it can be interpreted by starting with the perspective of the critical perception of the idleness characteristic of Russian culture in the sixteenth and seventeenth centuries: curiosity is a direct consequence of this idleness.

Whereas the pilgrim on his journeys noted in the first instance religious practices and churches on his travels, and this was his "business," the diplomat concentrated on political questions. The area of "work" was defined by an order and for the moment had quite a narrow scope. Muscovite Russia's sphere of political interest was still undeveloped, as was its political language. However, Gubin's digests contain several points that allow us to define the image of the Other that he saw.

First, he very clearly delimits "their holiday" and does not even say what it was called. For him, this holiday is completely foreign and needs no description, as a description is the first step to understanding and perhaps to an integration into his cultural landscape. Precisely to prevent that, "their holiday" is decisively placed in the sphere of the unnamed, which means it is undistinguished and therefore nonexistent.

Second, Gubin uses two terms in his descriptions of the political rituals: kornysh and "conference" (s"ezd). Here, too, we face various strategies. He translates the name of one Nogai Horde power institution into Russian, whereas

---

52 Ibid.
53 Ibid., 146, 147.

he does not provide a Russian equivalent for the other, and, significantly, he does not even seek one. Proceeding from the text of the digests, a kornysh is an audience, and not only before a bey but before any Nogai aristocrat. Thus, he mentions a kornysh before Sheikh-Mamai, which did not occur, and a kornysh before Ismail, which did. A conference, on the other hand, was of a general nature, and all the mirzas were expected to attend. To Daniil Gubin's mind, it was the conference that was particularly important as it reflected the unity of the Nogai Horde.

Interestingly, all the work of creating these descriptive strategies took place in a rich flow of Turkic names, names of rivers, mentions of nomadic encampments, and much else, which shows that Russian culture did not have a strict taboo against what was Turkic or Tatar. In other words, we may assume that the sphere of the Other did not include all Tatars but only certain facets of their life and culture.

In that regard, the sustained untranslatability of a series of political and social terms is noteworthy. Thus, in addition to the kornysh or *korniush*, traditionally understood as a reception held by the head of a Tatar dynasty,[54] other words left untranslated included court and state titles and ranks, both Tatar and Ottoman: *cheush, bashmakchei, sanchak*, and so on. These titles were sometimes briefly glossed, but more often they were not only not translated but were perceived as names, as occurred in the Russian-Ottoman diplomatic correspondence with the Azov *dezdar*, when the missives would either replace a name with a title or merge a name and title.[55] The fact that concepts were left untranslated could be less a sign of assimilation of this terminology[56] or a "conspiracy of silence"[57] than a marker of "otherness" and the desire not to accept the words and phenomena he recorded.[58]

In this context, it makes sense to remember the instruction of Bernhard Waldenfels: "Otherness and Response make up a single whole but in a way in which the other challenges us by escaping our grasp and going beyond the

---

54 M. V. Moiseev, ed.; *Posol'skaia kniga po sviaziam Moskovskogo gosudarstva s Krymom: 1567–1572 gg* (Moscow: Fond "Russkie vitiazi," 2016), 70–72, 74–75, 89, 92–93, 104, 160, 162, 167, 173, 227.

55 The 1571 missive is addressed "To the Azov *dizdarzefer*," see RGADA, f. 89, op. 1, kn. 2, l. 154.

56 Mikhail Khodarkovskii, *Stepnye rubezhi Rossii: kak sozdavalas' kolonial'naia imperiia: 1500–1800* (Moscow: Novoe literaturnue obozrenie, 2019), 79.

57 K. Iu. Erusalimskii, "Obrazy rossiiskogo orientalizma (Obzor)," *Novoe literaturnoe obozrenie* 161, no. 1 (2020): 378–91.

58 Moiseev, *Posol'skaia kniga po sviaziam Moskovskogo gosudarstva s Krymom. 1567–1572 gg.,* 70–72, 74–75, 89, 92–93, 104, 160, 162, 167, 173, 227.

limits of our understanding."[59] In other words, developing these observations and applying them to the real political situation, we can note that a rather extensive layer of political reality and culture of post-Horde states went, as it were, "unobserved." They are recorded, described in little detail, but remain beyond the boundaries of "Ours," and the failure to translate here is precisely a medium of such exclusion, that very same "response" of Waldenfels. The mechanism of the "response" was to leave the "Other" beyond the threshold of understanding, and diplomats who found themselves in the midst of a stream of that "Other," when foreign phenomena surrounded them and represented normative practice, were forced to ascribe to them the nature of "the extra-orderly, which by various means reaches the surface along the edges of and in gaps within all possible orders."[60] Under these condition, the usual topoi used in describing the Tatars—as cruel, aggressive, and treasonous—are far from being in the foreground, if they exist at all. What does come to the fore are features of everyday interaction and ceremonies, questions of organizing the content of the legation, and conflicts with the functionaries of the receiving side, the gathering of information, and negotiations. Coming in contact with the local diplomatic custom, with the structure of local officialdom, Russian diplomats record them and more often than not leave them untranslated, thereby sealing their belonging to the sphere of the "Other."

Image of the Tatars in the Reports of Border Voivodes

The voivodes' digests present another interesting group of sources. The voivodes of border towns actively corresponded not only with the capital but also with each other and with the authorities in foreign border cities. The entire complex of the local policy of these voivodes (in the regions of Astrakhan, Terek, Siberia, and others) can be defined as lesser or border diplomacy. In their dispatches to Moscow, the voivodes described the local situation in standard, recognized descriptive language. At the same time, the voivodes' chancelleries stored the digests of local fur tribute [yasak] collectors, sentries, and investigators, which contained a highly interesting body of data that can be viewed as the forerunner of Russian ethnography. Ultimately, it was the provincial powers who established the traditions of demography that, although revised in the eighteenth century, nevertheless came to form the basis of Russian ethnography.

---

59 Bernhard Waldenfels, *Motiv chuzogo* (Minsk: Propilei, 1999), 123.
60 Ibid., 124.

Let us examine some letters missive (*gramoty*) issued by the Astrakhan authorities in the early seventeenth century. A descriptive strategy close to that developed by Russian envoys in the Tatar states was characteristic of these texts. For example, when describing the Nogais, the Astrakhan voivodes aimed at describing their affiliation with a specific Nogai mirza as accurately as possible: "Odnash Bazarov of the Ishterekov ulus" or "Korakelmametev of Bayzigit Ucheshev's ulus."[61] A geographic nomenclature had already been formed, but the presence of an alternative one, which is even recognized in secondary cases, is acknowledged: "they were sent from Yaik, from Sol'ianaia Gora, which is called Inder in Tatar."[62] The ethnic situation in Astrakhan was described in the following ways: "Russian people [. . .] Nogai and Yurt Tatars" or "in the city, in the fortress, and on the squares, and in the yurts."[63]

We may suppose that the terms "Yurt Tatars" and "Nogai" allowed the Russian powers to define the population of the Astrakhan region and environs when borders were porous, and the nomadic way of life remained. In any event, such a distinction is presupposed in the digest of the Samara voivode Prince Dmitrii Pozharskii:

> And the Nogai and Ishcherekov Tatars will run out of Astrakhan, but the Yurt Tatars with their wives and children all ran out of Astrakhan to the Nogai Horde, and the old Tatars, who had been born in Astrakhan and had always lived there—all these Tatars fled to the Nogai.[64]

Thus, in this text we see that everything "Tatar" (from the Russian voivode's perspective at the start of the seventeenth century) is divided into three groups. The first group is the Nogais of the Great Nogai Horde, who temporarily found themselves in the city. The second group is the Yurt Tatars, who quite possibly made up a nonlocal element; at any rate, they had not "always" lived there. The third group is the old Tatars who, clearly, made up the core group of the Astrakhan population. Consequently, we can confidently say that the voivode gave a fully correct description of the complicated ethnic picture that had formed in the lower Volga region and that he describes it using three terms— namely, "Ishterekov Nogais," Yurt Tatars, and old Tatars. Unfortunately, we do

---

61 *Akty istoricheskie* (St. Petersburg: V tipografii P-go Otdeleniia Sobstvennoi E. I. V. kantseliarii, 1841), 3:25.
62 Ibid.
63 Ibid., 216, 282.
64 Ibid., 422.

not now have the analytical perspective to allow us to clarify this terminology further, but we can acknowledge that Russian thought in the early seventeenth century had already formed a conceptual apparatus that was more precise than it had been at the turn of the fifteenth and sixteenth centuries, even if it was far from being as precise as the refined analytics of subsequent centuries.

Conclusion

The description of the Other in Russian thought went through several stages; in the course of this process, the sphere of this Other acquired details. Before the Mongol conquest, we see very general perceptions of the East, which is thought of exclusively in geographic terms; we see a division among the peoples of the east into Ishmaelite nomads and *busurman* Muslims. In this picture, the nomads were heralds of the end of the world, and Muslims were a Judeo-pagan sect. The Mongol invasion and subsequent dependence, first on the Mongol state and then on the Golden Horde, led to a merging of the images of nomads and Muslims, and in the end the concept of "Tatars" emerged, a treasonous and highly aggressive people. During the period of dependence on the Golden Horde, Russian thought was not prepared to perceive the "East" outside the framework of a concrete political formation, the Golden Horde. However, as liberation from this dependence progressed, the picture of the "East" starts to become more complex. The topos of treason became definitive in descriptions of the Tatars and spread from text to text. Russian thought did not develop other descriptive strategies, either under the Golden Horde or later, following liberation from it. However, whereas literary descriptions come to a halt on this level, the descriptive model becomes more complex in the everyday practice of contacts, which was reflected in official writing, such as the reports of diplomats and the correspondence of voivodes. In these conditions, the customary topoi used to describe the Tatars as cruel, aggressive, and treasonous were, if present, far from at the forefront. Traits of everyday socializing and ceremonies, organizational matters of the maintenance of the embassy, disputes with functionaries of the host country, information gathering, and negotiations came to the fore. When Russian diplomats encountered a local ambassadorial custom and the local rank structure, they recorded them and most often left them untranslated, thus cementing their belonging to the sphere of the "Other." In the voivodes' practices, however, this sphere of the "Other" turned out to be a working area, which is why an apparatus of categories was born that became the basis for a nascent ethnography. Gradually, the "Other" is assimilated and appropriated, and its boundaries are blurred and "thinned." The concept of allegiance became the decisive factor for the appropriation of the "Other." Now, every person is first and foremost a loyal subject of the Orthodox tsar, and if that is true, then all traits of "otherness" fall into the background. Thus, in the sixteenth and seventeenth centuries, the image of the "Other" is subject less to reinterpretation than inflation: in losing its attributes, it nevertheless retained them, first and foremost in terms of religious culture.

Works Cited

Archival Sources

Rossiiskii gosudarstvennii arkhiv drevnikh aktov (RGADA). Fond 89 (Snosheniia Rossii s Turtsiei). Op. 1, kn. 2.

Rossiiskii gosudarstvennii arkhiv drevnikh aktov (RGADA). Fond 123 (Snosheniia Rossii s Krymom). Op. 1, kn. 2.

Printed Sources and Literature

Akty istoricheskie. Vol. 3. St. Petersburg: V tipografii Vtorogo Otdeleniia Sobstvennoi Ego Imperatorskogo Velichestva kantseliarii, 1841.

Amel'kin, A. O. "Natsional'naia katastrofa v obshchestvennom soznanii pravoslavnogo naseleniia v epokhu srednevekoviia." In *Nashestvie Batyia i ustanovlenie ordynskogo iga v obshchestvennom soznanii Rusi XIII–XVII vekov.* Edited by A. O. Amel'kin and Yu. A. Seleznev, 7–11. Voronezh: Tipografiia IP Aleinikova, 2004.

Andreicheva, M. Iu. *Obrazy inovertsev v Povesti vremennykh let.* St. Petersburg: Nestor-Istoriia, 2019.

Bakhtin, A. G. *XV–XVI veka v istorii Mariiskogo kraia.* Ioshkar-Ola: Mariiskii poligraficheskо-izdatel'skii kombinat, 1998.

Brikner, A. G. "Russkie diplomaty-turisty v Italii v XVII stoletii." *Russkii vestnik* 128: 5–31. Moscow: V universitetskoi tipografii (M. Katkov) na Strastnom bul'vare, 1877.

———. "Russkie diplomaty-turisty v Italii v XVII stoletii." *Russkii vestnik* 130: 5–62. Moscow: V universitetskoi tipografii (M. Katkov) na Strastnom bul'vare, 1877.

———. "Russkii turist v Zapadnoi Evrope v nachale XVIII v." *Russkoe obozrenie* 1 (1892): 5–38.

Erusalimskii, K. Iu. *Sbornik Kurbskogo.* Vol. 2: *Issledovanie knizhnoi kul'tury.* Moscow: Znak, 2009.

———. "Obrazy rossiiskogo orientalizma (Obzor)." *Novoe literaturnoe obozrenie* 161, no. 1 (2020): 378–91.

Halperin, Charles. *Tatarskoe igo. Obraz mongolov v srednevekovoi Rossii.* Translated by M. E. Kopylova. Voronezh: Izdatel'stvo Voronezhskogo gosudarstvennogo universiteta, 2012.

Khodarkovskii, Mikhail. *Stepnye rubezhi Rossii: kak sozdavalas' kolonial'naia imperiia. 1500–1800.* Moscow: Novoe literaturnoe obozrenie, 2019.

Khudiakov, M. G. *Ocherki po istorii Kazanskogo khanstva.* Moscow: INSAN, 1991.

Kuntsevich, G. Z. "Dva rasskaza o pokhodakh tsaria Ivana Vasil'evicha Groznogo na Kazan' v 1550 i 1552 godakh." *Pamiatniki drevnei pis'mennosti i iskusstva 30. Otchety o zasedaniiakh imperatorskogo obshchestva liubitelei drevnei pis'mennosti v 1897–1898 gody s prilozheniiami.* St. Petersburg: Tipografiia V. S. Balasheva i Ko, 1898.

Likhachev, D. S. "Povesti russkikh poslov kak pamiatniki literatury." *Puteshestviia russkikh poslov XVI–XVII vv.* Edited by D. S. Likhachev, 319–46. St. Petersburg: Nauka, 2008.

Lur'e, Ia. S and D. Rykov, eds. *Perepiska Ivana Groznogo s Andreem Kurbskim.* Moscow: Nauka, 1993.

Makarii arkh. (Veretennikov). *Iz istorii russkoi ierarkhii XVI veka.* Moscow: Podvor'e Sviato-Troitskoi Sergievoi Lavry, 2006.

Moiseev, M. V., ed. *Posol'skaia kniga po sviaziam Moskovskogo gosudarstva s Krymom. 1567–1572 gg.* Moscow: Fond 'Russkie vitiazi', 2016.

Moiseev, M. V. Sviatye protiv Kazanskogo khanstva: 'chudesnaia' istoriia kazanskoi voiny." *Evropa sviatykh. Sotsial'nye, politicheskie i kul'turnye aspekty sviatosti v Srednie veka.* Edited by S. Iatsyk, 273–84. St. Petersburg: Aleteiia, 2018.

———. "Azov (Azak) v 1570 g. v donesenii russkogo poslannika Ivana Novosil'tseva." *Srednevekovye tiurko-tatarskie gosudarstva* 11 (2019): 60–66.

Pamiatniki diplomaticheskikh snoshenii drevnei Rossii s derzhavami inostrannymi. Vol. 1. Part 1. St. Petersburg: pechatano v tipografii II Otdeleniia Sobstvennoi Ego Imperatorskogo Velichestva kantseliarii, 1851.

Demkova, N. S., ed. "Povest' o Timofee Vladimirskom." Text prepared, translated, and annotated by N. S. Demkova. *Biblioteka literatury Drevnei Rusi*, Vol. 9, 106–13. St. Petersburg: Nauka, 2000.

Polnoe sobranie russkikh letopisei (PSRL). Vol. 13. Moscow: Iazyki russkoi kul'tury, 2000.

Puteshestviia russkikh poslov XVI–XVII vv. St. Petersburg: Nauka. 2008.

Rogozhin, N. M., ed. *Posol'skie knigi po sviaziam Rossii s Nogaiskoi Ordoi. 1489–1549.* Makhachkala: Dagestanskoe knizhnoe izdatel'stvo, 1995.

Rudakov, V. N. *Mongolo-tatary glazami drevnerusskikh knizhnikov serediny XIII–XIV vv.* Moscow: Kvadriga, 2009.

Schimmelpenninck van der Oye, David. *Russkii orientalizm. Aziia v rossiiskom soznanii ot epokhi Petra Velikogo do Beloi emigratsii.* Moscow: Politicheskaia entsiklopediia, 2019.

Seleznev, Iu. V. "Ideino-religioznaia otsenka sovremennikami russko-ordynskikh otnoshenii 1240–1270 gg." In *Nashestvie Batyia i ustanovlenie ordynskogo iga v obshchestvennom soznanii Rusi XIII–XVII vekov.* Edited by A. O. Amel'kin and Iu. A. Seleznev, 34–51. Voronezh: Tipografiia IP Aleinikova, 2004.

———. *Russkie kniaz'ia v sostave praviashchei elity Dzhuchieva ulusa v XIII–XV vv.* Voronezh: Tsentral'no-Chernozemnoe knizhnoe izdatel'stvo, 2013.

Shaposhnik, V. V. *Tserkovno-gosudarstvennye otnosheniia v Rossii v 30–80-e gody XVI veka.* St. Petersburg: Izdatel'stvo S.–Peterburgskogo universiteta, 2006.

Volkova, T. F. ed., *Kazanskaia istoriia.* Translated by T. F. Volkova. Vol. 10. St. Petersburg: Nauka, 2000.

Waldenfeld, Bernhard. *Motiv chuzogo.* Minsk: Propilei, 1999.

Zimin, A. A. *I. S. Peresvetov i ego sovremenniki. Ocherki po istorii russkoi obshchestvenno-politicheskoi mysli serediny XVI veka.* Moscow: Izdatel'stvo AN SSSR, 1958.

———. *Formirovanie boiarskoi aristokratii v Rossii vo vtoroi polovine XV–pervoi treti XVI v.* Moscow: Nauka, 1988.

4

From *Inozemtsy* to *Inovertsy* and *Novokreshchenye*: Images of Otherness in Eighteenth-Century Russia

Ricarda Vulpius

Abstract

This chapter focuses on the different categories of otherness that the Russian elite created in the eighteenth century while ruling over the southern and eastern peripheries of the tsarist empire. We will examine how the construction of otherness changed in the seventeenth century, and how the perceived differences were subsequently perpetuated resulting in the creation of a new legal category in 1822, the *inorodtsy*. In spite of a general assimilatory policy, non-Russians in the east and south remained delineated as "Foreign believers" (*inovertsy*) from "natural Russians" (*prirodnye Rossiiane*). Even after conversion to Russian orthodoxy the "Foreign believers" (inovertsy) did not become "Russians" but were labelled "Newly converted" (*novokreshcheny, novokreshchennye*). This category is of particular interest: it was, in the first place, a category with social and cultural traits, but gradually it also received legal features. At the end of the eighteenth century the description inorodtsy gained acceptance, shifting the emphasis away from differences in religion, lifestyle and customs to less changeable criteria. The new category inorodtsy represented difference that was supposed to wane by means of assimilatory politics or politics of acculturation.

Introduction

The eighteenth century represents a key turning point in Russian ideas about who in Russia was to be regarded as "Other" and how they were to be designated. With the conquest of the Baltic provinces, the expansion into the Far East and Russian America, and the acquisition of the southern Steppe, the Crimea, and domains in partitioned Poland, the tsarist empire not only made decisive territorial gains. This was also a period of profound change in traditional ways of thinking and in how power politics was practiced by Russia's elites. Only at this point did the change in mindset result in the formation of an all-encompassing imperial consciousness.[1]

Since Otherness does not exist in its own right but arises only as a result of projection, the construct of "Other" is closely connected with the construct of one's own collective.[2] It therefore stands to reason that the shift in how the elites in eighteenth-century Russia saw themselves also influenced the criteria they used to decide who was to be regarded as "Other," for example, as foreign.

The terminology used to denote "internal others," in other words, those who were subjects of the tsar but who were not counted as core people of the Russian empire, mirrors very precisely these changes in images of Other and self. This chapter will focus, firstly, on how the term inozemtsy ("those originating from other lands")—a term used from the fifteenth century until roughly 1720—was replaced by the designation inovertsy ("those of other faiths," c. 1680–1820).[3] Secondly, it will examine the term novokreshchenye ("newly baptized"), which was used from the fifteenth century until the second half of the nineteenth, but became widespread only in the eighteenth century.[4]

---

1   The following is based largely on my recently published monograph: Ricarda Vulpius, *Die Geburt des Russländischen Imperiums. Herrschaftskonzepte und -praktiken im 18. Jahrhundert* (Vienna: Böhler Verlag, 2020).

2   S. V. Sokolovskii, *Obrazy Drugikh v rossiiskoi nauke, politike i prave* (Moscow: Put', 2001), 41–82.

3   It was not until the early nineteenth century that the term *inovertsy* was gradually replaced by *inorodtsy* (alien/of foreign origin, 1790–1917) and for those in Russian Alaska by *kreoly* (indigenous). John W. Slocum, "Who, and When, Were the Inorodtsy? The Evolution of the Category of 'Aliens' in Imperial Russia," *Russian Review* 57 (1998): 173–90; Ilya Vinkovetsky, "Circumnavigation, Empire, Modernity, Race: The Impact of Round-the-World Voyages on Russia's Imperial Consciousness," *Ab Imperio* 1–2 (2001): 191–210.

4   Andreas Kappeler, "Kak klassifitsirovali russkie istochniki 16-serediny 19vv etno-religioznye gruppy Volgo-Ural'skogo regiona?," in *Ispovedi v zerkale. Mezhkonfessional'nye otnosheniia v tsentre Evrazii (na primere Volgo-Ural'skogo regiona XVII–XXI vv.)*, ed. Stefan A. Dyuduan'on (Nizhnii Novgorod: Nizhegorodskii gosudarstvennyi lingvisticheskii universitet, 2012); Leonid A. Taimasov, "From 'Kazan's Newly Converted' to 'Orthodox Inorodtsy': The Historical Stages of the Affirmation of Christianity in the Middle Volga Region," in *Imperiology:*

The most suitable sources for tracing how the construct of Otherness changed over time are those in which Russia's imperial elites defined the legal and administrative coordinates for the coexistence of the many peoples of the empire.[5] Documents of the executive likewise capture well the perceptions of government representatives on the periphery of the empire regarding the administrative, military, economic, and religious spheres. The type of source chosen underlines the fact that the images of Otherness addressed here are, without exception, *attributions*. By their very nature, they do not say anything about how those perceived as "Other" saw themselves. Yet these official attributions by state officials were certainly of great relevance, irrespective of the question of whether those identified as "Other" internalized this status or not. The attributions were representations, perceptions, and conceptualizations of social life; they reflected the interaction between the Russian elite and non-Russians; and they helped to form these perceptions but were also transformed by them. As categories of legal significance, they were fundamentally important for the life chances of individuals and collectives. They defined the rights and obligations of subjects, their access to education, their right to own property and to trade, and their access to production opportunities and to both material and personal resources.[6]

As the change in terminology from inozemtsy to inovertsy suggests, over the centuries the Russian elites came to see Otherness from different points of

From Empirical Knowledge to Discussing the Russian Empire, ed. Kimitaka Matsuzato (Sapporo: Slavic Research Center, 2007); A. Iu. Konev, "Pravovoe polozhenie 'novokreshchenykh inovertsev' Sibiri. XVII–XVIII veka," *Vestnik Novosibirskogo Gosudarstvennogo Universiteta 5, Seriia: Istoriia, filologiia 3: Arkheologiia i etnografiia*: 20–25. Paul W. Werth, *At the Margins of Orthodoxy: Mission, Governance, and Confessional Politics in Russia's Volga-Kama Region, 1827–1905* (Ithaca: Cornell University Press, 2002); Sokolovskii, *Obrazy Drugikh v rossiiskoi nauke, politike i prave*, 55–61; Michael Khodarkovsky, "'Ignoble Savages and Unfaithful Subjects': Constructing Non-Christian Identities in Early Modern Russia," in *Russia's Orient: Imperial Borderlands and Peoples, 1700–1917*, ed. Daniel R. Brower and Edward J. Lazzerini (Bloomington: Indiana University Press, 1997); Michael Khodarkovsky, "Four Degrees of Separation: Constructing Non-Christian Identities in Muscovy," in *Cultural Identity in Muscovy, 1359–1584*, ed. A. M. Kleimola and G. D. Lenhoff (Moscow: ITZ-Garant, 1997); Andreas Kappeler, *Rußlands erste Nationalitäten. Das Zarenreich und die Völker der Mittleren Wolga vom 16. Bis 19. Jahrhundert* (Vienna: Böhlau Verlag, 1982); Hans-Heinrich Nolte, "Verständnis und Bedeutung der religiösen Toleranz in Rußland 1600–1725," *Jahrbücher für Geschichte Osteuropas* 17, no. 1 (1969): 494–530.

5 Fundamental here are the forty-eight volumes of the Complete Collection of Laws of the Russian Empire, *Polnoe sobranie zakonov Rossiiskoi Imperii* (hereafter cited as PSZRI), which, however—despite what their name suggests—were far more than just legislative texts and as such constitute numerous sources of the executive with the character of legal norms.

6 Elise K. Wirtschafter, "Social Categories in Russian Imperial History," *Cahiers du monde russe* 50, no. 2–3 (April-September 2009): 213–50.

view. The categories of difference used to construct Otherness were nonetheless closely linked. Hardly any of them were wholly replaced; rather, depending on the respective historical and situational context, they simply changed their relative ranking within the list of criteria. In most cases, as this chapter posits, the categories merged into one another, reinforcing each other in the process. The concept of intersectionality, first applied in gender and diversity research but subsequently also used by historians, would seem particularly appropriate for describing the definition of Early Modern parameters of Otherness.[7] This approach seeks not only to capture constructs of social, economic, and cultural differences over time and in the relationship between societal structures and individual action, but goes further: using an intersectional analysis it also focuses on the reciprocal effects of the respective perceptions of difference in the various categories and on how they reinforced or complemented one another and/or consigned other characteristics to the background.[8]

Inozemtsy ("Those Originating from Other Lands")

A central focus of this chapter is the Russian imperial elite's images of non-Russians within the tsarist empire who were subjects of the tsar but who were not Christians. Up to and including the first two decades of the eighteenth century these people were called inozemtsy—a word comprising the prefix *ino*- meaning "different/other" and the suffix *zemtsy*, which is closely related to the word "land" (*zemlia*). Thus, from Moscow's point of view, the inozemtsy were

---

7 Matthias Bähr and Florian Kühnel, ed., *Verschränkte Ungleichheit. Praktiken der Intersektionalität in der Frühen Neuzeit* (Berlin: Duncker & Humblot: 2018); Moritz Florin, Victoria Gutsche, and Natalie Krentz, ed., *Diversität historisch. Repräsentationen und Praktiken gesellschaftlicher Differenzierung im Wandel* (Bielefeld: Transcript, 2018); Birgit Emich, "Normen an der Kreuzung. Intersektionalität statt Konkurrenz oder: Die unaufhebbare Gleichzeitigkeit von Amt, Stand und Patronage," in *Normenkonkurrenz in historischer Perspektive*, ed. Arne Karsten and Hillard von Thiessen (Berlin: Duncker & Humblot, 2015), 83–100; Andrea Griesebner and Susanne Hehenberger, "Intersektionalität. Ein brauchbares Konzept für die Geschichtswissenschaft?," in *Intersectionality und Kritik: Neue Perspektiven auf alte Fragen*, ed. Vera Kallenberg, Jennifer Meyer, and Johanna M. Müller (Wiesbaden: Springer Verlag, 2013), 105–24.
8 See Emich's critical modification of the intersectional model (Emich, "Normen an der Kreuzung. Intersektionalität statt Konkurrenz oder: Die unaufhebbare Gleichzeitigkeit von Amt, Stand und Patronage"); Julia Obertreis, "Intersektionalität im Russischen Reich? Wechselwirkungen zwischen Kategorien sozialer Differenz im 19. Jahrhundert und der *spatial turn*," in *Diversität historisch. Repräsentationen und Praktiken gesellschaftlicher Differenzierung im Wandel*, ed. Moritz Florin, Victoria Gutsche, and Natalie Krentz (Bielefeld: Transcript Verlag, 2018), 161–92.

those who did not originate in the Russian core territory (*russkaia zemlia*) and whose origins were instead connected with other countries or territories.

The term inozemtsy therefore had a double meaning: on the one hand, it referred to "external foreigners," including those who came mainly from other European states and who resided in the tsarist empire; on the other, to "internal foreigners," who as subjects of the tsar had originally lived not in the "core territory of Russia" but in "other territories" and who together with these had successively been incorporated into Muscovy. They include former inhabitants of the Tatar-Mongolian Khanates of Kazan, Astrakhan, and Sibir' together with Kalmyks and Buryats who had migrated from Mongolia and many other ethnic groups who had settled or were itinerant in Siberia and the Far East.

What both groups, the "external" and the "internal" foreigners, had in common was that they did not belong to the Russian Orthodox Church, or at least had not done so since birth. The inozemtsy in the sense of "internal foreigners" were either Muslims (Muslim Crimean Tatars, originating from Central Asia), Buddhists (Kalmyks and Buryatians) or, in the case of the autochthonous people of Siberia, nature worshippers.

Conversely, linking geographical origin in the "core land of Russia" with the religious marker of membership of the Orthodox Church had for centuries been considered the most important criterion for deciding whether a person could be counted as Russian.[9] The intersectionality of geographical, ethno-social, and religious aspects—a typical phenomenon of pre-Modern societies—had been around since the Middle Ages and also found expression in the Russian word for "peasant" (*krest'ianin*), which literally translated means "one who belongs to the cross," a Russian Orthodox Christian, in other words.[10]

But what were those inozemtsy called who had converted either from Islam or from Buddhism or from nature religions to Orthodoxy and hence as both "those originating from other lands" *and* "those of other faiths" became adherents of the Russian Orthodox faith? In late fifteenth-century Spain, every group of converts became a social group with its own designation. Thus, the Spanish authorities called Jews who had converted to Christianity *conversos*, whereas converts from Islam were called *moriscos*. Even generations after their conversion these groups retained their official designations and, as such, were subject to discrimination.[11]

---

9 Nolte, "Verständnis und Bedeutung," 503–4.
10 Khodarkovsky, "Four Degrees of Separation," 265; Nolte, "Verständnis und Bedeutung," 503.
11 Kevin Ingram, "Introduction," in *The Conversos and Moriscos in Late Medieval Spain and Beyond. Vol. 1: Departures and Change*, ed. Kevin Ingram (Leiden: Brill, 2009), 1–21.

In the secondary literature, the view is still widespread that in the tsarist empire until well into the nineteenth century converting to Orthodoxy was tantamount to becoming a member of the Russian people.[12] With reference to Arnold van Gennep's model of "Rites of Passage," Michael Khodarkovsky gives a more nuanced account of the transition phase in the course of which inozemtsy could become "natural Russians" (*prirodnye russkie*). He divides it into three phases,[13] the first of which involved swearing an oath and giving hostages (in the case of collective entry), thus becoming subjects of the tsar and receiving a new political identity.[14] The second phase, the transition phase, entailed a change in economic status, expressed above all in the payment of a tribute called a *yasak*, for which only non-Christians who had been incorporated into the empire were liable.[15] Yasak is a word of Turkish origin used to describe the tribute that the principalities of Rus' and natives of Tatar khanates had to pay to the Mongols and essentially means "law or ordinance."[16] The subjugated were obliged to pay this tribute to the victor and it was strictly separated from the more or less voluntary payment of offerings and gifts (*pomniki*). In most cases, especially in much of Siberia and the Far East, the yasak was paid in the form of furs; elsewhere, such as in the Kazan region, it was sometimes paid in cash, at other times in goods.[17]

Accordingly, all those liable for the yasak were denoted "yasak-payers" (*iasachnye liudi*). In legal texts this term is often found as a synonym for inozemtsy. On the other hand, those who were not yet subjects of the tsar and were therefore not yet liable for the yasak—but in line with government wishes soon would be—were described as "inozemtsy who are not yet payers of the yasak" (*neiasachnye inozemtsy*)—prospective inozemtsy subjects, so to speak.

12 Liudmila I. Sherstova, *Tiurki i russkie v iuzhnoi Sibiri: Etnopoliticheskie protsessy i etnokul'turnaia dinamika XVII–nachala XX veka* (Novosibirsk: Institut arkheologii i etnografii SO RAN, 2005), 118–19; Nolte, " Verständnis und Bedeutung," 504; V. M. Gessen, *Poddanstvo, ego ustanovlenie i prekrashchenie*, vols. 1–2 (St. Petersburg: Pravda, 1909), 203–6. A more differentiated view is taken by Kappeler, "Kak klassifitsirovali russkie istochniki"; Khodarkovsky, "Four Degrees of Separation"; Werth, *At the Margins*.

13 Arnold van Gennep, *The Rites of Passage* (Chicago: University of Chicago Press, 1960); Victor Turner, *The Ritual Process: Structure and Anti-Structure* (Ithaca: Routledge, 1977); Khodarkovsky, "Four Degrees of Separation."

14 For more details on the modalities of becoming a Russian subject, see Vulpius, *Die Geburt des Russländischen Imperiums*, 53–73.

15 An exception were those non–Russians who had not been subjects of the Khanate of Kazan (Udmurts and West Mordvinians). These were not included in the group of *yasak*-payers, but instead integrated into the category of Russian peasants and assigned either to the "black," "court," or "monastery peasants." Kappeler, "Kak klassifitsirovali russkie istochniki," 20–22.

16 Sergei V. Bakhrushin, "Iasak v Sibiri v XVII v." *Nauchnye Trudy*, (Moscow: Akademiia Nauk SSSR, 1955), 3:49.

17 Ibid., 49–65.

In both cases, whether inozemtsy or iasachnye liudi, the terms emphasized that they were to be distinguished from the Russian majority population.[18]

The third stage identified by Khodarkovsky involved converting to the Orthodox faith and served as a final rite of incorporation which was followed by a change in customs as well as legal and economic integration.[19] Did this, then, mean for non-Christians that their conversion to Orthodoxy finally made them members of the core people of the tsarist empire? At first glance, there is much to suggest that this was the case: anyone who decided to be baptized in the seventeenth century was immediately exempted from paying the yasak. The idea was that those who decided to adopt the faith of their conquerors should no longer have to pay a tribute and therefore no longer belonged to the group of iasachnye liudi. But did this change in economic circumstances also mean becoming a member of the Russian majority population?

Categories of differentiation that continued to exist in the late seventeenth and early eighteenth centuries indicate that this was by no means always the case. Andreas Kappeler and Michael Khodarkovsky have already discovered that in early Muscovy, only the very top and the very bottom strata of society rapidly became assimilated. Thus, provided that they converted following their conquest in the sixteenth century, members of the Chinggisid dynasty of Astrakhan, the Crimea, Kazan, and Siberia, were allowed to carry Russian aristocratic titles and received many compensations in the form of land and money in return for military service.[20] At the other end of the social scale, it was often those converts who had to work as servants in Russian households who assimilated.[21] The overwhelming majority of all other Muslims or other non-Christians on the other hand continued to be called "newly baptized" (novokreshcheny, novokreshchennye) long after their conversion.[22] In most cases, they passed on this status to the next or even further generations. Legal texts from the late seventeenth and early eighteenth centuries also use formulations such as "newly baptized inozemtsy" or "baptized and unbaptized inozemtsy," indicating that their conversion by no means meant that the "newly baptized" became Russians,

---

18 Sokolovskii, *Obrazy Drugikh v rossiiskoi nauke, politike i prave*, 58–61.
19 Khodarkovsky, "Four Degrees of Separation," 249.
20 There are a number of examples where after two generations no non-Russian origin could be identified even in the names entered in the genealogy of the Russian aristocracy. Khodarkovsky, "Four Degrees of Separation," 261–62.
21 Ibid., 263.
22 The term "newly baptized" already appears in the mid-sixteenth century. Taimasov, "From 'Kazan's Newly Converted"; Kappeler, *Rußlands erste Nationalitäten*, 101.

but rather that—despite their change of confession—they often continued to be counted among the group of inozemtsy.[23]

Thus, it becomes clear that the attribute "new" said nothing about when an individual had converted. Rather, the imperial elite sought to form a special group who were expressly not to be merged with the core Russian people but were to be kept in a clearly identifiable transition phase. The intention was to demarcate this group both from the "natural Russians" and from members of their own ethnic group who had retained their original faith. The feature that distinguished the "newly baptized" from those in their society of origin was above all a socioeconomic one: without being baptized, the yasak-payers remained in the group of inozemtsy, paid yasak and in sociocultural and legal terms had far less to do with the Russian core population than the "newly baptized."

The Moscow authorities' terminological distinction between the inozemtsy, "the newly baptized," and the yasak-payers was not, however, founded on any kind of moral judgment:[24] the "Others" were allowed to remain different. While they were encouraged to convert, as a rule—until the 1680s—they did not suffer any disadvantages if they decided to remain true to their own faith. The only government stipulation that was a cause of socioeconomic pressure was the rule that "unbaptized people originating from other lands" (*nekreshchenye inozemtsy*) were not allowed to employ Orthodox servants in their households. The source language, however, testifies to the fact that this ruling was intended primarily to protect the Orthodox believers rather than to punish those of other faiths.[25] What is more, the Russian nobility was likewise not permitted to hold non-Christian serfs on their lands. It thus becomes clear that the main purpose of these regulations was to separate those of different faiths. It was only at the end of the seventeenth century under Tsar Fedor and the Regent Sof'ia that this long-term policy of tolerance was abandoned. Yet their attacks on exclusively Muslim estate owners were soon retracted again.[26]

Given, however, that in numerous cases, neither being a long-term subject of the tsar (a political change of identity) nor being a member of the Russian

---

23 PSZRI 2, no. 1117 (April 5, 1685), 662–63; PSZRI 3, no. 23 (February 18, 1696), 244–45; PSZRI 6, no. 3636 (November 1, 1720), 234–35.

24 Yuri Slezkine, "The Sovereign's Foreigners: Classifying the Native Peoples in Seventeenth-Century Siberia," *Russian History* 19, no. 1–4 (1992): 475–86; Yuri Slezkine, *Arctic Mirrors: Russia and the Small Peoples of the North* (Ithaca: Cornell University Press, 1994), 11–46.

25 PSZRI 1, no. 823 (May 21, 1680), 267; PSZRI 2, no. 867 (May 16, 1681), 312–13; PSZRI 2, no. 870 (May 24, 1681), 315; PSZRI 2, no. 955 (September 23, 1682), 467–68; T. A. Oparina and S. P. Orlenko, "Ukazy 1627 i 1652 godov protiv 'nekreshchennykh inozemtsei,'" *Otechestvennaia istoriia* 1 (2005): 22–39.

26 Kappeler, *Rußlands erste Nationalitäten*, 246–48.

Orthodox Church—despite its major importance as a criterion for the Russian collective perception—helped those in question to become members of the Russian majority society, it became clear that the perception of *ethnic* Otherness had a major role to play in the continuing demarcation. Here "ethnic" or "ethnic group" should be understood as a collective whose members saw themselves as cohesive on account of a shared past manifested in historical traditions, customs, language, and lifestyle. Indeed, the majority of the "newly baptized" had retained their former customs and their mostly Tatar identity. Many were baptized purely for economic motives and did not intend to relinquish their former way of life.[27]

At the beginning of the eighteenth century, at any rate, two things may be ascertained: firstly, although the Russian imperial elite defined Otherness primarily in terms of religion, ethnic-cultural markers also had a role to play. Secondly, the fragmented structure of early modern Russian society was conducive to the formation of socioeconomic groups with a special status, like that of the "newly baptized." One lexicon for Muscovite Russia records almost five hundred separate social categories to denote different ranks and statuses.[28] With so little legal cohesion, the formation in the sixteenth century of a new social group known as the "newly baptized" was nothing out of the ordinary but very much in keeping with Muscovy tradition.

With the beginning of Petrine rule in the eighteenth century, it was not only the self-perception of the Russian elite that changed dramatically but also their construct of Otherness. None of the earlier attributes lost its importance. Yet now a completely new attribute rose dramatically in significance and brought with it not only a new measure of Otherness but also new terminology.

A New Criterion and *Inovertsy*

In June 1700, Tsar Peter I instructed the newly appointed Metropolitan in Tobol'sk to ensure that "impenitents persisting in the blindness of idolatry and other forms of unbelief" should be led "to recognize, serve, and worship the true living God."[29] Learned monks from Kiev circles should "tackle superstition

---

27 Michael Khodarkovsky, "The Conversion of Non-Christians in Early Modern Russia," in *Of Religion and Empire. Missions, Conversion, and Tolerance in Tsarist Russia*, ed. Robert P. Geraci and Michael Khodarkovsky (Ithaca: Cornell University Press, 2001), 115–43.

28 G. E. Kochin, *Materialy dlia terminologicheskogo slovaria drevnei Rossii* (Moscow: Izdatel'stvo Akademii nauk SSSR, 1937), 436–39.

29 PSZRI 4, no. 1800 (June 18, 1700), 59–60.

at the roots and with solid proof of the Holy Gospels lead many souls out of the realm of Satanic darkness and towards the light of the true knowledge of Christ, our God."[30]

Never before in Muscovy, in times of peace and, what is more, decades *after* the incorporation of foreign ethnic groups by the state, had someone at the head of this state spoken of these groups as "impenitents persisting in the blindness of idolatry," of souls that were to be led to the light "out of the Satanic darkness." On the contrary, in the many decades since their incorporation, the beliefs of the Siberian ethnic groups had played no role whatsoever for the state. With these words, Tsar Peter I drew a connection between the concerns of the early West European Enlightenment and those of Christian missionaries.[31] By taking up a moral position, setting that imagined to be good against that imagined to be evil ("Satanic"), he ended the phase of relative religious tolerance in Muscovy that had lasted for more than a century. Within a few years, he paved the way for a discourse and a policy to gain the upper hand in the tsarist empire that signaled contempt on the part of Christians for nature religions and, in later decrees, asserted a conviction of the superiority of Christians over other, non-Christian religious communities (Muslim and Buddhist).[32]

Around the turn of the century the neologisms *politichnyi* ("civilized") and *liudskost'* (initially meaning "civility," later "civilization") had come to the Russian empire via Polish-Lithuanian and Ukrainian.[33] For the first time in the tsarist empire, these neologisms were used to form a hierarchy of collective forms of life and a perception that some ethnic groups were more civilized than

---

30 Ibid.

31 On the term "Early Enlightenment" coined by Eduard Winter and more generally on the division of the Enlightenment in Russia into periods, see Eduard Winter, *Frühaufklärung: Der Kampf gegen den Konfessionalismus und die deutsch-slawische Begegnung* (Berlin: Akademie Verlag, 1966); Marc Raeff, "The Enlightenment in Russia and Russian Thought in the Enlightenment," in *The Eighteenth Century in Russia*, ed. G. Garrard (Oxford: Oxford University Press, 1973); Elise K. Wirtschafter, "Thoughts on the Enlightenment and Enlightenment in Russia," *Journal of Modern Russian History and Historiography* 2 (2009): 1–26; Michael Schippan, *Die Aufklärung in Russland im 18. Jahrhundert* (Wiesbaden: Harassowitz Verlag, 2012).

32 *Pis'ma i bumagi imperatora Petra Velikogo* 1, no. 227 (St. Petersburg, Leningrad, Moscow, 1887–2003), 694–95; Vulpius, *Die Geburt des Russländischen Imperiums*, 300–302.

33 The word *liudskost'* is an East Slav equivalent of the Latin term *humanitas*, which was translated into the Western European vernaculars as *humanité* (French), *humanity* (English) and *Humanitet, Menschlichkeit* or *Menschheit* (German). Hans Erich Bödeker, "Menschheit, Humanität, Humanismus," in *Geschichtliche Grundbegriffe. Historisches Lexikon zur politisch-sozialen Sprache in Deutschland*, ed. Otto Brunner, Werner Conze and Reinhart Koselleck (Stuttgart: Klett Cotta Verlag, 1982), 3:1074–77; Vulpius, *Die Geburt des Russländischen Imperiums*, 209–12.

others. The driving force in establishing the new terminology in the Russian political-social lexicon was Tsar Peter I and his confidantes. Right from the start, the meaning of civilized was defined in two contexts: the behavior of the individual and the condition of an entire ethnic group. The notion of civility became a central tenet in the vision of a "new" Russian empire. From then on, the tsarist empire not only counted itself among the "civilized" nations but also used this new claim as a justification for renaming the state an "empire."[34]

The introduction of this new terminology and the dual application of the notion of civilized (individual and collective), together with the assertion of the claim that Russia itself was a "civilized" state at the same time, provided the basis for using the concept to initiate a Russian discourse about civilizing non-Christian ethnicities and, by extension, developing a civilizing policy. As the quotations above revealed, both the discourse and the policy began during Tsar Peter's lifetime and manifested themselves in aggressive missionizing campaigns. While motivated to some extent by the adoption of cameralist concepts and the ideal of a well-ordered police state,[35] Peter I saw in the dissemination of the Russian Orthodox religion a vehicle for spreading education and moral principles. He believed he had a duty to instruct non-Christian ethnic groups in a belief system that was judged to be more civilized.

The conversion of individuals was now replaced by an attempt to carry out ethnically based mass missionizing campaigns and to make conversion more sustainable through religious schooling.[36] In this respect, the Petrine attacks on the belief and value systems of non-Christians constituted only the beginning of a much more comprehensive "civilizing" policy. Religion was only the starting point for Peter's measures, for in the subsequent systematic process of missionizing under Peter's successors—Anna and especially Elizabeth—in the first half of the eighteenth century, the policy was extended to embrace many other spheres such as ways of living and working, language, and the

---

34 PSZRI 6, no. 3840 (October 22, 1721), 445–46.
35 Marc Raeff, *The Well-Ordered Police State. Social and Institutional Change through Law in the Germanies and Russia, 1600–1800* (New Haven: Yale University Press, 1983), 1221–43.
36 A. N. Grigor'ev, "Khristianizatsiia nerusskikh narodnostei kak odin iz metodov natsional'no-kolonial'noi politiki tsarizma v Tatarii (s poloviny XVI v. po fevral' 1907g.)," *Materialy po istorii Tatarii*, vol. 1 (Kazan': Tatgosizdat, 1948); F. G. Islaev, *Islam i pravoslavie v Povolzh'e v XVIII v.: Ot konfrontatsii k terpimosti* (Kazan': Izdatel'stvo Kazanskogo universiteta, 2001); Joseph Glazik, *Die russisch-orthodoxe Heidenmission seit Peter dem Großen* (Münster: Aschendorfesche Verlagsbuchhandlung, 1954); Nolte, "Verständnis und Bedeutung"; Khodarkovsky, "The Conversion of Non-Christians in Early Modern Russia," in *Of Religion and Empire. Missions, Conversion, and Tolerance in Tsarist Russia*, ed. Robert P. Geraci and Michael Khodarkovsky (Ithaca: Cornell University Press, 2001); Keemia V. Orlova, *Istoriia khristianizatsii Kalmykov: seredina XVII–nachalo XX v.* (Moscow: Nauka, 2006).

everyday culture of non-Russians.[37] In that respect, when Catherine II came to power—despite the halt to the previous policies vis-à-vis other religions of the empire—this did not mark the beginning of an entirely new era of political rule. Rather, Catherine's efforts to promulgate a sedentary life represented a continuation of a policy initiated by Peter I that judged non-Russian ethnic subjects in terms of Russian perceptions of "civilized."

The social shifts outlined above, the Russians' new self-image, and the use of a new characteristic to denote "Other" in the tsarist empire are reflected in changes in terminology. The term inovertsy—consisting of the prefix ino- ("other") combined with the suffix *vertsy*, derived from *vera* ("faith")—had already emerged in the second half of the seventeenth century. Nonetheless, for the first two decades of the eighteenth century, this term continued to play a secondary role vis-à-vis inozemtsy as a designation for non-Christian subjects.[38] This was to change at the peak of the Petrine missionizing campaigns. Russian rule over the former Khanates of Kazan, Astrakhan, and Sibir' was considered to have been consolidated long since. In place of the geographic marker used to construct the notion of Otherness, which still resonated strongly in the term inozemtsy despite its heavily religious connotations, the emphasis now shifted to the notion of "those of another faith." It is ironic that religion acquired an enhanced significance as a criterion for the classification of Otherness at precisely the point when Peter I abolished the office of patriarch as the head of the Russian Orthodox Church and thus greatly reduced the influence of religion on state policy. The contradiction can only be understood if one realizes that the religiously defined demarcation of non-Christian people since the Petrine era and in the decades to come was connected less with an inherent religious deficit than with a perceived lack of education and "civilization."[39]

When inovertsy replaced inozemtsy as the term used to denote "internal others," the original double meaning of inozemtsy was reduced to a single meaning—namely, non-Orthodox subjects originating from other countries who were in the service of the tsar. In 1722, Peter I defined as inozemtsy "those who have come from foreign states and have entered the service [of the tsar]," whereas previously it had also been applied to all non-Orthodox inhabitants of

---

37 For more details, see Vulpius, *Die Geburt des Russländischen Imperiums*.

38 One of the earliest uses is recorded in 1684: PSZRI 2, no. 1099 (December 16, 1684), 644–45.

39 The terminological turning point came in 1720, even though the old term *inozemtsy* continued to be used informally in Siberia for several decades, similarly to the older term for being a subject (*kholopstvo* instead of *poddanstvo*). Some examples: PSZRI 5, no. 3410 (1719), 727; 6, no. 3697 (1720), 279; 7, no. 4556 (August 28, 1724).

the empire.[40] The new definition included not only western Europeans but also subjects of the Ottoman and Persian empires.[41]

The characteristic of Otherness among "internal others" previously contained in inozemtsy continued to apply to them in the new term inovertsy, in which the ethnic and socioeconomic aspects overlapped alongside the allegedly lesser degree of civilization and the religious marker. The ethnically loaded nature of this term is illustrated by the fact that legislation distinguished not between "those of other faiths" and Russian Orthodox subjects, but instead between "Muslims," inovertsy, and "peoples of Russia";[42] elsewhere "Others" were defined not as "Muslims and others of other faiths" but as "Tatars and other inovertsy."[43] How little the attribution "of other faiths" was tied to individuals and how closely it was connected with ethnic criteria is shown by the clarification issued in 1728 of which "subjects of Russia's empire were to be counted as inovertsy" (*v Rossiiskoi Imperii mnogie poddannye obretaiutsia inovertsy, a imenno*): "Mordvinians, Chuvash, Chermissy, Ostyaks, Votyaks, Lopari, and other similar peoples whose names are not known."[44]

In socioeconomic terms, the distinction that had already been drawn between inozemtsy and "natural Russians" continued to be applied to "those of other faiths": as before, only inovertsy were liable to pay the yasak, but they in turn were not liable for military service. There was, however, one significant exception: while at no point were "natural Russians" obliged to pay the yasak, from 1703 onwards, those who had had themselves baptized, and therefore should not really have been counted as "those of other faiths"; were obliged to go on paying it nonetheless.

Novokreshchenye ("the Newly Baptized") in the Eighteenth Century

In line with the seventeenth-century practice of freeing subjects from the yasak payments once they had been baptized, the process of mass-state

---

40 PSZRI 6, no. 3937 (1722), 535.

41 See PSZRI 12, no. 9249 (January 13, 1746), 3, 504.

42 "Magomentane ili drugie inovertsy, kotorye [. . .] kogo iz Rossiiskikh narodov v svoiu veru prevratiat [. . .]," PSZRI 8, no. 5333 (September 12, 1728), 94ff., here 100.

43 *"Tatar i prochikh inovertsev, kotorye krestilis."* PSZRI 7, no. 4556 (August 28, 1724), 342. See also the categorization of "Russians," "Muslims," and *inovertsy* in PSZRI 12, no. 9446 (October 8, 1747), 764.

44 PSZRI 8, no. 5333 (September 12, 1728), 100.

Christianization launched by Peter I would logically have meant considerable losses for the state coffers. This could not possibly have been in the interests of a tsar in need of funds to wage numerous and protracted wars, first against the Ottomans, subsequently against the Swedes. Added to this were two further aspects: as decades of rule over ethnic groups in the south and east of the tsarist empire went by, it became increasingly difficult to justify the yasak as a tribute to be paid by conquered people; instead, it came to be regarded as a specific form of tax.[45] Just as "natural" Orthodox Russians were obliged to pay taxes, it seemed opportune to demand from inozemtsy continued payment of the yasak even after their baptism. What is more, Metropolitan Filofei (Leshchinskii), who led the Christianization offensive from Tobol'sk under Peter I, was probably motivated by a desire to ensure that the wish to convert to Christianity was genuine and therefore to decouple it from any financial incentives.

Filofei Leshchinskii's request to the tsar in 1702 to end exemption from the yasak for those who decided to be baptized received a positive response: a year later, the Siberian order (*Sibirskii prikaz*) announced that converted Christians would no longer be freed from paying the yasak as a matter of principle.[46] What is more, in 1719 Peter I wanted to combine countless different social groups into a single levy of state peasants, and in 1723 the Senate, with the tsar present, discussed the question of who all should be included under "state peasants." In this context, Peter I argued for the inclusion of the yasak-payers (*yasachniki*) in addition to the so-called single homesteaders (*odnodvortsy*), the Mordvinians and Chermissy.[47] In other words, for a short time, it looked as if all the former "internal others" would—in the wake of Petrine efforts to standardize the state—become part of a single state people structured according to social estates. Just as Peter I had introduced a standard term (*poddanstvo*) for the whole of the population for being a subject of Russia regardless of ethnic, social, or religious affiliation, the earlier term kholopstvo as a term was replaced for non-Christian subjects.[48]

Ultimately, however, the perception that the difference between "natural Russians" and yasak-payers was too large for them to be amalgamated into a single group gained the upper hand: although the tsar's ruling of June 1724 bracketed together a small group of yasak-payers (unbaptized service people,

---

45 Konev, "Pravovoe polozhenie," 20–26.

46 Ibid., 23.

47 Evgenii V. Anisimov, *Podatnaia reforma Petra I. Vvedenie podushnoi podati v Rossii 1719–1728 gg* (Leningrad: Nauka, 1982), 179.

48 Elena N. Marasinova, *Vlast' i lichnost': Ocherki russkoi istorii XVIII veka* (Moscow: Nauka, 2008), 257–63; Vulpius, *Die Geburt des Russländischen Imperiums*, 90–92.

so-called "Tatars"[49]) and yasak peasants (from the ranks of the Tatars, Chuvash, Mordvinians, Mari, and Udmurts) with the already existing state peasants and the so-called single homesteaders to form a new category of state peasants;[50] another group—namely Tatars from Astrakhan and Ufa, Bashkiria and "Siberian yasak-payers of other faiths" (*sibirskie iasachnye inovertsy*)—were explicitly exempted from the poll tax introduced for the general population.[51] Moreover, when Prince Ivan V. Solntsev-Zasekin—sent to "count souls" following the "revision"—nonetheless dared to include newly baptized yasak-payers in the list of those who had to pay the poll tax as well, the Senate in 1726 decided once and for all that Tatars from Astrakhan and Ufa, Bashkirians, and all groups of the Siberian yasak population would be freed from the poll tax, whereas all of them—irrespective of whether they had been baptized or not—had to go on paying the yasak as before.[52]

Who were those whom the Russian elite still considered to be "too different" to form a single social category together with Russian state peasants and pay a poll tax instead of the yasak? The words used by the Senate in 1726 to denote "Others" provide some clues here: they stated, namely, that they were "Siberian yasak-payers of other faiths who had been newly baptized" (*sibirskie iasachnye inovertsy novokreshchenye*).[53] Thus, a geographical category (Siberian) was combined with a socioeconomic category (yasak-paying) and with the marker that superficially appeared to denote religious status but actually stood for the degree of "civilization."[54] However, this still leaves open the question of how the oxymoron "newly baptized people of other faiths" is to be understood.

The above analysis has shown that—already in the late seventeenth century— the designation "newly baptized" no longer referred to the religious act of baptism. By the eighteenth century, this was even more the case. In fact, the term in combination with the designation inovertsy was so strongly ethnically charged that there was no longer a fundamental difference between it and the racial

---

49 On the issue of ethnic designations in the tsarist empire see Kappeler, "Kak klassifitsirovali russkie istochniki," 13–39.

50 Kappeler, *Rußlands erste Nationalitäten*, 262–63.

51 PSZRI 7, no. 4533 (June 26, 1724), 18, 318.

52 PSZRI 7, no. 4860 (March 26, 1726), 595–96. Nevertheless, after 1720 those willing to be baptized were exempted for three years from the state *yasak* tribute as a reward. PSZRI 6, no. 3637 (1720): 234–35.

53 Ibid.

54 The geographical term "Siberian" should be very broadly understood here, since at that time it also included the Far East and in the course of the eighteenth century also came to include parts of steppe regions inhabited by Kazakhs. In Speransky's statute of 1822, for example, the Kazakhs of the former Middle Horde were renamed "Siberian Kirgiz." PSZRI 38, no. 29127 (July 22, 1822), 394–433.

categories of the nineteenth century. If there was a difference, it was only a matter of degree. Numerous legal texts now echoed the Russian imperial idea according to which "newly baptized" and "those of other faiths" were no longer to be regarded as mutually exclusive categories, as they had originally been conceived. As early as 1722, a tsarist instruction to the governor of Kazan speaks of "those of other faiths, among them the newly baptized"; in 1724, the Senate refers to an order to "Tatars and other people of other faiths who had themselves baptized" and a Senate resolution of 1740 states that "many newly baptized people of other faiths" lived together with unbaptized.[55] In other words, in the perception of the Russian administration, a change of religion did not lead to any significant change in the degree of Otherness. In reality, the origin of a converted subject remained a key factor in the identity assigned to him or her.

In this context, Tsarina Anna's instruction to the Senate in 1740—according to which an Archimandrate should travel with several clerics to various provinces to instruct the newly baptized in Christian teachings and, above all, to find Russians to help in this task—is very revealing: In the case of the baptism of children of the newly baptized, "long-established Russians" (*starinnye Russkie liudi*) were to make themselves available as "godfathers or godmothers" (*vospriemniki i vospriemnitsy*). And if even they did not have a precise idea of what they should be teaching the children of "newly baptized people of other faiths," guidelines were to be disseminated throughout the state and in all churches on how to treat baptized children of the "newly baptized." Of equal importance, however, was that "the newly baptized should marry Russians and via this circumstance renew their friendship with one another."[56] With a Russian daughter- or son-in-law in the house, the "newly baptized" would gradually be able to leave behind and forget their former "erroneous" ways.[57]

The nominal adoption of the Russian Orthodox faith was apparently not sufficient for these people to escape their Otherness. They were also required to adopt Orthodox customs and practices and as far as possible form blood ties via marriage or at least by taking established Russians as godparents. The Otherness that in the Russian perception was derived from the "other" origins of the "newly baptized" could not be discarded by individuals through their modes of behavior during their lifetime. Rather, the categories of difference were officially so numerous and so extensive that only several generations later at the earliest

---

55 PSZRI 6, no. 4123 (November 2, 1722), 792; PSZRI 7, no. 4556 (August 28, 1724), 342–43; PSZRI 11, no. 8236 (September 11, 1740): 248–56.
56 PSZRI 11, no. 8236 (September 11, 1740), 248–56, here 250.
57 Ibid., 250.

and only through enormous missionizing and cultural efforts as well as mixed marriages could they be overcome.

But what in the Russian view could serve as a measure of the success of efforts to overcome Otherness? From what point on could "newly baptized" free themselves from their assigned identity and officially become "Russians"? In the eighteenth century, there was no standard rule for this. Whereas Peter I had clearly defined who from then on was to be regarded as an inozemets in the sense of an "external foreigner"; until the very end of the century there was no legal definition of who belonged to the socio-ethnic group of "those of other faiths" (inovertsy) and who should be included in the category of the "newly baptized" (novokreshchenye) and for how long.

It was precisely this deficit that came back to haunt the Senate when, in September 1760, it had to decide whether the "baptized" or "newly baptized" Tatars, Cheremissy, Chuvash, Mordvinians, and Votyaks from the former Khanate of Kazan should be called up to serve as soldiers on the same basis as (Russian) state peasants. The recruitment obligation did not apply to the "newly baptized" since they had been exempted in 1722.[58] However, the Senate proved to be inventive: it stipulated that the criterion for deciding who was on a par with Russian state peasants with respect to military service should be the length of time for which the "newly baptized" had held this status. Suddenly, the first census of 1722 was deemed suitable as the cut-off point: anyone who had been baptized prior to this date, and hence almost for four decades previously and had been listed in the more recent census as "newly baptized," was now no longer to be seen as "newly baptized" (*ikh novokreshchenymi uzhe i pochitat' ne dolzhno*). Nevertheless, this still did not mean that they were now considered "Russians." Rather, those affected were now to be entered in the records as "baptized before the last census" (*pisat'sia kreshchenymi do prezhnei perepisi*)![59] Rather than repealing this category of differentiation, it was merely adapted for the purpose of military recruitment.

Even the Senate found this relatively arbitrary adaptation of the definition to require legitimation. The Senate therefore retrospectively justified this arbitrary adaption with the argument that the right moment had come to put the baptized and named on a par with "other State peasants," because the once "newly baptized" had given Russian names to their children born since the last census.[60] It remained unclear whether giving children Russian names was a

---

58 PSZRI 6, no. 4123 (1722), 792.
59 PSZRI 15, no. 11099 (September 11, 1760), 506–7.
60 Ibid.

necessary condition for recruitment or whether it was simply supposed to serve as a retroactive legitimation for the decision to put formerly "newly baptized" on a par with state peasants. At any rate, the Senate's decision demonstrated what a creative approach could be taken to undoing and reconstructing categories of difference and how much change the characteristics were subject to over time.[61] Moreover, the creative solutions born of necessity also proved to be long-lived: from then on the tsarist administration divided Christian non-Russians into "newly baptized" and "formerly baptized" (*starkokreshcheny*)—a distinction designed to divide those (mainly Tatars) who had, in some cases, converted two hundred years ago from those who had gone over to Russian Orthodoxy in the course of the mass missionizing campaign that had taken place under Peter I and the Empresses Anna and Elizabeth.[62]

In the 1760s, the Senate's optimism that an assimilation of the newly baptized "Tatars" had been virtually achieved and that therefore other adaptive steps could be taken was by no means shared by the whole of the imperial elite. In 1766, the governor of Orenburg, Prince Avram A. Putiatin, brought an appeal to the contrary before the Senate: according to him, among those who had newly settled in his province were many "people of other faiths" (inovertsy), and among them "newly baptized" (primarily Tatars' and Chuvash) who were neither suitable nor reliable enough (*neudobny i beznadezhny*) were to be entrusted with household duties or with arable farming. "Those of other faiths" and "newly baptized" should, he argued, therefore in the future be settled exclusively in "internal provinces" among the Christian population. So far, not one of the "newly baptized Tatars [...] had had themselves baptized voluntarily," unless they had been facing punishment for robbery. Indeed, they had returned to their old dwellings, as had the Chuvash, "so that they would not have to live in Christian reverence but remain in unbelief and idolatry (*v idolopoklonstve*)." "Great Russians" were therefore required, he continued, to apprentice the Bashkirs in arable farming and "to teach them other great Russian customs."[63]

---

61 The "doing difference" approach comes from gender research and was applied by Candace West and Sarah Fenstermaker to intersectionality research. See their "Doing Difference," *Gender and Society* 9 (1995): 8–37.

62 The first cases of such neologisms appeared in the 1760s: *Sbornik Imperatorskogo rossiiskogo istoricheskogo obshchestva* (St. Petersburg, 1903), 115:443 (1767); (St. Petersburg, 1869), 4:129; (September 4, 1767); see Kappeler, *Rußlands erste Nationalitäten*, 357. Around the middle of the nineteenth century, the "formerly baptized" Tatars already regarded themselves as a new ethnic group in their own right, called *kryasheny* in Tatar. See ibid., 498.

63 "Donoshenie orenburgskogo gubernatora kn. A. A. Putiatina v Senat," in *Materialy po istorii Bashkirskoi ASSR* 4, no. 496 (March 21, 1766): 472.

Perceptions of Otherness depended on context and were mutable: the Senate's urgent need for recruitment was one thing; Putiatin's concern to make the periphery of the empire fruitful for crop cultivation and to distribute land to "Great Russians" was quite another. The crucial point here was what benefits whom. The governor's accusation that the "newly baptized" had proven to be "unsuitable and unreliable" for household duties and arable farming also concealed a further criterion that became increasingly relevant for the construction of difference in the second half of the eighteenth century: the thesis of the Swiss legal philosopher Emer(ich) de Vattel, who had further developed the thinking of John Locke, according to which the ownership of land carried with it the obligation to use it as effectively as possible. This thesis had also become known in the tsarist empire.[64] The topos of using intensive cultivation of the land became an issue that dominated the imperial discourse of the waning eighteenth century. The way that the nomads of the steppe treated land increasingly came to be considered "irresponsible" and, hence, the practice of driving them onto other or smaller territories was seen as legitimate. Against this background, under Catherine II, a sedentary lifestyle and engagement in arable farming rose to the top of the list of criteria for measuring the degree of "civilization." Conversely, a lack of these characteristics became a new important criterion for defining Otherness. In Putiatin's eyes, being a "Great Russian" meant being engaged in productive arable farming, whereas being "newly baptized" and hence a non-Russian was tantamount to a wasteful and hence irresponsible treatment of land.[65]

Even though the hierarchy of categories used for measuring Otherness constantly changed over the course of the eighteenth century, it is nonetheless possible to identify basic lines of demarcation vis-à-vis other groups for the term "newly baptized" over the centuries. In the sixteenth century, the category of "newly baptized" was based on religious and ethnic characteristics and initially referred to a small group of baptized Tatars. This retained its currency even 150 years *after* the first forced baptisms, emphasizing not only the relative nature of the attribution "new" but, above all, making it clear that the act of

---

64 John Locke, *Two Treatises of Government. The Second Treatise of Government. An Essay Concerning the True Origin, Extent, and End of Civil Government* (London: Amen-Corner, 1690), second treatise, sec. 37; Emeric de Vattel, *Le droit de gens ou principes de la loi naturelle, appliqués à la conduite et aux affaires des nations et des souverains*, ed. Albert de Lapradelle (Washington: University of Michigan Library, 1916 [1758]), 81, 78. On the reception of the topos of "unused" and "empty" land in the tsarist empire see Vulpius, *Die Geburt des Russländischen Imperiums*, 357–65.

65 "Donoshenie orenburgskogo gubernatora kn. A. A. Putiatina v Senat," 464–73.

baptism did not, and could not, make fully-fledged Christians and, hence, "natural Russians" out of "heathens." The policy of difference intensified even further in the wake of the mass Christianization campaign that had begun under Peter I and was stepped up considerably under his successors Tsarinas Anna and Elizabeth. The oxymoron of "newly baptized people of other faiths," found so often in official sources in the eighteenth century, reveals that the religious aspect of conversion came to play only a superficial role in the definition of "newly baptized" over the course of the eighteenth century. By contrast, the term "other" primarily connoted ethnically characteristics gained in relevance. As the perception of Russians of themselves as a civilized people increased, an alleged lack of civilization among "people of other faiths" and "newly baptized" became an especially important marker of difference, which was judged in terms of a knowledge and practice of Russian Orthodox customs and traditions and an established sedentary lifestyle associated with arable farming.

Given that the hierarchy of categories that the Russian elite used to measure Otherness could change not only diachronically but also, depending on the context, synchronically and that the criteria of Otherness usually intensified each other, it would not appear to make much sense to separate out the latter into categories of political identity and socioeconomic, religious, linguistic, and civilizational difference. It would likewise be impossible to discern a complete replacement of one category by another. Instead, as the example of the Orenburg governor Putiatin illustrates, a complex interaction can be observed: in the perception of ethnically constructed Otherness, religious difference had a certain role to play, and socioeconomic differences became merged with criteria for measuring the degree of civilization. In turn, these differences were strengthened by the perception of religious deviance.

The most important finding is that the thesis—according to which in the Russian Empire of the eighteenth century determined the categories used by the state to delineate differences between "native Russians" and "Others"— was predominantly based on religion is no longer tenable.[66] The attribution common in the eighteenth century of "newly baptized people of other faiths" (*novokreshchenykh inovertsev*) shows that "newly baptized" were for the most part unable to rid themselves of their status as "Others," despite their adoption of Christianity. As a rule, those who were referred to as Others not only remained encumbered with this category until the end of their lives but were also forced

---

66 See, for example, Sherstova, who does not recognize any colonial tendencies in Russian policy, underlining what for the Russians was allegedly an organic process of assimilation, and asserts that there was no special transitional category. Sherstova, *Tiurki i russkie*, 126.

to pass it on to their children. Whereas at the beginning of the century the intention of Petrine policy had appeared to be long-term amalgamation with other non-Christian parts of the empire—nominally, administratively, and with respect to religion—the construction of the categories of "people of other faiths" and "newly baptized" did precisely the opposite. Later in the nineteenth century, the term "people of other origins" (*inorodtsy*) was likewise used as a collective attribution for non-Russians who—in terms of origin and social status had nothing in common—were bracketed together solely through the perceptions of the Russian elite. This perception had grown since the beginning of the eighteenth century and assumed that ethnic groups in the east and south of the empire were inferior to the Russian majority society "in their degree of civilization and in their current way of life."[67]

The gulf between, on the one hand, the intention of bringing about acculturation that would in some cases have had an assimilating effect and, on the other hand, the de facto perpetuation of the differences between the indigenous and non-indigenous population was not peculiar to Russia. The situation was similar in other empires. The historians Jane Burbank and Frederick Cooper conclude that "all empires were to some degree reliant on both incorporation and differentiation."[68] In this respect, one could say, analogously to Homi Bhabha's analysis of the colonial discourse, for the majority of the inovertsy und novokreshchenye of the eighteenth century and as precursors for the inorodtsy of the early nineteenth century in the tsarist empire, they became "white but not quite."[69]

Works Cited

Primary Sources

"Donoshenie orenburgskogo gubernatora kn. A. A. Putiatina v Senat." *Materialy po istorii Bashkirskoi ASSR* 4, no. 496 (March 21, 1766). Moscow: Izdatel'stvo Akademii nauk SSSR, 1936.

---

67 This formulation is taken from the foreword to the Statute for the non-Russians of Siberia and the southern Steppe regions. PSZRI 38, no. 29127 (July 22, 1822), 394–433, here 394.

68 Jane Burbank, Frederick Cooper, *Empires in World History: Power and the Politics of Difference* (Princeton: Princeton University Press, 2010), 13.

69 Homi K. Bhabha, "Of Mimicry and Man. The Ambivalence of Colonial Discourse," *Discipleship: A Special Issue on Psychoanalysis* 28 (Spring 1984): 125–33.

Locke, John. *Two Treatises of Government. The Second Treatise of Government. An Essay Concerning the True Origin, Extent, and End of Civil Government.* London: Amen-Corner, 1690.

Pis'ma i bumagi imperatora Petra Velikogo. Vols. 1–13. St. Petersburg, Leningrad, Moscow: n.p, 1887–2003.

Polnoe sobranie zakonov Rossiiskoi Imperii (PSZRI). 1. Ser., Vols. 1–46. St. Petersburg: Tipografiia II Otdeleniia Sobstvennoi Ego Imperatorskogo Velichestva Kantseliarii, 1830.

Sbornik Imperatorskogo rossiiskogo istoricheskogo obshchestva. Vols. 1–148. St. Petersburg, 1876–1916.

de Vattel, Emeric. *Le droit de gens ou principes de la loi naturelle, appliqués à la conduite et aux affaires des nations et des souverains.* Edited by Albert de Lapradelle. Washington: University of Michigan Library, 1916.

Secondary Sources and Literature

Anisimov, Evgenii V. *Podatnaia reforma Petra I. Vvedenie podushnoi podati v Rossii 1719–1728 gg.* Leningrad: Nauka, 1982.

Bakhrushin, Sergei V. "Iasak v Sibiri v XVII v." *Nauchnye Trudy* 3, no. 2 (1955): 49–85.

Bähr, Matthias, and Florian Kühnel, eds. *Verschränkte Ungleichheit. Praktiken der Intersektionalität in der Frühen Neuzeit.* Berlin: Duncker & Humblot, 2018.

Bhabha, Homi K. "Of Mimicry and Man. The Ambivalence of Colonial Discourse." *Discipleship: A Special Issue on Psychoanalysis* 28 (1984): 125–33.

Bödeker, Hans Eric. "Menschheit, Humanität, Humanismus." In *Geschichtliche Grundbegriffe. Historisches Lexikon zur politisch-sozialen Sprache in Deutschland.* Edited by Otto Brunner, Werner Conze, and Reinhart Koselleck, 1063–128. Vol. 3: Stuttgart: Klett Cotta Verlag, 1982.

Burbank, Jane, and Frederick Cooper. *Empires in World History: Power and the Politics of Difference.* Princeton: Princeton University Press, 2010.

Emich, Birgit. "Normen an der Kreuzung. Intersektionalität statt Konkurrenz oder: Die unaufhebbare Gleichzeitigkeit von Amt, Stand und Patronage." In *Normenkonkurrenz in historischer Perspektive.* Edited by Arne Karsten and Hillard von Thiessen, 83–100. Berlin: Duncker & Humbolt, 2015.

Florin, Moritz, Victoria Gutsche, and Natalie Krentz, eds. *Diversität historisch. Repräsentationen und Praktiken gesellschaftlicher Differenzierung im Wandel.* Bielefeld: Transcript, 2018.

Gennep, Arnold van. *The Rites of Passage*. Chicago: University of Chicago Press, 1960.

Gessen, V. M. *Poddanstvo, ego ustanovlenie i prekrashchenie*. Vols. 1–2. St. Petersburg: Pravda, 1909.

Glazik, Joseph. *Die russisch-orthodoxe Heidenmission seit Peter dem Großen*. Münster: Aschendorfesche Verlagsbuchhandlung, 1954.

Griesebner, Andrea, and Susanne Hehenberger. "Intersektionalität. Ein brauchbares Konzept für die Geschichtswissenschaft?" In *Intersectionality und Kritik. Neue Perspektiven auf alte Fragen*. Edited by Vera Kallenberg, Jennifer Meyer, and Johanna M. Müller, 105–24. Wiesbaden: Springer Verlag, 2013.

Grigor'ev, A. N. "Khristianizatsiia nerusskikh narodnostei kak odin iz metodov natsional'no-kolonial'noi politiki tsarizma v Tatarii (s poloviny XVI v. po fevral' 1907g.)." *Materialy po istorii Tatarii* (1948): 226–85.

Ingram, Kevin. "Introduction." In *The Conversos and Moriscos in Late Medieval Spain and Beyond*. Vol. 1: *Departures and Change*, 1–21. Leiden: Brill, 2009.

Islaev, F. G. *Islam i pravoslavie v Povolzh'e v XVIII v.: Ot konfrontatsii k terpimosti*. Kazan: Izdatel'stvo Kazanskogo Universiteta, 2001.

Kappeler, Andreas. *Rußlands erste Nationalitäten. Das Zarenreich und die Völker der Mittleren Wolga vom 16. Bis 19. Jahrhundert*. Vienna: Böhlau Verlag, 1982.

———. "Kak klassifitsirovali russkie istochniki 16-serediny 19vv etno-religioznye gruppy Volgo-Ural'skogo regiona?" In *Ispovedi v zerkale. Mezhkonfessional'nye otnosheniia v tsentre Evrazii (na primere Volgo-Ural'skogo regiona XVII–XXI vv.)*. Edited by Stefan A. Dyuduan'on, 13–39. Nizhnii Novgorod: Nizhegorodskii gosudarstvennyi lingvisticheskii universitet, 2012.

Khodarkovsky, Michael. "Four Degrees of Separation: Constructing Non-Christian Identities in Muscovy." In *Cultural Identity in Muscovy, 1359–1584*. Edited by A. M. Kleimola and G. D. Lenhoff, 248–66. Moscow, Ohio: ITZ-Garant, 1997.

———. "'Ignoble Savages and Unfaithful Subjects': Constructing Non-Christian Identities in Early Modern Russia." In *Russia's Orient: Imperial Borderlands and Peoples, 1700–1917*. Edited by Daniel R. Brower and Edward J. Lazzerini, 9–26. Bloomington: Indiana University Press, 1997.

———. "The Conversion of Non-Christians in Early Modern Russia." In *Of Religion and Empire. Missions, Conversion, and Tolerance in Tsarist Russia*. Edited by Robert P. Geraci and Michael Khodarkovsky, 115–43. Ithaca: Cornell University Press, 2001.

Kochin, G. E. *Materialy dlia terminologicheskogo slovoria drevnei Rossii*. Moscow: Izdatel'vstvo Akademii Nauk SSSR, 1937.

Konev, A. Iu. "Pravovoe polozhenie 'novokreshchenykh inovertsev' Sibiri. XVII–XVIII veka." *Vestnik Novosibirskogo Gosudarstvennogo Universiteta* 5, no. 3 (2006); 20–25.

Marasinova, Elena N. *Vlast' i lichnost': Ocherki russkoi istorii XVIII veka*. Moscow: Nauka, 2008.

Nolte, Hans-Heinrich. "Verständnis und Bedeutung der religiösen Toleranz in Rußland 1600–1725." *Jahrbücher zur Geschichte Osteuropas* 17 (1969): 494–530.

Obertreis, Julia. "Intersektionalität im Russischen Reich? Wechselwirkungen zwischen Kategorien sozialer Differenz im 19. Jahrhundert und der *spatial turn*." In *Diversität historisch. Repräsentationen und Praktiken gesellschaftlicher Differenzierung im Wandel*. Edited by Moritz Florin, Victoria Gutsche, and Natalie Krentz, 161–192. Bielefeld: Transcript Verlag, 2018.

Oparina, T. A. and S. P. Orlenko. "Ukazy 1627 i 1652 godov protiv 'nekreshchennykh inozemtsev.'" *Otechestvennaia istoriia* 1 (2005): 22–39.

Orlova, Keemia V. *Istoriia khristianizatsii Kalmykov: seredina XVII–nachalo XX v*. Moscow: Nauka, 2006.

Raeff, Marc. "The Enlightenment in Russia and Russian Thought in the Enlightenment." In *The Eighteenth Century in Russia*. Edited by G. Garrard, 25–47. Oxford: Oxford University Press, 1973.

———. "The Well-Ordered Police State and the Development of Modernity in Seventeenth- and Eighteenth-Century Europe: An Attempt at a Comparative Approach." *The American Historical Review* 80 (1975), no. 5: 1221–43.

Schippan, Michael. *Die Aufklärung in Russland im 18. Jahrhundert*. Wiesbaden: Harassowitz Verlag, 2012.

Sherstova, Liudmila I. *Tiurki i russkie v Iuzhnoi Sibiri: Etnopoliticheskie protsessy i etnokul'turnaia dinamika XVII—nachala XX veka*. Novosibirsk: Institut arkheologii i etnografii SO RAN, 2005.

Slezkine, Yuri. "The Sovereign's Foreigners: Classifying the Native Peoples in Seventeenth-Century Siberia." *Russian History* 19 (1992): 475–86.

———. *Arctic Mirrors: Russia and the Small Peoples of the North*. Ithaca: Cornell University Press, 1994.

Slocum, John W. "Who, and When, Were the *Inorodtsy*? The Evolution of the Category of 'Aliens' in Imperial Russia." *Russian Review* 57 (1998): 173–90.

Sokolovsky, S. V. *Obrazy Drugikh v rossiiskoi nauke, politike i prave*. Moscow: Put', 2001.

Taimasov, Leonid A. "From 'Kazan's Newly Converted' to 'Orthodox Inorodtsy': The Historical Stages of the Affirmation of Christianity in the Middle Volga Region." In *Imperiology: From Empirical Knowledge to Discussing the Russian Empire*. Edited by Kimitaka Matsuzato, 111–38. Sapporo: Slavic Research Center, 2007.

Turner, Victor. *The Ritual Process. Structure and Anti-Structure*. Ithaca: Routledge, 1977.

Vinkovetsky, Ilya. "Circumnavigation, Empire, Modernity, Race: The Impact of Round-the-World Voyages on Russia's Imperial Consciousness." *Ab Imperio* 1–2 (2001): 191–210.

Vulpius, Ricarda. *Die Geburt des Russländischen Imperiums. Herrschaftskonzepte und Praktiken im 18. Jahrhundert*. Vienna: Böhler Verlag, 2020.

Werth, Paul W. *At the Margins of Orthodoxy. Mission, Governance, and Confessional Politics in Russia's Volga-Kama Region, 1827–1905*. Ithaca: Cornell University Press, 2002.

West, Candace, and Fenstermaker, Sarah. "Doing Difference." *Gender and Society* 9 (1995): 8–37.

Winter, Eduard. *Frühaufklärung. Der Kampf gegen den Konfessionalismus und die deutsch-slawische Begegnung*. Berlin: Akademie Verlag, 1966.

Wirtschafter, Elise K. "Social Categories in Russian Imperial History." *Cahiers du Monde russe* 50 (2009): 213–50.

——. "Thoughts on the Enlightenment and Enlightenment in Russia." *Journal of Modern Russian History and Historiography* 2 (2009): 1–26.

Part Two

CLASSIFYING THE "INTERNAL OTHERS"

Section Summary

Michael Khodarkovsky

The concept of Otherness is not new. In one form or another, it is found in Plato and was elaborated in philosophy by Georg Hegel and Edmund Husserl before making its way into other disciplines. It was only in the last fifty years that the concept of Otherness migrated from sociology, anthropology, and literature into the field of history. In some sense, anything and anyone could be considered Other in different contexts and circumstances. After all, throughout much of Russian history, a Russian peasant was very much the Other to a Russian noble, just as a resident of Novgorod was to the resident of Astrakhan. In other words, Otherness may be defined through various characteristics: social, economic, cultural, geographic, linguistic, and so on.

Because it could be a vague and elusive concept, it is important to establish the basic parameters of Otherness discussed in this chapter. The following five chapters consider a very specific Other, the one that was distinct, clearly visible, and located at the margins of the imperial core. These were non-Russian and non-Christian peoples who, in today's terms, would be characterized as belonging to a different race, ethnicity, religion, and civilization. The following chapters discuss Russia's perceptions and some policies towards this Other in the empire's Asian borderlands: Siberia, Central Asia, and the Caucasus. Chronologically, the chapters cover the entire imperial period from the seventeenth to the early twentieth centuries.

Throughout most of Russian imperial history, one could distinguish two different sets of perceptions: those of the Russian government and those of the ordinary Russians who came into contact with the indigenous population along the expanding frontiers. Among several markers of difference, two were of particular importance to the Russian government. The first one was political loyalty, as Moscow considered, whether a certain people had agreed to profess allegiance to a tsar and to pay tribute in furs, as happened in Siberia (*mirnye iasachnye liudi*), or whether they remained independent or subjects to other rulers (*nemirnye neiasachnye liudi*). The second critical marker that in the eyes of the government separated the non-Christians from Russians was their "law," the term used to define their religion: Islam, Buddhism, and Judaism, or the lack of any "law," when it concerned the animists. Geopolitical, political, and religious markers were understood broadly and were closely linked with conversion to the Orthodox Christianity seen by the government as an ultimate marker of inclusion and loyalty.

But for the Russians who found themselves in the frontier regions and in direct contact with the local population, the markers were more personal and tangible: smell, food, dress, and local customs all seemed exotic and puzzling. It was only in the late eighteenth and early nineteenth century that St. Petersburg began to show interest in these issues, or what one would describe today as ethnography and culture of the Other.

In the early modern times, the Muscovites referred to foreigners in the West as *inozemets*, (a calque from the German "Ausländer)" or by the word *nemets* (then and now a designation for the Germans), which was applied to any foreigner, the way Ottomans used *frengi* (literally, French) to designate a generic European. In Asia, while sometimes using inozemets, the authorities did not have a general, all-encompassing term for the newly encountered peoples. They usually referred to the indigenous peoples by their tribal name, if it was known, or by the name of their specific ruler. In the eighteenth century, as more indigenous peoples came under government control and a religious marker acquired greater significance, the authorities deployed a more general term to refer to the indigenous population as non-Christians *inovertsy* (literally meaning of a different faith), similar to how the Ottomans referred to non-Muslims (*gayr-i Müslim*).

In the nineteenth century, St. Petersburg relied on a general term to encompass all non-Christian peoples of the empire, both east and west. *Inorodtsy* (literally meaning of a different kin, race), a term that blended both racial and religious differences, was initially introduced by the Russian official Mikhail Speransky in his 1822 statute in relation to the indigenous population of Siberia. By the end of the century, it came to include empire's non-Christian population: animists, Buddhists, most of the Muslims, and Jews. Ironically, this was also a time of rapid and self-conscious rise of ethnic identities among the empire's numerous non-Christian peoples.

While the following chapters are preoccupied with the Other, they also beg a question about the Self. Should not examining the ways in which Russians perceived 'Others' also tell us something about the Russians themselves? It seems that historically the most constant separation marker between the Russians and Others was a religious one. After all, to be a Russian was synonymous with being an Orthodox Christian. As such, converts to the Orthodox Church were considered Russian regardless of their racial or other characteristics. Even when the concept of race became a common coin in the nineteenth century, there is no indication that it served as an official marker of difference and discrimination. Anyone could become a Russian if they converted to Orthodoxy. And because historically religious conversion was driven by the Russian state, "the innate tolerance" sometimes attributed to the Russian Orthodox Church had nothing to do with the church itself and had everything to do with the government policies. For most of Russian history, the Orthodox church was indeed a handmaiden of the state.

Yet again, the official perception of Russianness and Otherness was not the same for those who resided in the borderland regions and encountered the Other in daily life. These Russians who lived in the proximity of the indigenous communities noted racial differences between the Slavic and Asian people and observed their different customs and ways of life. Here, even those indigenous people who became converts to the Orthodoxy continued to be seen for a long time as racially different from their Russian neighbors.

The following five chapters shed light on Russia's perceptions of the Other in different regions and at different times. The first chapter by Yuri Akimov considers Muscovite-Russian expansion in Siberia during the seventeenth and eighteenth centuries. He suggests that during this time, Russians perceived the indigenous people in a medieval sense, as representatives of "the anti-world," while in the eighteenth century they began to see them through the lens of the Enlightenment. And because the former did not immediately disappear, it created a sense of double Otherness of the Siberian native population. If in the first stage of the Siberian conquest, the Russian authorities had little concern for converting the natives, after Peter I's reforms in the early eighteenth century, conversion became one of the main issues.

No doubt this change was due in part to Russia's new attitudes and perceptions brought about by Peter I's reforms and a growing awareness of the Western attitudes towards the Native Americans. Peter I's contemporary, Russian polymath Ivan Pososhkov, chastised Russia's feeble efforts to convert the natives in contrast to the success of the Spanish and the Catholic Church in the Americas. He advocated a full assimilation of the indigenous population, erasing their tongues, and taking their children away from the parents who refused to convert. The latter sounded similar to the Ottoman policy of the *devshirme*, which was about seizing young boys from the Christian population of the Balkans and bringing them to Istanbul to be converted and raised as Ottoman Muslims. In one form or another (local schools for hostages, resettlement of converts, educating native young men in Petersburg), many Russian officials proposed and implemented some of the same ideas throughout the eighteenth and nineteenth centuries.

Yet unlike the organized missionary activity of the Catholic church, Russia had neither missions in the Western sense nor a specific missionary arm of the church until the nineteenth century. Conversion to the Orthodox Christianity was a matter administered by the government. Peter I deployed full repressive powers of the state to force non-Christians to convert. Those who did were offered tax breaks and privileges, those who refused faced additional burdens and, in the case of the Tatar nobles in the Volga region, had their lands confiscated.

Another wave of forced conversion took place in the mid-eighteenth century, with the founding of The Agency for Convert Affairs charged with converting the natives. The Agency claimed to convert tens of thousands mostly in the mid-Volga region. Not surprisingly, conversion by force with little effort to explain the precepts of Christianity meant that most of the new converts remained Christians only on paper, something that several churchmen who arrived in the region decades later reported to their astounded superiors. The Agency was abolished by Catherine II who radically changed the course by embarking on a policy of religious tolerance, particularly toward her Muslim subjects.

Different perceptions of the indigenous population were not the only reason for Russia's changing attitudes and policies in Siberia. In the seventeenth century, collecting *yasak*—a tribute in furs expected from the indigenous peoples—was the government's top priority. But because religious conversion was less a matter for the church and more for the government to decide, Moscow offered new converts an exemption from taxes or tribute for three to five years. Large number of converts in Siberia would have seriously undermined the collection of valuable furs, and conversion at the time proceeded at a slow pace.

Moscow's cautious approach toward conversion in the seventeenth century was also due to the fact that despite its rapid expansion in Siberia, Moscow had only tenuous control of the newly claimed lands and peoples. While some natives were accustomed to submitting yasak as a tribute from the days of the Golden Horde, others viewed it as a mutual trade with the newcomers. Indeed, Russian officials often reported that the natives refused to submit their furs until they received various desired tools and items from the Russians. In time, however, with the expansion of Russian forts, natives' dependence on Russian trade, and the declining value of furs, Russia authorities were finally able to apply pressure to convert the natives. As such, Russia's growing efforts to convert the non-Christians in the eighteenth century were not only a function of changing perceptions but also of Russia's growing resources, expanded control of the region, and changing priorities.

In addition to religion, there was another long-lasting marker of difference between Russia and the indigenous peoples—a level of social organization. The newly encountered peoples were seen as non-sovereign and not state-organized, a collection of tribes and clans with disparate social structures and no single ruler. From Moscow's point of view, a non-sovereign people could only be considered subjects of the Russian tsar. No wonder that from their initial encounter and with little knowledge about their counterpart, Russian envoys to the indigenous rulers immediately insisted on their oath of allegiance to the tsar (*shert*), submission of yasak, and surrender of hostages (*amanat*). All three principals were borrowed from the times of the Golden Horde and for centuries remained the key conditions on which Russia built its relationship with the non-Christians peoples as the empire expanded east and south.

Reaction to Moscow's preposterous claims varied. Some peoples who were previously the subjects to the khans of the Golden Horde accepted Russia's suzerainty. Others, who were traditionally independent declined, and on some occasions, when Russian envoys were seen as arrogant and insulting, envoys were put to death. But most of the time when the Russians and the indigenous chiefs came to terms, their agreement involved misunderstandings and mutual misperceptions. If for Russians shert, yasak, and amanat were the articles of submission to the tsar, the natives regarded the shert as a treaty of mutual military aid, yasak as a reciprocal trade, and their amanats as Russia's honorable guests. These false expectation of each other continued for a long time. When Russian military governors failed to send the troops to assist the local chiefs against their enemy, they considered their arrangement with Moscow null and void and felt free to switch sides in search of new allies. The Russians, in turn, considered such behavior treacherous and a violation of the chiefs' allegiance to the tsar.

One issue that so far received little attention in the chapter and in general historiography is a matter of translation. After all, both sides—Russians and native peoples—knew little of each other and had few opportunities to learn more. Prior to the late eighteenth century, when Western, mostly German scholars began traveling and describing empires' different peoples and lands, Russians had little interest in understanding the natives' mores and ways of life. The indigenous people too had limited communication with the Russian frontier towns and forts. Any communication required a presence of interpreters and translators. But most interpreters were illiterate with a bare-bone knowledge of one of the dialects of the Turkic languages, which were the *lingua franca* throughout much of Asia. Translators were literate but always in short supply, as attested by numerous complaints from the Russian military governors bemoaning the lack of translators.

Apart from a shortage of interpreters and translators and their dubious competence, a deliberate mistranslation was another serious issue that distorted mutual perceptions. Russian translators were under strict instructions to translate the letters from the indigenous rulers only in a form of petition to their suzerain, the tsar. In several cases when both the original letters from a local ruler and a Russian translation are preserved, the original addressed the tsar as an equal and a military ally, while the translation abounded in submissive terms of a humble subject to the tsar. Likewise, when charged by Moscow with violating their obligations, the indigenous chiefs often complained that this was not what they believed they were committing to, when they had signed a written shert.

The same set of perceptions, policies, and mutual misconceptions applied elsewhere along the imperial frontiers of Asia. One such frontier in the seventeenth and eighteenth centuries was in southern Siberia, where Russians encountered the Oirats, a nomadic people of Inner Asia. This is the topic of the chapter by V. D. Puzanov. The main difference with the natives of Siberia was that the Oirats were not expected to pay yasak because they were a powerful nomadic confederation and a formidable adversary. As always, Russia's main goals were military and geopolitical, in this case, using the Oirats against Russia's potential foes, the Qing China and neighboring nomadic peoples. And as elsewhere, the relationship with the Oirats was articulated in terms of the Oirat subjects versus a Russian suzerain.

In the early seventeenth century, a large group of Oirats moved further west, eventually arriving in the Caspian steppe. They became known as Kalmyks. In dealing with the Kalmyks, Kazakhs, or other nomadic peoples, the Russian authorities believed that their nomadic lifestyle was the main barrier toward them becoming Russia's loyal and civilized subjects. Once the Russian government no longer had the need in the nomadic cavalry as a military force against Russia's enemies, its policies were directed at settling the nomadic peoples, and whenever possible, ascribing them to the Cossack estate and converting them to Christianity.

The fate of the Oirats was sealed in the mid-eighteenth century, when squeezed between expanding Russia on the one hand and Qing China on the other, they ceased to be a military threat and were finally subdued and incorporated into China. The conquest of the Oirats brought an end to a great nomadic age that witnessed periodic explosive migrations of nomadic warriors who through the millennia brought to the knees more than one Eurasian empire and civilization.

The chapter by Nikita Khrapunov carries one into a recently conquered Crimea circa 1800. Khrapunov examines various travelogues, both by Russians and foreigners and how they reflect the changing image of the Crimean Tatars. Given a history of the Crimean Tatars' raids against the Slavic population and capture and enslavement of hundreds of thousands over the centuries, Russians naturally, developed a very negative image of the Crimean Tatars. The first years following Crimea's conquest and its ultimate annexation into the Russian empire in 1783 witnessed much destruction of the Tatar cultural monuments. But within a few decades, with increasing colonization of the Crimea by Slavic settlers, the image of the villainous Tatars has morphed into a harmless people living in a perfect Rousseauian communion with nature.

Some Russian and foreign travelers bemoaned Russia's destruction of the mosques and palaces and exoticized the Tatars, similar to Alexander Pushkin's romantic image of "a friend of the steppe, Kalmyk" introduced in his famous poem of 1836, a description that would have been impossible only a few decades before. But there were also others who, like Peter Simon Pallas, saw the Tatars as lazy and wanted to have them replaced with the Armenians and Georgians. Or a Russian playwright, Alexander Sumarokov, who suggested to move the Tatars to the Volga River and to bring instead the Greeks and Georgians, so that Christians would replace Muslims. Such suggestions were not unusual, and, in fact, such relocations and deportations did take place throughout the Caucasus.

Caucasus is a place where Dominik Gutmeyr-Schnur's chapter takes the reader to discuss the photographic images from the region in the late nineteenth and early twentieth centuries. To demonstrate how official imperial photography served as a means of visual integration of the Other into the empire, he focuses his attention on two critical developments of photography in Russia: the 1867 All-Russian Ethnographic Exhibition in Moscow and the album *Views in the Caucasus and the Black Sea* by celebrated photographer Sergei Prokudin-Gorskii.

Not surprisingly, Russia's primary concerns were military, and the first images of the Caucasus were taken in the 1850s by the graduates of the Military Topographical Department. Ethnography remained subservient to other state interests: geopolitical, military, and in the case of the 1867 Ethnographic Exhibition that showcased Russian nationalist and pan-Slavic agenda, also political.

Less than half a century later, Prokudin-Gorskii, with a generous support from the government and personal interest of the tsar, created images of a diverse empire in the Caucasus and elsewhere. All along, argues Gutmeyr-Schnur, photography was placed in the service of the imperial authorities and helped to transform a mental appropriation of the region from an external and exotic into an internal province of the empire.

The last chapter in this section by Marina Shcherbakova discusses the emergence of the ethnographic studies of Russia's Jews by Russian Jews in the early twentieth century. Originally, the focus of such ethnography was the shtetl-world within the Pale of Settlement. In time, these studies also began to include the old Jewish communities of the Crimea, Caucasus, and Central Asia. Shcherbakova's focus is the ethnographer, Isaak Lur'e who dedicated his life to the study of the Jews of Central Asia. Lur'e believed that the Bukhara and other Jews of Central Asia were more backward and less civilized than the Ashkenazi Jews of European Russia but that eventually a religious unity of both groups will help to erase the backwardness of the former. Shcherbakova concludes that Lur'e's views were a combination of European Orientalist ideas and those of the Jewish national movement. One might add that in the late nineteenth and early twentieth century, similar developments had commonly taken place throughout the imperial borderlands. They involved Russified indigenous literary elites creating ethnographic and literary traditions for their respective peoples, and thus forging new ethnic and national identities among empire's non-Christian population.

In sum, this section creates a rich tapestry of Otherness in the Russian empire. In contrast to the primarily commercial interests of the Western European empires in the New World, Moscow's principal concerns upon encountering the non-Christian peoples were geopolitical. The Russian government first claimed the natives as its subjects, and only in the eighteenth century, it began to perceive them as savages, whose wild state of nature could be tamed by Christianity and civilization. In other words, Russia first considered indigenous peoples as unfaithful subjects, then wild and ignoble savages, before romanticizing them as noble savages in the nineteenth century.

The insistence on a political allegiance of the native population was a result of both Moscow's political theology as well as its expanding frontiers towards potentially hostile neighboring peoples and empires. Like most other empires and states, religious identity remained a principal marker of difference. In Russia, however, it was also highly malleable. Unlike the West European empires but like Russia's Eurasian counterparts (Ottoman, Persian, and Chinese empires), race played little role in official views of Otherness. Anyone could become a Russian, provided they converted to Orthodoxy and eventually assimilated into a Russian culture and way of life. Both religious conversion and Russian culture were equated with civilization (*grazhdanstvennost*), which the Russians tried to inculcate into the non-Christians throughout the nineteenth century.

Equally malleable was the notion of ethnicity, which burst onto a late imperial scene. One the eve of the Russian empire's demise, the tension between the imperial and national identities as well as ethnic and religious ones settled into an uneasy co-existence. Clearly, perceptions of Otherness in Russia were inseparable from Russia's own self-image and its continuous search for reconciling the notions of empire and a nation-state.

5

From "Sovereign's Foreigners" to "Our Savages": Otherness of Siberian Indigenous Peoples in Seventeenth- and Eighteenth-Century Russia[1]

Yuri Akimov

Abstract

This chapter examines Russians' perceptions of the indigenous population of Siberia in the seventeenth and eighteenth centuries, especially under Peter the Great. Since the beginning of the conquest of Siberia, Russians perceived their indigenous population first as "foreigners" (*inozemtsy*), then as "strangers" (*inorodtsy*). At the same time, in the pre-Petrine era, the Russian administration demanded that the indigenous communities recognize the power of the tsar, yield and surrender by paying the fur tribute (*yasak*), extraditing hostages (*amanats*), and taking the oath (*shert'*). However, it did not purposefully seek to change their beliefs, customs, mores, and everyday life. The situation changed dramatically in the early eighteenth century, when Peter ordered a campaign to convert "foreigners" to Orthodoxy without changing their "non-Russian" status as yasak payers. Since the 1710s, Christianization had been carried out with the help of the local civic authorities, often by force. At the same time, indigenous Siberians were beginning to be considered not merely as adherents of the "wrong" faith ("idolaters") but as "wild," "backward," "unenlightened,"

---

1   This work is an output of a research project implemented as part of the Basic Research Program at the National Research University Higher School of Economics (HSE University).

and "poor" people in a state of "childhood," who were accordingly opposed to those who were "civilized" and whose care they needed. It can therefore be stated that under Peter the Great the otherness of indigenous Siberians attained a new quality. This chapter will reveal the factors that contributed to this transition. The similarities and differences between the Russian perception of the indigenous peoples of Siberia as others and the perception of non-European peoples by Europeans will be considered separately.

Introduction

The conquest, exploration, and colonization of Siberia are among the most important milestones in Russian history. They made Russia a great Eurasian power, extending to the Arctic and Pacific Oceans, the borders of which remain to this day. For historians of different historical schools and perspectives, Siberian expansion was also of great importance for the formation of Russian self-consciousness. Mikhail Gefter claims that Russia only became Russia "when it absorbed Siberia."[2]

Meanwhile, Russian expansion in northern Asia became a turning point in the destiny of its numerous indigenous peoples. They became subjects of the Russian tsars and were incorporated into imperial legal, political, and socioeconomic structures. From the first contacts, the Russians regarded them as foreigners (*inozemtsy*—literally, inhabitants of another land), as others in contrast to themselves. During the seventeenth and eighteenth centuries, Russians' perception of indigenous Siberians evolved. The most radical changes occurred in the Petrine epoch, when they began to regard Siberia's indigenous peoples not only as inozemtsy but as savage people who needed to be civilized and Christianized.[3]

This chapter focuses on the "Otherness" of Siberian natives in seventeenth- and eighteenth-century Russia. It covers the pre-Petrine, Petrine, and post-Petrine periods. Each is considered in the context of the period's European colonial experience. Correspondingly, Siberia is regarded as a colony similar to the overseas possessions of Spain, England, France, and so on (according to Wolfgang Reinhard, colonialism is "one people's control over another people through the economic, political, and ideological development gap between

---

2   Mikhail Gefter, *Iz tekh i etikh let . . .* (Moscow: Progress, 1991), 383.

3   For categories and changes in defining Otherness, see also Vulpius, "From *Inozemtsy* to *Inovertsy* and *Novokreshchenye*: Images of Otherness in Eighteenth-Century Russia," in this volume.

the two").[4] Special attention is paid to the cultural, political, legal, ideological, religious, and ethnic factors that transformed Siberian natives into others in the eyes of Russia, as well as the origins of these factors.

I appeal to Tzvetan Todorov's idea that highlighting existing differences in reality implies a distinction between at least three problematic axes: the value axis, the axis of human action, and the projection of the other's image.[5] It is also based not only on Yuri Lotman's semiotic methods in general but also on his thesis of two types of culture (content-oriented and expression-oriented), his statement that a culture creates not only its own type of internal organization but also its own type of external "disorganization."[6]

In this chapter, I hypothesize that the reforms of the early eighteenth century created a double otherness of Siberian natives (in Russian eyes). Although the Muscovite perception of them did not disappear, it combined with the perception of overseas peoples (Amerindians, Africans, and so on) imported to Russia from Europe under Peter the Great.

"Sovereign's Foreigners" (*Gosudarevy inozemtsy*): Cultural Encounters in Siberia

After the conquest of the Khanate of Sibir' in the late sixteenth century, the Russians began to move rapidly into Northern Asia. The main goal of Russian expansion was not only (or even not so much) the opening of new lands as such but the imposition of fur tribute (yasak) on their native inhabitants in favor of the tsar (yasak had a material expression, but at the same time it was a symbol of submission to Russian power). This process lasted for the entire seventeenth century. Some regions and their inhabitants (for example, the Chukotka and the Chukchis) were subordinated only in the eighteenth century.

The Russians referred to the native population of Siberia as *inozemtsy*. As established by Andrei Zuev and Pavel Ignatkin, the term was first applied to indigenous Siberians in 1565. It then gradually began to enter the clerical

---

4   Wolfgang Reinhard, *A Short History of Colonialism*, trans. Kate Sturge (Manchester: Manchester University Press, 2011), 1.

5   Tzvetan Todorov, *The Conquest of America: The Question of the Other*, trans. Richard Howard (New York: Harper & Row, 1984); Claudia Costin, "Diversity: An Image of the Difference Regarding the Other," in *Contextual Identities: A Comparative and Communicational Approach*, ed. Emilia Parpala and Leo Loveday (Newcastle-upon-Tyne: Cambridge Scholars Publishing, 2015).

6   Yuri Lotman, *Semiosfera* (St. Peterburg: Iskusstvo-SPB, 2000), 495–97.

practice and vocabulary of the Siberian administration. From the beginning of the seventeenth century, it became ubiquitous, becoming "a universal name for the natives of Siberia in the business and everyday language of Muscovite Russia in the seventeenth century." The collective term *iazytsy*, people who did not speak Russian, was also used (though less often), as were (even less often) "Siberians" (*Sibirtsy*) and "Siberian people." The broader (and neutral) term "yasak people"—people who paid yasak—could also be applied to indigenous Siberians.[7]

The use of the term inozemtsy (especially its increasing frequency in the seventeenth century) is associated with the specifics of Russian expansion in Siberia. In the first stage, during the war with the Khanate of Sibir' and the subsequent exploration and conquest of Western Siberia, the Russians initially encountered peoples who were already familiar to them—the Tatars (the Tatars were not regarded as inozemtsy), the Khants, the Mansis, the Nenets, and the Selkups—who were considered to be at a higher stage of development compared with some peoples of Northeastern Siberia. These peoples were considered by the Russians as "others," yet contact with them was not associated with deep differences of understanding. The latter was due to the fact that all the peoples in question were in varying degrees familiar with the institutions Russians used and on which the Russian colonization of Siberia in the late sixteenth to mid-eighteenth centuries was based: the collection of fur tribute (yasak), the oath of allegiance (*shert'*), and the taking of hostages (*amanats*) as guarantees of payment of tribute and submission to Russian power.

A similar situation was observable in the southern part of Eastern Siberia—the Baikal region, Transbaikalia, Dauria, and so forth, where the local population was familiar with the idea of tribute paying and overlordship. So, having met with the Buryats for the first time, the Russians noted with surprise that this people "not only does not pay yasak to anybody but takes it from other peoples."[8]

The picture was different in Northeastern Siberia, Chukotka, and Kamchatka. There the Russians encountered peoples who, first, had had no previous contact with them (that is, they were unknown to the Russians); second, were at a significantly lower stage of development (with a primitive communal system, an appropriating economy, and primitive technologies); and third, lacked any knowledge of the yasak tribute, shert' oath, and amanats

7 Andrei Zuev and Pavel Ignatkin, "'Inozemtsy'—'Their' and 'Other': Terminological Classification for Social and Political Status of Siberian Natives in the Moscow State (End of the 16th–Beginning of the 18th Century)," *Vestnik NGU. Seriia: Istoriia, filologiia* 15, no. 8 (2016): 67–85.
8 Mikhail Bogdanov, *Ocherki istorii buriat-mongol'skogo naroda: s dopolnitel'nymi stat'iami B. B. Baradina i N. N. Koz'mina* (Verkhneudinsk: Buriat-Mongol'skoe izdatel'stvo, 1926), 29.

hostages. In the mid-1640s, the Russians were therefore surprised to find that the Tungus did "not know that people must pay yasak to the sovereign."[9] Some peoples of Eastern Siberia considered the amanats prisoners, and the latter in turn considered themselves dead and that their fate was of no interest to their relatives. It was therefore initially difficult to capture amanats from such natives. When they found themselves in a hopeless situation, they allegedly committed murder and then suicide—the men stabbed the women and children and then themselves.[10] Second, captives often also sought to take their own lives—"they choked themselves and stabbed each other to death."[11] Third, they were useless for the Russians because they did not perform their main function of ensuring the payment of yasak and maintaining loyalty to the Russian government.

In the pre-Petrine era, several interrelated processes took place in Siberia. On the one hand, the conquest by the Russians, the subjugation of its peoples to Russian power (it generally ended by the middle of the seventeenth century), and the formation of a system of colonial government continued. At the same time, Siberia was regarded not as a periphery but as a "remote state, which is located among the lands of paganism and other faiths."[12] On the other hand, the aboriginal communities that faced Russian expansion had been witnessing dramatic and sometimes tragic changes. Even though there was no organized resistance, there was opposition to the Russians, with consequences.[13] Aborigines died in clashes with Cossacks and the servicemen (*sluzhilye liudi*), were subjected to violence by the yasak collectors, suffered from epidemics of infectious diseases brought in from outside, and were deprived of part of their lands. All of this resulted in a decline in the number of aboriginal communities, in forced migrations, and in the decay of traditional cultures.

According to Dittmar Schorkowitz, Russia's state colonialism was not based on trade or a plantation economy.[14] Indeed, until the early eighteenth century, the main—and, in fact, the only—goal of Russian policy regarding the Siberian aborigines was to ensure their obedience and regular flow of yasak. The

9 Andrei Zuev, *Russkie i aborigeny na krainem severo–vostoke Sibiri vo vtoroi polovine XVII–pervoi chetverti XVIII v.* (Novosibirsk: NGU, 2002), 120.
10 Ibid., 161.
11 Vladimir Bogoraz, *Chukchi* (Leningrad: Izdatel'stvo instituta narodov Severa, 1944), 44.
12 *Polnoe sobranie zakonov Rossiiskoi imperii.* In 45 volumes, (St. Petersburg, 1830), 2:663 (hereafter cited as PSZRI).
13 Alan Wood, *Russia's Frozen Frontier: A History of Siberia and the Russian Far East: 1581–1991* (London: Bloomsbury Academic, 2011), 30.
14 Dittmar Schorkowitz, "Was Russia a Colonial Empire?," in *Shifting Forms of Continental Colonialism: Unfinished Struggles and Tensions*, ed. Dittmar Schorkowitz, John R. Chávez, and Ingo W. Schröder (London: Palgrave Macmillan, 2019), 124.

authorities constantly ordered local administrators to "protect tributary people" and "treat them gently."[15] However, the order was ignored on the ground, and there was lots of abuse, violence, and "unmotivated cruelty."[16] Even at the official level, it was constantly admitted that tributary people suffered "need, losses, and great insults" from Cossacks and the service class.[17] Nevertheless, as Valerie Kivelson noted, "Muscovite attitudes toward people and property, geography and typology, created a fundamental belief that the indigenous population had to be geographically fixed and reified in its difference, rather than assimilated or eradicated."[18]

The Russian government did not set the goal to convert the Siberian natives to Christianity, "civilize" them, instill new skills, or introduce them to a settled lifestyle à la russe. The Russians considered all the native inhabitants of Siberia subjects of the tsar: the "sovereign's inozemtsy" (what the natives themselves understood by this is another matter).[19] However, not only did they differ from the Russians, but they were opposed to them in religion, legal status, lifestyle, language, and other key respects. Russians believed they professed the only "true" and correct faith (Orthodoxy), while foreigners adhered to the "wrong" faith (paganism/idolatry) or completely lacked it. Different versions of the *Esipov Chronicle*[20] stated that indigenous Siberians were people who did "not know the Almighty God and His divine law." It further specified that "the Skewbald Horde [the Selkups], the Ostyaks [Khants], and the Samoyeds do not have the divine law, but they worship idols and offer sacrifices to demons as

---

15 Gerhard Friedrich Müller, *Istoriia Sibiri* (Moscow: Vostochnaia Literatura RAN, 2005), 3:365, 366.

16 Cf. Yuri Akimov, *Severnaia Amerika i Sibir' v kontse XVI–seredine XVIII v.: ocherk sravnitel'noi istorii kolonizatsii* (St.Petersburg: Izdatel'stvo Sankt-Peterburgskogo universiteta, 2010); Andrei Zuev, "'Konkvistadory imperii': russkie zemleprokhodtsy na Severo-Vostoke Sibiri," in *Region v istorii imperii: istoricheskie esse o Sibiri*, ed. Sergei Glebov (Moscow: Novoe izdatel'stvo, 2012).

17 Müller, *Istoriia Sibiri*, 372.

18 Valerie Kivelson, "Claiming Siberia: Colonial Possession and Property Holding in the Seventeenth and Early Eighteenth Centuries," in *Peopling the Russian Periphery: Borderland Colonization in Eurasian History*, ed. Nicholas B. Breyfogle, Abby Schrader, and Willard Sunderland (London: Routledge, 2007), 36.

19 Michael Khodarkovsky, "'Ignoble Savages and Unfaithful Subjects': Constructing Non-Christian Identities in Early Modern Russia," in *Russia's Orient: Imperial Borderlands and Peoples, 1700–1917*, ed. Daniel R. Brower and Edward J. Lazzerini (Bloomington: Indiana University Press, 1997), 12–13.

20 "Esipov Chronicle" *(Esipovskaia letopis')* is an early chronicle of Siberian history written by Savva Esipov in 1636.

to God."[21] In relation to various groups of foreigners, it was also often claimed that they had "no faith and no literacy."[22] As "The Chronographic Tale"[23] put it:

> There are many people with different languages in this vast Siberian tsardom. These same people, though resembling men, have the temper and life of a beast, as they do not have the divine law: some worship a stone, some worship a bear, some worship trees or birds. They carve birds, beasts, and snakes from wood and worship them.[24]

Also, *Pogodin's Chronicler*,[25] describing *Vogulichy* (the Mansi), claimed that they "worship soulless idols."[26]

From the legal perspective, inozemtsy were a special category of the population (tributary people, payers of yasak), isolated from those classes to which the Russians belonged. The latter, accordingly, did not pay any yasak but either paid taxes or offered a service.[27] A similar situation occurred in Spanish America, where all the indigenous peoples were considered subjects of the crown and carried certain duties in its favor (*tributo*), but their status differed radically from that of the Spaniards.

The natives were perceived by the Russians as belonging to the nomad world, the opposite of their settled world. In fact, this perception was not true: some of the natives did lead a nomadic life, while some were sedentary. But the Russians wanted to see them as nomadic, pastoral Siberians. Here one can draw a parallel with English America, where the British stubbornly refused to notice Indian agriculture—however, on different grounds. This ignorance helped them justify their rights to supposedly "no-man's" land.[28] The Russians perceived the

21 Aleksei Okladnikov and Boris Rybakov, "Sibirskie letopisi," in *Polnoe sobranie russkikh letopisei* (Moscow: Nauka, 1987), 36:107.

22 Ibid., 75.

23 "Chronographic Tale" (*Khronograficheskaia povest'*) is an extract from a universal "Chronology" of world history compiled circa 1650–60.

24 Elena Dergacheva-Skop, ed., *Letopisi Sibirskie* (Novosibirsk: Novosibirskoe knizhnoe izdatel'stvo, 1991), 44–45.

25 "Pogodin's Chronicler" (*Pogodinskii letopisets*) is part of an anonymous compilation of world history, written at the end of the seventeenth century.

26 Okladnikov and Rybakov, *Sibirskie letopisi*, 129.

27 Kivelson, "Claiming Siberia: Colonial Possession and Property Holding in the Seventeenth and Early Eighteenth Centuries," 27.

28 Wilbur Jacobs, "British-Colonial Attitudes and Policies toward the Indian in the American Colonies," in *Attitudes of Colonial Powers toward the American Indian*, ed. Howard Peckham and Charles Gibson (Salt Lake City: University of Utah Press, 1969), 85.

appropriating economy of the Siberian inozemtsy as contrasting with their producing economy. They also highlighted the differences in everyday matters, including diet, marital and family relations, clothing, and housing.

Finally, there was a language barrier between the two communities, which had two aspects. The first was practical, since there was a problem in communication: foreigners "spoke their own language,"[29] and therefore "one could not do without a Russian interpreter."[30] The second was symbolic because pre-Petrine Russia's attitude to foreign languages was, in the words of Yuri Lotman, "irreconcilable": they were "considered a means of expressing foreign culture," and a foreign religion.[31] Accordingly, the "Orthodox language" of the Russians was contrasted with the "non-Orthodox languages" of the indigenous peoples.

All these differences between Russians and indigenous people—confessional, class, household, linguistic—divided the two worlds. From the perspective of the Russians, their correct, ordered, well-organized world ("we") was opposed to the "anti-world" of the inozemtsy—the incorrect and other ("they"). This also contributed to the further consolidation of the perception of the Russians of themselves.

Siberians as Others in the Eyes of Seventeenth-Century Muscovites

What was the attitude of Russians to this "otherness"? What was their assessment of the Siberian "others": positive, negative, or neutral? It is certainly difficult to answer this question unambiguously because in practice all three attitudes were combined. Moreover, the attitudes of the representatives of different social groups could vary. Obviously, the perception of the indigenous groups by Cossacks and fur traders (*promyshlenniki*) could have been different from that of priests or administrators. On the maps of Semen Remezov, which were intended primarily for the authorities, the local native communities "were not only presented in visual terms as political units [. . .] but were granted that stature even in the face of evidence to the contrary."[32]

---

29 Okladnikov and Rybakov, *Sibirskie letopisi*, 129.
30 Anna Liutsidarskaia, "Tolmachi v Sibiri. Period nachala kolonizatsii territorii," *Gumanitarnye nauki v Sibiri* 3 (2011): 27.
31 Lotman, *Semiosfera*, 495–96.
32 Kivelson, "Claiming Siberia: Colonial Possession and Property Holding in the Seventeenth and Early Eighteenth Centuries," 34.

Meanwhile, in pre-Petrine Russia, most of the information about Siberia and its inhabitants came from one source—reports and interrogatories (*skaski*) of Russian explorers (that is, Cossacks and the service class). There were simply no alternative channels for obtaining information—again, unlike the case with the European colonies in the New World (for example, the native people of Canada were represented differently in the descriptions of French explorers and the famous *Jesuit Relations*).

Compared with Europeans in the New World, the Muscovites of the seventeenth century were alien to extremes. Far from considering the natives of Siberia "noble savages," they did not admire them. Yet, neither did they perceive them unambiguously in a dark manner, as was the case in many Spanish (and not only Spanish) descriptions of Amerindians, where the latter appeared as "savages" who practiced "terrible cruelties"; their faith was seen as serving "demons" and "forces of evil" (idols "with diabolical countenances"), and the activities of their priests as murderous and "preaching all kinds of evil."[33]

Viktor Zemskov, in comparing the chronicles of *La Conquista* and the chronicles of the conquest of Siberia, noted the "insufficient surprise of Russians when they encountered Siberian religious rites and accordingly, the immeasurably less attention paid to 'wooden chump prayers' and idol worshippers (*shaitanshchiki*), and the rather everyday tone of the narratives (compared with the descriptions of the American chronicles)."[34] This is partly because at the initial stage of the colonization of Siberia there were very few priests who could pay attention to this, while Cossacks and the service class literally ignored pagan rituals. However, even in Russian documents and chronicles that are clearly of ecclesiastical origin, value judgments in relation to the religious beliefs of indigenous people were rare.

As Yuri Slezkine has noted, the Russians clearly had a negative perception of two aspects of the life of Siberian inozemtsy: their food and accepted relations between the sexes: *skarednaia iad'* (unclean food), including eating dogs, and "bad lust."[35] Indeed, in speaking of the natives, the Russians often noted that "all they eat is very brutal and repulsive in their mouths, and they are foul and

---

33 Bernal Díaz del Castillo, *The True History of the Conquest of New Spain* (Farham: Hakluyt Society, 2010).

34 Viktor Zemskov, "Khroniki konkisty Ameriki i letopisi vziatiia Sibiri v tipologicheskom sopostavlenii (k postanovke voprosa)," in *Svobodnyi vzgliad na literaturu: Problemy sovremennoi filologii*, ed. Andrei Mikhailov (Moscow: Nauka, 2002), 178.

35 Yuri Slezkine, *Arctic Mirrors: Russia and the Small Peoples of the North* (Ithaca: Cornell University Press, 1994), 45.

unclean in the extreme"; "they eat the raw meat of beasts and snakes, and drink their blood like water, and they also eat grass and roots."[36]

At the same time, the Russians in general had a neutral or, more precisely, an indifferent attitude to the Siberian natives in the pre-Petrine era. They were foreigners, they were different, and the differences between them and the Russians were therefore taken for granted. It is very significant that, until the beginning of the eighteenth century, the Russians made almost no effort to convert Siberian natives to Orthodoxy. This is even more surprising given that the Russians considered their arrival in Siberia, its conquest, and its colonization as the fulfilment of a divine mission and the realization of the will of Providence. The annexation of the Siberian Khanate by Moscow was considered a "heavenly gift" to the Russian monarch: Siberia, as *Pogodin's Chronicler* argues, "was taken by God's command";[37] *Stroganov Chronicle* claims that "God granted the Siberian state to the tsar."[38]

As they moved deeper into Siberia, exploring and populating it, the Russians saw themselves as completely transforming the territories that fell into their orbit, radically altering the religious landscape. *Pogodin's Chronicler* continues: "The sun of the Gospel enlightened the Siberian land. And by God's command, towns, and villages where many Orthodox inhabitants live appeared in many places."[39] *Esipov Chronicle* tells, "the Orthodox Christian faith has spread"; "previously, the Siberian land was marred by idolatry; now it is beaming with piety."[40]

Moreover, in the views of both the Russian colonizers and the Russian authorities, all this quietly and peacefully coexisted with the fact that on the territory where "the Sun of the Gospel" shone, the natives continued to be pagans and freely confessed their faith. Indeed, the conversion of foreigners to Orthodoxy was allowed and nominally approved, but it was in no way encouraged.

Historians (especially Soviet ones) have pointed out that since the baptism of indigenous people automatically led to a reduction in the number of payers of yasak, it was unprofitable for the state, which was therefore not interested in converting pagans.[41] This is partly true, of course. In Siberia, Moscow first

---

36 Okladnikov and Rybakov, *Sibirskie letopisi*, 107, 179, 235.
37 Dergacheva-Skop, *Letopisi Sibirskie*, 60.
38 Ibid., 108.
39 Ibid., 96, 98.
40 Okladnikov and Rybakov, *Sibirskie letopisi*, 51.
41 Natal'ia Apollova, *Khoziaistvennoe osvoenie Priirtysh'ia v kontse XVI–pervoi treti XIX v.* (Moscow: Nauka, 1976), 104.

and foremost needed tributary people. However, it should be noted that in the history of European colonialism at that time, there were cases in which the interests of secular colonial expansion conflicted with its religious goals. For example, in the New France of the mid-seventeenth century, the Jesuits' missionary activity among the Indians sometimes ran counter to the interests of the fur trade, which was the main branch of the colony's economy.

Concerning the religious situation in Siberia in the seventeenth century, Valerie Kivelson has noted that the Russians, in fulfilling their imperial mission, "adhered to a program of *Christianization without conversion*. [. . .] God wholeheartedly supported the Russian enterprise, because it promised to spread His name and glory to the ends of the earth, but He was content with Christianizing the land and landscape in ways that did not necessarily rely on conversion of the pagan population."[42] In these circumstances the "dissemination of God's word took place more through the extension of Russian settlement than through any concerted evangelical campaign." Thus, "Muscovites systematically presumed and imposed a hierarchy of faiths and relegated their new Muslim, pagan, and shamanist subjects to the bottom strata of the religious ladder."[43]

In my view, it should be added that this approach corresponded to the peculiarities of pre-Petrine Russian culture, which, as Yuri Lotman has noted, aimed "primarily at expression, where the main opposition was the juxtaposition of 'right' and 'wrong,'" and which "may not have any desire for expansion. [. . .]. Non-culture is equated here with anti-culture and thus, in its very essence, cannot be perceived as a potential area of cultural dissemination."[44] (Lotman uses "the glossemantic categories of plane of expression [signifier, *signifiant*] and plane of content [signified, *signifié*].")[45] This corresponded to the medieval idea of the world as a finite, closed, and hierarchically organized space in which the Christian was contrasted with the non-Christian idolater.[46]

The religious situation in pre-Petrine Siberia resembled the religious situation in English America. Officially, all the English colonies on the Atlantic coast—as stated in their charters—were created to spread the true faith (not to mention the colonies of New England, where the Puritans conducted their

42 Valerie Kivelson, *Cartographies of Tsardom: The Land and Its Meanings in Seventeenth-Century Russia* (Ithaca: Cornell University Press, 2006), 150.
43 Ibid.
44 Lotman, *Semiosfera*, 495–97.
45 Renate Lachmann, "Value Aspects in Jurij Lotman's 'Semiotics of culture/semiotics of text,'" *Dispositio* 12, no. 30–32 (1987): 15–16.
46 Svetlana Luchitskaia, *Obraz Drugogo: musul'mane v khronikakh krestovykh pokhodov* (St. Petersburg: Aleteia, 2001).

"great experiment" of creating a "New Israel"). However, in the seventeenth century, the English engaged in scarcely any missionary activities among the "poor savages," although they were convinced that they were performing a "divine mission."

Another confirmation of the predominance of neutral and indifferent attitudes of Muscovites to the "otherness" of Siberian natives is that, in the seventeenth century, Russians had little information about inozemtsy, and they did not seek to expand their knowledge of them. Of course, Russian explorers, officials, and merchants noted certain features of the social structure, economy, and everyday household life of natives, their beliefs, culture, and language, but they did not seek to study or comprehend all this in depth, considering it unnecessary, a fact that the Europeans, who were in this way unlike the Russians, noticed in the early seventeenth century. For example, Isaac Massa wrote, "the gods they [the Tungus] worship and the religious rites they perform are unknown and remain so, since Muscovites are not interested in such things."[47] Similarly, Lotman argues that "The function of any boundary [. . .] is to limit the penetration, filtering and adapting the processing of the external into the internal."[48] The next question concerns how rigid or flexible and, accordingly, how surmountable or insurmountable the borders between the worlds of Russians and foreigners were.

One of the most important indicators here is the movement from the world of the inozemtsy to the world of the Russians (the question of reverse transitions is beyond the scope of this study). As noted above, a native could convert to Orthodoxy; this was not prohibited, though it was not encouraged. The ban only applied to the practice of forced baptism, or "baptism in captivity," as a result of which the new convert actually became a slave.[49] The native who converted to Orthodoxy both legally and mentally ceased to be an inozemets and became "Russian." He ceased to be considered a payer of yasak and was included in a "Russian" class or estate. He also ceased to be perceived as one of his own people by his former relatives. When several converted natives were offered the possibility "to live on their lands and in their yurts as before," they replied that they had "left their faith, and they [would] not be allowed in their land because they [were] baptized."[50]

47 Mikhail Alekseev, ed., *Sibir' v izvestiiakh zapadno-evropeiskikh puteshestvennikov i pisatelei, XIII–XVII vv.* (Novosibirsk: Nauka, 2006), 265.

48 Lotman, *Semiosfera*, 265.

49 Aleksei Konev, "Shertoprivodnye zapisi i prisiagi sibirskikh 'inozemtsev' kontsa XVI–XVIII vv.," *Vestnik arkheologii, antropologii i etnografii* 6 (2019): 172–77.

50 Iosif Ogryzko, *Khristianizatsiia narodov Tobol'skogo Severa v XVIII v.* (Leningrad: Uchpedgiz, 1914), 16–17.

In the seventeenth century, natives who converted to Orthodoxy and thus became "Russian" experienced no discrimination from the society that accepted them. As early as the nineteenth century, historians noted the "absence of tribal hostility" between Russians and indigenous peoples.[51] It was not important whether they were baptized voluntarily or accepted baptism because of a combination of circumstances (the latter applies primarily to women who were taken captive and married Russians). However, there were generally few such transitions from inozemtsy to "Russians." Aleksei Konev and Roman Poplavskii demonstrate that the motives for voluntary conversion were caused by extraordinary circumstances,[52] which in turn were not frequent. For example, in the whole of Yakutia in 1701 there were only twenty-five converted aboriginals.[53]

Although the Russians viewed the indigenous world as "other," irregular, and disordered, the latter was in fact, of course, also an organized space, though organized differently. Accordingly, there was "a permanent exchange, the development of a common language, Koine (Κοινή), a formation of creolized semiotic systems" on the border between the two worlds.[54] For instance, Russians had to take into account the fact that the natives (especially in the east and northeast of Siberia) considered yasak, first, not a tribute but an element of commodity exchange or exchange of gifts and, second, not a symbol of submission to Russians but a symbol of union with them. Accordingly, the salary and gifts "from the sovereign" that were intended for the inozemtsy as subjects became remuneration in their eyes, even if it was not equivalent, for their furs and military alliance. This did not suit the central authorities, and the collectors of yasak were instructed to remind foreigners that they "must not cheat [because] they pay yasak as tribute to the sovereign and do not sell it."[55] However, the reality was different. Maxim Perfiliev reported of the Tungus: "The Tungus [...] request [...] gifts of tin and beads, and feed, flour, and butter and fat, and as they get all of it, they on demand give a sable from two or three families. And they do not want to give anything without gifts."[56]

---

51 Nikolai Firsov, *Polozhenie inorodtsev severo-vostochnoi Rossii v Moskovskom gosudarstve* (Kazan: Universitetskaia tipografiia, 1866), 233.

52 Aleksei Konev and Roman Poplavskii, "Dar v politike i praktike khristiianizatsii sibirskikh 'inovertsev' (po materialam Zapadnoi Sibiri kontsa XVI–XVIII v.)," *Vestnik arkheologii, antropologii i etnografii* 4, no. 43 (2018): 168.

53 Mikhail Fedorov, *Pravovoe polozhenie narodov Vostochnoi Sibiri: XVII–nachalo XIX veka* (Iakutsk: Knizhnoe izdatel'stvo, 1978), 85.

54 Lotman, *Semiosfera*, 267.

55 Sergei Bakhrushin, "Iasak v Sibiri," *Nauchnye trudy* 3, no. 2 (1955): 75.

56 Nikolai Stepanov, "Prisoedenenie Vostochnoi Sibiri v XVII v. i tungusskie plemena," in *Russkoe naselenie Pomoria i Sibiri (Period feodalizma)*, ed. Aleksei Okladnikov (Moscow, Nauka: 1973),

The Russians had to adapt their practices of taking the oath of allegiance to the tsar to the religious and legal beliefs of the natives. This oath (*shert'*) was a very important legal and symbolic element, meaning the acceptance of a particular people as Russian citizens. The taking of the oath by the natives of Siberia was accompanied by various rites that were intended to "fix" it. These rites were borrowed from the natives themselves: drinking dog's blood, eating soil, pronouncing the words of the oath on a bearskin where knives and axes lay, walking between the halves of a dog cut in two, drinking from a vessel in which golden objects lay, and so on.[57] By doing so, in the eyes of the Russians, shert' had "the same legal meaning as kissing the cross—the oath of Orthodox subjects."[58] There was therefore a symbiosis of "own" and "theirs," formed on the "border" between two "worlds" (or between the "world" and the "anti-world").

In the European colonies of that time, a similar symbiosis can be found at the institutional level. The Spaniards used indigenous institutions in Mexico and Peru. However, outside the zone of high civilizations, including North America, there was nothing like this. There, the Europeans forced the indigenous peoples to play by their rules—that is, to sign (put totem symbols on) documents (treaties, agreements) drawn up according to European rules, even though the indigenous peoples did not understand them. As for the "symbolic acts" borrowed from the Amerindians, they had no legal force (in general, the Amerindians were not recognized as legal proprietors of the land, for example).

Thus, in the pre-Petrine era, the Russians formed an image of the Siberian natives as "others." The markers of this "otherness" were designated or formulated, the borders between the world of Russians and the world ("anti-world") of foreigners were drawn, a certain evaluative attitude to the latter was formed, and the possibilities of overcoming borders and moving from one world to another were established. At the same time, the borders between the two worlds were mainly geographical in nature and quite tangible. Russians and Siberian natives entered the eighteenth century with this baggage.

108; see also Khodarkovsky, "'Ignoble Savages and Unfaithful Subjects': Constructing Non-Christian Identities in Early Modern Russia," 15–16.

57 Grigorii Popov, *Ocherki po istorii Iakutii* (Iakutsk: Izdatel'stvo Narkomprozdrav Ia. ASSR., 1924), 29; Fedor Kudriavtsev, *Istoriia buriat-mongol'skogo naroda. Ot XVII v. do 60-kh godov XIX v. Ocherki* (Moscow: Izdatel'stvo Akademii nauk SSSR, 1940), 52.

58 Konev, "Shertoprivodnye zapisi i prisiagi sibirskikh 'inozemtsev' kontsa XVI–XVIII vv.," 172.

Changes in Russian Policy toward Siberian Natives under Peter the Great

The transformations of the stormy Petrine era affected all corners and peoples of the Russian state without exception. Siberia was also affected. At the outset of his reign, Peter raised the issue of the necessity of converting Siberian pagan natives to Orthodoxy. In the late 1690s, in a conversation with Patriarch Adrian, the tsar spoke of the need for "evil-believers [. . .] to get to know the Lord and his divine law."[59]

The need to baptize the native inhabitants of Siberia, and to spread Orthodoxy to China and Mongolia, was apparently mentioned in an unpreserved letter Peter the Great wrote to the head of the Siberian prikaz, Andrei Vinius, on March 11, 1698. This was followed by Vinius's response on April 22 of the same year, in which he reported that "a decree has been issued to the Siberian bishop, to the effect that, after finding [. . .] learned men, he should send them there to preach and baptize, [. . .] [so that] in the future the apostolic work would constantly expand."[60]

In June 1700, the tsar personally decreed the selection of a "good and learned" person in Ukraine who could become metropolitan of Tobolsk and head of the Siberian diocese.[61] According to the tsar, he had to "gradually bring to baptism in China and Siberia people obdurate in the blindness of idolatry and other infidelities." In Siberia, this above all concerned "yasak peoples, [. . .] living near Tobolsk and other Siberian cities."[62]

Peter's decree clearly indicates that a radical transformation had begun in Russians' perception of the faith of Siberian natives. While before Peter their paganism and idolatry were accepted by the Russians as wrong but at the same time expected and "normal" for inozemtsy, now they were perceived not merely negatively but as an abnormal and intolerable phenomenon that must be eradicated.

In 1701, in the severest initial phase of the Great Northern War, a decree was issued for the establishment of a minor seminary (spiritual school) in Tobolsk. It was intended to train priests who "could teach people and numerous foreigners in Siberia who do not know the Lord, bring them to the knowledge of the True

---

59 Konstantin Kharlampovich, *Malorossiiskoe vliianie na velikorusskuiu tserkovnuiu zhizn'* (Vol. 1. Kazan: Izdatel'stvo knizhnogo magazina M. A. Golubeva, 1914), 404.

60 *Pis'ma i bumagi imperatora Petra Velikogo*, tom 1, *(1688–1701)* (St. Petersburg: Gosudarstvennaia tipografiia, 1887), 616–17.

61 PSZRI, 4:60.

62 Ogryzko, *Khristianizatsiia narodov Tobol'skogo Severa v XVIII v.*, 25.

Faith, and then seek the expansion of Holy Baptism to the Chinese state itself."[63] In 1702, Filofei Leshchinskii (Filoteusz Leszczyński), an enlightened man from Malorossiia and a graduate of the Kiev theological academy (with many other figures of the Russian Orthodox Church of the Petrine era), was appointed the new Siberian metropolitan. In the same year, he received a very important instruction from the tsar to baptize inozemtsy without exempting them from paying yasak—that is, without changing their status and becoming Russian.[64]

The edicts and orders of the early 1700s stated that natives should be induced to accept baptism voluntarily ("gradually," "by their own will"). Initially, the Russian clergy sought to act in this way—they persuaded inozemtsy to accept Orthodoxy voluntarily without threats but promising nothing in return. However, the missions of Filofei and his men to the Khants, Kets, Selkups, and Mansi in the middle of the second half of the eighteenth century were unsuccessful. Archimandrite Martinian's mission to Kamchatka in 1705 also failed.[65]

Faced with this situation, the authorities decided to resort to a proven carrot and stick policy, and the stick, as often happens, was considerably more powerful. In 1710, Peter ordered the forcible baptism of the Khants (Ostyaks) and the burning of their idols and destruction of their place of worship, and "if any Ostyaks commit to resist this decree, the death penalty shall be imposed."[66] Those baptized were promised a "benefit" (discount) in the payment of yasak (an exemption for several years—usually between three and ten) and gifts of shirts, bread, and so on. Similar orders were issued in subsequent years. Thus, a decree was issued on December 6, 1711 "on the destruction of idols of the Voguliches, Ostyaks, Tatars, and Yakuts, and on the baptism of these peoples into the Christian faith."[67]

The missionary activity was supported by the secular authorities. As early as 1710, Filofei was informed that the Tobolsk voivode Ivan Bibikov had been told to give him everything that was "needed for the journey." The Siberian metropolitan now repeatedly received permission to take "from the treasuries of cities all he needs for that conversion," and the commandants of all Siberian cities in turn were obliged to "give what is needed without any deduction."[68]

In 1711, Filofei was succeeded in the Diocese of Tobolsk by another native of Malorossiia, Ioann (Maksimovich), but Filofei remained in Siberia and

---

63 Fedorov, *Pravovoe polozhenie narodov Vostochnoi Sibiri: XVII–nachalo XIX veka*, 85.
64 Ogryzko, *Khristianizatsiia narodov Tobol'skogo Severa v XVIII v.*, 25.
65 Slezkine, *Arctic Mirrors: Russia and the Small Peoples of the North*, 50.
66 Ogryzko, *Khristianizatsiia narodov Tobol'skogo Severa v XVIII v.*, 26.
67 PSZRI, 4:133.
68 Ibid.

continued to engage in missionary activities. His first successful mission trip was in 1712, when the first Siberian governor, Prince Matvei Gagarin, arrived in Tobolsk and took over its organization. The missionaries were given a boat, food, money, and gifts for converts, and armed guards and interpreters were assigned to them. Local officials (yasak collectors) had gathered the natives in advance at the place where the missionaries were to arrive,[69] and the first mass baptism took place.

During the first decade of the eighteenth century, several missionary trips were undertaken by Filofei and his associates to various regions of Siberia and the Far East, as a result of which a significant number of the natives (mostly adult men) were baptized. However, there is no exact data on the number of converts. In 1721, Filofei himself spoke of thirty thousand; Peter congratulated him on the conversion of "forty thousand and more"—this figure is widespread and can be found in many works, though it is difficult to say on what it is based.[70]

Clearly, several reasons dictated the decision of Peter, the reformer tsar, to launch a campaign to convert Siberian natives to Orthodoxy. First, it introduced Russians to the European practice of missionary activity among pagans carried out by missionary monks (before Peter, there was no mission as an institution in Russia, and monks were not engaged in missionary activity). Second, Peter desired rationalization, order, and uniformity on a national scale. Third, the tsar viewed the Orthodox Church as part of the state apparatus and an instrument for educating good subjects. Fourth, he was intolerant of superstition and mysticism, and thus he had a negative attitude toward paganism as the most primitive and crude form of religion. All this was dictated by considerations of state policy.[71]

A comprehensive study of the territories beyond the Urals and their population (geographical, ethnographic, archaeological, botanical, and zoological, and so on) also began under Peter. The tsar's attention was drawn to Siberia as a source of curiosity—unusual animals and birds, plants, objects, and people. In 1721, Turinsk commandant Stepan Kazimerov was ordered to buy and send to St. Petersburg via Tobolsk "various kinds of live animals and birds and natural crystal in blocks," and "mammoth horns and bones."[72] On several occasions,

---

69 Ogryzko, *Khristianizatsiia narodov Tobol'skogo Severa v XVIII v.*, 33.

70 Viacheslav Sofronov, *Svetochi zemli sibirskoi: Biografii arkhipastyrei Tobol'skikh i Sibirskikh (1620–1918 gg.)* (Ekaterinburg: Ural'skii rabochii, 1998).

71 See also Vulpius, "From *Inozemtsy* to *Inovertsy* and *Novokreshchenye*: Images of Otherness in Eighteenth-Century Russia" in this volume.

72 *Pamiatniki sibirskoi istorii XVIII veka: Kniga vtoraia, 1713–1724* (St. Petersburg: Tipografiia ministerstva vnutrennikh del, 1885), 292–93.

Peter ordered that "the best shamans who cure diseases and seem to guess the reasons for them" be brought from Siberia with "those with embroidered faces from the Tungus and Lamutsk peoples"—that is, people with faces tattooed by piercing their cheeks.[73]

Daniel Gottlieb Messerschmidt's 1719 expedition is considered the starting point for the scientific study of Siberia under Peter. Initially, it was conceived primarily as botanical, but Messerschmidt went far beyond the initial instructions given to him, exploring not only Siberia's flora and fauna but its geography, climate, monuments of past and present material and spiritual culture, and the languages, customs, and beliefs of its inhabitants. He was interested in "shaitans, objects from burials, ancient Tatar manuscripts," and much more.[74] He compiled a table of numerals in twenty different languages of the Siberian peoples and conducted "surveys" (interviews) of the population on a variety of topics.[75] Messerschmidt was the first to collect information about the Evenks, Kets, Selkups, and Buryats. He described their appearance, clothing, homes, decorations, weapons, and lifestyle.

In studying and describing Siberia, the people of Peter's era began to consider it an "out-of-Europe periphery" like the colonial possessions of European powers and its inhabitants as "savages" and "uncivilized" people who lagged in their development, who should be "enlightened" and "civilized." Many apologists for Peter's reforms spoke of the need for this. Vasilii Tatishchev argued that among non-Russian peoples, "it is very necessary to arrange such schools so that [. . .] their infants can learn Russian literacy, the language and the law of God, and through it soon to conveniently convert them to Christianity and a pious life and teach them to live in a house."[76]

Ivan Pososhkov proposed a radical and very strict program of Christianization and russification of natives in his "Paternal Testament." Its first stage was to be conversion to Christianity, not only through preaching but through an entire system of incentives for the baptized and restrictions for the unbaptized. He even suggested that converted natives should be required to wear identification marks on their clothing: "And for the sake of clear knowledge, all those who are baptized should sew circles on their clothes on both the upper and underwear, and on their shirts, on the right shoulder." The conversion was to be followed

---

73 Ibid., 365–66.
74 Natal'ia Kopaneva, "Nauchnoe puteshestvie D. G. Messerschmidt'a kak chast' proektov Petra I po opisaniiu Rossiiskogo gosudarstva," *Ural'skii istoricheskii vestnik* 2, no. 51 (2016): 49.
75 Mariia Novlianskaia, *Daniel Gottlieb Messerschmidt i ego raboty po issledovaniiu Sibiri* (Leningrad: Nauka, 1970), 19.
76 Vasilii Tatishchev, *Izbrannye proizvedeniia* (Leningrad: Nauka, 1979), 104.

by compulsory study of the Russian language and the refusal to use all native languages: "and if their languages are not destroyed, then they cannot be perfect Christians, but they will be half-believers: with a Christian name and rank, but not Christian in their deeds." Pososhkov proposed the main channel for the dissemination of Russian should be through children, whom he proposed to remove from their parents if they had not learned Russian by the age of ten.[77]

In the Petrine era, indigenous Siberians (who were previously only the object of exploitation—payers of yasak) acquired several new "hypostases": they became the object of missionary activity, the object of study, and (potentially) the object of education and introduction to civilization. Accordingly, the attitude toward them became different on every axis: axiological (as the estimates of natives changed), gnoseological (as new information about them appeared), and praxeological (as the policy toward them changed). In general, the attitude became more complex than in the seventeenth century.

The native inhabitants of Siberia remained *iasachnye inozemtsy*—that is, foreigners and payers of yasak; they were not subject to the duties borne by Russians in that they did not pay a poll tax and were not conscripted.[78] Unlike the pre-Petrine era, converting indigenous Siberians to Christianity now did not mean changing their social status or "turning" them into Russians. Their otherness began to be twofold: if physical and spatial borders had previously lain between the Russian and indigenous worlds, the borders of "civilization" now began to overlap with them. Natives thus became others to Russians not only because of the differences that the latter observed in the seventeenth century but because they had become "wild" and "backward" in Russian eyes. In other words, differences had acquired a qualitative historical dimension.

"Our Crude Peoples": The Russian Perception of Siberian Natives in the First Half of the Mid-Eighteenth Century

In the post-Petrine period, Russian policy toward Siberia and its indigenous population continued to follow the directions outlined under Peter the Great, but there was also a partial return to the pre-Petrine order. Thus, Siberia was included in the unified system of state administration under Peter, and the same

---

77 Ivan Pososhkov, *Zaveshchanie otecheskoe* (St. Petersburg: Sinodal'naia tipografiia, 1893), 325–26.

78 Fedorov, *Pravovoe polozhenie narodov Vostochnoi Sibiri: XVII–nachalo XIX veka*, 87.

institutions operated there as in other parts of Russia. However, in 1730, under Anna Ioannovna, the Siberian prikaz was restored, to which the functions of several nationwide departments dealing with Siberia were transferred. This situation was maintained until 1763, when the prikaz was finally abolished under Catherine the Great.

In the second half of the 1720s and in the 1730s, the missionary activity of the Russian Orthodox clergy among the natives of Siberia continued, though its intensity diminished somewhat. A decree of September 11, 1740 acknowledged that "not everything is done as it should be with such infidels, especially the newly baptized, and some things are completely forgotten; many newly baptized infidels live with non-Christians in the same villages, and seeing temptations from them, they prefer to adhere to them and remain in their former delusion."[79] Meanwhile, the authorities did not abandon the idea of converting the Siberian natives to Orthodoxy. A Senate decree was issued in 1735 on "allowing" the priests from the Diocese of Tobolsk to "go to the newly converted [...] with the rites of the church."[80] In the 1730s and 1740s, the state regularly allocated funds for gifts designed for new converts and the construction of churches, and the conversion of the Yakuts to Orthodoxy continued; the Buryats and the Evenks also began to get baptized.[81] According to the clergy themselves, most of the newly converted natives were "weak" in their faith, had a scant knowledge of Christian doctrine, and sometimes did not even remember the names given them at baptism.

In official Russian documents of the first half of the eighteenth century, Siberian natives continued to be called inozemtsy. At the same time, this term ceased to be used in relation to other non-Russian peoples of the Russian Empire (for example, the peoples of the Urals and the Volga region) who had previously, in the seventeenth century, also been called foreigners. According to Aleksei Konev, "this is one of the signs of a significant difference in the position of the peoples of the Volga region and Siberia, which was the result of the pace and degree of their integration into Russia's socioeconomic system."[82] In our opinion, a civilizational or cultural component should be added to this understanding of the Petrine transformation of the relationship between the Russian and the Siberian peoples.

---

79 Ibid.
80 PSZRI, 4:550.
81 Ibid.
82 Aleksei Konev, "Fenomen 'inozemchestva', iasak i daroobmen: narody Povolzh'ia, Urala i Sibiri v Rossii kontsa XVI – nachala XVIII vekov." Zolotoordynskoe obozrenie/Golden Horde Review 7, no. 4 (2019): 769.

Despite the conversion of some Siberian natives to Orthodoxy, the boundary that separated them from Russians did not disappear. In the set of criteria defining the otherness that distinguished inozemtsy from Russians in the seventeenth century, baptism can be considered a step toward the reduction of the gap, or distance, between "us" and "them." But in the eighteenth century, even if they were baptized, other differences remained where they were, and most importantly, they were loaded with new meaning, resulting in a huge step backward, a deepening of the gap, and a qualitative change in its character in the form of the recognition of Siberian natives as "wild," "crude," and "backward" peoples. This perception was developed, spread, and consolidated in the first half and middle of the eighteenth century.

This perception was greatly influenced by the study of Siberia and its population on the one hand and the translation and/or imposition of European knowledge of the Age of Enlightenment on the other. The process that had begun under Peter the Great continued successfully under his successors. As a result of research by Gerhard Friedrich Müller, Georg Wilhelm Steller (Stöller), Johann Georg Gmelin, Stepan Krasheninnikov, Peter Simon Pallas, and others, information about the languages, lifestyle, customs, and beliefs of the Siberian natives was not merely collected, but their level of development was assessed, and they were accordingly placed at the lowest level in the hierarchy of peoples. At the same time, their similarity to the indigenous inhabitants of the territories that became the object of European colonial expansion was emphasized. Johann Gottlieb Georgi wrote, "The similarity of lifestyle, manners, and characteristics of our crude peoples with many other wild peoples in other parts of the world is tangible. There are similarities in dress between some North Americans and our Ostyaks, as well as in lifestyle, furnishings, and other things."[83]

In the descriptions of the eighteenth century, natives were contrasted with Russians using almost the same criteria as in the seventeenth century: diet (Russians ate boiled fish, natives ate it dry), housing (Russians lived in houses, natives in yurts), marital and family relations, and so on. However, all aspects of indigenous life now began to be perceived very negatively, with descriptions of their "filth," "stench," "rudeness," "stupidity," "ignorance," and so on.[84] All this was interpreted as "the absence of civilization," which meant the Russians' European model of behavior and European culture.

---

83 Johann Gottlieb Georgi, *Opisanie obitaiushchikh v Rossiiskom gosudarstve narodov* (St. Petersburg: pri Imperatorskoi Akademii nauk, 1799), 10–11.
84 Slezkine, *Arctic Mirrors: Russia and the Small Peoples of the North.*

The Russian Empire positioned itself as "a glorious state" accepted in the community of "political peoples" and colonial powers. As Mark Bassin observes, "Like Spain or England, the Netherlands or Portugal, on the largest scale Russia as well could be divided into two major components: on the one hand, a homeland or metropolis that belonged within European civilization, and, on the other, a vast, but foreign, extra-European colonial periphery."[85] Siberian natives were residents of this colonial periphery, becoming the Russians' "own legal savages" (hence the spread of the term *inorodtsy*—peoples of another origin or another kin, a term that by the end of the eighteenth century would gradually replace the term inozemtsy). The Russians thus began to believe that they had a mission to lead them to civilization.

Now, in contrast to the seventeenth century, they could set themselves such a task because they not only had the necessary tools but had also changed their own worldview and attitude. Although in the pre-Petrine era, as has already been observed, Russian culture was broadly directed primarily at expression, it was now directed primarily at content. According to Yury Lotman, such a culture opposes itself to entropy (chaos) and thus, for it, "the main opposition [. . .] is the contraposition of 'ordered' and 'disordered.'" Such a culture "always thinks of itself as an active essence that should spread and considers non-culture as the sphere of its potential spread." In such a culture, "the spread of knowledge occurs through its expansion into the realm of ignorance," whereas "in the conditions of the opposite type of culture, the spread of knowledge is possible only as a victory over lies."[86]

For the seventeenth-century Russian, Siberians were "anti-people," residents of the "anti-world," adherents of "anti-religion," and exponents of "anti-behavior" ("they consider the forbidden to be allowed"), whom it was pointless and unnecessary to reform. One could only "escape" from the anti-world through baptism (that is, "defeat the lie"). For the eighteenth-century Russian, Siberians became the "wrong" people with the "wrong" behavior, appearance, lifestyle, and customs because of their lack of knowledge. This situation could and should be corrected by "disseminating knowledge" and eventually making Siberians "correct" people. Accordingly, the transition from the "wrong" to the "right" world was not made immediately but by long and painstaking work requiring effort from both Russians and natives. The former had to teach and

---

85 Mark Bassin, "Russia between Europe and Asia: The Ideological Construction of Geographical Space," *Slavic Review* 50, no. 1 (1991): 5.
86 Lotman, *Semiosfera*, 496–97.

set an example; the latter had to learn and rebuild many aspects of their lives in a Russian fashion.

However, in practice, the implementation of this scheme was very slow and complicated. In the first half of the eighteenth century, Siberian natives, as in pre-Petrine times, were contacted primarily by yasak collectors and merchants, who were far from being the best teachers or bearers of a positive—that is, civilized—example. The clergy's opportunities and the extent of their influence on the native congregation were limited. Most converts were nominally Christian but preserved pagan customs, rituals, and worldviews. Siberian natives began to use Russian metal products and tools, buy some products from the Russians (mostly flour, bread, and tea), and become addicted to alcohol and tobacco. There were no other changes in their life in the eighteenth century.

Siberian inozemtsy/inorodtsy remained "others" to the Russians; only the content of their otherness and attitude toward it had changed. If in the seventeenth century the Siberian natives were considered others by Russians in the medieval sense, in the eighteenth century they became others in the Enlightenment sense. The difference between "us" and "them" acquired a historical and civilizational dimension.

No such transformation of otherness occurred in any other European colonial empire of that time because no colonial power experienced such a radical political, cultural, and mental transformation as Russia in the Petrine era. Of course, European countries developed and evolved, but they remained within the same civilizational and cultural paradigm. Accordingly, the evolution of their perception of the other—for example, of the indigenous peoples during *La Conquista*—were influenced only by the processes that took place in the New World contact zone and their perception in the metropolis. In Spain, Portugal, England, France, and Holland, there was no "invasion of foreign ideas" from any third party as there was in Russia from Europe in the early eighteenth century.

Conclusion

Between the seventeenth century and the first half of the eighteenth, the otherness of the Siberian natives in the eyes of the Russians underwent a significant transformation. This transformation differed from that which occurred at the same time in the colonies of other European powers. The differences above all concerned the praxeological level. Starting with Columbus, Europeans in the New World did not see in the native someone "truly other,

[. . .] capable of being not merely an imperfect state of oneself."[87] In contrast, seventeenth-century Russians considered Siberian inozemtsy representatives of the "anti-world"—that is, as others in the fullest sense of the word. This was due first to the peculiarities of Russian culture aimed at expression and the Russian mindset of the time. It also resulted from the fact that seventeenth-century Russian society was still a fully medieval premodern society, in contrast with European societies. In other words, the Russians saw indigenous Siberians as others partly because they shared the medieval idea of the opposition between Christians and non-Christian idolaters. Outside the Christian world, there was a space that was not covered by God's ordinances, where Christian customs and prohibitions did not apply.[88]

Axiologically and partly epistemologically, the Russian approach was more in line with the European. Natives may have received a positive or negative assessment in some situations, though the prevailing one was neutral, which was again due to the previously mentioned understanding, recognition, and awareness of their otherness.

Peter the Great's modernization of Russia led to a change in how Siberian natives were perceived. Praxeologically, Russians adopted the European approach "grounded in egocentrism, in the identification of our own common values with values in general, of our *I* with the universe—in the conviction that the world is one."[89] Siberia's indigenous inhabitants were thus not considered representatives of the "anti-world" but as "wild" and "backward" people—ignorant, superstitious, and uncultured. From that point, and looking to the future, they needed to be converted to Christianity and introduced to civilization. Meanwhile, they were different because they were considered to be at a stage of development that had long been passed by Europeans. "They" had corresponded to "us" in the past and should become "us" in the future: the idea of the other was based on time.

Simultaneously, there were changes in the perception of Siberian natives as the other at the axiological and epistemological levels. The backwardness and ignorance of inozemtsy caused a negative attitude and was condemned. Information collected about them by the scientists of the eighteenth century confirmed the need for their baptism, training, and eventual russification. At the same time, while in the eighteenth century the Europeanized elite's view of Siberia and its inhabitants changed quite radically, at the local level many

---

87 Todorov, *The Conquest of America: The Question of the Other*, 42.
88 Aron Gurevich, "Kategorii srednevekovoi kul'tury," *Izbrannye trudy* 2 (1999): 76–79.
89 Ibid.

attitudes and perceptions characteristic of the pre-Petrine era were preserved. Siberian natives' otherness was now dual. Moreover, these two realities were scarcely related. This perhaps explains why the indigenous peoples of Siberia did not disappear but have survived and preserved their identity to the present day.

Works Cited

Akimov, Yuri. *Severnaia Amerika i Sibir' v kontse XVI–seredine XVIII v.: ocherk sravnitel'noi istorii kolonizatsii.* St. Petersburg: Izdatel'stvo Sankt-Peterburgskogo universiteta, 2010.

Alekseev, Mikhail, ed. *Sibir' v izvestiiakh zapadno–evropeiskikh puteshestvennikov i pisatelei, XIII–XVII vv.* Novosibirsk: Nauka, 2006

Apollova, Natal'ia. *Khoziaistvennoe osvoenie Priirtysh'ia v kontse XVI–pervoi treti XIX v.* Moscow: Nauka, 1976.

Bakhrushin, Sergei. "Iasak v Sibiri." *Nauchnye trudy* 3, no. 2 (1955): 49–85.

Bassin, Mark. "Russia between Europe and Asia: The Ideological Construction of Geographical Space." *Slavic Review* 50, no. 1 (1991): 1–17.

Bogdanov, Mikhail. *Ocherki istorii buriat-mongol'skogo naroda: s dopolnitel'nymi stat'iami B. B. Baradina i N. N. Koz'mina.* Verkhneudinsk: Buriat-Mongol'skoe izdatel'stvo, 1926.

Bogoraz, Vladimir. *Chukchi.* Leningrad: Izdatel'stvo instituta narodov Severa, 1934.

Costin, Claudia. "Diversity: An Image of the Difference Regarding the Other." In *Contextual Identities: A Comparative and Communicational Approach.* Edited by Emilia Parpala and Leo Loveday, 12–24. Newcastle-upon-Tyne: Cambridge Scholars Publishing, 2015.

Dergacheva-Skop, Elena, ed. *Letopisi Sibirskie.* Novosibirsk: Novosibirskoe knizhnoe izdatel'stvo, 1991.

Díaz del Castillo, Bernal. *The True History of the Conquest of New Spain.* Farnham: Hakluyt Society, 2010.

Fedorov, Mikhail. *Pravovoe polozhenie narodov Vostochnoi Sibiri: XVII–nachalo XIX veka.* Iakutsk: Knizhnoe izdatel'stvo, 1978.

Firsov, Nikolai. *Polozhenie inorodtsev severo-vostochnoi Rossii v Moskovskom gosudarstve.* Kazan': Universitetskaia tipografiia, 1866.

Gefter, Mikhail. *Iz tekh i etikh let . . .* Moscow: Progress, 1991.

Georgi, Johann Gottlieb. *Opisanie vsekh obitaiushchikh v Rossiiskom gosudarstve narodov*(St. Petersburg: pri Imperatorskoi Akademii nauk, 1799.

Gurevich, Aron. "Kategorii srednevekovoi kul'tury." *Izbrannye trudy* 2 (1999): 17–262.

Jacobs, Wilbur. "British-Colonial Attitudes and Policies toward the Indian in the American Colonies." In *Attitudes of Colonial Powers toward the American Indian*. Edited by Howard Peckham and Charles Gibson, 81–106. Salt Lake City: University of Utah Press, 1969.

Kharlampovich, Konstantin. *Malorossiiskoe vliianie na velikorusskuiu tserkovnuiu zhizn'*. Vol. 1. Kazan': Izdatel'stvo knizhnogo magazina M. A. Golubeva. 1914.

Khodarkovsky, Michael. "'Ignoble Savages and Unfaithful Subjects': Constructing Non-Christian Identities in Early Modern Russia." In *Russia's Orient: Imperial Borderlands and Peoples, 1700–1917*. Edited by Daniel R. Brower and Edward J. Lazzerini, 9–26. Bloomington: Indiana University Press, 1997.

Kivelson, Valerie. *Cartographies of Tsardom: The Land and Its Meanings in Seventeenth-Century Russia*. Ithaca: Cornell University Press, 2006.

———. "Claiming Siberia: Colonial Possession and Property Holding in the Seventeenth and Early Eighteenth Centuries." In *Peopling the Russian Periphery: Borderland Colonization in Eurasian History*. Edited by Nicholas B. Breyfogle, Abby Schrader, and Willard Sunderland, 21–40. London: Routledge, 2007.

Konev, Aleksei. "Shertoprivodnye zapisi i prisiagi sibirskikh 'inozemtsev' kontsa XVI–XVIII vv." *Vestnik arkheologii, antropologii i etnografii* 6 (2006): 172–77.

———. "Fenomen 'inozemchestva', iasak i daroobmen: narody Povolzh'ia, Urala i Sibiri v Rossii kontsa XVI – nachala XVIII vekov." *Zolotoordynskoe obozrenie/ Golden Horde Review* 7, no. 4. (2019): 760–83.

Konev, Aleksei, and Roman Poplavskii. "Dar v politike i praktike khristiianizatsii sibirskikh 'inovertsev' (po materialam Zapadnoi Sibiri kontsa XVI–XVIII v.)." *Vestnik arkheologii, antropologii i etnografii* 4, no. 43 (2018): 165–74.

Kopaneva, Natal'ia. "Nauchnoe puteshestvie D. G. Messerschmidt'a kak chast' proektov Petra I po opisaniiu Rossiiskogo gosudarstva." *Ural'skii istoricheskii vestnik* 2, no. 51 (2016): 44–52.

Kudriavtsev, Fedor. *Istoriia buriat-mongol'skogo naroda. Ot XVII v. do 60–kh godov XIX v. Ocherki*. Moscow and Leningrad: Izdatel'stvo Akademii nauk SSSR, 1940.

Lachmann, Renate. "Value Aspects in Jurij Lotman's 'Semiotics of Culture / Semiotics of Text.'" *Dispositio* 12, no. 30–32 (1987): 13–33.

Liutsidarskaia, Anna. "Tolmachi v Sibiri. Period nachala kolonizatsii territorii." *Gumanitarnye nauki v Sibiri* 3 (2011): 27–31.

Lotman, Yuri. *Semiosfera*. St. Petersburg: Iskusstvo-SPB, 2000.

Luchitskaia, Svetlana. *Obraz Drugogo: musul'mane v khronikakh krestovykh pokhodov*. St. Petersburg: Aleteia, 2001.

Müller, Gerhard Friedrich. *Istoriia Sibiri*. 3rd ed. Moscow: Vostochnaia Literatura RAN, 2005.

Novlianskaia, Mariia. *Daniel Gottlieb Messerschmidt i ego raboty po issledovaniiu Sibiri*. Leningrad: Nauka, 1970.

Ogryzko, Iosif. *Khristianizatsiia narodov Tobol'skogo Severa v XVIII v.* Leningrad: Uchpedgiz, 1941.

Okladnikov, Aleksey, and Boris Rybakov, eds. "Sibirskie letopisi." *Polnoe sobranie russkikh letopisei*. Vol. 36 (Moscow: Nauka, 1987).

Pamiatniki sibirskoi istorii XVIII veka: Kniga vtoraia, 1713–1724. St. Petersburg: Tipografiia ministerstva vnutrennikh del, 1885.

Pis'ma i bumagi imperatora Petra Velikogo. Tom pervyi (1688–1701). St. Petersburg: Gosudarstvennaia tipografiia, 1887.

Popov, Grigorii. *Ocherki po istorii Iakutii*. Iakutsk: Izdatel'stvo Narkomprozdrav Ia. ASSR., 1924.

Pososhkov, Ivan. *Zaveshchanie otecheskoe*. St. Petersburg: Sinodal'naia tipografiia, 1893.

Polnoe sobranie zakonov Rossiiskoi imperii (PSZRI). *Pervoe sobranie*. In 45 vols. St. Petersburg, 1830.

Reinhard, Wolfgang. *A Short History of Colonialism*. Translated by Kate Sturge. Manchester: Manchester University Press, 2011.

Schorkowitz, Dittmar. "Was Russia a Colonial Empire?" In *Shifting Forms of Continental Colonialism: Unfinished Struggles and Tensions*. Edited by Dittmar Schorkowitz, John R. Chávez, and Ingo W. Schröder, 117–50. London: Palgrave Macmillan, 2019.

Slezkine, Yuri. *Arctic Mirrors: Russia and the Small Peoples of the North*. Ithaca: Cornell University Press, 1994.

Sofronov, Viacheslav. *Svetochi zemli sibirskoi: Biografii arkhipastyrei Tobol'skikh i Sibirskikh (1620–1918 gg.)*. Ekaterinburg: Ural'skii rabochii, 1998.

Stepanov, Nikolai. "Prisoedenenie Vostochnoi Sibiri v XVII v. i tungusskie plemena." In *Russkoe naselenie Pomoria i Sibiri (Period feodalizma)*. Edited by Aleksei Okladnikov, 106–24. Moscow: Nauka, 1973.

Tatishchev, Vasilii. *Izbrannye proizvedeniia*. Leningrad: Nauka, 1979.

Todorov, Tzvetan. *The Conquest of America: The Question of the Other*. Translated by Richard Howard. New York: Harper and Row, 1984.

Wood, Alan. *Russia's Frozen Frontier: A History of Siberia and the Russian Far East: 1581–1991*. London: Bloomsbury Academic, 2011.

Zemskov, Viktor. "Khroniki konkisty Ameriki i letopisi vziatiia Sibiri v tipologicheskom sopostavlenii (k postanovke voprosa)." In *Svobodnyi vzgliad na literaturu. Problemy sovremennoi filologii*. Edited by Andrei Mikhailov, 173–83. Moscow: Nauka, 2002.

Zuev, Andrei. *Russkie i aborigeny na krainem severo-vostoke Sibiri vo vtoroi polovine XVII–pervoi chetverti XVIII v*. Novosibirsk: NGU, 2002.

———. "'Konkvistadory imperii': russkie zemleprokhodtsy na Severo-Vostoke Sibiri." In *Region v istorii imperii: istoricheskie esse o Sibiri*. Edited by Sergei Glebov, 17–46. Moscow: Novoe izdatel'stvo, 2012.

Zuev, Andrei, and Pavel Ignatkin. "'Inozemtsy'—'Their' and 'Other': Terminological Classification for Social and Political Status of Siberian Natives in the Moscow State (End of the 16th–Beginning of the 18th Century)." *Vestnik NGU. Seriia: Istoriia, filologiia* 15, no. 8 (2016): 67–85.

6

The Russians and the Oirats (Dzungars) in Asia in the Seventeenth and Eighteenth Centuries: Contacts and Images of the "Other" in the Era of Empire Building

Vladimir Puzanov

Abstract

Between the sixteenth and eighteenth centuries, the Russians encountered numerous eastern peoples. In the seventeenth century, the Russians met the Oirats (Dzungars), a nomadic ethnic group that had previously belonged to the Mongol Empire. During that time, their territory spread from the upper Ob river to the Volga. The Oirats waged war from China to Austria, participated in military actions near Beijing in 1644, and fought against the Turks for Vienna in 1683. During the second half of the seventeenth century, most of the Oirats were united under the rule of the Dzungarian Khanate. Diplomatic, military, and trade contacts with the Oirats were very important for the Russians of Siberia. The Russian state had longstanding contacts with the nomadic world. Both the Russians and Oirats perceived each other according to their own political and cultural traditions. Later, Dzungarian rulers tried to modernize their army with the help of imported Russian technologies and innovations during their confrontation with the warlike Qing China. However, Russia did not wish to share new weapons with nomads. Technological expansion nevertheless occurred through frequent contact between the Russians and Oirats.

First Contacts

As it expanded eastwards between the sixteenth and eighteenth centuries, the Russian state and the Russian people encountered many states, peoples, and tribes. Some of these were already known to the Russians, and some were new to them. Of these contacts made within that time, those with the nomadic peoples—with whom the Russians came into contact in the south of their area of settlement—were of special significance. These centuries, when the Russians annexed swathes of Asia, were the last period in which the nomadic peoples were still able to have a significant influence on the neighboring peoples.

The eastern Slavs and then the Russians came into contact with the nomadic eastern Iranians, as well as Turkic peoples and Ugrians in the south and east of the Eastern European plain. Later, following the Mongol conquest of the thirteenth century, the world of Muscovite Russia was primarily in contact with the already familiar nomads of the White Horde (which later historiography would call the Golden Horde). Between the sixteenth and eighteenth centuries, the Russians entered into relations with those hordes of whom they knew very little.

The Oirats are related to the western Mongols by descent and language. As the monk Hyacinth (Bichurin) noted, the ethnonym "Oirat" first denoted close relatives.[1] The nobility and then the simple nomads of these people would later call themselves Oirats. The Kalmyk ethnonym was used by the Turkic peoples of Siberia and elsewhere to describe the Oirats. The Russians borrowed this ethnonym from the Turkic peoples between the sixteenth and eighteenth centuries. The term Kalmyk (in the sense of "separated" from the main group) was adopted by a Volga group of Oirats that had finally freed itself from the rest of the Mongols in the seventeenth century.

The Russian official and translator of Kalmyk language, secretary of Kalmyk affairs at the Board of Foreign Affairs V. M. Bakunin, noted that the Dzungars and Khoshouts called themselves Oirats, and the Torgouts on the Volga River in the eighteenth century, taking the ethnonym Kalmyks, believed that they were so called by the Russians. According to the official, in fact, the ethnonym

---

1   Nikita Iakovlevich Bichurin [Iakinf, O.], "Istoricheskoe obozrenie Oiratov ili Kalmykov s XV veka do nastoiashchego vremeni," *Zhurnal Ministerstva vnutrennikh del* 8 (1833): 538.

came from the Tatar language and meant "backward."[2] G. F. Miller—one of the most prominent historians of Russia of the eighteenth century and a major researcher of Siberia, as well as the leader of a government-commissioned scientific expedition to the east of the Russian Empire between 1733 and 1743—noted that the Turkic peoples of Siberia who lived between the Rivers Ob and Volga called the Oirats Kalmyks, whereas the Tatars to the east of them in the Krasnoyarsk and Kuznetsk *uezdy* called this people "Uirats, and no other name."[3]

The Oirats were one of the Mongol tribes already known in the eleventh and twelfth centuries. The Oirats separated themselves from the sphere of Mongol tribes in the fifteenth century, forming a distinct political entity. In 1552, the Mongols inflicted a heavy defeat on the Oirats and drove them westwards out of the nomadic zone on the River Orkhon. After 1562, the Oirats were forced to leave for the basin of the River Irtysh.[4] At the end of the sixteenth century, the Oirats' political crisis, caused by defeats and loss of land, led to their migration to the east, west, and south. In the seventeenth century, the largest khanate of Central Asia, that of Bukhara, was dependent on the Oirats for their payments of the tribute.[5] Juraj Križanić—a Croat, Catholic priest, pan-Slavist and proponent of unity with Rome, who arrived in Russia in 1659 and then spent a long spell, from 1661 to 1676, in exile in Tobolsk—noted in the middle of the seventeenth century that the people of Bukhara were good traders and farmers, but at the same time "a rather unwarlike people; to avoid invasion they are forced to pay tribute to the Kalmyks."[6]

In the seventeenth century, the Oirat world encompassed a vast territory from Lake Qinghai to the Volga River. Groups of armed Oirats fought in a territory stretching from China to Austria. Volga Kalmyks took part in military events on the side of the Manchurians near Beijing in 1644, and on the side of the Poles and Austrians in battles with the Turks for Vienna in 1683.[7] In the second half

2 Vasilii Mikhailovich Bakunin, *Opisanie kalmytskikh narodov, a osoblivo iz nikh torgoutskogo, i postupkov ikh khanov i vladel'tsev* (Elista: Kalmytskoe knizhnoe izdatel'stvo, 1995), 22.

3 G. F. Miller, *Opisanie Sibirskogo tsarstva* (St. Petersburg: Izdanie Imperatorskoi Akademii Nauk, 1750), 20.

4 N. V. Ustiugov, ed., *Ocherki istorii Kalmytskoi ASSR* (Moscow: Nauka, 1967), 70.

5 V. V. Bartol'd, *Sochineniia* (Moscow: Nauka, 1968), 5:538–40; P. P. Ivanov, *Ocherki po istorii Srednei Azii (XVI–seredina XIX v.)* (Moscow: Vostochnaia literatura, 1958), 34; A. I. Tsepkov, ed., *Angliiskie puteshestvenniki v Moskovskom gosudarstve v XVI v.*, trans. Iu. V. Got'e (Riazan': Aleksandriia, 2006), 221–23.

6 A. Titov, *Sibir' v XVII v.* (Moscow: Izdanie G. Iudina, 1890), 186.

7 N. N. Pal'mov, *Etiudy po istorii privolzhskikh kalmykov* (Astrakhan': Izdanie Kalmytskogo oblastnogo ispolnitel'nogo komiteta, 1926), 1:3.

of the seventeenth century, the strongest Dzungar Khanate united most Oirat tribes and groups.

In the sixteenth and seventeenth centuries, the Russians in Asia encountered the Oirats, a nomadic people who had formerly been part of the Mongol Empire. In the seventeenth century, bands (*ulus*) of Oirats traveled west and occupied new lands between the Rivers Irtysh and Volga. As a result, the Oirats became the Russian state's main neighbors in southern Siberia and in the Volga basin. Siberia was to the north of the Eurasian Steppe, where several nomadic alliances fought each other during the Russian conquest of the khanate of Sibir'. These alliances included Oirats, Kazakhs, and Nogai. From the late sixteenth century, Oirats from Mongolia gradually occupied territories in southern and western Siberia. In a letter from Ivan IV to merchants of the Stroganov family in 1574 about Siberia, the Oirats are listed among the nomadic peoples of Asia.

In the sixteenth century the Oirats carried out raids on the Kazakhs and Nogai westwards as far as the Volga River. In 1556, the Nogai on the Volga River prepared to rebuff a raid by the Kalmyks.[8] In the 1620s, the Torghuts (numbering about fifty thousand yurts), led by the *taishi* (leader) Kho Orluk (whom the Russians called Urliuk) advanced through the southern Siberian lands towards the Volga River.

The first contacts of men serving Russian military needs in Siberia with the Oirats took place at the end of the sixteenth century, when the Russians were only securing their control of the khanate of Sibir'.[9] In 1598, Voeikov, the warlord of the Tara uezd, learned that a detachment of five hundred Oirats had migrated towards the Ob River from the south.[10] The first encounters between the Russians and the Oirats took place on the lands of the southern Siberian Tara uezd.[11] There would later be several disputes between the Russian authorities and the Oirats about the ownership of territories between the southern Siberian provincial towns and the Kalmyk encampments. According to the *Remezov Chronicle*,[12] the Oirats nomadically occupied the area west of the Siberian rivers Ishim, Om, and Kamyshlov, which were known as the "Kalmyk border." The

---

8 V. V. Trepavlov, *Istoriia Nogaiskoi ordy* (Moscow: Vostochnaia literatura RAN, 2002), 372; S. K. Bogoiavlenskii, "Materialy po istorii kalmykov v pervoi polovine XVII v," *Istoricheskie zapiski* 5 (1937): 1, 60.

9 Rossiiskii gosudarstvennyi arkhiv drevnikh aktov (The Russian state archive of ancient acts), f. 113 (Dzungar files), 1595, d. 1, ll. 1–3 (hereafter cited as RGADA).

10 RGADA, f. 214 (Sibirskii prikaz), kn. 11, l. 57.

11 RGADA, f. 214, kn. 11, l. 98; G. F. Miller, *Istoriia Sibiri*, vol. 2. (Moscow: Izdatel'stvo Akademii Nauk SSSR, 1941), appendices, 228.

12 A chronicle on Siberia, compiled by a Russian historian Semen Remezov in the late seventeenth century.

chronicle referred to the upper reaches of the River Irtysh and Lake Zaysan as the "Kalmyk land," where the Sibir Khan Kuchum conducted his final raid for horses.[13]

The Oirats' acceptance of the status of Russian subjects in 1608 did not lead to their actual dependence on the Russian state.[14] V. V. Grigor'ev correctly observed that "living inside Russian borders, the Kalmyk khans behaved not as subjects, but as allies of Russia."[15] In the seventeenth century, the Kalmyks on the Volga formed political relations with other groups of Kalmyks, the Dzungar Khanate. The khans and the taishis of the Kalmyks received Chinese ambassadors without the consent of the Russian government as late as the time of Peter the Great.

In 1616, the government in Moscow, the Boyar Duma, decided to exchange ambassadors and gifts with the Oirats with the aim of bringing them under the Russian tsar's control. Warlords sent ambassadors southwards from Tobolsk, which was the main center of contact with the Oirats. Oirat ambassadors who arrived in Tobolsk frequently continued to Moscow.[16] In 1623, Tsar Michael I ordered the reception of the Oirat ambassadors in the southern cities, such as Ufa, and the centers of southern Siberia of Tobolsk and Tara. He also ordered that they not be sent to Moscow, "and that they be refused in that because they are numerous and warlike."[17]

In 1630, a group led by Kho Orluk reached the River Ural and River Volga and subjugated a group of nomads living there.[18] Later historical writings by the Kalmyks would recall that Kho Orluk's band reached the banks of the Volga River, which were ruled by the White Tsar, that is, the Russian ruler. Kho Orluk occupied the new lands without the consent of the Russian state.[19]

By the seventeenth century, the Russian state was experienced in dealing with the nomads. At the same time, it viewed the institutions and traditions

---

13 Bogoiavlenskii, "Materialy po istorii kalmykov v pervoi polovine XVII v.," 1, 51.

14 Shiran Bodievich Chimitdorzhiev, *Vzaimootnosheniia Mongolii i Rossii XVII–XVIII vv.* (Moscow: Nauka, 1987).

15 V. V. Grigor'ev, *Russkaia politika v otnoshenii Srednei Azii* (St. Petersburg: Sbornik gosudarstvennykh znanii, 1874), 10.

16 I. Ia. Zlatkin and N. V. Ustiugod, ed. *Russko–mongol'skie otnosheniia 1607–1636. Sbornik dokumentov* (Moscow: Vostochnaia literatura, 1959), 1:54–56.

17 Ibid.,1:128.

18 RGADA, f. 119 (Kalmytskie dela), op. 2, d. 1630 g., l. 1; N. V. Kiuner, *Kitaiskie izvestiia o narodakh Iuzhnoi Sibiri, Tsentral'noi Azii i Dal'nego Vostoka* (Moscow: Vostochnaia literatura, 1961), 69; A. V. Badmaiev, ed., *Kalmytskie istoriko-literaturnye pamiatniki v russkom perevode* (Elista: Izdatel'stvo Kalmytskogo nauchno–issledovatel'skogo instituta iazyka i kul'tury, 1969), 51.

19 *Kalmytskie istoriko-literaturnye pamiatniki v russkom perevode*, 52; Bartol'd, *Sochineniia*, 593.

of the nomadic world through the lens of its own systems. The nomads also understood the Russian systems by analogy with their own traditions.

In December 1616, two men who served the military needs of the Russian state in Siberia—Tomila Petrov, a native of the Grand Duchy of Lithuania, and the Cossack Ivan Kunitsyn—were questioned in the Ambassadorial Chancellery in Moscow about their journey to the Oirats. The warlord and boyar I. S. Kurakin had sent the Russian ambassadors from Tobolsk in April 1616 to make an appeal to Taishi Talai and other taishis of the Oirats, so that they would "[...] serve the tsar and be upright in everything, and to visit the tsar's Siberian cities with all kinds of goods."[20] According to Petrov's and Kunitsyn's short description, the Oirats "live [...] in their own land as nomads, they have no cities, and their huts are all made of fabric and transported on camels."[21] The important taishis lived in more expensive and comfortable Bukharian tents.

Furthermore, the men noted that the Oirats "fought with bows, spears and sabre, and harquebuses, but had little gunpowder."[22] The nomads acquired gunpowder in Bukharan lands: "they raided the Bukharians and took their gunpowder."[23] The Oirats fought in good armor, "in iron armor and lobster-tailed pot helmets, and their armor consisted of iron plates half the width of a palm, against which arrows and sabres are not effective."[24] The nomads started a battle by showering their opponent with the "first volley of arrows," after which they would attack "with spears," and after that, "with sabres."[25]

In the 1620s, the Oirats continued to move westwards. As a result, the Oirat alliance occupied the territories from the River Irtysh to the River Volga. The Oirats were now the Russians' main nomadic neighbors in the south of western Siberia. The Oirats lacked a unitary state in the seventeenth century. The chief leader, the "grand taishi," was the head of the *ulus*, the political unions of the Oirats. Talai led the Dörbets, Baibagish led the Khoshuts, Kharakhulla led the Dzungars, and Kho Orluk led the Torghuts. According to the Bukharians, the grand taishis formed a military alliance in 1633 under which Taishi Kho Orluk defended the Oirats from the Nogai, Taishi Talai controlled Bukhara, Taishi Kuisha controlled the Kazakhs, and Taishi Batur controlled the Mongols. The alliance allowed the Oirats to combine their military forces.

---

20 Zlatkin and Ustiugov, *Russko-mongol'skie otnosheniia 1607–1636*, 52.
21 Ibid.
22 Ibid.
23 Ibid.
24 Ibid., 53.
25 Ibid.

In the 1630s, the main problem for the Russian state in Siberia was represented by the Khoshouts. Their Taishi, Kuisha—the younger brother of the famous "big taishi" Baibagish—became related to the descendants of Khan Kuchum by marriage and organized a series of campaigns to the southern Siberian cities Tara and Tyumen, where the taishi sent their closest relatives.

In 1637, the Kuisha taishi ulus, which had five thousand *kibitkas*,[26] was located on the Yamyn River, six weeks south of the Russian military center of the city of Tara. Earlier in August 1630, Ambassador Kuisha Kultaiko arrived in Ufa, and was sent to Moscow. However, since 1623, the Oirat ambassadors were not allowed to Moscow and so Kultaiko was detained in Ufa. The Ambassadorial Order did not attach any importance to this embassy at all, without sending a response to the request of the *voivode* of Ufa I. G. Zhelyabuzhsky about the embassy until December 6, when the *voivode* had to write to Moscow for the second time. Such a practice, usual for the order of Moscow, was offensive to the Oirat nobility[27].

According to Chinese sources, from 1636 to 1638 the Khoshouts of Kuisha abandoned their old pastures and moved far to the southeast to Kukonor Lake. Relations between the Oirats and the Mongols played an important role here. The events of 1636–1638 had great consequences both for the Oirat world and for relations with the Russians in Siberia. In the first third of the seventeenth century, the Russian state dealt with several independent uluses, of which the Derbet ulus was the most powerful. Later, the political situation changed: the Khoshouts left the Derbets. The Torgouts managed to remain independent from the power of the Derbets and found the western center of the Oirat world on the Volga River. In the east, the Dzungars began to play an increasing role in the nomadic world; they subjugated part of the Oirats' uluses. Finally, in the 1670s, the struggle among the Oirats led to the victory of the Dzungar Khanate on the Irtysh River and the Kalmyk Khanate on the Volga River. After the defeat of the Hoshouts, the Dzungars became Russia's neighbors in Siberia in the area from the Yenisei to Ishim Rivers.

The rise of the Dzungars was caused by the policy of Kharkhulla's son, Batur, who ruled from 1635 to 1653. Batur counted on receiving arms from the Russian state, in the form of harquebuses, as well as domestic animals for his court.

In 1679, the Siberian Chancellery asked the Boyar Duma what was to be done with the Oirats. Should they be made Russian subjects and compelled to pay tribute, as the tsar required of other peoples of Siberia, or should efforts

---

26 A Russian name for a portable dwelling used by nomads, called a *yurt* in Turkic languages.
27 A military and administrative leader appointed by a tsar.

simply be made to protect the lands of the Siberian uezdy from the Oirats by demanding they encamp themselves at a distance? On December 15, 1679, Tsar Fedor III ordered that Oirats be made Russian subjects, but at the same time required them to make their camps far away from the Russian uezdy to avoid conflict with the Russians and the tributary population.[28]

S. V. Bakhrushin noted that the entire seventeenth century in southern Siberia was marked by a conflict between the Russians and nomadic Kalmyks and Mongols for the right to extract tribute from the Turkic population.[29] In the south, the Russian state and the Dzungars *de facto* accepted a situation of dual subjecthood in which the Turkic peoples were forced to pay tribute to both the Russians and the Oirats, and thus be subjects of two states simultaneously.

At the same time, the Russian powers had to make do with constant underpayment of tribute. This led to frequent conflicts in southern Siberia between the Russian population of the Kuznetskii, Tomsk, and Tara uezdy and the Dzungars, Kyrgyz, Teleuts, and other peoples of the region.[30] The Russian powers attempted to end this situation. However, the Turkic population in southern Siberia continued to pay tribute to the Dzungars until the Dzungar Khanate was conquered by the Chinese in 1755–1758.[31]

The rulers of the Dzungar Khanate considered many *volosti* populated by Turkic groups in the Tara and Kuznetskii uezdy of Siberia their subjects and collected tribute from them.[32] In 1755, the Russian Senate learned from the materials of the Siberian Chancellery that the tributary populations of the Tara and Kuznetskii uezdy of Siberia were also paying tribute to the Dzungar Khanate. When the Senate asked the Siberian Chancellery when and on what basis that payment began, the Chancellery was unable to furnish any materials in response.[33]

The image of the Oirats in the era of their first contacts with the Russians in Siberia was one of a warlike, nomadic people. Russian ambassadors perceived the Oirats through their concepts of their own political cultural and other familiar societies. Tomila Petrov and Ivan Kunitsyn spent a month living with the band of Talai, the grand taishi of the Derbets, an authoritative and influential

---

28 N. F. Demidova, ed., *Russko–mongol'skie otnosheniia 1654–1685. Sbornik dokumentov* (Moscow: Vostochnaia literatura, 1996), 3:354.

29 S. V. Bakhrushin, "Iasak v Sibiri v XVII v.," *Nauchnye trudy* 3, no. 2. (1995): 50.

30 RGADA, f. 130 (Sibirskie dela), op. 1, d. 4, 1658 g., ll. 1–11.

31 Oleg Valer'evich Boronin, *Dvoedannichestvo v Sibiri XVII–60–e gg. XIX vv.* (Barnaul: Azbuka, 2002), 156–68.

32 RGADA, f. 199, p. 481, ch. 4, l. 48.

33 RGADA, f. 113, god 1647, d. 1, l. 11–27; f. 199, p. 478, ch. 3, d. 14, ll. 3–6; f. 214, op. 1, ch. 8, d. 6299, ll. 1–3; f. 248, op. 8, kn. 473, l. 127.

representative of the Oirat elite. Petrov and Kunitsyn decided that Talai was a tsar, the main ruler of all the Oirats. "The main taishi of the entire Kalmyk land is that hero, Taishi Talai. And the entire Kalmyk land calls him tsar, but he does not style himself a tsar."[34]

The ambassadors called the grand taishi of the Oirats, Kho Orluk ruler of the Torghuts, and Chokur, ruler of the Dzungars, who at that time were in an alliance with Talai, the "elite advisers close to the taishi," by analogy with the Russian boyars. During their questioning the ambassadors even called representatives of the Oirat elite *pashas* in the Turkish manner.[35]

Image of the Oirats in Russia in the Seventeenth Century

According to the Russian chronicles, the population of Siberia was distinct in its ethnic diversity. According to the *Chronicle of Savva Esipov*, the Russians met speakers of "many languages" as early as in the basin of the River Ob.[36] As the *Stroganov Chronicle* states, Siberia was the site of "many and varied languages: Tatar, Ostyak, Kalmyk, Samoyed, the Skewbald Horde, and many other unnamed languages—each had its own ruler."[37] The neighbors in the south of Siberia were the states of the Oirats, Mongols, Manchus, Kazakhs, Bukhara and the khanate of Khiva, as well as the Chinese Empire.

Moreover, in the early *Rumiantsevskii Chronicle*, evidently composed in the early seventeenth century, the author distinguished the Oirat-Kalmyks from the Muslim Tatars and the pagan Ostyaks and Samoyeds. At the same time, the chronicle noted of the Kalmyks: "It is unknown what law they obey or what the testaments of their fathers are, as I found nothing written on the topic and could not ask anyone about it."[38]

In the *Chronographic Tale*, written around the middle of the seventeenth century, the Kalmyks are noted among other people of the Siberian kingdom— namely the Tatars, Voguls (today's Mansi), Ostyaks, Samoyeds, Lopans, Tungus, Kyrgyz, Yakuts and others—with the explanation: "many people of various

34 Zlatkin and Ustiugov, *Russko-mongol'skie otnosheniia 1607–1636*, 52.
35 Ibid., 53.
36 "Esipovskaia letopis'," *Polnoe sobranie russkikh letopisei* (Moscow: Nauka, 1987), 36:36, 45.
37 E. I. Degacheva-Skop, ed., *Letopisi sibirskie* (Novosibirsk: Novosibirskoe knizhnoe izdatel'stvo, 1991), 126.
38 Ibid., 11.

languages in that unpeopled stretch of the Siberian land."[39] The *Chronographic Tale* listed a total of seventeen "languages" (peoples) in the Siberian kingdom.[40] The *Tale* states that "even though these people have a human form, they are in manner and shape like wild animals, as they have no religion: some worship stones, others worship bears, and yet others a tree or birds. They make birds, beasts, or snakes out of a tree and worship it."[41] However, the author then goes on to sort the peoples of the territory according to the presence of a writing system. The *Tale* notes that most peoples of Siberia lacked a writing system, except for the Muslim Tatars and the Oirat-Kalmyks, who were "taught by the lamas of the Chinese kingdom."[42]

Later, the Russian population of Siberia became more closely acquainted with the Oirats' culture. Russian military servants in Siberia noted the Kalmyks' high level of competence in the arts of war. A detailed description of this people based on stories of the Russian military servants in Siberia was given by Juraj Križanić, who arrived in Russia in 1659 and then spent a long spell, from 1661 to 1676, in exile in Tobolsk.

By the mid-seventeenth century, the "Kalmyk steppes," the lands of the Kalmyks, stretched from the Chinese borders to Astrakhan *oblast'*. At that time, the Oirats' bands were on the banks of the Rivers Tobol and Ishim, immediately next to the southern uezdy of Siberia.[43] As Juraj Križanić notes, the Kalmyks drove their herds to new pastures here: "the Kalmyks stay in one place until their herds have eaten their fill; then, when all the grass is eaten, they drive their herds to a new location."[44] In the summer, the Kalmyks encamped themselves in the south of their lands, near China and Bukhara, and in the autumn moved northwards towards Siberia "because of the abundance of fuel there."[45] As a result, the Kalmyk elite was forced to stop making attacks on Russian settlements and make frequent promises of tribute to the tsar.[46]

Juraj Križanić wrote that relations with the Kalmyks were very important for the Russian lands in Siberia. At the time, the Kalmyks were a powerful and large nomadic people that owned lands from the Ob River to the Volga River.

---

39 Ibid., 45.

40 Ibid., 50.

41 Ibid., 45.

42 Ibid., 51.

43 RGADA, f. 214, st. 455, l. 1; f. 1111, op. 2, d. 737, l. 1; Demidova, *Russko-mongol'skie otnosheniia 1654–1685*, 205.

44 Titov, *Sibir' v XVII v.*, 180.

45 Ibid.

46 M. P. Alekseev, *Sibir' v izvestiiakh zapadnoevropeiskikh puteshestvennikov i pisatelei* (Irkutsk: Oblastnoe izdate''stvoe, 1941), 558.

The Kalmyk grand taishi strove for friendly coexistence with the Russians, supporting trade between the Siberian cities, Bukhara, and China, as well as Russian expeditions to Iamish Lake. The nomads on Iamish Lade and in the Russian cities traded in livestock and slaves with the Russians. The cultural and economic connections of the Russian population of Siberia with the peoples of the East had deep consequences.

Križanić argues that "people tell us wonders" about the military capabilities of the Oirat-Kalmyks and the Mongols.[47] He states that they "enter battle perfectly armed" in helmets, with spears and in chain mail, and fought with arrows and spears, known as *sulims*, shorter than the ones then in use by Europeans.[48] It is curious that Križanić compares these sulims of the Kalmyks with the ancient Romans' weapons.

Križanić compared the military formation of the cavalry of the Oirat-Kalmyks to the Hussar formation adopted in Eastern Europe in the seventeenth century, especially in Hungary and Poland, noting that the Oirats carried a spear, sabre, bow, and armor, "covering their elbows and hips with armor, or wearing chain mail."[49] In the seventeenth century, the Hussars were the heavy cavalry of Europe. In battle, the Oirats could drive livestock ahead of them, breaking up their opponent's military formation.

At that time, harquebuses became widespread among the nomads of the east. According to Križanić, the Mongols of southern Siberia had harquebuses and traditional nomadic arms. Russians in Siberia noted in the 1670s that the Kalmyks' main weapon was still the bow; however, they were now also using harquebuses. According to Križanić, the Oirats' military formation was one of the best and most famous, one that he recommended for adoption by Russian soldiers, as well as the military formations of the Mongols, Samoyeds, Scots, Hussars, dragoons, musketeers, armor-bearers "and to retain as an example at least one division of each formation."[50] Križanić explained the victories of the ancient Romans, the contemporary Poles over the Germans, and the contemporary Austrians over the Swedes primarily through the fact that the victors had varying troops with various armor.

According to a Russian geographical work in the second half of the seventeenth century, "Description of Siberia" (*Opisanie Sibiri*) by an unknown author, Kalmyks, ruled by various taishis, lived in the south of the territory

---

47 J. Krizhanich, *Politika* (Moscow: Nauka, 1965), 429.
48 Titov, *Sibir' v XVII v.*, 180.
49 Krizhanich, *Politika*, 429.
50 Ibid., 428.

along the River Irtysh beyond the Tara uezd, "and those Kalmyks do not pay tribute in kind to the great rulers; they simply live by their own customs, trade between themselves and send their representatives to the Russian cities of Tobolsk, Tara, and Tomsk to trade."[51] Lake Iamish played a large role in relations with the Kalmyks. It took five weeks to reach the lake from Tara by boat on the Irtysh River. In summer the lake was the site of trade between the Bukharians and Kalmyks, who arrived "with horses, all sorts of livestock and prisoners and trade freely with the Russians via their hostages."[52]

At the same time, the bands of the "Kalmyks' tsar," Khan Boshokty on the "great lake" of Zaysan were a journey of two months by boat on the River Irtysh from Iamish Lake. According to the Russians the Dzungar khan and "his comrades" the taishis could in fifteen days gather a hundred thousand "military servants" in their bands, and all of them horsemen.[53] Archers were of the most importance ("they fight with bows"); however, by that time some nomads already had harquebuses, albeit only "with fuses."

According to "Description of Siberia," "they have a great deal of livestock in their bands [. . .] camels, good horses, cattle of many breeds, big sheep, small horses, that is to say, of the breed of donkeys." The Kalmyk lands were the habitat of many animals and fish: beavers, leopards, foxes, white birds and a "whole multitude of all types of birds." Agriculture was developed: "all types of spring crops grow: millet and spelt wheat."[54]

In the Russian state in the seventeenth century, the power and size of the Kalmyk bands was the subject of wonder. As Križanić noted, "this people is very great in number; it thus is no less numerous than the Scythians or Tatars."[55] The Russians noted that just a few decades previously, when they entered Siberia, there had been many fewer Kalmyks, "or they were not sufficiently well known." However, later, "they multiplied in such a number that they were barely possible to count."[56]

The Russians considered that the Oirats had previously lived under the control of one "taishi or prince." By the middle of the seventeenth century, they already had many princes whom they styled taishi.[57] The taishi had "numerous

---

51 L. N. Maikov and V. V. Maikov, eds., *Sibirskie letopisi* (St. Petersburg: Izdanie Arkheograficheskoi komissii, 1907), 380.

52 Ibid.

53 Ibid., 381.

54 Ibid.

55 Titov, *Sibir' v XVII v.*, 181.

56 Ibid.

57 Ibid., 182.

troops" and waged war on one another. At the same time, the taishi strove to live with the Russians "as friendly neighbors, on the one condition that their ambassadors be favorably received."[58] The Russian state also aimed to support peace with the Oirats, accepting their ambassadors and trading with them, "as, furthermore, it was not expensive for them."[59]

In the cities of Siberia and on Lake Iamish, where the Russian military servants of Siberia collected salt, trade with the Oirats took place. The nomads brought "horned livestock and beasts of burden, their sweetmeats and Chinese tobacco," as well as selling slaves: "relatives and their own children." The Oirats comforted those sold into slavery by telling them that they would not be as hungry as they had been during the nomadic wanderings.[60] As a result, Križanić wrote, everyone in Siberia, even those of modest means, had one or "more Kalmyk slaves."[61]

In another work, Križanić compared the Kalmyks with the ancient Scythians, noting that "the ancient Scythian people lived off mere pasture and livestock, which is how the Kalmyks live now."[62] According to Križanić, the dwellers of the Hungarian land were "of untold wealth," where they had fields used only for livestock, which sold annually "about a hundred thousand oxen and many horses." Such husbandry needed to be launched in southern Siberia with the aid of the Kalmyks. "Attempts could be made to agree with the Kalmyks so they would permit our people to put a few hundred or thousand head of livestock out to pasture, and so that we had their hostages. Or it would be better to agree with the taishi so that he sent us a few hundred or thousand head of livestock and horses at an agreed price."[63]

Peter the Great's ambassadors to China between 1692 and 1695, Eberhard Isbrand Ides and Adam Brand, suggested that the Kalmyks, Kyrgyz and Mongols were the "main Tatar people" living in Siberia. The diplomats noted that the Kalmyks lived between the sources of the Tobol and Ob Rivers in the north, along the course of the Irtysh River above Iamysh Lake, where they met with Siberian Tatars and Russians.[64]

---

58 Ibid.
59 Ibid.
60 Ibid., 186.
61 Ibid.
62 Krizhanich, *Politika*, 410.
63 Ibid.
64 Eberhard Isbrand Ides and Adam Brand, *Zapiski o russkom posol'stve v Kitai (1692–1695)* (Moscow: Nauka, 1967), 88, 277.

The image of the Oirats in the seventeenth century was one of a terrifying, warlike people that could end the history of civilization in Russia and Europe. Križanić noted that at this time "many tried to guess [...] what we should expect from this people as God's imponderable fates would have it."[2] Previously, "some dark peoples, such as Goths, Vandals, Herules, Slavs, Huns, Saracens, Tatars, Turks and others" had been sent as punishment for the sins of other peoples.[65] The politics, lives, and leaders of the Oirat-Kalmyks in the seventeenth century aroused great interest among the elites of the Russian state. The boyar Boris Morozov—an important political figure and West-leaning Russian of the seventeenth century—in Križanić's description "a man enjoying a rather significant influence and one of the main Moscow grandees," asked him, as a man well versed in the European tradition, whether he knew from conversation or from reading the names of the tsar Altyn, the taishis Kon, Ablai or other Oirat taishis. When Križanić replied that he had never heard of these names before, Morozov was surprised that "such a large and warlike people as the Kalmyks had been passed over in silence by European historians."[66]

Image of the Oirats in Russia in the Eighteenth Century

Semen Remezov, a military servant and the greatest Russian geographer and historian of Siberia in the late seventeenth and early eighteenth centuries, wrote a legend according to which the Oirats' history was connected to an expedition to Asia by Alexander the Great. According to the legend, the homeland of the Oirats was Greater India, whence—after the expedition of Alexander the Great, who ordered them to guard their herds—they ran to Lake Sain-nor on the upper River Irtysh, from whence "their ancestors had come," and where they occupied large spaces "to Altai, to the Rivers Kamen', Ishim and Ural."[67] This legend, reflecting the perceptions of educated Russians, was later entered into the *Chronicle of Cherepanov* in Tobolsk. According to the *Remezov Chronicle*, the nomadic peoples of Siberia, the Kalmyks, Mongols, and Cossack horde lived on the steppe: "they travel on camels and feed off their livestock."[68]

According to the *Chronicle of Cherepanov*, written in Tobolsk in the middle of the eighteenth century, the "main wealth" of the Oirats was livestock, primarily

---

65 Ibid.
66 Ibid., 182.
67 RGADA, f. 196, op. 1, d. 1542, l. 125.
68 Maikov and Maikov, *Sibirskie letopisi*, 316.

horses, camels, cattle, and sheep. In addition to rearing livestock, the nomads also hunted and tilled the land. "Their steppes contain several wild and forest beasts [...] Saiga antelopes, red deer and boars, as well as some, albeit inferior, foxes, martens, beavers, otters, stoats and corsac fox."[69] The Oirats planted cereals in the river valleys, "near rivers and small rivers," "for the most part barley, millet, spelt, wheat, oats, peas, and vegetables."[70]

According to a "Description of Siberia" (*Opisanie Sibiri*) in the 1680s, the Oirats' army numbered as many as eighty to a hundred thousand men.[71] By 1715, according to the Colonel Bukhol'ts, the troops of the kontaishi, the ruler of the Dzungar Khanate, alone numbered more than sixty thousand men.[72] The Russian envoy Ivan Unkovskii wrote that by 1722 the kontaishi of the Dzungar Khanate commanded the forces of a "good army" numbering around sixty thousand. If necessary, more could be commanded, up to around one hundred thousand, "all cavalry." The warriors used bows, spears 7.5 *arshins* long, sabers, "and many have harquebuses, all with linstocks."[73] Remezov, a Russian military servant, historian, and geographer of Siberia, wrote that the Oirat-Kalmyks fought only on horseback, "and they are so unused to horseless battle that they know not how to do it." Their usual weapons were bows, spears. And sabers, but "for the most part their dress is military": chain mail, armor, lobster-tailed pot helmets, and handles. The Oirats' tactics assigned a great role to the first attack: "in battle they are quite violent in the first assault, and if they cannot initially attain victory, they are quite amenable."[74]

In the eighteenth century, Russia exercised a considerable political and cultural influence on the Dzungars. In 1715, Peter I sent Ivan Bukhol'ts on an expedition in search of gold along the River Irtysh to the Dzungar lands.[75] By 1720, as a result of the expeditions of Bukhol'ts, Stupin and Likharev on the Irtysh River, five Russian fortresses had been built.[76] The Kontaishi Tsewang Rabtan (1697–1722) organized the manufacture of arms, copper, and iron,

69 RGADA, f. 196, op. 1, d. 1542, l. 125.
70 Ibid.
71 Maikov and Maikov, *Sibirskie letopisi*, 381.
72 RGADA, f. 9, r. 23, l. 32.
73 I. S. Unkovskii, *Posol'stvo k Ziugarskomy Khun–Taichzhi Tsevan–Rabtanu i putevoi zhurnal za 1722–1724 gg.* (St. Petersburg: tipografiia V. Kirshbauma, 1887), 194.
74 RGADA, f. 196, op. 1, d. 1542, l. 123; Maikov and Maikov, *Sibirskie letopisi*, 381; Alekseev, *Sibir' v izvestiiakh zapadnoevropeiskikh puteshestvennikov i pisatelei*, 357; N. I. Nikitin, *Sluzhilye liudi v Zapadnoi Sibiri* (Novosibirsk: Nauka, 1988).
75 RGADA, f. 9, p. 23, ll. 30–36.
76 RGADA, f. 248, op. 7, kn. 373, l. 317.

from which "armor and lobster-tailed pot helmets"[77] were made. Besides, Tsewang Rabtan encouraged the Oirats to organize ploughed fields with wheat, millet, barley, and rice, where the Bukharians, subjected to the Oirats, worked, and later even some of the Oirats themselves.[78]

A small Russian colony of dwellers of Siberia who had come to trade or were taken prisoner was formed in the Dzungar Khanate. After 1716, this colony was supplemented by Swedish prisoners. The kontaishi tried, with the help of the Russians and Swedes, to modernize the military forces of the Dzungar Khanate, using European arms and even tactics. According to the *Chronicle of Cherepanov*, in 1716 in a caravan from Tobolsk the Oirats captured a Swedish *styckjunkare* (warrant officer) Iagan Renat (Johan Renat) and the arms master and Siberian Zelenovskoi, whom the kontaishi "with the promised mercy and not insignificant rewards brought over to his side."[79] Johan Renat manufactured cannons and "trained them somewhat in artillery."[80] Zelenovskoi taught the Oirats how to make firearms, "with which they learnt to shoot, albeit badly, and their guns lacked locks," with fuses.[81] The arrival of Johan Renat in the Dzungar Khanate led to large changes in the Oirats' life. Later, Renat would teach the Oirats how to smelt iron ore, make cannons and bombs, and was appointed by the kontaishi as commander of the forces of the Dzungar Khanate in the new war of the nomads with China.

By 1724, Renat had made six "small copper cannons" and three mortars for the kontaishi. Apart from that, the Swedish captives built "a small broadcloth factory," and the Russians captured in 1716 started leather factories. Christina, widow of the Swedish officer Sims, married the Swedish lieutenant Johan Debish in Oirat captivity, and made "golden braided trimmings and the like, and taught the daughters of the kontaishi and other maidens her craft."[82] In 1732, Johan Renat told the Russian envoy, Major Ugrimov, that he had made a total of twenty cannons and twenty nine-pound mortars for the Oirats.[83] In 1733, following the victories over the Chinese army, Johan Renat, with a large fortune in gold silver and precious items, was released by the Oirats back to Sweden.[84]

---

77 RGADA, f. 196, op. 1, d. 1542, l. 124.
78 I. Ia. Zlatkin, *Istoriia Dzhungarskogo khanstva* (Moscow: Nauka, 1983), 218.
79 RGADA, f. 196, op. 1, d. 1542, l. 124.
80 Ibid.
81 Ibid.
82 Unkovskii, *Posol'stvo k Ziungarskomu Khun-Taichzhi Tsevan-Rabtanu i putevoi zhurnal za 1722–1724 gg.*, 232.
83 Ibid., 234.
84 Miller, *Istoriia Sibiri*, 3: 487.

On December 18, 1716, Peter the Great sent the kontaishi a letter from Amsterdam and noted that the Dzungar Khanate was on Russian land; however, the tsar, showing mercy to the kontaishi, was prepared to leave the Oirats on their old land and even defend them from other peoples:

> And we, the great ruler, our royal highness, taking mercy on you, wishing for you and the Khan Aiuka and other Kalmyk rules to remain in our mercy, allow you and your subjects to freely retain their dwellings in those lands, although they are part of our Siberian kingdom [...]. But most of all we command for you to be protected and defended against other enemies.[85]

In 1722, Peter the Great sent an envoy with Ivan Unkovskii to the kontaishi of the Dzungar Khanate with the proposal of going over "to our protection," as Khan Aiuka of the Volga Kalmyks had done. After the acceptance by the kontaishi of Russian subjecthood, Peter the Great promised to protect them with Siberian troops from all opponents, including from the Chinese khan.[86] At that time, the Oirats were in a difficult situation: they were fighting China in the east and the Kazakh Horde in the west. The Oirats' war with China lasted from 1712 to 1722.[87] Apart from the Chinese, the kontaishi from the start of his rule constantly had to fight the Kazakh Horde, against which he maintained a force of around thirty thousand soldiers.[88]

The kontaishi Tsewang Rabtan told the Russian envoy Unkovskii that he had previously requested the construction of new Russian fortresses in the Dzungar Khanate for defense from Chinese attacks. However, in December 1722, the belligerent old emperor Xuanye (who ruled under the title of the Kangxi Emperor), who had ruled since 1662, died, and his successor sent ambassadors to the Oirats so that they would live "in friendship." The Oirats consequently no longer needed Peter I's military help and protection, and in the words of the kontaishi, "I do not need the cities for that now."[89]

---

85 B. P. Gurevich and V. A. Moiseev, eds., *Mezhdunarodnye otnosheniia v Tsentral'noi Azii, XVII–XVIII vv., kniga 1* (Moscow: Nauka, 1989), 1, 240.

86 Unkovskii, *Posol'stvo k Ziungarskomu Khun-Taichzhi Tsevan-Rabtanu i putevoi zhurnal za 1722–1724 gg.*, 36–45.

87 Ibid., 192.

88 Ibid., 193.

89 Ibid., 113.

The kontaishi's power was based on the Oirat elite: "the kontaishi does not carry out great deeds without the advice of the councils of elite advisers."[90] According to Unkovskii, in the summer of 1723, the kontaishi convened in Urgu "all the elite advisers' ulus and the best Kalmyks" to discuss whether to be under the protection of the Russian emperor. A "great dispute" began at the meeting, with the elite dividing into two camps.[91]

The kontaishi's son Galdan Tseren and his cousin "the first *zaisan* (elite adviser)" Tseren Donduk led the group opposed to subjecthood, and it appears that they may have wanted to kill all the Russian envoys.[92] Sederchap, the kontaishi's second wife and daughter of the Khan Aiuki, was in color of accepting the tsar's protection. The Oirats told Unkovskii that Tseren Donduk told the kontaishi's wife, "Are we really to live as servants, as your father did?" The Oirats valued their independence and did not wish to accept even a rather soft form of "protection" from a foreign ruler.

The elite of the Dzungar Khanate collected information about Russia, its military forces, the recently ended war with Sweden, its relations with Turkey, Peter I's reforms and his behavior.[93] The kontaishi was interested in why Peter I had assumed a new title: "He was formerly known as the Great Tsar; why do we now call him Emperor?" The reforms in Russia also aroused interest in the Dzungar Khanate. News of them had reached the khanate from Siberia. The kontaishi asked: "You do everything in a new style nowadays, and write books in a new way?"[94]

It is typical that the kontaishi Tsewang Rabtan asked a Russian envoy where the emperor currently "liked to abide," whether his navy's ships were large, how many troops they could transport, how many cannons they had, whether Russian ships sailed to America and how to reach that continent, how many patriarchs there were in Russia and why there was currently no patriarch, and so on.[95]

The Oirats were particularly interested in Russia's relations with China, whose rulers said that "there were no stronger or braver people, and all pay them tribute."[96] The kontaishi asked whom the Russians considered stronger: the Turkish sultan or the Chinese khan. Unkovskii replied that the Russians sent

---

90 Ibid., 194.
91 Ibid., 105–109.
92 Ibid., 119.
93 Ibid., 57.
94 Ibid.
95 Ibid., 41.
96 Ibid., 60.

the Chinese khan "gifts" and not tribute, that the Russians considered Turkish warriors brave, and that "the Chinese were bad at warfare."[97]

On August 25, 1736, the authorities in the Siberian governorate and the Siberian Chancellery reported to the Senate that, in the event of war with the kontaishi, even when accounting for the new regiments in Siberia, sending "a large corps of regiments" would be necessary and that, without it, defending the governorate would be impossible as "the opponent has a rather large army." As a result, according to the Siberian authorities, "if regiments are not sent to the Siberian governorate as a precaution against the ruler Galdan Tseren, [. . .] an alliance should be sought with him."[98]

In his *Lexicon* written between 1733 and 1745, the important Russian eighteenth-century administrator and historian V. N. Tatishchev wrote: "the Dzungars are a Kalmyk people, great and rather strong."[99] At the same time he noted that the Dzungars had been divided into "many taishis or princes, and because of their internal conflicts were not very able to create much of an elite."[100] However, after the migration of a "great part" of the Oirats to the Volga River during the reign of Tsar Michael I, the head of the Dzungars, that is, "the kontaishi styled himself khan and made himself an authoritarian ruler," subjugating all the other Oirat taishis to him.[101]

The kontaishi Tsewan Rabtan waged "great wars" with China, Bukhara and the Kazakhs and having secured victory over the latter, "made some of them pay tribute and conquered many Bukhara cities."[102] Tsewan Rabtan's successor continued wars with China and successful wars with the Kazakhs and "made a great proportion of the Kazakhs his subjects." The Great Horde of the Kazakhs recognized the Dzungars' power.[103]

In 1732, the Russian ambassador to the Oirats, Major Ugrimov, wrote that "nowadays the Kalmyk people encamp themselves in the Altai mountains on the right bank of the Irtysh River."[104]

The Om River, a tributary of the Irtysh River, was then considered the boundary of Russia and the Oirats. At the same time, the Oirats considered the

---

97 Ibid.
98 RGADA, f. 248, op. 3, kn. 135, ll. 651–52.
99 V. N. Tatishchev, *Leksikon Rossiiskoi istoricheskoi, geografricheskoi, politicheskoi i grazhdanskoi* (Leningrad: Nauka, 1979), 291.
100 Ibid.
101 Ibid.
102 Ibid., 292.
103 Ibid., 307.
104 Unkovskii, *Posol'stvo k Ziungarskomu Khun-Taichzhi Tsevan-Rabtanu i putevoi zhurnal za 1722–1724 gg.*, 236.

Ob River to be the boundary, as they considered the Kuznetskii and Krasnoyarsk uezdy of Russian Siberia their own lands.[105]

Tatishchev, in his argument with the Swedish researcher Strahlenberg, attempted to demonstrate that the disputed lands in the south belonged to Russia by dint of their conquest after the victory in 1582 over the Khan Kuchum and his children: "The Russian Empire has the right to all those lands, which were previously ruled by the Siberian khans."[106] The Oirat-Kalmyks, "under various taishis, warring among themselves," occupied some of the southern lands at a time when Russia had not yet built all the cities in the new territory, and there was a "shortage of Russian soldiers in Siberia."[107] When Russia had the troops and means, "the Russians built cities closer to them along the Irtysh."[108] Here, Tatishchev means Ivan Bukhol'ts' and others' expeditions to the River Irtysh during the reign of Peter the Great.

In 1727, Kontaishi Tsewan Rabtan died. According to Tatishchev, the new Kontaishi Galdan Tseren (1725–1745) had "a dispute with Russia in Siberia" over land, "but never entered real war; rather, he corresponds with the governor and makes claims for justice in an offended manner."[109]

Regarding the construction of the fortresses on the Irtysh River as far as the Altai Mountains, the kontaishi "considered this an insult and arrived with troops; however, he did not put up a large resistance and rather sought concord with Russia, and above all retreated voluntarily for great political reasons."[110]

In his 1736 work *Obshchee geograficheskoe opisanie vsei Sibiri* (General geographical description of all of Siberia), Tatishchev wrote that, according to the Russians' information, the boundary of the Dzungars and the Mongols was the upper course of the Ob River, noting, however, that in reality, the Dzungars collected tribute in kind east of the upper Ob and Televskoe Lake from the "peoples" living in the Sayan Mountains.[111] The Altai Mountains separated the Russian possessions from the Dzungar Khanate.[112] Moreover, in 1740, the upper River Tobol formed the boundary between the "Dzungar Kalmyks," that is, Oirats, and the Kazakhs.[113]

---

105 Ibid., 237.
106 Tatishchev, *Sobranie sochinenii* (Moscow: Ladomir, 1995), 8:411.
107 Ibid.
108 Ibid.
109 Tatishchev, *Leksikon Rossiiskoi istoricheskoi, geograficheskoi, politicheskoi i grazhdanskoi*, 292.
110 Ibid.
111 V. N. Tatishchev, *Izbrannye trudy po geografii Rossii* (Moscow: Gosudarstvennoe izdatel'stvo geograficheskoi literatury, 1950), 48.
112 Ibid., 49, 161.
113 Ibid., 130.

In his 1744 work *Vvedenie k gistoricheskomu i geograficheskomu opisaniu Velikorossiiskoi imperii* (Introduction to a historical and geographical description of the Great Russian Empire), Tatishchev noted, in a chapter entitled "On the peoples of the Great Russian Empire," that among the ancient peoples who had previously dwelt in the region were the "Dzungar-Kalmyk idol worshippers, living beyond the Altai and Bulana Mountains, whom the Russians named the Kontaishnitsy, after their former ruler, the *kontaishi*, and now his son Galdan Tseren, but they are unaware they are named after him."[114] Tatishchev also noted another group of Oirat-Torghuts: "Kalmyks living near the River Volga who voluntarily arrived to be ruled by the Russians in 740 with their ruler Aiuka, after whom they are called Aiukiny."[115]

Tatishchev lived in an era of political and military decline of the nomadic world and wrote of one generation of Oirats: "The Khoshuts were also strong, but now they are rather diminished."[116] The rulers of the nomadic empires, the khans who had conquered Asia, "were divided into different states and had fallen into internal conflict; they lost most of the regions they had conquered and became objects of contempt."[117] Tatishchev recalled that on the orders of the Russian empress he handed over the symbols of power and subjecthood, a sabre and banner, in 1738 to the khan of the Kazakhs, Abul Khair, and in 1741 to the Kalmyk Khan Dunduk Dashi, "and they followed my instructions, given to me by Her Majesty, perfectly."[118]

In his work, G. F. Miller divides the Oirats into three "main generations," of which the Elets lived in the south, from the Altai Mountains, between "grand Bukhara" and the Mongol possessions "as a separate autocratic state."[119] It is characteristic that the historian understood the Oirat political system in the Dzungar Khanate as a form of autocratic monarchy. Tatishchev also strove to understand Oirat-Kalmyk society through the prisms of Russian culture, calling the *aimak* land possession "the possession of one *zaisang*, that is, nobleman," and an *ulus* (band) the possession of Oirat princes.[120]

According to Miller, Torghuts was the name for the Kalmyks living on the Volga River and "subject to the Russian state." He wrote about a prediction of the Buryats of Siberia according to which they were "a single nature" with the

114   Ibid., 177.
115   Ibid., 181.
116   Tatishchev, *Sobranie sochinenii*, 8:439.
117   Ibid.
118   V. N. Tatishchev, *Sobranie sochinenii* (Moscow: Ladomir, 1994), 1:365.
119   Miller, *Opisanie Sibirskogo tsarstva*, 20.
120   Tatishchev, *Leksikon Rossiiskoi istoricheskoi, geograficheskoi, politicheskoi i grazhdanskoi*, 156.

Elet-Oirats in ancient times and noted that both the Oirats and Buryats spoke dialects of Mongolian.[121] Tatishchev and Miller laid the foundation for the scientific study of the Oirats in Russian historiography. However, at that time the Oirats' state, the Dzungar Khanate was already in deep political crisis. The last great kontaishi, Galdan Tseren, died in 1745, after which a power struggle began between his children and the Oirat elite. In 1755, Chinese troops exploited Galdan Tseren's succession dispute and invaded the Dzungar Khanate, destroying the Oirat state. Hundreds of thousands of Oirats were killed between 1755 and 1758, with thousands fleeing to Russian Siberia. The Chinese invasion and subsequent collapse of the Dzungar Khanate in 1757 and 1758 caused relations between the Russian Empire and China to be further strained.[122]

In the western territory of the Oirat alliance in 1655, the eldest son of Kho Orluk, Daichin, sent ambassadors to Tsar Alexis I and promised that the Oirats would henceforth cease attacking Russian cities and be subject to the White Tsar.[123] Daichin's grandson, Aiuka, swore to the tsar that the Kalmyks would not attack Russian cities, and that they would not form friendships with Turkey, Crimea, or Persia. Aiuka maintained independent diplomatic relations with Eastern states such as Persia, the khanate of Khiva and even distant China, sending and receiving ambassadors.[124] At the same time, Khan Aiuka called his letters to the warlords of Astrakhan orders (*ukazy*), and these orders of the khan were accepted by the Russian warlords until 1719, when Peter the Great sent the first governor, A. P. Volynskii, to Astrakhan.

Here, too, on the Volga River, the Oirats long maintained an independent foreign policy.[2] In 1690, the taishi of the Torghuts, Aiuka, accepted the highest nomadic title, khan, without notifying the Russian tsar. In the 1680s the Volga Oirats fought as part of the Holy League against the Ottoman Empire. In 1685, the ruler of the Polish-Lithuanian Commonwealth, John III Sobieski, invited the Kalmyks to send a detachment for a new campaign against the Turks, noting the nomads' valor in previous years.[125]

G. V. Vernadskii rightly noted that even the rulers of the Volga Kalmyks in the seventeenth century considered themselves independent rulers and viewed their relations with the Russian tsar as a military alliance.[126] At the same time, from 1655 the Russian rulers considered the Volga Kalmyks their vassals;

121 Miller, *Opisanie Sibirskogo tsarstva*, 21.
122 Zlatkin, *Istoriia Dzhungarskogo khanstva*, 289.
123 *Kalmytskie istoriko-literaturnye pamiatniki v russkom perevode*, 58.
124 Pal'mov, *Etiudy po istorii privolzhskikh kalmykov*, 8.
125 *Kalmytskie istoriko-literaturnye pamiatniki v russkom perevode*, 62.
126 G. V. Vernadskii, *Moskovskoe tsarstvo* (Tver: Agraf, 2001), 2:74–76.

however, the Ambassadorial Chancellery handled relations with both them and the Don Cossacks.

Grigorii Kotoshikhin, a functionary in the Ambassadorial Chancellery who in 1664 fled to Poland and then to Sweden, wrote in his notes that Russian tsars wrote letters to European rulers and other "potentates" with lists of all their titles. At the same time, the Kalmyks styled the tsar in an abbreviated fashion: either "to the White Tsar of all Russia, Aleksei Mikhailovich, a greeting," or simply "to the White Tsar," without name or title. Similarly, the Kalmyks wrote "about their and others matters briefly in their letters," preferring to discuss the main matters verbally with ambassadors.[127]

Even the Volga Oirats considered themselves representatives of a Far Eastern culture and foreign to their new neighbors. It is telling that although the Russian tsars sent several ambassadorial missions to China in the seventeenth century, the first ambassadorial mission from China only arrived in Russia at the headquarters of the Torghuts' Khan Aiuka, who was considered a subject of the Russian tsar, in 1714. When he met the Chinese ambassadors, Khan Aiuka said: "Although I live far from your state, you see in my hat and clothing that I am barely different from you. Compare us to the Russians and see how great the difference is between us and them in dress, hats, language, and our entire ways of life."[128]

Conclusion

Russian culture in the seventeenth and eighteenth centuries saw big changes in the formation of the image of the Oirat-Kalmyks. The image of the Oirats in Russian culture in the seventeenth century was one of a large, warlike people on the border of the European world that presented a potential threat. In their way of life, warlike nature, and vast numbers, the educated thinker Juraj Križanić compared this people to the ancient Scythians and Tatars. In the words of the boyar Boris Morozov, educator of Tsar Alexis I, the Kalmyks were a "large and warlike people." Eschatologically, the mysterious Oirats could put an end to the European world, as the Barbarians had done during the Great Migration.

---

127   G. O. Kotoshikhin, *O Rossii v tsarstvovanie Alekseia Mikhailovicha* (St. Petersburg: Izdanie Arkheograficheskoi komissii, 1884), 42.

128   N. N. Pal'mov, *Ocherk istorii kalmytskogo naroda za vremia ego prebyvaniia v predelakh Rossii* (Astrakhan': Izdanie Kalmytskogo oblastnogo ispolnitel'nogo komiteta, 1922), 32.

However, at the same time, the Russians noted that the Kalmyks in the second half of the seventeenth century were independent of Russia, yet not its enemy. They lived with the Russians with "unneighborly custom" and were closely connected by trade. The power dynamics changed in the eighteenth century, however. Russia became a powerful empire, and the Oirats gradually lost their military and political influence in the east. The image of the Oirats in Russian culture lost its religious and eschatological dimensions, but at the same time became more concrete and scientific in the works of the first historians of the Russian Empire, G. F. Miller and V. N. Tatishchev.

Russians perceived the Oirats both through their concepts of their own political cultural and other familiar societies. Russian military servants called some Oirat rulers tsars and others "elite advisers close to the taishi," by analogy with the Russian boyars, or in the Turkish manner, pashas.[129]

Was the Dzungar Khanate, the Oirats' state, merely a land of barbarity? Such an approach is widespread in the historiography. William McNeill argued that the victory of China over the Dzungar Khanate, the "confederacy of Kalmyks," in 1757 was a final step in that era of world history, when barbarism retreated under the pressure of civilization on less advanced societies.[130]

According to Michael Khodarkovsky, both in Kievan Rus' and later, after the Europeanizing reforms of Peter I in the eighteenth century, the nomads were generally perceived by functionaries, the representatives of power, as wild and childlike.[131] It was only in the 1830s that the great poet Aleksander Pushkin, in the new Romantic tradition, called the Kalmyks a "peaceful and good people" who came from the Chinese border from the start of the seventeenth century "under the protection of the White Tsar" and who, in 1771, persecuted by government officials, were forced to flee the Volga basin for the east.[132]

However, similar discussions were had in Russia as early as the seventeenth century. In his tract *Politika* (Politics or Policy) Juraj Križanić wrote about the relations of the Russians in the seventeenth century with the "wild" and "backwards" peoples of Asia:

> Why do we get arrogant and boast that the Samoyeds, Ostyaks and Kalmyks seem rude, inhuman, and barbaric compared to us?

129 Zlatkin and Ustiugov, *Russko–mongol'skie otnosheniia 1607–1636*, 53.
130 William McNeill, *Voskhozhdenie Zapada* (Moscow: Nika-Tsentr, 2004), 831.
131 Michael Khodarkovsky, *Stepnye rubezhi Rossii* (Moscow: Novoe literaturnoe obozrenie, 2019), 262–27.
132 A. S. Pushkin, "Istoriia Pugachevskogo bunta," *Sochineniia* (St. Petersburg: Izdanie Tipografii ekspeditsii zagotovleniia gosudarstvennikh bumag, 1838), 5:8–10.

For us, that should be grounds not for arrogance, but for humility and enlightenment. For insofar as these people seem wild and bestial compared to us, equally as much do we in comparison to other nations seem rude and ignorant, as our ignorance leads other nations to consider us wild, too.[133]

The author concludes: "We deceive ourselves when we hide our own shortcomings from ourselves."[134] In Križanić's dialogue, Khervoi, who stands for the author, considers the Slavs "our people—in the middle between civilized and backwards people."[135]

Juraj Križanić justly considered that relations with the Kalmyks were of very great significance for the Russian state in Siberia in the seventeenth century. The Kalmyks were then a powerful and large nomadic people that owned lands from the River Ob to the River Volga. Semen Remezov wrote, in the early eighteenth century in Tobolsk, that the Oirat-Kalmyks were "accepted in brotherhood and friendship, and loyal in their neighbourliness."[136]

It must be noted that the Oirats of the Dzungar Khanate and other nomadic alliances in the seventeenth century and first half of the eighteenth century were an important military and political neighbor of the Russians in Siberia. As a result, in the first years of contacts with the Oirats, the Russians were interested in information about the Oirats' military strength, as well as their political structure. In the first half of the seventeenth century, the image of the Oirats was noted in Russian chronicles among many other peoples living in the "boundless expanse" of the Siberian land. The early Siberian chronicles of the time noted that the Kalmyks were not Muslims or pagans, but their cultural tradition, their "law," was unknown to Russian scribes. Later, by the middle of the seventeenth century, the Kalmyks were noted in the Russian chronicles as a people with a sufficiently developed written tradition and a culture that was linked to China's.

The Oirat-Kalmyks who arrived in the Volga basin in the first half of the eighteenth century lost their political independence. The Oirat-Dzungars remained independent until the military storm by China between 1755 and 1758. The rulers of the Dzungar Khanate strove to modernize their military and economy with Russian and Swedish help. The Russians respected the Oirats' military and political force. Russian military servants, envoys, and functionaries

133 Krizhanich, *Politika*, 493.
134 Ibid.
135 Ibid.
136 RGADA, f. 196 "Rukopisnoe sobranie F. F. Mazurina," op. 1, d. 1542, l. 123.

noted in their descriptions of the Dzungar Khanate its political and social aspects, comparing them with society in the Russian Empire. This was a trait of the military servant Semen Remezov, the exile Juraj Križanić, the envoy I. S. Unkovskii, the historian and functionary V. N. Tatishchev, and the historian G. F. Miller. At the same time, for these Russian authors, the Oirats of the Dzungar Khanate were not representatives of the barbaric world, but of another, interesting and distant culture.

Works Cited

Archival Sources

Rossiiskii gosudarstvennyi arkhiv drevnikh aktov (RGADA), f. 113 (Ziungorskie dela), god 1595, d. 1, 1647.

Rossiiskii gosudarstvennyi arkhiv drevnikh aktov (RGADA), f. 130 (Sibirskie dela).

Rossiiskii gosudarstvennyi arkhiv drevnikh aktov (RGADA), f. 199, "Portfeli G.F. Millera."

Rossiiskii gosudarstvennyi arkhiv drevnikh aktov (RGADA), f. 214 (Sibirskii prikaz).

Rossiiskii gosudarstvennyi arkhiv drevnikh aktov (RGADA), f. 248 "Pravitel'svuiushchii Senat."

Rossiiskii gosudarstvennyi arkhiv drevnikh aktov (RGADA), f. 119 (Kalmytskie dela), op. 2, d. 1630.

Rossiiskii gosudarstvennyi arkhiv drevnikh aktov (RGADA), f. 9 "Kabinet Petra I."

Rossiiskii gosudarstvennyi arkhiv drevnikh aktov (RGADA), f. 196 "Rukopisnoe sobranie F. F. Mazurina," op. 1, d. 1542, 1543.

Printed Sources and Literature

Alekseev, M. P. *Sibir' v izvestiiakh zapadnoevropeiskikh puteshestvennikov i pisatelei.* Irkutsk: Oblastnoe izdatel'stvoe, 1941.

Badmaev, A. V., ed. *Kalmytskie istoriko-literaturnye pamiatniki v russkom perevode.* Elista: Izdatel'stvo Kalmytskogo nauchno-issledovatel'skogo instituta iazyka i kul'tury, 1969.

Bakunin, Vasilii Michailovich. *Opisanie kalmytskikh narodov, a osoblivo iz nikh torgoutskogo, i postupkov ikh khanov i vladel'tsev. (Sochinenie 1761 goda.* Elista: Kalmytskoe knizhnoe izdatel'stvo, 1995.

Bakhrushin, S. V. "Iasak v Sibiri v XVII v." *Nauchnye trudy* 3, no. 2. (1995): 49-85.

Bartol'd, V. V. *Sochineniia.* Vol. 5. Moscow: Nauka, 1968.

Bichurin, Nikita Yakovlevich [Iakinf, O.]. "Istoricheskoe obozrenie Oiratov ili Kalmykov s XV veka do nastoiashechego vremeni." *Zhurnal Ministerstva vnutrennikh del* 8 (1833): 283-303, 371-413.

Bogoiavlenskii, S. K. "Materialy po istorii kalmykov v pervoi polovine XVII v." *Istoricheskie zapiski* 5 (1937): 48-101.

Boronin, Oleg Valer'evich. *Dvoedannichestvo v Sibiri XVII–60-e gg. XIX vv.* Barnaul: Azbuka, 2002.

Chimitdorzhiev, Shiran Bodievich. *Vzaimootnosheniia Mongolii i Rossii XVII–XVIII vv.* Moscow: Nauka, 1987.

"Esipovskaia letopis'." *Polnoe sobranie russkikh letopisei.* Vol. 36. Moscow: Nauka, 1987.

Degacheva-Skop, E. I., ed. *Letopisi sibirskie.* Novosibirsk: Novosibirskoe knizhnoe izdatel'stvo, 1991.

Demidova, N. F., ed. *Russko-mongol'skie otnosheniia 1654–1685. Sbornik dokumentov.* Vol. 3. Moscow: Vostochnaia literature, 1996.

Grigor'ev, V. V. *Russkaia politika v otnoshenii Srednei Azii.* St. Petersburg: Sbornik gosudarstvennykh znanii, 1874.

Gurevich, B. P. and V. A. Moiseev, ed. *Mezhdunarodnye otnosheniia v Tsentral'noi Azii, XVII—XVIII vv. Kniga 1.* Moscow: Nauka, 1989.

Ides, Eberhard Isbrand, and Adam Brand. *Zapiski o russkom posol'stve v Kitai (1692-1695).* Moscow: Nauka, 1967.

Ivanov, P. P. *Ocherki po istorii Srednei Azii (XVI–seredina XIX v.).* Moscow: Vostochnaia literatura, 1958.

Khodarkovsky, Michael. *Where Two Worlds Met: The Russian State and the Kalmyk Nomads, 1600-1771.* Ithaca: Cornell University Press, 1992.

———. *Stepnye rubezhi Rossii.* Moscow: Novoe literaturnue obozrenie, 2019.

Kiuner, N. V. *Kitaiskie izvestiia o narodakh Iuzhnoi Sibiri, Tsentral'noi Azii i Dal'nego Vostoka.* Moscow: Vostochnaia literatura, 1961.

Kotoshikhin, G. O. *Rossii v tsarstvovanie Alekseia Mikhailovicha.* St. Petersburg: Izdanie Arkheograficheskoi komissii, 1884.

Krizhanich, J. *Politika.* Moscow: Nauka, 1965.

Maikov, L. N, and V. V. Maikov, ed. *Sibirskie letopisi.* St. Petersburg: Izdanie Arkheograficheskoi komissii, 1907.

McNeill, William. *Voskhozhdenie Zapada.* Moscow: Nika-Tsentr, 2004.

Miller, G. F. *Opisanie Sibirskogo tsarstva.* St. Petersburg: Izdanie Imperatorskoi Akademii Nauk, 1750.

———. *Istoriia Sibiri.* Vol. 2. Moscow and Leningrad: Izdatel'stvo Akademii Nauk SSSR, 1941.

———. *Istoriia Sibiri.* Vol 3. Moscow: Vostochnaia literatura, 2005.

Nikitin, N. I. *Sluzhilie liudi v Zapadnoi Sibiri.* Novosibirsk: Nauka, 1988.

Pal'mov, N. N. *Ocherk istorii kalmytskogo naroda za vremia ego prebyvaniia v predelakh Rossii.* Astrakhan': Izdanie Kalmytskogo oblastnogo ispolnitel'nogo komiteta, 1922.

———. *Etiudy po istorii privolzhskikh kalmykov.* Vol 1. Astrakhan': Izdanie Kalmytskogo oblastnogo ispolnitel'nogo komiteta, 1926.

Pushkin, A. S. "Istoriia Pugachevskogo bunta." *Sochineniia.* Vol 5. St. Petersburg: Izdanie Tipografii ekspeditsii zagotovleniia gosudarstvennikh bumag, 1838.

Schorkowitz, Dittmar. *Die soziale und politische Organisation bei den Kalmücken (Oiraten) und Prozesse der Akkulturation vom 17. Jahrhundert bis zur Mitte des 19. Jahrhunderts: Ethnohistorische Untersuchungen über die mongolischen Völkerschaften.* Frankfurt am Main: Peter Lang, 1992.

Tatishchev, V. N. *Izbrannye trudy po geografii Rossii.* Moscow: Gosudarstvennoe izdatel'stvo geograficheskoi literatury, 1950.

———. *Leksikon Rossiiskoi istoricheskoi, geograficheskoi, politicheskoi i grazhdanskoi.* Leningrad: Nauka, 1979.

———. *Sobranie sochinenii.* Vol. 1. Moscow: Ladomir, 1994.

———. *Sobranie sochinenii.* Vol. 8. Moscow: Ladomir, 1995.

Titov, A. *Sibir' v XVII v.* Moscow: Izdanie G. Iudina, 1890.

Trepavlov, V. V. *Istoriia nogaiskoi ordy.* Moscow: Vostochnaia literatura RAN, 2002.

Tsepkov, A. I., ed. *Angliiskie puteshestvenniki v Moskovskom gosudarstve v XVI v.* Translated by Iu. V. Got'e. Riazan': Aleksandriia, 2006.

Unkovskii, I. S. *Posol'stvo k Ziungarskomu Khun-Taichzhi Tsevan-Rabtanu i putevoi zhurnal za 1722–1724 gg.* St. Petersburg: tipografiia V. Kirshbauma, 1887.

Ustiugov, N. V., ed. *Ocherki istorii Kalmytskoi ASSR.* Moscow: Nauka, 1967.

Vernadskii, G. V. *Moskovskoe tsarstvo.* Vol. 2. Tver: Agraf, 2001.

Zlatkin, I. Ia. *Istoriia Dzhungarskogo khanstva.* Moscow: Nauka, 1983.

Zlatkin, I. Ia. and N. V. Ustiugov, ed. *Russko-mongol'skie otnosheniia 1607–1636. Sbornik dokumentov.* Vol. 1. Moscow: Vostochnaia literatura, 1959.

7

"In a Menagerie of Nations": Crimean Others in Travelogues, c. 1800[1]

Nikita Khrapunov

Abstract

The famous Edward Clarke once compared Crimea to a menagerie in which "contrasted specimens of living rarities are singularly associated."[2] After its unification with Russia in 1783, Crimea became an attraction for travelers seeking to study and describe the empire's new province. The travelers represented the multiethnic and multilingual imperial political and cultural elite. Sometimes, their mother tongue was not Russian. This chapter seeks to uncover how Russian intellectuals described and used the various features of Crimean Others from Muslim, Jewish, and Christian cultures. For example, travelers believed that peoples from antiquity such as the Scythians, Sarmatians, Huns, and Cimbrians still existed. Rousseau's "noble savages" were to be found in the "natural paradise" on the southern coast, maintaining the prehistoric virtues of hospitality and honesty, simplicity, and laziness, and living a simple life close to nature. In contrasting the Karaites and Jews, the travelers supported the former's desire to escape discriminatory legislation. The Tatars, Karaites, and

---

1   This chapter has been prepared with support from the Russian Foundation for Basic Research, project no. 18-09-00053 "Crimea as Viewed by the English in the Late Eighteenth and Early Nineteenth Century."
2   Edward Daniel Clarke, *Travels in Various Countries of Europe, Asia, and Africa. Part 1: Russia, Tahtary, and Turkey*, 4th ed. (London: T. Cadell and W. Davies, 1816), 2:221–22.

Jews were described as "Eastern" nations, featuring exotic religions, primitive cult practices, irregular town planning, dirt, superstitions, a lack of medicine, and specific ethics, and thus as the antithesis of Western civilization.

General Background

Russia never developed such a specific attitude to travel as a source of knowledge and a method of education as the Westerners, especially Britons, did. However, in the eighteenth century, the swiftly Europeanized Russian nobility learned the western tradition of Grand Tour and travel writing[3]—sometimes with a zeal worthy of a better cause. For example, a satiric play published in the English journal *The Bee* (1792) described a Russian gentleman traveler in Paris, who from his experience abroad learned only the customs of squandering money and exchanging mistresses like gloves.[4] Apart from journeys to Western, Central, and Southern Europe, Russian tourers made different trips throughout their vast and diverse empire, which offered a great deal of opportunities for scientific and educative observations. An example could be the case of Pavel Stroganov (1772–1817), a young Russian noble, who in a company of his French tutor Gilbert Romme (1750–1795) traveled in various parts of Russia, from Petersburg to the Urals and from the White Sea to Crimea.[5]

In 1783, Catherine the Great liquidated the Crimean Khanate and incorporated its territories into the Russian Empire. The Crimean Peninsula thus became an attraction for foreign and Russian travelers. In the first twenty-five years of its new history, no fewer than thirty travelogues describing Crimea and its populations appeared.[6] The Crimean Peninsula was still an almost unknown space, and Russia had to work on routine administrative and economic problems as it explored its new province.[7] The latter task was undertaken by

---

3 See Sara Dickinson, *Breaking Ground: Travel and National Culture in Russia from Peter I to the Era of Pushkin* (Amsterdam and New York: Rodopi, 2002).

4 Anthony Cross, *U temzskikh beregov: rossiiane v Britanii v XVIII veke* (St. Petersburg: Akademicheskii proekt, 1996), 255–56.

5 Aleksander Chudinov, *Zhil'ber Romm i Pavel Stroganov: istoriia neobychnogo soiuza* (Moscow: Novoe literaturnoe obozrenie, 2010), 160–70.

6 See Arsenii Markevich, "Taurica: opyt ukazatelia sochinenii, kasaiushchikhsia Kryma i Tavricheskoi gubernii voobshche," *Izvestiia Tavricheskoi uchenoi arkhivnoi komissii*, 20 (1864), 104–160; 28 (1898), 17–24; (1902), 58–62. Anthony Cross, *In the Land of the Romanovs: An Annotated Bibliography of First-hand English-language Accounts of the Russian Empire (1613–1917)* (Cambridge: Open Book Publishers, 2014), 91–148.

7 For details see Nikita Khrapunov and Denis Konkin, eds., *Problemy integratsii Kryma v sostav Rossii, 1783–1825* (Sevastopol: Al'batros, 2017), 37–91.

travelers, some commissioned by the government, others on their own initiative. Researchers, adventurers, diplomats, tutors, sentimental writers, and civil and military officers visited Crimea and reported their observations, feelings, and reflections. Their writings—sometimes translated into foreign languages and distributed throughout Europe and North America—laid the foundation for the generally accepted image of Crimea that still exists in the public mind.[8]

For a century, Crimea was not considered "purely Russian" in the historical and cultural sense. For example, in his oration on the centenary of Crimea's unification with Russia, Bishop Germogen (Dobronravin, 1820–1893) bitterly regretted that instead of Russifying Crimea, its new Russian inhabitants imitated the "Asiatic" population: "O Crimea, Crimea, our beloved Crimea! How many non-Russian you still have, how many non-Orthodox you still have! How few, few traces of our century-long possession of you remain!"[9]

The peninsula therefore remained Russia's "own East," allowing Russian intellectuals to understand their belonging to "Western civilization" and apprehend the historical mission of their empire.[10] Crimea's image in travelogues was therefore ambivalent: travelers perceived it as a land that was both their own and alien. Moreover, most attempted to learn about Crimea from the books of their predecessors or armchair researchers before starting their journeys. On arrival on the peninsula and in acquainting themselves with it, they remembered already known historical facts and circumstances, like the adventures of Agamemnon's daughter Iphigenia among the Taurians or King Mithridate VI's wars with Rome, the baptism of Rus' under Prince Vladimir the Great, or Catherine the Great's Crimean journey, and "identified" them with what they saw. The journey thus became one of recognition and recollection.

---

8 For alternative Russian, Ukrainian, and Crimean Tatar narratives see Gwendolyn Sasse, *The Crimea Question: Identity, Transition, and Conflict* (Cambridge, MA: Harvard University Press, 2007), 65–126; for the different aspects of Crimea's representation see Andrei Zorin, *By Fables Alone: Literature and State Ideology in Late Eighteenth- and Early Nineteenth-Century Russia* (Boston: Academic Studies Press, 2014), 92–120; Andreas Schönle, "Garden of the Empire: Catherine's Appropriation of the Crimea," *Slavic Review* 60, no. 1 (2001): 1–23; Sara Dickinson, "Russia's First 'Orient': Characterizing the Crimea in 1787," *Kritika: Explorations in Russian and Eurasian History* 3, no. 1 (2002): 3–25; Vladimir Orekhov, *V labirinte krymskogo mifa* (Veliky Novgorod, Simferopol, and Nizhny Novgorod: Rastr, 2017), 84–420; Khrapunov and Konkin, *Problemy integratsii Kryma*, 75–91, 30–52, 369–82; Jürgen Osterhammel, *Unfabling the East: The Enlightenment's Encounter with Asia*, trans. Robert Savage (Princeton: Princeton University Press, 2018), 314–21.

9 Bishop Germogen, *Tavricheskaia eparkhiia* (Pskov: Tipografiia gubernskogo pravleniia, 1887), 506.

10 Dickinson, "Russia's First 'Orient': Characterizing the Crimea in 1787," 3–25; Nikita Khrapunov, "'Vostok v Evrope': Krym posle prisoedineniia k Rossiiskoi imperii glazami inostrantsev," *The New Past* 1 (2018): 63–78.

Famous courtier and wit Charles-Joseph de Ligne (1735–1814), who visited Crimea in 1787 in Catherine's retinue, expressed this better than others:

> I expected to elevate my soul on arriving in the Taurica[11] through all the great things, true and false, that have happened here. My mind was ready to turn itself, with Mithridates, to the heroic, the fabulous with Iphigenia, the military with the Romans, the fine arts with the Greeks, to brigandage with the Tartars, to commerce with the Genoese. All those personages and nations are somewhat familiar to me; but lo! here comes another, and they have severally disappeared before the Arabian Nights.[12]

In contrast with Western Europe, separated from the "Eastern" countries by thousands of miles, Russian residents never apprehended the "East" as something distant and exotic. Contact with these peoples and countries had existed since time immemorial. The establishment of the Rus'ian state in the ninth century as a mediator in east-west trade; the Mongol invasion in the thirteenth century and the later domination of the Golden Horde; Ivan the Terrible's expansion into the Volga region and Siberia in the sixteenth century; the conflicts of many centuries with the Crimean Khanate—all these factors made the East or Islamic world a kind of habitual experience for Russians. In the eighteenth century, residents of St. Petersburg, Moscow, or Nizhny Novgorod could meet Persians, Bukharans, or Kalmyks who came to trade in their cities. However, Russia always lacked reliable information about the state structure or economy, religious principles, and legal system of neighboring countries.

Returning to the subject of this chapter, travel revived the problem of the Other by variously directing the voyager to strange peoples and cultures. The famous British traveler Edward Daniel Clarke (1769–1822) explained why Crimea became an important stage in the European Grand Tour:

> The variety of different nations which are found in the Crimea, each living as if in a country of its own, practicing its peculiar customs, and preserving its religious rites, is one of the circumstances which renders the Peninsula interesting to a

---

11 The ancient name of Crimea in Greek and Roman sources.

12 Charles-Joseph de Ligne, *The Prince de Ligne, His Memoires, Letters, and Miscellaneous Papers,* trans. Katherine Prescott Wormeley (Boston: Hardy, Pratt & Company, 1902), 2:17.

stranger: at Baktcheserai,[13] Tahtars and Turks; upon the rocks above them, a colony of Karaite Jews; an army of Russians at Akmetchet;[14] in other towns, Anatolians and Armenians; in the steppes, Nagays, Gipsies, and Calmucks: that in a very small district of territory, as in a menagerie, very opposite specimens of living curiosities are singularly contrasted.[15]

Both western and Russian cultures considered ethnic variety an inalienable feature of the East, regardless of the region where it was observed. As Catherine the Great wrote in her letter to Voltaire on May 18–29, 1767 from Kazan, "Now I am in Asia; I wanted to see it with my own eyes. In this city there are twenty different peoples who are nothing like each other."[16] A hundred years later, in 1868, Russian writer Gleb Uspenskii visited the North Caucasus and concluded:

What in Russia should be studied as separate regions of Great Russia, Little Russia, Volhynia, or Kazan Tatary, all this could be seen here as if there are samples grouped within small spaces of the area, as in a museum.[17]

The presence of Muslim, Jewish, and Christian cultures within a small area allowed travelers to Crimea to find various Others and use their image for various purposes. In describing non-Russian peoples, educated visitors often revealed the consequence of their own phobias, stereotypes, and complexes. Indeed, the genre itself led the writer to underline the strange and unusual features of the Other Country and the exoticism of its population that differed from the world with which they were familiar.

This chapter's aim is to discover the particular features of the images of Others in the Crimean context. Apart from the Russian-speaking noblemen who came to the Crimea for pleasure or education, some of the travelogue authors analyzed below were connected with Russia by service and represented

---

13 No stable spelling of Crimean place names then existed in western languages. I have therefore used today's forms in the chapter's text and have left the original spellings in direct citations from sources.

14 Today's Simferopol.

15 Clarke, *Travels*, 221–22.

16 Voltaire, *Oeuvres complètes. Nouvelle* édition, ed. Léon Thiessé (Paris: Pourrat frères et companie, 1831), 3:21.

17 Gleb Uspenskii, *Sobranie sochinenii v deviati tomakh* (Moscow: Gosudarstvennoe izdatel'stvo khudozhestvennoi literatury, 1957), 7:327.

the Empire's polyethnic elite. Indeed, some were of non-Russian origin, and some wrote in German or French. I have deliberately included persons of non-Russian culture and language in this list, in contrast with the tradition that describes "Russian travelogues" as those written only in Russian.[18] However, I will set aside Crimean verses of the Russian court poets of the period, who in their own ways praised the region and probably often reflected the state ideology.[19] Nor will I discuss the drawings of voyagers and traveling painters who populated the Crimean landscapes with exotic persons in the bright clothes known from distant countries.[20] The chronological frame of this chapter starts from the Russian annexation of Crimea and finishes with the inflaming of the Napoleonic Wars, which during the turn of the first and second decades of the nineteenth century temporary stopped Crimean tours. It was the period that determined some principal features of the image of Crimea in Russian culture. A few references to later travelogues are made from time to time in case when they seem appropriate, for example, to show the longevity of stereotypes.

A Land between East and West

The travelers of the Enlightenment knew that the classical Graeco-Roman tradition placed the border between Europe and Asia along the Strait of Kerch, between Crimea and Taman Island (or Peninsula, as it is now called). The sentimental writer Pavel Sumarokov (1767–1846) visited Crimea twice, publishing three famous volumes of travelogues in which he attempted to apply many of Laurence Sterne's methods to Russian soil. Having reached Kerch on the easternmost tip of the Crimean Peninsula, Sumarokov wrote: "Here Crimea ends, which itself is the border of Europe."[21] Although Russia viewed the peninsula as its own East, it was actually located *to the south* of St. Petersburg and Moscow. Mental maps often differed from geographical ones. Thus, in 1787, when Mozart was leaving Vienna for Prague (actually located *to the northwest* of the Austrian capital), he considered that he was traveling

---

18 See Andreas Schönle, *Authenticity and Fiction in the Russian Literary Journey, 1790–1840* (Cambridge, MA: Harvard University Press, 2000); Dickinson, *Breaking Ground*.

19 See Zorin, *By Fables Alone*, 92–120.

20 See Ol'ga Sosnina and Aleksandr Val'kovich, eds., *Orientalizm. Turetskii stil' v Rossii. 1760–1840-e* (Moscow: Kuchkovo pole, 2017), 125–52.

21 Pavel Sumarokov, *Puteshestvie po vsemu Krymu i Bessarabii v 1799 godu* (Moscow: Universitetskaia tipografiia, 1805), 73.

to the land of an unknown language to the East.[22] In *Ukraine between East and West*, the outstanding modern Byzantinist Ihor Ševčenko acknowledges that Ukraine's geographical *West* was Poland, located in the northwest, though its *East* was in Byzantium in the south and in Moscow in the north.[23] Be that as it may, geographically Crimea was in Europe, though the Muslim heritage visibly revealed the Eastern component of its nature.

Crimea was physically separated from mainland Russia. To its north was an at least three-hundred-kilometer strip of flat, dreary, woodless, and sparsely populated steppe. The narrow isthmus of Perekop connected the peninsula with the continent. It was also possible to come from the east by crossing the sea at the Strait of Kerch. These natural obstacles both underlined that Crimea was a specific country and made voyagers "wait for miracles." A similar feeling was experienced by those who crossed the Ural Mountains to get from Europe into Asia.[24]

Matthew Guthrie (1743–1807), a Scottish physician in Russian service and a person of encyclopedic interests, wrote an account of an imagined journey to Crimea, using information on the peninsula from various published sources.[25] In his words, the peninsula consisted of two parts:

> The saline grassy stept, or plain, on the North [. . .] [and] fine mountainous country to the South, the admiration and abode of polished commercial nations for upward of two thousand years, who filled its ports with ships and merchandize, till the barbarous Turks shut up the Thracian Bosphorus, and turned the busy Euxine[26] into a watery desert.[27]

---

22 Larry Wolff, *Inventing Eastern Europe: The Map of Civilization on the Mind of the Enlightenment* (Stanford: Stanford University Press, 1994), 106–7.

23 Ihor Ševčenko, *Ukraine between East and West: Essays on Cultural History to the Early Eighteenth Century* (Edmonton and Toronto: Canadian Institute of Ukrainian Studies Press, 1996), 1–11.

24 See David Schimmelpenninck van der Oye, *Russian Orientalism: Asia in the Russian Mind from Peter the Great to the Emigration* (New Haven: Yale University Press, 2010), 112.

25 For his authorship of the travelogue published under the name of his late wife see Nikita Khrapunov, *Angliiskie puteshestvenniki i Krym. Konets XVIII–pervaia tret' XIX v.* (Sevastopol: Al'batros, 2022), 95–100 (with bibliography).

26 Ancient name of the Black Sea.

27 Matthew Guthrie, *A Tour, Performed in the Years 1795–6, through the Taurida, Or Crimea, the Ancient Kingdom of Bosphorus, the Once-Powerful Republic of Tauric Cherson, and All Other Countries on the North Shore of the Euxine, Ceded to Russia by the Peace of Kainardgi and Jassy* (London: T. Cadell, Jun., and W. Davies, 1802), 54.

There are two key elements in this passage: the opposition of civilization, trade, and Europeanness with barbarism, Islam, and Asianness; and admiration for the picturesque landscapes of southern Crimea.

An Earthly Paradise and Its Dwellers

Tired by the long journey through the steppe, travelers were enchanted to discover mountains, fertile valleys, rivers, and forests, and they emotionally described Crimea as an earthly paradise. They located this Eden in different nooks: some preferred the Mediterranean southern coast, though Guthrie found it to the north of the Crimean mountains: the first "earthly paradise" in the vicinity of Bakhchisarai, and the "Tauric Arcadia" in the valley of Baydar encircled by mountains in the southwest.[28] Later, the German officer in Russian service Pierce-Balthazar von Campenhausen (1746–1808) derided these exalted words: "The oval valley of Baydar [. . .] is indebted a good deal for its captivating appearance to the sterility of the surrounding country, and does not by any means deserve to be compared with the vallies of Switzerland."[29]

The search for paradise in remote areas was typical of the period: travelers "discovered" it in Greece, Switzerland, Scandinavia, South America, and the Pacific islands.[30] Although the *topos* of paradise is traditional in travelogues, voyagers could supply it with different nuances. When Catherine the Great visited Bakhchisarai, the former Khanate's capital in 1787, she wrote a verse to her favorite Grigory Potemkin, the governor of South Russia: "Oh, miracles of God! Who of my ancestors / Slept quietly because of their[31] hordes and Khans? / But I cannot sleep amidst Bakhchisarai / Because of tobacco smoke and cries [. . .] Is it not a place of paradise?"[32] Here paradise signifies the triumph of the conqueror, who takes possession of a very important place, the land of promise. However, those who came after the Empress may have had another opinion.

Many years later Aleksandr Kaznacheev (1788–1880), an ex-governor of Crimea, wrote in a private letter:

28 Ibid., 70, 116.
29 Pierce-Balthazar von Campenhausen, *Travels through Several Provinces of the Russian Empire; With an Historical Account of the Zaporog Cossacks, and of Bessarabia, Moldavia, Wallachia, and the Crimea* (London: Richard Phillips, 1808), 52.
30 Khrapunov and Konkin, *Problemy integratsii*, 347–48.
31 Tatar.
32 Viacheslav Lopatin, ed., *Ekaterina II i G.A. Potemkin. Lichnaia perepiska, 1769–1791* (Moscow: Nauka, 1997), 216.

> The endless sky is before me, mirroring the universe! Surrounded by mountains and fine nature, I feel my nothingness and elevate my soul. Admiring the beauties of sky and earth, I become better and gentler. In the capital everything is the other way [...]. The thought often comes to my mind: is not this the promised land? A fragment of the ancient paradise, or its antechamber?[33]

Following the ideas of Jean-Jacques Rousseau, such a natural Eden was understood as a place to which to escape from the depraved life of European capitals and avail of the simple pleasures of rural life. Vladimir Izmailov (1773–1830) made Crimea a stage of his southern journey of 1799, in which he combined emotional reflections with an interest in Russian history. Somewhere in eastern Crimea he met a Tatar princess, a sister of the last Crimean Khan, who preferred a happy life in the bosom of nature to the temptations of St. Petersburg, where the Russian government "showered her with flattering symbols of honor."[34] According to Izmailov: "It was Venus on Earth wearing Tatar dress, with only a shadow of her heavenly image." This new acquaintance said to the traveler: "I have seen both St. Petersburg and Moscow [...]. I prefer this unknown spot of the world to magnificent cities."[35] But she could not escape "envy and slander," so some "angry persons" even compared her with the most famous courtesans of Ancient Greece. Importantly, Izmailov observed that "of all her people's customs, she retained only the clothes"—that is, only the Enlightenment (Europeanization) could allow a person to follow the Rousseauian ideal consciously.[36]

Fascinated by Crimea's landscapes, seascapes, gardens, and orchards, many travelers did not notice its darker side—exotic diseases, for example. Sumarokov knew that "merely the words 'Crimean fevers' inspire fear."[37] He observed that "those who travel to Crimea decorate its cemeteries with numerous tombstones,"[38] and that these tombstones contradicted his pictures of a terrestrial paradise. The victims did not follow "precautions proper in this country, acting in accordance with previously rooted habits."[39] In contrast, the

---

33 Yurii Bartenev, ed., "Yurii Nikitich Bartenev. 1840–1842," *Russkii arkhiv* 1 (1898): 111.
34 Vladimir Izmailov, *Puteshestvie v poludennuiu Rossiu. V pis'makh. Novoe izdanie* (Moscow: Tipografiia Khristofora Klaudiia, 1805), 3:61.
35 Ibid., 62.
36 Ibid., 63.
37 Pavel Sumarokov, *Dosugi krymskogo sud'i, ili vtoroe puteshestvie v Tavridu* (St. Petersburg Imperatorskaia tipografiia, 1805), 2:2.
38 Ibid., 3.
39 Ibid.

Tatars as autochthonous inhabitants knew that cleanliness and appropriate clothing prevented many of these diseases. There were almost no disabled or those with physical defects among them.[40] The Others were therefore better fitted to the Other region.

A certain parallel could be found with the Russian image of Siberia. Like Crimea, it featured a paradoxical combination of the features of "paradise" (a promised land) and "hell" (a terrible climate). However, in the image of Siberia, the former was imbued with freedom from serfdom and arbitrary officialdom, the latter with the presence of exiled criminals.[41]

Patriarchal and Exotic: Ta(r)tars and Karaites

Although travelers certainly knew of the Armenians, Greeks, Jews, and Karaites, the principal Other was the Tatar. Alexander von Benckendorff (1782–1844) came to Crimea in 1804 as a member of a secret mission sent by Tsar Alexander I to study the provinces of Russia. Many years later, under the next Tsar, Nicholas I, von Benckendorff became the head of the Russian secret police and an odious figure in Russian literature. However, his diary exemplifies a sober fixation with what he saw. Its author had no illusion about the Russian government. Von Benckendorff wrote of the eternal conflict between the Russians and the Tatars. The latter "were long the masters of Russia,"[42] but times had changed, and the Russians had conquered the Tatars and devastated their once flourishing land.

> But the eternal shame for the conquerors and for the reign of Catherine [the Great] will be that the whole of Crimea became uninhabited; this beautiful province, the breadbasket of Constantinople and Asia Minor, covered with cities with blossoming gardens, which fed more than a million hardworking people, was made a desert. [. . .]. When in Caffa,[43] you feel shame: the Tatars were skillful there, and the Russians destroyed everything.[44]

---

40 Ibid., 4–5.
41 Vadim Trepavlov, ed., *Obrazy regionov v obshchestvennom soznanii i kul'ture Rossii (XVII–XIX vv.)* (Tula: Grif i K, 2011), 42–43.
42 Alexander von Benckendorff, *Vospominaniia 1802–1837* (Moscow: Rossiiskii fond kul'tury, 2012), 80.
43 Modern Feodosia.
44 Benckendorff, *Vospominaniia*, 80–81.

The famous Russian poet Aleksandr Griboedov (1795–1829) formed a similar opinion after visiting Caffa in 1825:

> At this torched site the Gothic customs of the Genoese used to dominate; they were replaced by the Mongols' pasturing with an admixture of Turkish luxury; we followed them, as universal heirs, and the spirit of destruction with us; no building survived, no part of the town remained unploughed, undug over.[45]

Travelers knew that Crimea's past was replete with heroic events and dramatic stories. According to von Benckendorff, "This entire country arouses the greatest interest with the fabulous history of its past, the turbulences it survived, the peoples who populated it, the history of the Greeks, Genoese, Tatars, and Russians, who subsequently possessed this land."[46]

It was considered that here, as everywhere in Eastern Europe[47], history crystallized and revealed the peoples of the past. As Izmailov put it, the "[n]atural residents of Crimea, the Tatars, are also known from the account of Herodotus, under the name of the Scythians."[48] Guthrie went further. Not only did he trace the Tatars to the Scythians but he interpreted the Crimean Karaites, or non-Talmidic Turkic-speaking Jews, as the possible descendants of the Melanchlaeni of antiquity. The ancient Cimmerians—through the Gauls and Celts—were not only Crimea's most ancient population, who had given it their name (Cimmerians—Cimmerium—Crim), but the forefathers of this Scottish doctor and his French (Gallic) spouse.[49] Guthrie saw history as continuity: ancient peoples never disappeared without a trace but simply changed their names. Logically, there was a need for modern parallels with the names known to the classical writers, thus uncovering centuries-long ethnic histories. Territory and faith mattered, too, but less than the ethnonym did. These ideas correspond to the proto ethnography of the Enlightenment.[50]

As was customary for the English speakers of the period, Guthrie spelt "Tatars" *Tartars*. This play on words was impossible in Russian, though in English it was

45 Aleksandr Griboedov, *Polnoe sobranie sochinenii* (St. Petersburg: Dmitrii Bulanin, 2006), 3:101.
46 Benckendorff, *Vospominaniia*, 82.
47 See Wolff, *Inventing Eastern Europe*.
48 Izmailov, *Puteshestvie*, 3:124.
49 Guthrie, *A Tour*, 9, 84, 195, 406.
50 See: Yuri Slezkine, "Naturalists versus Nations: Eighteenth–Century Russian Scholars Confront Ethnic Diversity," *Representations* 47 (1994): 173–74.

quite revealing. It connected the Ta(r)tars to *Tartarus*, the underworld of Greco-Roman mythology. This tradition reflected the ancient fear of invasion by the thirteenth-century Mongols, who were seen as heralds of the end of days, as the Christian prophets had predicted.[51] Westerners viewed the Tatars as archetypical savages and barbarians.[52] Meanwhile, the Russians' many centuries' history of conflict with the Golden Horde and its successor states caused them to consider the Tatars[53] as the Other, the embodiment of every negative feature, especially anger, guile, and cruelty.[54] The annexation of Crimea drastically changed this view: the Crimean Tatars were now described as a gentle and harmless people living in the bosom of nature like Rousseau's noble savage. One of the best examples appears in the book by French couple Adèle (1819–1883) and Xavier (1812–1848) Hommaire de Hell, who visited Crimea in 1841.

> When looking at today's Tatars, who will see in these simple persons with modest merits the descendants of the arrogant Mongols, who in former times established their dominance over part of western Europe? Their active life in camps, long campaigns, wild customs, and haughty character were replaced by indifferent limpness and a philosophical fatalism, which seemed to help them as they worked in the fields, vineyards, and beautiful orchards.[55]

The contrast with descriptions of the peoples of the Caucasus is demonstrative: in the same age, the latter were commonly interpreted as martial savages and eternal predators.[56] Perhaps the reason was that Crimeans remained peaceful subjects of the Empire, though the war with indigenous tribes of the Caucasus lasted to the 1860s.

Russian patriots saw Catherine the Great's success in Crimea as a symbol of military fame. Poet and dramatist Dmitry Gorchakov (1758–1824), who served

---

51 Aleksandr Filiushkin, "Kak Rossiia stala dlia Evropy Aziei?" in *Izobretenie imperii: iazyki i praktiki*, ed. Il'ia Gerasimov, Marina Mogilner, and Aleksandr Semenov (Moscow: Novoe izdatel'stvo, 2011), 13, 39 note 16.

52 Osterhammel, *Unfabling the East*, 303–14.

53 In the Russian imperial usage the word "Tatar" signified all the Turkic-speaking Muslims living in the wide tract from Crimea and the Caucasus to Central Asia and Siberia.

54 Mark Batunskii, "Islam i russkaia kul'tura XVIII veka. Opyt istoriko-epistemologicheskogo issledovaniia," *Cahiers du monde russe et soviétique* 27, 1 (1986): 56.

55 Orekhov, *V labirinte krymskogo mifa*, 442.

56 Vladimir Bobrovnikov, "Orientalizm v literature i politike na Severnov Kavkaze," In *Aziatskaia Rossiia: liudi i struktury imperii* (Omsk: Izdatel'stvo OmGU, 2005), 26–29.

as the prosecutor of the Taurida (i. e. Crimean) Governorate between 1807 and 1810, wrote a poem about the thoughts of a Russian standing at the foot of Chatyr-Dag, "the king of the Tauric mountains."[57] On the eve of Napoleon's Russian campaign, he remembered the former victories of the Russian armies, lamenting the position of Alexander I, who followed the orders of the French leader. In this context, the unmentioned Tatars stand for Russia's enemies and the reason for her former triumph.[58]

The Others certainly had an exotic appearance. Traveling through southern Crimea, where the roads were poor and there was no Russian-speaking population, required guides and translators. Sumarokov hired a Turkish interpreter "with the biggest moustache, which reached his eyes, like horns. Indeed, I had said I needed simply the Tatar language, but it was supplied with a titled moustache."[59] Peter Simon Pallas (1741–1811), a natural historian of German origin, became a widely recognized researcher after his learned travels to Siberia sponsored by the Russian Academy of Sciences. Catherine the Great sent him to investigate the south of Russia in 1793 and 1794, and later gave him estates in Crimea. There, he wrote a general description of the peninsula. Studying the southern coast, he described its population, who "though regarded as Tartars, are nevertheless the offspring of other nations, who had either landed here, or had been driven thither from the interior."[60] Their physical appearance was remarkable: "Faces of uncommon length, as well as arched, exceedingly long noses, and high heads compressed with a view to render them unusually flat, all contribute to produce diverse caricatures."[61] Pallas compiled a special appendix to his book discussing the inhabitants of the Crimean Peninsula. Their physical appearance was that of the Other: they had other haircuts, other style of makeup, other clothes, other customs, other houses fueled by other materials, other languages, and other food. Some of these resembled, for example, the features of other exotic peoples like the Turks, Circassians, or Cossacks.[62]

In describing the peoples living in Crimea, educated writers often contradicted one another. In such accounts a single trait signified civilization, though its alternative was barbarism. Among such oppositions was cleanliness-dirtiness. When, after a journey along the southern coast, Griboedov saw a

---

57 Gorchakov, "Russkii u podoshvy Chatyrdaga," *Russkii arkhiv* 7–8 (1871): 1285.
58 Ibid., 1285–88.
59 Sumarokov, *Puteshestvie po vsemu Krymu i Bessarabii v 1799 godu*, 49.
60 Peter Simon Pallas, *Travels through the Southern Provinces of the Russian Empire in the Years 1793 and 1794* (London: John Stockdale, 1812), 2:149–50.
61 Ibid., 148.
62 Ibid., 342–61.

Greek church in the vicinity of Balaklava, he wrote in his journal: "the church is white, a fine view after the dirty mosques."[63] Contrasting Karaites with Talmudic Jews, Guthrie mentioned that "Here, to the surprise of those acquainted with the Polish or Northern Jews, the children of Israel are found with an air of cleanliness and prosperity seldom seen among the former."[64] Thus, according to Guthrie, the Karaites were much closer to "civilized nations" than their Polish Talmudic brethren. In another passage, he wrote that the Tatars also understood the "known industry" of the Karaites and therefore allowed them to live in the town atop a cliff not far from their capital, where there was no water spring. The industrious Karaites collected rainwater and brought water up from the plain.[65] Von Campenhausen disagreed with "praising the cleanliness of these Israelites."[66] However, he stated that "they are tolerated by the Tatars on account of their industry."[67] It seems the oppositions industry-laziness and cleanliness-dirtiness were understood as differences between Us and Them, and between different kinds of Other.

Travelers remarked on Tatar hospitality: Sumarokov was so fascinated with it that he returned to this subject several times.

> I have heard much praise of their hospitality and seen its examples; but I should render justice to the Crimean Tatars, who in this respect, as well as in unselfishness and sincere services, may be an example to many enlightened peoples.[68]

The German Johann Christian von Struve (1768–1812) entered Russian service and spent some months in Crimea in 1792, awaiting the beginning of an embassy to Constantinople. Von Struve visited the peninsula's different towns and places. One day, he lost his way when returning to Simferopol. Suddenly, he heard a dog barking and arrived at a Tatar village. A *murza*, or nobleman, "after receiving me with great civility, invited me to sit near the fire, ordered me a good bed, and the following morning sent a guide with me to Sympheropol."[69] This and other adventures convinced the traveler that the Tatars had retained their patriarchal

---

63 Griboedov, *Polnoe sobrabie sochinenii*, 2:328.
64 Guthrie, *A Tour*, 83.
65 Ibid., 85.
66 Campenhausen, *Travels*, 51.
67 Ibid., 51–52.
68 Sumarokov, *Puteshestvie po vsemu Krymu i Bessarabii v 1799 godu*, 153.
69 Johann Christian von Struve, *Travels in the Crimea* (London: G. and J. Robinson, 1802), 25; see also: Sumarokov, *Puteshestvie po vsemu Krymu i Bessarabii v 1799 godu*, 89; Izmailov, *Puteshestvie*, 3:85–87.

virtue: "I have had opportunities of remarking frequently among them traits of sublime generosity and mildness, a noble and truly patriarchal simplicity, and an eagerness of hospitality that deserves the highest commendation."[70]

However, hospitality was also typical of other Crimeans. Sumarokov described an encounter on the south-eastern coast with a Greek officer, who welcomed the stranger, offered him exotic meals, and showed him his gardens and picturesque beach where he used to fish. The Russian traveler was delighted with this Edenic country and his noble host, so he began to think of leaving the "vain and empty"[71] world of St. Petersburg, where no true friendship and no sincere feeling was possible, and settling in Crimea.[72] Evidently, kindness and sincerity were inseparable in his perception from this natural paradise, far from civilization.

However, some of the Others' customs looked less pleasant to European travelers. Sumarokov enjoyed the unaccustomed food the Tatars offered him— simple dishes that differed from the food to which he was accustomed in the Russian capital. However, he wrote:

> I found the eastern habit of eating like brothers from a single bowl very unpleasant; [. . .] I also considered it disgusting that every dish was taken with bare hands. I [. . .] separated my portion in a corner and ate with a fork in the European manner.[73]

Local eating traditions were thus also interpreted as a marker of the Other.

Unfamiliar Towns and Worship

Another marker was the unusual appearance of local towns. Their irregular system, with narrow crooked streets and the blind walls of houses encircled by high fences, the exotic structures of mosques, public baths, caravanserais, coffee houses, and fountains surprised people as different as Sumarokov, the sentimental dreamer, and Pallas, the realistic scientist.[74] These strange structures reflected an

---

70 Struve, *Travels in the Crimea*, 23–24.
71 Sumarokov, *Puteshestvie po vsemu Krymu i Bessarabii v 1799 godu*, 92.
72 Ibid., 90–93.
73 Ibid., 50.
74 Sumarokov, *Puteshestvie po vsemu Krymu i Bessarabii v 1799 godu*, 51–53, 129–31; Sumarokov, *Dosugi krymskogo sud'i, ili vtoroe puteshestvie v Tavridu* (St. Petersburg: Imperatorskaia tipografiia, 1803), 1:116; Pallas, *Travels*, 2:17–18, 27, 249–50.

alternative way of life and adaptation to specific cultural and religious norms. However, foreigners recognized the picturesqueness of Oriental towns against the background of mountains and cliffs. The contrast between regular European and irregular Oriental towns is clear in Guthrie's description of Sevastopol:

> The old Tartar houses here, as well as everywhere else in the peninsula, are small and ill-built; but we find along the quay some new buildings in a much better taste, the natural consequence of its being the station of the great Euxine fleet, and, of course, the chief residence of the flag and other naval officers.[75]

The most striking symbol of Oriental Others was certainly their mosques. However, their lack of understanding of Islamic culture prevented travelers from recognizing their aesthetic value. Describing the magnificent structure in Yevpatoria, a port city on the western Crimean coast, Izmailov stated: "Here is the mosque, for which, they say, that of Mecca was the model. Much splendor, but little beauty."[76] Another marker of otherness was the public baths, whose function resembled European clubs. Sumarokov contrasted Tatar ladies' love of bathing with what was normal for Russian women:

> Certainly, every people has its own customs: our lady with a fan open and a lorgnette before her eyes would die of boredom in your bathhouse antechamber with chorba and pilau;[77] alike, your Tatar lady would yawn from our officers' addresses.[78]

Many travelers could not avoid watching the ritual performed by the dervishes, especially those living in the former Khan's capital in Bakhchisarai. They found this ritual strange and surprising. Dmitrii Tarasov (1792–1866), a physician of Alexander I, followed the tsar on his last journey to Crimea in 1825. He was

> very surprised with how these Turkish monks delivered prayers. The ritual was that, in the middle of the mosque, they, fifty persons in number, stood in a circle and started, with visible

---

75 Guthrie, *A Tour*, 93; see also: Sumarokov, *Dosugi krymskogo sud'i*, 1:193–94.
76 Izmailov, *Puteshestvie*, 3:98.
77 Traditional Crimean Tatar dishes: *chorba* is a soup of lamb and vegetables; *pilau* a dish of rice (or millet, for rice was very expensive in the period in question), meat, and vegetables stewed in a cauldron.
78 Sumarokov, *Dosugi krymskogo sud'i*, 1:155.

effort, bowing very fast and low, making exclamations, in unison and in harmony, much resembling the oinking of pigs, and continued this until some started fainting from tiredness.[79]

However, Sumarokov concluded his description of the dervishes:

> Different peoples, different customs! What seems laughable to one, another finds important; one understands as normal [a thing] from which another flinches with shame. [...] There is no common good or evil, and everyone has the same goal: everyone seeks to acknowledge his Creator, to resign himself before Him, and to bring some offering to Him in gratitude.[80]

Exaggerating their own aesthetic standards, travelers apprehended Muslim religious rites as primitive and indecent aping. In 1827, the Briton James Webster (1802–1828) visited Bakhchisarai and witnessed the ritual of dervishes in the same mosque as Sumarokov, but his conclusion was considerably more critical: "To call this affair ridiculous, horrid, and incredible, is nothing; to form any conception of its disgusting absurdity, one must have witnessed it."[81] Perhaps this was a general feature of the "Western" mind: there are many similarities here with accounts of Egypt by Napoleonic soldiers.[82] Yet not all travelers' reflections were so negative. When Sumarokov witnessed another dervish ceremony, his conclusion was: "However, we should agree that rituals unintelligible or unpleasant to God's glory are found not only among the Mohammedans," and compared them to ancient Roman and pagan Slavic rites.[83] Only a century later, Émile Durkheim would recognize: "Men cannot celebrate [religious] ceremonies for which they see no reason, nor can they accept a faith which they in no way understand."[84]

Some travelers thought that even Christianity could change in a distant land. Izmailov described a medieval "cave town" in Inkerman, featuring

---

79 Dmitrii Tarasov, *Imperator Aleksandr I. Poslednie gody tsarstvovaniia, bolezn' i pogrebenie* (Moscow: Kuchkovo pole, 2013), 185–86.

80 Sumarokov, *Puteshestvie po vsemu Krymu i Bessarabii v 1799 godu*, 136.

81 James Webster, *Travels through the Crimea, Turkey, and Egypt* (London: Henry Colburn and Richard Bentley, 1830), 1:87.

82 Evgeniia Prusskaia, *Frantsuzskaia ekspeditsiia v Egipet 1798–1801 gg.: vzaimnoe vospriiatie dvukh tsivilizatsii* (Moscow: ROSSPEN, 2016), 146, 156–67.

83 Sumarokov, *Dosugi krymskogo sud'i*, 2:180–81.

84 Émile Durkheim, *The Elementary Forms of the Religious Life*, trans. Joseph Ward Swain (London: George Allen & Unwin Ltd., 1915), 430.

several artificial caverns carved into a mountain's rocky slope. He connected this monument with Genoese colonists who had fled there from danger. "Approaching the church, [we saw] it consisted of two chapels. The altar, where the blood of innocent victims sacrificed by superstition was shed, existed intact. Above it, there was a stone cross."[85] Izmailov probably saw this unthinkable human sacrifice in a Christian sanctuary as an indication that a strange country could influence traditional Christian ritual.

The Eastern Romance

The East was considered a romantic place, in which other morals and sexuality flourished,[86] and the most unbelievable adventures could happen, as in the *Arabian Nights* or the *Abduction from the Seraglio*.[87] When von Benckendorff saw the former Khan's residence in Bakhchisarai, with its romantic chambers, fountains, baths, and harem, he wrote in his diary: "In this palace, more than in any other place, one would dream of finding a beauty, and here the Khan should rule a harem full of pretty slaves."[88] Guthrie told a story of the Tatars mistaking a noble Greek lady, the wife of a Russian general, who spoke Turkish, for "a fair daughter of Mahomet, held in Christian bondage by the right of war, and secretly opened a subscription among themselves to purchase her liberty."[89] A Tatar gentleman offered a thousand ducats for this purpose, because he wanted "to open once more the door of paradise to this lovely hourie,[90] possibly by the way of recommending himself to her favour, at an after period."[91] Although Guthrie may have fabricated this episode, he believed his readers would take it for the truth.

Travelers evinced gender stereotypes in explaining Muslims' strict control of the behavior of women as the result of men's jealousy. According to von Campenhausen: "The Crimean Tatars are extremely addicted to jealousy, but that does not prevent their wives from being gallant—'Tout comme

---

85 Izmailov, *Puteshestvie*, 3:15.
86 Edward Said, *Orientalism* (London: Penguin, 1977), 185–91.
87 For the romantic image of the Turk/Muslim see Larry Wolff, *The Singing Turk: Ottoman Power and Operatic Emotions on the European Stage from the Siege of Vienna to the Age of Napoleon* (Stanford: Stanford University Press, 2016).
88 Benckendorff, *Vospominaniia*, 82.
89 Guthrie, *A Tour*, 65.
90 In Muslim tradition, *houris* are eternally young girls who delight the faithful in paradise.
91 Guthrie, *A Tour*, 66.

chez nous.'"[92] Guthrie wrote that Tatar houses had no windows onto the street because of "polygamy, and its natural consequence, jealousy, having turned the façade of Tauric dwellings to the inner court."[93] Unlike many of his contemporaries, Izmailov did not like the exotic appearance of Crimean towns, because their structures were literally jails for poor women.

> Tatar houses enclosed with stone fences higher than their very roofs, and concealed from sight; the khans, or hotels, obstructed with high walls, and the mosques which add nothing to decoration make the town something like a state prison, casting a sad shadow on nature. The valley flowers are less lovely, and the streams of the river murmur less nicely when you imagine that these stone walls conceal living creatures and beautiful captives. [...]. The sin only and the evil only should hide in the darkness.[94]

These appraisals are unsurprising for the European culture of the period: for example, the statements of Frenchmen who visited Egypt during Bonaparte's campaign were very similar.[95] They therefore reflect a general *topos* of the Islamic treatment of women.

According to Guthrie, his wife was shocked by the difficult conditions endured by Tatar women, who were "only accessible to their own masters, who are literally so in Mahometan states, though we right Christian wives only call you so to laugh at your lordship."[96] Pallas saw harems as a cause of great vice, because they cultivated the idleness of children: "if at work, to make long pauses, and above all to do nothing, constitute their supreme enjoyments: for this mode of life, a foundation is probably laid by educating their boys in the harems."[97] In contrast, Sumarokov saw some positive features in these guidelines: "This custom may be unbearable for femininity, but for men it is very well invented."[98] In another instance, he stated that "between two persons one should necessarily take preference, despite all Europeans' propagations of matrimonial equality."[99]

---

92 Everything as with us (French). Campenhausen, *Travels*, 54.
93 Guthrie, *A Tour*, 215; see also ibid., 217.
94 Izmailov, *Puteshestvie*, 3:76–77.
95 Prusskaia, *Frantsuzskaia ekspeditsiia v Egipet*, 82, 108–9.
96 Guthrie, *A Tour*, 217.
97 Pallas, *Travels*, 2:356.
98 Sumarokov, *Puteshestvie po vsemu Krymu i Bessarabii v 1799 godu*, 69.
99 Sumarokov, *Dosugi krymskogo sud'i*, 1:155.

He envied his Muslim guide, because "he has two pretty wives, uses their charms according to a schedule, passes from one embrace to another, when some cannot find a single wife."[100]

Lazy Natives

The Crimean landscape differs significantly from that of Central Russia, and the Crimeans therefore had different occupations and a different attitude to labor. When Sumarokov traveled along the southern coast, he observed there were no large fields with crops of corn or haystacks, and even the workers in the fields worked differently from their Russian counterparts.

> I do not hear the workers' loud-voiced singing [. . .]. Morose husbands work with their sickles in silence, the wives and daughters are leaving for faraway furrows, and around them languor and inactivity reign.[101]

It was assumed that Russians enjoyed their labor, but the Tatars did not. The rich Mediterranean environment caused travelers to regard the Crimeans as idlers and loafers, who had neither the stimulus nor desire to work. Sumarokov informed his readers that Crimea received provisions and different goods used in daily life from neighboring Ukraine and even faraway Russia. The reason was the Tatars' behavior, which he interpreted in moral terms: "Muslims, spoilt by laziness, on finding pearls scattered at their feet do not want to bend to collect them. They can be compared to a dissolute son who is spending his father's treasure."[102] The treasure here implies the natural riches of the peninsula. This is certainly reminiscent of the philosophical classics of the Enlightenment: Montesquieu and Rousseau identified laziness as a mark of the rich and fructiferous south.[103]

The greatest critic of Tatar laziness was Pallas, who spent many years in Crimea as a local landowner and therefore could refer to his own (negative) experience. As researchers have already noted, Pallas's initial enthusiasm

---

100   Sumarokov, *Puteshestvie po vsemu Krymu i Bessarabii v 1799 godu*, 154–55.
101   Sumarokov, *Dosugi krymskogo sud'i*, 2:202.
102   Ibid., 1:164–65; see also ibid., 2:10–11, 198–99.
103   Charles Montesquieu, *The Spirit of Laws*, trans. Thomas Nugent (New York: The Colonial Press, 1899), 1:332; Jean-Jacques Rousseau, *Emile, or On Education*, trans. Allan Bloom (New York: Basic Books, 1979), 52.

for Crimea was replaced by skepticism, especially because he was engaged in disputes with his neighbors about land properties.[104] Be that as it may, his travelogue is replete with harsh words. Among the obstacles to the economic development of Crimea, he listed the fact "that the most beautiful mountain-tracts are [. . .] inhabited by slothful Tartars; whose rural economy exhibits a passion for devastation peculiar to that people."[105] His suggestion was simple: idle Tatars should be expelled from fertile regions to the hinterland and replaced with a much more industrious population. However, this was not Tatarophobia. For Pallas, it was a universal method of economic development, because he proposed doing the same to Russian landowners and western adventurers incapable of properly developing Crimean lands and manufacturing.

> Should the Crimea, at some future period, be so fortunate as to receive a few thousand Georgian and Armenian colonists, who might prosper and live here [. . .] there is no doubt but many hundreds of poods[106] of silk could, from this neighborhood, be brought to commercial markets [. . .]. It is, however, to be regretted, that all these fine, warm dales of the southern coast are inhabited partly by useless, inactive, and, in certain cases, dangerous Tartars, who understand the art of destroying better than that of rearing; and, on the other hand, that the crown-lands have been granted to such proprietors, as possess neither the ability nor the good-will of establishing colonies for the public good, in situation thus favoured by nature.[107]

However, not all the travelers considered this "laziness" a natural feature of the Tatars; nor did they consider forced deportation necessary. For them, the reason lay in Tatars' modest needs and the problems of Russian government.[108] A son of a French emigrant, Paul Guibal (1795–1834), who studied Crimea and the Caucasus between 1818 and 1819, possibly on the appointment of the administration of the southern Russian provinces,[109] mentioned that the Tatars

---

104 Khrapunov and Konkin, eds., *Problemy integratsii Kryma*, 48–49.
105 Pallas, *Travels*, 2:362.
106 Old Russian measure of weight equal to 16.38 kg or 36.08 British pounds.
107 Pallas, *Travels*, 2:262.
108 Osterhammel, *Unfabling the East*, 320–21.
109 Concerning this person and his treatise, see Nikita Khrapunov, "Obraz Kryma v zapiskakh frantsuzskogo emigranta Polia Gibalia," *Annuaire d'études françaises* (2018): 437–52.

residing in the Crimean Mountains differed from the Tatars of the steppe by race, economy, and customs. The mountaineers

> know well how to cultivate the ground but are lazy by their nature, and live enjoying their life, as they understand it, not caring about getting rich. In this regard they are possibly wiser than Europeans.[110]

Some travelers could thus distinguish between different kinds of Other by their attitude to labor.

Like Pallas, Sumarokov also suggested the resettlement of the Tatars in faraway lands in the Volga and Ural regions, and if this was impossible, at least on the Crimean steppe, replacing them with "foreign newcomers,"[111] or Greeks and Armenians. However, his arguments differed from Pallas's. First, it would ensure the security of Crimea: clearly, Sumarokov viewed the Tatars as potential allies of the Ottomans. Second, in a new location, where Russia would retain the Tatar's traditional self-government, they would better adapt themselves to the new imperial realities.[112] However, Tatar conservatism still had some good benefits, as their morality and manners were undamaged by civilization:

> The preservation of ancient customs and the removal of evil caused by the Enlightenment are the reasons for the uncorrupted character of the Tatars. They are honest, simple-hearted, complacent, non-mammonish, naturally gifted with wit and very hospitable, but disposed to severity and revenge. Theft, not indulged by abundance, and drinking, prohibited by Muslim law, are scarcely known here.[113]

Of course, this idea was closely connected with his notion of Crimea as an earthly paradise and a Rousseauian *topos* of noble savages.

According to Pallas, "Tatar sloth" had an impact on their society. Combined with their usual manner of dressing their women in Turkish "silks and staffs, embroidered with gold," the extreme idleness of the laboring class produced

---

110 Paul Guibal, *Obozrenie Kryma, Novorossii i Kavkaza v dnevnike puteshestviia iz Odessy v Tiflis, 1818–1819*, trans. T. P. Peters (Moscow: Russkii Mir, 2017), 57.

111 Sumarokov, *Dosugi krymskogo sud'i*, 1:168.

112 Sumarokov, *Dosugi krymskogo sud'i*, 1:167–69; see also: Sumarokov, *Puteshestvie po vsemu Krymu i Bessarabii v 1799 godu*, 181–88.

113 Sumarokov, *Puteshestvie po vsemu Krymu i Bessarabii v 1799 godu*, 180.

only "very few wealthy individuals among the Tatars."[114] In Sumarokov's view, the lack of distinction between Tatar nobles and ordinary people distinguished them from Russian society, with its marked contrast between landlords and peasants.[115] According to Pallas, laziness also left a physical mark on the Tatars: "any disorders prevail among them, except the itch arising from sloth or infection, and rheumatic complaints."[116]

Two issues require comment: first, "Laziness" as a marker of Otherness appears in western accounts of remote countries, from Ireland and Greece to Egypt and Southeast Asia. Russian intellectuals adopted this discourse to describe Ukraine, Georgia, and Russian America. It made the mission of the colonizers/civilizers noble, presenting them as teachers of childish aborigines.[117] In the modern age landlords, economists, and sociologists have used the concept of the idleness of dependent populations (European peasants or North American slaves) to explain low incomes in the agricultural sphere.[118] Second, in the imagination of Crimean travelers, Tatar laziness was connected with the idea of an extraordinarily rich natural bounty supplying the locals with all the fruit and material necessary for a careless life. It was no accident that the discourse of idlers was always related to the fertile part of the country. Descriptions of its population change with the landscape. An example is Sumarokov's account of his journey to the Kerch Peninsula in eastern Crimea. It was a flat steppe "where you can but rarely see any kind of eminence, and there is neither a river, nor a spring, nor the smallest trace of wood."[119] This natural poverty changed the Tatars' character. "This lack of necessary things overcomes the idleness of the Tatars, and there, where another people may probably refuse to live, they have replaced natural poverty with industry."[120] Kaznacheev may have followed a similar logic in 1833, when, as the governor of a Crimea experiencing starvation, he organized public works for different ethnic groups, and the Tatars in particular. "Although the Tatars are not work lovers, the indigence will habituate

114   Pallas, *Travels*, 2:356.
115   Sumarokov, *Dosugi krymskogo sud'i*, 1:185–87.
116   Pallas, *Travels*, 2:361.
117   Khrapunov and Konkin, eds., *Problemy integratsii Kryma*, 337–39; Mircea Eliade, *Myths, Dreams and Mysteries: The Encounter between Contemporary Faiths and Archaic Realities* (New York: Harper & Row, 1967), 39–56; Syed Hussein Alatas, *The Myth of the Lazy Native* (London: Frank Cass, 1977); Ter Ellingson, *The Myth of the Noble Savage* (Los Angeles: University of California Press, 2001).
118   Alexander Etkind, *Priroda zla. Syr'e i gosudarstvo* (Moscow: Novoe literaturnoe obozrenie, 2020), 45, 52, 62, 280, 369–70.
119   Sumarokov, *Dosugi krymskogo sud'i*, 2:95.
120   Ibid.

them to labor, if not permanent, then temporary. One should be surprised by this people's love of idleness."[121]

Conclusion

Travelers viewed Crimea as the ideal place for an educational, romantic, or research journey. They were able there to reflect on the variety of human cultures, and racial and ethnic types. In the eyes of travelers, Crimean peoples evinced various traces of Otherness. Although the Tatars, Jews, Karaites, and Greeks could not be confused, they all had much in common. According to Sumarokov:

> The eastern peoples have firmly preserved everything related to their beliefs, rituals, and customs. After the passage of many centuries, we see among the Turks the same attire and costumes, as well as the same morals and oddities; among the Jews scarcely one fine button was added or removed on the cloth, and it well could be that their songs differ somewhat. Why does this happen? Because their clans do not mix, the rules of their lawmakers are strictly followed, and every kind of reasoning is removed. Like a woman of fashion, enlightenment likes changes; ignorance adheres to stability; enlightenment places vices in a row; ignorance is rooted in previous ones.[122]

The main features of the Other were conservatism, backwardness, and traditionalism. Travelers considered themselves men of the Enlightenment, dynamic and progressive; Crimeans were the opposite, though they still possessed some attractive and Romantic features.

Two important features of the descriptions of Crimean Others are analyzed above. First, I examined the similarity of topics discussed and the interpretation of Russian and western travelers who visited Crimea in the first decades of Russian rule.[123] The reason for this similarity may be the westernization of the Russian elite, who were familiar with foreign languages, read western literature,

---

121 Aleksandr Kaznacheev, *Partikuliarnye pis'ma grafu M.S. Vorontsovu 1828–1837 gg.* (Moscow: Novy khronograf, 2015), 188.

122 Sumarokov, *Dosugi krymskogo sud'i*, 1:109.

123 For the latter, see Khrapunov and Konkin, eds., *Problemy integratsii Kryma*, 329–52; Khrapunov, "Vostok v Evrope," 63–78.

and thus apprehended the achievements of the Enlightenment culture and its stereotypes and way of thinking. Second, I examined the enduring *topoi* which formed around 1800. An example is "Tatar laziness." In the second half of the nineteenth century, Dmitrii Semenov (1835–1902) compiled a popular reader for students that was republished several times. It describes Russia "according to travelers' accounts and scholarly research."[124] In the chapter on the Crimean Tatars, first published by Gustav Radde (1831–1903) in 1856, there is a passage on their "outstanding laziness."[125] However, this laziness was a wider marker: it was considered an attribute of Muslim Others, as one can see from the wide distribution of this *topos* in accounts of the Turks suggested by Russian publications during the Russo-Turkish war of 1877–78.[126]

Works Cited

Alatas, Syed Hussein. *The Myth of the Lazy Native*. London: Frank Cass, 1977.

Bartenev, Yurii, ed. "Yurii Nikitich Bartenev. 1840–1842." *Russkii arkhiv* 1 (1898): 100–24.

Batunskii, Mark. "Islam i russkaia kul'tura XVIII veka. Opyt istoriko-epistemologicheskogo issledovaniia." *Cahiers du monde russe et soviétique* 27, no. 1 (1986): 45–69.

Benckendorff, Alexander von. *Vospominaniia 1802–1837*. Edited by M. V. Sidorova and A. A. Litvin. Translated by O. V. Marinin. Moscow: Rossiiskii fond kul'tury, 2012.

Bobrovnikov, Vladimir. "Orientalizm v literature i politike na Severnov Kavkaze." In *Aziatskaia Rossiia: liudi i struktury imperii*. Omsk: Izdatel'stvo OmGU, 2005.

Campenhausen, Pierce-Balthazar von. *Travels through Several Provinces of the Russian Empire; With an Historical Account of the Zaporog Cossacks, and of Bessarabia, Moldavia, Wallachia, and the Crimea*. London: Richard Phillips, 1808.

---

124 Dmitrii Semenov, *Otechestvovedenie. Rossiia po rasskazam puteshestvennikov i uchenym issledovaniiam* (Moscow: Salaev, 1879), 2.
125 Ibid., 196–97.
126 Kati Parppei, "'This Battle Started Long Before Our Days . . .' The Historical and Political Context of the Russo-Turkish War in Russian Popular Publications, 1877–78," *Nationalities Papers* 49, no. 1 (2021): 171–73.

Chudinov, Aleksandr. *Zhil'ber Romm i Pavel Stroganov: istoriia neobychnogo soiuza*. Moscow: Novoe literaturnoe obozrenie, 2010.

Clarke, Edward Daniel. *Travels in Various Countries of Europe, Asia, and Africa. Part 1: Russia, Tahtary, and Turkey*. 4th ed. Vol. 2. London: T. Cadell and W. Davies, 1816.

Cross, Anthony. *U temzskikh beregov: rossiiane v Britanii v XVIII veke*. Translated by N. L. Luzhetskaia. St. Petersburg: Akademicheskii proekt, 1996.

———. *In the Land of the Romanovs: An Annotated Bibliography of First-Hand English-Language Accounts of the Russian Empire (1613–1917)*. Cambridge: Open Book Publishers, 2014.

Dickinson, Sara. "Russia's First 'Orient': Characterizing the Crimea in 1787." *Kritika: Explorations in Russian and Eurasian History* 3, vol. 1 (2002): 3–25.

———. *Breaking Ground: Travel and National Culture in Russia from Peter I to the Era of Pushkin*. Amsterdam and New York: Rodopi, 2006.

Durkheim, Émile. *The Elementary Forms of the Religious Life*. Translated by Joseph Ward Swain. London: George Allen & Unwin Ltd, 1915.

Eliade, Mircea. *Myths, Dreams, and Mysteries: The Encounter between Contemporary Faiths and Archaic Realities*. New York: Harper & Row, 1967.

Ellingson, Ter. *The Myth of the Noble Savage*. Los Angeles: University of California Press, 2001.

Etkind, Aleksandr. *Priroda zla. Syr'e i gosudarstvo*. Moscow: Novoe literaturnoe obozrenie, 2020.

Filiushkin, Aleksandr. "Kak Rossiia stala dlia Evropy Aziei?" In *Izobretenie imperii: iazyki i praktiki*, Edited by Il'ia Gerasimov, Marina Mogilner and Aleksandr Semenov, 10–48. Moscow: Novoe izdatel'stvo, 2011.

Geissler, Christian. *Byt i nravy russkogo naroda na rubezhe XVIII–XIX vekov*. Translated by V. V. Akunov, M. D. Bulycheva, and T. A. Grablevskaia. Moscow: Kuchkovo pole, 2015.

Germogen, Bishop. *Tavricheskaia eparkhiia*. Pskov: Tipografiia gubernskogo pravleniia, 1887.

Gorchakov, Dmitry. "Russkii u podoshvy Chatyrdaga." *Russkii arkhiv* 7–8 (1871): 1285–1288.

Griboedov, Aleksandr. *Polnoe sobrabie sochinenii*. Vol. 2. St. Petersburg: Notabene, 1999.

———. *Polnoe sobrabie sochinenii*. Vol. 3. St. Petersburg: Dmitry Bulanin, 2006.

Guibal, Paul. *Obozrenie Kryma, Novorossii i Kavkaza v dnevnike puteshestviia iz Odessy v Tiflis, 1818–1819*. Translated by T. P. Peters. Moscow: Russkii Mir, 2017.

Guthrie, Matthew. *A Tour, Performed in the Years 1795–6, through the Taurida, Or Crimea, the Ancient Kingdom of Bosphorus, the Once-Powerful Republic of Tauric Cherson, and All Other Countries on the North Shore of the Euxine, Ceded to Russia by the Peace of Kainardgi and Jassy; by Mrs. Maria Guthrie*. London: T. Cadell, Jun., and W. Davies, 1802.

Izmailov, Vladimir. *Puteshestvie v poludennuiu Rossiu. V pis'makh. Novoe izdanie*. Vol. 3. Moscow: Tipografiia Khristofora Klaudiia, 1805.

Kaznacheev, Aleksandr. *Partikuliarnye pis'ma grafu M.S. Vorontsovu 1828–1837 gg*. Moscow: Novyi khronograf, 2015.

Khrapunov, Nikita. "Obraz Kryma v zapiskakh frantsuzskogo emigranta Polia Gibalia." *Annuaire d'études françaises* (2018): 437–52.

———. "'Vostok v Evrope': Krym posle prisoedineniia k Rossiiskoi imperii glazami inostrantsev." *The New Past* 1 (2018): 63–78.

———. *Angliiskie puteshestvenniki i Krym. Konets XVIII–pervaia tret' XIX v.* Sevastopol: Al'batros, 2022.

Khrapunov, Nikita, and Denis Konkin, eds. *Problemy integratsii Kryma v sostav Rossii, 1783–1825*. Sevastopol: Al'batros, 2017.

Ligne, Charles-Joseph de. *The Prince de Ligne, His Memoires, Letters, and Miscellaneous Papers*. Translated by Katherine Prescott Wormeley. Vol. 2. Boston: Hardy, Pratt & Company, 1902.

Lopatin, Viacheslav, ed. *Ekaterina II i G.A. Potemkin. Lichnaia perepiska, 1769–1791*. Moscow: Nauka, 1997.

Markevich, Arsenii. "Taurica: opyt ukazatelia sochinenii, kasaiushchikhsia Kryma i Tavricheskoi gubernii voobshche." *Izvestiia Tavricheskoi uchenoi arkhivnoi komissii*, 20 (1864): 104–60; 28 (1898), 17–24; 32–33 (1902), 58–62.

Montesquieu, Charles. *The Spirit of Laws*. Vol. 1. Translated by Thomas Nugent. New York: The Colonial Press, 1899.

Orekhov, Vladimir. *V labirinte krymskogo mifa*. Veliky Novgorod, Simferopol, and Nizhny Novgorod: Rastr, 2017.

Osterhammel, Jürgen. *Unfabling the East: The Enlightenment's Encounter with Asia*. Translated by Robert Savage. Princeton: Princeton University Press, 2018.

Pallas, Peter Simon. *Travels through the Southern Provinces of the Russian Empire in the Years 1793 and 1794.* Translated from German. 2nd ed. Vol. 2. London: John Stockdale, 1812.

Parppei, Kati. "'This Battle Started Long Before Our Days...' The Historical and Political Context of the Russo-Turkish War in Russian Popular Publications, 1877–78." *Nationalities Papers* 49, no. 1 (2021): 162–79.

Prusskaia, Evgeniia. *Frantsuzskaia ekspeditsiia v Egipet 1798–1801 gg.: vzaimnoe vospriiatie dvukh tsivilizatsii.* Moscow: ROSSPEN, 2016.

Rousseau, Jean-Jacques. *Emile, or On Education.* Translated by Allan Bloom. New York: Basic Books, 1979.

Said, Edward. *Orientalism.* London: Penguin, 1977.

Sasse, Gwendolyn. *The Crimea Question: Identity, Transition, and Conflict.* Cambridge, MA: Harvard University Press, 2007.

Schimmelpenninck van der Oye, David. *Russian Orientalism: Asia in the Russian Mind from Peter the Great to the Emigration.* New Haven: Yale University Press, 2010.

Schönle, Andreas. *Authenticity and Fiction in the Russian Literary Journey, 1790–1840.* Cambridge, MA: Harvard University Press, 2000.

———. "Garden of the Empire: Catherine's Appropriation of the Crimea." *Slavic Review* 60, no. 1 (2001): 1–23.

Semenov, Dmitrii. *Otechestvovedenie. Rossiia po rasskazam puteshestvennikov i uchenym issledovaniiam.* 2nd ed. Vol. 2. Moscow: Salaev, 1879.

Ševčenko, Ihor. "Ukraine between East and West." *Harvard Ukrainian Studies* 16, no. 1–2 (1992): 174–83.

Slezkine, Yuri. "Naturalists versus Nations: Eighteenth-Century Russian Scholars Confront Ethnic Diversity." *Representations* 47 (1994): 170–95.

Sosnina, Ol'ga and Aleksandr Val'kovich, eds. *Orientalizm. Turetskii stil' v Rossii. 1760–1840-e.* Moscow: Kuchkovo pole, 2017.

Struve, Johann Christian von. *Travels in the Crimea.* Translated from German. London: G. and J. Robinson, 1802.

Sumarokov, Pavel. *Puteshestvie po vsemu Krymu i Bessarabii v 1799 godu.* Moscow: Universitetskaia tipografiia, 1800.

———. *Dosugi krymskogo sud'i, ili vtoroe puteshestvie v Tavridu.* Vol. 1. St. Petersburg: Imperatorskaia tipografiia, 1803.

———. *Dosugi krymskogo sud'i, ili vtoroe puteshestvie v Tavridu.* Vol. 2. St. Petersburg: Imperatorskaia tipografiia, 1805.

Tarasov, Dmitrii. *Imperator Aleksandr I. Poslednie gody tsarstvovaniia, bolezn' i pogrebenie.* Moscow: Kuchkovo pole, 2013.

Trepavlov, Vadim, ed. *Obrazy regionov v obshchestvennom soznanii i kul'ture Rossii (XVII–XIX vv.).* Tula: Grif i K, 2011.

Uspenskii, Gleb. *Sobranie sochinenii v deviati tomakh.* Vol. 7. Moscow: Gosudarstvennoe izdatel'stvo khudozhestvennoi literatury, 1957.

Voltaire. *Oeuvres complètes. Nouvelle édition.* Edited by Léon Thiessé. Vol. 3. Paris: Pourrat frères et companie, 1831.

Webster, James. *Travels through the Crimea, Turkey, and Egypt.* Vol. 1. London: Henry Colburn and Richard Bentley, 1830.

Wolff, Larry. *Inventing Eastern Europe: The Map of Civilization on the Mind of the Enlightenment.* Stanford: Stanford University Press, 1994.

———. *The Singing Turk: Ottoman Power and Operatic Emotions on the European Stage from the Siege of Vienna to the Age of Napoleon.* Stanford: Stanford University Press, 2016.

Zorin, Andrei. *By Fables Alone: Literature and State Ideology in Late Eighteenth- and Early Nineteenth-Century Russia.* Boston: Academic Studies Press, 2014.

8

Visually Integrating the Other Within: Imperial Photography and the Image of the Caucasus (1864–1915)

Dominik Gutmeyr-Schnur

Abstract

This chapter focuses on the formation and development of the visual image of the Caucasus in the era of photography. Relating to discourses on knowledge production and dissemination within the visual construction of the Caucasus as part of imperial Russia, it shows how early photography produced a multiplicity of images that allowed a representational transition of a region from an external "other" to an internal periphery. Drawing on the argument that the Russian nation-building project distinguished between the Empire and Russian national territory, the author asks for the place of the Caucasus within a differentiation between nationalized and colonial space. For this purpose, I investigate the 1867 All-Russian Ethnographic Exhibition and Sergei Prokudin-Gorskii's album *Views in the Caucasus and Black Sea Area* (1905–1915) and underscore that strategies of visualizing the empire eventually contributed to the ambiguity of the image of the Caucasus in imperial Russia that goes beyond a binary understanding of "Russianness" and colonial "other."

Introduction

Scholarly work on both the Caucasus in the nineteenth century and the development of photography in imperial Russia is rich, but they have been little addressed together.[1] However, visualization through photography played an important role in the state's attempt to define the conventions for the representation of the Russian Empire and how it was intended to be imagined by the contemporary audience. I therefore focus my analysis in this chapter on the formation and development of the visual image of the Caucasus in the era of imperial photography. Drawing on the argument that the Russian nation-building project distinguished between the empire and Russian national territory,[2] I investigate the place of the Caucasus within the imperial project in the second half of Europe's long nineteenth century.

To do this, I investigate two cornerstones of the development of photography in the Russian Empire: first, the 1867 All-Russian Ethnographic Exhibition; and second, Sergei Prokudin-Gorskii's album *Views in the Caucasus and Black Sea Area* (undated but produced between 1907 and 1915; title devised by the staff of the Library of Congress). I argue that photography in imperial service produced an archive that allowed the mental appropriation of a region through its representational transition from an external exotic other to an internal province. The two cornerstones bridge half a century, from the mandatory incorporation of the "most important works of Russian photography"[3] to the collections of the Imperial Public Library in St. Petersburg in 1856 to the Russian Revolution of 1917 and the fall of the empire, which pulled the carpet from under Prokudin-Gorskii's epic project. In this period the invention—commonly dated with Daguerre's 1839 presentation at the Parisian Academy of Sciences—and global circulation of photographic technology and practices coincided with the Russian Empire's

1 See, for example, Sergei V. Boglachev, *Pervye fotografy Kavkaza* (Piatigorsk: Sneg, 2013); Svetlana Gorshenina and Heather S. Sonntag, "Early Photography as Cultural Transfer in Imperial Russia: Visual Technology, Mobility and Modernity in the Caucasus and Central Asia," *Khazar Journal of Humanities and Social Sciences*, Special Issue (2018): 322–44. Karina Solovyova and Inessa Kouteinikova, "A Different Caucasus: Early Triumphs of Photography in the Caucasus," in *Slaviane Evropy i narody Rossii. K 140-letiiu pervoi etnograficheskoi vystavki 1867 goda*, ed. Nataliia M. Kalashnikova (St. Petersburg: Slaviia, 2016).

2 Alexei Miller, *The Romanov Empire and Nationalism* (Budapest: Central European University Press, 2008), 175–76.

3 Jelena Barchatowa, "Die erste nationale Fotosammlung," in *Bilder eines Reiches*, ed. Boris Groys and Peter Weibel (Berlin: Kehrer, 2012), 50.

expansion towards the Caucasus and Central Asia, which eventually provided the basis for a photographic archive as "a form of collective colonial memory"[4] in these imaginative geographies.

My chapter thereby follows the present volume's overall theme to engage with the fluctuation of images of the "other" in the Russian Empire and their relationship to the process of colonializing expansion across Eurasia. Building on Edward Said's blind spot toward Russia's colonialism, the past twenty years' prominent scholarly debate on "Russian Orientalism" has shown its particularly fluctuant nature, both in its display and in its geographical location, dependent on the stage of Russia's imperial project and expansion.[5] The associated visual representation of the Russian Empire's "others" has so far been unequally investigated in regard to its geographic localization. Central Asia has received the most scholarly attention, which reflects the Russian state's prominent adoption of photography as an instrument of rule and representation during the empire's military campaigns in the region throughout the 1860s to 1880s.[6] For the Caucasus, it mostly remains a scholarly desideratum for which I address the state's similar ambition to turn the Caucasus from an "external other" and a source of Romantic reveries into an internal province. Concerning discourses on knowledge production and dissemination within the visual construction of the Caucasus as part of the Russian Empire, I explore the political-national co-option of the photograph against the backdrop of two columns of the attempt to establish an imperial photographic archive. However, I do not argue that this was uncontested, and I agree with the postcolonial criticism that "the Saidian picture of a unidirectional manifestation of cultural power"[7] does not inevitably result in an exclusive image of an "imperial Caucasus," arguing that the photographic history in the empire's southern borderlands is more complex in terms of reciprocal influences and amalgamation processes. The

---

4   James S. Ryan, *Picturing Empire: Photography and the Visualization of the British Empire* (London: Reaktion, 1997), 12.

5   See, for example, David Schimmelpenninck van der Oye, *Russian Orientalism: Asia in the Russian Mind from Peter the Great to the Emigration* (New Haven: Yale University Press, 2010).

6   See, among many, Margaret Dikovitskaya, "Central Asia in Early Photographs: Russian Colonial Attitudes and Visual Culture," *Slavic Eurasian Studies* 14 (2007): 99–133; Kate Fitz–Gibbon, "Emirate and Empire: Photography in Central Asia 1858–1917," *SSRN*, September 29, 2009, https://ssrn.com/abstract=1480082; Heather S. Sonntag, "Genesis of the Turkestan Album 1871–1872. The Role of Russian Military Photography, Mapping, Albums & Exhibitions on Central Asia" (PhD diss., University of Wisconsin-Madison, 2011).

7   Alexander Etkind, "Orientalism Reversed: Russian Literature in the Times of Empires," *Modern Intellectual History* 4, no. 3 (2007): 621.

study of vernacular photographic traditions thereby remains another scholarly desideratum.[8]

Photography and the Romantic Caucasus in the Public Empire

A feature of Europe's long nineteenth century (1789–1914) was that it was an era of the growth of the "public" domain and was related to new practices of owning "public things."[9] Elites across the continent not only developed an interest in their nation's history but especially pursued the survey of its manifestation in the form of historic monuments. As early as 1826, the Russian Ministry of Internal Affairs disseminated an order among provincial governors to compile lists of all "monuments of architecture" in their provinces, add a visual survey of the facades of historical buildings, and prevent their demolition.[10] It thereby sought to establish an all-empire register of architectural antiquities. Although this first attempt at an official survey failed because of unclear instructions and the governors' concern about additional expenses entailed by state monuments, it testifies to the state's increasing ambition to collect and categorize its territories and history while relying on visual documentation.

The potential of photography for surveying historic monuments was therefore explored from the technology's earliest days. When François Arago presented the daguerreotype to the French Chamber of Deputies, he praised "the extraordinary advantages which could have been derived from so exact and rapid a means of reproduction," because it needed only one photograph "to copy the millions of hieroglyphics which cover even the exterior of the great monuments of Thebes, Memphis, Karnak, and others."[11] The ensuing years

8 See, for example, Dominik Gutmeyr, "The Oil Boom and the Beginnings of Photography in Imperial Baku: Co-Constructing Knowledge in an Industrial City," in *Migration, Knowledge Exchange and Academic Cultures: Europe and the Black Sea Region before WWI*, ed. Biljana Ristovska-Josifovska (Skopje: Institute of National History, 2021).

9 Ekaterina Pravilova, *A Public Empire: Property and the Quest for the Common Good in Imperial Russia* (Princeton: Princeton University Press, 2014).

10 Ibid., 135.

11 François Arago, "Report [on the daguerreotype, presented to the French Chamber of Deputies]," trans. from the French cit. *History of Photography*, ed. Josef Maria Eder (New York: Dover, 1978), 234.

and decades saw a steady increase in state-sponsored recording and surveying projects based on photography.[12]

In attempting to collect, categorize, and eventually exhibit its territories, the Russian Empire could build on the enormous symbolic capital of some of its realms such as Crimea[13] or the Caucasus. The first time a camera focused on the southern borderlands along the Caucasus mountain range was in 1843, when the chemist Carl Julius Fritzsche, an associate of the Imperial Academy of Sciences in St. Petersburg, was commissioned for an expedition to investigate mineral springs in the south of the empire. He was accompanied by Sergei L. Levitskii, who would one day become one of the most famous photographers in the Russian Empire but was then still an amateur with a camera. Levitskii was assigned to take photographs of Caucasus vistas around the spa towns of Piatigorsk and Kislovodsk. The first series of photographs of the Caucasus, and the first prominent series of Russian landscape photography, built on a contemporary understanding of the Caucasus as an exotic borderland within a romantic imagination of the region as an external other. Into the first decades of the Caucasian War (1817–1864) the region played the role of "the Oriental muse"[14] in Russia's imperialist imagination, for which the image of the Caucasus and its native population as an exotic other was strongly shaped by Russian Romanticism.[15]

Levitskii's mountain vistas would therefore not have come into being, nor would they have sparked much interest, were it not for a complex network of political, cultural, and economic relationships. If Aleksander S. Pushkin had not "discovered the Caucasus" in the sense that he had "securely fixed the territory on the readership's cultural horizon in 1822"[16] with his narrative poem *The Captive of the Caucasus* (*Kavkazskii plennik*)—a poem through which "Russian society made the acquaintance of the Caucasus for the first

12 Elizabeth Edwards, *The Camera as Historian. Amateur Photographers and Historical Imagination, 1885–1918* (Durham: Duke University Press, 2012), 4–5.

13 See, for example, Sara Dickinson, "Russia's First 'Orient': Characterizing the Crimea in 1787," in *Orientalism and Empire in Russia*, eds. Michael David-Fox, Peter Holquist, and Alexander Martin (Bloomington: Slavica 2006); Kerstin S. Jobst, *Die Perle des Imperiums. Der russische Krim-Diskurs im Zarenreich* (Konstanz: UVK, 2007).

14 Schimmelpenninck van der Oye, *Russian Orientalism: Asia in the Russian Mind from Peter the Great to the Emigration*, 60–74.

15 See, for example, Susan Layton, *Russian Literature and Empire: Conquest of the Caucasus from Pushkin to Tolstoy* (Cambridge: Cambridge University Press, 1994); Katya Hokanson, *Writing at Russia's Border* (Toronto: University of Toronto Press, 2008); Harsha Ram, *The Imperial Sublime: A Russian Poetics of Empire* (Madison: University of Wisconsin Press, 2003).

16 Layton, *Russian Literature and Empire: Conquest of the Caucasus from Pushkin to Tolstoy*, 5.

time"[17]—Levitskii's photographs would not have been able to automatically build on a rich cultural capital. Furthermore, the photographer was equipped with one of Russian daguerreotypist Aleksei F. Grekov's cameras, which had one of Charles Chevalier's combined glass lenses. This made it interesting for the latter to exhibit the images at industrial expositions in France. Had the poetic conceptualization of the Caucasus as a "new Parnassus," international technological innovation, imperialist expansionism, and government support for topographic documentation combined with an understanding of photography as a craft rather than an art not converged, Levitskii would not have released his shutter vis à vis the mountain range, the images would not have circulated widely and been acclaimed, and no one would consider the region "a cradle of Russian photography."[18]

However, the romanticized representation of a Caucasus inspired by the fascination for the alpine sublime and drawing on the rich Caucasus genre in Russian literature was supplemented and partly supplanted by the output of an increasingly institutionalized academia that again turned to (visual) surveys of the regions the affiliated scholars sought to explore. Photography was considered a medium of objective representation, appearing to constitute an ideal method of documentation to meet the desire to gather and impart knowledge of the Russian Empire's various provinces and peoples. At the nexus of travel literature, the disciplines of geography, ethnography, and anthropology, and the technological progress of photography, the imagination of the imperial peripheries changed, which ultimately also affected the image of the Caucasus.

Ethnographers' Delayed Embrace of Photography

The lack of universities and branches of the Academy of Sciences outside the imperial centers led to the establishment of new societies that articulated a particular interest in the exploration of the empire's new provinces. The (Imperial) Russian Geographical Society (Russkoe geograficheskoe obshchestvo, (I)RGO) was established in 1845. It represents the nineteenth-century encouragement of people to organize according to their interests and fields of study. The first years of the society's work were shaped by various visions of "ethnography" because, on the one hand, the RGO co-founder and

---

17 Vissarion G. Belinskii, *Polnoe sobranie sochinenii* (Moscow: Akademiia nauk, 1953–59), 7:372.
18 Solovyova and Kouteinikova, "A Different Caucasus: Early Triumphs of Photography in the Caucasus," 135.

naturalist Karl Ernst von Baer understood the discipline as a science of empire with an emphasis on the diversity of the human race (physical anthropology) and, on the other, the long-term chairman and folklorist Nikolai I. Nadezhdin envisioned a study of nationality (*narodnost'*) with a particular focus on the study of the Russian people rather than of the peoples of Russia. Although divided in its disciplinary orientation, the RGO was united in its ambition to collect, order, and preserve data on the Russian Empire. A first ethnographic survey resulted in more than two thousand responses, with descriptions from all over the empire and information about a broad variety of places and groups.[19] By the mid-nineteenth century—and in response to both the era of Great Reforms and the RGO's success and prestige—reports and expeditions to the Russian Empire's provinces had become booming enterprises.[20]

The increase in the scientific exploration of the empire did not immediately result in an embrace of photography. The dominant faction around Nadezhdin in the RGO remained true to the tradition of European humanism and linguistic analyses in addressing the meaning of texts as visual representation, which continued to be regarded as an aesthetic side product.[21] Although the RGO had already opened a branch in Tbilisi in 1851, engagement with photography as a means of documenting the Caucasus was at first primarily confined to the military, where graduates from the Military Topographical Department (Voenno-topograficheskii otdel, VTO) were instructed to take photographs of the landscape and the lives and customs of the native population within the framework of military interests—in parallel with photography in Central Asia, given the background of the famous "Turkestan album."[22] The early publications of the RGO are therefore visibly devoid of illustrations—both drawings and prints based on photography—and a properly constituted committee even rejected proposals that sought to undertake photographic expeditions to the provinces of the empire.[23] The lesser influence of Baer and the natural sciences at the RGO meant that visual practices were subordinated to Nadezhdin and

19 See, for example, Nathaniel Knight, "Science, Empire, and Nationality: Ethnography in the Russian Geographical Society, 1845–1855," in *Imperial Russia: New Histories for the Empire*, ed. Jane Burbank and David L. Ransel (Bloomington: Indiana University Press, 1998), 125.

20 See, for example, Catherine B. Clay, "Russian Ethnographers in the Service of Empire, 1856–1862," *Slavic Review* 54, no. 1 (1995): 45–61.

21 Nathaniel Knight, "Russian Ethnography and the Visual Arts in the 1840s and 1850s," in *Visualizing Russia: Fedor Solntsev and Crafting a National Past*, ed. Cynthia Hyla Whittaker (Leiden: Brill, 2010), 141.

22 See, for example, Dikovitskaya, "Central Asia in Early Photographs: Russian Colonial Attitudes and Visual Culture": 104–8.

23 Knight, "Russian Ethnography and the Visual Arts in the 1840s and 1850s," 127–30.

the humanistic approach to the disciplines, for which it needed a new circle and institution to emerge with a sustainable influence on the use of photography and the public imagination of the empire.

Photography at the 1867 All-Russian Ethnographic Exhibition

By the 1860s the RGO faced institutional competition in the field of ethnography when the Society of Devotees of Natural Science, Anthropology and Ethnography (Imperatorskoe obshchestvo liubitelei estestvoznaniia, antropologii i etnografii, IOLEAE) was established in Moscow in 1863, followed by a separate anthropology section on the initiative of zoologist Anatolii P. Bogdanov a year later. Like Baer, he came from the natural sciences and conducted research into physical anthropology, which brought an openness to visual practices that influenced the newly established society. It quickly conceptualized its first major project in the 1867 All-Russian Ethnographic Exhibition (*Vserossiiskaia etnograficheskaia vystavka*), where the active use of visual material dominated both the preparation and execution from the outset.

The 1867 Exhibition constituted the first attempt to order, visualize, and present knowledge about the entire Russian Empire, while its planning coincided with the end of the conquest of the southern borderlands. Photography played a major role in production and presentation, for it became a medium of knowledge exchange with the conveners of the 1851 Great Exhibition at London's Crystal Palace, which hosted the first world fair, and whose anthropological section inspired Bogdanov and his committee to plan and realize an exhibition in the Russian Empire intended to compensate for the lack of a display of the peoples of Russia in London. Bogdanov thereby sought to confront the audience with representations of the various ethnic groups' "characteristic features" and eventually bridge a significant gap in the awareness of the Russian public, which to him appeared to know more about the populations of Africa and Australia than about the indigenous peoples inhabiting their own empire.[24] The organizing committee further decided to use photography as a tool for the documentation of the empire's ethnic groups—photographs that themselves became both

---

24 "Etnograficheskaia vystavka 1867 goda Imperatorskago Obshchestva Liubitelei Estestvoznaniia, Antropologii i Etnografii," *Izvestiia Imperatorskago Obshchestva Liubitelei Estestvoznaniia, Antropologii i Etnografii* 29 (1878): 1.

exhibited objects and allegedly objectifying blueprints for the mannequins at the center of the exhibition.[25]

For two months in 1867, the Moscow Manege became a panopticon that guided the visitor across the vast landmasses of the Russian Empire, spanning from Poland in the west to Russian America in the east. The regions and peoples who inhabited this vast space were exhibited and viewed by thousands of visitors, who flocked to the exhibition center to see what Bogdanov had conceptualized in an event with a didactic dimension, which in his view had a greater potential to reach out to the masses than public lectures or popular writings.[26] The exhibition finished with an anthropological section, compiled of as many as five hundred skulls and brains pickled in formaldehyde and a rich assortment of craniological measuring instruments, and a display of the ethnographic composition of the empire following the logics of geographical space. The visitor could follow a path within a recreated map of the empire and encounter representations of ethnic groups in the form of more than three hundred mannequins, sorted into almost sixty national and regional groups, along their corresponding place on that map.[27]

Although the exhibition's published protocols have repeatedly attracted scholarly interest, Ewa Manikowska has only recently documented the difficulty of accessing the photograph collections preserved today in the archives of the Russian Museum of Ethnography in St. Petersburg[28]—an experience shared by the author—for which an in-depth analysis of the set of two thousand photographs (and drawings) accumulated by that first all-Russian photographic survey remains another scholarly desideratum. We know from the protocols and the press coverage accompanying the exhibition that the use of photography, and what Nathaniel Knight calls the "imperative of authenticity,"[29] limited the organizers' concern by expressing the primacy of "Russianness" in the empire. While the state and its institutions were interested in collecting, ordering, and exhibiting knowledge of the empire, the 1867 organizers also had to cope with coexisting conceptions of identity derived from either an imperial or an ethnic belonging. Furthermore, a purely exoticizing display of non-Slavic

25 Ibid., 4–6.
26 Ibid., 1.
27 See, for example, Nathaniel Knight, *The Empire on Display: Ethnographic Exhibition and the Conceptualization of Human Diversity in Post-Emancipation Russia* (Washington, DC: NCEEER, 2001), 1–11.
28 Ewa Manikowska, *Photography and Cultural Heritage in the Age of Nationalisms: Europe's Eastern Borderlands (1867–1945)* (London et al.: Bloomsbury, 2019), 19.
29 Knight, *The Empire on Display: Ethnographic Exhibition and the Conceptualization of Human Diversity in Post-Emancipation Russia*, 21.

peoples—similar to the London Exhibition's conceptualization of "primitive non-European peoples"—would have thwarted the approach to an integrative display, with ethnic Russians as one nation among many in the empire. The exhibitions eventually overachieved in this ambition; contemporary commentators were especially critical of the ethnic Russian mannequins as subpar or even ugly, and thus by no means adequately or favorably presenting this group's cultural achievements.[30] The exhibition used a photographic survey to produce a visual framework that supported the idea of a diverse, multi-ethnic Russian Empire that integrated formerly exoticized provinces like the Caucasus in a pan-imperial narrative, but which also led to a conflict of interest with an increasingly important ethnic nationalism.

Studies by Ewa Manikowska[31] and Božidar Jezernik[32] have shown that the attempts to visualize (Slavic) peoples within and outside the Russian Empire had long-lasting implications for the (self-)representation of the groups on display in Moscow, often constituting a milestone in the development of regional photographic practices.[33] The photographic types from Poland that were used to support the narrative of imperial diversity were eventually reproduced in Polish scholarly books and exhibitions with the aim of underscoring a distinct Polish identity.[34] The display of these images in Moscow had furthermore underlined a second dimension that went beyond the pan-imperial narrative and extended into the Austro-Hungarian Empire. The society's scholarly ambitions were thereby supplemented by the Russian state's political aim of showcasing Slavic unity under Russian patronage: the event coincided with the Second Slavic Congress, which took place in Moscow and St. Petersburg, comprising not only Polish subjects but Montenegrins and Bulgarians, and culminated in the distribution of an informative German-language handbook containing guidelines for the collection of ethnographic objects among the Austro-Hungarian Slavs and the eventual production of twelve photographs of

---

30 Roland Cvetkovski, "Empire Complex: Arrangements in the Russian Ethnographic Museum, 1910," in *An Empire of Others: Creating Ethnographic Knowledge in Imperial Russia and the USSR*, ed. Roland Cvetkovski and Alexis Hofmeister (Budapest: Central European University Press), 215–16.

31 Manikowska, *Photography and Cultural Heritage in the Age of Nationalisms: Europe's Eastern Borderlands (1867–1945)*.

32 Božidar Jezernik, "The Moscow Ethnographic Exhibition of 1867," *Zbiór Wiadomości do Antropologii Muzealnej* 6 (2019): 7–28; Božidar Jezernik, "The Priest Matija Majar and the Moscow Ethnographic Exhibition of 1867," *Traditiones* 40, no. 2 (2011): 45–76.

33 See, for example, for Lithuania, Dainius Junevičius, "Lietuvos fotografų nuotraukos pirmojoje Rusijos etnografijos parodoje 1867 m," *Lietuvos kultūros tyrimai* 10 (2018): 142–62.

34 Manikowska, *Photography and Cultural Heritage in the Age of Nationalisms: Europe's Eastern Borderlands (1867–1945)*, 41.

four men and two women as models for wax figures that were presented at the Moscow Exhibition, designated as "Slovenians from the Zilja Valley."[35]

In Poland, reservation concerning pan-Slavism under Russian patronage paved the way for a reinterpretation of the photographs once the exhibition had concluded. As a directorial expression of power and rule, the exhibits from Poland were designated by their provenance rather than by their ethnonym,[36] while the mannequins from the Austro-Hungarian Empire were referred to as Slovenians.[37] The latter case irritated the Austrian press, which condemned the exhibition as a "Slavic national demonstration," presenting it as follows on the title page of the Viennese newspaper *Die Debatte und Wiener Lloyd* on April 25, 1867: "A pan-Slavic fraternization is a conspiracy against Austria—whoever participates in it—challenges all of Austria, and a cry of outrage is the only conceivable answer the peoples of Austria can give to those who participate in such an outrageous assassination attempt on Austria's existence." Meanwhile, the Slovenian writer France Jaroslav Štrukelj gladly referred to the exhibition as a milestone in national consciousness when calling on his compatriots not to "give away a single shack to the foreigners anymore!"[38]

Despite its central symbolic capital in nineteenth-century Russian culture, the Caucasus was poorly portrayed by comparison. The society's 1878 volume on the exhibition addresses the fact that in contrast with the region's famed diversity, the exhibition only managed to include thirteen mannequins from the Caucasus and concentrated almost exclusively on the territories south of the mountain range, omitting presentations of peoples like the Ossetians or Chechens. For the latter, the society included an explanatory footnote that the late arrival of costumes from the Caucasus had made the timely production of mannequins impossible. However, as long as photographs of the peoples in question compensated for the lack of mannequins, the exhibition's organizers' ambition to provide both scholars and the public with visual aids in the study of the empire's ethnography was satisfied.[39] Indeed, the photographs and drawings gave the audience a much more comprehensive image of the southern borderlands of the Caucasus. More than three hundred pictures, including views

---

35 Jezernik, "The Priest Matija Majar and the Moscow Ethnographic Exhibition of 1867," 48, 63.

36 *Ukazatel' Russkoi etnograficheskoi vystavki*, (Moscow: Universitetskaia tipografiia, 1867), 63–68.

37 Ibid., 73–76.

38 Cited in Jezernik, "The Priest Matija Majar and the Moscow Ethnographic Exhibition of 1867," 70.

39 "Etnograficheskaia vystavka 1867 goda Imperatorskago Obshchestva Liubitelei Estestvoznaniia, Antropologii i Etnografii," 29, 45–46.

from the Georgian Military Highway, Tiflis (Tbilisi), and two series amassing more than one hundred and thirty Caucasus "types" were thought to confront the visitors with a broad overview of the lands along the empire's southern mountain and the *inorodtsy* inhabiting them.[40]

The committee had elaborated a set of clear rules for the production and use of these photographs, which everyone contributing to the exhibition was asked to follow. An image of the sitter's face and his or her profile had to be taken, both for the production of the mannequin's head and the establishment of a photographic collection.[41] This requirement and the intention of establishing a corpus of comparable images was underlined by the decision of the exhibition's planning committee to offer a gold medal to anyone providing at least fifty pairs of portraits in a larger format between twenty-two and twenty-seven centimeters in length.[42] At least the Nizhny Novgorod based photographer Baptiste Barrault (B. Barro), who was also one of the few to be named in the catalogue and minutes of the 1867 exhibition, is known to have informed the organizers of his intention to produce at least fifty portraits and to have advertised his business by referring to the prize he received after the exhibition.[43] He and the other photographers interested in contributing were asked to search for "typicality" as the most central feature of the images and to submit their works by January 1, 1867 at the latest.

However, the committee was forced to realize that they could not rely on the services of enough photographers for several regions on display, so they were forced to include local governors, whom they asked to organize photographic portraits through their clerks.[44] The Caucasus was one of the regions for which this was the case: the organizers relied on the viceroy's financial co-contribution for the acquisition of ethnographic objects[45] and on the services of the Moscow-based studio "Caucasus Photography" by the Simonenko brothers. In 1865, following the death of his brother Aleksandr who had founded the studio, Petr Fedorovich Simonenko had continued to run the business and had thereby become one of the many early examples of "Caucasus photographers" who had mastered photography with the Caucasus army.[46] These professional ties

---

40 Ibid., 65–67.
41 Ibid., 4.
42 Ibid., 86.
43 Ibid., 91.
44 Ibid., 79–80.
45 Ibid., 37.
46 Tat'iana Shipova, *Moskovskie fotografy 1839–1930. Istoriia Moskovskoi fotografii* (Moscow: Planeta, 2012), 322.

to the southern borderlands were also probably the background for the name of the studio, but the career of Petr Simonenko is also representative of the first photographers in the region who had a military career. The graduates of the VTO, working for military interests, and the Caucasus army's photographic unit, which had been established in 1862 were thus sought to support the collection of topographical and ethnographic data on the region. The names of those who eventually conducted the assigned works therefore often remain unknown, which is also the case for many of the 1867 exhibition's Caucasus photographs, which bear an imprint of the VTO instead of a private studio—with exceptions such as Petr Simonenko, who was awarded a silver medal for his contribution.

The All-Russian Ethnographic Exhibition of 1867 is the first example of a large-scale project to create a public image of the Russian Empire. It is also the first example of such an initiative relying on a photographic survey in both its planning and implementation. The photographs produced were thought of as a medium of documentation but were simultaneously a medium of knowledge circulation, actively contributing to the reimagination of space for co-option for political purposes. The exhibition's goal, and that of learned societies such as the organizing IOLEAE, was to promote Russia in a sense that "the study of foreign lands can only be a supplement to the study of our own."[47] It thus contributed to a new mental appropriation of imperial provinces such as the Caucasus, which had until then been primarily understood as an external other. One of the exhibition's results was the creation of a first national photo collection, for it had been a precondition that the contributing photographers donated their works to the newly established Dashkov Museum of Ethnography within the Rumiantsev Museum, Moscow's first public museum. This collection was eventually complemented by a photographic survey by Torvald Mitreiter (also Mitreyter), a Danish photographer in service of the imperial court, who was commissioned to produce a set of about two hundred and fifty photographs of the 1867 mannequins on display in the Dashkov Museum in the 1880s.[48] The production of such a set of photographs, taken against an identical background, constituted the last step towards the exhibition's ambition to publicly collect

---

47 Address by co-founder Grigorii E. Shchurovskii to an 1867 IOLEAÈ meeting. Cited in Joseph Bradley, "Pictures at an Exhibition: Science, Patriotism, and Civil Society in Imperial Russia," *Slavic Review* 67, no. 4 (2008): 941.

48 Manikowska, *Photography and Cultural Heritage in the Age of Nationalisms: Europe's Eastern Borderlands (1867–1945)*, 25–26; Karina Iu. Solov'eva, "Obrazy narodov Rossiiskoi imperii 1860-kh godov. Po materialam Etnograficheskoi vystavki 1867 goda," in *Slaviane Evropy i narody Rossii. K 140-letiiu pervoi etnograficheskoi vystavki 1867 goda*, ed. Nataliia M. Kalashnikova (St. Petersburg: Slaviia, 2008), 60.

and display imperial space as united in diversity, thereby including formerly exoticized realms in the borderlands.

Supported by the Tsar: The Colorful Caucasus of Sergei Prokudin-Gorskii

A second column of the Russian Empire's photographic archive was constituted by the color images of the Russian Empire taken by Sergei Prokudin-Gorskii (1863–1944) between around 1904 and 1915. A pioneer of Russian color photography, Prokudin-Gorskii proposed the systematic documentation of the Russian Empire, for which he eventually gained Tsar Nicholas II's support in 1909. He was assigned to document the peripheral territories of the Russian Empire. His photographs, today kept at the Library of Congress in Washington, DC, span the empire from Karelia to Central Asia and from Siberia to the Caucasus, at a time of sociopolitical and technological change in the Russian Empire's last decade.[49] Unlike the scarcely known images from the 1867 exhibition, the digitization of the photographs by the Library of Congress[50] and its website's open accessibility have led to a profusion of coffee table books, making Prokudin-Gorskii's works the most known and widespread nineteenth-century photographs from the Russian Empire.

However, most titles that engage with the photographer's work emphasize the photographs' aesthetic dimension and high-resolution reproduction,[51] whereas a systematic in-depth analysis of the vast majority of the one thousand nine hundred glass-plate negatives and fourteen albums with identifications of images, which had survived the post-1918 journey into Parisian exile, has yet to be conducted. Furthermore, the images from the Caucasus often appear of peripheral interest within the photographer's corpus.[52] Using visual content

---

49 For more background see, for example, Véronique Koehler, *Voyage dans l'ancienne Russie. Les photographes en couleurs de Serguei Mikhaïlovitch Procoudine-Gorsky* (Paris: Albin Michel, 2013).

50 See Harold Leich, "The Prokudin–Gorskii Collection of Early 20th Century Color Photographs of Russia at the Library of Congress: Unexpected Consequences of the Digitization of the Collection, 2000–2017," *Slavic and East European Information Resources* 18, no. 3–4 (2017): 223–30.

51 See, for example, Robert Klanten, *Nostalgia: The Russian Empire of Czar Nicholas II Captured in Color Photographs by Sergei Mikhailovich Prokudin–Gorskii* (Berlin: Gestalten, 2012).

52 See, for example, William Craft Brumfield, *Journeys through the Russian Empire: The Photographic Legacy of Sergey Prokudin–Gorsky* (Durham: Duke University Press, 2020).

analysis,[53] I grouped the 255 single images of Prokudin-Gorskii's album *Views in the Caucasus and Black Sea Area* (for two more images only captions but no photographs are preserved, while a photograph of a small oil manufacturing building is reproduced twice in the album) into recurring motifs, which were then systematically grouped by types—a type differing from a motif in its degree of abstraction, effectively reducing the denotation of individual motifs to their pictorial statement. The formation of such types and subsequent image type analysis suggests that the representation of the Caucasus followed an implicit imperial agenda and primarily served four purposes.

Firstly, and based on Vera Tolz's suggestion of a state-framed Russian policy aimed at nation building fostering a sense of community and unity rather than the imperial domination of minorities,[54] the album's selection of ethnographic photographs represents an inclusive imagery of a multi-ethnic empire, offering a collective identity not only to Russians but the empire's minorities. Seventeen of the album's photographs—four of which constitute one page of the album with the page title "Types of Dagestan" (cf. fig. 1)—address the region's multi-ethnic composition. All are meticulously staged in the tradition of the nineteenth-century visual construction of Russianness and non-Russianness,[55] with national attire at the center of the viewer's attention. The portrayed clothes allowed certain groups to display the cultural traditions and national character of their respective imagined communities, especially the Georgians and the Armenians. The displayed clothing of these two groups also suggests their noble status. The caption "Georgian" is used exclusively for the former, contradicting earlier imperial policies that depicted the territory as ethnically heterogeneous by stressing its affiliation to Kartvelian tribal groups such as Svans, Mingrelians, and others in the 1897 census, for example.[56] For the latter, Prokudin-Gorskii chose to include Armenians from Artvin in the contested Russian-Ottoman borderlands rather than from the Erivan Governorate or the

---

53 See, for example, Elke Grittmann, "Methoden der Medienbildforschung in der Visuellen Kommunikationsforschung," in *Handbuch Visuelle Kommunikationsforschung*, ed. Katharina Lobinger (Wiesbaden: Springer, 2019); Elke Grittmann and Ilona Ammann, "Quantitative Bildtypenanalyse," in *Die Entschlüsselung der Bilder*, ed. Thomas Petersen and Clemens Schwender (Cologne: Halem, 2011).

54 Vera Tolz, "Orientalism, Nationalism, and Ethnic Diversity in Late Imperial Russia," *The Historical Journal* 48, no. 1 (2005): 132–36.

55 Elena Vishlenkova, "Strategies of the Visual Construction of Russianness and Non-Russianness, 1800–1830," in *Defining Self: Essays on Emergent Identities in Russia: Seventeenth to Nineteenth Centuries*, ed. Michael Branch (Helsinki: Finnish Literature Society, 2009).

56 Juliette Cadiot, "Searching for Nationality: Statistics and National Categories at the End of the Russian Empire (1897–1917)," *The Russian Review* 64, no. 3 (2005): 449–50.

city of Tbilisi, where Armenians constituted the single largest group in the early twentieth century. Prokudin-Gorskii also chose to portray the Black Sea coast's significant Greek minority as tea pickers with the plantation's Chinese foreman Lau Džen-Džau, showing a Russian medal on his vest, probably awarded for his contribution to the successful cultivation of tea in the Russian Caucasus. The type photographs also indicate a strong integration into the empire, for the portrayed Lezgin is shown wearing a medal of honor on his chest with a bust of Tsar Alexander III. In the interest of the state, which funded Prokudin-Gorskii's work, the ethnographic photographs in the album created an image of visual cohesion supporting the empire's territorial integrity.

Secondly, this collective identity is underscored by the region's presentation as a source of idyll and inspiration—a remnant of Romanticism—that accompanied Prokudin-Gorskii's ambition to "arouse love for the motherland, interest in studying its beauties and inexhaustible riches"[57] with his photographs.

FIGURE 1. Types of Dagestan. Library of Congress, Prints & Photographs Division, Prokudin-Gorskii Collection [LOT 10336, p. 43].

---

57 Cited in Dikovitskaya, "Central Asia in Early Photographs: Russian Colonial Attitudes and Visual Culture": 112.

Of particular importance is the visualization of the garden, an oft-stressed allegory of paradise across confessional boundaries.[58] More than a quarter of the photographs (71 out of 255) prominently emphasize a (botanical) garden, plantation, or (subtropical) plant (see fig. 2). The "metaphor of a mountainous landscape as a space of diversity"[59] thereby strengthened the first aim to visualize the region as an ethnically diverse space, used in particular by a page with the caption "In the Mountains of Dagestan." It is no coincidence that this is opposite the "Types of Dagestan" page. It is notable that despite the prominent caption "Caucasus" on the first page of the album, Prokudin-Gorskii took most of his images along the Black Sea coast and its direct hinterlands. The renowned views of the snow-capped peaks such as Kazbegi, Elbrus, and Ushba are therefore omitted, whereas the only views of rocky Caucasus peaks come from its western

FIGURE 2. Bamboo in Chakva [Bamboo. Chakva]. Library of Congress, Prints & Photographs Division, Prokudin-Gorskii Collection [LC–DIG–prokc–21517].

58 Dževad Karahasan, *Knjiga vrtova. O jeziku i strahu* (Zagreb: Antibarbarus, 2002).
59 Oksana Sarkisova, *Screening Soviet Nationalities: Kulturfilms from the Far North to Central Asia* (London and New York: I. B. Tauris, 2017), 147.

spur in Dagestan. Despite his prominent support by the Ministry of Railway Transport, it remains unknown whether he had access to the mountains.

Thirdly, the included photographs documenting the growth of industrial infrastructure—for example, drying ovens for tea, a glass factory in Borjomi on the railway tracks (see fig. 3), or a steam room for the treatment of bamboo poles—need to be understood against the backdrop of the narrative of Russia being a source of progress and innovation, despite its belated industrialization. These images build on the prominent series of Baku oil wells, the building of the Georgian Military Highway, or the laying of the Caucasus railway tracks (for example, by Aleksandr Mishon, Dimitrii Ermakov, and Vladimir Barkanov), establishing a visual contrast between periphery and progress—a contrast the imperial policy it is suggested can bridge. Hence, Prokudin-Gorskii does not place the romanticized landscape in a contradictory juxtaposition with his industrial-technological photographs but supports the narrative of the transition of the Caucasus into a malleable province through the latter. These two aspects also converge in the conceptualization of the Caucasus landscape as a source of

FIGURE 3. A Glass Factory in Borjomi [Glass factory in Borzhom]. Library of Congress, Prints & Photographs Division, Prokudin-Gorskii Collection [LC–DIG–prokc–21571].

recreation, also visible in the prominent genre of spa town photography, as in Prokudin-Gorskii's photographs of the Borjomi Gorge. This is connected with the narrative of the imperial state, enabling a re-conceptualization of wilderness as recreational space, for the image shows a gorge with roads, railway tracks, and telegraph poles instead of an untouched side valley.

Fourthly, the album visually presents the historical past preserved in ancient monuments, which correlates to Austin Jersild's analysis of nineteenth-century scholars' obsession with antiquity, resulting in a vision of a "dormant and degraded land long after its fall from grace."[60] Driven by the idea that photography would be able to produce "exact" representations, archaeologists addressed their ambition to objectify the documentation of their research and thus make use of photography, which increasingly began to supplant other processes of reproduction. However, an image is no simple reproduction of a certain circumstance or matter but co-constructs knowledge by modifying, organizing, or even creating it.[61] At a time when photography was emerging as an increasingly important mode of data capture and transmission,[62] Prokudin-Gorskii's interest in photographing the remains of a Byzantine church or eleventh- to fourteenth-century monastic complexes like the Timotesubani Monastery (see fig. 4) reflects the attempt to connect with a premodern period of prosperity. According to the photographer's memoirs, it was exactly these photographs of antiquities and ancient monuments that prompted most attention from the tsar.[63]

The official support of Prokudin-Gorskii's photography had foreseen the establishment of a public visual archive in response to a hegemonic project. The types represented in the *Views in the Caucasus and Black Sea Area* album correlate with the initial ambition of incorporating the entire collection of images into the curriculum and offering an imperial patriotism in reply to any national, social, or political tensions in the early twentieth century. However, these plans were never enacted, and while some photographs were prominently integrated in the celebration of the Romanov Tercentenary in 1913, the outbreak of World

---

60 Austin L. Jersild, *Orientalism and Empire: North Caucasus Mountain Peoples and the Georgian Frontier, 1845–1917* (Montreal: McGill–Queen University Press, 2012), 68.
61 Geimer, "Einleitung," in *Ordnungen der Sichtbarkeit. Fotografie in Wissenschaft, Kunst und Technologie*, ed. Peter Geimer (Frankfurt/Main: Suhrkamp, 2002), 7.
62 Christopher Pinney, *Photography and Anthropology* (London: Reaktion, 2011), 21.
63 See, for example, Svetlana Garanina, "Sergei Mikhailovich Prokudin–Gorsky," *The World of 1900–1917 in Color/Mir 1900–1917 v tsvete*, published 2003; accessed June 12, 2022, http://www.prokudin-gorsky.ru/download/Prokudin-Gorsky%20Biography.pdf, 19.

FIGURE 4. Timotesubani Monastery [Timotis-Ubanskii Monastery]. Library of Congress, Prints & Photographs Division, Prokudin-Gorskii Collection [LC–DIG– prokc–21673].

War I eventually put an end to the project.[64] While Prokudin-Gorskii suggested presenting his audience with the "real Russia and its ancient monuments,"[65] his works offer an insight into a commissioned documentation with blanks of sociopolitical questions and economic shortcomings. The album therefore reveals more about the photographer's understanding of his role in the process and the Russian perception of its southern borderlands than about the region *per se* at the turn of the century. His take on color photography as the most accurate means of protocolary reproduction of its time[66] supported the ambition of

---

64 See e.g. Henning Lautenschläger, "Prokudin-Gorskij," in *De Gruyter Allgemeines Künstlerlexikon. Die bildenden Künstler aller Zeiten und Völker*, edited by Andreas Beyer (Berlin: De Gruyter, 2018), 97:69.

65 Cited in Svetlana Garanina, "Delo Kantseliarii Soveta Ministrov o priobretenii v kaznu kollektsii fotograficheskikh snimkov dostoprimechatel'nostei Rossii S. M. Prokudina-Gorskogo, 1910–1912 gg," *Rossiiskii Arkhiv: Istoriia otechestva v svidetel'stvakh i dokumentakh XVIII–XX vv.* IX (1999): 468.

66 Prokudin-Gorskii, "Pamiatniki stariny Mariinskoi sistemy i verkhnego Povolzh'ia i neskol'ko slov o znachenii tsvetnoi fotografii," in *Trudy IV s'ezda russkikh zodchikh*, ed. Viktor V. Eval'd (St. Petersburg: Gosudarstvennaia tipografiia, 1911), 593.

reimagining the Russian Empire within a narrative of cohesion. Consequently, the entanglement with the state and the prominence of Prokudin-Gorskii's work complicated the late imperial image of the Caucasus, for it constituted a production and reframing of a once Orientalized realm with high symbolic capital which could still be built into a constituent of the empire. *Views in the Caucasus and Black Sea Area* reflects this process of negotiating the image of the Caucasus, and the idea of state and empire in the periphery.

Conclusion

It was not only the literary Caucasus that evolved throughout the long nineteenth century—from Pushkin's genre-building *The Captive of the Caucasus* to Lev N. Tolstoy, who was masterfully portrayed on the occasion of his eightieth birthday by none other than Sergei Prokudin-Gorskii, and his final take on the region in *Hadzhi Murat*—but photography also played a key role in the imperial project to mentally appropriate the empire's peripheral provinces in a narrative of imperial cohesion and the empire's supremacy regarding national identities. With this aim, the Russian state actively fostered surveys of the empire that sought both to create a visual archive of a coherent empire and engage with the public. The All-Russian Ethnographic Exhibition of 1867 and Prokudin-Gorskii's generously supported tour through the Russian Empire's provinces combined these ambitions, underscoring the state's intention of visually integrating the other within.

Works Cited

Arago, François. "Report [on the daguerreotype, presented to the French Chamber of Deputies]." Translated from the French, cit. *History of Photography*. Edited by Josef Maria Eder (1978), 232–45. 4th ed. New York: Dover, 1932.

Barchatowa, Jelena. "Die erste nationale Fotosammlung." In *Bilder eines Reiches*. Edited by Boris Groys and Peter Weibel, 50–55. Berlin: Kehrer, 2012.

Belinskii, Vissarion G. *Polnoe sobranie sochinenii*. Vol. 7. Moscow: Akademiia nauk, 1959.

Boglachev, Sergei V. *Pervye fotografy Kavkaza*. Piatigorsk: Sneg, 2013.

Bradley, Joseph. "Pictures at an Exhibition: Science, Patriotism, and Civil Society in Imperial Russia." *Slavic Review* 67, no. 4 (2008): 934–66.

Brumfield, William Craft. "The Color Photographs of Sergei Mikhailovich Prokudin-Gorskii." *Visual Resources* 6, no. 3 (1990): 243–56.

———. *Journeys through the Russian Empire: The Photographic Legacy of Sergey Prokudin-Gorsky*. Durham: Duke University Press, 2020.

Cadiot, Juliette. "Searching for Nationality: Statistics and National Categories at the End of the Russian Empire (1897–1917)." *The Russian Review* 64, no. 3 (2005): 440–55.

Clay, Catherine B. "Russian Ethnographers in the Service of Empire, 1856–1862." *Slavic Review* 54, no. 1 (1995): 45–61.

Cvetkovski, Roland. "Empire Complex: Arrangements in the Russian Ethnographic Museum, 1910." In *An Empire of Others: Creating Ethnographic Knowledge in Imperial Russia and the USSR*. Edited by Roland Cvetkovski and Alexis Hofmeister, 211–51. Budapest: Central Eastern University Press, 2014.

Dickinson, Sara. "Russia's First 'Orient'. Characterizing the Crimea in 1787." In *Orientalism and Empire in Russia*. Edited by Michael David-Fox, Peter Holquist, and Alexander Martin, 85–106. Bloomington: Slavica, 2006.

Dikovitskaya, Margaret. "Central Asia in Early Photographs: Russian Colonial Attitudes and Visual Culture." *Slavic Eurasian Studies* 14 (2007): 99–133.

Edwards, Elizabeth. *The Camera as Historian. Amateur Photographers and Historical Imagination, 1885–1918*. Durham: Duke University Press, 2012.

Etkind, Alexander. "Orientalism Reversed: Russian Literature in the Times of Empires." *Modern Intellectual History* 4, no. 3 (2007): 617–28.

"Etnograficheskaia vystavka 1867 goda Imperatorskago Obshchestva Liubitelei Estestvoznaniia, Antropologii i Etnografii." *Izvestiia Imperatorskago Obshchestva Liubitelei Estestvoznaniia, Antropologii i Etnografii* XXIX (1878).

Fitz-Gibbon, Kate. "Emirate and Empire: Photography in Central Asia 1858–1917," SSRN, September 29, 2009. https://ssrn.com/abstract=1480082.

Garanina, Svetlana. "Delo Kantseliarii Soveta Ministrov o priobretenii v kaznu kollektsii fotograficheskikh snimkov dostoprimechatel'nostei Rossii S. M. Prokudina–Gorskogo, 1910–1912 gg." *Rossiiskii Arkhiv: Istoriia otechestva v svidetel'stvakh i dokumentakh XVIII–XX vv.* IX (1999): 466–92.

———. "Sergei Mikhailovich Prokudin-Gorsky." *The World of 1900–1917 in Color/Mir 1900–1917 v tsvete*. 2003. Accessed June 12, 2022. http://www.prokudin-gorsky.ru/download/Prokudin-Gorsky%20Biography.pdf.

Geimer, Peter. "Einleitung." In *Ordnungen der Sichtbarkeit. Fotografie in Wissenschaft, Kunst und Technologie*. Edited by Peter Geimer, 7–25. Frankfurt/Main: Suhrkamp, 2002.

Gorshenina, Svetlana and Heather S. Sonntag. "Early Photography as Cultural Transfer in Imperial Russia: Visual Technology, Mobility and Modernity in the Caucasus and Central Asia." *Khazar Journal of Humanities and Social Sciences*, Special Issue (2018), 322–44.

Grittmann, Elke. "Methoden der Medienbildforschung in der Visuellen Kommunikationsforschung." In *Handbuch Visuelle Kommunikationsforschung*. Edited by Katharina Lobinger, 527–46. Wiesbaden: Springer, 2019.

Grittmann, Elke and Ilona Ammann. "Quantitative Bildtypenanalyse." In *Die Entschlüsselung der Bilder*. Edited by Thomas Petersen and Clemens Schwender, 163–78. Cologne: Halem, 2011.

Gutmeyr, Dominik. "The Oil Boom and the Beginnings of Photography in Imperial Baku: Co-Constructing Knowledge in an Industrial City." In *Migration, Knowledge Exchange and Academic Cultures: Europe and the Black Sea Region before WWI*. Edited by Biljana Ristovska-Josifovska, 271–96. Skopje: Institute of National History, 2021.

Hokanson, Katya. *Writing at Russia's Border*. Toronto: University of Toronto Press, 2008.

Jersild, Austin L. *Orientalism and Empire. North Caucasus Mountain Peoples and the Georgian Frontier, 1845–1917*. Montreal: McGill-Queen University Press, 2012.

Jezernik, Božidar. "The Priest Matija Majar and the Moscow Ethnographic Exhibition of 1867." *Traditiones* 40, no. 2 (2011): 45–76.

———. "The Moscow Ethnographic Exhibition of 1867." *Zbiór Wiadomości do Antropologii Muzealnej* 6 (2019): 7–28.

Jobst, Kerstin S. *Die Perle des Imperiums. Der russische Krim-Diskurs im Zarenreich*. Konstanz: UVK, 2007.

Junevičius, Dainius. "Lietuvos fotografų nuotraukos pirmojoje Rusijos etnografijos parodoje 1867 m." *Lietuvos kultūros tyrimai* 10 (2018): 142–62.

Karahasan, Dževad. *Knjiga vrtova. O jeziku i strahu*. Zagreb: Antibarbarus, 2002.

Klanten, Robert. *Nostalgia: The Russian Empire of Czar Nicholas II Captured in Color Photographs by Sergei Mikhailovich Prokudin-Gorskii*. Berlin: Gestalten, 2012.

Knight, Nathaniel. "Science, Empire, and Nationality: Ethnography in the Russian Geographical Society, 1845–1855." In *Imperial Russia: New Histories for the Empire*. Edited by Jane Burbank and David L. Ransel, 108–41. Bloomington: Indiana University Press, 1998.

——. *The Empire on Display: Ethnographic Exhibition and the Conceptualization of Human Diversity in Post-Emancipation Russia*. Washington, DC: NCEEER, 2001.

——. "Russian Ethnography and the Visual Arts in the 1840s and 1850s." In *Visualizing Russia. Fedor Solntsev and Crafting a National Past*. Edited by Cynthia Hyla Whittaker, 127–44. Leiden: Brill, 2010.

Koehler, Véronique. *Voyage dans l'ancienne Russie. Les photographes en couleurs de Sergueï Mikhaïlovitch Procoudine-Gorsky*. Paris: Albin Michel, 2013.

Lautenschläger, Henning. "Prokudin–Gorskij." In *De Gruyter Allgemeines Künstlerlexikon. Die bildenden Künstler aller Zeiten und Völker*. Edited by Andreas Beyer. Vol. 97, 69–70. Berlin: De Gruyter, 2018.

Layton, Susan. *Russian Literature and Empire: Conquest of the Caucasus from Pushkin to Tolstoy*. Cambridge: Cambridge University Press, 1994.

Leich, Harold. "The Prokudin-Gorskii Collection of Early 20th Century Color Photographs of Russia at the Library of Congress: Unexpected Consequences of the Digitization of the Collection, 2000–2017." *Slavic and East European Information Resources* 18, no. 3–4 (2017): 223–30.

Manikowska, Ewa. *Photography and Cultural Heritage in the Age of Nationalisms. Europe's Eastern Borderlands (1867–1945)*. London: Bloomsbury, 2019.

Miller, Alexei. *The Romanov Empire and Nationalism*. Budapest: Central European University Press, 2008.

Pinney, Christopher. *Photography and Anthropology*. London: Reaktion, 2011.

Pravilova, Ekaterina. *A Public Empire: Property and the Quest for the Common Good in Imperial Russia*. Princeton: Princeton University Press, 2014.

Prokudin-Gorskii, Sergei. *Views in the Caucasus and Black Sea Area*. Library of Congress. Accessed June 12, 2022. https://www.loc.gov/item/2001696385.

——. "Pamiatniki stariny Mariinskoi sistemy i verkhnego Povolzh'ia i neskol'ko slov o znachenii tsvetnoi fotografii." In *Trudy IV s'ezda russkikh zodchikh*. Edited by Viktor V. Eval'd, 591–94. St. Petersburg: Gosudarstvennaia tipografiia, 1911.

Ram, Harsha. *The Imperial Sublime: A Russian Poetics of Empire*. Madison: University of Wisconsin Press, 2003.

Ryan, James S. *Picturing Empire: Photography and the Visualization of the British Empire*. London: Reaktion, 1997.

Sarkisova, Oksana. *Screening Soviet Nationalities: Kulturfilms from the Far North to Central Asia*. London: I. B. Tauris, 2017.

Schimmelpenninck van der Oye, David. *Russian Orientalism: Asia in the Russian Mind from Peter the Great to the Emigration.* New Haven: Yale University Press, 2010.

Shipova, Tat'iana N. *Moskovskie fotografy 1839–1930. Istoriia Moskovskoi fotografii.* Moscow: Planeta, 2012.

Solov'eva, Karina Iu. "Obrazy narodov Rossiiskoi imperii 1860–kh godov. Po materialam Etnograficheskoi vystavki 1867 goda." In *Slaviane Evropy i narody Rossii. K 140-letiiu pervoi etnograficheskoi vystavki 1867 goda.* Edited by Natal'ia M. Kalashnikova, 58–63. St. Petersburg: Slaviia, 2008.

Solovyova, Karina and Kouteinikova, Inessa. "A Different Caucasus: Early Triumphs of Photography in the Caucasus." *Venezia Arti* 25 (2016): 133–49.

Sonntag, Heather S. *Genesis of the Turkestan Album 1871–1872. The Role of Russian Military Photography, Mapping, Albums & Exhibitions on Central Asia.* PhD diss., University of Wisconsin-Madison, 2011.

Tolz, Vera. "Orientalism, Nationalism, and Ethnic Diversity in Late Imperial Russia." *The Historical Journal* 48, no. 1 (2005): 127–50.

Ukazatel' Russkoi etnograficheskoi vystavki. Moscow: Universitetskaia tipografiia, 1867.

Vishlenkova, Elena. "Strategies of the Visual Construction of Russianness and Non-Russianness, 1800–1830." In *Defining Self. Essays on Emergent Identities in Russia: Seventeenth to Nineteenth Centuries.* Edited by Michael Branch, 173–92. Helsinki: Finnish Literature Society, 2009.

9

Perception of Others within One Ethnic Minority: Jewish Ethnographic Studies in the Late Russian Empire

Marina Shcherbakova

Abstract

This chapter addresses the issues of the ethnographic studies of Jewish culture in the periphery of the Russian Empire conducted by Russian Jewish intellectual elites from the center. Discussions started by Jewish scholars after the Russian Revolution of 1905 provide insights into the perception of Jewish otherness, the revision of persistent identity structures, and the production of a narrative of ethnographic cosmopolitanism between imperialism and modernization. Initially focusing on the shtetl world in the Pale of Settlement, the interest of scholars expanded to Jewish communities in Crimea, the Caucasus, and Central Asia. This scholarship demonstrates the encounter between "our" civilized and "their" primitive social and cultural forms among Jews. The construction of ethnographic knowledge about Georgian, Crimean, and Bukharan Jews was based on the models of Russian and European Orientalism on the one hand and the ideas of the Jewish national movement on the other. By drawing together the collective social and subethnic identities of Jews as they were imagined by Russian Jewish researchers, this chapter seeks to reflect critically on the construction of the Jewish national affinity on the eve of 1917 and its manifestation in early Soviet policies.

Introduction

The ethnographic description of Jewish culture in the Russian Empire by Jewish researchers began to be developed in the early twentieth century. As an academic discipline, Jewish ethnography was formed in the context of the political debates of 1905–1917. The significance of an ethnic culture was reconceptualized during a quest for ways to overcome the crisis in which Russian Jews found themselves. Supporters of Jewish autonomism and a stronger diaspora in the Russian Empire appealed to the themes of national identity and cultural memory with the aim of fixing them in the Jewish people's consciousness and preparing Jews for receptiveness to the ideas of a new Jewishness.[1]

The Jewish Society for History and Ethnography (JSHE) (Evreiskoe istoriko-etnograficheskoe obshchestvo), founded in 1909 in St. Petersburg by the theoretician of autonomism Simon Dubnov and his associates, was closely connected to this cultural and historical project.[2] Studies and publications in the journal *Evreiskaia starina* (Jewish Antiquity) were followed by the formation of collections of Judaica, which were exhibited in the museum of the society opened in 1915 and which vividly displayed the methodology and perspective of the Jewish researchers of St. Petersburg.[3] The contemporary literature takes a critical view of the fact that these ethnographic activities fell outside the anthropological discourse that in the 1910s defined the academic perception of the cultural development of nations, despite the enthusiasm of Lev Shternberg, member of the St. Petersburg Academy of Sciences, for the work of the JSHE and the cooperation with Samuil Vaysenberg.[4]

---

1 For the history of Jewish autonomy, see, for example, Robert Seltzer, *Simon Dubnow's New Judaism: Diaspora Nationalism and the World History of the Jews* (Leiden: Brill Academic Publishers, 2014); Anke Hilbrenner, *Diaspora-Nationalismus: Zur Geschichtskonstruktion Simon Dubnows* (Göttingen: Vandenhoeck and Ruprecht, 2007).

2 For the foundation and work of the JSHE, see Viktor Kel'ner, "Vremia sobirat' kamni (K istorii Evreiskogo istoriko-etnograficheskogo obshchestva i ego kollektsii)," *Voprosy muzeologii* 10, no. 1. (2019): 10, 1, 43–55; Irina Sergeeva, "Istoriia Muzeia i Arkhiva Evreiskogo istoriko–etnograficheskogo obshchestva posle oktiabria 1917 goda," *Judaic-Slavic Journal* 1, no. 2 (2019): 13–43; Jeffrey Veidlinger, *Jewish Public Culture in the Late Russian Empire* (Bloomington: Indiana University Press, 2009), 229–61.

3 For a more detailed account of the history of the journal *Evreiskaia starina*, see, for example, Kerstin Armborst-Weihs, "Die Zeitschrift 'Jevrejskaja starina': Wissenschaftlicher Kommunikationsort und Sprachrohr der Jüdischen Historisch–Ethnographischen Gesellschaft in St. Petersburg," *Zeitschrift für Religions- und Geistesgeschichte* 58, no. 1 (2006): 29–48.

4 Marina Mogilner, "Between Scientific and Political: Jewish Scholars and Russian–Jewish Physical Anthropology in the Fin-de-Siècle Russian Empire," in *Going to the People: Jews*

Furthermore, the JSHE was focused basically on East European Jews: this was dictated by the crisis in which the Jews in the Pale of Settlement found themselves. These Jews were seen as a target audience for the autonomist project and reflecting the cultural links of the St. Petersburg Jewish intelligentsia, which primarily consisted of natives of the Pale of Settlement. Nevertheless, in spite of Dubnov's appeals in his theoretical work to the Jews of Russia as a whole, the treatment of Jews who traditionally lived in Central Asia, the Caucasus, and Crimea and the construction of a complex Jewish diaspora in the Russian Empire remained a peripheral activity for those working in the JSHE.[5] Before the Russian Revolution, the pages of *Evreiskaia starina* contained just a few ethnographic overviews of non-Ashkenazi Jewish ethnic groups, written by Vaysenberg, the pioneer of Jewish racial studies, following his expeditions.[6] The policy of the journal, edited by Dubnov, allows us to think of the self-identification of the Ashkenazim as the ideological leader in the autonomist national project and of imperial patterns in the interactions of the center and periphery on the map of the Jewish diaspora in Russia.

Against that background, the many years of work of the secretary of the JSHE, Isaak Lur'e, who devoted himself to the study of Jews in Central Asia and went on to establish the Indigenous Jewish Museum in Samarkand, are particularly noteworthy. As the permanent assistant to Dubnov in the JSHE and the right-hand man of the founder of Jewish ethnography, S. An-sky (whose real name was Shloyme Zaynvl Rapoport), in the affairs of the Jewish Museum in Petrograd, in his own research Lur'e followed his mentors' methods.[7] However, his engagement with the culture of the Bukharan, Persian, and Caucasic Jews, as well as his expedition to Palestine, which concentrated on the folklore of Yemenite Jews in Jerusalem, demonstrated his capability of action in accordance with his own academic interests and political convictions. What remains fragmentarily of Lur'e's legacy, who died in repressions in Central Asia, allows us to track the

and the Ethnographic Impulse, ed. Jeffrey Veidlinger (Bloomington: Indiana University Press, 2016), 45–46.

5 Armhorst-Weihs, "Die Zeitschrift 'Jevrejskaja starina': Wissenschaftlicher Kommunikationsort und Sprachrohr der Jüdischen Historisch-Ethnographischen Gesellschaft in St. Petersburg," 31.

6 Samuil Vaysenberg, "Evrei v Turkestane: otchet o letnei poezdke," *Evreiskaia starina* 4 (1913): 390–406; Samuil Vaysenberg, "Istoricheskie gnezda Kavkaza i Kryma: Iz otcheta o letnei poezdke 1912 g," *Evreiskaia starina* 6 (1913): 51–60; Semen Dubnov, "Istoricheskaia taina Kryma: 1; Periody krymskoi istorii, 2. Pamiatniki Mangup-Kale," *Evreiskaia starina* 7 (1914): 1–21.

7 For more information on him, see, for example, Gabriela Safran, *Wandering Soul: The Dybbuk's Creator, S. An-sky* (Cambridge, MA: Harvard University Press, 2010).

formation of the Jewish intelligentsia's knowledge of Central Asian Jews in the early twentieth century. The perspectives adopted in that ethnographic work make an analysis of certain questions of the construction of the Jewish nation in diaspora possible. What factors affected the hierarchy in the multicultural Jewish community in Russia? What role did ethnic-political interests play in research practices? How was the East-West dichotomy unpacked in the Jewish ethnographic discourse and in museum representations?

This article seeks to contribute to the discussion in this volume constructed around the image of Others in the Russian Empire from the perspective of the Christian majority by exploring the practice of distinction within the great Russian Jewish community.[8] Along with the large Ashkenazic community, this diaspora encompassed several subgroups of Jews in the Caucasus and Central Asia. United by shared values of Judaism, the Georgian Jews, the Mountain Jews, and the Central Asian Jews had significant cultural and ritual differences as well as different approaches to national self-identification and acculturation. Each group was attached to local languages and maintained inconsistent relationships to the Jewish world outside the local community.

The case study of Lur'e's ethnographic exploration and museumization of Bukharan Jewish culture provides a micromodel of the construction of a national idea in an empire. It shows how images of others were formed and circulated within a multicultural society and a geographically extended territory. Of special interest are the subjects of antagonism and factors of unification that would be applied in a museum exhibition or in historiographical publications as tools of propaganda. The aspects that shaped the perception of different groups within the Russian Jewish diaspora and the mental images derived from it determined the collective identification processes, which parallels some patterns of imperial rule in Russia.

Jews in the Russian Empire: Framework of the Collective Experience

The policies of the Russian Empire in the Middle Ages and in the early modern period were defined by hostility toward Jews. The perception of Jews by the Russian authorities was based on profound and traditional Christian neglect of the Jewish others in Russian society. Until the 1720s, there were no Jews in

---

8   See Charles Halperin, "Varieties of Otherness in Ivan IV's Muscovy: Relativity, Multiplicity, and Ambiguity" and Oleg Minin, "The Self and the Other: Representations of the Monarchist Foe and Ally in the Satirical Press of the Russian Right (1906–1908)" in this volume.

the Russian Empire, aside from the few travelers and migrant merchants, who would not be considered part of the state's population.[9] As a result of the reforms of Peter I and his political successors in the eighteenth century, especially Catherine II, Russia turned from its historical eastward expansion to the west. The political and cultural contacts with European countries that followed, as well as the annexation of the territories between Muscovy and the Baltic Sea under Peter I and, even more so, the division of the Polish-Lithuanian Commonwealth under Catherine II in 1772, 1773, and 1795, increased the Jewish population in the country from zero to the largest in the world. The Russian Empire received about seven hundred fifty thousand Jews along with the territories of central and eastern Poland and Lithuania. The annexed territories delivered new ethnic groups and communities to the Russian Empire, including their collective identities rooted in the predominantly Catholic political and cultural system and the history of a relationship with Jews.

The political interaction of the Russian administration with Jews was based on insecurity and a lack of experience, which led to contradictory regulations.[10] The tsarist approach to the Jewish question could be described as "unresolved tension between integration and segregation."[11] The policies of Catherine II drifted from the ideas of the European Enlightenment and legal equality for the national minorities to the traditional issues of Russian society and its rigid social hierarchy, into which the Jewish population could not be easily integrated. The latter resulted in the first discriminatory laws in the early nineteenth century, when the authorities attempted in 1808 and in 1823 to expel Jews from the countryside into towns. More important was the implementation of the Jewish Pale of Settlement in 1791, which was originally developed in order to protect Moscow merchants while prohibiting Jewish merchants from Belarus from settling and trading in the centers of the Russian Empire.

However, the Pale of Settlement became the fundamental framework for the historical experience of Jews in the Russian Empire and was elevated to a cornerstone of Jewish identity in the twentieth century and of the image of Russian Jewry.[12] The impoverishment of people in the Jewish "Dark Continent,"

---

9   See, for example, Michael Stanislawski, "Russia: Russian Empire," *YIVO Encyclopedia of Jews in Eastern Europe*, 2010, accessed June 13, 2022, https://yivoencyclopedia.org/article.aspx/Russia/Russian_Empire.

10 Michael Brenner, *Kleine jüdische Geschichte* (München: C. H. Beck Verlag, 2008), 216.

11 Stanislawski, "Russia: Russian Empire."

12 Elissa Bemporad, "Bemporad on Deutsch, 'The Jewish Dark Continent: Life and Death in the Russian Pale of Settlement,'" *H–Judaica*, April 2013, accessed June 13, 2022, https://networks.h-net.org/node/28655/reviews/30942/bemporad-deutsch-jewish-dark-continent-life-and-death-russian-pale.

as Semen Dubnov labeled it, due to uneven economic development and limitations, as well as the overconcentration of the Jewish population in fixed provinces, predetermined the tension between two worlds that interacted on a daily basis but perceived each other as distant and dangerous.[13] The inconsistent Jewish policies of Alexander I, whose well-intentioned ideas were challenged by his later ignorant despotism, gave way to the clear and tough line of Nicholas I. The policies of Nicholas I and the resulting reality were deemed by the Jews to be formal persecution of Judaism in Russia. The perspective of the authorities was based on a neglect of Jewish religious, cultural, and visual distinctiveness, and a willingness to absorb and assimilate the Jewish primarily religious otherness rather than to develop an awareness of the differences and to embrace it as part of a multicultural framework. Most crucial was the government's requirement for Jewish communities to deliver several men for twenty-five years of military service. This measure was aimed at detaching Jewish men from the sources of their national institutions and to convert them to Christianity so that they would be lost to their communities. The abolition of the kahal[14] in 1844 eliminated the autonomy of the Jewish communities, which were placed under the control of local authorities. However, this law lacked a distinction between the secular and the religious spheres for it to be regarded as a final solution of the Jewish question in tsarist Russia.

The late imperial period was marked by a swing from retained and intensified restrictions against Jews in the first thirteen years of Nicholas II's reign to granting certain liberties to Jews. The major Kishinev pogrom in 1903 shook the government into an awareness of the social challenges coming from the troubled position of Jews in the state. Followed by the Revolution of 1905, the tsar was faced with the importance of liberalizing the existing restrictive laws and providing a constitutional foundation for Jewish civic rights, as well as abolishing the Pale of Settlement in 1916. The permission to vote in the new parliamentary elections and to create political parties gave Jews political rights before their legal emancipation and encouraged the national movement that shaped the Russian Jewish world in the first decades of the twentieth century. At the same time, the Jewish national renaissance was a reaction to the rise of right-wing political movements after 1905 that defended the "Russian idea" and Orthodoxy. They disseminated Jewish stereotypical images as nonproductive

---

13 Ibid.
14 Autonomous governments of Jewish communities in the Polish-Lithuanian Commonwealth and the Russia Empire.

exploiters and such traditional Christian anti-Jewish motifs as ritual murder and the threat of worldwide Jewish conspiracy.

The profound Jewish otherness was what determined the predominantly negative perception of Jews in the Russian Empire and influenced the cultural aspect of the interaction with Jews. Slavic folklore provides an insight into the concept of the Jewish Other, which is rooted in Christian and pre-Christian images and morphed into a system of folktales and myths referring to common stereotypes about Jews. In one representative Slavic narrative, for example, Jews were associated with demons that did not belong to the real world and mediated between the two worlds of people and the supernatural sphere.[15] As Minin shows in his chapter in this volume, the Russian right-wing Black Hundreds movement applied these folklore motifs widely in their propaganda and used them in the satirical press and visualizations in caricatures as "the source of all evil in holy Russia,"[16] which was meant to undermine the existing order based on Orthodox tradition and autocracy.

Following the Polish partitions, blood libels[17] appeared in the Russian Empire as well. During the last two decades of the nineteenth century and in the early twentieth century, accusations of ritual murders and, according, trials delivered an agenda that was part of the rise of antisemitism in the late Russian Empire, including the mass killing of Jews during several waves of pogroms in the Pale of Settlement. The accusations of ritual murder took place in the colonies of the Russian Empire outside the Pale of Settlement as well, which might have been influenced by the presence of antisemitic Russian authorities. The most significant case took place in 1879 in the Georgian town of Kutaisi, known for its large Jewish community, where nine Hasidic Jews were accused of murdering a young Georgian peasant girl. The Jews were acquitted, but this case received extensive coverage and generated a new wave of discussion.[18]

Jewish communities in the Russian Empire represented a multicultural composition that was dominated by a majority of the Ashkenazic Jews in the European part of the state. The Caucasic and Asian territories of the empire that

---

15 Semen Reznik, "Krovavy navet v Rossii. Istoriko–dokumental'nye ocherki," *Vestnik* 24, no. 231 (November 1999), cited in *Ldn-Knigi-Lib*, accessed June 14, 2022, http://ldn-knigi.lib. ru/JUDAICA/R_Chvolson.htm.

16 See Minin, "The Self and the Other: Representations of the Monarchist Foe and Ally in the Satirical Press of the Russian Right (1906–1908)" in this volume.

17 False accusations of Jews murdering Christians, especially children, to use their blood in religious rituals.

18 Hillel J. Kieval, "Blood Libels and Host Desecration Accusations," *YIVO Encyclopedia of Jews in Eastern Europe*, 2016, accessed June 13, 2022, https://yivoencyclopedia.org/article.aspx/ Blood_Libels_and_Host_Desecration_Accusations.

were conquered mainly in the nineteenth century included groups of Jews that can be described as Oriental Jews, or Mizrahi. The presence of the communities of Georgian Jews, Mountain Jews, Bukharan Jews, and Mashhadi Jews on the Russian ethnographic map reflected the colonization dynamics of the Russian Empire in the Caucasus and in Central Asia. The policies of the Russian government toward Oriental Jews in the new territories were predetermined by the perception of these Jews as indigenous peoples similar, for example, to local native ethnicities in the colonies who were as other as the Muslim ethnicities in Central Asia. The Jews of Central Asia and the Caucasus were indeed more assimilated than Ashkenazic Jews in Ukraine, Belarus, and Lithuania.

Oriental Jews were therefore regarded by Russian rulers as an efficient and useful group. This fact contributes to Halperin's argumentation about the Jews as the most "other" in the Russian Empire, whereas Muslims were perceived by the Russian authorities as mentally less distant and hostile. The Bukharan Jews who were visually and culturally similar to the Muslim population of Turkestan, as well as the Georgian Jews who reached a certain level of cultural assimilation in Georgia, were regarded as less opposed to Christians. The positioning of these groups in opposition to the Ashkenazic communities would enhance the malicious image of the latter and the stereotypes linked to that image.[19] The Bukharan and Caucasic Jews were subject to the general regulation of Jews in the Russian Empire, albeit in a more liberal way. The areas of tolerated residence of the Bukharan, Georgian, and Mountain Jews were not considered part of the Pale and were not governed by its provisions.[20]

These contradictions point out the multilayered perspective on the category "Russian Jewry" and the internal experiences in the Russian Jewish diaspora. The Oriental Jews differed not only in general characteristics from the European Jews, but there were major differentiations in language, rituals, and everyday practice between communities in the Caucasus and in Central Asia. As a result, the relationships between the subgroups within the diaspora were shaped by cultural, geographical, economical, and historical factors. The categories of Jewishness and of otherness were interconnected in the collective identity of the Russian Jewish diaspora. This particular otherness challenged the intellectuals of Ashkenazic origin to explore the distant Oriental communities ethnographically and historically in the course of the Jewish national

---

19 Albert Kaganovich, *Druz'ia ponevole: Rossiia i bukharskie evrei 1800–1917* (Moscow: Novoe literaturnoe obozrenie, 2016), 20.

20 John Klier, "Pale of Settlement," *YIVO Encyclopedia of Jews in Eastern Europe*, 2010, accessed June 13, 2022, https://yivoencyclopedia.org/article.aspx/Pale_of_Settlement.

renaissance on the eve of the Revolution of 1917. These attempts at a critical examination of the diaspora became a source for constructing self-identifying concepts and images during major political transitions and a troubled position of Jews in the Russian Empire. The ethnographic and museological approach to Oriental Jewry by Isaak Lur'e, who himself belonged to the Russian Jewish intellectual elite engaged in academic work in St. Petersburg, originated within this framework. His studies constituted a critical examination of Bukharan Jews as an exotic and conservative Jewish group. The resulting production of a visual narrative by Lur'e in the museum of Samarkand through objects of material culture and historical artifacts would establish a sense of national awareness about them and contribute to the explanation of us during a time of political upheavals and national revisions.

Isaak Lur'e: The Making of a Researcher

Lur'e was born in Novgorod in 1875, the son of a merchant from Vitebsk. Between 1902 and 1911, Lur'e studied at universities in Paris and St. Petersburg.[21] To receive permission to live in St. Petersburg, he was forced to register as a tailor in the Chamber of Trades in the capital. That allowed him to study in the Faculty of Oriental Studies of St. Petersburg University and attend the Higher Courses in Oriental Studies. The latter was the first secular Jewish educational institution in Europe and played a significant role in the Jewish sociopolitical and national movement of the time.[22]

In the pre-revolutionary period, Lur'e's career was closely connected with organizations that adhered to ideas of the national modernization of Russian Jewry. The main such organization was the JSHE, in which Lur'e served as archivist, as editorial secretary for *Evreiskaia starina*, and as curator of the collection in the society's museum. Lur'e fully devoted himself to ethnographic and historiographic research, which developed rapidly due to the rise of a national movement that sought a bedrock in traditional culture. Lur'e was ascetic in his personal life, while his professional activities mere marked by a passion for his work and great zeal, which Dubnov recorded in his memoirs:

---

21 "Lur'e Isaak," *Elektronnaia evreiskaia entsiklopediia*, 2003, accessed June 13, 2022, https://eleven.co.il/jews-of-russia/education-secular-culture/12513/.

22 David Schimmelpenninck van der Oye, *Russian Orientalism: Asia in the Russian Mind from Peter the Great to the Emigration* (New Haven: Yale University Press, 2010), 171–98.

He was a sort of Jewish Diogenes. A man of about thirty, not handsome, dressed carelessly, with a stutter and a chronic cold, Lur'e had no family or thoughts of one, lived a solitary life, ate poorly, but for all that he had an insatiable intellect. A typical bookworm, he read everything indiscriminately in both Jewish languages and in some European ones, in particular about Oriental studies. [. . .] He lived on a paltry monthly salary and even managed to put something aside from it to fund his excursions to Palestine.[23]

Dubnov's memoirs demonstrate that he highly valued Lur'e's conscientious help in archive work and research, as well as his faithfulness to the aims and tasks of the JSHE.[24] Lur'e adopted the JSHE's approach to the role of historical knowledge and was convinced that study of the collective Jewish cultural experience and the reinforcement of a national culture amounted to an important contribution to the modernization of Russian Jewry. Dubnov wrote in his memoir, *Buch des Lebens* (Book of Life), that his assistant, an "ardent nationalist,"[25] who used Hebrew in his correspondence until the 1930s, reproached him for publishing *Evreiskaia starina* in Russian rather than Hebrew. Lur'e's political views were overall socialist. Despite his work in the JSHE, his cooperation with Zionist publications and his interest in Hebraic studies showed that he was not indifferent to the ideas of uniting and reviving the Jewish nation in its ancestral homeland. Later, in the Soviet period, Lur'e spoke of several transformations in his convictions in the framework of socialist doctrine. Like most Soviet sociologists and culturologists working during Stalinism, in 1931 Lur'e publicly came out as a long-time adherent of dialectical Marxism and set aside his nationalist ideas in the interests of internationalism and the class struggle.[26] However, his museum work gives but superficial evidence of such a change. On the contrary, his work followed the pre-revolutionary lodestars of the JSHE until his final days.

Whereas Dubnov was a mentor in matters of political education and Jewish historiography in terms of the development of Jewish scientific activity in the diaspora, An-sky was the main example to be followed in ethnographic field work, the collection of ancient Jewish artefacts, and museum activities. An-sky's

---

23 Simon Dubnow, *Buch des Lebens: Erinnerungen und Gedanken. Materialien zur Geschichte meiner Zeit* (Göttingen: Vandenhoeck and Ruprecht, 2005), 116.
24 Ibid., 117.
25 Ibid., 116.
26 Central State Archive of the Republic of Uzbekistan, f. 94, op. 5, d. 842, l. 27.

view of research into Judaic practices was based on the conception of a collective Jewish autoethnography that aimed at awakening a national self-awareness and at constructing a usable past and renaissance of traditions in a renewed format in concord with the age.[27] In similar fashion to Dubnov's efforts to make historical knowledge the basis for the national life of Russian Jews, An-sky strove for the emergence of a mass ethnographic movement. The collection, description, and popularization of elements of the national cultural heritage were intended to stimulate an identity, alongside the rabbinic tradition of Torah teaching.[28] In 1914, An-sky published a Jewish Ethnographic Program for Field Studies, in the development of which Lur'e played a key role.

The scholarly interests of Lur'e, who believed in the populist nationalism of the ideologues of the Jewish Renaissance, were thus formed at the intersection of history and ethnography. In his 1908 programmatic article "Evreiskoe narodnoe tvorchestvo" (Jewish popular creative work), An-sky criticized the prominent Russian Jewish ethnologists Lev Shternberg, Vladimir Bogoraz, and Vladimir Iokhel'son for their failure to concentrate their research on Jews.[29] This nationalist approach may also be observed in Lur'e. For example, in a letter to the folklorist Sof'ia Maggid, he wrote, "Unfortunately, talented Jews for the most part study anything else but Jewishness. The words from the 'Song of Songs,' 'my own vineyard I have not kept,' remain true today."[30]

The Perspective of the Jewish Research Ethnographer in the Political Context

Lur'e was a member of the young generation of the liberal Jewish intelligentsia in St. Petersburg whose national worldview was formed against the backdrop of the political disenchantments of its teachers and by the revolutionary moods in

---

27 For the history of the Jewish ethnographic movement in the Russian Empire, see, for example, Jeffrey Veidlinger, ed., *Going to the People: Jews and the Ethnographic Impulse* (Bloomington: Indiana University Press, 2016); Veniamin Lukin, "Akademiia, gde budut izuchat' folklor: An-skii—Ideolog Evreiskogo muzeinogo dela," in *Evreiskii muzei*, ed. Valerii Dymshits and Viktor Kelner (St. Petersburg: Simpozium, 2004), 281–307; Nathaniel Deutsch, *The Jewish Dark Continent: Life and Death in the Russian Pale of Settlement* (Cambridge, MA: Harvard University Press, 2010).
28 Deutsch, *The Jewish Dark Continent: Life and Death in the Russian Pale of Settlement*, 35.
29 Ibid., 28.
30 Archive of the Institute of the Oriental Manuscripts of the Russian Academy of Sciences, f. 85, op. 2, d. 438, l. 1.

Russian society between 1905 and 1917.[31] Dissatisfaction with the status of the educated Jewish elite of the older generation, who until the 1880s had argued for integration and acculturation, was initially caused by political changes in the 1870s and 1880s and the antisemitic Great Reforms of Alexander II.[32] The Jewish elite's move from positivism to nationalism was accompanied in 1901 by a discussion on the necessity of founding a national Jewish school system and a Jewish National Committee in Odessa, where many Jewish intelligentsia members lived in accordance with the settlement law.[33] Jews finally lost all optimism regarding state policy between 1903 and 1905, when a wave of pogroms swept across Kishinev (Chisinau), Odessa, and other cities. The Jewish intelligentsia's reaction showed that they saw these pogroms as a turning point in the history of Russian Jews. Dubnov wrote, "In contrast to my weak reaction in my youth to the April pogroms of 1881, which seemed but a temporary reaction to the assassination of the tsar on March 1, this time the new era of bloody pogroms was a great shock to me."[34] Furthermore, the political views of many Jewish activists were shaken by the revolutionary tension around 1905 and by the prospects of the political emancipation of Russian Jews.

Both the political rise of the 1900s and 1910s and the national cultural renaissance of opponents of emigration from Russia as a model for the future characterized the Jewish intelligentsia of this period.[35] Before 1905, the educated Jewish elite could be characterized as Russian Jews. This imagined community was distinguished by the use of Russian as a literary language and was concentrated primarily in St. Petersburg. Within the context of the nationalist movement, the self-identifier "Russian Jew" proved incompatible with the ideas of autonomism, and it was replaced by a conception of spiritual leadership of the Jewish intelligence as a basis for the modernization of Jewish culture beyond the Russian capital.[36] This phenomenon was reflected in the social and cultural forms of differentiation within the Jewish macrosociety in the Russian Empire;

---

31 Verena Dohrn, *Jüdische Eliten im Russischen Reich: Aufklärung und Integration im 19. Jahrhundert* (Cologne: Böhlau Verlag, 2008), 400.

32 For the status of Jews under Alexander III, see, e.g., John Klier, *Russians, Jews, and the Pogroms of 1881–1882* (Cambridge: Cambridge University Press, 2011); Natan Meir, "'The Sword Hanging over Their Heads': The Significance of Pogrom for Russian Jewish Everyday Life and Self-Understanding," in *Anti–Jewish Violence: Rethinking the Pogrom in East European History*, ed. Jonathan Dekel-Chen (Bloomington: Indiana University Press, 2011), 114.

33 Seltzer, *Simon Dubnow's New Judaism: Diaspora Nationalism and the World History of the Jews*, 138–39.

34 Ibid.

35 Hilbrenner, *Diaspora–Nationalismus: Zur Geschichtskonstruktion Simon Dubnows*, 38.

36 Anke Hilbrenner, "Simon Dubnov's Master Narrative and the Construction of Jewish Collective Memory in the Russian Empire," *Ab imperio* 4 (2003): 151.

these forms had a significant influence on Jews' scholarly research of their own people.

Following the development of a concept of national autonomy and the foundation of a Jewish "Folkspartei" in 1906, supporters of autonomism started to perceive the nation not only as a subject of study and a source of inspiration but also as a subject of political struggle.[37] The autonomist program aimed for the formation in Russia of a national ethnic community that would serve as a form of national state in the framework of a multi-ethnic empire. Dubnov theorized about a synthesis of tradition and modernity that would demand the adaptation of Western modernity to east European reality and the secularization of Jewish culture. In these respects, historical memory was responsible for the formation of a national self-awareness.[38]

As a historian and ethnographer, Lur'e was thus formed among people who cared about the political future of Jews in the Russian Empire. An inseparable part of this nation-building project was the reborn interest in the Jewish nation's cultural heritage, a topic that had in the previous decades lost ground to the preoccupation with ideas of Jewish enlightenment and assimilation. In the JSHE manifesto published in the first issue of *Evreiskaia starina* in 1909, Dubnov discussed the paths of the Jewish nation's development, constructing as he did a dichotomy between the intellectual elite and the common people. This opposition was an echo of the populist movement, which gave rise to many early twentieth-century ethnographers. At the same time, this opposition predefines the perspective of Jewish ethnographic research, the subject of which a priori remained the "common masses," unable to systematize their cultural experience and therefore doomed to weakness:

> The common masses unconsciously weave the long thread of the centuries, but if a people's brain, its intelligentsia, does not do the same with a reliance on its clear historical consciousness, will that thread not snap, will that historical continuity that is the nation's soul not vanish, will the great chain not shatter into separate links?[39]

---

37 Semen Dubnov, *Folkspartei: Evreiskaia narodnaia partiia* (St. Petersburg: C. Kraiz, 1907).
38 Semen Dubnov, *Pis'ma o starom i novom evreistve* (St. Petersburg, Obshchestvennaia pol'za, 1907); Semen Dubnov, *Grundlagen des Nationaljudentums* (Berlin: Jüdischer Verlag, 1905).
39 N.a., "Uchreditel'noe sobranie i publichnye zasedaniia Evreiskago Istoriko-Etnograficheskago Obshchestva," *Evreiskaia starina* 1 (1909): 157.

The term *Jewish masses* pervades like a red thread through the activities and publications of the scholars in the JSHE. The common people's cultural world was revealed by the Russian Jewish intelligentsia as an unconscious bearer of the national memory, the guardian of which would be the intelligentsia.[40] The view of the common people as a subject of study was defined by the intelligentsia's civilizing approach, so that the educated elite perceived the Jews from the Pale of Settlement and other remote regions of tsarist Russia from a colonial perspective. However, the Jewish ethnography paradox, a source of internal tension, was that the Pale of Settlement was the birthplace of many Jewish artists, political activists, and intellectuals and contained a primitive authenticity of Jewish culture that the theorists of autonomism lacked. In the words of Nathaniel Deutsch, the scholarly approach to the lower strata of the Jewish people followed the Hassidic principle of "descent in order to ascend."[41] In other words, stooping to the common people's level meant the righteous man's path to spiritual growth, an idea that precisely describes the goal of the Jewish ethnographic movement.

The image of the common people as a bearer of the spiritual continuity of the national culture also arose from the contradiction of tradition and enlightenment, primitiveness and progress. This outlook was connected to the cultural and geographical polarization of East and West, which consequently gave a condescending hue to the term "eastern Jew" (*Ostjude*), which in Europe originally meant the Ashkenazic Jews of Poland and the Russian Empire.[42] Russian figures in the Jewish national renaissance brought that discourse to the Russian Empire, rediscovering for themselves as they did so the narratives of the Jewish East and recognizing the value of these sometimes exotic traditions. The starting point for the historians and ethnographers of the JSHE was the need to find a new collective identity for Jews in the Russian Empire that would accord with various Jewish groups that took the concept of Russian Jewishness as the basis for their self-perception.[43] The study of a living tradition, which presupposed the description of Jewish communities untouched by modernization, brought the Jewish intellectuals of St. Petersburg not only to the Pale of Settlement, some parts of which were geographically west of the Russian capital, but also to Central Asia, Crimea, and the Caucasus.[44] In this regard, apart from the Western

40 Ibid., 154.
41 Deutsch, *The Jewish Dark Continent: Life and Death in the Russian Pale of Settlement*, 29.
42 Hilbrenner, *Diaspora-Nationalismus: Zur Geschichtskonstruktion Simon Dubnows*, 12.
43 Veidlinger, *Jewish Public Culture in the Late Russian Empire*, 273.
44 Vaysenberg, "Evrei v Turkestane: otchet o letnei poezdke," 390–406; Vaysenberg, "Istoricheskie gnezda Kavkaza i Kryma: Iz otcheta o letnei poezdke 1912 g.," 51–60; Dubnov, "Istoricheskaia taina Kryma: I; Periody krymskoi istorii, II. Pamiatniki Mangup–Kale," 7, 1–21.

modernist projection on the Jews of the East, Russian Jewish ethnographic studies developed Oriental studies traditions in Russian scholarship that went back to the romanticization of the eastern colonies of the Russian Empire and, after 1917, turned into the phenomenon of Soviet Orientalism.[45]

From Ethnography to the Museum

The growing interest of the JSHE in the public display of its collection of objects of Jewish material culture led Lur'e to think theoretically about a Jewish museum. The museum was in general regarded by the Jewish nationalists as an important tool of communicating political ideas from us to the others—from the national and scholarly leaders to the broad public—and of visualizing an identity fostering values. The concept of the museum was basically rooted in the dichotomy of ruler and followers. Lur'e's article "On a Jewish Museum" was published in the St. Petersburg Zionist weekly *Rassvet* (Dawn) in 1913.[46] In it, Lur'e wrote about questions of Jewish museology, a topic that before him only Samuil Vaysenberg had addressed in his survey article.[47] Strictly speaking, the discussion of a conceptual construction of a Jewish museum was not continued until 1931 by the representative of Soviet Judaica and Leningrad ethnographer Isaiah Pul'ner.[48]

Two arguments in Lur'e's article sounded very innovative and brought his perception of a Jewish museum beyond the discursive boundaries of the Jewish historical and ethnographic movement in Russia. First, he formed an idea that would become the guiding principle of the work of Jewish museums in the years of revolutionary struggle: "Now, as we stand at a watershed, when the old way of life is ever more intensively being replaced by new forms, we need to take more measures than ever before to secure for posterity and history the monuments of our present daily life, the life that is fading into the depths of the ages."[49]

---

45 Aliya Abykayeva-Tiesenhausen, *Central Asia in Art: From Soviet Orientalism to the New Republics* (London: I. B. Tauris, 2016), 151.

46 Isaak Lur'e, "O evreiskom muzee," *Rassvet* 50 (1914): 31–34.

47 Samuil Vaysenberg, who had studied medicine in Heidelberg, was the first Jewish researcher of race theory and anthropology. Vaysenberg addressed the theoretical questions of ethnographic research and museology in the following work: Samuil Vaysenberg, "Jüdische Museen und Jüdisches in Museen: Reiseeindrücke," *Mitteilungen zur jüdischen Volkskunde* 3 (1907): 77–88. For Vaysenberg's anthropological activities, see, e.g., Efron, *Defenders of the Race: Jewish Doctors and Race Science in Fin-de-Siècle Europe* (New Haven: Yale University Press, 1994), 91–122.

48 Isai Pul'ner, "Voprosy organizatsii evreiskikh etnograficheskikh muzeev i evreiskikh otdelov pri obshchikh etnograficheskikh muzeiakh," *Sovetskaia etnografiia* 3–4 (1931): 156–63.

49 Lur'e, "O evreiskom muzee," 32.

This was a turning point marked in the principles of Jewish salvage ethnography, which in light of the destruction of the Jewish milieu by pogroms strove to save objects of national material culture and secure them in a museum.[50] Lur'e experimented with a methodology that a few years later became more widespread in Soviet research, placing cultural and social changes in ethnic groups during and immediately after the Revolution at the center of attention. However, in contrast to Soviet scholarly projects, which on the whole served as part of the state's management of ethnic policy, Lur'e's ideas were in no way connected with the ruling political regime. On the contrary, the author joined ranks with the opposition wing of Russian Zionists, whose views were published in *Rassvet*, regardless or even in spite of his cooperation with the main platform of the autonomists and diaspora nationalists.

Lur'e's view developed from his thoughts on the national interests of the Jewish community, which, to his mind, could not be fully achieved under autonomy. His theoretical thoughts on museology were an attempt to understand cultural and social changes as a transformation of the contradiction between modernization and revolution. In this context, he appealed to the importance of contemporary history, which, alongside the past, was part of the entirety of Jewish cultural experience and needed to remain at the center of attention of historians. Lur'e held that everyday Jewish cultural and social practices, which were exclusively representative of the present day, required conscious scholarly understanding. He believed that the documentation of the Jewish community's political life after 1905 deserved special focus, as before that there had been no precedents of political activity among the Jewish population in the Russian Empire. Lur'e moved away from the Dubnov program of a historical discipline of Judaism and instead advocated a synchronized recording of social transformations and their effects on ethnic communities.

Lur'e's second important argument was directly connected to the concept of the display in a museum of the cultural diversity of Jews, which, in his opinion, could only take place in Jerusalem, as the single site of unification of various Jewish groups:

> For us, believers in the unity and revival of the Jewish nation, there cannot be any other site of a Jewish museum than Jerusalem. One does not even need to be a Zionist to direct one's

---

50 For more on salvage ethnography, see, for example, Jack Kugelmass, "The Father of Jewish Ethnography?," in *The Worlds of An-sky: A Russian Jewish Intellectual at the Turn of the Century*, ed. Gabriela Safran and Steven Zipperstein (Palo Alto: Stanford University Press, 2006), 348.

gaze thither in any attempt to do a common national deed, one that is not local or of the moment but that is of eternal historical importance.[51]

This approach also contradicted the JSHE's idea of a museum and to a large extent matched the basic tenets of cultural Zionism.[52] Lur'e's thesis put in the forefront the fundamental cultural unity of the Jewish nation, which was fueled in its spiritual center, Palestine. Lur'e developed his ethnographic projects from this position, which explains his interest in the eastern branch of Jewish culture and the Central Asian Jewish communities, which were in contact with the ancestral homeland. The diverse results of Lur'e's Palestinian expedition became the basis for his ethnographic and museum work in Samarkand in the 1920s.

The First Experience of Studying the Eastern Jews

After developing a Jewish ethnographic program, which was published by An-sky in 1914, Lur'e traveled to Palestine, where he studied the folklore of Yemenite Jews on the example of An-sky's renowned expeditions to the Pale of Settlement. This first attempt at an independent ethnographic field study aroused his interest in eastern groups of Jews, some of whom lived in a state of social oppression and were less studied than Ashkenazic Jews. In Jerusalem, Lur'e succeeded in recording one hundred wax cylinders with two hundred folk songs, as well as gathering some artifacts of the material culture of Yemenite, Persian, Baghdadi, and other Jewish communities.[53] Through this fieldwork, Lur'e aimed to familiarize himself with these, exotic to him, Jewish groups from an ethnographic perspective, aiming to expand the JSHE's collections with the aid of a corpus of rare sources and to collect new research materials. Lur'e was particularly proud that he had "even" contacted an Abyssinian Jew and received from him a transcription of popular songs, something that characterizes the perspective of a European ethnographer seeking the rarest and most exotic objects.

This rather general expedition already revealed the Orientalist approach in which Lur'e aimed to describe a world unknown and exotic to him. This

---

51 Lur'e, "O evreiskom muzee," 33.
52 Andreas B. Kilcher, "Jüdische Renaissance und Kulturzionismus," in *Handbuch der deutsch-jüdischen Literatur*, ed. Hans Otto Horch (Berlin: De Gruyter, 2015), 99–121.
53 Archive of the Institute of the Oriental Manuscripts of the Russian Academy of Sciences, f. 85, op. 2, d. 438, l. 1ob.

distinctive trait would later gain a fresh impulse during Lur'e's work in Central Asia. His journey to Jerusalem was carried out using this approach and reflected a Western researcher's Eurocentric view of groups of the Jewish populace in the Middle East. Yemenite Jews, who had emigrated en masse to Palestine between 1881 and 1918, constituted the central subject of his study.[54] Lur'e directed his attention to this community, which was culturally very exotic and socially subordinate to the Ashkenazic Jews in Palestine.[55] The status of Yemenite Jews pointed to poverty and cultural primitiveness, which in ethnographic research was considered a source of authentic information. This journey allowed Lur'e to take the revolutionary step in his research of the Jewish world of going beyond the boundaries of Dubnov's discourse, which had been primarily aimed at Jews in eastern Europe. In contrast to An-sky and many other Russian researchers of Jewish ethnography, Lur'e traveled to Asia and gathered materials that made possible the expansion and even transformation of existing knowledge of the Jewish world that was contemporary for scholars in the 1910s. The audio recordings of the folklore of Jerusalem's Jews were entered in an accession book in St. Petersburg; however, despite Lur'e's stated intentions, no publications based on them followed.

Imagined Worlds: Central Asian Jews and the Diaspora of Russian Jews

In 1915, Lur'e traveled to Turkestan and published an article, "Jews in Central Asia," which he had written in Tashkent.[56] It gives an insight into the perception of the world of Central Asian Jews through the prism of relations between the center and the periphery, between a Jewish ("European") progressive elite and conservative communities. Lur'e contrasted the Central Asian Jewish communities with the Pale of Settlement as the center of Jewish life, the representatives of which occupied, in his opinion, a higher rung of development. At the same time, Lur'e saw the link between the conservative Bukharan Jews

---

54 Bat-Zion Klorman, *Traditional Society in Transition: The Yemeni Jewish Experience* (Leiden: Brill Academic Publishers, 2014), 89–90.

55 Klorman describes the Yemenite Jews' social status as follows: "In Palestine they made numerous efforts to become part of the Zionist enterprise. But the Zionist establishment's response to their needs was never sufficient. Resources allocated to them were usually inferior to those given to immigrants from European countries, leaving them behind in comparison to Ashkenazi Jews" (ibid., 191).

56 Isaak Lur'e, "Evrei v Srednei Azii," *Rassvet* 8 (1915): 25–28.

and the Yishuv and consequently with the most important source of spiritual life for the Jewish nation as a great potential for the consolidation of Jewish national forces in Russia. Given the crisis facing Jews in the Pale of Settlement, overcoming the cultural abyss between Bukharan and European Jews was a political necessity. Contacts between these communities were expected to be a positive influence on the cultural status of the Bukharan Jews and the weakened national self-identification of the largely assimilated Ashkenazic Jews. Through this argument, Lur'e presented a fundamentally new model for perceiving the Bukharan Jews. Despite his elitist and considerably Orientalist tone, his views defined in a pragmatic way the role of Bukharan Jews in the diaspora of Russian Jews.

Lur'e described the Central Asian Jews through the prism of the national political needs of the Jewish community in Russia in the early twentieth century and during the First World War. Lur'e thought of the diaspora in terms of the East-West paradigm well-known in Jewish historiography, a paradigm he transferred to the Jewish cultural map of the Russian Empire.[57] He constructed a national discourse by counterposing Bukharan and Ashkenazic Jewish features, which signified the normative categories of the perception of Jews. The characteristics of national authenticity that Lur'e presented in his article go beyond the framework of the stereotypes of Oriental studies not only when he tries to describe the specifics of the culture and daily life of the peripheral Jewish community in Central Asia but also when he marks its functional location on the map of the diaspora. The daily practices of Bukharan Jews, which differed markedly from the Jewish world that Ashkenazic Jews in the "center" considered normal and orderly, gained a new significance in the context of political searches, although he did not claim himself to be a spiritual leader. Lur'e's concept presupposed a cultural exchange between Bukharan Jews and Ashkenazic Jews in Russia, behind which is suggested an attempt to smooth mutual discord and the unequal status of the two communities. At the same time, the role of the Bukharan Jews was nonetheless viewed from the standpoint of the interests of the Jewish national future, one being prepared and implemented by educated Ashkenazim:

> Now, when the "Pale," for decades the center of cultural and national life of Russian Jewry, faces incredibly difficult trials, it is more important than ever to rally and unite the Jews scattered

---

57 For the discourse of East and West in Jewish philosophy and historiography, see, for example, Hilbrenner, *Diaspora-Nationalismus: Zur Geschichtskonstruktion Simon Dubnows*, 11.

across central Russia. In an age of difficulties for the center, the periphery gains a special meaning and is burdened by new, important tasks. The time has come for Jews in the Russian interior to feel more clearly and emphasize more strongly their connection with the rest of Russian Jewry. Jews "beyond the Pale" are suffering the horrors of war significantly less [...] Jews "beyond the Pale" apparently do not feel the full importance and gravity of the moment when, on the one hand, we stand on the threshold of great events, both on the path of the implementation of our national ideal and on the path to transforming the legal framework of our daily life, and, on the other hand, we have been overwhelmed with disasters of the kind we had not experienced for a long time. Jews beyond the Pale have somehow grown unaccustomed to living by "national interests," even in the meaning of those words that a normal "common" Jew in the Pale would give them.[58]

In this statement on the political aims and intentions of his study of Bukharan Judaism, Lur'e defined the role of researchers, that is, the Jewish intelligentsia, and of himself: the elites, who culturally and intellectually surpassed the "Jewish mass," had to act as an invisible hand for the purpose of enabling qualitative changes in the diaspora. This self-perception was connected to the ideas of the Narodnik movement, which also influenced Jewish intellectual revolutionaries of the 1900s (such as An-sky and Shternberg).[59] Lur'e's appeal to Central Asian Jews characterizes him as a leader, educator, and peace-making force acting in the interests of Jewish national life and prosperity in the diaspora: "We need to shake off our passivity and apathy and begin to live by our national interests. We need to fix the mistake of the past decades, when Jews 'beyond the Pale' were almost entirely the stronghold of assimilation."[60]

The literature on Bukharan Jews during the empire period contains much evidence of discrimination. However, the general opinion was that antisemitism first came to Central Asia with the Russian conquest, whereas before that antisemitism was not characteristic of Muslim-Jewish relations, regardless of legal inequality in comparison with others. The population was atypical.

---

58 Lur'e, "Evrei v Srednei Azii," 25.
59 For An-sky's connections to the Narodnik movement, see, e.g., Lukin, "Akademiia, gde budut izuchat' folklor: An-skii—ideolog evreiskogo muzeinogo dela," 57.
60 Lur'e, "Evrei v Srednei Azii," 26.

Lur'e showed that he occupied precisely the same position and did not intend to make the interethnic tension and discrimination against Jews in Turkestan more difficult. He saw a restraining force in this "new" region and brilliantly contrasted its situation with that of eastern Europe, where enmity toward Jews was historically determined:

> That entire mass of various tribes lives side by side rather peacefully. In Turkestan, as everywhere, one feels slight antisemitism, but only slightly. The traditional antisemitism present in the Pale of Settlement, Poland, the Baltic region, or even in parts of the interior of Russia is absent here. Turkestan is a new region. Tashkent was only conquered 51 years ago, and the other cities even later. There are no social traditions here, and antisemitism here is therefore imported, light, brought in personally by every arrival from the interior of Russia or the western fringes.[61]

The position of Bukharan Jews in Central Asia could not be considered equal, given various legal restrictions and the arbitrariness of the Muslim rulers. However, in the eyes of Jews in Persia and Afghanistan, as well as Ashkenazim who had suffered from pogroms at the start of the twentieth century, Central Asian Jews were subjected to less official violence. This angle could be observed in Lur'e's essay, in which the author perceived modern antisemitism in the countries of eastern Europe as a threat to Jewish existence. In his opinion, the status of Bukharan Jews was formed by their relatively safe location in the multiethnic coexistence of the peoples of Central Asia.

The museum's collections thus primarily presented the question of legal discrimination and marginalization of Bukharan Jews in Central Asia in the collections of documents of the Russian government in Turkestan, which included copies of government files, statistical research, and literature. Bukharan Jews were also identified through materials on policy toward Jews in the Emirate of Bukhara, as well as toward *chala* Jews who had adopted Islam (*chala* is Tajik for "neither one nor the other"), who, socially and anthropologically, formed a border group. Dubnov selected out these materials in accordance with his principles of Jewish historical research: the community replaced the individual as a subject of national history and bearer of collective historical experience. This approach, which arose in the context of pre-Revolutionary national research of east European Jews, was

---

61 Ibid.

characterized by a focus on state policy and legislation as a historical actor whose object the Jews were. Like Dubnov, Lur'e studied the community of Bukharan Jews, who represented a nation and its collective experience.

In general, the view of the cultural heritage of Bukharan Jews may be characterized as a semantization of Bukharan Jews as peripheral or border members of the Jewish nation in diaspora. Social and cultural digressions were seen in this context as productive for the continuation of Jewish national life, as these changes shed light on the existing national order and facilitated its further existence. When Lur'e included Bukharan Jews in the pan-Jewish national discourse and observed this border group in the framework of the Jewish diaspora, he did so with an eye on Ashkenazic self-identification, which needed to be reinforced through differentiation and a comparative analysis of the various ends of the Jewish spectrum. In summarizing his ethnographic observations in Turkestan, Lur'e stated, "Unfortunately, there is almost no Jewish life in the region; there is the life of Jews, who try all they can to melt into the background and forget their nation and their national ideals."[62] He thereby drew a boundary between "belonging" and "not belonging" and set standards for national self-awareness and a national renaissance of the Jews.

The ethnographic aspect played a secondary role in this article about Central Asian Jews. Lur'e's perspective was aligned with the shared idea, current in the central regions of Russia, that the daily practices and rituals of Bukharan Jews "differed little from those of Muslims"[63] from an Ashkenazic perspective. Yet the expressed connection of Bukharan Jewish culture with the values and rituals of Judaism and strong national identification of Bukharan Jews, in particular, their unbroken connection with the Holy Land, earned close attention on the part of the Ashkenazic community. In Lur'e's words, this was because east European Jews' identity had no direct connection with native Jewish culture. This aspect reveals Lur'e's Zionist leanings and their integration in his methodology, a rare example of the confluence of Zionist ideas and Jewish diaspora ethnography.

Western Semantization of the Ethnography of Middle Eastern Jews

In Lur'e's collection and curatorial work, Bukharan Jews' cultural and historical narratives were related through artefacts of particularly valuable

---

62 Ibid., 28.
63 Ibid.

ethnological and aesthetic expressiveness. The visual representation of the cultural connection of Bukharan Jews with the Holy Land was also important. An example is a collection of ritual garments brought from Palestine to Samarkand for a woman's postnatal period and for men's prayer at Yom Kippur.[64] On the other hand, the artefacts made by Jewish textile dyers characterized the traditional local crafts of Bukharan Jews and the economic conditions of the Jewish minority in the multi-ethnic setting of Central Asia. At the same time, in the Jewish Museum opened by Lur'e in Samarkand in 1922, these artefacts told the story of the social status of the Jews before the Revolution since dyeing, a despised occupation, was forbidden to the Muslim population and could only be practiced by the poorest Uzbeks temporarily.[65]

Social narratives were communicated by typical Bukharan Jewish clothing, which could be distinguished from Tajik and Uzbek clothing in Samarkand through individual, almost invisible traits. A man's kaftan in the museum's collection could only be identified as Jewish by its silk lining: Muslims were forbidden by religious law from making linings from materials other than cotton.[66] Such artefacts also spoke to a low level of antisemitism among the native populations of Central Asia, as Lur'e noted during his first journey to Turkestan, yet a highly relevant issue for Ashkenazim.[67] In addition to Jewish markings on outerwear, which encouraged a discussion of rights and ethnic segregation, the external similarity of clothing worn by Jews, Uzbeks, and Tajiks from Central Asia pointed to a stronger interethnic connection, in contrast to the social chasm between Ashkenazic Jews and the majority of the population in the east European part of Russia, of which one form of evidence was the special clothing practices of Ashkenazic Jews, who lived in a similarly traditional fashion.

Overall, the range of fabrics and clothing demonstrates the view of the Europeanized curator of the Jewish Museum who had arrived in Samarkand from the capital of the Russian Empire. The choice of artefacts and stories on which the exhibition focused illustrates what Lur'e found socially and culturally noteworthy in the daily life of Bukharan Jews. His museum displays aimed, as a rule, at the construction of a "useful past" and a cultural and historical context for the development of a national dynamic in society. However, his observations and interpretations spoke to themes and problems of his own identity—that is,

---

64 Tat'iana Emel'ianenko, "Pamiatniki traditsionno-bytovoi kul'tury bukharskikh Evreev v muzeinikh sobraniiakh: osobennosti komplektovaniia," *Etnograficheskoe obozrenie* 3 (2010): 70.
65 Ibid.
66 Ibid.
67 Lur'e, "Evrei v Srednei Azii," 28.

they functioned autoethnographically. Moreover, the items chosen for display in the museum illustrated the single-faceted and limited nature of perception of an outsider in a rather closed traditional society.

All the garments in the museum collection were made of high-quality materials, including imported materials such as brocade, with luxurious gold and silver embroidery.[68] These objects represent a connection with medieval European documents from Central Asia that referred to the fact that the Bukharan Jews were wealthier and their standard of living was higher than their neighbors. The museum repeated this interpretation uncritically and placed aesthetics and regional exoticism in the foreground. This view omits the fact that the young generation of the Bukharan Jewish elite in Samarkand in the first two decades of the twentieth century strove to look European.[69] This approach to the choice of material artefacts for display in the museum became the reason for insufficient attention to the diversity of social and religious groups in the community.

The tendency to study Central Asian Judaism through the prism of Orientalist tradition was even more obvious in the method Lur'e practiced in his research. He used a pre-revolutionary collection of anthropological photographs of Central Asia as a template for his ethnographic research in Samarkand—in particular, a collection of Jewish types from the collections of the JSHE in St. Petersburg. In 1925, Lur'e wrote to Shternberg about how he used the photographs he had brought with him:

> The photographs of Bukharan Jews I brought with me from Leningrad were, as it turns out, taken in Samarkand, and it was a great pleasure for me when a 70-year-old Bukharan Jew warmly thanked me for the chance to see again his father, who had died 43 years before. It is a pity that I was unable to bring the other photographs of Bukharan Jews with me. I asked Yudovin to send them to me. Please remind him to do so when you see him.[70]

---

68 Emel'ianenko, "Pamiatniki traditsionno-bytovoi kul'tury bukharskikh Evreev v muzeinikh sobraniiakh," 71.

69 For the acculturation of wealthy Jews in Turkestan, see, for example, Kaganovich, *Druz'ia ponevole: Rossiia i bukharskie evrei 1800–1917*, 371–74.

70 St. Petersburg Division of the Archive of the Russian Academy of Sciences, f. 282, op. 2, d. 178, l. 2. The mention of Iudovin indicates that the collection of photographs of Central Asian Jews belonged to the Jewish Museum under the JSHE. In 1925, Yudovin was appointed curator of the collections of the Jewish Museum, which reopened following the Revolution of 1917 in 1923 (Aleksandr Ivanov, *Opyty molodogo cheloveka dlia fotograficheskikh rabot: Solomon Iudovin i russkii piktorializm*, [St. Petersburg: Center "Petersburg Judaica," 2005]).

In addition to the national educational ideas for the Jewish Museum, Lur'e brought objects with him which, as museum exhibits, transmitted his personal narrative, which he had prepared before he ever arrived in Samarkand. These exhibits also affected the construction of the self-representation of the local informants with whom Lur'e interacted in using these artefacts. Lur'e clearly followed an established model of behavior, as a similar subject was later described in the satirical novel *The Golden Calf* by Il'ia Il'f and Evgenii Petrov. The novel is about Muscovites who travel to Central Asia on the newly opened Turksib railway line with a tsarist-era travel guide and getting exclusively colonial impressions of their journey, which, to their pleasure, are confirmed by encounters with the local population.[71] The photographic collection created under Lur'e's leadership contained images that were clearly constructed under the influence of existing artistic and photographic images.[72] Aside from the research project, these observations by Lur'e and his colleagues facilitated the semantization of social and cultural differences among Bukharan Jews, the role of which in national design was determined by Lur'e's Western perspective.

Lur'e's attempts to capture the spiritual world of Bukharan Judaism and put it on museum display are still evident in the collections of religious artefacts, including Torah cases, several Hanukkah candlesticks, Passover Seder dishes, and other attributes of Jewish religious holidays.[73] In the museum, these religious artefacts became multi-layered sources that could primarily transmit the spiritual bases of Central Asian Jewish culture through the story of the local religious practices. Additionally, the religious artefacts of a spiritual life illuminated the basis of Judaism as a transnational cultural system that shattered regional boundaries and revealed deep connections.

The Torah case from 1728 gave an important understanding of the Samarkand community's history and way of life, with the aim of reinforcing the national self-perception of Bukharan Jews by presenting the Jewish framework its meaning established by religious law. The artefact explained the meaning of the religious ritual and the most important events in the Jewish year and life cycle. What is more, the origin, material, and technical completion of this metallic Torah case, decorated with filigreed engraving in the Persian style, contained a message

---

71 Il'ia Il'f and Evgenii Petrov, *Zolotoi telenok* (St Petersburg: Azbuka, 2018), 2:248–49.

72 This refers to characteristic photographs of anthropological types, as well as to photographs of Bukharan Jews in traditional indoor settings; see the Photographic Archive of the European Museum in Samarkand, a copy of which is stored in the St. Petersburg Institute of Jewish Studies.

73 Emel'ianenko, "Pamiatniki traditsionno-bytovoi kul'tury bukharskikh Evreev v muzeinikh sobraniiakh," 70.

about cultural contacts and migratory paths, as well as about the interaction of Bukharan Jews with the outside world, and the inclusion of Bukharan Jews in the social and economic life of Central Asia. All these themes were important for the researcher as material for the construction of a map of the diaspora and the positioning of Central Asian Jews on it.

Lur'e had similar aims when he formed a collection of Jewish manuscript translations into the Jewish Tajik language and books that he acquired for the future museum's library, of which he later exhibited a selection in the permanent collection.[74] In the context of the museum, the book as the central reflection of Jewish culture and the symbol of the "people of the book" was not only a material but also a spiritual and a linguistic source for the story of Jewish civilization. The museum's library catalogue consisted of around three hundred cards, the majority of which were printed in Hebrew in Europe in the nineteenth century.[75] Some had markings indicating their ownership at some time by Jewish families in Samarkand. Of particular interest were earlier editions, which made it possible to reconstruct a cultural heritage of the diaspora and its influence in Central Asia. Lur'e strove to study the intellectual cultural heritage of Bukharan Jews, which was supposed to contain spatial and temporal aspects. In this context, Lur'e collected and researched Persian Jews' manuscripts, which had already attracted his attention in St. Petersburg, and through the leadership of te Samarkand community he contacted the British Museum to obtain from London copies of the illustrated manuscripts of Persian Jews.[76] His intention in this, evidently, was to study the unique features of the liturgy of Bukharan Jews, who in the eighteenth century had transitioned from the Persian to the Sephardic ritual.[77] The intended result of this research was

---

74 An annotated inventory of manuscripts from the museum's collection was compiled in the 1990s by a research group from Russia, the United States, and Israel. Mikhail Nosonovskii, "Biblioteka i arkhiv Tuzemno-evreiskogo muzeia," in *Evrei v Srednei Azii: Proshloe i nastoiashchee*, ed. Il'ia Dvorkin (St. Petersburg: St. Petersburg Jewish University, 1995); Leonard Gertsenberg and Mikhail Nosonovskii, "Teksty na evreisko-tadzhikskom iazyke iz Tuzemno-evreiskogo muzeia v Samarkande," in *Evrei v Srednei Azii: Proshloe i nastoiashchee*, ed. Il'ia Dvorkin (St. Petersburg: St. Petersburg Jewish University, 1995), 160–76.

75 Nosonovskii, "Biblioteka i arkhiv Tuzemno-evreiskogo muzeia," 188.

76 Archive of the Institute of the Oriental Manuscripts of the Russian Academy of Sciences, f. 85, op. 2, d. 72, l. 2.

77 E. N. Adler began examining these questions during his expedition to Central Asia, of which Lur'e was very well aware. Adler visited Jews' houses with an interpreter in Bukhara and thus gathered information about private libraries. He acquired the most valuable items for his collection. Based on the publication dates of the discovered Persian and Sephardic prayer books, Adler reconstructed a chronology of changes in liturgical practice in the Bukharan community. Alanna Cooper, *Negotiating Identity in the Context of Diaspora, Dispersion and Reunion: The Bukharan Jews and Jewish Peoplehood* (PhD diss., Columbia University, 2000), 45.

a topography of eastern groups of Jews whose living spaces were immediately adjacent to each other.

The numerous translations and printed books from other Sephardic and Ashkenazic regions of the diaspora in Lur'e's collection present information on the participation of Bukharan Jews in the transregional Jewish scholarly discourse and the routes of knowledge transfer between Europe and Asia, which took place thanks to Jewish trade contacts and migration.[78] Lur'e's selection is his subjective reconstruction of this aspect of history. However, the multifaceted character of reading cultivated in the Jewish communities of Central Asia is striking. This fact contradicts the established Western concept of the cultural isolation and backwardness of Bukharan Jews. With the help of these studies, Lur'e approached questions regarding the structure of relations between separate Jewish groups in the global Jewish community and the meaning of the local historical and cultural experience complementing the rules of life laid down by Judaism.

Ethnographic Research as an Element of the Diaspora's Hierarchy

The subjective view of a St. Petersburg researcher on the culture of Bukharan Jews and his unspoken mission of political enlightenment of Central Asian Jews and bringing them closer to the national movement were even more obvious in his work with historical narratives. These aspects were exposed in the 1920s at an exhibition of the Samarkand Jewish Museum through the lens of basic events in the history of east European Jews. The exhibition related in detail the history of the Zionist movement, the participation of the Jew G. Perets in the Decembrists' Revolt of 1825, as well as the history of the Jewish socialist party, the Bund.[79] For this purpose, images and texts were used (copies of historical documents, newspaper clippings, and so forth), the aim of which was educating museum visitors about the class struggle of Jews in Russian society before 1917. While the historical experience of Central Asian Jews was being portrayed via primitive regional artefacts of material culture and traditional crafted items, the themes and subjects of the Ashkenazic world spoke of a dynamic unconnected with Bukharan Jews.

---

78 Nosonovskii, "Biblioteka i arkhiv Tuzemno-evreiskogo muzeia," 188.
79 Central State Archive of the Republic of Uzbekistan, f. R–94, op. 5, d.842, l. 6.

The museum exhibition was built on the sociopolitical narrative of the Jewish people in diaspora, a people whose driving force were the Ashkenazim. Also on display were materials related to the pre-Soviet past of Ashkenazic culture, which had roots in the religious aspects of Jewish life. The exhibition displayed exemplary images of Ashkenazic scholars and rabbis who represented the sources of the Jewish Orthodox movement in eastern Europe: the Vilna Gaon, the rabbi Yitzchak Elchanan Spektor, and others. There were photographs of synagogal plate from An-sky's collection in St. Petersburg, engravings with depictions of ornaments from headstones, and the interiors of synagogues in the Pale of Settlement that were researched during JSHe expeditions. These depictions were part of the exhibition's plan to reconstruct a model of the Jewish diaspora and collective identity of Ashkenazic Jews interactively. In this context, the east European synagogue symbolized the center of Jewish political life and stood in opposition to the Central Asian synagogue, which did not bear the same function.

The zoning of the Jewish world and the construction of the map of the diaspora also illustrate the migration of national ideas and objects from Europe to Asia. Lur'e went to Samarkand with ideas of Jewish national enlightenment and the diaspora that he had formed at the interface of the autonomist and Zionist national movements. During his work in Samarkand, his views were adjusted following the victory of the socialist revolution and the Soviet rise to power. In his 1915 article, Lur'e wrote that a great cultural and social divide lay between Ashkenazic and Bukharan Jews.[80] However, in the 1920s he tried to unite these two groups, turning the museum space and the exhibition into a site of multicultural contacts between Asian and European Jews. This project was intended to make possible the functioning of the diaspora, on the map of which Central Asia was essentially seen as a periphery for the conservation of conservative values necessary for the support of the national movement at its "center." This approach made it possible to include the border groups of Bukharan Jews in the map of the Jewish future. The empirical ethnography (documents and artefacts of spiritual culture, rituals, customs, folklore) also laid the basis for the ethnological and social semanticization of Bukharan Jews in the national context, illustrated the relations between different poles of the Jewish world, and was intended to facilitate their cultural exchange.[81]

---

80 Lur'e, "Evrei v Srednei Azii," 28.
81 Iulia-Karin Patrut, "'Zigeuner' als Grenzfigur deutscher Selbstentwürfe," *Geschichte und Gesellschaft*, 39 (2013): 298.

Conclusion

Lur'e's research reflected a national movement aimed at reinforcing the cultural and social self-perception of various Jewish groups via cultural memory. Lur'e's methodology went beyond the theory and practice of the St. Petersburg JSHE: in addition to the narratives of the nation's past necessary for the renewal of national life, Lur'e researched the transformation of national culture in the new political context. He was moved by a desire to highlight the present and study the borders between old and new Jewry. He stood for the innovative documentation of Jewish cultural heritage and ethnography, both from the diachronic and historiographical perspectives and from that of a synchronous analysis, which he had already formulated in his programmatic article of 1913. Lur'e's research shows a striving to create a model of collective Jewish identity that could combine Jews in Turkestan, the Caucasus, and Russia, relying as it did on the transnational religious component of Jewish culture. However, in this regard the attempt to connect the experience of Ashkenazic and Central Asian Jews reflected the Jewish social hierarchy in the Russian Empire and defined the spheres of influence of certain Jewish groups in a single Jewish whole.

Lur'e's research provides an understanding of the practice of transferring cultural practices, knowledge, and political ideas from the center to the peripheral regions of the Russian Empire and then the Soviet Union. Lur'e followed in the footsteps of Western scholars in Central Asia, whose massive scale was established by imperialist stereotypes and Orientalist models of perceiving the nations inhabiting the East. The category of "otherness" determined the motivation of such studies, tinting both scientific and political knowledge. The collection of material artefacts of Jews native to Central Asia collected by Lur'e contained many items that hearkened back to Russian colonial culture at the time of the conquest of Central Asia. With that, Lur'e's research directly illustrates the perspective of the Russian Jewish elite, which felt its separation from national roots and from the groups that formally made up the entirety of Russian Jewry.

The collection and exhibition of the museum of Bukharan Jewish culture created by Lur'e in the Sovietized Samarkand in 1922 provided an insight into the practice of imagining and stereotyping the "other" as well as the role of visual experiences in the public communication of national ideas. The photographical work and the assembled bulk of objects of the material culture of Bukharan Jews was a result of a semantic selection within the framework of a certain political and cultural agenda. It involved Orientalist objectivization by a Western scholar, elitist perspective on the indigenous culture linked to the imperial center-periphery relations, as well as Jewish nationalist populism fostering the concept of an imagined community that needs a sufficient number of people to identify with it in order to become real. Ironically, this approach reflected a swing between segregation and integration that characterized the policies of the Russian Empire toward Jews. In his approach, Lur'e drifted from the appreciation of the Bukharan Jewish conservative distinctiveness as a threshold of authentic and pure Judaic values to stereotyping the backwardness of Oriental Jews and attempts to acculturate them to the Ashkenazic culture as a source of reflected national self-identification.

The Jewish cultural and political discourse that arose at the center of the empire at the intersection of the Jewish national renaissance, Jewish emancipation, and revolutionary rise, upon being transferred to Turkestan underlined the semanticization of the peripheral community of Bukharan Jews as a border point in the Jewish national project. Lur'e's activities highlighted the hierarchical structure of the Jewish community in the Russian Empire, which was in many ways formed on the model of interaction between the Russian elite and the colonized peripheries. The image of the other and the concept of otherness, based in many ways on the researcher's ethnic stereotypes, were used to form an idea of collective identity, as well as to reflect the ethnographer's personal self-awareness. His ethnographic expeditions, for which he set the tasks of studying culture and bringing the intelligentsia closer to the people as part of the Jewish autonomist national movement, that is, entry into a cultural dialogue, illustrate the characteristic duality of perceiving a group of "others." For example, Lur'e pointed out the developmental backwardness of Bukharan Jews compared to the Ashkenazic Jews, that is, he contrasted them with his own "Westernist" ideas of the civilized nature of the nation. However, this very characterization is revealed as conservatism and faithfulness to the traditions of Judaism, which are valued more highly than the emancipated nature of Jews in the Russian capital. It is precisely by this that Lur'e recognizes the superiority of a group of Jews that is other to him in a certain category, while not denying the superiority of Ashkenazim in more important social and ethnic-political areas. This model of interaction between the Jewish elite and peripheral communities corresponds to the stereotyping between ethnic groups lacking close blood ties and copies the perspective of the populist (Narodnik) movement and of colonial ethnography. A diaspora constructed by Jewish autonomists on the basis of the opposition between "our" and "other," "civilized" and "backward," was destined to collide with the social and cultural distance between the former and the latter, the overcoming of which was utopian, even given their shared religion.

Works Cited

Archival Sources

Archive of the Institute of the Oriental Manuscripts of the Russian Academy of Sciences, f. 85, op. 2, d. 438, ll. 1–2.

Central State Archive of the Republic of Uzbekistan, f. R–94, op. 5, d. 842, ll. 6, 27.

St. Petersburg Division of the Archive of the Russian Academy of Sciences, f. 282, op. 2, d. 178, l. 2.

Printed Sources

Dubnov, Semen. *Grundlagen des Nationaljudentums.* Berlin: Jüdischer Verlag, 1905.

——. *Pis'ma o starom i novom evreistve.* St. Petersburg: Obshchestvennaia pol'za, 1907.

——. *Folkspartei: Evreiskaia narodnaia partiia.* St. Petersburg: C. Krayz, 1907.

——. "Istoricheskaia taina Kryma: 1. Periody krymskoy istorii, 2. Pamiatniki Mangup-Kale." *Evreiskaia starina* 7 (1914): 1–21.

Lur'e, Isaak. "O evreiskom muzee." *Rassvet* 50 (1914): 31–34.

——. "Evrei v Srednei Azii." *Rassvet* 8 (1915): 25–28.

"Uchreditel'noe sobranie i publichnye zasedaniia Evreiskago Istoriko-Etnograficheskago Obshchestva." *Evreiskaia starina* 1 (1909): 154–60.

Vaysenberg, Samuil. "Evrei v Turkestane: otchet o letnei poezdke." *Evreiskaia starina* 4 (1913): 390–406.

——. "Istoricheskie gnezda Kavkaza i Kryma: iz otcheta o letnei poezdke 1912 g." *Evreiskaia starina* 6 (1913): 51–60.

Wajsenberg, Samuil. "Jüdische Museen und Jüdisches in Museen: Reiseeindrücke." *Mitteilungen zur jüdischen Volkskunde* 3 (1907): 77–88.

Literature

Abykayeva-Tiesenhausen, Aliya. *Central Asia in Art: From Soviet Orientalism to the New Republics.* London: I. B. Tauris, 2016.

Armhorst-Weihs, Kerstin. "Die Zeitschrift 'Jevrejskaja starina': Wissenschaftlicher Kommunikationsort und Sprachrohr der Jüdischen Historisch-Ethnographischen Gesellschaft in St. Petersburg." *Zeitschrift für Religions- und Geistesgeschichte* 58, no. 1 (2006): 29–48.

Bemporad, Elissa. "Bemporad on Deutsch, 'The Jewish Dark Continent: Life and Death in the Russian Pale of Settlement.'" *H-Judaica*, April 2013. https://networks.h-net.org/node/28655/reviews/30942/bemporad -deutsch-jewish-dark-continent-life-and-death-russian-pale.

Brenner, Michael. *Kleine jüdische Geschichte*. München: C. H. Beck Verlag, 2008.

Cooper, Alanna. *Negotiating Identity in the Context of Diaspora, Dispersion and Reunion: The Bukharan Jews and Jewish Peoplehood*. PhD diss., Columbia University, 2000.

Deutsch, Nathaniel. *The Jewish Dark Continent: Life and Death in the Russian Pale of Settlement*. Cambridge, MA: Harvard University Press, 2010.

Dohrn, Verena. *Jüdische Eliten im Russischen Reich: Aufklärung und Integration im 19. Jahrhundert*. Cologne: Böhlau Verlag, 2008.

Dubnow, Simon. *Buch des Lebens: Erinnerungen und Gedanken. Materialien zur Geschichte meiner Zeit*. Göttingen: Vandenhoeck and Ruprecht, 2005.

Efron, John M. *Defenders of the Race: Jewish Doctors and Race Scientists in Fin-de-Siècle Europe*. New Haven: Yale University Press, 1994.

Emel'ianenko, Tat'iana. "Pamiatniki traditsionno-bytovoi kul'tury bukharskikh evreev v muzeinikh sobraniiakh: osobennostı komplektovaniia." *Etnograficheskoe obozrenie* 3 (2010): 66–76.

Gertsenberg, Leonard and Nosonovskii, Michail. "Teksty na evreisko-tadzhikskom iazyke iz Tuzemno-evreiskogo muzeia v Samarkande." In *Evrei v Srednei Azii: Proshloe i nastoiashchee*. Edited by Il'ia Dvorkin, 160–76. St. Petersburg: St. Petersburg Jewish University, 1995.

Hilbrenner, Anke. "Simon Dubnov's Master Narrative and the Construction of Jewish Collective Memory in the Russian Empire." *Ab imperio* 4 (2003): 143–64.

Hilbrenner, Anke. *Diaspora-Nationalismus: Zur Geschichtskonstruktion Simon Dubnows*. Göttingen: Vandenhoeck and Ruprecht, 2007.

Il'f, Il'ia, and Evgenii Petrov. *Zolotoi telenok*. Vol. 2. St. Petersburg: Azbuka, 2018.

Ivanov, Aleksandr. *Opyty molodogo cheloveka dlia fotograficheskikh rabot: Solomon Iudovin i russkii piktorializm*. St. Petersburg: Center "Petersburg Judaica," 2005.

Kaganovich, Albert. *Druz'ia ponevole: Rossiia i bukharskie evrei 1800–1917.* Moscow: Novoe literaturnoe obozrenie, 2016.

Kel'ner, Viktor. "Vremia sobirat' kamni (K istorii Evreiskogo istoriko-etnograficheskogo obshchestva i ego kollektsii)." *Voprosy muzeologii* 10, no. 1. (2019): 43–55.

Kieval, Hillel J. "Blood Libels and Host Desecration Accusations." *YIVO Encyclopedia of Jews in Eastern Europe,* 2016. Accessed June 13, 2022. https://yivoencyclopedia.org/article.aspx/Blood_Libels_and_Host_Desecration_Accusations.

Klier, John. "Pale of Settlement." *YIVO Encyclopedia of Jews in Eastern Europe,* 2010. Accessed June 13, 2022. https://yivoencyclopedia.org/article.aspx/Pale_of_Settlement.

———. *Russians, Jews, and the Pogroms of 1881–1882.* Cambridge: Cambridge University Press, 2011.

Klorman, Bat-Zion. *Traditional Society in Transition: The Yemeni Jewish Experience.* Leiden: Brill Academic Publishers, 2014.

Kugelmass, Jack. "The Father of Jewish Ethnography?" In *The Worlds of An-sky: A Russian Jewish Intellectual at the Turn of the Century.* Edited by Gabriela Safran and Steven Zipperstein, 346–61. Palo Alto: Stanford University Press, 2006.

Lukin, Veniamin. "Akademiia, gde budut izuchat' folklor: An-skii—Ideolog Evreiskogo muzeinogo dela." In *Evreiskii muzei.* Edited by Valerii Dymshits and Viktor Kelner, 57–94. St. Petersburg: Simpozium, 2004.

"Lur'e Isaak." *Elektronnaia evreiskaia entsiklopediia,* 2003. Accessed 13 June, 2022. https://eleven.co.il/jews-of-russia/education-secular-culture/12513/.

Meir, Natan. "'The Sword Hanging over Their Heads': The Significance of Pogrom for Russian Jewish Everyday Life and Self-Understanding (The Case of Kiev)." In *Anti-Jewish Violence: Rethinking the Pogrom in East European History.* Edited by Jonathan Dekel-Chen, 111–28. Bloomington: Indiana University Press, 2011.

Mogilner, Marina. "Between Scientific and Political: Jewish Scholars and Russian-Jewish Physical Anthropology in the Fin-de-Siècle Russian Empire." In *Going to the People: Jews and the Ethnographic Impulse.* Edited by Jeffrey Veidlinger, 45–63. Bloomington: Indiana University Press, 2016.

Nosonovskii, Mikhail. "Biblioteka i arkhiv Tuzemno-evreiskogo muzeia." In *Evrei v Srednei Azii: Proshloe i Nastoiashchee.* Edited by Il'ia Dvorkin, 188–92. St. Petersburg: St. Petersburg Jewish University, 1995.

Patrut, Yulia-Karin. "'Zigeuner' als Grenzfigur deutscher Selbstentwürfe." *Geschichte und Gesellschaft* 39 (2013): 286–305.

Pul'ner, Isai. "Voprosy organizatsii evreiskikh etnograficheskikh muzeev i evreiskikh otdelov pri obshchikh etnograficheskikh muzeiakh." *Sovetskaia etnografiia* 3–4 (1931): 156–63.

Reznik, Semen. "Krovavy navet v Rossii. Istoriko-dokumental'nye ocherki," *Vestnik* 24, no. 231, (November 23, 1999), cited in *Ldn-Knigi-Lib*. http://ldn-knigi.lib.ru/JUDAICA/R_Chvolson.htm.

Safran, Gabriela. *Wandering Soul: The Dybbuk's Creator, S. An-sky*. Cambridge, MA: Harvard University Press, 2010.

Schimmelpenninck van der Oye, David. *Russian Orientalism: Asia in the Russian Mind from Peter the Great to the Emigration*. New Haven: Yale University Press, 2010.

Seltzer, Robert. *Simon Dubnow's New Judaism: Diaspora Nationalism and the World History of the Jews*. Leiden: Brill Academic Publishers, 2014.

Sergeeva, Irina. "Istoriia Muzeia i Arkhiva Evreiskogo istoriko-etnograficheskogo obshchestva posle oktiabria 1917 goda." *Judaic-Slavic Journal* 1, no. 2 (2019): 13–43.

Stanislawski, Michael. "Russia: Russian Empire." *YIVO Encyclopedia of Jews in Eastern Europe*, 2010. Accessed June 13, 2022. https://yivoencyclopedia.org/article.aspx/Russia/Russian_Empire.

Veidlinger, Jeffrey. *Jewish Public Culture in the Late Russian Empire*. Bloomington: Indiana University Press, 2009.

Veidlinger, Jeffrey, ed. *Going to the People: Jews and the Ethnographic Impulse*. Bloomington: Indiana University Press, 2016.

Part Three

THE OTHER IN TIMES OF CONFLICT AND CRISIS

Section Summary

Stephen M. Norris

In May 1904, Nikolai Georgevich Garin-Mikhailovskii, a fifty-two-year-old travel writer, hit the road again. Known for a 1898 book about his journey around the world, this time he ventured to Chita. A major transit hub because one of the first Siberian segments on the Trans-Siberian Railroad connected the city with Irkutsk, 550 miles to the west, and a point where travelers could either continue to Vladivostok or change to journey to Harbin, Chita was a bustling steppe city. At the time the writer visited, Chita saw an influx of Russian soldiers: Garin-Mikhailovskii was there to get a sense for how the war that had broken out between Russia and Japan was unfolding. Upon arriving, the writer and his companions rushed to the newsstand to gobble up the latest news only to discover the papers were the same editions they had just read in Irkutsk.

Then a Russian officer approached. Garin-Mikhailovskii described the soldier as thin and raggedy, wearing a shabby uniform, fresh from battle and fresh from witnessing a defeat. Garin-Mikhailovskii and his companions pressed the officer for answers about his recent battle—he fought for seven hours straight at one point before receiving a wound—and about the Japanese enemy. The officer described them as brave, worthy opponents, even if he thought his fellow Russians were braver. The officer went on to dispel rumors his interlocutors had about the Japanese—they fought in a sophisticated fashion, not as beasts. The encounter ended with Garin-Mikhailovskii asking how the Russian officer felt about the Japanese before the war. "I thought they were monkeys," came the reply.[1]

A few days later, Garin-Mikhailovskii finally got new newspapers from Moscow. By that time, he had become hopeful that the Russians would prevail in the war because the impressions "our" troops held about the enemy had also changed in the way the officer first told them about. "No longer do you hear the words 'monkeys' or 'yellow-skins,'" he observed, but now the view of the enemy is one of respect. Russian armies could win, in other words, because they had stopped seeing their enemy as caricatures. Now that they knew they were fighting worthy opponents, the war could be won.[2]

A couple of months before Garin-Mikhailovskii encountered the attitudes about the Japanese, the noted newspaper publisher Aleksei Suvorin—whose papers Garin-Mikhailovskii no doubt read while in Irkutsk and Chita—received a visit from Sergei Tatishchev, the diplomat and historian, who was acting on behalf of Viacheslav von Plehve, the minister of the interior. Suvorin had been in the newspaper business for a long time: his paper, *Novoe vremia* (New Times), was particularly popular and influential. It was also avowedly nationalistic, supporting first Alexander III's and then Nicholas II's policies of Russification. *Novoe vremia* had even advocated for the imperial ventures in the Far East that Garin-Mikhailovskii would want to observe. In his editorials, Suvorin would insult the Japanese "yellow Lilliputians" and "devils with horns," among other slurs.[3] Before his visitor arrived, Suvorin had discussed an article with one of his journalists that called the Japanese "devils with green eyes."[4] The writer worried that the article was more like a *lubok*, a popular print, than a newspaper piece. Suvorin didn't mind, noting that a good visual lubok needed talent just like an article but both could drive home a clear point about the nature of Russia's enemy.[5]

Then his visitor arrived. Tatishchev's trip to Suvorin in March 1904 confirmed the paper's significance. As the power of the press grew, and with it the expansion

---

1 Garin-Mikhailovskii's diary is available through the remarkable *Prozhito* project run by the European University of St. Petersburg. This entry is located here: Nikolai Garin-Mikhailkovskii, "Zapis' dnevnika," *Prozhito*, accessed June 22, 2022, https://prozhito.org/note/90269. He uses the word "macaque" (*makaka*).

2 Garin-Mikhailovskii's entry: Nikolai Garin-Mikhailkovskii, "Zapis' dnevnika," *Prozhito*, accessed June 22, 2022, https://prozhito.org/note/90278.

3 See Zachary Hoffman, "Subversive Patriotism: Aleksei Suvorin, *Novoe vremia*, and Right-Wing Nationalism during the Russo-Japanese War," *Ab Imperio* 1 (2018): 76.

4 Suvorin's diary entry also available through the *Prozhito* site: Aleksei Surovin, "Zapis' dnevnika," *Prozhito*, accessed June 22, 2022, https://prozhito.org/note/202439.

5 Ibid.

of a public sphere in the Russian Empire, Nicholas II began to realize he needed to court the right sort of journalism. Tatishchev told Suvorin the tsar wanted to meet with a newspaper delegation. Nicholas II had three conditions for its composition: it should consist of three people, one had to be Suvorin, and no one could be Jewish. "The sovereign loves you,"[6] Tatishchev told Suvorin. The message that passed between editor and tsar was one that Suvorin belonged; Jews did not. The newspaperman was excited yet anxious, pleased that the tsar himself read the paper but worried that a summons to court might affect its popularity.[7] He went anyway.

These two episodes from 1904 may not be directly related, but they are connected in important ways. Both capture sentiments about war. Both note the significance of media—newspapers, but also popular prints—within the Russian Empire. Both highlight the enemies of this empire, often understood crudely and in national terms. Garin-Mikhailovskii's travels and talks and Suvorin's meetings and musings reveal how discussions of enemies, both external and internal, involved people from random Russian soldiers, well-known travel writers, newspaper magnates, and the tsar himself. The views about enemies— whether Japanese opponents in war or the fear of Jewish journalists—stemmed from the rise of nationalism within and outside the Russian Empire.

Russia had begun to experience significant problems with nationalism prior to 1904, a byproduct of longstanding developments stretching back at least to 1812, when the war against Napoleon awoke of a strand of Russian national identity.[8] After the defeat in the Crimean War (1853–56), the empire faced challenges produced from it and the subsequent era of Great Reforms, which in turn introduced new ways of participating in the political system and with it, new categories of difference within the diverse empire. Booming interest in ethnography and in history fueled these differences, in part by promoting and then categorizing notions of "Russianness" and its preeminence against peoples within the Empire deemed less civilized.[9] Russia went to war in 1877 against the Ottoman Empire in part because of public demands that the "Great Russians" do something to help their "brother Slavs," the Bulgarians, living under a "Turkish

---

6 Ibid.
7 Ibid.
8 A subject I cover in my book *A War of Images: Russian Popular Prints, Wartime Culture, and National Identity, 1812–1945* (DeKalb: Northern Illinois University Press, 2006). For the early development of this trend, see Hans Rogger's classic study: *National Consciousness in Eighteenth-Century Russia* (Cambridge, MA: Harvard University Press, 1960).
9 Olga Maiorova covers this subject in her excellent book, *From the Shadow of Empire: Defining the Russian Nation through Cultural Mythology, 1855–1870* (Madison: The University of Wisconsin Press, 2010).

yoke." National, imperial, and religious imaginings collided here, seen in popular prints at the time and in the emerging popular press, including Suvorin's: he would even recall this connection when recounting his 1904 meeting.

Under Alexander III and his son, Nicholas II, these developments came together in a campaign of Russification and a reification of all things "Russian," powered by "a fervent love for ethnic Russia and its imperial ambitions."[10] Tensions naturally followed, not least because the imperial state "engaged in both discriminating as well as nationalizing policies," but also "maintained vital distinctions between Russians and non-Russians, Orthodox and non-Orthodox peoples, as well as between social estates."[11] The Russian Empire, in other words, tried to act like an empire and nation all at once.

As the imperial state engaged in these policies, the tsar and his officials began to worry more about national groups within the empire and not just those outside its borders. Troublesome groups such as the Poles became even more pernicious in the eyes of tsarist administrators and Russian nationalists: they were not just rebellious, but poisonous and contagious.[12] National movements in Finland and Ukraine also seemingly threatened the very fabric of the nationalizing empire, causing consternation and further discriminatory policies. "Older hierarchical categories based on social estate or religion," Valerie Kivelson and Ronald Suny have written, "steadily gave way to new loci of identity based on class, occupation, and ethnicity."[13]

We could also add race to this list, as that term and concept began to filter into the empire and fuel further tensions. As Eugene Avrutin has demonstrated, the "deep conservatism and pessimism" of the time meant that "Jews emerged as the most visible 'others' who were often perceived as a threat to the health and prosperity of the imperial 'nation.'"[14] The Russo-Japanese War of 1904–5 and revolution within Russia that followed defeat brought these trends out clearly.

---

10 Valerie Kivelson and Ronald Grigor Suny, *Russia's Empires* (Oxford: Oxford University Press, 2017), 199.

11 Ibid., 201. See also Mikhail Dolbilov's study of the earlier unevenness of Russification in the western borderlands, "Russification and the Bureaucratic Mind in the Russian Empire's Northwestern Region in the 1860s," *Kritika* 5, no. 2 (Spring 2004): 245–71. Dolbilov's massive study is also instructive: *Russkii krai, chuzhaia vera: Etnokonfessional'naia politika imperii v Litve i Belorussii pri Aleksandre II* (Moscow: NLO, 2010).

12 Kivelson and Suny, *Russia's Empires*, 205. These issues are also covered in Aleksei Miller's book, *Imperiia Romanovykh i natsionalizm* (Moscow: NLO, 2010). The image of the "rebellious Poles" and how it shaped Russian national identity is covered in Mal'te Rol'f, *Pol'skie zemli pod vlast'iu Peterburga: ot Venskogo Kongressa do Pervoi Mirovoi* (Moscow: NLO, 2020).

13 Kivelson and Suny, *Russia's Empires*, 223.

14 Eugene Avrutin, "Racial Categories and the Politics of (Jewish) Difference in Late Imperial Russia," *Kritika* 8, no. 1 (Winter 2007): 14–15.

Russian popular prints and newspaper reports frequently cast the Japanese enemy in racially inferior terms—often as monkeys—while the explosion of new publications during and after 1905 included nationalist journals that would denounce Jews in particular as harmful to the nation.[15]

The two episodes above provide telling snapshots of these tendencies. The soldier who spoke to Garin-Mikhailovskii had obviously imbibed the racist sentiments circulating about the Japanese, while Suvorin and Nicholas II shared a racist belief about Russia's Jewish population.[16] In fact, the two episodes may be more connected than they seem. In a 1906 issue of the nationalist, anti-Semitic journal *Pliuvium*, the cartoonist Luka Zlotnikov drew a gross caricature of a Jewish man and a Japanese officer linked arm-in-arm, both holding bags of money from their alliance.[17] External and internal enemies were now more or less the same in the eyes of extreme nationalists.

This section's chapters also draw links between imagined enemies of the Russian Empire in the later imperial period. We might read the contributions that follow as further episodes of the kind Garin-Mikhailovskii and Suvorin recounted, further explorations of the nationalizing trends and pressures within the Empire Zlotnikov's cartoon visualizes.

Between 1890 and 1905, as Anna Rezvukhina, Alena Rezvukhina, and Sergey Troitskiy discuss in their contribution, the media ecosystem that existed in Russia prior to 1905 produced a dizzying array of images depicting Russian enemies, rivals, and even friends. This imagined "bestiary" acted as a zoo of sorts, with an assortment of national stereotypes grafted onto representations of animals. Great Britain could be drawn in several guises, with a hungry lion emerging as the most common depiction of that country. Similarly, Russian image makers took the French cockerel—a national symbol within France, just as the British lion was within the UK—and adapted it, making it appear more arrogant. Given that France and Russia entered an alliance in this period, the animalistic representations of that country proved to be less insulting than those featuring the British lion. Germany was most frequently portrayed as a dog, China as a dragon, while the United States—a newer country without a well-established animal symbol—proved harder to pin down visually. And,

---

15 I cover the popular prints of the war in *A War of Images*. For the right-wing journals, see my article *"Pliuvium's* Unholy Trinity: Russian Nationhood, Anti-Semitism, and the Public Sphere after 1905," *Experiment* 19 (2013): 87–116.

16 Suvorin was himself a notorious anti–Semite. See Benjamin Nathans, *Beyond the Pale: The Jewish Encounter with Late Imperial Russia* (Los Angeles: University Press of California, 2002), 285–92.

17 L. Zlotnikov, "Allies (A Jew and a Japanese)," *Pliuvium*, no. 8 (Nov. 25, 1906), 1.

of course, Russian caricaturists depicted Japan in various zoomorphic guises, including monkeys.

Examining a roughly similar chronology, Immo Rebitschek takes us deep into the making of internal others based on ethnicity and with it, the role of otherness within an empire such as Russia's. Focusing on famines in the Volga region between 1891 and 1907, Rebitschek explains how tsarist officials initially could only conceive of famines as a "peasant" matter, thinking in terms of social estate, thus exacerbating its effects among the Tatar populations. Moreover, widespread belief on the ground that the Tatars had received better plots after serfdom's end, failed to pay for their land, and still shirked their work meant that General Mikhail Annenkov, sent by the Ministry of Interior to deal with the famine in 1892, cared little for the suffering of Tatars, stating coldly that "The Tatar economy will collapse—that is the judgment of history, and it is scarcely beneficial to support them at the expense of the Russian population."[18] Here we can see national difference at work: "Russians" belong in the Volga region and within the Empire; Tatars, who had lived in this region longer, do not.

The concept of an enemy from one nation or group that threatens the dominant hold of another, as Johanna Wassholm writes in her fascinating contribution, could also be turned against Russians. The Grand Duchy of Finland had enjoyed relative autonomy within the Russian Empire after its 1809 incorporation, but the pressures of nationalism noted above led Nicholas II to issue a February Manifesto in 1899 that ramped up heavy Russification policies within Finland. Edvard Isto's well-known painting *Attack* (at least well-known to those of us who regularly use it in classes to illustrate this episode) perfectly captures the Finnish response: a blonde Finnish maiden dressed in a white dress with a blue shawl (the national colors) fends off a rapacious double-headed eagle trying to rip her book of laws from her hands. Isto could therefore redirect the bestial imaginary that Russian image makers drew about other groups against Russia. And as Wassholm writes, after 1899 the Finnish press had a field day depicting itinerant Russian peddlers—common traveling salesmen across the empire who often carried the newspapers and popular prints that spread other stereotypes—as hostile agents working to further undermine Finnishness. These Russians were cast on the pages of Finnish papers as weeds, parasites, and harmful creatures.

The proliferation of enemy images of the kinds described above, including bestial imaginaries and concepts of parasites needing to be eliminated, proliferated in Russian right-wing publications after 1905. Oleg Minin notes in his chapter that journal titles themselves reflected this nasty turn: examples

---

18 See Rebitschek's chapter in this volume.

include publications such as *Knout* and *Rope*. The national, ethnic, and racial lenses that had been crafted and employed to view others since the 1890s (if not before) could be retooled after 1905 to peer at any number of internal and external enemies who were deemed unsupportive of the monarchy. Minin analyzes the Zlotnikov image mentioned above as part of this rightward, and more ominous, focus on enemies. The text of the cartoon acknowledged defeat in the Russo-Japanese War but vowed to win the greater national war against enemies: "They defeated us," it asked, "but will they also rule over us?"[19] These journals answered that question, as Minin notes, by regularly featuring images of the heroic *bogatyr*, a medieval knight, who always stood ready to crush Russia's foes.

The repertoire of enemies would expand after 1905. A. A. Avdashkin analyzes how the Russian acquisition of Far Eastern territories and with them, an influx of Chinese laborers into Russia, further cemented a Russian version of the notorious "yellow peril" concept. Focusing on Chinese workers in the Ural region through a close reading of archival documents, Avdashkin reveals how the new workers provoked consternation among other laborers and tsarist officials alike, reinforcing at local, regional, and national levels the emerging racialized discourses about "others." A further influx of Chinese laborers during the Great War only inflamed tensions further. As Avdashkin effectively argues, the attitudes expressed by ethnic Russians in Perm powerfully capture the surprising speed in the spread and depth of resentment based on ethnic stereotypes in late imperial Russia. External enemies, when brought inside the Empire, remained enemies nonetheless, delineated along racial and religious lines.

Identifying, categorizing, and castigating enemies of course did not end in 1917, as the empire experienced the tumult of revolution. Instead, the Bolsheviks and their enemies sought to mobilize support through their own views of who was and who was not against them. Amid this revolutionary moment, as I. S. Rat'kovskii writes, someone such as Lavr Kornilov, the tsarist general best known for the "affair" from August and September 1917 that bears his name, acts as a perfect encapsulation of the way othering developed in the late empire and how it transferred into the Soviet period. A Siberian Cossack with Asian heritage, Kornilov could be viewed as "one of ours," an "other," or just "an outsider" depending on who was writing about him. As Russia descended into political chaos and violence, Kornilov's supporters turned him into an almost saint-like figure, a true "Russian" patriot. His detractors would see him as an 'outsider' who was devilish in his intentions. This either/or othering built on the concepts developed in the late imperial era, notions bandied about in

---

19 See Minin's chapter in this volume.

Garin-Mikhailovskii's and Suvorin's recollections that open this introduction. It also ensured that depictions of enemies could be reused yet again, forming an important component of the Soviet era.

Works Cited

Avrutin, Eugene. "Racial Categories and the Politics of (Jewish) Difference in Late Imperial Russia." *Kritika* 8, no. 1 (Winter 2007): 13–40.

Dolbilov, Mikhail. "Russification and the Bureaucratic Mind in the Russian Empire's Northwestern Region in the 1860s." *Kritika* 5, no. 2 (Spring 2004): 245–71.

———. *Russkii krai, chuzhaia vera: Etnokonfessional'naia politika imperii v Litve i Belorussii pri Aleksandre II.* Moscow: NLO, 2010.

Garin-Mikhailovskii, Nikolai Georgevich. *Zapis' dnevnika*, 1904. Accessed June 15, 2022. https://prozhito.org/note/90269.

Hoffman, Zachary. "Subversive Patriotism: Aleksei Suvorin, *Novoe vremia*, and Right-Wing Nationalism during the Russo-Japanese War." *Ab Imperio* 1 (2018): 69–100.

Kivelson, Valerie and Suny, Ronald Grigor. *Russia's Empires*. Oxford: Oxford University Press, 2017.

Maiorova, Olga. *From the Shadow of Empire: Defining the Russian Nation through Cultural Mythology, 1855–1870.* Madison: The University of Wisconsin Press, 2010.

Mal'e. Rol'f. *Pol'skie zemli pod vlast'iu Peterburga: ot Venskogo Kongressa do Pervoi Mirovoi.* Moscow: NLO, 2020.

Miller, Aleksei. *Imperiia Romanovykh i natsionalizm*. Moscow: NLO, 2010.

Nathans, Benjamin. *Beyond the Pale: The Jewish Encounter with Late Imperial Russia.* Los Angeles: University Press of California, 2002.

Norris, Stephen M. *A War of Images: Russian Popular Prints, Wartime Culture, and National Identity, 1812–1945.* DeKalb: Northern Illinois University Press, 2006.

———. "*Pliuvium's* Unholy Trinity: Russian Nationhood, Anti-Semitism, and the Public Sphere after 1905." *Experiment* 19 (2013), 87–116.

Rogger, Hans. *National Consciousness in Eighteenth-Century Russia.* Cambridge, MA: Harvard University Press, 1960.

Zlotnikov, L. "Allies (A Jew and a Japanese)." *Pliuvium*, no. 8 (St. Petersburg, Nov. 25, 1906), 1.

10

The Russian Imagological Bestiary: The Zoomorphic Image of the Enemy ("Other") at the Turn of the Century, 1890–1905

Anna Rezvukhina, Alena Rezvukhina, and Sergey Troitskiy

Abstract

Based on the material of caricatures from satirical magazines of the Russian Empire's period of decline (*Budil'nik, Shut*, and so on), as well as postcards and posters, this chapter reveals the visual rhetorical mechanisms for the "other" on the eve of the Russian Revolution of 1905. The period between 1890 and 1905 was one of active development of new methods of image formation and changes in iconology and iconography under the influence of new technologies in the media space, and a lively rapprochement of the fine arts with everyday social and political life. New ways of image shaping were developing both with the reduction of space due to the development of the media and expansion of geographical space, mainly to the East—to China and Japan. The revised world map and its construction through the concept of oneself and others is the main theme of the analyzed caricatures. They represent the local visual images of the enemy that existed during the period, in which the image of the "other" found both its toponymic localization and personification through fusion with the innate image of the other country. The representation of the world as a "bestiary"—the development and use of zoomorphic images of "others" (as octopi, snakes, monkeys, and so on)—is especially emphasized. Other ways of depicting otherness are also considered: the semantics of color, scale, associative array, and posture.

Introduction

The concept of space has often been visualized through anthropomorphic or zoomorphic images. These images not only convey knowledge about the population of specific regions, but communicate regional political and cultural preferences, as well as expectations, about these locations.[1] Motivated by the desire to explore the world around them, people looked for the features of familiar creatures, animals, or people with whom they could "come to an agreement" in the uncontrollable environment, whether they were constellations, forces of nature, or new territories. This iconic interpretation is found in the earliest maps and became especially popular during the Age of Discovery. In the Middle Ages, it replaced descriptions of regions in cartography, reflecting the prevailing cultural trend of visualization for the illiterate (for example, the system of ecclesiastical visual images known as "the Bible for the Illiterate" by Gregory the Great [590–604]). Maps and atlases not only show the relative geographical positions of different areas—they also provide reference information and reflect cultural relations between the recorded area and the region where the map (or atlas) was made. Mapmaking still follows the same principle: "Only after the 'own' spaces have been dealt with, the 'rest' can be understood, but often in less detail. This order fundamentally affects young people's worldviews."[2] The cartographer's own region is the reference point, the center of the world.

Visual anthropomorphic or zoomorphic images used to characterize a certain location reflected stereotypical ideas about it. In other words, these images had to have their own unique language, serve as markers or "icons," so that readers could successfully interpret the information they conveyed. A map (or atlas) could therefore only be interpreted in one way, determined by the cartographer and his or her specific cultural values and stereotypes. All other interpretations of maps were rejected. "As a result, the map-reader easily falls into the habit of

1 Special thanks to Maria Bumakova and Irina Nagovitsyna for their translation of this chapter to English.
2 Severin Halder et al., eds., *This Is Not an Atlas: A Global Collection of Counter-Cartographies* (Bielefeld: Transcript Verlag, 2018), 11.

seeing 'the map as a precise portrayal of reality.'"[3] Thus, the boundaries on maps (or atlases) were much more effective than real ones. The symbolic stratification of space performed by cartographers confirmed and/or set clear cultural roles, distinguishing between the "self" and the "other." As parts of this book demonstrate, such space stratification can be found in any period of Russian history.

This chapter analyses how visual images that reflect cultural stereotypes also determine borders on the cultural map. Our objective is to recreate the cultural map of a short period in the history of Russian culture—the heyday of Romantic nationalism, that is, the last decade of the nineteenth century, ending with the Russo-Japanese War (1904) and the first Russian Revolution (1905). That period was entitled also imperialism. The Russian media was subject to censorship, making it especially revealing. The government's concession to the revolutionary public, the October Manifesto (October 17, 1905), declared the freedom of the press, stimulating almost uncontrolled publishing activity. Magazines were prohibited only after they had been published. We are especially concerned with the period before the publishing boom.

Moreover, the fine arts were at their zenith between 1890 and 1905 because of the increased public interest in art and artists' desire to marry high art with sociopolitical (everyday) life. Established and generally accepted mechanisms of image creation were modified and updated. New technologies determined new conditions and limitations for the iconology and iconography of images. It was now possible to distribute printed images, which benefited artistically from the very popular Russian *lubok* print. This possibility encouraged the development of caricature in magazines, newspapers, posters, and postcards. Although each media type had its technical limitations that affected the construction of the image, the general principles of visual caricature rhetoric had already begun to form in the late nineteenth-century media space.

Stereotypes in Caricatures

Like the images in atlases, caricatures also deal with stereotypes. A stereotypical caricature causes laughter because its aim is to convey cultural stereotypes, exaggerating them or placing them in an unusual context. Zachary Hoffman, who studied the caricature in 1900–1905 Russian publications of *Russkoe*

---

3   John Pickles, *A History of Spaces. Cartographic Reason, Mapping and the Geo-Coded World* (London: Routledge, 2004), 35.

Slovo (Russian Word) and *Novoe Vremia* (The New Times), points out that "stereotypical representations perpetuated these depictions but also built narratives of purportedly typical European and Asian behaviors [. . .] these visual narratives articulated specific ideas about Europeanness and Asianness."[4] At the same time, caricatures are a follow-up to the cultural or political discourse they convey. Caricatures therefore allow the researcher to identify the typical (stereotypical) features of everyday culture (at the level of everyday consciousness), describe the cultural and political discourse[5] of a given period, or highlight any changes in stereotypes. It should be noted, however, that such changes can only occur in the wake of major events, such as revolutions.[6]

The very structure of a caricature makes it a perfect political tool. In most cases a caricature is a combination of visual (an image) and verbal (writing that accompanies the image, such as a character's speech, a caption, or a title) elements. Yet its most important element is the current and retrospective cultural context—its relationship with cultural stereotypes and common historical, cultural, political, mythological, religious, and everyday realia. Since the caricature refers to up-to-the-minute high-profile personalities and events, and simultaneously relies on stereotypes, images, and associations established in the cultural code, the context complements the information compressed and encrypted in the caricature, giving it a broader perspective. The story depicted in the caricature thus fits the reader's available knowledge system and worldview. The expressiveness of the caricature—its humorous basis—does not appeal to logical arguments of reason but to the emotions. The caricature leaves no room for multiple interpretations and gives an unambiguous and categorical assessment—it denounces, exposes, condemns, or ridicules. The moment when the "truth" is "suddenly" revealed and "lies" are fiercely exposed repeats itself in the caricature. This is especially true for the visual component, where the essence is revealed by deforming the external appearance. The external appearance thus reinforces the inner meaning, making it obvious.

The caricature is always relevant (it deals with current issues and alludes to a specific person or event) and convincing (it refers to the context, well-known facts, and established elements of the cultural code). Its images are recognizable, understandable, and easy to interpret, which makes the caricature an effective

---

4   Zachary Hoffman, "Drawing Stereotypes: Europe and East Asia in Russian Political Caricature, 1900–1905," *Sibirica* 19 (2020): 87.

5   Evgeniia Artemova, *Karikatura kak zhanr politicheskogo diskursa* (PhD diss., The Volgograd State Pedagogical University, 2002).

6   John Richard Moores, "Revolution," in *Representations of France in English Satirical Prints 1740–1832*, ed. John R. Moores (London: Palgrave Macmillan, 2015), 151–76.

political tool. Depending on *what* exactly is emphasized, and *how* it is depicted in the caricature, public opinion based on a certain political position is formed, and the actions of the ruling elite are legitimized in the world arena. For example, the image of the "other" is used to model the world and divide the existing geopolitical map into the "self," "our allies," and "our enemies." The image of the "self" is clearly outlined; the "other" is defined as the opposite of the "self," and vice versa, the image of the "self" is clarified through the "other."

Zoomorphic Images in Caricature: The Historical Background

In the late nineteenth and early twentieth centuries, Russian magazines and newspapers tended to mix serious articles and caricature. Moreover, special satirical magazines focused on the humiliation of the "other" or "others." There was a need to find a place for new images on the map of the "other" or "others" in addition to the already established caricature iconography of Russia's former international opponents. European, and especially Russian, ideas of the world map broadened—mainly towards the East (Japan, China, and Korea). With advances in technology that made communication over long distances easier, this encouraged people to seek new ways of description.

Media caricature was now a tool to overcome cultural aphasia—it created a new language for exploring and assimilating space. Cultural aphasia, a concept proposed by Roman Jakobson[7] and developed by Serguei Oushakine[8] in relation to the 1990s, quite accurately describes the period under study and the cultural processes in Russia at that time. The last years of Alexander III's reign were marked by a particularly conservative cultural and political life; chauvinist attitudes became ever more pronounced, and the reforms were completely reversed. The sovereign's desire to achieve and maintain ultimate stability gave rise to censorship and isolationist tendencies. The beginning of Nicholas II's reign did not bring the expected changes; on the contrary, he declared he would follow a similar path. Until the First Russian Revolution and the October Manifesto, despite the huge changes that took place in culture, the economy, technology, foreign policy, public life, and their associated

7 Roman Jakobson, "Two Aspects of Language and Two Types of Aphasic Disturbances," in *Fundamentals of Language*, ed. Roman Jakobson and Morris Halle (Hague: Mouton & Co, 1956).
8 Serguei Alex Oushakine, "Byvshee v upotreblenii: Postsovetskoe sostoianie kak forma afazii," *Novoe literaturnoe obozrenie* 100 (2009): 760–92.

expectations, official policy praised traditionalism and opposed innovation in artistic expression. Policies of suppression led to what Jacobson defines as the characteristics of aphasia—the disintegration of discourse practices and a regression to earlier descriptive models.[9] Yet "discourse losses are combined with discourse compensations."[10] External changes, which forced changes both in culture as a whole and in the practice of discourse, came into conflict with cultural policies that aimed to assert stability. People therefore needed new tools to produce new content; however, creating new forms as a method of cultural production was suppressed. The only way to compensate for this was to turn to earlier (stereotypical, now stable) forms. Caricature based on zoomorphic physiognomy simultaneously combined elements of cultural aphasia (stable visual and interpretative forms, symbolic substitution) and elements that could overcome it. A humorous reinterpretation of stable forms undermined their authority and created a humorous visual rhetoric—a language that made an apophatic discussion of change possible.

Visual representations from this period reveal an identification based on the distinction between the "self" and the "other," while the image of the "stranger" (the "enemy") radicalized the "other." "The animalization of the enemy is, at times, intensified, especially during extreme internal or external social tension."[11]

The "other" becomes an enemy when he or she is depicted as the "stranger," that is, when the "other" is radicalized and marginalized. This is when a zoomorphic image becomes useful, largely because humans identify animals as "others." Moreover, humans are often believed to have conquered nature. By their knowledge and power, humans subdued nature and drew a dividing line between humanity and the animal kingdom. Humans are natural beings. However, they perceive themselves as indisputably superior to animals because they are alleged to be the only living creatures with minds. The animal is therefore always a step lower in the intelligent/unintelligent dichotomy.[12] References to the animal kingdom in caricature therefore show other countries and peoples as "strangers," discrediting their position and actions by bringing them down to the level of animals. A zoomorphic image indicates the marginal state of a person or group of people at the edge of losing human dignity and violating cultural and

---

9 Roman Jakobson, *Studies on Child Language and Aphasia* (Berlin: de Gruyter, 1971), 13.

10 Oushakine, "Byvshee v upotreblenii: Postsovetskoe sostoianie kak forma afazii," 765.

11 "Cette animalisation de l'adversaire est périodiquement avivée lors des plus fortes tensions, internes ou externes à la société" (Eric Baratay, "Le zoo: lieu politique, XVIe–XXe siècles," in *L'Animal en politique*, ed. P. Bacot and E. Baratay [Paris: L'Harmattan, 2003], 16).

12 See Tom Regan, *The Case for Animal Rights* (Los Angeles: University of California Press, 1983).

social rules. In the first place, it emphasizes those characteristics of personality, behavior, and intelligence that indicate a certain inferiority and inconsistency with a typical representation of a human being, pushing the portrayed person into the realm of the unreasonable, wild, and different.

The result is that animality becomes synonymous with the nonhuman, and even anti-human. Zoomorphic images are thus a tool for excluding and displacing certain people from the universal social community (which usually means the "self/us" community) when the "other/others" are no longer perceived as autonomous subjects but as objects driven by irrational motives. When a zoomorphic "stranger" becomes part of the worldview, and the distinction between the "self" and the "other" is emphasized, a certain hierarchy— geopolitical, racial, gendered, or social—emerges. Alongside this, a green light is given to violence and aggression towards the "stranger" as a dangerous, wild, and unreasonable entity.[13] Zoomorphic images (as an antipode to people or the "self") justify the exploitation and humiliation of the enslaved, contempt for and violence towards enemies, and even afford "reasonable" justification for the extermination of the latter.

An animal that is used to portray a country or a people as the "stranger" is never chosen accidentally. On the contrary, it strictly depends on a specific cultural code. It defines the characteristics of each animal and its relationships with other animals. National "bestiaries" and differences in how they assign various, even opposite, meanings and associations to the same animal, are related to the country's history, geographical location and climate, economy, use of domestic animals and game, patterns of interaction with wild animals and their abundance, and the diversity of species. Ideas about the animal world were not objective and depended solely on human perception; by observing animals, people determined their value and usefulness, or possible danger and harm. People also attributed to animals' habits and appearance qualities that were originally characteristic of humans. Animals were brave or cowardly, cunning or stupid, good or evil, because people saw them as such and assigned these characteristics to them.

The subsequent comparison of a person's actions and character with the animal's behavior through a zoomorphic image is a double transfer, the return of human qualities to the person. However, the use of the animal's image seems to indicate that a quality is innate and natural, while "human" qualities are subject

---

13 Imanol Zubero, "The Construction of the Stranger and Social Violence," in *Violence and Communication*, ed. Jose Antonio Mingolarra, Carmen Arocena, and Rosa Martin Sabaris (Reno: Center for Basque Studies University of Nevada, 2011), 33–50.

to correction. This fact finally places the person alienated by a zoomorphic image into the impenetrable category of "strangers," who are denied any opportunity to become closer to the "self." However, the innate nature of qualities can be interpreted positively—for example, if a zoomorphic metaphor is used for self-description, either opposing the "stranger" or independently. In this case, a dignified and worthy animal that evokes positive associations is chosen for a metaphorical comparison.

Animals communicate certain qualities, which make it possible to design an animal typology.[14] Generally, the animal kingdom in any culture can be divided into a group of noble animals (used in emblems and heraldry, which strengthens positive associations with them as worthy animals) and a group of impure, harmful, or dangerous animals (used as the basis for expletives and curses and viewed as indicators of base and negative qualities). Another common classification is the distinction between predators and livestock. Both groups have a predominantly negative connotation. For example, the predator's image was used to portray those who posed a threat. It suggested they should either be "domesticated" or "exterminated," while livestock animals were perceived as a resource, inferiors devoid of their own will and individuality. The zoomorphic image of livestock in caricature is therefore used to portray lower social classes, not those with more power and wealth, or at the international level, conquered and subjugated lands and peoples or colonies.[15] Contrary to the submissive domesticated animals that were part of everyday life, less common animals were chosen to portray an enemy as the "stranger." The more alien and incomprehensible an enemy (its language, traditions and customs, appearance, way of life), the less familiar was the animal chosen to depict it. It could be an exotic animal from an unknown country or a fantastic beast.

The most popular zoomorphic images used to portray an enemy as the "stranger" are exotic or fantastic animals, as well as predators or monsters, their extreme embodiment. Moreover, the line between the fantastic and the monstrous is quite thin; we can therefore say that there is a single way to represent the "stranger" as *a beast*, in which predatory, fantastic, exotic, and monstrous qualities are shown in different shades, or rather gradations. Thus, while exotic traits merely indicate the significant otherness, foreignness, and strangeness of the "other," a fantastic image represents its fundamental

---

14 See, for example, Kenneth Lai, "Masked as Beasts: An Analysis of Zoomorphism in the Cultural Imaginary of Hybridity," *Aisthesis* 3 (2014): 1–13.

15 See, for example, the images of Panama as a cow and Tibet as an ibex: *Strekoza*, no. 51 (1892), 5; *Strekoza*, no. 12 (1893): 1; *Oskol'ki*, no. 37 (1904): 1; *Shut*, no. 22 (1904): 1; *Budil'nik*, no. 19 (1904): 1.

otherness, and a predatory image reflects its fundamental strangeness and danger. These intermediate shades identify someone who is "closer than 'the stranger'" and "more like 'us'," whereas a monster represents the ultimate degree of otherness, strangeness, and danger associated with the "other." The "other" becomes the "stranger" through demonization. At the core of the different facets of the "stranger" is potential or direct danger—fantastic and exotic creatures are unknown and therefore dangerous, while predators and monsters are obviously aggressive and hostile. A beast embodies violence and force; it personifies cruelty and insatiability. Unlike a human criminal, a beast cannot be negotiated with, appeased, or bought off; its conscience or mercy cannot be appealed to. Only two tactics can therefore be applied in relation to the "stranger" as a dangerous or even predatory animal—taming and extermination, because the "stranger is the harbinger of possible harm and as such is the embodiment of a psychic archetype across the animal kingdom."[16]

Nevertheless, the predatory characteristic is twofold—it can be present both in the image of an unreasonable and cruel monster, guided by uncontrollable instincts and bloodlust, and in the image of a strong and independent, but dangerous creature that has a right to prey on weaker animals. The image of a predator is therefore associated with a food chain—a hierarchy of zoomorphic images used in caricature, for example. In this case, aggression, suppression, and dominance can be perceived as the natural order of things; however, it is only possible in the representation of the "self" in the image of a noble predator. Moreover, when "strangers" are portrayed as bloodthirsty or dangerous predators, their aggression—the aggression of the "other"—looks baseless, without motive, and unfair.

It should therefore be noted that the principles of ambivalence, semantic plasticity, and, to a certain extent, reversibility are preserved in zoomorphic caricature, despite its radicality. The political situation is rarely stable and is subject to frequent change, so the images that describe the balance of forces on the world political arena—current allies and enemies—change accordingly. The same applies to zoomorphic images. The list of qualities associated with a particular animal is quite extensive, so the same zoomorphic image can be used in different political contexts to accent different things, allow for different judgements, draw attention to certain stereotypes (a set of negative stereotypes can be replaced by more condescending or even positive ones), and emphasize different characteristic features. If it is difficult or impossible to reverse an

---

16 Maxine Sheets-Johnstone, "The Enemy: A Twenty-first Century Archetypal Study," *Psychotherapy and Politics International* 8, no. 2 (2010): 148.

established negative image, a new zoomorphic image can be constructed to reflect the new balance of forces. However, it is often the case that several zoomorphic images circulate simultaneously: a certain country will have leading and several subordinate representations. Self-representation (the image of "us") can also be diverse, because different zoomorphic images can embody the different virtues a nation attributes to itself. They are sometimes difficult to combine in one image, such as peace and courage in combat. The circulation of several zoomorphic images thus makes the use of caricature tools more effective.

The "Other" as the Enemy

Contrary to the *lubok* print, the caricature focuses on the nonlocal *topos*, so the images of the "stranger" ("other") acquire their *topos* localization. Caricaturists use two main methods to build the image of the "stranger":

1. deconstructing (we avoid the word *deconstruction* here deliberately to avoid associations with the method proposed by J. Derrida) of the heroic semantics in the already existing image, using comic hyperboles, anti-symmetrization, litotes, and satire;
2. image construction (the language of visualization, discourse construction).

The discourse about the "stranger" was constructed through local visual images of the enemy in relation to such peoples as the British, Germans, Austrians, Turks, and Japanese.[17] The process of forming the enemy's image[18] in relation to these peoples was mutual. According to Hannes Hofbauer,[19] who studies image construction related to Russia, the enemy portrayal and imagological iconography of the "Moscovite monsters"[20] is the result of tough geopolitical

---

17 It became base for the iconology of Erwin Panofsky (Erwin Panofsky, *Studies in Iconology: Humanistic Themes in the Art of the Renaissance* [New York: Harper & Row, 1972]).

18 Denis Denisov, "Identifikatsiia obraza vraga v politicheskoi kommunikatsii," *Vestnik RGGU: Politologiia. Istoriia. Mezhdunarodnye otnosheniia* 1 (2009): 113–26.

19 Hannes Hofbauer, *Feindbild Russland: Geschichte einer Dämonisierung* (Vienna: Promedia Verlag, 2016).

20 "Moscovite (Muscovite) monsters" is a medieval collective designation for the inhabitants of Muscovy (Russia), reactualized in nineteenth-century British literature and journalism in relation to the historical period before the reign of Peter the Great, often specifically in relation to the reign of Ivan the Terrible. See further: Karl-Heinz Ruffman, *Das Rußlandbild im England Shakespeares* (Göttingen: Musterschmidt, 1952); Charles Halperin, "The Double Standard:

competition. Constructing the enemy's image to radicalize the "stranger" is necessary to legitimize all political decisions regarding the object of this radicalization and gain social support.[21]

As mentioned earlier, there are two main methods for creating a zoomorphic caricature: image construction and disintegration. Constructing a caricature without a primary image that could be further presented comically begins with the analysis of the common knowledge concerning the object. Public attention is diverted to recognizable qualities and features, which simultaneously represent the object clearly, succinctly, and concisely. These qualities are so closely associated with this object that, if necessary and with a certain effort, it is possible to replace the object as a whole with this single feature, reduce it to one detail, and still preserve more concisely the general meaning and related connotations. An emphasis on the object's characteristic features and the selection of its typical qualities comprises the primary material for a caricature. This process occurs within a certain cultural and semantic field that is based on current demands. Later, the perception of this material may change and become comical, which in turn produces new meanings and corresponding forms with the help of caricature tools such as visual and verbal methods, as well as playing with context. An image is therefore constructed through its isolation from common knowledge, and its further formation and fixation in a concise and succinct format.

The construction method can be broken down into the following steps: (1) a current political event generates a need to portray a particular country; (2) the caricaturist actualizes the available common knowledge about the country, based mainly on stereotypes about its population and its national mindset concerning attributed patterns of behavior and character traits, as well as appearance, traditional clothes, and so on; (3) the most catchy and typical features recognizable to the broadest audience are selected as the primary material; (4) the material is processed and placed in a certain context to give it comic effect—in our case, with the help of a zoomorphic image that combines emphasized features and associations related to a country or its people, and stable ideas and associations related to an animal; (5) the visual image is an end product and is incorporated into the caricature composition. It may include anthropomorphic or other zoomorphic images, a combination of visual and verbal components.

Livonian Chronicles and Muscovite Barbarity during the Livonian War (1558–1582)," *Studia Slavica et Balcanica Petropolitana* 1, no. 23 (2018): 126–47; Svetlana Koroleva, *Britanskii mif o Rossii* (Berlin: Direkt-Media, 2016).

21 Dieter Senghaas, *Rüstung und Militarismus* (Frankfurt: Suhrkamp Verlag, 1972). See also Gustave Doré, *Die äußerst anschauliche, fesselnde und seltsame Histoire vom Heiligen Rußland* (Gütersloh: Bertelsmann, 1970).

Deconstructing also deals with the established social knowledge and stereotypes about the object of caricature. However, the process of deconstructing is the reverse of construction. The key difference is that the primary material in deconstructing is already available—a formed and fixed visual image often marked by elevated or heroic semantics. The starting point of deconstructing is therefore the deconstruction of an existing image into component elements to change its configuration and add new details. Deconstructing results in a reversed image. It has clearly recognizable features of the original image with completely transformed semantics. During image construction, isolated and not yet closely related stereotypes are selected and then further synthesized in a single semantic unit. On the other hand, during deconstructing, a complete image is first deconstructed, and only then are comically charged elements selected. Essentially, deconstructing is a critical inversion of the existing image. It diminishes and discredits its meaning in an ironic key, ridicules through mimicking and reinterpretation, and transforms the heroic into the comic.

The original image, which must undergo deconstructing and transformation into a zoomorphic one, is usually a stereotype of another country about itself (an autostereotype). It can be either anthropomorphic or already zoomorphic. Anthropomorphic country images or personifications were mainly allegorical. They were represented by stylized ancient goddesses (for example, France, Great Britain, Germany, Italy) or generalized images of the mother/Virgin Mary with noticeable national symbols—a national costume, battle armor, a traditional hairstyle, or recognizable everyday items and cultural artefacts (mainly typical of peasants or villagers). Male figures are also used in personifications of the "national spirit," not as members of an ancient pantheon, but as generalized images of common people or the warrior.

The late eighteenth-century physiognomic works of P. Camper,[22] J. K. Lavater,[23] and F. J. Gall[24] place man, beasts, and God on an equal footing, making

---

22 Petrus Camper, *Dissertation sur les variétés naturelles qui caractérisent la physionomie des hommes des divers climats et des différens ages: suivie de réflexions sur la beauté, particulièrement sur celle de la tête: avec une manière nouvelle de dessiner toute sorte de têtes avec la plus grande exactitude* (Paris: Chez H.J. Jansen, 1791) and *Discours prononçés par feû Mr. Pierre Camper, en l'Académie de dessein d'Amsterdam, sur le moyen de représenter d'une manière sûre les diverses passions qui se manifestent sur le visage, sur l'étonnante conformité qui existe entre les quadrupèdes, les oiseaux, les poissons et l'homme, et enfin sur le beau physique* (Utrecht: B. Wild and J. Altheer, 1792).

23 Johann Caspar Lavater, *L'art de connaître les hommes par la Physionomie* (Paris: L. Prudhomme, Levrault, Schoell et C.nie, 1809).

24 Franz Josef Gall, *Anatomie et physiologie du système nerveux en général et du cerveau en particulier, avec des observations sur la possibilité de reconnaître plusieurs dispositions intellectuelles et morales de l'homme et des animaux par la configuration de leurs têtes* (Paris: F. Schoell, 1810).

the transformation from one state to another quite easy. The transformation of form and its visualization stimulated academic research into evolution, and vice versa, the research in physiology contributed to the development of visual rhetoric.[25] It was widely used during the French Revolution; for example, when a certain public figure was compared by their supporters with a "heroic" animal in a serious and dramatic manner, their image was instantly transformed by the opponents into a parody in caricature.[26] This created a virtual realm of animal-like characters in real history, which was constructed and maintained by professional caricaturists in a visual (rhetorical) battle.[27] Caricature developed after the late eighteenth century as a key tool of social criticism and protest.[28] Its most frequent device was the zoomorphic transformation of a person, mainly due to the popularity of the "zoomorphic physiognomy tables"[29] that provided detailed descriptions of how an animal might be transformed into a human and back. During the nineteenth century, political fauna became quite prominent in journalism; essentially, animalistic caricature implemented the Romantic idea of comparing "fauna with a national or a social group, with a 'realistic' image of a person."[30]

Zoomorphic caricature encouraged the development of national languages used to define the "stranger" and their transformations in relation to the space occupied on the mental map. In the context of romantic nationalism, this was especially important for national self-identification and a stable identity model. Driven by a social demand for humorous (satirical) images of the "stranger,"

---

25 Zoomorphic physiognomy is also used in the journalism and fiction of that time (for example, by H. Balzac) to describe characters while preserving the visual effect; thus, a comparison with an animal or an enumeration of characteristic zoomorphic features refers to the visual source, assuming that the reader is familiar with the physiognomic tradition.

26 Andre Blum, *La caricature révolutionnaire* (Paris: Jouve et Cie, 1916); Richard Taws, "The Currency of Caricature in Revolutionary France," in *The Efflorescence of Caricature, 1759–1838*, ed. Todd Porterfield (Aldershot: Ashgate, 2011).

27 Furthermore, special recommendations and rules are written and published to facilitate the caricaturist's work. See, for example, Francis Grose, *Rules for Drawing Caricaturas with an Essay on Comic Painting* (London: Samuel Hooper, 1789).

28 In the nineteenth century the caricature became so institutionalized that special works on the history of caricature were published (Thomas Wright, *A History of Caricature and Grotesque in Literature and Art* [London: Virtue Brothers & Co, 1865]; Champfleury, *Histoire de la caricature antique* [Paris: E. Dentu, 1865]).

29 See, for example, the "Lavater's table" (Johann Caspar Lavater, *Gradation de la tête de grenouille jusqu'au profil d'Apollon, d'après les idées du célébre Lavater* [Paris: Chéz Joubert fils et Charles Bance, 1793–1810], accessed June 15, 2022, https://www.loc.gov/resource/cph.3b35221/).

30 Jurgis Baltrushaitis, "Zoofiziognomika," in *Mir obrazov. Obrazy mira. Antologiia issledovanii vizual'noi kul'tury*, ed. Nataliia Mazur (St. Petersburg, Moscow: Novoe izdatel'stvo, 2018), 239; Ian Haywood, *Romanticism and Caricature* (Cambridge: Cambridge University Press, 2013).

the art of caricature flourished in France, Britain, the US, Russia, and other countries.[31] It also made a noticeable contribution to the development of national stereotypes. Caricaturists from such magazines as *Puck* (the US),[32] *La Caricature* (France), *Punch* (Britain),[33] and many more developed the iconography that reflected the nineteenth-century global political fauna and assigned an image to each country. Caricatures usually featured captions to explain the image. However, this was redundant because of the stereotypical nature of the images. Considering that magazines borrowed caricature stories from one another, as well as repeating previous stories with minor modifications, it is unsurprising that images were common and recognizable, regardless of the magazine and country of its origin. There were stable or relatively stable images such as a bear (Russia), a bald eagle (the US), an eagle (Germany), a Gallic cockerel (France), a double-headed eagle (Austria), and a dragon (China).

Some images depended on the caricature storyline, especially images depicting countries whose position was undergoing change, or generally unstable countries: a monkey, dog, wolf (Italy); a leopard (Japan); a turkey (Turkey); a dog, fox (France); a donkey (Spain); a dog, boar, fox (Germany); a cat (Austria/Germany). Due to the active exploration of Asia, especially China and Japan, their images were added to those already established by the end of the Napoleonic Wars. Historian E. Baratay described this process, and its specifics as follows: "Mockery of people leads to social criticism and creates human stories played out by beasts serving as a mirror and a screen. They allow a more brutal satire, because they are free from any threat of censorship or outrage due to the comic nature of the story."[34]

Marianne and John Bull are examples of well-established anthropomorphic autostereotypes. John Bull is a generalized ironic self-personification of Britain,

---

31 Todd Porterfield, *The Efflorescence of Caricature, 1759–1838* (Aldershot: Ashgate, 2011); Elise K. Kenney and John M. Merriman, *The Pear: French graphic arts in the golden age of caricature* (New York: Worldwide Books, 1991); Mary Dorothy George, *English political caricature; a study of opinion and propaganda* (Oxford: Clarendon Press, 1959); Francis Donald Klingender, *Hogarth and English Caricature* (London: Transatlantic Arts, 1944); Tat'iana Alent'eva, *Raziashchee oruzhie smekha. Amerikanskaia politicheskaia karikatura XIX veka (1800–1877)* (St. Petersburg: Aleteia, 2020).

32 "*Puck* magazine pages online," *Library of Congress*, accessed June 15, 2022, https://www.loc. gov/pictures/search/?q=ap101.p7&sp=1&st=gallery.

33 *Punch* magazine volumes online, accessed 15 June, 2022, https://sites.google.com/site/ punchvolumes/

34 "La dérision des hommes mène à la critique sociale avec la création d'histoires humaines jouées par des bêtes servant de paravent et de miroir. Elles permettent une satire plus féroce car libérée de tout danger de censure ou d'outrance grâce au comique de la situation" (Baratay, "Le zoo: lieu politique, XVIe–XXe siècles," 6).

depicted as a stout middle-aged man with sideburns and a sly face. He is dressed in a tailcoat, frock coat, and top hat. Any item of his outfit may feature the pattern or copy the image of the British flag. The image is completed with a cane or a pipe. Marianne is a personification of the French Republic, depicted as a young woman whose most recognizable accessory is the Phrygian cap—a hat worn in the Roman Empire by freed slaves. Later, it became a symbol of liberty, associated with the French national motto "*Liberté, Egalité, Fraternité*," which emphasizes liberty as a fundamental principle of the French national identity. Marianne represents a common woman. However, sometimes she is depicted wearing an antique tunic. In addition to the Phrygian cap, Marianne has frequently been portrayed with the French flag, the French cockade, or a weapon, because her image appeared during the French Revolution. Marianne and John Bull were created as a self-representation by French and British artists respectively. Anthropomorphic images are sometimes supplemented with zoomorphic ones. For example, Marianne may be depicted with a Gallic cockerel, and John Bull with a bulldog.

If countries used a zoomorphic image in their self-representation, it was a noble animal. The choice of the animal depended on the heraldic or symbolic tradition of a particular country. For example, the Gallic cockerel, mentioned earlier as a French national symbol, refers to the Latin ethnonym *gallus*, which could mean both a cockerel and a Gaul—a resident of Gallia, the Roman province inhabited by the Celtic peoples who were ancestors of the modern French people. It is believed that the Romans compared Gauls with cockerels, probably in mockery, because of their bright red hair arranged in a hairstyle resembling a cockerel's comb. The Gauls treated this bird with respect, because it was associated with the solar cult of the sunrise. The cockerel thus evoked positive associations in the French and gradually became part of their self-identification, especially after the French Revolution, when this zoomorphic image acquired new meanings such as bravery, determination, pugnacity, courtesy, chivalry, and a quick temper. The British bulldog, meanwhile, was originally bred for bull baiting and dog fighting, becoming a national symbol of Britain and the embodiment of strength, endurance, and bravery after the breed was approved in Britain in 1865. The bulldog became John Bull's companion and resembled him both in character and appearance. It gradually adopted features that were attributed to a true gentleman, such as composure, conservatism, a presentable appearance, confidence, and a certain phlegmatic nature. As a result, this animal itself became associated with "good old England."

Before analyzing a zoomorphic caricature, it is therefore necessary to determine whether the image was constructed or deconstructed from another image. The next step is to determine the image's components—the specific visual elements involved in the caricature. Special attention should be paid to the following:

- *"what is shown"*—deliberately emphasized elements in the foreground that act as the core of the image;
- *"what is said"*—verbal elements that complement the visual image; how verbal and visual elements are interrelated in the caricature;
- *"how it is shown"*—expressive means that build up a visual composition of the caricature, and how these means connect its elements; the relationship between the elements and their configuration created by expressive means; the dynamics and effect they produce;
- *"what is implied"*—stereotypes and concepts woven into the image, ideas referred to by the caricature as a whole and by its elements separately; the relationship between zoomorphic and national stereotypes; specific historical events to which the caricature refers; a broader context in which the caricature is placed;
- *"what is meant"*—an emotional response and effect created by the zoomorphic image in the caricature as a whole and the idea behind this image.

The Image of the "Stranger" in Satirical Magazines

This chapter considers how the methods previously analyzed were used in caricatures to create and replicate zoomorphic images of foreign countries in Russian magazines between 1890 and 1905. The research material was obtained from the most popular illustrated satirical magazines published during this period—*Shut* (Jester), *Budil'nik* (Alarm clock), *Oskolki* (Fragments), and *Strekoza* (Dragonfly).

Britain

Among European countries, Britain stands out with its many zoomorphic images. This number indicates both the country's role as a leading global power promoting its interests around the world and the great demand for caricatures (including zoomorphic images) because of the negative perception of British imperial ambitions. At the turn of the twentieth century, the struggle for colonies and dependent territories intensified; Russia and Britain had conflicting interests in many regions such as the Far East, Central Asia, Turkey, and the Balkans. Britain was therefore portrayed as the "stranger" in view of a possible clash and an attempt to defend Russia's interests, mainly in the Far East; thus, undisguised British aggression in the Far East was opposed to the supposedly beneficial Russian influence on Asian countries. However, since the tension did not escalate into an open conflict, almost no caricatures depict a direct confrontation between the two countries, while existing caricatures focus on denouncing and condemning foreign aggression against third countries and express skepticism and contempt for foreign imperial ambitions.

Britain is presented as a cruel, cunning, greedy, and predatory country, posing a threat to weaker nations. Special emphasis is often placed on greed and gluttony to show that Britain's claims on new territories are illegal. To do this, the caricaturists use images such as an octopus with tentacles stretching in every direction,[35] a giant crocodile with an open mouth,[36] a bulldog attacking a goat (Tibet),[37] and the most common zoomorphic image—a lion with an exaggerated appetite.[38]

The lion, as the most popular zoomorphic image, is a vivid example of a deconstructing autostereotype. It is one of the British symbols whose origins are in heraldry. The heroic zoomorphic self-representation emphasized such leonine qualities as strength, courage, a royal appearance, and dignity. After deconstructing, the only original quality left, if any, was strength. The lion in the caricatures is never royal or dignified; its face, habits, and movements reflect intensely base emotions, mainly anger or greed. It never fights an equal opponent. If it is necessary to emphasize the victim's weakness and the power imbalance, the caricature shows a larger predator attacking a weak herbivore that cannot fight back or defend itself. If Britain's exorbitant claims are ridiculed, the caricature shows a ferocious and violent large animal confronted by calm people who show no fear or concern for the proximity of a dangerous predator; for example, one caricature shows a lion clutching a map of Africa in its claws and anthropomorphic images of other countries dragging the lion by its tail.

---

35 *Budil'nik*, no. 32 (1900): 5.
36 *Budil'nik*, no. 25 (1900): 5.
37 *Budil'nik*, no. 19 (1904): 1.
38 *Strekoza*, no. 22 (1899): 2.

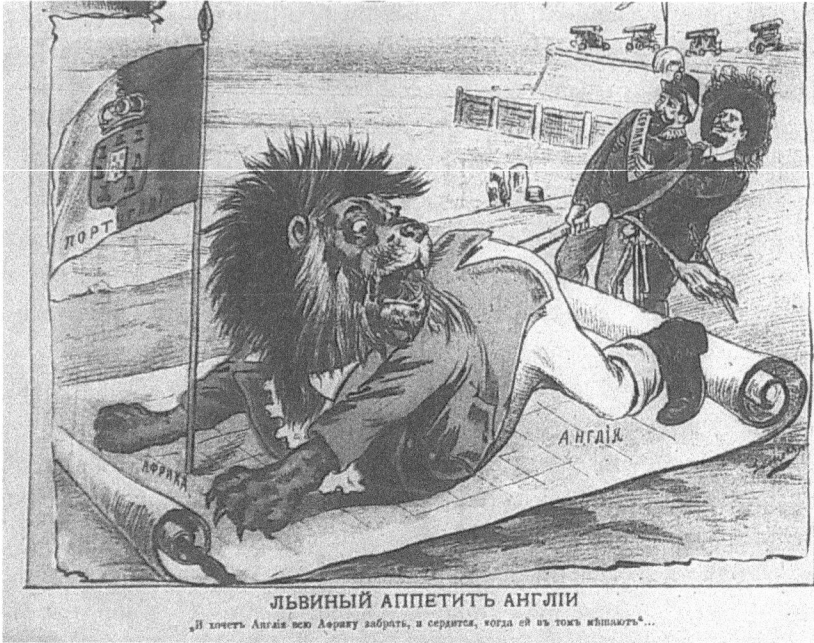

ЛЬВИНЫЙ АППЕТИТЪ АНГЛІИ

„Й хочетъ Англія всю Африку забрать, и сердится, когда ей въ томъ мѣшаютъ"...

FIGURE 1. The Appetite of the British Lion, 1890. Illustration in *Budil'nik* (*Satiricheskii zhurnal s karrikaturami*) 26, no. 12: 12. Moscow: N. A. Stepanov, courtesy of the National Library of Russia.

Along with the images of a powerful animal driven by base instincts, the caricature often uses an image of a ragged, emaciated, and frightened lion. This implies the former power and the early decline of the British Empire. The Anglo-Boer War (1899–1902) had an especially strong influence on the development of this image. During the war, most Russians sympathized with Britain's opponent. Britain's enemy was significantly weaker. However, Boer resistance was strong and caused serious damage to Britain's reputation on the world arena. The situation itself provided ample opportunities to create a comic effect. Caricatures exaggerated the imbalance of power, showing a lion attacked by mosquitoes or midges.[39] The lion's wounds or signs of exhaustion, its decrepitude, and feebleness were often deliberately emphasized or depicted with a repulsive naturalism that is generally not typical of caricatures.[40]

Furthermore, Britain is often portrayed as a bulldog or an aquatic creature, for example, an octopus or a crocodile. The bulldog's image was also deconstructed from an existing autostereotype that emphasized such typically British features of

---

39 *Strekoza*, no. 40 (1900): 2; *Shut*, no 17 (1900): 1.
40 *Oskolki*, no. 47 (1899): 1; *Shut*, no. 40 (1899): 3; *Strekoza*, no. 6 (1901): 6.

the dog as its phlegmatic nature, calmness, perseverance, and fighting skills. The deconstructing of this image in Russian caricatures was significantly influenced by the fact that dogs are associated with rather negative qualities in Russian culture, and the Russian word for a female dog is a swear word. The caricature image of the bulldog is excessively ugly—the legs are too short; the body is disproportionate; the face is distorted with anger or has a meaningless stupid expression.[41] The images of aquatic creatures are new image constructions. They are based on the associations of Britain as a seafaring nation. In constructing aquatic zoomorphic images, caricaturists emphasized the features that could cause disgust and fear. The body and skin structure of aquatic creatures differs greatly from that of terrestrial creatures, and they look disgusting or shapeless. Reptiles and aquatic creatures are perceived as cold-blooded slippery beasts that ambush other creatures, enhancing the repulsive effect.

Caricatures based on zoomorphic images often feature additional elements associated with Britain. The most popular elements are a map of the world or the part that shows the scale of British imperial ambitions, and a pith helmet, which refers to the British status as the most powerful colonial empire. In general, both elements refer to colonialism and represent negative symbols of western civilization.

FIGURE 2. *"Civilization" in the English Style*, 1900. Illustration in *Budil'nik* (*Satiricheskii zhurnal s karrikaturami*) 36, no. 32: 5. Moscow: N. A. Stepanov, courtesy of the National Library of Russia.

---

41 *Oskolki*, no. 14 (1904): 1; *Oskolki*, no. 15 (1904): 1; *Budil'nik*, no. 19 (1904): 1; *Shut*, no. 22 (1904): 1.

France

France and Germany and their zoomorphic images frequented the pages of satirical magazines less than Britain, yet they made their mark in the period under study. Unlike British zoomorphic images, which continued to be actively developed, reinterpreted, modified, and given new features, the images of France and Germany were characterized by stability. In most cases, France was represented as the Gallic cockerel,[42] its traditional national symbol. Interestingly, the image offered limited possibilities for deconstructing. Caricatures exaggerate traits associated with the original image, like arrogance and cockiness, or ridicule its excessive aggressiveness by showing a scared cockerel battered in a fight. However, the cockerel's image is never crudely comic. Moreover, in many caricatures it is more positive and/or stronger than the zoomorphic images of other countries in the same storyline. For example, the caricature of the Entente Cordiale shows a striking contrast between the self-confident and proud Gallic cockerel and the ugly and despondent English bulldog, tied to the cockerel by its paw.[43] Moreover, no attempt was made to create an alternative zoomorphic image that represented France as a beast or a monster. It can be assumed that such a delicate deconstructing and the lack of monstrosity in the French zoomorphic image are a result of the largely friendly relations between Russia and France during this period. Russian society perceived France as an ally much more than an enemy.

Germany

The zoomorphic image of Germany was also quite stable; the great majority of caricatures portray it as a dog. It should be noted that another traditional image—the black eagle—which stems from heraldry and serves as the basis for the German autostereotype, was used much less often; in caricatures, the proud eagle was usually diminished and transformed into a predatory kite.[44] Between 1890 and 1905, the wolf was not typically used as a self-representation of Germany. This image may seem more heroic yet is still proximate to a dog. Instead, the country opted for a comparison with the eagle which, among other things, was associated with the continuity of the imperial tradition. Thus, in the

42 *Shut*, no. 17 (1901): 7; *Budil'nik*, no. 18 (1899): 8; *Budil'nik*, no. 34 (1899): 5.
43 *Oskolki*, no. 15 (1904): 1.
44 *Shut*, no. 17 (1901): 7.

case of Germany, the choice was made in favor of constructing a new image rather than deconstructing the existing one. However, as mentioned earlier, the dog has more negative connotations in Russia than in Europe. For example, the expression 'dog's loyalty' can be used in both a positive and derogatory sense. In the latter meaning, it indicates the degrading and servile feeling inferiors have towards their superiors. Germany's zoomorphic image as a dog also implies this. In most cases the dog is depicted as tired, sad, submissive, and with a dark coat.[45] The general impression of passivity and weakness is emphasized by a lack of movement—the dog appears at a standstill or waiting. To make it look old and weak, the dog's face is given the thick gray eyebrows and moustache of German Chancellor Otto von Bismarck, who resigned in 1890.[46]

The United States

There were few zoomorphic representations of the United States during the studied period. Instead, the focus was on the anthropomorphic image of Uncle Sam, borrowed from the Americans. It is possible that Russia did not perceive the United States as an enemy because it was only gaining momentum in the world political arena at the time. However, despite its limited representation in caricatures, the first attempts to construct a zoomorphic image of the United States as the "stranger" were being made. The country was mostly portrayed as predatory and ravenous (like the United Kingdom), as well as foreign and exotic; for example, the United States was depicted as a shark with a giant mouth or a bloated boa constrictor digesting its prey. The snake probably refers to the cartoon *"Join, or Die"*[47] by Benjamin Franklin, created during the United States struggle for independence from Britain.

The East in Russian Caricature

During the analyzed period, caricaturists could in most cases draw on the existing zoomorphic images of western countries, even if these images, as shown above, were used as the basis for deconstructing or construction. Zoomorphic representations of eastern countries were only emerging during the period under

---

45 *Strekoza*, no. 11 (1890): 1; *Strekoza*, no. 14 (1890): 2.
46 *Strekoza*, no. 15 (1891): 1.
47 N.a., "Join, or Die," *Pennsylvania Gazette* (May 9 1754): 2.

FIGURE 3. *Far Away by the Yellow Sea. Leave Me Alone, Geisha!* 1904. Illustration in *Shut* (*Khudozhestvennyi zhurnal s karikaturami*) 26, no. 6: 7–8. St. Petersburg: A. A. Grigor'ev, courtesy of the National Library of Russia.

study, and their development was therefore quite intense. The development of images was partly a way of charting the "discovery" and "appropriation" of eastern countries on an imaginary world map. Appropriation was in turn integrated into a broader process of development and reinforcement of the very notions of "Europeanness" and "Asianness"—that is, typically European and Asian behavior, lifestyle, and mindsets. The backbone of the dichotomy is the idea of their essential opposition across such categories as "strong/weak," "male/female," "light/dark," "positive/negative," "pure/filthy," "active/passive," and so on. These oppositions became a major tool for demarcating the world. In Russia, the European/Asian dichotomy was inevitably linked to the challenges of the nation's self-positioning as a land between East and West. Unlike other colonial powers, Russia's border with Asia, its permeability, and even its presence was a matter of perspective. Many Europeans therefore viewed Russia as an Asian rather than a European country, whereas Russians themselves were unanimous concerning Russia's European/Asian status and in their attitude towards Asia.

Russia's influence in the Far East naturally meant the caricature of the studied period showed a prevalence of zoomorphic images of Far Eastern countries, namely China and Japan. Other eastern countries, such as India,[48] Tibet,[49] and Persia,[50] did not feature in the pages of satirical magazines, and the use of their zoomorphic images was situational. In contrast, Turkey was often depicted as a sick old man.[51]

As previously discussed, the creation of an anthropomorphic image precedes the construction of a zoomorphic one. In the cases of China and Japan, the human characters have the grotesque, emphatically Asian facial features, traditional hairstyles, and clothes that appeared exotic to the European eye, and often feature such attributes as oriental hand-painted fans. Caricaturists tend to depict China as a public servant[52] and show Japan as a geisha.[53] Moreover, even the public servant image is emphatically feminine because of his long, layered clothes and braided hair—a way of presenting him as weak, stupid, and cowardly and simultaneously cunning and devious. Interestingly, as Japan underwent modernization and borrowed "European," that is, "proper" traits, the

---

48 India as a dog: *Shut*, no. 36 (1897): 2; as an elephant: *Budil'nik*, no. 11 (1905): 8.
49 Tibet as an ibex: *Oskolki*, no. 37 (1904): 1; *Shut*, no. 22 (1904): 1; *Budil'nik*, no. 19 (1904): 1.
50 Persia as an old lion: *Shut*, no. 24 (1899): 3.
51 *Strekoza*, no. 31 (1891): 5; *Strekoza*, no. 42 (1896): 1; *Strekoza*, no. 42 (1901): 1; *Oskolki*, no. 21 (1904): 8; *Budil'nik*, no. 46 (1895): 7.
52 *Strekoza*, no. 32 (1894): 1; *Strekoza*, no. 23 (1898): 2; *Oskolki*, no. 45 (1900): 10; *Shut*, no. 30 (1891): 4.
53 *Strekoza*, no. 10 (1904): 3; *Strekoza*, no. 21 (1905): 4; *Shut*, no. 4 (1904): 3; *Budil'nik*, no. 9 (1904): 1; *Budil'nik*, no. 32 (1904): 1.

femininity of its image gradually decreased. First, the image of geisha gave way to a samurai, and then to a serviceman in a European-style military uniform. From the outset of the developing of both Chinese and Japanese images, caricaturists used a technique that gradually facilitated the transition to the zoomorphic image as such: faces were grotesquely disproportionate and beastlike; hands often had claws instead of nails (partial zoomorphism).[54]

China

Since the two oriental countries were exotic and little known, preference in the construction of their zoomorphic images was given to fantastic and exotic traits. Thus, the construction of China's zoomorphic image was based on the most revered fantastic creature of Chinese bestiary—the dragon[55] (Long or Lung), a traditional symbol of the Celestial Empire. This may appear to be a direct borrowing of an established autostereotype, but the approach is considerably more complex. It was a unique transformation made possible by essential differences in the European and Chinese systems of symbols. Europeans borrowed an external appearance and imbued it with a completely different meaning. In Chinese cosmology, the dragon is not only a symbol of sovereignty and the emperor's power but the most senior of the five sacred animals—patrons of the elements and the world at large. The dragon embodies the ideas of sanctity, wisdom, kindness, dignity, and nobility, which makes it the greatest of the benevolent mythological creatures. In contrast, the European tradition treats the dragon as the most fearful of mythical monsters, a symbol of ferocity, brutality, and malice, while the Christian tradition places the dragon on an equal footing with the serpent—an incarnation of Satan. Defeating a dragon in Europe was traditionally seen as an act of heroism. Even a direct borrowing of the exterior appearance of the sacred Chinese patron with no further deconstructing therefore resulted in a fully-fledged image of the "other," with all its negative associations.

The further development of China's zoomorphic image occurred primarily through the comic depreciation of the dragon's strength and power. Despite a relatively detailed depiction of the mighty predator's physique, the dragon is in most cases small, on a par with human figures or even smaller. Even if the dragon

---

54 *Strekoza*, no. 36 (1894): 1; *Strekoza*, no. 21 (1895): 1; *Strekoza*, no. 26 (1900): 5; *Strekoza*, no. 21 (1904): 10; *Shut*, no. 2 (1904): 1.

55 *Strekoza*, no. 28 (1905): 5; *Budil'nik*, no. 27 (1900): 1.

FIGURE 4. *In Front of the Chinese "Dragon,"* 1900. Illustration in *Budil'nik* (*Satiricheskii zhurnal s karrikaturami*) 36, no. 27: 1. Moscow: N. A. Stepanov, courtesy of the National Library of Russia.

exceeds humans in size or is depicted as aggressive, attacking, or threatening, it does not instill fear in the other characters in the storyline. Caricaturists usually showed the dragon as defeated, immobilized, being chased into a cage, chained, or with a muzzle on its snout.[56] Yet the caricature created an ambiguous attitude to the beast. Some caricatures featured grotesquely ugly dragons or images resembling illustrations from medieval bestiaries; others showed a weak and humiliated dragon that evoked sympathy rather than disdain. In the latter case the dragon's appearance and the expression of its eyes are humanlike rather than beastly, while the European characters are depicted as excessively rude and cruel to the already defeated creature.

Japan

Japan is represented by a significant number of zoomorphic caricatures, rivaled only by Great Britain in quantity. The formation of its zoomorphic image as "other" was particularly relevant during the studied period against the backdrop of the worsening conflict between Russia and Japan over areas of influence in the Far East, which climaxed in the Russo-Japanese War of 1904–1905. An unstable transitional perception of Japan gave way to caricatures with a multitude of zoomorphic images that coexisted with or succeeded one another. A remarkable illustration of such a coexistence of competing multiple images in the transition phase is a caricature depicting Japan as three creatures at once: a shark, a lobster, and a macaque.[57] Japan's geographical location and its naval confrontation with Russia meant that many of the zoomorphic images represented various aquatic creatures and reptiles: a crab-eating frog,[58] a shark, an octopus,[59] and a snake. Such instances emphasize the voraciousness and disproportionate appetite of the "other," as well as its outlandish nature, given that even the snakes and the frogs symbolizing Japan belong to exotic species.

Caricaturists often accentuated the difference in size between Japan and other countries, including the considerably larger Russia and China. To illustrate this contrast, they depicted Japan as a swarm or plague of small but irksome creatures, like mosquitoes or rats.[60] One of the caricatures featured Japan as a mosquito

---

56 *Strekoza*, no. 15 (1899): 2; *Strekoza*, no. 27 (1900): 2; *Strekoza*, no. 38 (1900): 2.
57 *Strekoza*, no. 31 (1904): 3.
58 *Budil'nik*, no. 6 (1904): 1.
59 *Strekoza*, no. 30 (1905): 4.
60 *Budil'nik*, no. 25 (1904): 1.

FIGURE 5. *A Talk Between a British Bulldog and a Japanese Puppy*, 1904. Illustration in *Shut* (*Khudozhestvennyi zhurnal s karikaturami*) 26, no. 6: 11. St. Petersburg: A. A. Grigor'ev, courtesy of the National Library of Russia.

on the nose of an anthropomorphic China.[61] Despite the emphasis on the imbalance of forces, Japan is still shown as aggressive, threatening, and offensive, not as a negligible or powerless creature. To illustrate the country's dependence on European powers, caricaturists resorted to the image of a dog[62] waiting for its master to throw it a bone, timid and obedient, restless, and exaggeratedly small compared with other characters, whether anthropomorphic or zoomorphic. An example is a grotesquely small Japan as a lapdog next to a large bulldog symbolizing Great Britain. However, this image may also be interpreted as a dog turning against its masters.

Another popular zoomorphic image of Japan is that of a monkey. This communicates the idea of Japan's dependent and imitative behavior. The construction of this image can be traced to the anthropomorphic stage when human characters resembled monkeys. The monkey[63] is a most effective tool for depicting Japan's dual position. It is an essentially inferior creature, yet it has a certain resemblance to those who are higher on the evolutionary ladder, so it is left only with mimicking their behavior. To underscore this duality, the monkeys are commonly shown as ugly and relatively small, with grimaces on their muzzles, dark or yellow hair and skin, but dressed in European clothes, often with military peaked caps or firearms, and busy with various human activities.

At the same time, to designate Japan as "other," caricaturists constructed chimaera-like images—half-human, half-monkey. They could also resort, though less frequently, to a different animal or mythical creature. In all, the mythical chimaera image became a popular and productive way of reflecting Japan's paradoxical nature within the European/Asian dichotomy as a combination of features perceived as diametrically opposite and confrontational. With Japan's continuous modernization and increasingly confident participation in global political affairs, it was increasingly represented as a unique amalgamation of its traditional Asian culture and successfully appropriated European borrowings. The image of a chimaera reflected the perception of this combination as unnatural, and characteristic of a cunning and devious beast trying to camouflage itself amidst its new "friends."

---

61 *Budil'nik*, no. 8 (1895): 1.
62 *Budil'nik*, no. 12 (1904): 7; *Oskolki*, no. 40 (1904): 1.
63 *Strekoza*, no. 45 (1904): 3; *Strekoza*, no. 2 (1905): 3; *Budil'nik*, no. 17 (1904): 6.

FIGURE 6. *Chief "Macaque" of the Japanese Navy. Triumphant Telegrams that Float on the Water*, 1904. Illustration in *Budil'nik* (*Satiricheskii zhurnal s karrikaturami*) 40, no. 12: 1. Moscow: N. A. Stepanov, courtesy of the National Library of Russia.

Conclusion

Our analysis has identified expressive, compositional, and contextual tools used to develop zoomorphic images of foreign countries through the methods of deconstructing and construction. The composition of a zoomorphic political caricature requires two figures—the "self" and the "other." The "self," or a national autostereotype, a self-representation, may be shown explicitly, or it may be implied. In any case, it is irrelevant whether the "self" is displayed directly or indirectly. What is paramount for a caricature is that it depicts the "self" in any available way, because it is the reference point, the conditional center of the world, that defines the rest of the imaginary world map populated by allies, enemies, and colonies—"others/other." The "other" (or the enemy, or stranger) is the second key element in the composition of the caricature. It reflects the image of the "other" shaped through foreign policy, and to some extent the image of the "self" as constantly opposed to the "stranger." A possible third compositional element is the stranger's autostereotype, their self-representation. It appears when a caricature uses the deconstructing method to show the "stranger," that is, if the deconstructed autostereotype of another country becomes the basis of a new zoomorphic image.

There is a range of visual tools for creating a comprehensive zoomorphic image and comic effect: the scale and size of the figures (to reflect a country's size, political role, and military strength); the relative proportion and location of figures; human and animal (anti-human) representations (countries shown as a beast/person); gestures and facial expressions (emotions), poses and behavior, actions and dynamics; accompanying markers such as attributes (clothes, flags, weapons, maps) and colors. During the reviewed period, technical limitations determined the following color sets used in printing: yellow, black, and red for the "stranger"; light and neutral tones for self-representation. Comic effect is based on false expectations and exposure. Deliberate exaggeration of characteristic features transforms the original object into a parody, while placing the resulting visual image in an unusual context exposes the ugly or funny sides of reality and other people's shortcomings, thus creating the conditions for mockery. A parody implements various tools, such as excessive or partial exaggeration or understatement, a metaphorical transfer based on similarity, a contrast based on differences, visual metonymy, puns, and wordplay, references to the national, or more broadly, European or world culture.

Contextual analysis should focus on the material included in the caricature, as well as on the material that is deliberately or accidentally omitted, that is, to the shifted focus of attention that highlights some details and obscures the others. Reconstructing stereotypes to "pack" them into a caricature can be time consuming because a stereotype is part of conventional and concrete knowledge. However, stereotypical images can be managed through a shift, that is, through additions that set a different perspective for what is known. This method is successfully implemented by combining ideas about a particular animal and a particular country or people and placing the resulting hybrid in a context that emphasizes the chosen elements. Zoomorphic images are thus an effective tool for indicating changes in the political situation. Our analysis has disproved the assumption that a longer and more intense history of interaction between countries results in a broader set of zoomorphic images compared to those with a shorter history of contact and unclear stereotypes. On the contrary, caricatures and zoomorphic images act as tools for exploring new locations on the map, and the encounter with the unknown boosts their creativity, resulting in a larger number of free variations.

Works Cited

Archival Sources

The Library of Congress, Washington, DC.
The National Library of Russia, Saint Petersburg

Journals

Budil'nik
Oskolki
Shut
Strekoza

Literature

Alent'eva, Tat'iana. *Raziashchee oruzhie smekha. Amerikanskaia politicheskaia karikatura XIX veka (1800–1877)*. St. Petersburg: Aleteia, 2020.
Artemova, Evgeniia. *Karikatura kak zhanr politicheskogo diskursa*. PhD diss., The Volgograd State Pedagogical University, 2002.

Baltrushaitis, Jurgis. "Zoofiziognomika." In *Mir obrazov. Obrazy mira. Antologiia issledovanii vizual'noi kul'tury.* Edited by Nataliia Mazur, 217–40. St. Petersburg, Moscow: Novoe izdatel'stvo, 2018.

Baratay, Eric. "Le zoo: lieu politique, XVIe–XXe siècles." In *L'Animal en politique.* Edited by P. Bacot and E. Baratay, 15–36. Paris: L'Harmattan, 2003.

Blum, Andre. *La caricature révolutionnaire.* Paris: Jouve et Cie, 1916.

Camper, Petrus. *Dissertation sur les variétés naturelles qui caractérisent la physionomie des hommes des divers climats et des différens ages: suivie de réflexions sur la beauté, particulièrement sur celle de la tête: avec une manière nouvelle de dessiner toute sorte de têtes avec la plus grande exactitude.* Paris: Chez H. J. Jansen, 1791.

———. *Discours prononçés par feû Mr. Pierre Camper, en 'Acadêmie de dessein d'Amsterdam, sur le moyen de représenter d'une manière sûre les diverses passions qui se manifestent sur le visage, sur l'étonnante conformité qui existe entre les quadrupèdes, les oiseaux, les poissons et l'homme, et enfin sur le beau physique.* Utrecht: B. Wild and J. Altheer, 1792.

Champfleury. *Histoire de la caricature antique.* Paris: E. Dentu, 1865.

Denisov, Denis. "Identifikatsiia obraza vraga v politicheskoi kommunikatsii." *Vestnik RGGU: Politologiia. Istoriia. Mezhdunarodnye otnosheniia* 1 (2009): 113–126.

Doré, Gustave. *Die äußerst anschauliche, fesselnde und seltsame Histoire vom Heiligen Rußland.* Gütersloh: Bertelsmann, 1970.

Gall, Franz Josef. *Anatomie et physiologie du système nerveux en général et du cerveau en particulier, avec des observations sur la possibilité de reconnaître plusieurs dispositions intellectuelles et morales de l'homme et des animaux par la configuration de leurs têtes.* Paris: F. Schoell, 1810.

George, Mary Dorothy. *English Political Caricature: A Study of Opinion and Propaganda.* Oxford: Clarendon Press, 1959.

Grose, Francis. *Rules for Drawing Caricaturas with an Essay on Comic Painting.* London: Samuel Hooper, 1789.

Halder, Severin, Karl Heyer, Boris Michel, Silke Greth, Nico Baumgarten, Philip Boos, Janina Dobrusskin, Paul Schweizer, Laurenz Virchow, and Christoph Lambio, eds. *This Is Not an Atlas: A Global Collection of Counter-Cartographies.* Bielefeld: transcript Verlag, 2018.

Halperin, Charles. "The Double Standard: Livonian Chronicles and Muscovite Barbarity during the Livonian War (1558–1582)." *Studia Slavica et Balcanica Petropolitana* 1, no. 23 (2018): 126–47.

Haywood, Ian. *Romanticism and Caricature*. Cambridge: Cambridge University Press, 2013.

Hofbauer, Hannes. *Feindbild Russland: Geschichte einer Dämonisierung*. Vienna: Promedia Verlag, 2016.

Hoffman, Zachary. "Drawing Stereotypes: Europe and East Asia in Russian Political Caricature, 1900–1905." *Sibirica* 19 (2020): 85–118.

Jakobson, Roman. "Two Aspects of Language and Two Types of Aphasic Disturbances." In *Fundamentals of Language*. Edited by Roman Jakobson and Morris Halle, 55–82. Hague: Mouton & Co, 1956.

———. *Studies on Child Language and Aphasia*. Berlin: de Gruyter, 1971.

Kenney, Elise K., and John M. Merriman. *The Pear: French Graphic Arts in the Golden Age of Caricature*. New York: Worldwide Books, 1991.

Klingender, Francis Donald. *Hogarth and English Caricature*. London: Transatlantic Arts, 1944.

Koroleva, Svetlana. *Britanskii mif o Rossii*. Berlin: Direkt-Media, 2016.

Lai, Kenneth. "Masked as Beasts: An Analysis of Zoomorphism in the Cultural Imaginary of Hybridity." *Aisthesis* 3 (2014): 1–13.

Lavater, Johann Caspar. *Gradation de la tête de grenouille jusqu'au profil d'Apollon, d'après les idées du célébre Lavater*. Paris: Chéz Joubert fils et Charles Bance, 1793–1810. Accessed June 15, 2022. https://www.loc.gov/resource/cph.3b35221/.

———. *L'art de connaître les hommes par la Physionomie*. Paris: L. Prudhomme, Levrault, Schoell et C.nie, 1809.

Moores, John Richard. "Revolution." In *Representations of France in English Satirical Prints 1740–1832*. Edited by John R. Moores, 151–76. London: Palgrave Macmillan, 2015.

Oushakine, Serguei Alex. "Byvshee v upotreblenii: Postsovetskoe sostoianie kak forma afazii." *Novoe literaturnoe obozrenie* 100 (2009): 760–92.

Panofsky, Erwin. *Studies in Iconology: Humanistic Themes in the Art of the Renaissance*. New York: Harper & Row, 1972.

Pickles, John. *A History of Spaces. Cartographic Reason, Mapping and the Geo-Coded World*. London: Routledge, 2004.

Porterfield, Todd. *The Efflorescence of Caricature, 1759–1838*. Aldershot: Ashgate, 2011.

Regan, Tom. *The Case for Animal Rights*. Los Angeles: University of California Press, 1983.

Ruffman, Karl-Heinz. *Das Rußlandbild im England Shakespeares.* Göttingen: Musterschmidt, 1952.

Senghaas, Dieter. *Rüstung und Militarismus.* Frankfurt: Suhrkamp Verlag, 1972.

Sheets-Johnstone, Maxine. "The Enemy: A Twenty-First Century Archetypal Study." *Psychotherapy and Politics International Psychother. Politics. Int.* 8, no. 2 (2010): 146–61.

Taws, Richard. "The Currency of Caricature in Revolutionary France." Todd Porterfield ed. *The Efflorescence of Caricature, 1759–1838.* 95–115. Aldershot: Ashgate, 2011.

Wright, Thomas. *A History of Caricature and Grotesque in Literature and Art.* London: Virtue Brothers & Co, 1865.

Zubero, Imanol. "The Construction of the Stranger and Social Violence." In *Violence and Communication.* Edited by Jose Antonio Mingolarra, Carmen Arocena, and Rosa Martin Sabaris, 33–50. Reno: Center for Basque Studies University of Nevada, 2011.

11

Hungry and Different— "Otherness" in Imperial Famine Relief: 1891–1892

Immo Rebitschek

Abstract

Between 1891 and 1907, a sequence of famines struck the diverse population of the Russian Empire. Hunger crises confronted the imperial administration with the social dimensions of ethnic and religious "otherness," because minorities were affected most severely by recurrent crop failures. By examining relief policies and the communication of government and *zemstvo* officials, including media coverage, in multi-ethnic territories, this chapter pursues how "otherness" was perceived within the larger framework of social crisis in late imperial Russia, and how this perception changed after the watershed of 1905. The chapter will show how the imperial premodern perception of "otherness" as a purely cultural ascription evolved into a modern, more distinctive, and complex view of the social background of non-Russians. In the eyes of the Russian public and the imperial administration, ethnic "otherness" had little or no social dimensions until the revolution of 1905. It was the combined potential of social and national unrest that unveiled the ambiguity of "otherness" to them.

Introduction

In June 1892, the Kazan Governorate was in the grip of famine. Most peasants were only surviving on grain loans and charitable funds organized by local officials. In the Spasskii district (*uezd*), Iulia Dmitrievna Gerken, the wife of the land captain (*zemskii nachal'nik*) Iuri Sergeevich, approached the Special Committee for Famine Relief in St. Petersburg asking for at least 1,200 rubles for the building of bakeries and soup kitchens. She explained the problem was that previous donations had been spent on the Russian part of the population, because the existing soup kitchens were in Russian villages and therefore too remote from Tatar settlements: "There is therefore no possibility to help the Tatars, which is now extremely necessary—crowds of poor people were coming to our farmstead on a daily basis. Their only hope was the land captain and regardless of his intentions, he was powerless to help them."[1] A month later, the committee arranged for the payment of 1,200 rubles to her husband's precinct. Another month later, another two payments were made, one directly to the precinct, the other "directly to Iulia Gerken."[2] The official channels apparently offered no solution to the problem described by the land captain's wife. More importantly, none of the communications between the committee members and another letter of her husband give any indication of the existence of the Tatars, mentioning only "peasants" and the "peasant economy" in the Spasskii district.[3]

The Gerken intervention reveals both the particular hardships for the Tatars during the famine and an awareness of local support networks. Yet it also illustrates that the central authorities were assisting with additional funds for the starving without acknowledging the issue itself: that a certain group was not profiting from relief funds in the first place. A problem concerning the Tatars in particular had become a general "peasant" matter. This verbal twist raises the question of the perceptive borders of "Russianness" and "otherness." Did the imperial administration possess a terminology to describe non-Russians' exposure to different economic circumstances? More generally, was there a perception and way of communicating about the social problems of "ethnic" minorities in the first place; and did the notion of ethnicity affect and correspond with social policy?

---

1 Rossiskii gosudarstvennyi istoricheskii arkhiv, f. 1204, op. 1, d. 62, l. 36 (hereafter cited as RGIA).
2 Ibid., l. 50.
3 Ibid., ll. 38–50.

"Otherness" usually (although not always) reflects an unequal relationship in which identities are constructed through the identification of desirable and undesirable characteristics among oneself and others ("othering").[4] Although this constructed difference can be articulated as "relatively neutral,"[5] it is based on the mutual opposition and mutually exclusive characteristics (cultural, social, biological, and so on) by which an individual or group distinguishes itself from others.[6] The ingroup describes the outgroup by emphasizing its fundamental differences to confirm its own role or identity. Empires are usually defined or at least systematized by their approach to cultural difference.[7] Thus, where late imperial Russia is concerned, the historical debate concerning "otherness" is tied to a cultural context and analyzed against the backdrop of nation building. "Otherness" appears as the flip side of "Russianness." While the historiographical view of the creation of "Russianness" acknowledges the social dimensions of this debate (such as the peasant commune as the nucleus of the Russian nation),[8] it usually grounds the notion of "otherness" within the imperial borders in the framework of faith and language, reflecting a pattern set by contemporary ethnography.[9] The perception of imperial subjects as "non-Russian" was constructed, and is therefore primarily examined in the light of

4   Mike Crang, *Cultural Geography* (London: Routledge, 1998), 61.

5   Lajons Brons, "Othering. An Analysis," *Transience* 6, no. 1 (2015): 71.

6   For biological othering see esp. Simone de Beauvoir, *Das andere Geschlecht. Sitte und Sexus der Frau* (Berlin: Volk & Welt, 1989), 11.

7   Jane Burbank and Frederick Cooper, *Imperien der Weltgeschichte. Das Repertoire der Macht vom alten Rom und China bis heute* (Frankfurt/Main: Campus, 2012), 16, 320; Alexander Morrison, "Review: Muslims and Modernity in the Russian Empire," *The Slavonic and East European Review* 9, no. 4 (2016): 718; see also Ulrike von Hirschhausen and Leonard Jörn, "Zwischen Historisierung und Globalisierung. Titel, Themen und Trends der neueren Empire-Forschung," *Neue Politische Literatur* 56 (2011): 391–97; Robert Crews, *For Prophet and Tsar. Islam and Empire in Russia and Central Asia* (Cambridge, MA: Harvard University Press, 2006).

8   Susanna Rabow-Edling, *Slavophile Thought and the Politics of Cultural Nationalism* (Albany: State University New York Press, 2006); for the Duma–Period see Igor V. Omel'ianchuk, "Krest'ianskii vopros v programmakh konservativno-monarkhicheskikh partii Rossii (1905–1914 gg.)," *Voprosy istorii* 7 (2006): 83–97.

9   See, for example, Roland Cvetkovski and Alexis Hofmeister, eds., *An Empire of Others: Making Ethnographic Knowledge in Imperial Russia and the USSR* (Budapest: Central European University Press, 2014); Norihiro Naganawa, "Transimperial Muslims, the Modernizing State, and Local Politics in the Late Imperial Volga-Ural Region," *Kritika* 18, no. 2 (2017): 417–36; Elena Campbell, *The Muslim Question and Russian Imperial Governance* (Bloomington: Indiana University Press, 2015), 137–56; Ingeborg Baldauf, "Akkulturation—Chance oder Gefahr für die Rußland-Muslime an der Wolga und in Mittelasien?" in *Leben in zwei Kulturen. Akkulturation und Selbstbehauptung von Nichtrussen im Zarenreich*, ed. Trude Maurer (Wiesbaden: Harrassowitz, 2000), 161.

religious and cultural differences. A Tatar's "otherness" is seen from the vantage point of cultural Russification.

Joshua Sanborn has demonstrated that noncultural aspects provide a more differentiated view of the relationship between "Russians" and "non-Russians," describing it as a complex "matrix of difference and similarity."[10] While cultural demarcation lines seem clear, social and political considerations (like the political imperative to draft beyond ethnic lines) were conducive to shifting the lines and categories of the "self" and "others." Those whom the Russians considered legally and culturally "alien" (*inorodtsy*) could still be seen as part of the imperial self.[11] This shift exemplifies the transcendence of "otherness," depending on the categories to which the "self" refers. It also raises the question of the influence of other perspective-changing events, such as a social crisis, on the perception of otherness.

This chapter focuses on the fate of the Volga Tatars during the 1891–1892 famine in Kazan and the Russian relief response. It contextualizes a relationship that has been analyzed through the lenses of mutual cultural opposition. Famines and epidemics could transcend cultural division lines, spawning policies and discourses within the imperial administration that provide an alternative view of the relationship between the empire and its subjects, and reconciling cultural claims and social requirements. For example, the 1892 cholera outbreak in Tashkent reinforced notions of cultural chauvinism among Russian elites, but also forced them to "recognize mutual dependencies" and the necessity of cooperating with a population they deemed "backwards" and "dirty."[12] It is worth asking if the demarcation lines of "us" and "them" were still visible during a time of famine, which provided so little opportunity for cultural ascriptions, but which could affect certain groups to a different extent. Did the Russian view of starving Tatars conform to or transcend the notion of "otherness"?

Although there is ample literature on charity organizations and the charitable traditions of Islamic institutions in the Russian Empire, the role of the imperial administration and the cooperation of Tatar and Russian institutions in this

---

10 Joshua A. Sanborn, *Drafting the Russian Nation: Military Conscription, Total War, and Mass Politics, 1905–1925* (DeKalb: Northern Illinois University Press, 2011), 94.

11 For the legal and cultural context of the term *inorodtsy* see John V. Slocum, "Who, and When, Were the Inorodtsy? The Evolution of the Category of 'Aliens' in Imperial Russia," *The Russian Review* 57, no. 2 (1998): 173–90, and Vulpius, "From *Inozemtsy* to *Inovertsy* and *Novokreshchenye*: Images of Otherness in Eighteenth-Century Russia," in this volume.

12 Jeff Sahadeo, *Russian Colonial Society in Tashkent. 1863–1925* (Bloomington, IN: Indiana University Press, 2007), 87–89; 107.

respect remained desirable.[13] Even the 1891–92 famine has received little attention in recent years, and only a few Russian-speaking scholars have paid attention to the regional dimensions of this crisis without elaborating on its ethnic dimensions.[14] The geographical scope alone of the famine indicates how virulent this dimension had to be, because it struck many provinces with a considerable Muslim population (Ufa, Kazan, Orenburg, and Astrakhan, for example).[15] The famine also confronted the imperial administration with the social dimensions of ethnic and religious "otherness," because of all the population segments the inorodtsy were often the most severely affected by recurrent crop failure. This article examines the relief operation in the Kazan Governorate, showing how the imperial administration defined and managed its relationship with its non-Orthodox population (mainly the Volga Tatars). First, it shows how institutional and standardized communication about relief and its operation was determined by estate-based views, because the higher echelons of the state bureaucracy, as well as charitable organizations and the press, entirely rejected any ethnic or religious differentiation. The system of relief addressed a peasant issue, neither excluding nor acknowledging the ethnic dimension to this crisis. Second, I analyze the individual narratives beyond the standardized relief framework. Various local and central actors perpetuated knowledge and an interpretation of Tatars as a risk group during the famine. Privateers and state officials identified this group as part of a peasantry that was especially exposed to economic hardship. In emphasizing either cultural deficits or structural (socioeconomic) conditions, they made no clear distinction between "Russians" and "non-Russians," but externalized the negative features of peasant life, framing them as a worse and more dependent version of a Russian peasant, yet still part of the estate. The analysis and observations are primarily based on

---

13 See, for example, the edited volumes and source collections by I. K. Zagidullin, ed., *Istoriia Kazani v dokumentakh i materialakh XIX vek. Naselenie, konfessii, blagotvoritel'nost'. Kniga 2.* (Kazan: Tatarskoe knizhnoe izdatel'stvo, 2004); Radik Salikhov, *Uchastie tatarskogo predprinimatel'stva Rossii v obshchestvenno-politicheskikh protsessakh vtoroi poloviny XIX–nachala XX veka* (Kazan: FEN, 2004), 206–57.

14 See especially Richard G. Robbins Jr., *Famine in Russia 1891–1892. The Imperial Government Responds to a Crisis* (New York: Columbia University Press, 1975); see also the more recent volume by Alfred Eisfeld ed., *Hungersnöte in Russland und der Sowjetunion, 1891–1947. Regionale, ethnische und konfessionelle Aspekte* (Essen: Klartext, 2017); for regional aspects, see Gennadii E. Kornilov, ed., *Golodovki v istorii Rossii XVIII–XX vekov. Sbornik statei VIII Mezhdunarodnoi nauchno-prakticheskoi konferentsii* (Orenburg: OGPU, 2013); Rustam R. Batyrshin, "Golod 1891–1892 v Kazanskoi gubernii. Prichiny i posledstviia," in *Rossiiskoe krest'ianstvo i sel'skoe khoziaistvo v kontekste regional'noi istorii,* ed. A. G. Ivanov and A. A. Ivanov (Ioshkar-Ola: FGBOU VO, 2018), 257–62.

15 See Robbins, *Famine in Russia,* 5.

relief reports and letters both from the Special Committee in the capital and the provincial relief committee in Kazan, and on the reports of special envoys from the Ministry of Internal Affairs (MVD) to the governorate, as well as on the internal communication of the ministry's Economic Department.

Institutions: Structure and Communication

Recent historiography has gotten past the notion of a "backward" rural Russia in decay, returning a more differentiated verdict of Russia's agricultural development in the late nineteenth century. Still, in the face of demographic change, the lack of arable land and the lack of innovative agricultural technology, Russia's rural economy was prone to crises and the rural population increasingly vulnerable and less adaptable to crop failures.[16] From the autumn of 1890 until the spring of 1892 the central black earth regions experienced repeated droughts, resulting in the smallest grain harvest in European Russia in a decade. Emergency stocks of grain and seeds in the central grain producer regions (Riazan, Kursk, and so on) and the Lower Volga area had been exhausted after a series of bad harvests in the preceding years.[17] Combined with the enormous area of the drought (it covered two dozen provinces), the lack of infrastructure for transporting grain and bureaucratic obstacles, these crop failures became a famine that lasted until the summer harvest of 1892.[18] The Kazan Governorate was especially affected by the crop failure, ranking highest among the provinces in its need for grain and seed loans. The net harvest of rye per inhabitant fell here by 80%. More than 40% of all the seeds came as loans from the Ministry of Internal Affairs. On average, Kazan peasants received twice the food funds peasants elsewhere did.[19]

---

16 Arcadius Kahan, *Russian Economic History. The Nineteenth Century* (Chicago: The University of Chicago Press, 1989), 108–44. On the condition of the peasantry see, for example, Boris Mironov and Gregory Freeze, eds., *The Standard of Living and Revolutions in Russia, 1700–1917* (Oxon: Routledge, 2012), 128–74.

17 For the emergency stocks balance see esp. Komitet Ministrov, ed., *Prodovol'stvennoe delo I. Pechatnye predstavleniia Ministerstv Vnutrennikh Del, Putei Soobshcheniia i Finansov, kopii s vypisok iz zhurnalo Komiteta Ministrov po prodovol'stvennym delam, i sostavlennye kantseliarieiu Komiteta Ministrov spravki k sim delam, raspolozhennym po zasedaniiam Komiteta* (St. Peterburg, n.p., 1891–1892), 128.

18 Robbins, *Famine in Russia*, 1–13; Nikolai M. Dronin and Edward G. Bellinger, *Climate Dependence and Food Problems in Russia 1900–1990. The Interaction of Climate and Agricultural Policy and Their Effect on Food Problems* (Budapest: Central European University Press, 2005), 31–44.

19 Ministerstvo vnutrennykh del, *Vremennik tsentral'nogo statisticheskogo komiteta Ministerstva vnutrennykh del. Statisticheskie dannye po vydache ssud po obsemenenie i prodovol'stvie naseleniiu,*

As even the overall death toll (including or excluding hunger-induced disease) is difficult to determine,[20] there is no specific data for Kazan. It is certain that the deaths from starvation were unprecedented, and that government officials saw the situation in the province as alarming.[21]

On one hand, the first to experience the effect of crop failure were the Volga Tatars. There is extensive historiographical knowledge concerning the crises of Tatar husbandry and the economic strains on Muslim life in the lower Volga area.[22] Many of the Tatars in this area (97 percent) were peasants (usually state peasants).[23] The agrarian reforms of the 1860s had increased the economic pressure they faced. Tatar state peasants ended up with smaller and poorer lots, while only a fraction of farmers was considered "independent," which contributed to further social and economic polarization in Tatar agriculture.[24] Tatar peasants had worse prospects, fewer financial or other reserves, and were generally more vulnerable to crop failure. Historiography mentions famine as the major push factor for a massive rural exodus in these communities.[25]

However, the Tatars' economic situation was entirely absent from official institutionalized and standardized communication about famine relief. Censorship allowed extensive coverage of the famine and relief operations.[26] Yet none of the major newspapers in Kazan identified this situation as noteworthy or articulated ethnicity as a particular dimension of the crisis. Only a handful of external commentators and published letters referred to the Tatars or inorodtsy

postradavshemu ot neurozhaia v 1891–1892 gg. (St. Petersburg: Tipografiia P. P. Soikina, 1894), 8 (hereafter cited as MVD).

20 Stephen G. Wheatcroft, "The 1891–92 Famine in Russia: Towards a More Detailed Analysis of its Scale and Demographic Significance," in *Economy and Society in Russia and the Soviet Union, 1860–1930: Essays for Olga Crisp*, ed. Linda Harriett Edmondson and Peter Waldron (London: MacMillan, 1992), 44–64.

21 Robbins, *Famine in Russia*, 126.

22 See, for example, Rustem M. Mullagaliev, *Sotsial'no-ekonomicheskaia zhizn' tatarskoi krest'ianskoi obshchiny Kazanskoi gubernii v poreformennyi period (60–90-e gg. XIX v.)* (PhD diss., Academy of Sciences of Tatarstan Republic, 2011); Christian Noack, *Muslimischer Nationalismus im Russischen Reich. Nationsbildung und Nationalbewegung bei Tataren und Baschkiren 1861–1917* (Stuttgart: Franz Steiner Verlag, 2000), 88–91.

23 Boris Veselovskii, *Istoriia zemstva za 40 let* (St. Petersburg: Izdatel'stvo O.N. Popovoi, 1911), 4:17.

24 Farida G, Zainullina, *Tatarskaia derevnia Kazanskoi gubernii: sotsial'no-ekonomicheskaia i etnokul'turnaia transformatsiia (1861–1917 gg.). Avtoreferat* (Kazan: Akademiia Nauk RT, 2008), 16.

25 I. K. Zagidullin, *Tatarskoe natsional'noe dvizhenie v 1860–1905 gg.* (Kazan: Tatarskoe knizhnoe izdatel'stvo, 2014), 286–97; N. A. Khalikov, *Promysly i remesla Tatar povolzh'ia i urala (seredina XIX—nachalo XX v.)* (Kazan: Institut Istorii, 1998), 73.

26 Robbins, *Famine in Russia*, 168.

as a distinct group in the agricultural context.[27] The Tatars were usually identified as such in the framework of court proceedings, religious matters, or sanitary issues during the subsequent cholera crisis.[28] Articles about the relief operations mostly reported loans and charitable activities. Some described the devastating situation of starving peasants; others linked the current crisis to the wider debate about the general lack of arable land.[29] Agriculture and famine relief were a peasant problem.

The official view focused on an estate in crisis, because the "peasant question" featured no ethnic division lines before 1905. Indeed, the public debate about the peasantry mirrored a somewhat monolithic view of a backward and silent peasant mass. Yanni Kotsonis has even argued that the debate on the economic perspective of the Russian countryside served the self-insurance of Russia's elites by "othering" the *narod* as a counter-concept to the "cultured people."[30] One could argue that many late nineteenth-century intellectuals emphasized their deeper connection with the peasantry rather than their mutual exclusion and opposition, although naive idealization gave way to a more critical and analytical view.[31] However, the estate as a legal and socioeconomic unit determined the scope of the debate on rural poverty. This estate-based view was also reflected in famine relief legislation. The entire relief system was designed to "secure the national provision" for the "rural dwellers" (*sel'skikh obyvatelei*) and "local residents."[32] "Rural dwellers" referred to the members of the pre-reform peasant estate that included sedentary inorodtsy (but excluded Jews, who came under the category of "local residents").[33] Estate and geography determined the legal framework for relief and thus its communication. Russian food and charity legislation did not differentiate along ethnic division lines

---

27 A man named Kamaliutdin Gimatutdinov was operating a soup kitchen for Muslims and Christians alike and called for donations in the *Kazanskii birzhevoi listok* (January 15, 1892).

28 Another newspaper reported Tatars were carrying "healing stones" against cholera. *Kazanskie vesti* (August 8, 1892). See also the article about the "peculiarities" of Islam (February 7, 1892) or the debate concerning bilingual schools for Tatars (January 20, 1892) in *Volzhskii vestnik*.

29 See, for example, *Kazanskii birzhevoi listok* (January 26, 1892).

30 Yanni Kotsonis, *Making Peasants Backward: Agricultural Cooperatives and the Agrarian Question in Russia, 1861–1914* (London: Macmillan Press, 1999), 1–11.

31 Cathy Frierson, *Peasant Icons: Representations of Rural People in Late Nineteenth Century Russia* (Oxford: Oxford University Press, 1993), 9.

32 *Svod zakonov Rossiiskoi Imperii, poveleniem Gosudaria Imperatora Nikolaia Pervogo. Tom trinadtsatyi. Ustavy o narodnom prodovol'stvii, obshchestvennom prizrenii i vrachebnii. Izdanie 1892 goda* (St. Petersburg: Izdanie khozaistvennogo departmenta MVD, 1893), 1–2.

33 F. A. Brokgaus and I. A. Efron, *Entsiklopedicheskii slovar': Sakhar—Sem' mudretsov* (St. Petersburg: Brokgaus-Efron, 1900), 29:9, 375–76.

but considered the administrative prerogatives of estate-based institutions, reflecting financial control and logistic concerns. The legislation allowed some religious organizations to operate through a relief infrastructure of their own,[34] but the relief systems usually identified no differences among those receiving aid or loans.

The MVD formally controlled all the donations and charitable activities in the empire. Only designated territories with a nomadic inorodtsy population came under the jurisdiction of the Ministry for State Domains.[35] Curatorships (*popechitel'stva*) organized all the charity groundwork in villages and towns. They constituted the main pillar of organized famine relief fundraising. Here, the local elite—teachers, clerics, judges, *zemstvo* officials, and other local authorities—collected and distributed charitable money. The Special Committee in St. Petersburg (controlled by the MVD) gathered information on charity work through them.[36] Most of their reports sent through the official relief infrastructure emphasized the vulnerability of certain areas—such as Mamadysh or other territories with a large Tatar population—which usually lay on the outskirts of the main infrastructure (such as the Volga waterways), where relief institutions were the exception.[37] The *popechitel'stva* reports listed these areas without acknowledging this particular demography.[38] At the same time, mullahs and priests were elected together in the popechitel'stva. Their reports indicate that mullahs took responsibility for distributing charitable funds in their community, and that soup kitchens were erected in ethnically mixed settlements and visited by both Tatars and Russians.[39] Yet, this reflected logistic and, in this case, clerical competences rather than perceptions of otherness.

The entire communication between charitable institutions, such as donation reports and other published material from the Red Cross or the Holy Synod, revolved around the "indigent" (*nuzhdaiushchikhsia*) people or "poor/poorest peasants." The concluding report by the Red Cross in Kazan described its

---

34 *Svod zakonov. Ustav o narodnom prizrenii*, 66. This applied to Jewish and Evangelical denominations in the western provinces, whereas Catholic organisations were not entitled to their own charity infrastructure.

35 *Svod zakonov. Ustav o narodnom prodovol'stvii*, 1–2.

36 The *zemstva* organized their own boards. RGIA, f. 1204, op. 1, d. 192, ll. 77–84; RGIA, f. 1005, op. 2, d. 32, l. 76.

37 This issue was often emphasised by Fanni Gangardt, a Swiss native who collected donations from St. Petersburg and Kazan, setting up food kitchens and bakeries in the most affected districts of Laishevsk and Mamadysh, focusing on the remote parts of the country beyond the reach of the Red Cross or the *popechitel'stva*. RGIA, f. 1204, op. 1, d. 61, ll. 190–91.

38 See the statistical overview for Kazan province: RGIA, f. 1287, op. 4, d. 2125, l. 154; see Nechaev–Maltsev's report, RGIA, f. 1204, op. 1, d. 2.

39 RGIA, f. 1204, op.1, d. 193, ll. 77–84.

activities as a "struggle against a national disaster."[40] Its popechitel'stva focused their work on the "rural peasant population" but also emphasized that relief was to be "distributed equally among the entire population of the province, regardless of religion or estate."[41] The Red Cross clarified its humanitarian stance. Human suffering transcended lines of cultural and social division. The Russian Orthodox Church not only participated in the popechitel'stva but organized its own relief programs through its clerical infrastructure, in eparchial committees, for example. Their public and internal communication mostly addressed the fate of starving Christians, placing the church's efforts and human calamities in a religious context. Local priests and theological thinkers preached about the "Christian obligation to help the miserable."[42] Non-Orthodox denominations simply did not exist in these readings, which did not mean these groups were deliberately excluded from help. The reach of clerical infrastructure was mostly within (but not exclusively) the parish. Meanwhile, at the provincial and ministerial level both the relief mechanisms and communication reflected logistical and financial considerations. The ministries involved were concerned about how much money was spent on what by whom. The lists of donors and recipients sent to and compiled by the MVD did not reveal specific ethnic backgrounds.[43] Although local officials found it noteworthy that some members of the Tatar community reached out to and supported starving Russian peasants, the state bureaucracy simply acknowledged the person's role by listing them as donors.[44]

This logic also applied to the entire system of loan distribution. In times of subsistence crisis, the village commune would communicate its loan demands to the parish (*volost'*) administration, which would pass the request to the district zemstvo executive board (*uprava*). Depending on the budget (and budgetary policy), the zemstvo, provincial, or ministerial officials approved these lists.[45] Grain loan legislation was differentiated along administrative and estate lines, mainly between zemstvo and non-zemstvo regions. It allowed for the imperial

---

40 Kazanskoe gubernskoe popechitel'stvo Krasnogo Kresta, ed., *Otchet o deiatel'nosti Kazanskogo gubernskogo popechitel'stva Krasnogo Kresta po okazaniiu pomoshchi postradavshchemu ot neurozhaia naseleniiu Kazanskoi gubernii, za vremia s 18-go sentiabria 1891 po 1-go ianvaria 1893 goda* (Kazan: Tipografiia okruzhnogo shtaba, 1893), 4.

41 Ibid., 9.

42 A. A. Tsarevskii, *O khristiianskoi obiazannosti pomogat' bedstvuiushchim ot goloda. Publichnoe chtenie v biblioteke sv. Vladimira* (Kazan: Tipografiia Imperatorskogo Universiteta, 1892).

43 RGIA, f. 1005, op. 2, d. 34, ll. 50–60.

44 RGIA, f. 1204, op. 1, d. 192, l. 11.

45 *Svod zakonov. Ustav o narodnom prodovol'stvii*, 16. See esp. Richard G. Robbins Jr., "Russia's System of Food Supply Relief on the Eve of the Famine of 1891–92," *Agricultural History* 45, no. 4, (1971): 260–61.

administration to assume control over grain funds and loan distribution in certain inorodtsy areas for nomadic people with little or no agricultural tradition (such as the Samoyedic people in the northern territories).[46] This did not apply to the Volga Tatars as sedentary inorodtsy, who were not a legally distinct group but part of the peasantry. After 1892, the MVD tried to assess the overall total of loans given out in the crisis and collect payments. Central to the assessment reports was the fact that many peasants contested the numbers presented to them, yet no distinction was made between Russian and non-Russian peasants. One can only assume their ethnic background based on the names and surnames on the list. Neither the MVD's internal and public reports about its relief operation nor the ministerial exchange in the Ministerial Committee give any indication of religious or ethnic background.[47]

Those at all levels of institutionalized famine relief focused on the "starving" as an abstract, peasant group. This did not mean that everyone was blind to cultural differences. The entire relief system was designed to feed or control the rural population as a structural response to the peasant question, which did not include cultural division lines, let alone distinctions of ethnicity, but focused on socioeconomic implications. The 1891–92 Provincial "Meetings for Securing the Population with Foodstuffs" in Kazan provide a remarkable example of how notions of cultural and ethnic difference were filtered through institutions.

At these meetings, in January 1892, the Kazan governor Poltoratskii and officials from the MVD evaluated strategies for the transportation of seeds to the lower Volga region. The Kazan zemstvo assembly had requested a seed loan of as much as 4.5 million *pud*[48] from the MVD, hoping that it could be transported down the Volga River. In response, the Ministry of Internal Affairs sent General Mikhail Annenkov and his staff officer Aleksandr Terekhov to the meetings to assess the situation. Annenkov, a highly decorated veteran of the Russo-Turkish war, oversaw the public works program and "an enthusiastic proponent of the Russian railroad construction,"[49] and as such an important authority in matters of transport. His and especially Terekhov's assessment of the logistical situation struck an unusual tone. Terekhov's report to Annenkov stated that 1.1 million of the little more than two million inhabitants of Kazan were inorodtsy.[50] Since the abolition of serfdom they had not only received

---

46 *Svod zakonov. Ustav o narodnom prodovol'stvii*, 37–44.
47 RGIA, f. 1287, op. 4, d. 2274; MVD, *Vremennik*.
48 One *pud* is a unit of mass equal to 36.11 pounds or 16.38 kg.
49 Robbins, *Famine in Russia*, 112–13.
50 The 1897 poll counted 633,024 "Muslims" in the Kazan Governorate (29.1 percent), while close to 69 percent were considered "Orthodox") (I. K. Zagidullin, *Perepis' 1897 goda i tatary*

better plots than "the Russians" but had never paid their redemption fees. They had wasted their plots, and because they did not own horses would have no use for seed loans. Additionally, they lived in settlements remote from the Volga River. Providing seeds to them would be an "irretrievable waste of state funds."[51] Terekhov predicted: "The Tatar economy will collapse—that is the judgment of history, and it is scarcely beneficial to support them at the expense of the Russian population."[52] Annenkov's official recommendation to the Kazan authorities was a more moderate summary of Terekhov's. Nevertheless, he identified the Tatars as a problematic group, because only every third homestead owned a horse. They had to sow by hand. Transport expenses would thus exceed the yield, which in turn made the Tatars an economic liability.[53]

At the next meeting, neither of Annenkov's and Terekhov's suggestions, much less the wording, was considered. Members of the provincial administration, the zemstva, the MVD, and the charity committees instead agreed to re-evaluate the precise need for seed loans and to organize horses and cattle for the peasants. Although the MVD had already arranged to buy thirty thousand horses for this purpose, the Kazan zemstvo, and later Governor Poltoratskii, filed a request for an additional five hundred thousand rubles to feed them, and two hundred rubles directly for horseless peasants so they could buy them.[54] Instead of marginalizing and excluding the Tatars as a distinct group from seed provision, both the zemstvo and the provincial administration emphasized the need to provide for all peasants—those with and "those without horses."[55] At no point in this communication did the officials use the words "Tatar" or inorodtsy. The zemstvo assembly even suggested that horse owners could pay back their loans by working the lands of their horseless neighbors, a reference to territories inhabited mostly by Tatars.[56] There is no indication that this suggestion was put into practice. However, the officials involved rejected any ethnic reading of this crisis and instead addressed the needs of a peasant population. The official, that is, institutionalized communication about famine relief only allowed notions of estate and geography. Famine was perceived and addressed as a peasant issue. Ethnic distinctions, let alone the perception of Tatars as the "other" or a

---

Kazanskoi gubernii [Kazan: Tatarskoe knizhnoe izdatel'stvo, 2000], 39). Although these numbers do not reflect the citizens' legal status, they do not support Terekhov's calculation either.

51 RGIA, f. 1287, op. 4, d. 2125, l. 197ob
52 Ibid.
53 Ibid., l. 194.
54 RGIA, f. 1204, op. 1, d. 2, ll. 110–1; RGIA, f. 1287, op. 4, d. 2125, ll. 197ob, 329.
55 RGIA, f. 1287, op. 4, d. 2125, ll. 197ob, 331.
56 Ibid., ll. 330–33.

particular group within this framework, were visible only beyond the channels of institutional communication.

Individual Narratives of "Tatar Misery" in 1892

Both historians and many contemporaries involved in agriculture knew of the vulnerability of the Tatars in times of crises. In 1894, the ethnologist Konstantin Lavrskii published his observations from the 1880s and his hypothesis about the situation of the Volga Tatars.[57] Unlike most of his peers in ethnography and anthropology, who focused on cultural customs and biological or "racial" features, he had conducted a study of the economic and social conditions of the Tatar peasantry. Lavrskii was interested in allotment shares, economic dependencies, and patterns of work migration—not in "biological inclinations" or skull shapes.[58] His conclusion left no doubt that the Tatars belonged to the poorest population segment. They lacked sufficient plots of arable land, forests, and pasture, which in turn produced new generations of migrant workers. Contrary to popular belief, the Tatars were not wasteful with their resources or their land but were eager to keep as much land as possible. In addition to his analysis, Lavrskii issued a warning:

> Their economy will at least not improve; indeed, the proletariat is growing with each year. With each crop failure the livestock is dying, and there is no guarantee that these crop failures will not be repeated and occur as often in the future as they did in the past: 1868, 1870, 1873, 1877, 1880, 1883 [. . .]. The Tatar misery [*Tatarskaia bednota*] will force the Russian and Chuvash population to assume the debt for food loans.[59]

The message was clear: the Tatar peasants were the weakest link in Kazan's rural economy, and they would become gradually more dependent on grain loans than any other group, making them the first victims of famine. To some extent,

---

57 Konstantin Lavrskii, *Tatarskaia bednota. Statistiko-ekonomicheskii ocherk dvukh tatarskikh dereven Kazanskoi gubernii* (Kazan: Tipografiia gubernskogo upravleniia, 1894).
58 See also Farida G. Zainullina, "K. Lavrskii, odin iz pervykh issledovatelei istorii Tatarskogo krest'ianstva," in *Problemy istorii, kul'tury i razvitiia iazykov narodov Tatarstana i Volgo-Ural'skogo regiona. (Materialy Nauchno-prakticheskoi konferentsii)*, ed. A. A. Burchanov (Kazan: Gumanitariia, 2003), 2:100–103.
59 Lavrskii, *Tatarskaia bednota*, 35–36.

his observations mirrored what local activists and officials were witnessing and reporting in 1891–92. Local elites produced knowledge about Tatars being the most vulnerable population segment in this crisis, but whereas Lavrskii's scientific approach assumed them to be a distinct but equally capable social group determined by socioeconomic dependencies, many contemporaries saw the Tatars as the lowest peasants. In describing Tatar poverty, they were partly externalizing negative features of the Russian peasant without "othering" them.

This narrative of the Tatars as extreme examples of the less capable peasant was especially prominent in complaints about peasant work ethics and the alleged negative moral effect of grain loans. By the end of the nineteenth century, many politicians and economists in Europe shared the neo-Malthusian view that aid and loans without interest would demoralize rather than support the poor.[60] This view was widespread at every level of the imperial administration and shared by many experts dealing with famine long before 1891. The famous historian and chronicler of the Ministerial Committee, Sergei Seredonin, gave various examples of Russian ministers warning that "free" (irretrievable) loans could be a "dangerous, harmful and demoralizing thing."[61] Peasants would become accustomed to them and lose their incentive to work, creating a vicious circle of impoverishment. This narrative was closely intertwined with the ongoing debate on the "peasant question," and the overall controversy concerning whether the Russian peasant could make rational and economic decisions. Not all experts were pessimistic about it, but as Cathy Frierson has shown, by the late 1880s the educated public had the "tendency [. . .] to consign the peasant to a position of perpetual tutelage."[62] The peasant needed guidance and control. The Tatars were not outliers, but the primary example of such reliance.

In their capacity as multipliers of relief information, land captains and district *zemstvo* officials regularly warned the provincial administration about the peasants being too reliant on grain loans. In the autumn of 1891, a land captain from Mamadysh reported to the provincial administration that other land captains "had noticed a certain apathy among the people [*v narode*] to better their existence by their own effort, and an unusual demand [*neobychnuiu trebovatel'nost'*] for external aid."[63] Those who were receiving aid would lose

---

60 James Vernon, *Hunger: A Modern History* (Cambridge MA: Harvard University Press, 2007), 12.

61 S. M. Seredonin, *Istoricheskii obzor deiatel'nosti komiteta ministrov. Komitet Ministrov v tsarstvov. Imp. Aleksandra Vtorogo 1855 g. Fevr. 19–1881 g. Marta 1* (St. Petersburg: Kantseliariia Komiteta Ministrov, 1902), 243–44.

62 Frierson, *Peasant Icons*, 182.

63 RGIA, f. 1287, op. 4, d. 2125, l. 45.

interest in work, leading to further impoverishment. This "impoverishment [*obednenie*] appeared in precisely those settlements, mainly Tatar, where grain loans had been given out in the preceding years, and where the debt situation was considerable."[64] Those loans had "accustomed the people to idleness."[65] He also emphasized that the current famine would "call for profound empathy, even for those who become lazy,"[66] and that it would be unreasonable to confront them about it now. Although the notion of "laziness" was often applied to the Tatars, the warning was not limited to them but must be seen as part of a broader argument applied by most government officials: that grain loans (especially without interest) would stifle every peasant's incentive to work.[67] A lazy peasant could jeopardize all relief efforts and therefore must suffer the consequences of his actions. The Tatars were again chosen as a vivid example in this respect.

Nikolai Troinitskii was one of two important envoys the Special Committee had sent to Kazan to provide details about the relief operation. He, too, emphasized on many occasions that "the majority of the population views this aid [grain loans, I. R.]" not as loans but as "mandatory feeding, especially the Tatars."[68] His elaborate assessment of this problem revealed that Tatars in particular bore negative characteristics usually ascribed to the peasantry in general. In June 1892, Troinitskii reported to the MVD that the peasants would be ignorant of the difference between loans and aid, which had a "corrupting influence" on the population's "energy for work."[69] Yet, while "the Russian population of the province endured the God-given test with Christian humility—the Tatars insistently demanded relief [...] and sometimes even tried to express their demands through unrest."[70] In the next line, Troinitski again generalizes this problem, stating that a "considerable part of the population in Kazan" would rely on secure food provision by the government, believing that "the government is obliged to give them free bread."[71] In this reading, the Tatars and Russians shared a problem, but there was a cultural hierarchy to consider. Troinitskii would explain a peasant issue and then point to the Tatars as a "special" example. During his journey through the countryside, he encountered

---

64 Ibid., l. 48.
65 Ibid., l. 45.
66 Ibid., l. 48.
67 On "laziness" as an attribute of Tatars, see also Nikita Khrapunov "'In a Menagerie of Nations': Crimean Others in Travelogues ca. 1800" in this volume.
68 RGIA, f. 1204, op. 1, d. 61, l. 55.
69 RGIA, f. 1287, op. 4, d. 2178, l. 206.
70 Ibid.
71 Ibid.

all kinds of people, but "mainly Tatar,"[72] who pretended to starve, but who were ultimately fine. Similarly, he stressed that a "considerable part of the peasant population, especially the Tatars, distract themselves from farming."[73] The Tatars, he said, were especially predestined to what defined Russian peasants as the unreliable (in Kotsonis's words "other") estate: morally weak and easily corrupted by free loans.

Troinitskii did not stop with these comparisons. He asked the MVD to intervene explicitly in the Tatar village structure, not only in Kazan but in "neighboring provinces" as well. To "spark the desire to work" and recover the debt from the Tatar population, he suggested the temporary removal of "the elective village authorities" in Tatar settlements and their replacement with "reliable people from the outside,"[74] chosen by the land captain. These new authorities would "train the population to work and convince them that the source of prosperity lies only in work."[75] Troinitskii pushed the political argument about lazy peasants to the extreme, all the while targeting Tatars as a particularly backward group in need of guidance and education. This did not mean that he argued that they should suffer discrimination or be penalized. On the contrary, he reported to his superiors how the image of destitution and hunger, that "awakens the special care by Your Excellency, as the compassion by all of Russia, is almost completely related to this part of the inorodtsy population in the province (often Chuvash and in almost all cases Tatar),"[76] which had long been accustomed to misery and which was now threatened by the famine as the final blow to their capacity to escape poverty. Troinitskii did not merely externalize the negative image of the peasantry but suggested a distinct policy to address the Tatar situation.[77]

The second envoy, Iuri Stepanovich Nechaev-Mal'tsev, instead emphasized the shared fate of Russian and Tatar peasants. Nechaev-Mal'tsev was a glass manufacturer and philanthropist who had traveled through Kazan between 1891 and 1892 on behalf of the Special Committee. He provided information about charity work and the local needs among the Kazan populace for the higher echelons of the administration.[78] In 1892 he wrote two comprehensive reports—the first about the situation of the population in the Kazan *uezd*, the

---

72 Ibid.
73 Ibid.
74 Ibid.
75 Ibid., l. 207.
76 RGIA, f. 1287, op. 4, d. 2125, l. 246.
77 Ibid., fol. 245.
78 RGIA, f. 1204, op. 1, d. 2, ll. 30–32.

second about the whole province suffering from crop failure. Like Lavrskii, he focused on the economic factors that contributed to poverty. The first report painted a devastating picture of the peasantry, among whom the Tatars were especially suffering the consequences of crop failure. They lacked firewood, oil, and above all cattle. Close to 70% of the Tatar peasantry did not own horses. They lived in little "box-huts," mostly without doors. Every part of the interior in these huts was sold and their owners were left with literally nothing but a shirt.[79]

According to Mal'tsev, the main reason for their misery was that most Tatars "had not been entirely successful in adjusting to the everyday system based on the decree of 19 February 1861, and their agricultural economy gradually fell into decay."[80] Additionally, their settlements were far from the state forests, meaning Tatar peasants had no access to charitable donations of firewood. He used the Tatars as an example to criticize the Kazan zemstvo for being miserly with grain loans for the "destitute population,"[81] allocating only 60% of the average amount of grain and seeds. He was referring to the Russian poor as well as the Tatars, and interestingly hinted at some of the structural problems of the Tatar peasantry, which were connected with the transformation of Russian agriculture.

The second report came three months later and was a comprehensive assessment of hunger and famine relief for the entire province. It went into print and addressed a wider audience in the government and members of the charity board—including the Tsarevich himself. He made clear that 60% of the Kazan peasantry had been affected by the famine, and many had died.[82] Again, the non-Russian population was especially vulnerable to agricultural crises: "The Tatar settlements are in general characterized by great poverty, which can partly be explained by their trait to work sloppily. By all accounts they live in misery for many years, due to repeated crop failures in these areas." As in Troinitskii's report, the text included small references to ethnic stereotypes, stating that the "the Tatars of the Kazan district are barely capable of farming"[83] [*malo sposobny k zemledeliiu*]. Unlike his colleague, however, Mal'tsev made it clear that the reason for their misery was not to be found in lifestyle or culture, but in the general deficits of Russian agriculture:

> The deficits of the existing system are most visible in the Tatar settlement, whose numbers make up a third of all the inhabitants

---

79 RGIA, f. 1005, op. 2, d. 35, ll. 3–35.
80 Ibid., l. 34.
81 Ibid., l. 34ob.
82 RGIA, f. 1005, op. 2, d. 32, ll. 207–8.
83 RGIA, f. 1005, op. 2, d. 32, l. 181.

of the Kazan Governorate. A considerable majority rents out its land for a paltry sum, insufficient to pay off their duties—or they abandon everything and leave for the cities to find work. This does not exist among the Chuvash and Cheremis people, who are divided into small settlements of three to six farms and do not allow repartition. The welfare of those nationalities has been less affected by the recent crop failures, and the number of farms without horses has not risen.[84]

The Tatars and other nationalities were part of a wider argument against communal agriculture. They had the least amount of cattle and horses and lived on the worst soil. The Tatars were the first and sometimes the only ones to suffer from crop failure, which made not just them but non-Russians in general a clear indicator of structural problems in rural areas: "The multi-ethnic composition [*raznoplemennyi sostav*] of the population, with either of those nationalities being predominant in some settlements and villages, reveals their economic and sanitary situation, and the great destitution of places with a Tatar population is striking."[85]

Philanthropists and experts alike voiced their concern about the Tatars as a considerably vulnerable segment of the population. It was known they were affected early and most severely by crop failures. There were two narratives. Some identified this vulnerability as the result of cultural or ethnical weaknesses, portraying the Tatars as the lowest among the peasantry. Others used this vulnerability as an example of the frailty of the entire rural economy and the fate of the estate in general. Both narratives stressed that the Tatars were part of the same estate and therefore depended on guidance, immediate aid, and to some extent even increased supervision. Officials like Troinitskii may have insisted on a cultural hierarchy, but not to affirm a contrasting positive image of the Russian peasantry. Rather, they did so to add the distinction of cultural supremacy within a shared community. This distinction did not question the Tatars' belonging to the estate. The individual narratives of Tatar poverty reveal the transcending nature of "otherness," because notions of cultural distance were secondary to a general premodern estate-based perception of social belonging. In the context of social crises, the Tatars were considered peasants before they were considered non-Russians.

---

84 RGIA, f. 1005, op. 2, d. 32, ll. 170–71.
85 Ibid., l. 183 ob.

Outlook

The economic situation of the Tatars during the 1891–1892 famine exemplifies an important difference between institutional communication and individual knowledge. Historians, anthropologists, and other observers of the time refer to this group as being especially exposed to the hardships of hunger and destitution during these years. However, since the relief institutions addressed an estate problem, no statistical records or analysis can be found to comprehensively to grasp this phenomenon. Only those who were engaged in local relief work and who came into contact with the Tatars found a reason and way to communicate that this group was exposed to circumstances that not merely differed from those of their Russian neighbors but were gradually worsening. This discrepancy shows that the imperial famine relief system at an institutional level did not acknowledge an ethnic dimension of this crisis but was designed to meet the needs of a social group. The perception of cultural differences was visible only beyond standardized forms of communication. These individual narratives reflected cultural chauvinism and deeply rooted stereotypes, yet neither viewed the Tatars in mutual opposition to the Russian peasantry, but as an example of its undesirable characteristics. Tatars and Russians were part of the same estate and, as such, came under the responsibility of an administration that entirely rejected ethnic notions in such crises. Even when officials like Terekhov sought to establish such notions, they did not stick. This perception—individually and institutionally is important for two reasons.

First, most Tatar peasants were in an economically less favorable position than their Russian neighbors. Ethnicity was probably a determining factor in economic success. Yet the notion of ethnicity could not and did not correspond with relief policies. The Russian Empire did not differentiate along ethnic lines in its famine relief. This underlines an important difference with the British Empire, whose colonial administration not only differentiated between ethnicities but used food aid to target and efface indigenous economic structures.[86]

Second, for the administration and the Russian public, hunger was considered a peasant problem, a social disaster with no distinct ethnic or religious connection. Until 1905, the general perception of "otherness" was materialized exclusively around cultural notions such as religious affiliation. There was no binary view

---

86 David Nally has shown that the British colonial administration used policies of food provisioning to destroy (indigenous) nonmarket safety nets and efface local "customary entitlements" as an expression of biopolitical engineering. See David Nally, "The Biopolitics of Food Provisioning," *Transactions of the Institute of British Geographers*, n.s., 36, no. 1 (2011): 37–53.

of starving peasants in imperial Russia. It was only after the revolution of 1905 that national protests and peasant uprisings in some regions began to merge, and the administration was confronted by the interdependence of national and social questions. Although the combined potential of social and national unrest foreshadowed the fracture of the Russian Empire, the administration failed to adjust to the situation and its view of it, and to learn about the social causes of national unrest.

Works Cited

Archival Sources

Rossiskii gosudarstvennyi istoricheskii arkhiv (RGIA), f. 1005 Fond Iu. S. Nechaeva-Mal'tseva

Rossiskii gosudarstvennyi istoricheskii arkhiv (RGIA), f. 1204 Special Committee on Famine Relief

Rossiskii gosudarstvennyi istoricheskii arkhiv (RGIA), f. 1287 Khoziaistvennyi departament MVD

Newspapers

Kazanskii birzhevoi listok
Kazanskie vesti
Volzhskii vestnik

Printed Sources and Literature

Baldauf, Ingeborg. "Akkulturation—Chance oder Gefahr für die Rußland-Muslime an der Wolga und in Mittelasien?" In *Leben in zwei Kulturen. Akkulturation und Selbstbehauptung von Nichtrussen im Zarenreich.* Edited by Trude Maurer, 143–61. Wiesbaden: Harrassowitz, 2000.

Batyrshin, Rustam R. "Golod 1891–1892 v Kazanskoi gubernii. Prichiny i posledstviia." In *Rossiiskoe krest'ianstvo i sel'skoe khoziaistvo v kontekste regional'noi istorii.* Edited by A. G. Ivanov and A. A. Ivanov, 257–62. Ioshkar-Ola: FGBOU VO, 2018.

Beauvoir, Simone de. *Das andere Geschlecht. Sitte und Sexus der Frau.* Berlin: Volk & Welt, 1989.

Brokgaus, F. A., and I. A. Efron, ed. *Entsiklopedicheskii slovar': Sakhar—Sem' mudretsov.* Vol. 29. St. Petersburg: Brokgaus-Efron, 1900.

Brons, Lajons. "Othering. An Analysis." *Transience* 6, no. 1 (2015): 69–90.

Burbank, Jane, and Frederick Cooper. *Imperien der Weltgeschichte. Das Repertoire der Macht vom alten Rom und China bis heute.* Frankfurt am Main: Campus, 2012.

Campbell, Elena. *The Muslim Question and Russian Imperial Governance.* Bloomington: Indiana University Press, 2015.

Crang, Mike. *Cultural Geography.* London: Routledge, 1998.

Crews, Robert. *For Prophet and Tsar. Islam and Empire in Russia and Central Asia.* Cambridge, MA: Harvard University Press, 2006.

Cvetkovski, Roland, and Alexis Hofmeister, ed. *An Empire of Others: Making Ethnographic Knowledge in Imperial Russia and the USSR.* Budapest: Central European University Press, 2014.

Dronin, Nikolai M., and Edward G. Bellinger. *Climate Dependence and Food Problems in Russia 1900–1990. The Interaction of Climate and Agricultural Policy and Their Effect on Food Problems.* Budapest: Central European University Press, 2005.

Eisfeld, Alfred, ed. *Hungersnöte in Russland und der Sowjetunion, 1891–1947. Regionale, ethnische und konfessionelle Aspekte.* Essen: Klartext, 2017.

Frierson, Cathy. *Peasant Icons: Representations of Rural People in Late Nineteenth Century Russia.* Oxford: Oxford University Press, 1993.

Hirschhausen, Ulrike von, and Leonard Jörn. "Zwischen Historisierung und Globalisierung. Titel, Themen und Trends der neueren Empire-Forschung." *Neue Politische Literatur* 56 (2011): 389–404.

Kahan, Arcadius. *Russian Economic History. The Nineteenth Century.* Chicago: The University of Chicago Press, 1989.

Kazanskoe gubernskoe popechitel'stvo Krasnogo Kresta, ed. *Otchet o deiatel'nosti Kazanskogo gubernskogo popechitel'stva Krasnogo Kresta po okazanii pomoshchi postradavshchemu ot neurozhaia naseleniiu Kazanskoi gubernii, za vremia s 18-go sentiabria 1891 po 1-go ianvaria 1893 goda.* Kazan: Tipografiia okruzhnogo shtaba, 1893.

Khalikov, N. A. *Promysly i remesla Tatar povolzh'ia i urala (seredina XIX—nachalo XX v.).* Kazan: Institut Istorii, 1998.

Kornilov, Gennadii E., ed. *Golodovki v istorii Rossii XVIII–XX vekov. Sbornik statei VII Mezhdunarodnoi nauchno-prakticheskoi konferentsii.* Orenburg: OGPU, 2013.

Komitet Ministrov, ed., *Prodovol'stvennoe delo I. Pechatnye predstavleniia Ministerstv Vnutrennikh Del, Putei Soobshcheniia i Finansov, kopii s vypisok iz zhurnalov Komiteta Ministrov po prodovol'stvennym delam, i sostavlennye kantseliarieiu Komiteta Ministrov spravki k sim delam, raspolozhennym po zasedaniiam Komiteta.* St. Petersburg, 1891–1892.

Kotsonis, Yanni. *Making Peasants Backward: Agricultural Cooperatives and the Agrarian Question in Russia, 1861–1914.* London: Macmillan Press, 1999.

Lavrskii, Konstantin. *Tatarskaia bednota. Statistiko-ekonomicheskii ocherk dvukh tatarskikh dereven Kazanskoi gubernii.* Kazan: Tipografiia gubernskogo upravleniia, 1894.

Ministerstvo vnutrennykh del (MVD). *Vremennik tsentral'nogo statisticheskogo komitet Ministerstva vnutrennykh del. Statisticheskie dannye po vydache ssud po obsemenenie i prodovol'stvie naseleniiu, postradavshemu ot neurozhaia v 1891–1892 gg.* St. Petersburg: Tipografiia P. P. Soikina, 1894.

Mironov, Boris, and Gregory Freeze, ed. *The Standard of Living and Revolutions in Russia, 1700–1917.* Oxford: Routledge, 2012.

Morrison, Alexander. "Review: Muslims and Modernity in the Russian Empire." *The Slavonic and East European Review* 9, no. 4 (2016): 715–24.

Mullagaliev, Rustem M. *Sotsial'no-ekonomicheskaia zhizn' tatarskoi krest'ianskoi obshchiny Kazanskoi gubernii v poreformennyi period (60–90-e gg. XIX v.).* PhD diss., Academy of Sciences of Tatarstan Republic, 2011.

Naganawa, Norihiro. "Transimperial Muslims, the Modernizing State, and Local Politics in the Late Imperial Volga-Ural Region." *Kritika* 18, no. 2 (2017): 417–36.

Nally, David. "The Biopolitics of Food Provisioning." *Transactions of the Institute of British Geographers,* n.s., 36, no. 1 (2011): 37–53.

Noack, Christian. *Muslimischer Nationalismus im Russischen Reich. Nationsbildung und Nationalbewegung bei Tataren und Baschkiren 1861–1917.* Stuttgart: Franz Steiner Verlag, 2000.

Omel'ianchuk, Igor V. "Krest'ianskii vopros v programmakh konservativno-monarkhicheskikh partii Rossii (1905–1914 gg.)." *Voprosy istorii* 7 (2006): 83–97.

Rabow-Edling, Susanna. *Slavophile Thought and the Politics of Cultural Nationalism.* Albany: State University New York Press, 2006.

Robbins Jr., Richard G. "Russia's System of Food Supply Relief on the Eve of the Famine of 1891–92." *Agricultural History* 45, no. 4, (1971): 259–69.

———. *Famine in Russia 1891–1892. The Imperial Government Responds to a Crisis.* New York: Columbia University Press, 1975.

Salikhov, Radik. *Uchastie tatarskogo predprinimatel'stva Rossii v obshchestvenno-politicheskikh protsessakh vtoroi poloviny XIX–nachala XX veka.* Kazan: FEN, 2004.

Sanborn, Joshua A. *Drafting the Russian Nation: Military Conscription, Total War, and Mass Politics, 1905–1925.* DeKalb: Northern Illinois University Press, 2011.

Sahadeo, Jeff. *Russian Colonial Society in Tashkent. 1863–1925.* Bloomington IN: Indiana University Press, 2007.

Seredonin, S. M. *Istoricheskii obzor deiatel'nosti komiteta ministrov. Komitet Ministrov v tsarstvov. Imp. Aleksandra Vtorogo 1855 g. Fevr. 19–1881 g. Marta 1.* St. Petersburg: Kantseliariia Komiteta Ministrov, 1902.

Slocum, John V. "Who, and When, Were the Inorodtsy? The Evolution of the Category of 'Aliens' in Imperial Russia." *The Russian Review* 57, no. 2 (1998): 173–190.

Svod zakonov Rossiiskoi imperii, poveleniem Gosudaria Imperatora Nikolaia Pervogo. Tom trinadtsatyi. Ustavy o narodnom prodovol'stvii, obshchestvennom prizrenii i vrachebnii. Izdanie 1892 goda. St. Petersburg: Izdanie khozaistvennogo departmenta MVD, 1893.

Tsarevskii, A. A. *O khristiianskom obiazannosti pomogat' bedstvuiushchim ot goloda. Publichnoe chtenie v biblioteke sv. Vladimira.* Kazan: Tipografiia Imperatorskogo Universiteta, 1892.

Vernon, James. *Hunger: A Modern History.* Cambridge, MA: Harvard University Press, 2007.

Veselovskii, Boris. *Istoriia zemstva za 40 let.* Vol. 4. St. Petersburg: Izdatel'stvo O. N. Popovoi, 1911.

Wheatcroft, Stephen G. "Crises and the Condition of the Peasantry in Late Imperial Russia." In *Peasant Economy, Culture, and Politics of European Russia, 1800–1921.* Edited by Esther Kingston-Mann and Timothy Mixter, 128–174. Princeton: Princeton University Press, 1991.

———. "The 1891–92 Famine in Russia: Towards a More Detailed Analysis of its Scale and Demographic Significance." In *Economy and Society in Russia and the Soviet Union, 1860–1930. Essays for Olga Crisp.* Edited by Linda Harriett Edmondson and Peter Waldron, 44–64. London: MacMillan, 1992.

Zagidullin, I. K. *Perepis' 1897 goda i tatary Kazanskoi gubernii.* Kazan: Tatarskoe knizhnoe izdatel'stvo, 2000.

———. *Istoriia Kazani v dokumentakh i materialakh XIX vek. Naseleniekonfessii blagotvoritel'nost'. Kniga 2.* Kazan: Tatarskoe knizhnoe izdatel'stvo, 2004.

———. *Tatarskoe natsional'noe dvizhenie v 1860–1905 gg.* Kazan: Tatarskoe knizhnoe izdatel'stvo, 2014.

Zainullina, Farida G. "*K. Lavrskii, odin iz pervykh issledovatelei istorii Tatarskogo krest'ianstva.*" In *Problemy istorii, kul'tury i razvitiia iazykov narodov Tatarstana i Volgo-Ural'skogo regiona. (Materialy nauchno-prakticheskoi konferentsii).* Edited by A. A. Burchanov, 100–103. Vol. 2. Kazan: Gumanitariia, 2003.

———. *Tatarskaia derevnia Kazanskoi gubernii: sotsial'no-ekonomicheskaia i etnokul'turnaia transformatsiia (1861–1917 gg.). Avtoreferat.* Kazan: Akademiia Nauk RT, 2008.

12

"Agitators and Spies": The Enemy Image of Itinerant Russians in the Grand Duchy of Finland, 1899–1900

Johanna Wassholm

Abstract

This chapter investigates the enemy image of itinerant Russians created in the Finnish press in 1899 1900, after the issuing of the February Manifesto, which according to Finnish constitutional thought revoked the autonomous status of the Grand Duchy of Finland within the Russian Empire. It illuminates the political context in which the image emerged, the mechanisms through which it was constructed, the recommended measures to counter the perceived enemy, and how the image was reproduced in later historiography. The sources consist of Finnish newspapers and the resistance writings of the Finnish constitutionalist underground press, which have previously not been noted in research on the topic. The analysis shows that the enemy image, including a proposed boycott of all things Russian, was a central element in the constitutionalist strategy of passive resistance. More generally, it reveals how political conflict can affect relations between a sedentary majority population and itinerant groups from the outside, and the mechanisms through which seemingly peaceful transnational activities and relations can easily become politicized in times of conflict.

Introduction

In March 1899, the Finnish press alleged that Russian agitators, supported by nationalist circles in Russia aiming to undermine local society, were flooding into the Grand Duchy of Finland. The accusations targeted all itinerant Russians and surfaced shortly after the Finnish Senate promulgated the Russian February Manifesto,[1] which, according to many Finns, revoked the autonomous status of the Grand Duchy within the Russian Empire. The manifesto started a period that Finnish national historiography would in retrospect name the first period of "oppression" or "russification," and which would last until 1905. The roots of the conflict can be traced back to the 1860s, when the idea of Finland as a state of its own, although within the Russian Empire, was formed. This idea clashed with growing nationalist sentiment in Russia, which began to question the Grand Duchy's autonomy and viewed Finland—with its own internal jurisdiction, Diet, central administration, and budget—as a "separatist" entity that threatened the empire's unity.[2] Similar tensions between Russian imperial interests and the interests of the empire's semi-autonomous borderlands were typical for the time, and they resulted in attempts from the side of the central administration to unify the empire.[3]

In this chapter, I investigate the enemy image of itinerant Russians that was created and reproduced in the Finnish press in the years 1899 and 1900, following the issuing of the February Manifesto. I describe the political context in which the image emerged and analyze how it was constructed. More specifically, I examine how the alleged enemy's hostile character and subversive agenda were portrayed, and the practical measures that newspaper writers recommended should be taken in "defense" of the Finnish nation and its independent status

---

1 "Hans Kejserliga Majestäts Nådiga Manifest, gifvet i St. Petersburg, den 3/15 Februari 1899," in *Storfurstendömet Finlands författnings-samling för 1899* (Helsingfors: Kejserliga senatens tryckeri, 1900).

2 Leonard C. Lundin, "Finland," in *Russification in the Baltic Provinces and Finland, 1855–1914,* ed. Edward C. Thaden (Princeton: Princeton University Press, 1981), 382–98; Osmo Jussila, *Suomen suuriruhtinaskunta 1809–1917* (Helsinki: WSOY, 2004), 270–83; Juhani Mylly, *Kansallinen projekti. Historiankirjoitus ja politiikka autonomisessa Suomessa* (Turku: Kirja-Aurora, 2002), 208–19.

3 On the process in the imperial context, see, for example, Alexei Miller, "The Romanov Empire and the Russian Nation," in *Nationalizing Empires,* ed. Stefan Berger and Alexei Miller (Budapest: Central European University Press, 2015); as for Finland and the Baltic provinces, see Edward C. Thaden, ed., *Russification in the Baltic Provinces and Finland, 1855–1914* (Princeton: Princeton University Press, 1981); Gert von Pistohlkors, "'Russifizierung' in den Baltischen Provinzen und in Finnland," *Zeitschrift für Ostmitteleuropaforschung* 33, *Jahrbücher für Geschichte Osteuropas* 33 (1984): 592–606.

in relation to the Russian Empire. In the last section, I investigate how the enemy image created around 1900 was reproduced and interpreted in Finnish historiography. The aim is to illuminate the motives and mechanisms underlying the construction of the enemy image and its short- and long-term consequences for those who were portrayed as enemies. The chapter also contributes new knowledge concerning how people pursuing an itinerant lifestyle can easily become suspect in times of political distress, and more generally concerning attitudes toward Russians in Finland around 1900.

My theoretical point of departure is the concept of enemy image, defined as a stereotypical negative evaluation of "the other." The image emanates from a perception of the unfamiliar or strange and is utilized to evoke negative emotions and attitudes such as fear, aversion, aggression, and hate.[4] "The other," be it a nation, group, or individual, is condemned or denounced for refusing to respect the essential values of the "threatened" group. Not only is the enemy accused of unfriendliness but, more importantly, of malicious and hostile intentions, including an ambition to harm, destroy, and stir unrest.[5] Another point of departure is that itinerant lifestyles have commonly been perceived as a threat to sedentary societies throughout history.[6] This has been especially evident in times of unrest and conflict, as itinerant people have been suspected of spreading harmful ideas and diseases, or of being agents or spies in the service of hostile foreign powers.[7]

The conflict surrounding itinerant Russians in Finland around 1900 has been studied to some extent, although not from the perspective of enemy images and mobility. Previous research has mainly focused on the events evolving in the spring of 1899, when the conflict peaked, although the conflict remained on the political agenda in the subsequent years. Päiviö Tommila deals with the topic in a chapter in his extensive book on the Great Petition of 1899, and it is also addressed in research on the crofter question in Finland. In this context, the

4   Kurt R. Spillmann and Kati Spillmann, "Some Sociobiological and Psychological Aspects of 'Images of the Enemy,'" in *Enemy Images in American History*, ed. Ragnhild Fiebig-von Hase and Ursula Lehmkuhl (Providence: Berghahn, 1997), 5–11.
5   Ragnhild Fiebig-von Hase, "Introduction," in *Enemy Images in American History*, ed. Ragnhild Fiebig-von Hase and Ursula Lehmkuhl (Providence: Berghahn, 1997), 2–3; William Eckhart, "Making and Breaking Enemy Images," *Peace Research* 21, no. 4 (1989): 11–12.
6   Antti Häkkinen, "Kiertäminen, kulkeminen ja muukalaisuuden kohtaaminen 1800–luvun lopun ja 1900–luvun alun maalaisyhteisöissä," in *Vieraat kulkijat—tutut talot. Näkökulmia etnisyyden ja köyhyyden historiaan Suomessa*, ed. Antti Häkkinen et al. (Helsinki: Suomalaisen Kirjallisuuden Seura, 2005), 226–27.
7   Tuula Rekola, "Romernas tidiga skeden i Finland: från 1500-talet till mitten av 1800-talet," in *De finska romernas historia från svenska tiden till 2000-talet*, ed. Panu Pulma (Helsingfors: Svenska litteratursällskapet i Finland, 2015), 23.

focus is on the rumors about land distribution that peddlers and other itinerant Russians were accused of spreading.[8]

The topic also features in research on peddlers from other parts of the Russian Empire, who played a prominent role in mobile trade in the Grand Duchy, with their number increasing in the last decades of the nineteenth century with growing consumption and improved communications. Not least, regular steamship routes along the Finnish coast and the expansion of the railway network, which in 1870 connected Finland to St. Petersburg, contributed to their growing numbers.[9] The most numerous group of peddlers were Russian Karelians from the Arkhangelsk and Olonets Governorates, commonly known as "Rucksack Russians" or "Arkhangelites" in Finland.[10] Other major groups included Muslim Tatars, mainly from the region of Nizhny Novgorod, who had emerged as itinerant traders in Finland in the 1870s, and bristle collectors from the Tver and Pskov Governorates.[11] While peddlers from various parts of the empire were a common sight in the Grand Duchy, their legal status was somewhat opaque. Finland had its own internal legislation, and the Finnish Trade Act of 1879 only allowed peddling for persons with citizenship rights in the Grand Duchy. As most peddlers from the outside lacked such, they were formally forbidden to peddle. In previous decades, however, their formally illicit trade had generally been ignored by the Finnish authorities, and they were popular with their customers.[12]

---

8 Päiviö Tommila, *Suuri adressi* (Porvoo: WSOY, 1999), 245–56; Viljo Rasila, *Suomen torpparikysymys vuoteen 1909. Yhteiskuntahistoriallinen tutkimus* (Helsinki: Suomen Historiallinen Seura, 1961), 180–91; Matti Peltonen, *Talolliset ja torpparit: vuosisadan vaihteen maatalouskysymys* (Helsinki: Suomen Historiallinen Seura, 1992), 257–65; Sami Suodenjoki, "Land Agitation and the Rise of Agrarian Socialism in South-Western Finland, 1899–1907," in *Labour Unions and Politics under the North Star: The Nordic Countries, 1700–2000*, ed. Mary Hilson et al. (New York: Berghahn Books, 2017), 175–80.

9 Johanna Wassholm, "Tatar Pedlars in the Grand Duchy of Finland in the Late Nineteenth Century," *Studia Orientalia Electronica* 8, no. 2 (2020): 13–14.

10 On the Russian Karelian peddlers in the conflict, see Mervi Naakka–Korhonen, *Halpa hinta, pitkä mitta* (Helsinki: Suomalaisen Kirjallisuuden Seura, 1988), 46–53; Pekka Nevalainen, *Kulkukauppiaista kauppaneuvoksiin. Itäkarjalaisten liiketoimintaa Suomessa* (Helsinki: Suomalaisen Kirjallisuuden Seura, 2016), 101–03, 108–14.

11 Wassholm, "Tatar Pedlars," 13–14; Aulis J. Alanen, *Suomen maakaupan historia* (Helsinki: Kauppiaitten kustannus, 1957), 187–88; Nevalainen, *Kulkukauppiaista kauppaneuvoksiin*, 21–22. The bristle collectors exchanged their trinkets for horsehair and hog bristles, which they sold to broom factories in Russia.

12 Naakka-Korhonen, *Halpa hinta*, 177–81; Johanna Wassholm and Anna Sundelin, "Emotions, Trading Practices and Communication in Transnational Itinerant Trade: Encounters between 'Rucksack Russians' and their Customers in Late Nineteenth- and Early Twentieth-Century Finland," *Scandinavian Economic History Review* 66, no. 2 (2018): 133.

The analyzed sources mainly comprise articles in the Finnish press dealing with mobile Russians. Newspapers are relevant sources for examining enemy images, as they played an important role in shaping public opinion in the nineteenth century and, therefore, in disseminating enemy images.[13] The newspapers have been accessed through the Finnish National Library's digitized newspaper archive, which also contains publications by the clandestine resistance press of the Finnish underground opposition.[14] The underground press evolved in the autumn of 1900, after censorship temporarily or permanently suspended several constitutional newspapers. The resistance writings, which also include clandestinely distributed pamphlets and brochures, have rarely been noted in previous research on the conflict, although Steven Duncan Huxley, in his doctoral dissertation on Finnish passive resistance, states that they reveal a "more or less fanatical concern with the Russian peddlers."[15] The main and longest-lived underground newspaper was *Fria Ord* (Free Words), published in Stockholm from September 1900, as the informal continuation of the suspended constitutional mouthpiece *Nya Pressen*.[16] In the last chapter, I examine works of history in order to illuminate how the enemy image of mobile Russians was reproduced and interpreted in later Finnish history writing.

Enemy on the Move

According to Finnish constitutional thought, the February Manifesto of 1899 formally revoked the autonomy that Alexander I had granted the Finns in 1809, when Finland was transformed from an integral part of the Swedish realm into a Grand Duchy of the Russian Empire.[17] The manifesto was met with broad

---

13 Fiebig-von Hase, "Introduction," 14; Laura Stark, *The Limits of Patriarchy: How Female Networks of Pilfering and Gossip sparked the First Debates on Rural Gender Rights in the 19th–Century Finnish–language Press* (Helsinki: Finnish Literature Society, 2011), 40–42.

14 The digitized newspapers of the Finnish National Library: https://digi.kansalliskirjasto.fi/search.

15 Steven Duncan Huxley, *Constitutionalist Insurgency in Finland: Finnish 'Passive Resistance' against Russification as a Case of Nonmilitary Struggle in the European Resistance Tradition* (Helsinki: Suomen Historiallinen Seura, 1990), 169. Censorship was an important tool in Governor-General Bobrikov's russification program in Finland.

16 Pirkko Leino-Kaukiainen, "Kasvava sanomalehdistö sensuurin kahleissa 1890–1905," in *Suomen lehdistön historia 1: Sanomalehdistön vaiheet vuoteen 1905*, ed. Päiviö Tommila et al. (Kuopio: Kustannuskiila, 1988), 550–52. *Fria Ord* was published four to six times weekly until 1905. The publication (circulation 2,500 copies) was financed by subscription fees.

17 The idea that Finland had become a state of its own in 1809 was a national construct cemented in the 1860s. In recent modern historiography it is viewed as myth. See, for example, Jussila, *Suomen suuriruhtinaskunta*, 270–71.

discontent in Finland, immediately evoking strong anti-Russian sentiment. Within weeks, the press reported that Russians with malicious intentions had been observed roaming around the Grand Duchy. The suspects included a variety of itinerant persons, such as knife grinders, castrators, rag and bristle collectors, and ice-cream sellers.[18] The prime suspects were peddlers, the most numerous and therefore most visible group of itinerant Russians that Finns encountered in their everyday life.[19]

The press mainly accused itinerant Russians of two offenses. First, they were allegedly spreading unfounded and subversive rumors about land division in rural regions, seeking to convince the landless population that land was to be confiscated from landowners and given to them.[20] Building on the Russian *mir*—a Russian system of communal land ownership of village land—similar rumors in various forms had circulated in the Russian Empire, including Finland, throughout the nineteenth century. The rumors often emerged in conjunction with heated debates about crofters and landownership, a question that was highly topical in Finland in the late nineteenth century.[21] The Russian imperial bureaucracy had also exploited rumors on land division in attempts to deepen the split between the elites and the peasants in its borderlands. In Poland, for example, rumors stating that the peasants would receive land from the emperor were strategically utilized as a means to marginalize the local elite, the *szlachta*, from the Polish nation-building process.[22]

Second, itinerant Russians were accused of collecting signatures for a petition of some sort, usually depicted as a countermeasure to the Great Petition, which had been collected in Finland in March in defense of autonomy.[23] This allegedly "false" counter-petition, the press asserted, was to be sent to high-ranking

---

18 See, for example, *Kansalainen* (January 13, 1899), 2; *Västra Finland* (March 15, 1899), 1; *Laatokka* (April 5, 1899), 2; *Uusi Savo* (April 13, 1899), 2; *Wiborgsbladet* (April 16, 1899), 2; *Wiborgs Nyheter* (April 17, 1899), 2.

19 Johanna Wassholm and Ann–Catrin Östman, "Introduktion. Plats och praktiker i handelsmöten i Finland 1850–1950," in *Att mötas kring varor. Plats och praktiker i handelsmöten i Finland 1850–1950*, ed. Johanna Wassholm and Ann-Catrin Östman (Helsingfors: Svenska litteratursällskapet i Finland & Stockholm: Appell Förlag, 2021), 10.

20 See, for example, Valfrid Spångberg, *Statskuppen i Finland 1899. Ur det moderna samhällslivet* 19 (Stockholm: Albert Bonniers förlag, 1899), 122–24; *Laatokka* (April 5, 1899), 2.

21 Tommila, *Suuri adressi*, 247–48; Sami Suodenjoki, *Kuriton suutari ja kiistämisen rajat. Työväenliikkeen läpimurto hämäläisessä maalaisyhteisössä 1899–1909* (Helsinki: Suomalaisen Kirjallisuuden Seura, 2010), 97. On such rumors in the 1890s, see, for example, *Tampereen Sanomat* (September 29, 1895), 2.

22 Miller, *The Romanov Empire and Nationalism: Essays in the Methodology of Historical Research* (Budapest: Central European University Press, 2008), 327.

23 Tommila, *Suuri adressi*, 248–49. The allegations were partly presented by Finns who were collecting signatures for the Great Petition.

officials in the empire's machinery of power, and possibly Tsar Nicholas II in person. Its aim was to afford an illusory impression of political sentiments in Finland.[24]

By extension, such allegations were linked to accusations of mobile Russians falsely trying to convince people that "Russian law" would be enforced in the Grand Duchy; this was something for the Finns to rejoice about, since they would no longer have to suffer heavy taxes and other "burdens."[25] In some of the more sensational versions of the rumors, the Russians allegedly asserted that all Finnish county police officers would be executed, or that those who had signed the Great Petition would be exiled to Siberia.[26]

The general unrest in the spring of 1899 alarmed both the Finnish and Russian authorities. The Finnish Senate, on the one hand, ordered the regional governors to investigate whether there was any truth to the allegations.[27] Russian peddlers and industrialists, on the other hand, complained about being persecuted in the Grand Duchy. In petitions sent to Governor-General Nikolai Bobrikov, they pleaded for him to make peddling legal for all imperial subjects in Finland. Bobrikov ordered the Senate to renew the legislation on migrant trade on short notice. When it refused, on the grounds that this could only be done in connection with a complete reform of the Trade Act of 1879, Bobrikov referred the matter to the Russian legislative apparatus.[28] The Ordinance on Migrant Trade, which made all imperial subjects equal to Finnish citizens with regard to itinerant livelihoods, was issued on July 2, 1900.[29] Around the same time, two other Russian ordinances were passed: the Language Manifesto, which sought to strengthen the role of the Russian language in Finland, and an ordinance that limited the freedom of assembly. All three conflicted with Finnish law and were perceived as severe threats to Finnish autonomy.

24 *Västra Finland* (March 15, 1899), 1; *Wasa Nyheter* (May 7, 1899), 3; *Wasabladet* (April 11, 1899), 2.
25 *Laatokka* (April 5, 1899), 2. On the rumors concerning Russian law, see Hannu Immonen, "Kun Venäjän laki tulee," *Historiallinen Aikakauskirja* 90, no. 2 (1992): 117–28.
26 *Österbottningen* (March 28, 1899), 2; *Åland* (April 5, 1899), 2.
27 *Västra Finland* (March 15, 1899), 1. See also Tommila, *Suuri adressi*, 245.
28 Tuomo Polvinen, *Imperial Borderland: Bobrikov and the Attempted Russification of Finland, 1898–1904* (Durham: Duke University Press, 1995), 171; Tommila, *Suuri adressi*, 255–56.
29 "Hans Kejserliga Majestäts Nådiga Förordning om handels idkande af ryska infödingar. Gifven i Helsingfors, den 2 Juli 1900," in *Storfurstendömet Finlands författnings-samling för 1900* (Helsingfors: Kejserliga senatens tryckeri, 1901).

Constructing the Enemy Image

The enemy image that the press created of mobile Russians portrayed them as a collective external threat to the unity of the Finnish nation. Essentially, they were perceived as "foreigners" and "suspect figures," engaged in a shady mission to divide and destroy it.[30] In this, they were said to act on behalf of a "subversive band" of "foreign nationality," commonly assumed to be Governor-General Bobrikov and his regime.[31] Bobrikov, in turn, was allegedly backed by nationalist "secret powers" in Russia that incited and supported his agenda of thwarting Finnish autonomy.[32]

The press offered no evidence of the identity of these shadow powers but did make assumptions about them. One alleged culprit was the Slavic Committee (slaviska kommittén, slaavilainen komitea), referred to as a politically influential Russian "Patriot League." The committee had appointed a section to deal with the "Finnish question" shortly before the issuing of the February Manifesto. Its secretary was M. M. Borodkin, recognized as the author of the "Finnish correspondence" in the Russian newspaper *Novoe Vremia*,[33] which was infamously hostile to the "separatist" tendencies of the Grand Duchy.[34] Another suspect was the Ober-Procurator of the Holy Synod, K. P. Pobedonostsev, one of the prime ideologues of Russian autocracy.[35]

Further suspicions were raised toward P. I. Messarosh, known as a "Finland-hater" and an avid supporter of Bobrikov's Russification measures. Messarosh had been a correspondent for the *Moskovskie Vedomosti* in Finland since 1897 and served as an informer for Bobrikov. After the Finnish press revealed his identity in March 1899, the hate toward him grew so strong that he was forced to leave Finland in the spring of 1900.[36] The connections between these secretive political forces and the itinerant Russians who acted on their behalf in Finland

---

30 See, for example, *Wasa Nyheter* (May 7, 1899), 3; *Wasabladet* (April 11, 1899), 2; *Vestra Nyland* (April 21, 1899), 2; *Kristinestads Tidning* (September 29, 1900), 2.

31 See, for example, *Åbo Tidning* (March 14, 1899), 1; *Kotka Nyheter* (March 18, 1899, 3) *Laatokka* (April 4, 1899), 2. See also Tommila, *Suuri adressi*, 248–49; Naakka-Korhonen, *Halpa hinta*, 46.

32 [Elis Furuhjelm], *Upprop till fosterlandets försvar* (Stockholm: K. B. Boströms Boktryckeri, 1901), 2–3.

33 *Nya Pressen* (February 1, 1899), 3; (February 14, 1899), 3. See also, Eino Parmanen, *Taistelujen kirja. Kuvauksia itsenäisyystaistelumme vaiheista. I Osa: Routakauden puhkeaminen ja sen ensimmäiset vuodet* (Porvoo et al.: Werner Söderström Osakeyhtiö, 1936), 264–65.

34 Polvinen, *Imperial Borderland*, 26, 28, 30.

35 [Furuhjelm], *Upprop till fosterlandets försvar*, 6; *Aftonbladet* (August 18, 1900), 2. On Pobedonostsev, see Polvinen, *Imperial Borderland*, 10.

36 Tommila, *Suuri adressi*, 252–53.

were often depicted as indirect, indicating the existence of middlemen—for example, Russian gendarmes or shopkeepers residing in Finland. The author of an article in the newspaper *Wasabladet* claimed in April 1899 that one Russian peddler had allegedly confessed to having received orders from "some gendarme," who in turn worked on commands from above.[37]

The press described itinerant Russians as hostile agitators, instigators, and spies, allegedly acting on someone else's orders.[38] This is reflected in how they were portrayed as sneaking around on side roads, hiding in forests, and swiftly disappearing when approached by the police.[39] The fact that they appeared to be avoiding the authorities supported the allegations of their enmity and malicious intent, a central building block in the creation of enemy images.[40] The mole, an animal primarily living underground, offered an apt metaphor to represent the Russians' shady and hostile mission to undermine Finnish society; in the spring of 1899, Finnish newspapers published numerous articles titled "mole work."[41]

The enemy image was further strengthened with other negatively charged metaphors, portraying mobile Russians as "wretched creatures," "pushy parasites," or "harmful weeds."[42] They were also linked with dirt, being collectively described as a "filthy sewer" that was "contaminating" Finnish society.[43] The association with dirt follows a stereotypical pattern of the late nineteenth century, used in depictions of "the other" with the aim to justify exclusionary practices.[44] Furthermore, they were accused of selling harmful substances, such as poison, and spreading pestilence, not least venereal diseases.[45] Although such

---

37 *Wasa Nyheter* (April 6, 1899), 3.
38 *Västra Finland* (March 15, 1899), 1; *Laatokka* (April 5, 1899), 2; *Wasa Nyheter* (May 7, 1899), 3.
39 See, for example, *Wasa Nyheter* (May 7, 1899), 3; *Wasabladet* (April 11, 1899), 2; *Vestra Nyland* (April 21, 1899), 2; *Kristinestads Tidning* (September 29, 1900), 2.
40 Fiebig-von Hase, introduction, 2–3; Eckhart; "Making and Breaking Enemy Images," 11–12.
41 *Västra Finland* (March 15, 1899), 1; *Laatokka* (April 5, 1899), 2; *Kristinestads Tidning* (September 29, 1900), 2. Swedish "Mullvadsarbete"; Finnish "Myyrän työ." See also Spångberg, *Statskuppen*, 122. The mole metaphor already figured in the Finnish press before 1899; see, for example, *Wiborgs Tidning* (March 7, 1868), 1; *Tammerfors* (February 1, 1896), 3. See also Nevalainen, *Kulkukauppiaista kauppaneuvoksiin*, 111.
42 *Laatokka* (April 5, 1899), 2; *Västra Finland* (March 15, 1899), 1; *Kotkan Uutiset* (April 23, 1899), 1.
43 *Laatokka* (April 5, 1899), 2.
44 Häkkinen, "Kiertäminen, kulkeminen," 226–27; Adeline Masquelier, "Dirt, Undress, and Difference: An Introduction," in *Dirt, Undress, and Difference: Critical Perspectives on the Body's Surface*, ed. Adeline Masquelier (Bloomington: Indiana University Press, 2005), 6–7. See also Wassholm, "Tatar Pedlars," 19–20.
45 *Laatokka* (April 5, 1899), 2; *Wiborgs Nyheter* (June 1, 1899), 2; *Finliandskaia Gazeta* (April 20 [May 3 according to the Gregorian calendar], 1900), 2.

allegations have been commonly directed toward mobile people throughout history, the political tensions around the turn of the century made the rhetoric more explicit. The Finnish nation was pictured as a living organism that needed to defend itself to survive. In accordance with the laws of nature, an organism that could not rid itself of something harmful and destructive that was invading its body was doomed.[46]

The aim of the subversive mission was described rather vaguely. On a general level, it centered around the idea that the mobile Russians were seeking to stir unrest in Finnish society by agitating its lower classes to revolt against the elite. Their means to reach this goal was to spread disinformation, which distorted the sense of justice and truth of the common people. In connection with the collecting of signatures for the secretive petition, itinerant Russians were accused of using a variety of deceptive methods to get people to sign. For instance, they would interrogate people in a village about the names of absent persons and record their names in their notebooks, or ask people to write their names with the explanation that they wanted to learn to spell Finnish names.[47] In a story that appears particularly imaginative, a Russian chimney sweep insisted that he could offer his services free of charge because the Emperor guaranteed him a high salary; he urged villagers who wished to have their chimney swept for free to sign his "sweeping book."[48] The Russian newspaper *Moskovskie Vedomosti* features an intriguing insight into how the rumors on signature collecting could arise. The article describes a Tatar peddler's encounter with two local men on the streets of Helsinki, who offered to sell him fox furs. The Tatar asked them to write down their address in his notebook so that he could later collect the furs from their homes; this led an aggressive passer-by to confront the peddler, accusing him of collecting signatures for a deceitful petition.[49]

The Finnish press commonly accused the "Russian spies" of targeting the most "defenseless" in society: the uneducated, easy to deceive, and children. In one such depiction, two peddlers follow a young schoolgirl, interrogating her about what she is learning in class. The girl refuses to answer but the peddlers encourage her to write something on a piece of paper.[50] In another story, a young boy tears up a paper, angrily reprimanding a Tatar who had promised him ten

---

46 Homén, "Passiivinen vastarinta," 10–12.
47 *Västra Finland* (March 15, 1899), 1; *Wasa Nyheter* (May 7, 1899), 3; *Tampereen Sanomat* (April 11, 1899), 3.
48 *Wasa Nyheter* (April 6, 1899), 3.
49 *Moskovskie Vedomosti* 1900, no. 272.
50 *Vestra Nyland* (April 21, 1899), 2. See also *Tampereen Sanomat* (April 11, 1899), 3; *Wiborgs Nyheter* (April 22, 1899), 3.

pennies for his signature.[51] Many similar stories end in the same way, with the people seeing through the mobile Russians attempts to deceive or bribe. These obviously served as a normative model for how all Finns should act when approached by an "enemy" with questionable objectives.

In 1899 and early 1900, the Finnish press described in a rather vague manner the political objective of the enemy, who allegedly threatened the unity of the nation. The press mainly sought to raise awareness of the fact that mobile Russians were seeking to stir unrest in Finnish society by spreading rumors about land division and the implementation of "Russian law," and that they were collecting signatures for a petition that was meant to present a false view of the political sentiment in Finland regarding the imperial bureaucracy. In the underground resistance writings that were published from the fall of 1900, the political objectives were formulated more explicitly. Resistance writers claimed that the ultimate objective of the secretive mission was the complete destruction of everything that the Finns had held sacred since time immemorial: their religion, their language, and the social system inherited from their ancestors.[52] The mobile Russians were now portrayed as a tool in the Russian nationalists' plan to Russify Finland by slowly replacing the Lutheran faith with the Orthodox one and by founding Russian language schools.

In this context, recent developments in the Baltic provinces were presented as a warning example. Resistance writers drew parallels with the Baltic provinces, claiming that a similar strategy had already succeeded there. Allegedly, Russian peddlers had managed to drive local merchants out of business with the support of Russian nationalists. Having settled down permanently as shopkeepers, the former peddlers had in turn prepared the ground for more Russians to settle in the provinces. The same was said to be the goal in Finland: after settling down, the Russian shopkeepers would bring their families and employ more people from their home region. Eventually, the Russians would be so numerous that they would require Orthodox churches and Russian language schools to be established.[53]

---

51 *Kristinestads Tidning* (September 29, 1900), 2. See also *Kotkan Uutiset* (April 23, 1899), 1.
52 [Furuhjelm], *Upprop till fosterlandets försvar*, 2.
53 *Aftonbladet* (August 18, 1900), 2; Homén, "Passiivinen vastarinta," 11–12. References to Livonia were also made in 1899. See, for example, *Uusi Savo* (April 13, 1899), 2; *Wiipurin Sanomat* (April 17, 1899), 1. On russification measures in the Baltic provinces, see Edward C. Thaden, "The Russian Government," in *Russification in the Baltic Provinces and Finland, 1855–1914*, ed. Edward C. Thaden (Princeton: Princeton University Press, 1981), 33–75.

Practical Measures to Counter the Enemy

The enemy image as such was not the ultimate goal of those who had a political motive to construct it. Its practical function was to incite the Finnish nation as a collective to counter the threat that itinerant Russians allegedly posed. Measures in this direction were to be taken in every sphere of Finnish society: in national politics, by the local authorities, by civil society (including the press), and, by every individual. In a circular that the regional authorities in Uusimaa sent out in April 1899, it was stressed that no measures to counter the enemy would succeed without the support of the Finnish people as a unified whole.[54]

The first concrete measures to counter the "enemy" were taken in April 1899, when the regional governors received an order from the Finnish Senate to investigate the reported agitation. The governors sent a circular to the rural police, who, to gather information, detained and interrogated itinerant Russians suspected of engaging in illicit trade or spreading subversive rumors.[55] The local authorities also took measures which were in line with a paragraph in a new law on local government, issued in early 1899, that strengthened the local administration's responsibilities for order and security. According to Nevalainen, the most common measure, taken in at least eighty-eight municipalities, was to offer monetary rewards to people who denounced Russian peddlers to the authorities. The municipality of Virrat even petitioned the governor to hire an extra police officer, whose sole task would be to curb illicit peddling and control potential agitators.[56] Notices encouraging readers to denounce peddlers were published in the newspapers.[57] The reward system provoked especially negative reactions in the Russian press, not least as the money was to be taken from funds normally used to reimburse people for killing harmful animals to protect harvests and people. In this context, Russian peddlers were metaphorically likened to predators and vultures.[58]

---

54 *Vestra Nyland* (April 14, 1899), 2.
55 Detainments are noted in short paragraphs in the newspapers. See, for example, *Kansalainen* (March 31, 1899), 2; *Wasabladet* (April 11, 1899), 2; *Vestra Nyland* (April 14, 1899), 2; *Wiborgsbladet* (April 16, 1899), 2. Nevalainen estimates that at least fifty-four Russian peddlers were detained in the spring of 1899. Nevalainen, *Kulkukauppiaista kauppaneuvoksiin*, 103.
56 Nevalainen, *Kulkukauppiaista kauppaneuvoksiin*, 102–3. See also, Tommila, *Suuri adressi*, 252; Alanen, *Suomen maakaupan historia*, 456–57.
57 See, for example, *Laatokka* (April 5, 1899), 2; *Karjalatar* (April 29, 1899), 2.
58 *Finliandskaia Gazeta* (April 20 [May 3 according to the Gregorian calendar], 1900), 2. Such rhetoric had already been used in the 1860s when the Finnish press depicted Russian peddlers as dangerous wolves. Nevalainen, *Kulkukauppiaista kauppaneuvoksiin*, 111.

Measures were also taken to correct the presumed disinformation spread by the "agitators"—in other words, to raise awareness of the perils Finland faced. The main responsibility for this rested with the nation's educated elite, including civil servants and students, supported by the press. Newspapers across the political map published articles that corrected misunderstandings of the *mir* and *obshchina* institutions.[59] In the summer of 1899, the same students who a few months earlier had collected signatures for the Great Petition returned to the villages to give talks intended to correct potential misunderstandings.[60] Priests were urged to read proclamations from the authorities to their congregations, warning people against believing in untruthful promises spread by "Arkhangelites and other persons of Russian origin."[61] To achieve maximum results, warning signs were to be distributed. Some newspapers even featured a warning text that could be cut out and hung on the walls of administrative buildings and other visible places.[62]

After the ordinance that legalized peddling for Russian subjects came into force in July 1900, the police could no longer detain Russian subjects on suspicion of illegal trade. However, suspicions were now raised on other grounds and detainments were occasionally made under the pretext that peddlers lacked proper documentation or traded in forbidden goods. Finnish newspapers occasionally reported such detainments well into the twentieth century.[63] Without the possibility to use a legal weapon, the struggle now took an even more ideological and programmatic turn, which underlined the role of patriotic sentiment and collective responsibility. The underground resistance writings (for example, a brochure by constitutional leader Victor Magnus von Born) stressed that it was every Finn's moral obligation to ensure that itinerant Russians were "ostracized" through "the pressure of general patriotic opinion": "No citizen can watch with indifference as natives of a foreign country rove in

59 *Vårt Land* (March 14, 1899), 1; *Östra Nyland* (March 15, 1899), 2; *Hufvudstadsbladet* (March 28, 1899), 4; *Mikkelin Sanomat* (April 22, 1899), 1–2. Such misconceptions had already been corrected before 1899. See also Tommila, *Suuri adressi*, 251–52.

60 Matti Klinge, *Studenter och idéer. Studentkåren vid Helsingfors universitet 1828–1960*. III: *1872–1917* (Helsingfors: Studentkåren vid Helsingfors universitet, 1978), 206–11; Immonen, "Kun Venäjän laki tulee," 125–26.

61 *Björneborgs Tidning* (April 18, 1899), 2. See also Alanen, *Suomen maakaupan historia*, 457–58; Naakka-Korhonen, *Halpa hinta*, 47–48.

62 See, for example, *Wiipuri* (April 21, 1899), 2–3.

63 *Österbottningen* (March 11, 1904), 2; *Västra Finland* (March 12, 1904), 3.

gangs throughout the country, spreading worthless trinkets, devastating diseases and dangerous doctrines that lead to the disintegration of society."[64]

The resistance writers made the battle against itinerant Russians' hostile intentions a central element of constitutional passive resistance, a political strategy that, despite its name, was all but passive. Quite the contrary, the doctrine built on the realization that Finnish autonomy could not be defended merely by passively demonstrating against Russian encroachments on Finnish law.[65] The protagonists of passive resistance portrayed it as a method of weaponless warfare, a metaphor used, for example, in the pamphlet *Upprop till fosterlandets försvar* (Appeal to defend the fatherland), portrayed by Huxley as an exemplary work of propaganda and "passionate patriotic spirit with calculated strategic argumentation."[66] In this ideological construct, Finland was at war with Russia, but it was a war without weapons; instead of using force, the sly enemy was "insidiously attempting to sneak in from the East."[67] The Russians were waging war by inundating the Grand Duchy with treacherous agitators attempting to befriend "unsuspecting and credulous Finns."[68]

By stressing that Finland was at war with Russia, the resistance writers turned itinerant Russians into full enemies. And—as in any war—the nation needed to defend itself. The constitutionalist ideologues thus utilized the enemy image they had created in a manner typical of political leaders to prepare the people for war.[69] As violent defense was not an option in this case, other methods had to be applied. The main defensive measure that the resistance writers propagated was that of a complete boycott of Russians and Russian commodities in Finland. Until a better defense plan was developed, a boycott was the most effective way to drive the enemy out, and, as a method that was collective by definition, it required the participation of every Finn to succeed.[70] Resistance writers also

---

64 Victor Magnus von Born, *Huomattavaa syntyperäisten venäläisten kaupan harjoittamisesta ja venäläisistä postimerkeistä* (Stockholm: Isaac Marcus' Boktryckeri, 1900), 1–2. Translation after Huxley, *Constitutionalist Insurgency*, 170. This pamphlet was not widely distributed according to Arne Cederholm, *Kagalens uppkomst och andra episoder* (Helsingfors, 1920), 5.

65 See, for example, Homén, "Passiivinen vastarinta," 10–12; *Fria Ord*, no. 1–2 (1900), 5–6.

66 Huxley, *Constitutionalist Insurgency*, 169–70; *Fria Ord*, no. 1–2 (1900), 3.

67 [Furuhjelm], *Upprop till fosterlandets försvar*, 2.

68 Ibid., 2.

69 Eckhart, "Making and Breaking Enemy Images," 11–12.

70 [Furuhjelm], *Upprop till fosterlandets försvar*, 6–7; *Fria Ord* no. 1–2 (1900): 5–6; Homén, "Passiivinen vastarinta," 11–12. The text in *Fria Ord*, titled "Försvarsåtgärder" (*"Defensive measures"*) is identical to Furuhjelm's pamphlet. It claims that practical measures could not be presented in the conventional press because of censorship. The section that deals with peddlers was also published in the Swedish newspaper *Aftonbladet* (August 18, 1900, 2).

presented economic incentives to enforce their argument. In his pamphlet on the core idea of passive resistance, Victor Th. Homén stated that support of domestic work and the consumption of domestic goods would strengthen the Grand Duchy's financial independence, which in turn was a prerequisite for political sovereignty.[71]

The boycott idea had already been featured in the press in the spring of 1899, though not as explicitly as it was expressed in the resistance writings. Readers had been urged to refuse itinerant Russians shelter and food, without mercy or compassion.[72] Those who offered shelter to itinerant Russians were to be viewed as unpatriotic and ran the risk of being accused of supporting their "criminal activities."[73] Such rhetoric follows a typical pattern in the construction of enemy images, namely, the injunction to deny empathy to the perceived enemy on the grounds that this might prove dangerous and self-destructive.[74]

The programmatic ideology of passive resistance broadened the enemy image; now, the Finns were not only discouraged from contact with itinerant Russians but from interacting with Russians in general, including those who permanently resided in Finland. Exceptions could only be made regarding Russian subjects who had proved to be "complete Finns and good patriots."[75] The idea behind the boycott was that if it succeeded, hostile Russians would be both unwilling and unable to settle in the Grand Duchy. Homén states that while this might seem harsh, the Finns were not to blame for the precarious situation that the Russian policy toward Finland had placed them in.[76] In the ensuing years, campaigns against Russians residing in Finland, primarily petty traders and merchants, were initiated. For example, a "committee for opposing Russianism" (Venäläisyyden vastustamiskomitea) was founded in Tampere in 1901, with the explicit ambition to render impossible the businesses of Russian peddlers and merchants in Finland. The methods to achieve this goal were to limit the consumption of Russian goods, to distribute pamphlets that discouraged trade with Russians, to establish networks between Finnish peddlers to support

---

71 Homén, "Passiivinen vastarinta," 13.
72 *Västra Finland* (March 15, 1899), 1.
73 *Vestra Nyland* (April 14, 1899), 2; *Wasa-Posten* (January 23, 1900), 2.
74 Spillman and Spillman, "Some Sociobiological Aspects," 51.
75 Homén, "Passiivinen vastarinta," 12.
76 Ibid., 11–12.

domestic trade, and to encourage Finns to take on professions commonly held by Russians.[77]

The press campaign as such reveals little about the actual consequences the enemy image had for Russians in the Grand Duchy. Previous research indicates that the propagated boycott caused some degree of damage, especially to Russian petty traders and merchants, at least in the short term. In the spring of 1899, many peddlers were evicted or voluntarily returned to their home regions in Russia, with only the most experienced daring to return in the next two years. There is also evidence to suggest that merchants with Russian names were openly mocked, and some Russian shopkeepers were forced to close their business. Aulis J. Alanen maintains that the mutual trust and support that the majority of Finnish people had previously shown to Russian peddlers were never fully restored. He also states that the popularity that the peddlers lost in conjunction with the conflict was the main cause for the diminishing number of Russian peddlers in Finland in the early twentieth century.[78] Interviews with former Russian peddlers conducted by Maiju Keynäs in the 1940s and 1950s also support the assumption that the events made circumstances harsher for Russians.[79]

On the other hand, even the ideologues of passive resistance themselves recognized that turning the attitudes of the Finns against Russian peddlers was a challenge. In his brochure, Homén stated that if the boycott was to succeed, the people had to be convinced that the peddlers—who had traditionally appeared to them as "decent," "good-natured," and "playful," and whom they had therefore often protected from the police—had betrayed the confidence shown in them by resorting to being the enemy's henchmen.[80] An article titled "Slapp moral" (Loose morals), published in the main underground newspaper *Fria Ord* in October 1900, indicates that the proposed boycott had failed. Its anonymous author states it as a "sad fact"[81] that the strong anti-Russian sentiments that the Finns had expressed in the preceding year had already weakened. While many people spoke about the necessity of avoiding contact with "all things Russian," most had continued to buy Russian goods from Russian peddlers and

---

77 Gabriele Schrey-Vasara, "Venäläisyyden vastustamiskomitea," *Historiallinen Aikakauskirja* 85, no. 1 (1987): 3; Sami Suodenjoki, "Kauppiasboikotista kansallisuusvihaan. Valtaväestön ja venäläisten suhteet Tampereella vuosina 1899–1981," in *Tampere kieliyhteisönä*, ed. Harry Lönnroth (Helsinki: Suomalaisen Kirjallisuuden Seura, 2009), 153–55.

78 Alanen, *Suomen maakaupan historia*, 456, 459–60; Tommila, *Suuri adressi*, 252.

79 Naakka-Korhonen, *Halpa hinta*, 47.

80 [Furuhjelm], *Upprop till fosterlandets försvar*, 2–3.

81 "Slapp moral," *Fria Ord*, no. 13 (1900), 1.

merchants in market squares, market halls, and their own homes like nothing had happened.[82]

The Enemy Image in Finnish Historiography

From 1901 on, more acute conflicts replaced those surrounding itinerant Russians; in particular, these included the tensions surrounding the implementation of a Russian conscript law in the Grand Duchy and the Finnish boycott of it.[83] However, as relations between the Grand Duchy and the imperial administration remained strained until Finland's independence in 1917, the press occasionally reminded readers of the Russians' "treacherous agitation" around the turn of the century.[84] The image was also actively reproduced in the decades following Finland's declaration of independence in 1917. While the Finnish strategy toward russification had by no means been unanimous, the ideology of passive resistance became a central building block in the teleological historical account of Finland's road to independence. The proponents of passive resistance had been relatively few in terms of absolute numbers, but in retrospect they were easy to portray as those Finns who had dared to defend the nation against the enemy's encroachments, and those who had refused to compromise and therefore led Finland toward independence.[85]

In the some of the history writing of the 1920s and 1930s, it is stated as a given fact that nationalist circles in Russia had hired itinerant Russians to agitate and stir unrest in the Grand Duchy in conjunction with the issuing of the February Manifesto.[86] As late as 1957, in his book on rural shopkeepers, Alanen claims that the majority of itinerant Russians in Finland around the turn of the century had been "henchmen of the oppressive government."[87] He maintains that the idea of using itinerant Russians as stooges was consciously included in Bobrikov's original plan to subdue Finnish

---

82 Ibid., 1.
83 Einar W. Juva, "Det olagliga värnpliktsuppbådet, värnpliktsstrejken och tjänstemännens avsked," in *Finlands ofärdsår 1899–1917*, ed. Päiviö Tommila (Stockholm: Wahlström & Widstrand, 1963).
84 See, for example, *Turun Sanomat* (April 15, 1906), 2; *Hämeen Sanomat* (November 21, 1906), 1; *Lahti* (January 19, 1907), 1; *Suomalainen* (January 23, 1907), 4; *Uusi Aura* (March 9, 1907), 3; *Social-Demokraten* (July 24, 1908), 2; *Savon Sanomat* (July 27, 1910), 1.
85 Päiviö Tommila, *Suomen historiankirjoitus. Tutkimuksen historia* (Porvoo et al.: Werner Söderström Osakeyhtiö, 1999), 194.
86 See, for example, Edv. Hjelt, *Itsenäinen Suomi. Unelmasta todellisuuteen* (Helsinki: Tietosanakirja, 1921), 66.
87 Alanen, *Suomen maakaupan historia*, 456.

autonomy. However, Alanen maintains that few of the agents were from White Sea Karelia, the home region of most Russian peddlers in Finland, and asserts that the majority of those who had been hired as spies and agitators originated from the Olonets Governorate.[88] This may have been an attempt by Alanen to disconnect White Sea Karelians, many of whom had successfully settled as shopkeepers in Finland both before and after 1917, from the enemy image.

An example of how Finnish history writing between the wars stressed national unity in the past is found in Eino Parmanen's book *Taistelujen kirja* (Book of battles), published in 1936. Although the Finns had been strongly divided socially, economically, and politically, Parmanen underlines that there had been unanimous participation in the struggle to evict all Russians from Finland in 1899 and 1900, forcing two thousand peddlers to flee. He recognizes that the evictions had been harsh and that they had caused suffering to some completely innocent Russian subjects, but stresses that it was something that the Finnish nation had been forced to do to defend itself.[89]

Some authors convey more nuanced interpretations of the events. In the first comprehensive historical overview of the Russian era, *Elva årtionden ur Finlands historia* III, published in 1923, Finnish historian Bernhard Estlander recognizes that while there was undoubtedly agitation in Finland in which Russians may have participated, it was not orchestrated from above.[90] Estlander's view is more or less consistent with modern research, which has found no evidence of organized agitation.[91] However, it is a fact that rumors were spread, addresses were collected, and agitation in favor of "Russian law," thought to improve the living standards of the poorest population, did occur in Finland.[92] While mobile Russians, especially peddlers, may have participated in the agitation, their motive was probably not political conviction. Rather, historians have emphasized the role of itinerant people as distributors of news and information in the era before modern communications.[93] Bringing intriguing news and rumors was one

88 Ibid., 456, 459.
89 Parmanen, *Taistelujen kirja*, 265.
90 B. Estlander, *Elva årtionden ur Finlands historia* III: *1898–1908* (Helsingfors: Söderström & Co Förlagsaktiebolag, 1923), 59–60. For a similar account, see J. N. Reuter, *"Kagalen": ett bidrag till Finlands historia 1899–1905*, Skrifter utgivna av Svenska litteratursällskapet i Finland 199 (Helsingfors: Svenska litteratursällskapet i Finland, 1928), 44–45. Reuter ascribes the phenomenon to a typical psychological reaction in a conflict situation.
91 Polvinen, *Imperial Borderland*, 170; Tommila, *Suuri adressi*, 254–55.
92 Immonen, "Kun Venäjän laki tulee," 126.
93 Häkkinen, "Kiertäminen, kulkeminen," 250; Pia Karlsson, "En officer och gentleman? De ryska sågfilarna och spionanklagelserna," in *Bröd och salt. Svenska kulturkontakter med öst*, ed. Roger Gyllin et al. (Uppsala: Uppsala universitet, 1998), 149.

way to secure a warm welcome from the sedentary population in local society, including shelter and food, which itinerant people were completely dependent on. It therefore seems plausible that itinerant Russians may have spread the kind of rumors that they knew their customers, often belonging to the lower strata of society, wished to hear.[94]

In recent years, historians have shifted the focus from the alleged agitation of Russians to the political disunity within the Grand Duchy of Finland. Such interpretations stress that the Finnish conservative elite consciously created the enemy image out of fear of potentially subversive forces that could have been set in motion if the lower classes of society did prove to be susceptible to false rumors. To counter such a development, they decided to divert attention from the lines of internal division by creating the image of an external enemy that threatened the unity of the Finnish people. The political left, in turn, had an interest in upholding or even strengthening the lines of division, and therefore lacked a motive to deny the potentially subversive rumors.[95] The agendas of both political factions resonate with the core function of an enemy image, which, according to Fiebig-von Hase, is to serve specific ideological purposes rather than objective truth.[96]

Conclusion

The enemy image of mobile Russians that the Finnish press created in conjunction with the Russo-Finnish conflict around 1900 followed a typical pattern for how such images are created. As "agents and spies" supported by nationalist anti-Finnish forces in Russia, the enemy's intention was claimed to be to divide the nation by spreading potentially subversive rumors, to agitate the lower classes of society against the higher classes, and to convey to Russian leaders a false impression of the political sentiments in Finland. Negatively charged metaphors, likening itinerant Russians to dirt, parasites, and harmful moles, were utilized to construct the image.

The function of the enemy image was to make the Finnish people act in a manner that would make itinerant Russians' allegedly harmful mission impossible and discourage more Russians from settling in the Grand Duchy.

---

94 Rasila, *Suomen torpparikysymys*, 143.
95 See, for example, Peltonen, *Talolliset ja torpparit*, 263; Tommila, *Suuri adressi*, 254–56; Suodenjoki, *Kuriton suutari*, 97; Polvinen, *Imperial Borderland*, 287–91.
96 Fiebig-von Hase, "Introduction," 15.

The goal of the constitutional opposition was that measures toward this would be taken at every level of society. The police detained Russians for illegal trading or on suspicion of spreading rumors, the local authorities discouraged people from interacting with suspected agitators, and information campaigns were launched to correct the subversive ideas and misunderstandings that itinerant Russians allegedly spread.

In the Finnish underground press, publishing from the fall of 1900, the struggle against itinerant Russians became more explicitly ideological, and it was made part of the program of passive resistance. The constitutionalist interpretation was that Russia was waging a war without weapons against Finland, which required defensive measures to be taken. The most important of these was a complete boycott of "all things Russian," seen as the moral duty of every patriotic Finn. The enemy image was now broadened to include Russians who resided in Finland permanently, as well as Russian consumer goods. While the boycott does not seem to have been the success the resistance writers had hoped for, there is evidence to suggest that the press campaign did to some extent negatively affect the existence of Russians, at least in the short term.

Although other more topical conflicts replaced the one surrounding mobile Russians by 1901, the enemy image created in the years 1899–1900 was reproduced in Finnish historiography. Especially in the early decades of independent Finland, official history writing was dominated by the constitutionalist interpretation of passive resistance as a successful strategy that had paved Finland's road to independence, and many historical works presented it as a fact that itinerant Russians had indeed been involved in subversive political agitation between 1899 and 1901. Later history writing has nuanced this picture; while not denying that agitation did occur, modern research has found no evidence that it was orchestrated from above. Rather, it has been suggested that the enemy image was a product of internal political struggles; the constitutionalists had an interest in stressing the existence of an external enemy to downplay lines of internal division. Furthermore, the analysis shows that the creation of this enemy image followed a typical pattern. It depicted Russians as "strangers" with hostile intentions, who posed an external threat to the internal unity of the Finnish nation and served ideological aims rather than objective truth. It also demonstrates how itinerant groups can easily become targets of suspicion in times of conflict and that the campaign against itinerant Russians was more politically programmatic than previous research has suggested.

Works Cited

Newspapers

Åbo Tidning
Aftonbladet
Åland
Björneborgs Tidning
Finliandskaia Gazeta
Fria Ord
Hufvudstadsbladet
Hämeen Sanomat
Kansalainen
Karjalatar
Kotka Nyheter
Kotkan Uutiset
Kristinestads Tidning
Laatokka
Lahti
Mikkelin Sanomat
Moskovskie Vedomosti
Nya Pressen
Österbottningen
Östra Nyland
Päivälehti
Savon Sanomat
Social-Demokraten
Suomalainen
Tammerfors
Tampereen Sanomat
Turun Sanomat
Uusi Aura
Uusi Savo
Vestra Nyland
Vårt Land
Västra Finland
Wasabladet
Wasa Nyheter
Wasa-Posten

Wiborgsbladet
Wiborgs Nyheter
Wiborgs Tidning
Wiipuri
Wiipurin Sanomat

Literature

Alanen, Aulis J. *Suomen maakaupan historia*. Helsinki: Kauppiaitten kustannus, 1957.

Born von, Victor Magnus. *Huomattavaa syntyperäisten venäläisten kaupan harjoittamisesta ja venäläisistä postimerkeistä*. Stockholm: Isaac Marcus' Boktryckeri, 1900.

Cederholm, Arne. *Kagalens uppkomst och andra episoder*. Helsingfors, 1920.

Eckhart, William. "Making and Breaking Enemy Images." *Peace Research* 21, no. 4 (1989): 11–16.

Estlander, B. *Elva årtionden ur Finlands historia* III: *1898–1908*. Helsingfors: Söderström & Co Förlagsaktiebolag, 1923.

Fiebig-von Hase, Ragnhild. Introduction to *Enemy Images in American History*. Edited by Ragnhild Fiebig-von Hase and Ursula Lehmkuhl, 1–40. Providence: Berghahn, 1997.

[Furuhjelm, Elis.] *Upprop till fosterlandets försvar*. Stockholm: K. B. Boströms Boktryckeri, 1901.

"Hans Kejserliga Majestäts Nådiga Förordning om handels idkande af ryska infödingar. Gifven i Helsingfors, den 2 Juli 1900." *Storfurstendömet Finlands författnings-samling för 1900*. Helsingfors: Kejserliga senatens tryckeri, 1901.

"Hans Kejserliga Majestäts Nådiga Manifest, gifvet i S:t Petersburg, den 3/15 Februari 1899." *Storfurstendömet Finlands författnings-samling för 1899*. Helsingfors: Kejserliga senatens tryckeri, 1900.

Hjelt, Edv. *Itsenäinen Suomi. Unelmasta todellisuuteen*. Helsinki: Tietosanakirja, 1921.

Homén, Victor Th. "Passiivinen vastarinta." In Victor Theodor Homén, *Passiivinen vastarintamme: politillisia kirjoituksia 1899–1904*, 8–21. Helsinki: Otava, 1906.

Huxley, Steven Duncan. *Constitutionalist Insurgency in Finland: Finnish 'Passive Resistance' against Russification as a Case of Nonmilitary Struggle in the European Resistance Tradition*. Helsinki: Suomen Historiallinen Seura, 1990.

Häkkinen, Antti. "Kiertäminen, kulkeminen ja muukalaisuuden kohtaaminen 1800-luvun lopun ja 1900-luvun alun maalaisyhteisöissä." In *Vieraat kulkijat—tutut talot. Näkökulmia etnisyyden ja köyhyyden historiaan Suomessa.* Edited by Antti Häkkinen, Panu Pulma, and Miika Tervonen, 225–62. Helsinki: Suomalaisen Kirjallisuuden Seura, 2005.

Immonen, Hannu. "'Kun Venäjän laki tulee': sivistyneistö, kansa ja helmikuun manifesti." *Historiallinen Aikakauskirja* 90, no. 2 (1992): 117–28.

Jussila, Osmo. *Suomen suuriruhtinaskunta 1809–1917.* Helsinki: WSOY, 2004.

Juva, Einar W. "Det olagliga värnpliktsuppbådet, värnpliktsstrejken och tjänstemännens avsked." In *Finlands ofärdsår 1899–1917.* Edited by Päiviö Tommila, 56–67. Stockholm: Wahlström & Widstrand, 1963.

Karlsson, Pia. "En officer och gentleman? De ryska sågfilarna och spionanklagelserna." In *Bröd och salt. Svenska kulturkontakter med öst.* Edited by Roger Gyllin, Ingvar Svanberg, and Ingmar Söhrman, 144–65. Uppsala: Uppsala universitet, 1998.

Klinge, Matti. *Studenter och idéer. Studentkåren vid Helsingfors universitet 1828–1960. III: 1872–1917.* Helsingfors: Studentkåren vid Helsingfors universitet, 1978.

Leino–Kaukiainen, Pirkko. "Kasvava sanomalehdistö sensuurin kahleissa 1890–1905." In *Suomen lehdistön historia 1: Sanomalehdistön vaiheet vuoteen 1905.* Edited by Päiviö Tommila, Lars-Folke Landgren, and Pirkko Leino-Kaukiainen, 421–626. Kuopio: Kustannuskiila, 1988.

Lundin, C. Leonard. "Finland." In *Russification in the Baltic Provinces and Finland, 1855–1914.* Edited by Edward C. Thaden, 357–457. Princeton: Princeton University Press, 1981.

Masquelier, Adeline. "Dirt, Undress, and Difference: An Introduction." In *Dirt, Undress, and Difference: Critical Perspectives on the Body's Surface.* Edited by Adeline Masquelier, 1–34. Bloomington: Indiana University Press, 2005.

Miller, Alexei. *The Romanov Empire and Nationalism: Essays in the Methodology of Historical Research.* Budapest: Central European University Press, 2008.

———. "The Romanov Empire and the Russian Nation." In *Nationalizing Empires.* Edited by Stefan Berger and Alexei Miller, 309–68. Budapest: Central European University Press, 2015.

Mylly, Juhani. *Kansallinen projekti. Historiankirjoitus ja politiikka autonomisessa Suomessa.* Turku: Kirja-Aurora, 2002.

Naakka-Korhonen, Mervi. *Halpa hinta, pitkä mitta. Vienankarjalainen laukkukauppa.* Helsinki: Suomalaisen Kirjallisuuden Seura, 1988.

Nevalainen, Pekka. *Kulkukauppiaista kauppaneuvoksiin: Itäkarjalaisten liiketoimintaa Suomessa.* Helsinki: Suomalaisen Kirjallisuuden Seura, 2016.

Parmanen, Eino I. *Taistelujen kirja: kuvauksia itsenäisyystaistelumme vaiheista sortovuosina.* I *Osa: Routakauden puhkeaminen ja sen ensimmäiset vuodet.* Porvoo et al.: Werner Söderström Osakeyhtiö, 1936.

Peltonen, Matti. *Talolliset ja torpparit: vuosisadan vaihteen maatalouskysymys Suomessa.* Helsinki: Suomen Historiallinen Seura, 1992.

Pistohlkors, Gert von. "'Russifizierung' in den Baltischen Provinzen und in Finnland im 19. und beginnenden 20. Jahrhundert." *Zeitschrift für Ostmitteleuropaforschung 33, Jahrbücher für Geschichte Osteuropas* 33 (1984): 592–606.

Polvinen, Tuomo. *Imperial Borderland: Bobrikov and the Attempted Russification of Finland, 1898–1904.* Durham: Duke University Press, 1995.

Rasila, Viljo. *Suomen torpparikysymys vuoteen 1909. Yhteiskuntahistoriallinen tutkimus.* Helsinki: Suomen Historiallinen Seura, 1961.

Rekola, Tuula. "Romernas tidiga skeden i Finland: från 1500-talet till mitten av 1800-talet." In *De finska romernas historia från svenska tiden till 2000-talet.* Edited by Panu Pulma, 20–82. Helsingfors: Svenska literatursällskapet i Finland, 2015.

Reuter, J. N. *"Kagalen": ett bidrag till Finlands historia 1899–1905.* Skrifter utgivna av Svenska litteratursällskapet i Finland 199. Helsingfors: Svenska litteratursällskapet i Finland, 1928.

Schrey-Vasara, Gabriele. "Venäläisyyden vastustamiskomitea Tampereella vuonna 1901." *Historiallinen Aikakauskirja* 85, no. 1 (1987): 3–8.

Spillmann, Kurt R., and Kati Spillmann. "Some Sociobiological and Psychological Aspects of 'Images of the Enemy.'" In *Enemy Images in American History.* Edited by Ragnhild Fiebig-von Hase and Ursula Lehmkuhl, 43–63. Providence: Berghahn, 1997.

Spångberg, Valfrid. *Statskuppen i Finland 1899.* Ur det moderna samhällslivet 19. Stockholm: Albert Bonniers förlag, 1899.

Stark, Laura. *The Limits of Patriarchy: How Female Networks of Pilfering and Gossip sparked the First Debates on Rural Gender Rights in the 19th-Century Finnish-language Press.* Helsinki: Finnish Literature Society, 2011.

Suodenjoki, Sami. "Kauppiasboikotista kansallisuusvihaan. Valtaväestön ja venäläisten suhteet Tampereella vuosina 1899–1981." In *Tampere kieliyhteisönä.* Edited by Harry Lönnroth, 147–74. Helsinki: Suomalaisen Kirjallisuuden Seura, 2009.

———. *Kuriton suutari ja kiistämisen rajat. Työväenliikkeen läpimurto hämäläisessä maalaisyhteisössä 1899–1909.* Helsinki: Suomalaisen Kirjallisuuden Seura, 2010.

———. "Land Agitation and the Rise of Agrarian Socialism in South-Western Finland, 1899–1907." In *Labour Unions and Politics under the North Star: The Nordic Countries, 1700–2000.* Edited by Mary Hilson, Silke Neunsinger, and Iben Vuyff, 175–96. New York: Berghahn Books, 2017.

Thaden, Edward C., ed. *Russification in the Baltic Provinces and Finland, 1855–1914.* Princeton: Princeton University Press, 1981.

———. "The Russian Government." In *Russification in the Baltic Provinces and Finland, 1855–1914.* Edited by Edward C. Thaden, 15–108. Princeton: Princeton University Press, 1981.

Tommila, Päiviö. *Suomen historiankirjoitus. Tutkimuksen historia.* Porvoo et al.: Werner Söderström Osakeyhtiö, 1999.

———. *Suuri adressi.* Porvoo: WSOY, 1999.

Wassholm, Johanna. "Tatar Pedlars in the Grand Duchy of Finland in the Late Nineteenth Century." *Studia Orientalia Electronica* 8, no. 2 (2020): 8–24.

Wassholm, Johanna, and Anna Sundelin. "Emotions, Trading Practices and Communication in Transnational Itinerant Trade: Encounters between 'Rucksack Russians' and their Customers in late Nineteenth- and Early Twentieth-Century Finland." *Scandinavian Economic History Review* 66, no. 2 (2018): 132–52.

Wassholm, Johanna, and Ann-Catrin Östman. "Introduktion. Plats och praktiker i handelsmöten i Finland 1850–1950." In *Att mötas kring varor. Plats och praktiker i handelsmöten i Finland 1850–1950.* Edited by Johanna Wassholm and Ann–Catrin Östman, 9–31. Helsingfors: Svenska litteratursällskapet i Finland & Stockholm: Appell Förlag, 2021.

Wassholm, Johanna. "'Threatening Livelihoods': Nordic Enemy Images of Peddlers from the Russian Empire." In *Forgotten Livelihoods: Encounters and Practices of Petty Trade in Northern Europe, 1820–1960.* Edited by Jutta Ahlbeck, Eija Stark & Ann-Catrin Östman, 329–57. London: Palgrave Macmillan, 2022.

13

The Self and the Other: Representations of the Monarchist Foe and Ally in the Satirical Press of the Russian Right (1906–1908)

Oleg Minin

Abstract

The promulgation of press freedom by the Imperial Manifesto of October 17, 1905 signified the emergence of a nascent public domain in autocratic Russia. The politicized satirical press that appeared as a result took full advantage of the new liberty. The proliferating left-leaning satirical journals deployed a potent apparatus of visual and verbal devices to ridicule the autocratic regime, its power structures, supporters, and even the tsar. The left-wing journals were countered by the less numerous yet visible right-wing satirical periodicals. In delineating the complexities of the political context as a backdrop against which the satirical battles of the period were played out, this chapter seeks to investigate the imagery and language the right-wing satirical press used to ridicule the monarchist "other"—the antithetical and multifaceted forces of liberalism and revolution—and construct a representation of the "self," or the forces sympathetic to the regime and representative of the right-wing of imperial Russia's political spectrum.

Introduction

An important outcome of the revolutionary mayhem that swept across Russia in the wake of Bloody Sunday in January 1905 was the emergence of a budding public domain. The period saw the formation of imperial Russia's first political parties, the growth of an affiliated press, and intense political dialogue during the months leading to the convocation of the first Duma in April 1906. Political battles were also played out in the pages of satirical periodicals, an unprecedented flowering of which Russia experienced after the promulgation of the Imperial Manifesto on October 17, 1905, which among other civil liberties provided for the freedom of the press. Like the print media in general, the satirical press of the revolutionary period reflected incipient political divisions. The object of study of this research is right-wing, pro-monarchist satirical periodicals, which, together with their liberal counterparts, represented a constituent, if in many respects contemptible, part of the nascent public sphere and Russia's nationhood.[1] This chapter especially seeks to explore the ways in which these right-wing publications advanced through image and word, and in keeping with the main tenets of right-wing ideology, the satirical "othering" of monarchist Russia's ideological opponents—radical revolutionaries, the liberal-bourgeois parliamentary opposition, and liberal ministers of the imperial government, while at the same time constructing a positive representation of the "self," or the forces sympathetic to and protective of autocratic government and the Russian Orthodox faith.

The Rise of the Russian Right

Before 1905, the supremacy of the Russian monarchy as the epitome of absolutist values was scarcely challenged in the public arena: the centuries-old tsarist Russia almost completely lacked monarchist political organizations. With the notable exception of the short-lived, aristocratic, and subversive Holy Brotherhood (Sviashchennaia druzhina, 1881–1883), before March and April 1905, there was only one noteworthy, organized group—the St. Petersburg-based Russian Assembly (Russkoe sobranie).[2] Right-leaning political parties

---

1   I borrow this term and its connotation from Stephen M. Norris. See his *"Pliuvium*'s Unholy Trinity: Russian Nationhood, Anti-Semitism, and the Public Sphere after 1905," *Experiment* 19 (2013): 87–116.

2   As its statute explained, the Russian Assembly acted as a kind of aristocratic literary–artistic club, which sought to "assist in clarifying and strengthening [. . .] as well as implementing in

and unions emerged at the end of 1904 and beginning of 1905 in response to the spread of the revolutionary movement and the consolidation of the forces of the liberal opposition. The end of that fateful year saw the emergence of a variety of right-leaning political entities, many of which rapidly developed into formidable national organizations capable of mobilizing their own publics to act in defense of Russia's monarchy.[3] The watershed spring months of 1905 witnessed the emergence of Count Pavel Sheremetev's Union of Russian Men (Soiuz russkikh liudei, Moscow, March 1905) and Vladimir Gringmut's Russian Monarchist Party (Russkaia monarkhicheskaia partiia, Moscow, April 24, 1905). In November, these were followed by the foundation of what was to become one of the most prominent ultra-conservative monarchist-orthodox mass organizations—the St. Petersburg-based Union of the Russian People (Soiuz russkogo naroda). The Russian Assembly also transformed itself into a full-fledged political party with a developed and well-articulated program. During the two years leading up to the opening of the third, conservative duma in November 1907, monarchist parties and unions, largely through the unification efforts of the Russian Assembly, came to represent a substantial, powerful, consolidated right-wing front.

Right-Wing Dogma and Satirical Discourse

The rapid political mobilization of monarchist forces was accompanied by the codification of right-wing ideology, which may be perceived in retrospect as a collective doctrine developed by monarchism's leading ideologues.[4] The turn-

---

real life the true creative beginnings and peculiar characteristics of the everyday life of the Russian people." See V. V. Shelokhaev, ed., *Programmy politicheskikh partii Rossii. Konets XIX–Nachalo XX vv.* (Moscow: Rosspen, 1995), 419. For more on the Holy Brotherhood see B. V. Anan'ich and R. S. Ganelin, *Sergei Iul'evich Vitte i Ego Vremia* (St. Petersburg: Dmitrii Bulanin, 1999), 17–37.

3   Iu. I. Kirianov, *Pravye partii v Rossii 1911–1917* (Moscow: Rosspen, 2001), 5; V. V. Shelokhaev, ed., *Politicheskie partii Rossii. Konets XIX–pervaia tret' XX veka. Dokumental'noe nasledie. Pravye partii. Dokumenty i materialy*, 2 vols (Moscow: Rosspen, 1998).

4   The modern proponents of monarchism, in turn, relied on an extensive corpus of apologetic literature on the subject of Russian absolutism, which included the writings of Nikolai Karamzin (see, for example, his "Notes on Ancient and Modern Russia" ["Zapiski o drevnei i novoi Rossii"]), Metropolitan Filaret (Vasilii Drozdov) and Sergei Uvarov, the minister of education in the government of Nicholas I. For a comprehensive overview and analysis of the development of the nineteenth-century monarchist ideology, see S. L. Firsov, "'Okhranitel'naia ideologiia' i Pravoslavnaia Tserkov' v Rossii, 1825–1861," in *Filosofiia i sotsial'no-politicheskie tsennosti konservatizma v obshchestvennom soznanii Rossii (Ot istokov k sovremennosti). Sbornik statei. Vypusk 1*, ed. I. N. Solonin (St. Petersburg: Izdatel'stvo Sankt–Peterburgskogo

of-the century iteration of monarchist dogma displayed a number of common slogans and beliefs, while the key and all-embracing principle lying at its core was the revitalized theory of "official nationality," succinctly expressed in the 1830s by Sergei Uvarov in the ternary formula: "Orthodoxy, Autocracy and Nationality." The formula served as the ideological foundation of many incipient right-wing organizations. In November 1905, to integrate itself into the country's political life, the Russian Assembly published its program, prefacing it with the epigraph "For the Faith, the Tsar and the Fatherland." The program thus propagated the supremacy of the Russian Orthodox Church and autocratic rule; the power of the tsar was to be absolute and based on his continuous unification (*postoiannoe edinenie*) with the Russian people.[5] Similarly, in section three of the program, the Russian Monarchist Party stated that it stood for the indivisibility of the Great Russian Empire governed by the unlimited autocratic power of the Russian monarch, augmented by the free and dignified existence of the Russian Orthodox Church.[6]

The right-wing press in general and the satirical journals in particular took their cues from the monarchist parties' programs. Published by the local chapter of the Union of the Russian People, the Kharkov-based newspaper *Glas naroda* (People's voice), for example, opened its inaugural issue of November 26, 1906 with an introduction to its program prefaced with the emphatic exclamation "For the Orthodox Faith, for the Autocratic Tsar, for the Russian People." The editors of the newspaper deemed their principal objective to be the strong union (*krepkii soiuz*) of all of Russia's faithful sons around the throne to pacify and rebuild the motherland.[7] Founded in Moscow in early 1906 by Black Hundreds activist and member of the local chapter of the Union of the Russian People Vladimir Olovenikov, the satirical weekly *Knut* (Knout) was one of Russia's first journals of political satire with a distinctly right-wing bent.[8] The inaugural issue

---

universiteta, 2004), 142–72; D. I. Raskin, "Ideologiia russkogo pravogo radikalizma v kontse XIX—nachale XX v.," in *Natsional'naia pravaia prezhde i teper'. Istoriko-sotsiologicheskie ocherki. Chast' 1. Rossiia i russkoe zarubezh'e,* ed. R. S. Ganelin (St. Petersburg: Institut sotsiologii RAN-SPb, 1992), 5–47.

5 See "Programma 'Russkogo sobraniia' (1905)," in V. V. Shelokaev, ed., *Programmy politicheskikh partii Rossii. Konets XIX-Nachalo XXvv.* (Moscow: Rosspen, 1995), 420–21.

6 Ibid., 427. For a comprehensive analysis of the right-wing ideology beyond the triad of "Autocracy, Orthodoxy, Nationality," see, for example, S. A. Stepanov, *Chernaia sotnia v Rossii (1905–1914 gg.)* (Moscow: Izdatel'stvo VZPI, A/O "Rosvuznauka," 1992), 9–32. For a succinct summary of the main tenets of the monarchist ideology see also Raskin, "Ideologiia russkogo pravogo radikalizma v kontse XIX—nachale XX v," 8–9.

7 See *Glas naroda* 1 (November 26, 1906), 2.

8 *Knut* was edited and published by Olovenikov's wife, A. Olovenikova, who was also in charge of the Moscow monarchist newspaper *Veche* (Popular Assembly). *Knut*'s close connection to

of the magazine opened with an anonymous front-page color illustration entitled *Likhoi iamshchik* (Deft coachman), which visually codified the "Orthodoxy, Autocracy, Nationality" formula as the central guiding principle of its discourse (fig. 1).

The picture depicted Russia's new minister of the interior, Petr Stolypin, steering a troika carrying a woman clad in a traditional Russian folk dress richly trimmed with ermine. The word "Russia" is written across her *kokoshnik*-styled headpiece, while the slogan "Orthodoxy, Autocracy, Nationality" adorns the Russian tricolor at the front of the coach. A brief caption to the image offers right-wing praise of Stolypin as a competent and selfless statesman capable of restoring the crumbling internal order:

> Laboring hard to the point of forgetting his leisure time, a thunderous enemy of those who are not right (*nepravykh*) and a friend to order, whether he is called on to reform or to deal with trouble—always and everywhere, he is right here riding his *troika*. He is the enemy of stagnation, but he does not rush [...] he rides when standing and sleeps when seated.[9]

A contemporary critic argues that political cartoons and caricatures represent an effective way of informing "the public of political figures and the meaning of events."[10] However, it is also true that the continuous development of the political life of a country unavoidably makes such images dated, while the historical context against which they are originally created, and the events and political figures on which they are commenting, gradually become obscure. This observation is arguably applicable to all graphic and textual material featured in the periodical press. The meaning of the caption and some of the nuances of the anonymous cartoon in *Knut* will therefore benefit from further historical contextualization.

In Russia of 1905, the emergence of a parliamentary political order during the post October Manifesto period was accompanied by continuing urban and rural unrest. The instability of the situation was aggravated by waves of what Anna Geifman has called "revolutionary terrorism"; that is, attempts to assassinate senior government and military officials, "bombings, ideologically

---

the Union was often emphasized by the incorporation of the words "the Union of the Russian People" in its cartoons.

9   *Knut* 1 (1906), 1.

10 Lawrence H. Streicher, "David Low and the Sociology of Caricature," *Comparative Studies in Society and History* 8, no 1 (October 1965): 1.

FIGURE 1. Anon., *Likhoi iamshchik* (Deft coachman), *Knut* 1 (1906), 1. (cover)

motivated robberies, incidents of armed assaults," and so on, perpetrated by members of the Socialist Revolutionary Party and anarchists.[11] The restoration of state authority and security matters were thus the burning issues Stolypin faced on his appointment, first as Russia's new minister of the interior and then, on the dissolution of the first Duma in July 1906, as Prime Minister. Likewise, these were the issues that significantly informed Stolypin's political legacy, for he acquired the reputation of being both an able reformer and a harsh disciplinarian. Stolypin deemed the reinstatement of order and state authority a necessary precondition for further reform. Unlike his penultimate predecessor, Sergei Witte, Stolypin succeeded in pacifying the country, if only through a series of extraordinary military measures taken under the aegis of Article 87 of the new Fundamental Laws.[12] One of Stolypin's most notorious and arguably most effective actions was the introduction during this period of special field courts-martial for civilians, which a variety of accounts indicate sentenced to death more than a thousand suspected revolutionary terrorists.[13] Against this historical setting, the caption of the *Knut* illustration (with the obvious omission of any direct reference to summary courts-martial) welcomes Stolypin as a "thunderous enemy" of the seditious disorder perpetrated by the

---

11 See Anna Geifman, *Thou Shalt Kill: Revolutionary Terrorism in Russia, 1894–1917* (Princeton: Princeton University Press, 1993), 4–5.

12 The broadly phrased provisions of Article 87 allowed the government (the premier and the Council of Ministers) to issue emergency laws ("if extraordinary circumstances necessitate such measures"), for example, to restore state authority in the volatile regions of the country. Recourse to Article 87 was possible only when the Duma was in recess, in which case the Council of Ministers would seek the ultimate approval of the measure by the tsar. Such emergency laws and decrees would become redundant within two months of the reconvening of parliament, unless "the minister responsible submits a bill regarding the special measure," and it was approved by both houses of parliament. See "Stat'ia 87," in *Glava deviataia. O zakonakh. Svod osnovnykh gosudarstvennykh zakonov. Razdel pervyi. Osnovnye Gosudarstvennye Zakony* (Kazan': Tipo-Litografiia Imperatorskogo Universiteta, 1907), 16. See also Richard Pipes, *The Russian Revolution* (New York: Alfred A. Knopf Publishers, 1990), 160; Abraham Ascher, *The Revolution of 1905: Authority Restored* (Palo Alto: Stanford University Press, 1992), 70. Sergei Witte deemed Stolypin's use of Article 87 irresponsible. See S. I. Vitte, *Vospominaniia* (Moscow: Skif Aleks, 1994), 3:277–78.

13 For a detailed discussion of the statistics and sources see Geifman, *Thou Shalt Kill: Revolutionary Terrorism in Russia*, 227, 346. Stolypin was taken to task for his actions by liberal politicians and satirists alike. For examples of the latter see V. Botsianovskii and E. Gollerbakh, *Russkaia satira pervoi revoliutsii 1905–1906* (Leningrad: Gosudarstvennoe izdatel'stvo, 1925), 121. This may be contrasted with the rightists' reception of Sergei Witte, who was criticized, among many other things, for his inability to restore state order. With time, the rightists' reception of Stolypin would also change for the worse. However, when this cartoon was published in *Knut*, the new premier was largely supported by the right.

revolutionary movement, and a "friend to order," something the premier had so vigorously worked to restore.

The Othering of the Monarchist Foe

In his article "On a Theory of Political Caricature," Lawrence H. Streicher suggests that caricatures are "negative definitions, stereotypes, which are aimed at dramatizing aggressive tendencies through the definition of targets, the collective integration of 'private' feelings into public sentiments of 'self-defense' and the training of hatred and debunking techniques."[14] Certainly, such a description gauges the caricaturist's most extreme intentions, which go beyond the realm of constructive humorous criticism, seeking, for example, to vilify and denigrate opponents within a framework of a fierce ideological contest. Although scarcely extendable to the social or light-hearted and witty varieties of caricature, which were in any event rare in the satirical press of 1905, Streicher's suggestion may nevertheless describe much of the visual and verbal content of the Russian right-wing satirical press.

The right-leaning satirical journals emerged during the period of intense post October Manifesto political dialogue, mostly in opposition to their popular and omnipresent left-wing counterparts.[15] In these publications, as in the right-wing press in general, the crown acquired welcome (if unauthorized) allies, given that they were not officially sanctioned to speak for the regime. By the time of their appearance, the targets of their satirical vitriol were already well defined and articulated. The taxonomy of the enemies of Orthodox and tsarist Russia was part and parcel of right-wing dogma and was provided for by the leading ideologues of monarchism. A case in point is Vladimir Gringmut, the founder of the Russian Monarchist Party, the editor-in-chief of its mouthpiece, the daily *Moskovskie vedomosti* (Moscow news), and one of the principal advocates of the

---

14 Lawrence H. Streicher, "On a Theory of Political Caricature," *Comparative Studies in Society and History* 9, no. 4 (July 1967): 438.

15 Speaking about two right-wing satirical periodicals in particular (for example, *Vittova Pliaska* [Witte's Dance] and the illustrated *Pliuvium* [see the discussion of both below]), the assistant minister of the interior and member of the State Council Vladimir Gurko recalled in his memoirs that a group of young right-wing activists decided to publish humorous journals of their own "to counterbalance numerous similar magazines of an openly revolutionary character." See V. I. Gurko, *Features and Figures of the Past: Government and Opinion in the Reign of Nicholas II*, ed. J. E. Wallace Sterling, Xenia Joukoff Eudin, and H. H. Fisher, trans. Laura Matveev (Palo Alto: Stanford University Press, 1939), 434.

Black Hundreds movement. In his programmatic *Rukovodstvo chernosotentsa-monarkhista* (Manual of a black hundredist-monarchist), Gringmut classified the internal enemies of Russia as those whose intention it was to limit the tsar's autocratic power. This category included the "constitutionalists," "democrats," "socialists," "revolutionaries," "anarchists," and "Jews."[16] With minor variations in terminology and further additions to these major groups,[17] this taxonomy was adopted by the right-wing satirical periodicals as a guide to the definition of the targets of their satirical othering: for example, Olovenikov's *Knut*, which promoted itself as a political, artistic, literary, and "hilariously humorous" journal, vowed to direct its satirical blows, "like any whip would, at the right, left and center, but primarily at the Jews, their sympathizers (*prikhvostnei*), the leftists (*levshei*), the Constitutional Democrats, the anarchists, the bomb throwers (*bombisty*), and other such trash."[18] Without explicitly stating it, other right-wing satirical journals maintained objectives and attacked targets similar to those of *Knut*.

The classification of monarchist opponents, as outlined by Gringmut and restated in *Knut*, was based on the degree of liberalism and revolutionary extremism displayed by the forces of the left-wing opposition. The liberals and revolutionaries who challenged the absolute power of the tsar and the supremacy of the Orthodox Church, the alleged exploiters of the Russian people (primarily and stereotypically, wealthy Jewish businessmen and capitalists), and the state bureaucracy, which monarchists believed hampered the lasting unification of the tsar and his subjects, were identified as the principal enemies of autocratic Russia.

Because of the relentless radicalism of their political objectives and programs and their unwavering commitment to fighting the monarchy, the Social Democrats and Socialist Revolutionaries were first in the hierarchy of targets of right-wing satirical vitriol. This is seen in the frequency with which these groups were parodied in the journals. The language and imagery employed to designate them also acted as one of the devices of their satirical ridicule. The Marxist-oriented Russian Social Democratic Workers' Party and the closely associated Jewish Bund[19] were habitually referred to in these satirical journals as *esdeki*

---

16 See V. A. Gringmut, *Rukovodstvo chernosotentsa-monarkhista* (Kremenchug: Izdatel'stvo SRN, 1906), 4.

17 For example, radicalized university students, who can be included in any of the major groups, were one of the most popular targets of right-wing satire.

18 See *Knut* 5 (1908), 4.

19 The Bund, or General Jewish Labor Bund in Lithuania, Poland and Russia (Vseobshchii Evreiskii Rabochii Soiuz v Litve, Pol'she i Rossii) had originated in the late 1890s, comprising

(Social democrats) and *bundisty* (members of the Bund). The revolutionary terrorists, or the members of the fighting brigades of the Socialist Revolutionary Party, were divided into *bombisty* (bomb throwers) and *ekspropriatory* (expropriators), while revolutionaries in general were labelled *krasnoflazhniki* (red flaggers).

The verbal mockery used to designate the revolutionaries was accompanied by their graphic renderings in caricatures, in which they were often portrayed either as otherworldly beings or as earthly creatures of the lower order (serpents, vultures, bats, frogs, crows, donkeys, and dogs). In the previously mentioned *Knut* cartoon, *Deft coachman,* in contrast with the images of Stolypin and Russia representative of the self, bundist and anarchist others are depicted as black crows—perhaps in keeping with the negative connotation associated with the Russian phrase "*staia voron,*" or "flock of crows." The Socialist Revolutionary bomb-throwing terrorists and the opposition parties of the left are portrayed in this cartoon as bulldogs—reminiscent of the Russian phrase "*zlye sobaki,*" or "rabid dogs" (fig. 1). There is similar imagery in a cartoon in the fourth (1907) issue of the Moscow right-wing satirical weekly magazine *Zhgut* (Rope).[20] Entitled *Izbavitel' blizko* (The savior is near), the cartoon shows a young maiden (Russia) besieged by a flock of vulture-like crows identified as "S. R." (Socialist Revolutionaries), bureaucracy, revolutionary expropriators, anarchy, and "K. D." (Konstitutsionnye Demokraty—the Constitutional Democrats or Kadets) (fig. 2).

The revolutionary adversaries of the tsarist regime were often anathematized collectively under the all-embracing term *kramola,* or sedition. Visually codifying *kramola, Zhgut* opened its inaugural 1907 issue with a cartoon diatribe that presented in a single composition the various antithetical entities of sedition, which, the monarchists argued, were ready to thrust the country into the hands

---

various Marxist Jewish worker groups. In 1898, the Bund became part of the Russian Social Democratic Workers' Party. For more on the Bund, its history and program (ca. 1905), see Shelokhaev, ed., *Programmy politicheskikh partii Rossii,* 23–40.

20 Like *Knut, Zhgut* originated in Moscow, albeit a year later, in the autumn of 1907. Billed as "the most venomous" and misleadingly, a nonaffiliated, publication, the journal was financed and edited by Ivan Klang, an artist who in the 1890s had worked for two of the Moscow-based literary-artistic journals, *Moskva* (Moscow) and *Volna* (Wave). See V. A. Giliarovskii, *Sobranie sochinenii v chetyrekh tomakh* (Moscow: Poligrafresursy, 1999), 2:86. Giliarovskii identifies Klang as the publisher of both *Moskva* and *Volna,* while other sources indicate that he was one of their artistic contributors. Apart from editing and publishing *Zhgut,* Klang also appears to have written for it, as many of the literary segments in the journal are identified in abbreviated forms such as "Iv. K-g." Although most of the artwork in *Zhgut* remained anonymous, it would not be unreasonable to suggest that Klang, himself an artist, was their principal, if not only, author.

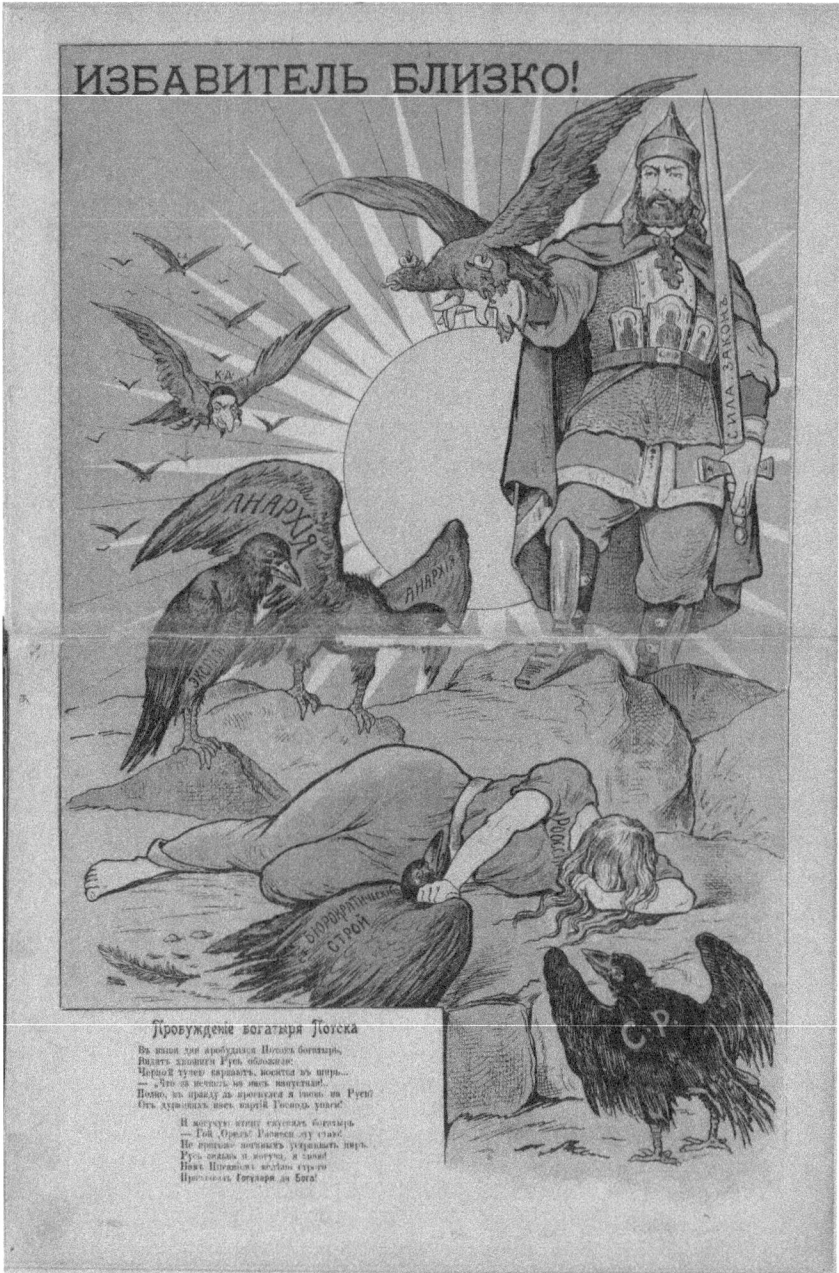

FIGURE 2. Anon, *Izbavitel' blizko* (The savior is near), *Zhgut* 4 (1907), 4–5.

of constitutional government and anarchy. The cartoon depicts a peasant carrying a monstrous witchlike creature on his back. The words "constitution" and "anarchy" are printed on the side of the creature's frock cloak. Despised by the right for being the instigator of the liberal reforms, the former premier Witte is easily identifiable by his physiognomy and a crown of gold—a reference to the title of count only recently bestowed on him by the tsar for the successful negotiation of the Treaty of Portsmouth in September 1905—which served both right- and left-wing satirists as a symbol and satirical device. In the *Zhgut* cartoon, Witte is portrayed as a befuddled large-breasted swamp mermaid, while the leaders of the Kadet party (Pavel Miliukov and Georgii L'vov) are depicted as green frogs. The speech bubble to the cartoon reads that a poor peasant (*muzhik*), hunched by the weight of anarchy, is running he knows not where; all around the grimy swamp creatures are croaking with various voices. Astonished and exhausted, he says, "I see, it's the Jewish witch" (fig. 3).

In identifying Jews with the accursed and subversive notions of "constitution" and "anarchy," *Zhgut* and other right-wing journals were adhering to one of the principal and ugly tenets of early twentieth-century Russian monarchist dogma—blatant antisemitism.[21] In the public realm there was scarcely a right-wing political program or Black Hundreds propaganda text that did not contain a set of limiting or accusatory anti-Jewish clauses, which were premised principally on the identification of Russia's Jews with revolution, rebellion, anarchy, and modern forms of capitalism.[22] Time and again, right-wing and Black Hundreds propaganda alleged that the Jews wished to overthrow the existing regime and divide the country, while striving for world domination.[23] In his exposition of the rise of the extreme right in Russia, Walter Laqueur succinctly addresses this Black Hundreds logic in averring that the monarchists' fire was concentrated against the Jews in particular because they were considered

---

21 Several seminal monographs treat the subject of the anti-Semitic nature of the monarchist ideology at length. See, for example, Walter Laqueur, *Black Hundred: The Rise of the Extreme Right in Russia* (New York: Harper Collins Publishers, 1993); Heinz-Dietrich Löwe, *The Tsars and the Jews: Reform, Reaction and Anti–Semitism in Imperial Russia, 1772–1917* (Langhorne: Harwood Academic Publishers, 1993); Steven Marks, *How Russia Shaped the Modern World: From Art to Anti-Semitism, Ballet to Bolshevism* (Princeton: Princeton University Press, 2003), 140–75; Hans Rogger, *Jewish Policies and Right-wing Politics in Imperial Russia* (Berkeley: University of California Press, 1986).

22 Hans Rogger discusses the origins of these beliefs in his *Russia in the Age of Modernization and Revolution, 1881–1917* (London: Longman, 1983), 199–207.

23 One of the Black Hundreds propaganda texts of the period, which advanced, among other preposterous notions, the conspiracy theory of Jewish world domination, was the "Protocols of the Elders of Zion." A useful discussion of the Protocols may be found in Marks, *How Russia Shaped the Modern World: From Art to Anti-Semitism, Ballet to Bolshevism*, 140–75.

FIGURE 3. Ivan Klang (attributed), *Anarkhiia, konstitutsiia* (Anarchy, constitution), *Zhgut* 1 (1907), 1. (cover)

the source of all evil in holy Russia. All Jews were revolutionaries and all revolutionaries were Jews. At the same time, all Jews were capitalists and all capitalists were either Jews or tools in the hands of Jews. The Jewish revolutionaries wanted to undermine and overthrow the existing order so as to facilitate the installation of the rule of the Jewish capitalists.[24]

The content of the right-wing satirical journal very much reflected this logic. By relying on a host of centuries-old hyperbolized Jewish stereotypes that were now admixed with freshly concocted political, economic, and social accusations, cartoons and verbal satire in the right-wing satirical journals strove to vilify the Jews, not only for their revolutionary activism but for many other unwarranted reasons: the Jews were satirized as purveyors of hard liquor and catalysts of the evil drinking habit, and often portrayed as capitalist exploiters and profiteers[25] and conduits of treason through the alleged cooperation of Jewish bankers with the Japanese during the recent war. The latter motif is presented in a cartoon entitled *Soiuzniki [Evrei i Iaponets]* (Allies [A Jew and a Japanese]), which opened the eighth issue of the arch-monarchist satirical weekly *Pliuvium* (November 25, 1906) (fig. 4).[26]

Authored by the artist and Black Hundreds activist Luka Zlotnikov, the monochrome image depicts caricature-like figures of a Japanese officer standing arm in arm with a Jewish businessman clad in a tuxedo, bow tie, and top hat. Both hold sacks of money identified as the English pound sterling, a detail

---

24 Laqueur, *Black Hundred: The Rise of the Extreme Right in Russia*, 26.
25 The brand of early nineteenth-century Russian antisemitism, which informed satirical portrayals of the Jews as despised capitalists trying to subjugate the Russian nation, represented, as Steven Marks points out, a function of the conservative anti-capitalist and anti–modern strain of right-wing ideology. In the eyes of some of the more conservative right-wing "capitalist rejectionists," to use Marks's terminology, the Jews were believed to pose a threat to the traditional system of values, because they were becoming closely identified with capitalism and the modern urban culture. See Marks, *How Russia Shaped the Modern World: From Art to Anti-Semitism, Ballet to Bolshevism*, 140–41. See also Raskin, "Ideologiia russkogo pravogo radikalizma v kontse XIX–nachale XX v.," 5–47. The conservative anti-modern strain of right-wing ideology also informed the right-wing satirical criticism of modernist Russian and European literature, which was perceived as a factor contributing to the moral degradation of the Russian nation.
26 *Pliuvium* was published in St. Petersburg. The first issue of this ugly anti-Semitic leaflet came out on October 7, 1906. It was edited by V. Liobel, and co-edited and published by V. Brevern, although these may not be the real names of the publication's producers. With the outward appearance of a newspaper, *Pliuvium* was billed as a literary journal. It contained an assortment of cartoons and caricatures, many of which were directed against the Jews.

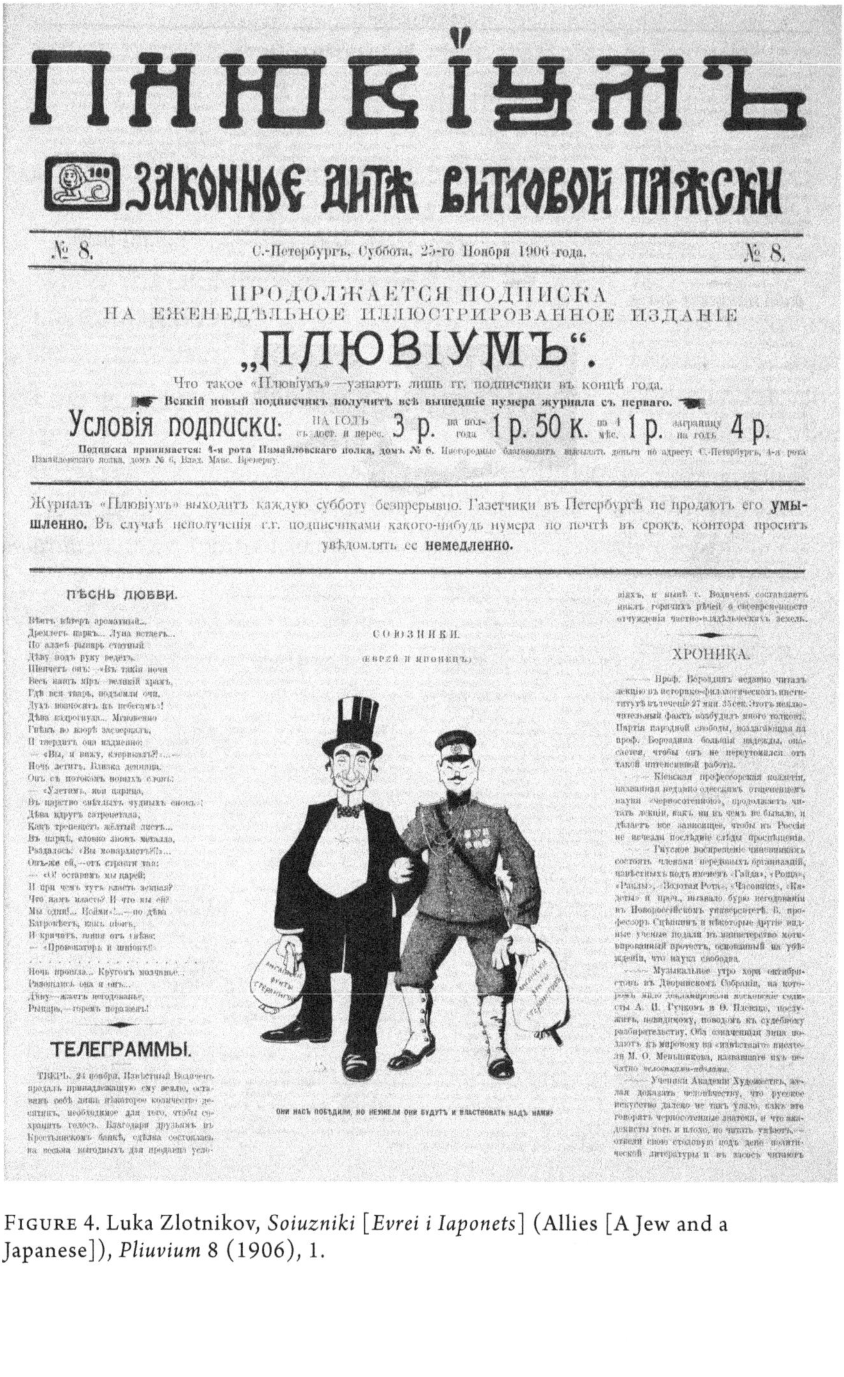

ПЛЮВІУМЪ

ЗАКОННОЕ ДИТЯ ВИТТОВОЙ ПИЯВКИ

№ 8. С.-Петербургъ, Суббота, 25-го Ноября 1906 года. № 8.

ПРОДОЛЖАЕТСЯ ПОДПИСКА
НА ЕЖЕНЕДѢЛЬНОЕ ИЛЛЮСТРИРОВАННОЕ ИЗДАНІЕ

„ПЛЮВІУМЪ".

Что такое «Плювіумъ»—узнаютъ лишь гг. подписчики въ концѣ года.

Всякій новый подписчикъ получитъ всѣ вышедшіе нумера журнала съ перваго.

Условія подписки: на годъ съ дост. и перес. 3 р. на полгода 1 р. 50 к. на 4 мѣс. 1 р. заграницу на годъ 4 р.

Подписка принимается: 4-я рота Измайловскаго полка, домъ № 6. Иногородные благоволятъ высылать деньги по адресу: С.-Петербургъ, 4-я рота Измайловскаго полка, домъ № 6, Влад. Макс. Бренеру.

Журналъ «Плювіумъ» выходитъ каждую субботу безпрерывно. Газетчики въ Петербургѣ не продаютъ его **умышленно.** Въ случаѣ неполученія г.г. подписчиками какого-нибудь нумера по почтѣ въ срокъ, контора проситъ увѣдомлять ее **немедленно.**

ПѢСНЬ ЛЮБВИ.

СОЮЗНИКИ.

(Еврей и японецъ.)

ТЕЛЕГРАММЫ.

ХРОНИКА.

FIGURE 4. Luka Zlotnikov, *Soiuzniki* [*Evrei i Iaponets*] (Allies [A Jew and a Japanese]), *Pliuvium* 8 (1906), 1.

which hints at Britain's role in financing the Japanese war effort.[27] The caption to the image—"They defeated us, but will they also rule over us?"—verbalizes the xenophobic division into "us" and "them," expressing the popular resentment toward the monarchist other prevalent in the wake of the Russo-Japanese war and rooted in the Black Hundreds patriotic, anti-capitalist, and anti-Semitic rhetoric.

The right-wing satirical othering of Jews as oppressive capitalists and revolutionaries, as well as of revolutionaries as a collective antagonistic and seditious body (for example, in the use of the term kramola), was accompanied by a similar treatment of the liberal-bourgeois parties, their leaders and political objectives, which, the monarchists believed, represented a formidable threat to the stability of the autocratic regime. Like the *Knut* cartoon, *Deft coachman*, which portrayed Stolypin as a tireless combatant against sedition, the anti-liberal bourgeois visual and verbal satire of the right-wing journals was steeped in the politics of the period between 1906 and 1908. In the history of tsarist Russia, this was the era of the painful emergence of a new constitutional order ushered in by several imperial manifestoes and decrees which established the Russian parliament (the Duma) and enabled the nation to hold parliamentary elections in March 1906, February 1907, and October 1907. Between the spring of 1906 and the autumn of 1907, the elections were followed by the convocation of the first, second and third Dumas.[28] For the Russian liberals, who were most strongly represented by the Constitutional Democrats (the Kadets) and led by one of the party's founding fathers, Pavel Miliukov, these developments resulted in a series of political victories over the regime. The most striking achievement, on a par with the October Manifesto and the establishment of the national parliament, was the Kadets' spectacular success in the first Duma elections and their prominent position, along with those of the socialist deputies, in the second Duma.[29] By contrast, the right-wing political parties did very poorly

---

27 Great Britain's financial aid to Japan before and during the war is explored more fully in the Australian Association for Maritime History's "British Assistance to the Japanese Navy during the Russo-Japanese War of 1904–5," *The Great Circle* 2, no. 1 (April 1980): 44–54.

28 The first Duma opened on 27 April 1906. It lasted only seventy-two days and was ultimately prorogued by the tsar in early July 1906. The second, "radical" Duma, which opened on 20 February 1907, was likewise prorogued, after only three months, in June 1907. Opening in early November 1907 and composed of mostly loyalist, upper class delegates (due to restrictions in the election law), the third, "conservative" Duma operated for the entire five-year period of its legal tenure.

29 For more on the composition of the second Duma, see Pipes, *The Russian Revolution*, 179; Abraham Ascher, *P. A. Stolypin: The Search for Stability in Late Imperial Russia* (Palo Alto: Stanford University Press, 2001), 174–75.

in the first two elections: in the first Duma their representation accounted for only 1% of the votes. Significant effort and some sizable gains in various parts of the country after the second elections ultimately garnered for the forces of the right a meagre 10% of the votes (fifty-seven deputies). This was minuscule compared with the more than 60% (322 deputies) shared by the opposition parties—the Kadets, the Laborites (*Trudoviki*), the Social Democrats, and the Socialist Revolutionaries.[30] It is hardly surprising, then, that against such a background the Kadets and their close political allies (the Union of October 17 [Soiuz 17-go Oktiabria]), the Party of Peaceful Renewal [Partiia mirnogo obnovleniia] and the Party of Democratic Reform [Partiia demokraticheskikh reform])[31] should become, next to the radical revolutionaries, the most prominent targets of right-wing satirical vitriol. The monarchists were vexed by essentially everything for which these liberal-bourgeois parties stood. Apart from the general indignation at the success of the opposition parties in the first two elections, the rightists contested the Kadets' radical proposals in the Duma, which included the abolition of the estate system, the granting of equal rights to Poles, Jews, and other minority groups and of political autonomy to the Polish Kingdom, and the restoration of the Finnish constitution. The Kadets' motion for the expropriation of private lands in favor of the landless peasantry (this being the liberals' paradoxical solution to Russia's persistent 'land' problem) also met with vigorous resistance from the right. In their illustrations and texts, the right-wing satirical journals emphasized these points of contention, reiterating the monarchists' overall antagonism to the liberal camp and the seditious ideas it promulgated in the Duma.

As was the government, right-wingers were especially annoyed by the obstinacy of the liberal-bourgeois opposition in the first two Dumas, its persistent unwillingness to cooperate with the regime, and its often ambiguous and changing position *vis-à-vis* the imperial administration, the socialist deputies and the rightists themselves.[32] These sentiments informed the references to the untrustworthy and shifty nature of the liberal bourgeois opposition, which became some of the more popular ways to debunk it in the right-wing satirical

---

30 For a comprehensive analysis of the conservatives' performance in the first three Dumas, see the section "Rightists and the Duma" in Don C. Rawson, *Russian Rightists and the Revolution of 1905* (Cambridge: Cambridge University Press, 1995), 152–225.

31 For some of the most recent sources on these parties' histories, programs and alliances, see Anna Geifman, ed., *Russia under the Last Tsar: Opposition and Subversion, 1894–1917* (Oxford: Blackwell Publishers, 1991), as well as Shelokhaev, ed., *Programmy politicheskikh partii Rossii.*

32 For more on the latter issue, see Ascher, P. A. *Stolypin: The Search for Stability in Late Imperial Russia,* 185, 200–201.

press. The liberal-bourgeois Duma deputies were habitually parodied and mocked as useless demagogues, idle talkers, traitors, and clowns. Illustrative of this line of right-wing satirical criticism is a *Knut* cartoon called *Dni smekha i zabavy* (Days of laughter and fun) (fig. 5). Intended to ridicule as much the very notion of the Russian parliament as the prominence of the left-wing coalition in the second Duma, the cartoon depicts the key opposition personalities as clowns and acrobats performing various juggling and balancing acts as part of the entertainment at the "Tavrichinelli Circus." The cartoon was designed as a poster advertisement, the full text of which read: "Sanctioned by the authorities. St. Petersburg. Tavrichinelli Circus! Only for several more days! Days of Laughter and Fun. Gala performance. Comic appearances of all the clowns."[33] Sustaining the ironic attitude, the accompanying caption explains that the performance will feature the director of the circus, Fedor Golovin (in real life the Kadet chairman of the second Duma), who "will balance a rotating plate" (identified as "the State Duma") "leaning it to the left." Also featured would be the audiences' favorite entertainer "Fedia" Rodichev (in reality, Fedor Rodichev, a Duma deputy and member of the Central Committee of the Kadet party), who would juggle balls, while the athlete Dolgorukov and the clown Aleksinsky demonstrated comic jumps and somersaults.[34]

---

33 See *Knut* 6 (1907), 8. The word "*Tavrichinelli*", and its intended comic effect, are created by combining two words, "*Tavricheskii*" and "*Chinizelli.*" The first designation refers to the "*Tavricheskii dvorets*" or the Tauride Palace—the official seat of the State Duma. The second word is the last name of Gaetano Chinizelli—the Italian actor, horseman and inspiration for the construction of the famous St. Petersburg circus (built in 1877), which bore his name until the 1917 Revolution.

34 Rodichev was a favorite target of the right-wing satirists, which was in no small measure due to his popularity and oratorical skills. He also gained notoriety (and was lampooned in the right-wing satirical journals) for the remark he made in the third Duma after Stolypin's report, in which the premier expressed his resolute intention of continuing to fight the revolution in Russia. In the ensuing debate Rodichev referred to the gallows used by Stolypin-instituted field courts as "Stolypin's neckties." Subsequently, for this "unconstitutional expression" Rodichev was banned from the Duma for fifteen sessions and challenged by Stolypin to a duel. The right-wing satirical periodicals satirized this incident in their cartoons. See, for example, an anonymous quip in Klang's *Zhgut*, which shows Rodichev being punished like a mischievous little boy with a broom by the Chairman of the Third Duma, the Octobrist Nikolai Khomiakov. The words "Fifteen-session ban" are inscribed on the broom, while the caption to the image has Rodichev plead with the "grown-up" Khomiakov: "Ouch, ouch, ouch! I will never do this again, Sir! I lied [. . .]. I will never mention the neckties again!" See *Zhgut* 4 (1907), 8. Pavel Dolgorukov was one of the original founders of the Constitutional Democratic Party and at the time of the publication of the *Knut* cartoon a deputy in the second Duma. Grigorii Aleksinskii was also a deputy in the second Duma, where he represented the radical Social Democratic Party.

FIGURE 5. Anon., *Dni smekha i zabavy* (Days of laughter and fun), *Knut* 6 (1907), 8.

Mockery of the liberal-bourgeois opposition was often conveyed by way of parodic interpretations of its parties' official names, acronyms, and popular nicknames. In common parlance the Party of Peaceful Renewal, for example, was known as "*obnovlentsy*" (renovators) or "*mirnoobnovlentsy*" (peaceful renovators), while the Kadets were referred to as "*kadety*."[35] In a piece entitled "Dialogue of Two Russian People" ("Dialog dvukh russkikh liudei"), featured in the first issue of *Knut* in 1907, the "peaceful renovators" were called, quite prosaically, "peaceful pigs" (*mirno-svin'i*), while the term "kadety" was transformed into "*kadiuki*"—an affront, the intended cheeky playfulness of which was based on the combination of two Russian words—"*gad*" (reptile, skunk) and "*gadiuki*" (vipers). The phonetic distortion was used to accommodate this right-wing satirical jab, which employed a rhyming pattern, for the words "kadiuki" and "gadiuki" rhymed exceptionally well. In this exchange the first speaker, the Bored One (*skuchaiushchii*), lamenting the dangers of the current political climate, exclaims: "I am alarmed, I lost my spirit (*ia v unyn'i*). The situation is dangerous: the reptilian Kadets (kadiuki) and the Peaceful Pigs (mirno-svin'i) have started to bark rather loudly!" His interlocutor, the Cheerful One (*veselyi*), advises him not to despair because happiness will befall them once the forces of evil are driven out of Russia. The Cheerful One also declares that he is not afraid of the Kadets, because they will soon drown in a swamp like worthless vipers: "Polno! Schast'e ulybnetsia! Ne boius' ia 'kadiuka!' On v bolote zakhlebnetsia, kak negodnaia gadiuka."[36]

This device of generating anti-liberal satire may be compared to a piece entitled "Material for a Dictionary of Contemporary Politics: Our Parties" ("Materialy dlia sovremennogo politicheskogo slovaria. Nashi partii"). It appeared around the same time in *Pliuvium*, one of the first conservative satirical publications, which often served as a source of puns and jokes for other right-wing satirical periodicals. In this mock dictionary, the acronyms of several left-wing political parties were spelled out satirically, if somewhat drolly; the Party of Peaceful Renovation, or the P. M. O. (Partiia mirnogo obnovleniia) was rendered as the Party of Almond Bran (Partiia Mindal'nykh Otrubei), while the Kadets, with its

---

35 In January 1906 the Kadets added to the original name of their party the new title of "Party of Popular Liberty" (Partiia narodnoi svobody). It was therefore often referred to by this new name in the right-wing satirical periodicals.

36 *Knut* 1 (1907), 6.

Russian acronym of P. K. D. (Partiia Konstitutsionnykh Demokratov), became the Party of the Wily Souls (Partiia Krivo-Dushnykh).[37]

Right-leaning satirical journals published in large provincial centers displayed an especially irreverent attitude towards the Kadets—something that undoubtedly reflected the intensity of political dialogue in the provinces and the rightists' anger across the country with the Kadets' prominence in the Duma. A case in point is the Kazan-based satirical journal *Kazanskii raeshnik* (Kazan barker). The pages of this rudimentary periodical are replete with satirical jibes of various types directed at the kadety, who were often depicted as reptiles, as in a drawing called *Mirnoe obnovlenie* (Peaceful renovation), in which the Kadets and the Party of Peaceful Renovation are shown in the guise of a venomous snake wrapped around a pole inscribed with the word "constitution" (fig. 6).[38] *Kazanskii raeshnik* also sought to stress deceitfulness and wiliness as the Kadets' principal political attributes. These traits are invoked in a short piece which appeared in the journal's first issue of 1907. Entitled "Ten Rules of 'Kadet' Cunning" (*Desiat' pravil 'ka-detskoi' khitrosti*), it provides such quasi-proverbial quips exposing the treacherous nature of the Kadet party as "say one thing, but think something completely different" (*govori odno, a dumai drugoe*), "do not forget your own kind" (*svoikh ne zabyvai*) and "prevaricate without limit" (*vri bez mery*).[39]

In addition to the political parties and leading personalities of the left, the taxonomy of right-wing targets for satirical castigation and othering was extended to include some of the liberally minded ministers of the imperial government. The State Councilor Vladimir Gurko recalled that the right-wing satirical periodicals criticized and caricatured the government, but in a manner that "was quite different from that of the scurrilous revolutionary organs: they criticized it for its spinelessness and lack of courage."[40] Perhaps like no other government official, Premier Witte was subjected to a constant barrage of both

---

37 See *Pliuvium* 17 (January 27, 1907), 4. This method of satirical ridicule appears to have been first used by the left-wing satirical journals. In its first issue in 1906 the satirical weekly *Leshii* (Wood Goblin), for example, published a segment that perhaps served as the model for the piece printed in *Pliuvium* a year later. Titled "Our Parties" (*Nashi partii*), it provided a list of conservative party acronyms interpreted in a satirical vein: the P. P. P., or the right-wing Party of Legal Order (Partiia pravovogo poriadka), was dubbed the Party of Complete Failure (Partiia polnogo provala). Standing for the monarchist Union of Russian Men (Soiuz russkikh liudei), the acronym S. R. L. was not even spelled out, because, as the journal explained, the Union's actual name was too obscene to be deciphered. See *Leshii* 1 (1906), 6.

38 See *Kazanskii raeshnik* 1 (January 1907), 16.

39 Ibid., 3.

40 Gurko, *Features and Figures of the Past: Government and Opinion in the Reign of Nicholas II*, 435.

Figure 6. Anon., *Mirnoe obnovlenie* (Peaceful renovation), *Kazanskii raeshnik* (January 1, 1907), 16.

left- and right-wing satirical ridicule, and not necessarily for his spinelessness and lack of courage. Gurko further notes in his recollections that in suffering patiently the insults of the revolutionary critics, Witte "could not reconcile himself to the criticism of the right. He often requested Durnovo to take steps to silence the satirists of the right; but Durnovo invariably turned a deaf ear, although he himself was frequently the butt of the caricatures and knew who their authors were."[41]

The liberals were dissatisfied with the limited and often contradictory character of Witte's political reforms. This dissatisfaction invariably found its satirical expression in pictorial and verbal mockery of the premier in the left-wing satirical press.[42] For their own reasons, Russia's monarchists and conservatives also nurtured a particularly potent dislike of Witte, so much so that a variant of the premier's last name was incorporated into the title of one of the right-wing humorous newspapers: *Vittova Pliaska* (Witte's Dance, 1905).[43] Satirical invective directed at the maverick premier in the cartoons and texts of right-wing satirical periodicals, especially those published in Moscow, was informed by the political charges brought against Witte. In a letter to his successor, Stolypin, in May 1910, Witte points out that it is sufficient to peruse "any 'truly right-wing' newspaper" in order to understand what fueled the rightists' hatred and desire to eliminate him.[44] In summarizing his impressions from the right-

---

41 Ibid., 435. Petr Nikolaevich Durnovo was minister of the interior.

42 For more on this, see Oleg Minin, *Art and Politics in the Russian Satirical Press: 1905–1908* (PhD diss., University of Southern California, 2008), 64–68. A compendium of left–wing visual and verbal jokes about Witte and other government ministers may be found in Botsianovskii and Gollerbakh, *Russkaia satira pervoi revoliutsii 1905–1906*, 114–30. For a recent collection of the period caricatures satirizing Witte, see Ella Saginadze, "*GLAVA PRAvitteL'STVA': Pervyi prem'er–ministr Rossiiskoi imperii Sergei Iul'evich Vitte v satiricheskoi grafike 1905–1908 godov: Al'bom–katalog karikatur*, ed. A.A. Rossomakhin (St. Petersburg: Evropeiskii universitet v Sankt–Peterburge, 2020).

43 *Vittova Pliaska* is a paraphrase of *Pliaska sviatogo Vita*—a Russian equivalent of the Latin name for the disorder "St Vitus's Dance" (*Chorea sancti viti*). The Russian name for the disorder is an almost exact phonetic equivalent of Sergei Witte's last name. In drawing on this similarity, the title of the newspaper was therefore designed to be a subtle pun insinuating that Russia had been struck with Witte–inspired constitutional reforms, which arrested its development just as the disorder of "St Vitus's Dance" would impede the movement of an afflicted person. Following its closure (after the seventh issue), *Vittova Pliaska* was revived in 1906 under the new title of *Russkaia Vittova Pliaska* (Russian Witte's Dance). It was ultimately replaced by *Pliuvium*, which bore the subtitle "*Zakonnoe Ditia Vittovoi Pliaski*" (A Legitimate Child of Witte's Dance) and which in turn served as a satirical prototype for the Moscow-published *Knut* and *Zhgut*.

44 See Sergei Witte, "Letter to P.A. Stolypin, the Chairman of the Council of Ministers, 3 May 1910," in A. Chernovskii, ed., *Soiuz russkogo naroda. Po materialam Chrezvychainoi sledstvennoi komissii Vremennogo Pravitel'stva 1917* (Moscow: Gosudarstvennoe izdatel'stvo, 1929), 128. In

wing press, Witte surmises that he is charged with being the chief conspirator betraying the tsar and the fatherland, as well as the architect of the constitution hated by all "true Russian people and patriots."[45] As H. D. Löwe points out, the latter charge was based on the conservatives' suspicion that the constitution was yet "one more indication that Witte actually was the great 'usurper,' hankering after the position of a Russian republic's first president."[46] Be that as it may, the monarchist press also alleged that Witte was a minister who achieved his high rank through the assistance of the Jews. He was also to blame for unleashing the entire liberal movement. Moreover, the monarchists were unhappy with Witte's insistence on pushing the reforms forward at the expense of restoring order and pacifying the country first. His philo-Semitic tendencies and the irretrievable loss of half of Sakhalin Island to Japan in the negotiated end to the Russo-Japanese War presented additional grounds for dislike and criticism. Indeed, a brief perusal of *Pliuvium* or *Glas naroda* strongly confirms Witte's assessment. In one of its issues, *Glas naroda* published a telegram appeal to the tsar composed by the council of the Kharkov Chapter of the Union of the Russian People. The appeal opened with a pathos-laden observation that the feelings of the Russian people had been hurt by Witte's return to Russia (from Portsmouth, where he had negotiated the treaty). Public opinion, the telegram continued, pointed to Witte as the principal perpetrator of all the horrid troubles that had befallen the Russian nation. To safeguard his faithful subjects from new troubles and unrest, the members of the council of the Union therefore beseeched the sovereign to stop the tormenter of the motherland and the servant of the Jews delivering new insults to the Russian people by his very presence in Russia and his future attempts to grant civil rights to Russia's Jews.[47] The right-wing satirical journals followed an analogous pattern in their treatment of Witte, ridiculing the premier for much the same reasons as did the Black Hundreds newspapers. Especially prolific in its mockery of the reform minister was Olovenikova's *Knut*. An anti-Witte diatribe not dissimilar to the one featured in *Glas naroda*, albeit reworked in a satirical vein and infused with a thick layer of irony, was featured in the first

---

his letter, Witte refers to a failed assassination attempt which took place on January 29, 1907, and which he claims was perpetrated by the Union of the Russian People, its leader, Alexander Dubrovin, his shady agents, and some high-ranking civil servants. Witte also describes this incident in his memoirs. See chapter 67 ('Attempt on My Life') in Vitte, *Vospominaniia*, 3:393–418.

45 See Witte, "Letter to P.A. Stolypin, the Chairman of the Council of Ministers, 3 May 1910," 128.

46 Löwe, *The Tsars and the Jews: Reform, Reaction and Anti-Semitism in Imperial Russia, 1772–1917*, 199.

47 *Glas naroda* 1 (November 26, 1906), 1.

issue of the journal in 1906. Composed by an anonymous writer hiding behind the pseudonym "Lord Khi," a piece entitled "Amusing St. Petersburg Feuilleton" (*Veselyi peterburgskii fel'eton*) reported that the Kiev branch of the Union of the Russian People was putting together a deputation to present Count V. Itte (sic) with an honorary gift for the special services he had rendered to the motherland."[48] Consisting of an artistically woven red silk noose, this "token of gratitude" was placed in a beautiful casket decorated with precious stones from Sakhalin Island.[49]

Witte's resignation as prime minister in April 1906 had little effect on the steady flow of *Knut* satires directed at him. As rich in the satirical treatment of Witte as were its past issues from the previous year, the first issue of the journal for 1908 featured several caricatures of the former premier, including a large centerfold storyboard-style cartoon entitled *Chudesnye prevrashcheniia* (Magic transformations). Masterminded by another anonymous artist called "*Pero*" (Feather),[50] and reminiscent of the tongue-in-cheek praise of Witte's conjuring skills coined by the liberal satirical weekly *Zritel'* (Spectator) (fig. 7), the *Knut* cartoon depicts a series of magical tricks that Witte performs using his bowler hat (fig. 8). Thematically, this sequence relies almost exclusively on the usual right-wing castigations of Witte for ceding half of Sakhalin Island to the Japanese, and for unleashing unrest and revolution in the country through the constitutional reforms. Harkening back to Witte's tenure as Russia's minister of finance (1893–1903), the bottom sequence, however, broadens the critical

---

48 This manner of spelling Witte's name was likely to have been devised to evoke its phonetic similarity with a Japanese-sounding name, in which case the pun acquired a political color suggestive of Witte's treachery and favoring of the Japanese during the Portsmouth Peace Treaty negotiations.

49 *Knut* 1 (1906), 4.

50 The great majority of the visual and verbal segments of the right-wing satirical journals were anonymous. They were either not signed at all or identified merely by obscure pseudonyms such as those found in *Knut* and *Zhgut* ('Ivan,' 'Stepan Chernyi,' 'Lord Khi,' 'Chernyi Voron,' 'Liutik,' 'Diadiushka Vlas,' 'Maksim Sladkii' and 'Emil' Zheltyi'). Apart from Ivan Klang, the publisher of *Zhgut*, it was hitherto possible to identify only one more artist, who worked under the penname "*Zlo*" (Evil). This was the aforementioned Luka Timofeevich Zlotnikov, who at one point was nominated to the Main Chamber of Vladimir Purishkevich's Russian People's Union of the Archangel Michael. In his artistic capacity, Zlotnikov collaborated with and contributed to a variety of monarchist periodicals, including *Russkoe znamia* (Russian Banner), *Zemshchina* (Local Self-Government), and the satirical *Pliuvium* and *Knut* (see his illustration for the back cover of *Knut* 12 [1907]). In March 1917, Zlotnikov surrendered to the revolutionary authorities, but was released several days later. According to A.S. Stepanov, Zlotnikov, along with a group of other staff members of *Russkoe znamia*, was executed by the Bolshevik government in Petrograd in June 1919. See P. S. Chkhartishvili, "Chernosotentsy v 1917 godu," *Voprosy istorii* 8 (1997): 134; Stepanov, *Chernaia sotnia: Vzgliad cherez stoletie*, 94.

FIGURE 7. Sergei Chekhonin (attributed), *Witte, the magician, sitting on an urn of incense to express his complete disposition and most sincere goodness toward someone, holds someone's sorrowful heart burning with a crimson flame. The indecent gestures [kukishi], in all likelihood, belong to anarchists who do not spare their wives and children, Zritel' 20 (1905), 3.*

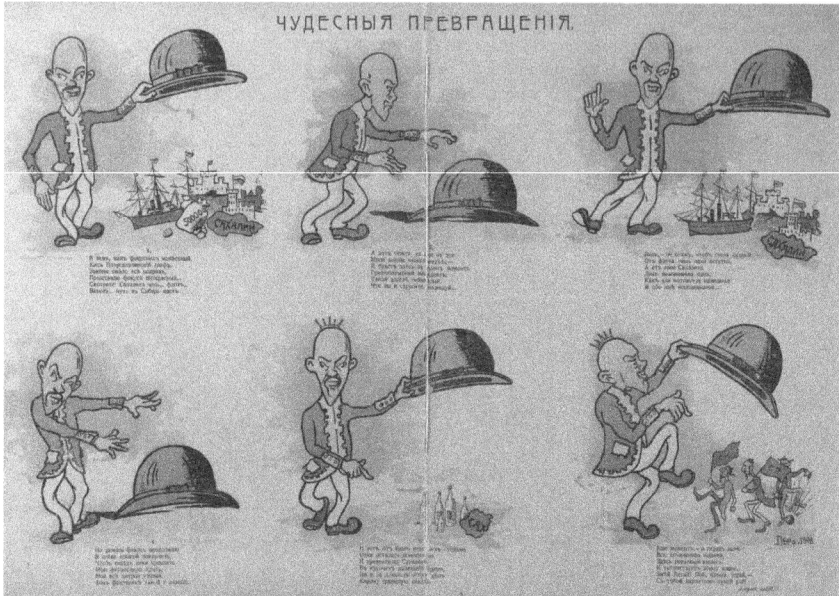

FIGURE 8. "Pero" (pseudonym), *Chudesnye prevrashcheniia* (Magic transformations), *Knut* 1 (1908), 4–5.

framework hitherto used to satirize the minister by blending the issue of the blame for the loss of Russian territory with that of Witte's economic innovations. Not unlike Boris Timofeev's "A Fairy-Tale about Cunning Sergei" (*Skazka o khitrom Sergee*), published in the leftist satirical weekly *Zhupel* (Bugbear), the *Knut* cartoon refers to the scheme of generating state revenues through a government monopoly on the distribution of alcohol, of which Witte was the chief architect.[51] Accordingly, the sequence shows Witte conjuring up from under his bowler hat a set of bottles positioned next to the remaining half of Sakhalin Island. The caption to this segment of the cartoon is a rhymed verse which reads: "Of all the good things of bygone days, only the state monopoly on vodka remains. And Sakhalin's become a tiny piece. Yet I received the count's crown for my wily tricks in doing this."[52]

Satirical castigations of Witte as the hated reformer, the treacherous diplomat and the mastermind of Russia's vodka monopoly also acquired a strongly anti-Semitic flavor as Russian monarchist dogma embraced the longstanding stereotype, to use Ben-Sasson's phrase, "of Jewish guilt for the drunkenness of

---

51 For more on this, see Patricia Herlihy, *The Alcoholic Empire: Vodka and Politics in Late Imperial Russia* (Oxford: Oxford University Press, 2002), 6.

52 *Knut* 1 (1908), 4–5.

the peasants."[53] Several such cartoons and texts appeared in *Zhgut* and *Kazanskii raeshnik*. For example, the first issue of *Zhgut* in 1907 featured a centerfold drawing with the ironic title of *Bogatyr'* (Epic Hero). It portrayed Witte, sporting his buffoonish crown, traversing the vast expanses of the Russian empire atop an old and raggedy nag and distributing shots of vodka to the already excessively intoxicated populace (fig. 9). A year later, a similar caricature was printed in the first issue of the provincial *Kazanskii raeshnik* in 1908. Echoing the *Chudesnye prevrashcheniia* sequence of *Knut* and unequivocally resembling the *Bogatyr'* picture in *Zhgut*, this cartoon shows Witte riding a horse and pulling from under his hat, as if by magic, a crown made of bottles of alcohol, which is not dissimilar to the one he himself is wearing (fig. 10).

The title *Bogatyr'* (Epic Hero) and the similarities in these cartoons' core ideas (for example, Witte either offering drinks or magically producing bottles of alcohol), the detail pertinent to the minister's attire (shabby and worn-out clothes), and Witte's designated mode of transport (an old nag) reveal that the two drawings were, in fact, illustrations of the texts they accompanied. In both cases, these were variously adapted versions of Count Aleksey Tolstoy's ballad

БОГАТЫРЬ.

FIGURE 9. Ivan Klang (attributed), *Bogatyr'* (Epic Hero), *Zhgut* 1 (1907), 4–5.

53 H. H. Ben-Sasson, "Wine and Liquor," in *Economic History of the Jews*, ed. Nachum Gross (New York: Schocken Books, 1975), 137.

FIGURE 10. Anon., *Slavny bubny za granitsei v bytnost' ikh v Rossii* (Celebrated aces abroad when they were in Russia), *Kazanskii raeshnik* 1 (1908), 9.

"Epic Hero" (*Bogatyr'*), which opens with a description of a strongman riding an overworked mare "back and forth and all around" the Russian tsardom.[54] Clad in torn garb and with a bottle of cheap vodka in his coat, he summons the young and old to come and try his wares, thus getting them addicted to the evil habit of drinking.

At the time of its original publication in 1867, Tolstoy's ballad was concerned with the perennial nineteenth-century Russian social problems of drunkenness and hunger in the countryside. In the ballad and in his correspondence, Tolstoy insinuated that these shortcomings resulted from the ill-balanced government emancipation policy. Tolstoy's indignation was especially directed at the government for generating revenues through the sale of alcohol and at the Russian people for their proclivity for drink rather than work.[55] Moreover, Tolstoy appeared to have disagreed with the system of *otkup* (private entrepreneurs "buying out" from the state the rights to sell alcohol) put into effect and refined through numerous mid-nineteenth-century reforms of the government monopoly on the distribution of alcohol. During his tenure as Russia's minister of finance, Witte took this revenue-generating system to a new level of efficiency.

However, in *Zhgut* Tolstoy's ballad was reproduced in a much-abridged version, reduced to a meagre eight stanzas from the original thirty-five.[56] Retaining enough of the original text to equate Tolstoy's strongman with the caricatured depictions of Witte, the editors of *Zhgut* reproduced only those passages of the ballad which contained racial slurs against the Jews as purveyors of spirits. Similarly, the editor of *Kazanskii raeshnik*, Prokofiev, chose to borrow selectively from Tolstoy's ballad so that in its final and much distorted version it would come across as a charge leveled against the Jews, who appeared to the reader to be the sole source of the evil drinking habit that besieged Russia. In both cases, the center of critical gravity moved from Tolstoy's focus on the alcohol problem and his criticism of the government, to Klang, and Prokofiev's focus on the stereotypical blaming of the Jews for the intoxication of the Russians.[57]

---

54 A. K. Tolstoi, *Sobranie sochinenii v chetyrekh tomakh* (Moscow: Biblioteka 'Ogonek', izdatel'stvo 'Pravda', 1969), 1:229.

55 A. K. Tolstoi, "B. M. Markevichu," in *Sobranie sochinenii* (Moscow: Khudozhestvennaia literatura, 1964), 4: 257–60.

56 *Zhgut* featured stanzas three, eight, twenty-nine, thirty, thirty-three, thirty-four, and thirty-five. Stanzas one, two, four, five, six, seven, nine to twenty-eight, and thirty-one were omitted. See *Zhgut* 1 (1907), 5–6.

57 For an overview of other examples of this phenomenon, see Ben-Sasson, "Wine and Liquor," 136–37. Anti-Semitic prejudice appears to be a clear line of convergence between Tolstoy's work and right-wing dogma—a factor that probably played a role in the choice of Tolstoy in

Constructing the Monarchist Self

The negative image of the multifaceted monarchist other, be it a bomb-throwing Socialist Revolutionary anarchist, a Constitutional Democrat, or a liberal minister in the imperial government, was counterbalanced in the right-wing satirical journals by the positive image of the self. Typically, and perhaps predictably, the right sought to represent itself through the pathos-laden figure of the positive patriotic hero. The graphic portrayal of the positive heroic self noticeably differed from that of the monarchist other. Caricatures and animal allegories rich in distortions and exaggerations were reserved for depicting the monarchist foe, while a less satirically oriented style of illustration-like renderings was employed to depict the positive personages representing the patriotic self.

The primary function of the patriotic hero was to combat sedition (kramola) and defend autocratic and Orthodox Russia from the omnipresent forces of subversion. One of the recurring means of verbal and pictorial portrayal of the patriotic defender, characteristic of the discourses of both central and peripheral right-wing satirical journals, was through the invocation of the historical and folk heroes of the past. Echoing in this instance the nationalist overtones in Viktor Vasnetsov's and Mikhail Vrubel's painterly depictions of the mythological epic heroes (bogatyri)[58] and the nationalism of turn-of-the-century sporting societies with the telling names "Russian Epic Hero" (*Russkii bogatyr'*) and "Russian Falcon" (*Russkii sokol*),[59] the right-wing satirical journals

---

particular by the editors and contributors of the right-wing satirical journals. Although the artistic integrity of Tolstoy's texts was significantly compromised, the xenophobic strain that was accentuated by such selective borrowing was still inherently present in them.

58 See, for example, Vasnetsov's canvas *Epic Heroes* (*Bogatyri*, 1898) and Vrubel's enigmatic *Epic Hero* (*Bogatyr'*, 1898).

59 The publication of right-wing satirical journals between 1906 and 1908 coincided with the establishment across the Russian Empire of the "falcon" (*sokol'skie*) sporting societies. During and after the 1905 Revolution many such societies leaned to the right, also adopting the motto "Orthodoxy, Autocracy, Nationality" as their guiding principle. Founded in the autumn of 1905, the St. Petersburg "falcon" sporting society "Gyrfalcon" (*Krechet*) indicated in its policy that it could be joined only by Russian citizens of the Orthodox faith, of all estates and incomes, who recognized "Orthodoxy, Autocracy, and Nationality" as the political foundation of the Russian state. At the same time, persons of Jewish faith or origin were precluded from becoming members of this society. In Moscow, the "First Russian Gymnastic Society" (renamed 'Falcon I' [*Sokol I*] in 1907) was chaired by the well-known Russian nationalist I. I. Kasatkin. Under his direction, the society was transformed into a powerful Black Hundreds organization of "truly Russian people." See T. Andreeva and M. Guseva, *Sport nashikh dedov. Stranitsy istorii rossiiskogo sporta v fotografiiakh kontsa XIX–nachala XX veka* (St. Petersburg: Liki Rossii, 2002), 40. Among the main prerogatives of the patriotic gymnastic society "Russian Epic Hero" (*Russkii bogatyr'*), which was founded in Kiev in June 1911 by a group of local nationalists, was the fostering of the physical and moral development of its members,

resorted to the heroic imagery of the epic warriors (bogatyri) from Russian folklore, Ilia of Murom and Potok. Frequent use was also made of the legend of the celebrated Grand Prince Vladimir—the original conduit of Byzantine Orthodox Christianity to Kievan Rus'.

Although the roots of the national hero rhetoric are traced to the *Primary Chronicle* and the Russian *byliny* epos, one of the most immediate sources available to the contributors and editors of turn-of-the-century right-wing satirical journals was again the stylized narratives of Count Aleksei Tolstoy. Especially popular were Tolstoy's ballads, written during the late 1860s and early 1870s, which featured Prince Vladimir, Ilia of Murom, Dobrynia Nikitich and Potok as their main protagonists.[60] *Knut* made use of Tolstoy's 1867 nationalist ballad "The Serpent Tugarin" ("Zmei Tugarin") and his short 1871 poem "Ilia of Murom" ("Il'ia Muromets"). To construct a positive image of the self, *Zhgut* also used Tolstoy's 1871 ballad "The Epic Hero Potok" ("Potok Bogatyr'"), presenting what amounted to an eccentric continuation of the original narrative.

Tolstoy's ballads and poems provided the editors of right-wing satirical journals with a convenient critical framework that allowed them both to accommodate the mockery of the ideological opponents of autocracy and to provide a commentary on the incongruities of life from the perspective of the monarchist *Weltanschauung*. At the same time, equating the heroic defender with the self, helped the journals to affirm the moral superiority of monarchism over the destabilizing effects of revolution. A device for attaining the latter objective was, first, to appropriate Tolstoy's noble and predominantly victorious protagonists and equate them either graphically or verbally (or through the confluence of both) with the monarchist movement in general or with a specific right-wing organization, and even personality. A simple editorial adjustment to the definition of the positive heroes' evil opponents (for example, through the substitution of a serpent in Tolstoy's narrative for that of a contemporary other, that is, the revolutionary) would result in the representation of the monarchists

---

as well as the development and strengthening of their patriotic sensibility. For more on the "Russian Epic Hero" see I. V. Omel'ianchuk, *Chernosotennoe dvizhenie na territorii Ukrainy (1904–1914 gg.)* (Kiev: Natsional'nyi institut ukrainsko-rossiiskikh otnoshenii, 2000), 50.

60 Relying heavily in his work on folklore and ancient Russian history and, in particular, on the legend of Prince Vladimir, Tolstoy was also the writer responsible for expanding the popular pantheon of the *byliny* and epic heroes of the past by placing the relatively little-known *bogatyr'* Potok among the household names of Ilia of Murom and Dobrynia Nikitich. In the Russian *byliny* epos, Tolstoy's Potok is known as Mikhailo Potyk. See I. M. Sokolov and V. Chicherova, eds., *Onezhskie byliny* (Moscow: Izdanie gosudarstvennogo literaturnogo muzeia, 1948), 134–47.

as victors over the forces of subversion.[61] This device is seen to operate, for example, in a full-page color illustration in the seventh issue of *Knut* in 1907. The cartoon shows the legendary Prince Vladimir confronting an enormous green dragon of many heads (fig. 11). The elderly, yet agile, prince is depicted clad in metal armor and holding an Excalibur-like sword with the words "the Union of the Russian People" inscribed on its blade.[62] Identified with the word kramola and symbolizing sedition, the dragon's largest head, adorned with massive spiky ears, is that of Premier Witte. The creature's numerous other heads, attached to Medusa-like snaking locks, represent a concatenation of the rightists' traditional others—progressive politicians, Jews, Kadets, and so on. Suggestive of the Greek myth of Perseus and the decapitation of the Gorgon, the pictorial rendering of the confrontation between the positive monarchist hero, Prince Vladimir, and the liberal-revolutionary opposition represented by the evil dragon, is accompanied in *Knut* by the nineteenth stanza from Tolstoy's ballad "The Serpent Tugarin." In the original narrative, Tolstoy depicted the legendary prince, surrounded by the boyars and the *byliny* heroes Ilia of Murom and Dobrynia Nikitich, feasting on the bank of the Dnieper River in the vicinity of Kiev. During the festivities, the entire party witnesses an old singer come forward to entertain the prince and his retinue. Instead of amusing the host and his guests, the singer delivers a threatening message concerning the troubled future of Russia, at which point he is confronted by the valiant Ilia and Dobrynia. Moreover, Dobrynia recognizes the old and ugly serpent Tugarin disguised as the singer and threatens to pierce him with his arrow. Magically transformed into a serpent, the singer flees the scene by way of the Dnieper. The stanza that follows the description of the serpent's hasty retreat in the concluding part of the ballad's original text was reproduced as a verbal commentary to Vladimir's encounter with the dragon in the *Knut* cartoon. Repulsed at the sight and smell of the wicked reptile, the prince rejoices at Dobrynia's heroic efforts to drive it away: "'What a vile creature!' says Vladimir, plugging his nose so as not to smell the awful stench; he spoke of all sorts of despicable things in his song,

---

61 Common in the right-wing satirical press of 1905, the device of substituting a traditional adversary with a more contemporary foe, as Hubertus F. Jahn has pointed out, was also used on a number of occasions in Russian patriotic war *lubki* produced at the outbreak of the Great War. See Hubertus F. Jahn, *Patriotic Culture in Russia during World War I* (Ithaca: Cornell University Press, 1995), 14.

62 In this picture, the image of the historical Prince Vladimir is transposed onto another Vladimir—Vladimir Vladimirovich Olovenikov—the founder of the journal and a staunch supporter of the monarchist cause. Making the ideological affiliation of the journal more transparent, this transposition is attested to by a footnote on the page featuring the cartoon.

FigURE 11. Anon., *T'fu, gadina! molvil Vladimir* (What a vile creature, Vladimir said), *Knut* 7 (1907), 4–5.

but fortuitously, the dog ran away from Dobrynia."[63] The juxtaposition of the positive hero with the caricatured image of all that represented a political threat to the Russian throne thus suggested the Union's moral victory over the collective forces of subversion.[64]

A similar confrontation of the positive monarchist hero with kramola, which culminated in the hero's ultimate triumph, was depicted in a large, annotated centerfold drawing published in the ninth issue of *Knut* in 1907 (fig. 12). Alluding, again, to Tolstoy and his poem "Ilia of Murom," the eponymous illustration presents Ilia risen from the dead and transplanted to turn-of-the-century Russia. Still under the impression that he is in Kievan Rus', the hero sets off to report to Vladimir in Kiev.[65] Along the way, the aged epic hero sees vessels decorated

---

63 *Knut* 7 (1907), 5.

64 A curious reverse adaptation of Tolstoy's ballad "The Serpent Tugarin" by Nikolai Faleev may be found in the first 1907 issue of the St. Petersburg left-wing satirical journal *Skomorokh* (Harlequin). Disgusted with the leaders of the right-wing parties (for example, Vostorgov and Dubrovin), Faleev's serpent Tugarin laments the absence of the imprisoned and exiled fighters for liberty—Ilia, Dobrynia and Aliosha. See *Skomorokh* 1 (1907), 4.

65 In the original text of Tolstoy's poem, Ilia, feeling hurt at being mistreated by Vladimir, is seen fleeing Kiev. Beyond this point, the narrative of *Knut* develops independently from Tolstoy's text.

FIGURE 12. Anon., *Il'ia Muromets* (Ilia of Murom), *Knut* 9 (1907), 4–5.

with red flags and people who, "like some fools," are also dressed in red. "Are they some foreign diplomats, who wish to present their gifts to the prince, or are they enemies?" Ilia ponders in amazement. On enquiring who these people might be, he is told they are from abroad, and that their mission is to save Russia, to initiate it into the culture of the West, to teach its people how to build barricades and sing revolutionary songs instead of Russian ones, to topple the tsarist regime, give power to the people, and permit the poor to rob the rich. Moreover, he is informed that there is no God in the heavens above. Amazed, startled, and completely unconvinced, Ilia responds forcefully and emphatically to the seditious speeches of his interlocutor, who undauntedly retorts that a conversation with a bomb-throwing *gimnaziia* student may be more convincing for the epic hero. After a short exchange between the old and wise Ilia and a fanatical young revolutionary, a bomb explodes, a piece of which strikes Ilia in the chest. However, the valiant knight is unharmed, but the toxic gases emitted by the bomb induce him to sneeze incessantly. Leaving no stone unturned, like the bomb itself, the power of Ilia's sneezing crushes all the revolutionaries, along with their red banners and boats.[66]

To construct its image of a positive monarchist hero, Klang's *Zhgut* employed a device distinctly different from that of *Knut*. The journal brought into play elements of the patriotic rhetoric that in the recent past had been invoked to drum

---

66 See *Knut* 9 (1907), 4–5.

up nationalism and popular support for the country's war effort. A case in point is the aforementioned large centerfold plate called *Izbavitel' blizko* (The Savior is near), printed in the fourth issue of *Zhgut* in 1907 (fig. 2). In it, the monarchist others, the antithetical forces of the revolution and sedition, are confronted by an epic warrior identified as Potok by the caption "Probuzhdenie Bogatyria Potoka" ("The Awakening of the Epic Hero Potok"). Alluding in its title to Tolstoy's acclaimed ballad "The Epic Hero Potok," this rendition of the epic hero visually employs the devices of the patriotic *lubki* posters produced during the opening months of the Russo-Japanese war. A decade later similar renderings would be seen in the war lubki mass-produced on the occasion of Russia's entry into the First World War.[67] As Yulia Mikhailova explains, the lubki posters from the time of the Russo-Japanese conflict were infused with symbolism and allegory "to build up the spirit of nationalism" in the Russian nation and "evoke anti-Japanese feelings."[68] Accordingly, on such posters, Russia was often portrayed as a valiant combatant ready to confront her enemies. For example, in a lubok poster entitled *K voine Rossii s Iaponiei* (On the War of Russia with Japan), Russia is depicted as a medieval warrior maiden clad in an ermine gown and decorated with Orthodox icons (fig. 13). Composed and self-confident, with a double-headed eagle on her left shoulder and an ethereal but armed guardian angel above her head, she is ready to defend herself from the belligerent fiery dragon signifying Japan. Although the olive branch in the maiden's right hand serves to symbolize Russia's peaceful intentions,[69] this image is noteworthy for the maiden's portrayal as a model Orthodox defender of the country who is ready to use her sword, for the moment resting peacefully on her left hip, when required.[70]

The *Zhgut* epic hero Potok is strikingly similar to the allegorical figure of Russia's Orthodox defender in this patriotic war poster, created to inspire loyalty and a sense of self-righteous verity. Decorated with an iconostasis, Potok of *Zhgut* sports chainmail armor identical to that of the warrior maiden of *On the War of Russia with Japan*. At the same time, like Prince Vladimir in the *Knut* cartoon, he wields an enormous sword with the words "power" and "law" inscribed on its blade. The warrior is accompanied by a double-headed eagle resting on his outstretched *right* hand. Fearless and self-confident, both

---

67 For more on these, see Jahn, *Patriotic Culture in Russia during World War I*, 11–29.
68 See Yulia Mikhailova, "Images of Enemy and Self: Russian 'Popular Prints' of the Russo-Japanese War," *Acta Slavica Iaponica* 16 (1998): 30–53.
69 Ibid.
70 In his seminal study of the Russian World War I *lubki* posters, Hubertus F. Jahn discusses a variety of important roles the depiction of Russia as a woman played in allegorical patriotic imagery, and the function of religious references it contained. See Jahn, *Patriotic Culture in Russia during World War I*, 24–28.

FIGURE 13. Anon., *K voine Rossii s Iaponiei* (On the war of Russia with Japan),
Popular war Lubok poster, ca. 1904.

are ready to defend autocratic Russia against its Constitutional Democratic, anarchist, Socialist Revolutionary, and bureaucratic adversaries, represented by a flock of black crows. Encircled by the forces of sedition, Russia herself is depicted as a defenseless young maiden who has fallen prey to her enemies.[71]

As this and other illustrations demonstrate, the national defender rhetoric of the right-wing satirical journals placed an especially strong emphasis on the masculinity of the positive hero, connecting it even more with the heroic male protagonists of Tolstoy's ballads. At the same time, the image of the perceived national adversary was again reinvented to correspond to the contemporaneous realities of the day; like the Japanese (and later, the Germans), the external enemies, although not disappearing completely, are by and large replaced or combined with the internal political and ideological opponents of the Russian right. Nor does the feminine imagery completely vanish, and such concepts as "Russia," "Duma," and "Constitution," perhaps due to the grammatical femininity of these words, continue to be allegorically portrayed as women in *Zhgut*, *Knut*, and other right-wing satirical journals.

To strengthen the impact of the visual image with a verbal caption and construct a specific ideological message, the editor of *Zhgut* (Ivan Klang) used Tolstoy's ballad "The Epic Hero Potok." However, instead of borrowing lines from the original text, he supplied a creative supplement to Tolstoy's narrative, in which the mid-nineteenth-century hero is transplanted to the Russia of the early twentieth century. Tolstoy's ballad thus becomes Klang's framework for commenting on the political issues of his day. It may be recalled that in the original text of the ballad the narrative ends when Potok, having traveled through time and witnessed the many incongruities of life in Russia (monarchical despotism, corruption in the courts, the "native soil" [*pochva*], communes and progress), decides to go back to sleep, hoping to wake during a more fortunate

---

71 *Zhgut* 4 (1907), 4–5. In 1914, in addition to the patriotic war *lubki*, in which Russia was depicted as a hallowed warrior maiden, the *Zhgut* rendition of Russia's defender as an Orthodox epic knight would inform the imagery of mass-produced postcards. Entitled *Velikaia voina* (The Great War) and designed by the period's popular illustrator, Elena Samokish-Sudkovskaia, this postcard depicts a male epic knight clad in medieval warrior gear, holding, like Potok of *Zhgut*, an enormous fairy tale-like sword and an elaborately decorated shield with the words *russkii bogatyr'* engraved on its front. A radiant cross, symbolizing Orthodoxy and imbuing the image with a degree of religious sanctity, is illuminated on the left of the warrior's chest. The caption to the image, an abridged quotation from the Imperial Manifesto of July 26, 1914 announcing the beginning of war between Russia and Austria-Hungary, reads: "Let all of Russia rise with iron in Her hands [and] a cross in Her heart." The complete citation from the manifesto has the following wording: "May Our Almighty Lord bless Our weapons and those of Our allies, and may all of Russia rise to the military undertaking (*ratnyi podvig*) with iron in Her hand [and] a cross in Her heart." See "Vysochaishii manifest ot 26 iulia 1914 g. ob ob'avlenii sostoianiia voiny Rossii s Germaniei," Lenta.ru, https://lenta.ru/news/2014/08/02/news01.

period in Russian history. Instead of the two hundred years of peaceful slumber projected for the hero by the author, in *Zhgut* Potok wakes only several decades later, in 1907. The epic hero can hardly believe that he is in Russia as he sees a country surrounded by predators (*khishchniki*). Appealing emphatically to God to spare his homeland from the proliferation of "foolish" political parties—"*ot duratskikh nas partii Gospod' upasi!*"—Potok lets the "mighty bird" (the double-headed eagle) fly from his hand to disperse the "dark cloud" of its adversaries. The narrative concludes with Potok's positive affirmation of the self—the might of monarchist Russia and the moral strength of the Russian people, who are ascribed by the scriptures to acknowledge and respect both the tsar and God.[72]

Conclusion

The Russian right-wing satirical press, like its ubiquitous left-wing counterpart, originated within the novel and necessarily divisive politics of 1905 Russia, characterized, on the one hand, by the nascent institutionalization of liberalism

---

72 Creative appropriations of Tolstoy's "The Epic Hero Potok" were popular in right-wing satirical journals, although they were not always used to construct a positive image of a national defender. For example, a year before *Zhgut* featured its cartoon *Awakening of the Epic Hero Potok*, the provincial satirical leaflet *Skvorets* (Starling) also provided a similar reference to Tolstoy's ballad. Composed by N. Zhelezniak, a regular contributor to the journal, and designed to comment on contemporary Russian political and social problems, this topical feuilleton was as critical of the government and the military as it was of the antithetical forces of the revolution. Awakening in Zhelezniak's narrative from his magical reverie only thirty-five years later, in 1906, Potok finds Russia a very different country and is startled by the changes: he hears that the press is censored, that the Russian peasant is often sick and hungry, that Russia is overtaken by ignorance, and that the regime has outlived itself. Concurring with the truthful nature of these statements, Potok surmises that these are all words, and that deeds are required. Accordingly, he unsheathes his sword and heads to the Far East to fight the Japanese. Once there, he observes a succession of Russian *voievodas* losing decisive land and sea battles and expresses the hope that the Russian people will take these criminal generals to task. When this does not happen, Potok flees to the Urals, where he witnesses a revolution. The Imperial Manifesto had granted the population various liberties and the tsar-loving crowds of peasants had morphed into hordes of *esdeki* (Social Democrats), *ka-de* (Constitutional Democrats), and *bundisty* (the Bund), loudly singing the *Marseillaise*, demanding equality for all and the tsar's abdication. Potok sees people being blown to pieces by bombs and the estates of the wealthy pillaged, while evil and rebellious *kramola* is everywhere. However, he is powerless to remedy the situation and having expressed his hopes that the future will be better, falls asleep again. Replicating Tolstoy's conclusion to his original "The Epic Hero Potok," the *Skvorets* narrative concludes with an authorial coda that could have been written by a revolutionary journalist: Potok has little time to rest, for the decisive battle has already begun, and Russia's bright new day is visible on the horizon. Potok will rise again when the "sun of truth" rises, peace and goodwill take root everywhere, and everyone finds happiness in life. See *Skvorets* 15 (1906), 114–15.

and, on the other, by the reactionary galvanization of the absolutist conservative forces. The right-wing satirical journals discussed in this chapter operated against a set of well-articulated targets which, in keeping with the taxonomy of autocratic Russia's enemies defined by the turn-of-the-century ideologues of monarchism, ran the gamut from liberal politicians and government ministers to radicalized revolutionaries. Conveyed through caricature, animal allegory, racial stereotypes, irony and verbal vitriol, the satirical othering of the monarchist foe was coupled in these journals with a representation of a patriotic self, portrayed graphically as the figure of an epic warrior whose task it was to defend monarchist and Orthodox Russia from the destabilizing forces of dissent, revolution, and sedition. In constructing the image of a national defender, the right-wing satirists relied on Russia's folklore, literary tradition, Orthodox heritage, and the patriotic imagery of the past, while the critical discourse of the right-wing satirical journals generally reflected the core principles of the monarchist dogma. The national defender rhetoric of publications like *Knut* and *Zhgut*, like the journals themselves, was brought to life by the exigencies of the day—the actual need felt by the conservatives, both politically and in critical-satirical terms, to defend autocratic Russia when revolution and liberalism were gaining ground in the arena of public politics and on the street.

The politicized satirical press of the left was to a great extent a clear indication of revolutionary gains and Russia's move in the direction of establishing a viable public sphere. In the more liberal atmosphere of the immediate post October Manifesto period, left-wing satirical journals took the lead in introducing their own iconography of heroes. Anticipating the socialist realist aesthetic of the Soviet era, Nikolai Shebuev's *Pulemet* (Machine Gun) and Yuri Artsybushev's *Zritel'* were especially keen to advance an iconography of the heroes of the revolution. The famous image of an angry worker yelling the emphatic, *"Doloi!"* (Away with!), which so incensed the tsar, opened the inaugural issue of the legendary *Pulemet*[73] (fig. 14). This was followed on the front cover of the second issue of the journal by Ivan Grabovskii's even more egregious *Ego Rabochee Velichestvo Proletarii Vserossiiskii* (His Working Majesty All-Russian Proletarian), which suggested the emergence of a new kind of political hegemony—that of the working class (fig. 15). Spread over several volumes of *Pulemet*, the gallery of new revolutionary heroes was summed up by Nikolai Shestopalov in his

---

73 Shebuev recalled Tsar Nicholas's irate reaction to the issue of the journal, which featured on its front cover a picture of an indignant worker with the suggestive caption, in his *Delo ob ego rabochem velichestve proletarii vserossiiskom* (Moscow: Izdatel'stvo politkatorzhan, 1931), 37–42.

FIGURE 14. Ivan Grabovskii, *Doloi!* (Away with!), *Pulemet* 1 (1905), 1. (cover)

FIGURE 15. Ivan Grabovskii, *Ego Rabochee Velichestvo Proletarii Vserossiiskii* (His Working Majesty All-Russian Proletarian), *Pulemet* 2 (1905), 1. (cover)

Soratniki (Brothers-in-arms), which opened the fourth (December 24) issue of *Zritel'* for 1905.[74] The image showed a soldier, a peasant, a worker-propagandist and a sailor united to form a new coalition of fighters for freedom depicted against the red dawn of a new era (fig. 16).

FIGURE 16. Nikolai Shestopalov, *Soratniki* (Brothers-in-arms), *Zritel'* 24 (1905), 1. (cover)

---

74 The subsequent issues of *Pulemet* featured on their front covers similar iconic images by Grabovskii: a revolutionary sailor was introduced in *"Russkaia svovoda rodilas' na more"* (Russian freedom was born at sea), which opened the third 1905 issue of *Pulemet*; a portrait of Father Gapon, with the caption *"Za mnoi!"* (Follow me!), was published on the cover of the journal's fourth issue; a compelling figure of a female revolutionary fighter, with a red flag in one hand and a revolver in another, was placed on the cover of the fifth issue of *Pulemet*. The caption to the image, *"U barrikady—Nachalo"* (At the Barricades—The Beginning), left no doubt as to Shebuev's intention to valorize a new breed of revolutionary fighters.

Despite a compelling effort on the part of the revolutionary fighters so cogently emblematized by *Pulemet* and *Zritel'*, the imperial government had ultimately prevailed, and the political outcomes of the 1905 Revolution, often described in the critical literature as abortive, were less than definitive. This signaled the allegorical victory of the monarchist defender from *Knut* and *Zhgut*, who, armed with the rhetoric of the Orthodox patriotic self, prevailed over his projected revolutionary opponents. However, after the success of the 1917 October Revolution, which accomplished what the first revolution failed to attain, the iconography of the defeated but not forgotten heroes of 1905, the foundation of which was laid in the satirical journals of the left, would be resuscitated to define Russian and Soviet art for years to come. There would no longer be any room for the iconography of the monarchist self and its emblematic heroic defender, which perished with the Orthodox and tsarist Russia they were called to protect in 1905.

Works Cited

Printed Sources

Glas naroda (Kharkov) 1 (November 26, 1906).
Kazanskii raeshnik 1 (January 1907).
Knut 1 (1906).
Knut 1 (1907).
Knut 6 (1907).
Knut 7 (1907).
Knut 9 (1907).
Knut 12 (1907).
Knut 1 (1908).
Knut 5 (1908).
Leshii 1 (1906).
Pliuvium 17 (1907).
Skomorokh 1 (1907).
Skvorets 15 (1906).
Zhgut 1 (1907).
Zhgut 4 (1907).

Literature

Anan'ich, B. V., and R. S. Ganelin. *Sergei Iul'evich Vitte i Ego Vremia.* St. Petersburg: Dmitrii Bulanin, 1999.

Andreeva, T., and M. Guseva. *Sport nashikh dedov. Stranitsy istorii rossiiskogo sporta v fotografiiakh kontsa XIX-nachala XX veka.* St. Petersburg: Liki Rossii, 2002.

Ascher, Abraham. *The Revolution of 1905: Authority Restored.* Palo Alto: Stanford University Press, 1992.

——— *P. A. Stolypin: The Search for Stability in Late Imperial Russia.* Palo Alto: Stanford University Press, 2001.

Australian Association for Maritime History. "British Assistance to the Japanese Navy during the Russo-Japanese War of 1904–5." *The Great Circle* 2, no. 1 (April 1980): 44–54.

Ben-Sasson, H. H. "Wine and Liquor." In *Economic History of the Jews.* Edited by Nachum Gross, 132–41. New York: Schocken Books, 1975.

Botsianovskii, V. and E. Gollerbakh. *Russkaia satira pervoi revoliutsii 1905–1906.* Leningrad: Gosudarstvennoe izdatel'stvo, 1925.

Chkhartishvili, P. S. "Chernosotentsy v 1917 godu." *Voprosy istorii* 8 (1997): 133–143.

Firsov, S. L. "'Okhranitel'naia ideologiia' i Pravoslavnaia Tserkov' v Rossii, 1825–1861." In *Filosofiia i sotsial'no-politicheskie tsennosti konservatizma v obshchestvennom soznanii Rossii (Ot istokov k sovremennosti). Sbornik statei. Vypusk 1.* Edited by I. N. Solonin, 142–72. St. Petersburg: Izdatel'stvo Sankt-Peterburgskogo universiteta, 2004.

Geifman, Anna, ed. *Russia under the Last Tsar: Opposition and Subversion, 1894–1917.* Oxford: Blackwell Publishers, 1991.

———. *Thou Shalt Kill: Revolutionary Terrorism in Russia, 1894–1917.* Princeton: Princeton University Press, 1993.

Giliarovskii, V. A. *Sobranie sochinenii v chetyrekh tomakh.* Vol. 2. Moscow: Poligrafresursy, 1999.

Gringmut, V. A. *Rukovodstvo chernosotentsa–monarkhista.* Kremenchug: Izdatel'stvo SRN, 1906.

Gurko, V. I. *Features and Figures of the Past: Government and Opinion in the Reign of Nicholas II.* Edited by J. E. Wallace Sterling, Xenia Joukoff Eudin, and H. H. Fisher. Translated by Laura Matveev. Palo Alto: Stanford University Press, 1939.

Herlihy, Patricia. *The Alcoholic Empire: Vodka and Politics in Late Imperial Russia.* Oxford: Oxford University Press, 2002.

Jahn, Hubertus F. *Patriotic Culture in Russia during World War I.* Ithaca: Cornell University Press, 1995.

Kirianov, Iu. I. *Pravye partii v Rossii 1911–1917.* Moscow: Rosspen, 2001.

Laqueur, Walter. *Black Hundred: The Rise of the Extreme Right in Russia.* New York: Harper Collins Publishers, 1993.

Löwe, Heinz-Dietrich. *The Tsars and the Jews: Reform, Reaction and Anti-Semitism in Imperial Russia, 1772–1917.* Langhorne: Harwood Academic Publishers, 1993.

Marks, Steven. *How Russia Shaped the Modern World: From Art to Anti-Semitism, Ballet to Bolshevism.* Princeton: Princeton University Press, 2003.

Mikhailova, Yulia. "Images of Enemy and Self: Russian 'Popular Prints' of the Russo-Japanese War." *Acta Slavica Iaponica*, 16 (1998): 30–53.

Minin, Oleg. *Art and Politics in the Russian Satirical Press, 1905–1908.* PhD diss., University of Southern California, 2008.

Norris, Stephen M. *"Pliuvium's* Unholy Trinity: Russian Nationhood, Anti-Semitism, and the Public Sphere after 1905." *Experiment* 19 (2013): 87–116.

Omel'ianchuk, I. V. *Chernosotennoe dvizhenie na territorii Ukrainy (1904–1914 gg.)* Kiev: Natsional'nyi institut ukrainsko-rossiiskikh otnoshenii, 2000.

Pipes, Richard. *The Russian Revolution.* New York: Alfred A. Knopf Publishers, 1990.

Raskin, D. I. "Ideologiia russkogo pravogo radikalizma v kontse XIX—nachale XX v." In *Natsional'naia pravaia prezhde i teper'. Istoriko–sotsiologicheskie ocherki. Chast' 1. Rossiia i russkoe zarubezh'e.* Edited by R. S. Ganelin, 5–47. St. Petersburg: Institut sotsiologii RAN-SPb, 1992.

Rawson, Don C. *Russian Rightists and the Revolution of 1905.* Cambridge: Cambridge University Press, 1995.

Rogger, Hans. *Russia in the Age of Modernization and Revolution, 1881–1917.* London: Longman, 1983.

———. *Jewish Policies and Right-wing Politics in Imperial Russia.* Berkeley: University of California Press, 1986.

Saginadze, Ella. "Glava praVITTEl'stva": *Pervyi prem'er-minister Rossiiskoi imperii Sergei Iul'evich Vitte v satiricheskoi grafike 1905–1908 godov: Al'bom-katalog karikatur,* ed. A. A. Rossomakhin (St. Petersburg: Evropeiskii universitet v Sankt-Peterburge, 2020).

Shebuev, N. *Delo ob ego rabochem velichestve proletarii vserossiiskom*. Moscow: Izdatel'stvo politkatorzhan, 1931.

Shelokhaev, V. V., ed. *Programmy politicheskikh partii Rossii. Konets XIX–nachalo XX vv.* Moscow: Rosspen, 1995.

———. "Programma Russkoi Monarkhicheskoi Partii (1905)." In *Programmy politicheskikh partii Rossii. Konets XIX–nachalo XX vv.* Moscow: Rosspen, 1995.

———. "Programma 'Russkogo sobraniia' (1905)." In *Programmy politicheskikh partii Rossii. Konets XIX–nachalo XX vv.* Moscow: Rosspen, 1995.

———. *Politicheskie partii Rossii. Konets XIX–pervaia tret' XX veka. Dokumental'noe nasledie. Pravye partii. Dokumenty i materialy*, 2 vols. Moscow: Rosspen, 1998.

Sokolov, I. M. and V. Chicherova, eds. *Onezhskie byliny*. Moscow: Izdanie gosudarstvennogo literaturnogo muzeia, 1948.

"Stat'ia 87." In *Glava deviatava. O zakonakh. Svod osnovnykh gosudarstvennykh zakonov. Razdel pervyi. Osnovnye Gosudarstvennye Zakony*. Kazan': Tipo-Litografiia Imperatorskogo Universiteta, 1907.

Stepanov, A. D. *Chernaia sotnia. Vzgliad cherez stoletie*. St. Petersburg: Tsarskoe delo, 2000.

Stepanov, S. A. *Chernaia sotnia v Rossii (1905–1914 gg.)*. Moscow: Izdatel'stvo VZPI, A/O "Rosvuznauka," 1992.

Streicher, Lawrence H. "David Low and the Sociology of Caricature." *Comparative Studies in Society and History* 8, no 1 (October 1965): 1–23.

—— "On a Theory of Political Caricature." *Comparative Studies in Society and History* 9, no. 4 (July 1967): 427–45.

Tolstoi, A. K. "B. M. Markevichu." In *Sobranie sochinenii v chetyrekh tomakh*. Vol. 4. Moscow: Khudozhestvennaia literatura, 1964.

———. *Sobranie sochinenii v chetyrekh tomakh*, vol. 1. Moscow: Biblioteka 'Ogonek', izdatel'stvo 'Pravda', 1969.

Vitte, S. I. *Vospominaniia*. Vol. 3. Moscow: Skif Aleks, 1994.

"Vysochaishii manifest ot 26 iulia 1914 g. ob ob'avlenii sostoianiia voiny Rossii s Germaniei." Lenta.ru. August 2, 2014. https://lenta.ru/news/2014/08/02/news01.

Witte, Sergei. "Letter to P. A. Stolypin, the Chairman of the Council of Ministers, 3 May 1910." In *Soiuz russkogo naroda. Po materialam Chrezvychainoi sledstvennoi komissii Vremennogo Pravitel'stva 1917*. Edited by A. Chernovskii. Moscow: Gosudarstvennoe izdatel'stvo, 1929.

14

The Construction of the Image of the "Other" in the Discussion of the "Yellow Peril": Chinese People in Late Imperial Russia

Andrey Avdashkin

Abstract

The expansion of the borders of Russian statehood and the formation of national identity in the late nineteenth and early twentieth centuries caused the emergence of a wide range of ideas about "other" ethnic communities. During the modernization and development of the vast lands in the east, the image of the "other" was supplemented by new outlines associated with representatives of the "yellow race." In the collective consciousness of Russian society, the image of the "yellow people" found no place in the familiar confessional continuum. A racial discourse therefore came to the fore. Representations of the "yellow race" were formed in a brief historical period and had no deep mental roots. This chapter discusses the question of how and under what circumstances the image of the "other" was supplemented by out-group bias or hostility toward representatives of the "yellow race." Concerning the Ural Mountains, the author describes how the image of the Chinese gained content in areas far removed from the Russian-Chinese frontier.

Introduction

When the Russian Empire's expansion reached the Far Eastern regions in the second half of the nineteenth century, it brought along a complex set of geopolitical, economic, and political issues. This was because the Far Eastern territory remained practically cut off from the demographic center of the empire until the opening of the Trans-Siberian Railway.[1] The empire's expanded borders required the assimilation of the new territories, but the shortage of Russian labor led to a massive influx of Chinese migrants; a Chinese community in Russia began to form. Thus, late imperial society required means for socially categorizing the Chinese and establishing daily practices of interaction with them. The small population of the Russians in the Far East keenly felt its remoteness from the imperial center and its defenselessness. The presence of migrant laborers from Asian countries caused increasing concern, as the Chinese were not only perceived as competitors but also as representatives of a foreign civilization, as it were, its "vanguard." In these conditions, both central and local government feared a "Sinicization" of the region and possible loss by Russia.

Against the background of phobias and the ambivalent attitudes of the Russian ruling elite and society, there was a desire for expansion into China, at the same time accompanied by the fear of "waking the dragon." The concerted modernization and strengthening of another dangerous neighbor in that region, Japan, aroused no less worrying expectations. For the most part, this set of problems was seen in the categories of "the yellow question," "the yellow problem," "yellow labor" and "the yellow danger." The rise of mass ethnophobia and the appearance and development of symbolic "enemies" in late imperial Russia became a reaction to modernizing processes and the dismantling of traditional societal institutions. The image of the enemy or the "other" became functionally necessary. It was a necessary, effective instrument of social consolidation that resulted from the destruction of the class-based social order.[2]

Sinophobia was fed by feelings of weak control over the Far Eastern periphery, fear of the Chinese as strong competitors in entrepreneurship, the husbandry of natural resources in that vast area, and so on.[3] The historical literature has

---

1 The construction of the railway began in 1891, and the final section to Vladivostok was completed in 1916.
2 Lev Gudkov, "Ideologema 'vraga': 'Vragi' kak massovy sindrom i mekhanizm sotsial'noi integratsii," in *Obraz vraga: sbornik*, ed. Lev Gudkov (Moscow: OGI, 2005), 17, 19.
3 Lewis Siegelbaum, "Another 'Yellow Peril': Chinese Migrants in the Russian Far East and the Russian Reaction before 1917," *Modern Asian Studies* 2 (1978): 307–30; Viktor Diatlov, "Migratsiia kitaitsev i diskussiia o 'zheltoi opasnosti' v dorevoliutsionnoi Rossii," *Vestnik*

already reconstructed the traits of labor migration during the First World War[4] in sufficient detail. At the same time, publications dedicated to the perception of the Chinese in late imperial Russia are still few and primarily composed on the basis of materials from the Russian Far East.[5]

The aim of the present chapter is to study, using the example of Chinese migrants, how the image of the "other" was constructed in Russia in the early twentieth century. After all, these perceptions were formed in historically short periods and outside the usual religious continuum without deep historical roots. For instance, Russia's German community formed over several centuries because of state protectionism. Jewish communities arose during the annexation of the territories in which they lived alongside Russia in the eighteenth century. The Chinese, in contrast, constitute the first "mass" labor migration in Russian history. Reaction to their presence therefore requires detailed analysis not only of the Russo-Chinese border but also of other regions where in the early twentieth century "yellow labor" was widely used; in our case, in the Urals.

At the same time, we emphasize that in this chapter it is impossible to comprehensibly cover such a multifaceted problem as the construction of images of the Chinese in late imperial Russia. Our task is to see the main plots around which this image was created and then reproduced far from the Russo-Chinese frontier in the documentation of the Ural factories. It is important to note that the sociopolitical discourse created the most understandable image of the Chinese for the layman. However, it was multifaceted and dynamic, changing depending on the domestic political situation in the Russian Empire and the events that took place in the international arena. But all the time these

Evrazii 1 (2000): 63–89; Yin Hsu Chia, "A Tale of Two Railroads: 'Yellow Labor': Agrarian Colonization, and the Making of Russianness at the Far Eastern Frontier, 1890s–1910s," *Ab Imperio* 3 (2006): 217–53; Mikhail Khodiakov, "Zheltorossiia kontsa XIX–XX veka v geopoliticheskikh planakh russkoi voennoi elity," *Noveishaia istoriia Rossii* 4 (2018): 880–97.

4 Vladimir Datsyshen, "Kitaiskaia trudovaia migratsiia v Rossii. Maloizvestnye stranitsy istorii," *Problemy Dal'nego Vostoka* 5 (2008): 99–104; Mikhail Kamenskikh, *Kitaitsi na Srednem Urale v kontse XIX–nachale XXI v.* (St. Petersburg: Izdatel'stvo Mamatov, 2011); Olga Alexeeva, "Experiencing War: Chinese Workers in Russia During the First World War," *The Chinese Historical Review* 1 (2018): 46–66; Mikhail Khodiakov, "Rossiiskoe zakonodatel'stvo nachala XX veka ob ispol'zovanii zheltogo truda v ekonomike Dal'nego Vostoka," *Vestnik Tomskogo gosudarstvennogo universiteta: Istoriia* 60 (2019): 78–83; Zifa Khasanova, "Kitaiskie rabochie v gody Pervoi mirovoi voiny na Iuzhnom Urale," *Voprosy istorii* 2 (2019): 133–39.

5 Iana Guzei, "Kategoriia 'zheltye' v kontekste rasovogo diskursa v Rossiiskoi imperii v kontse XIX–nachale XX v.," *Izvestiia Irkutskogo gosudarstvennogo universiteta: Seriia Politologia: Religiovedenie* 2 (2013): 167–78; Viktor Diatlov, "Ekzotizatsia i 'obraz vraga': sindrom 'zheltoi opasnosti' v dorevoliutsionnoi Rossii," *Idei i idealy* 2 (2014): 23–41; Viktor Diatlov, Iana Guzei and Tat'iana Sorokina, *Kitaiskii pogrom. Blagoveshchenskaia 'Utopiia' 1900 goda v otsenke sovremennikov i potomkov* (St. Petersburg: Nestor-Istoriia, 2020).

images remained a vivid embodiment of the "other," the instrumental function of which was the formation of collective identities among the general population. An important place was given to the visual and anthropological characteristics of the Chinese. At the same time, stereotypical ideas about the abstract "Other" that existed among the population of the empire even before mass contacts with the Chinese were actively involved. These patterns were strengthened and expanded, built into a new historical context from various regional angles.

The sources for the study consist of pre-revolutionary texts in periodicals, travelers' notes, and archive documents. When selecting and analyzing sources, I was interested not in all subject lines and political platforms of discussions on the "yellow peril" but rather only in problems connected with the presence of migrant laborers from China in the Russian Empire. When we delve into the texts of the pre-revolutionary period, we see that people of the time wrote a great deal, with pleasure and skill, including about the Chinese. Ideologemes and multiple texts that revealed the image of the "other" had more influence than the authors expected, including on people's worldview. It was not even important who the enemy was: Finns, Jews, Chinese, or someone else.[6] In this context, nationalist maxims that reflected the tensions of modernization and the formation of a national identity were incorporated into the mass consciousness of late imperial society.

Various texts copiously expressed, described, and formulated Russians' experience of the Chinese and the attitudes they developed toward them. The ideological tendencies of "Russia's special mission in the East," "the yellow peril," and "the yellow question" thus entered the sociopolitical space of the Empire.[7] The elite's high humanist culture, their taste for narrative and analysis of described phenomena, received in school, and their simple ability to intelligently construct texts played an important role in the construction of a solid stratum of sociopolitical thought about the presence of the Chinese in the Empire.

6   Alla Petukhova, "'Skazhi mne, kto tvoi vrag': antifinliandskii diskurs v prostranstve obshchestvenno-politicheskoi kommunikatsii Rossiiskoi imperii kontsa XIX–nachala XX vv.," *Ab Imperio* 3 (2010): 195–227; Pål Kolstø, "Competing with Entrepreneurial Diasporians: Origins of Anti-Semitism in Nineteenth-Century Russia," *Nationalities Papers* 42, no. 4 (2014): 691–707; Diatlov, "Ekzotizatsia i 'obraz vraga': sindrom 'zheltoi opastnosti' v dorevoliutsionnoi Rossii."

7   Anton Kireev, "'Yellow Peril' and the Development of the Russian Far East in the 1850s–1900s," *Sotsial'nye i gumanitarnye nauki na Dal'nem Vostoke* 1 (2010): 182–88; Alena Eskridge-Kosmach, "Russian Press and the Ideas of Russia's 'Special Mission in the East' and 'Yellow Peril'," *Journal of Slavic Military Studies* 4 (2014): 661–75.

The Boxer Rebellion and the Russo-Japanese War of 1904–1905 substantially expanded the use of the term "yellow" in the public sphere of the Empire.[8] This term was virtually absent from the St. Petersburg and Russian Far East press until the start of the twentieth century. Of 128 texts identified by Iana Guzei dated between 1895 and 1914 containing the concept of "yellow," only four dates to before 1900.[9] It is not by chance that precisely from 1900 onward the concept of the "yellow peril" first appeared and gained wide usage in the Russian public sphere as an allegory for "the surge of the yellow race into Europe."[10]

The Ural archives allow us to trace the perception of the authorities and factory administrations of the presence of the Chinese. The archival documents pertaining to the chancellery of the governor of Perm[11] contain a great deal of information on the status of the Chinese in the Perm Guberniia. These documents show us the specific characteristics of the daily life of Chinese laborers daily life and allow us to trace how the problems of their presence in the Urals were resolved. The documents of the Ural Mining Administration[12] and of the Administrations of the Bogoslovskii,[13] Nizhnii Tagil, and Lun'evka Mining Districts[14] are useful for gathering information about hired workers categorized as "yellow," their general position, patterns of behavior, relations with the administration, and other details important for the reliable reconstruction of the image of the "other."

The files of the fond of the special plenipotentiary for protection of the Ekaterinburg and Verkhotur'e Counties[15] contain information about measures used to control the Chinese in the Urals. The documents of the plenipotentiary of the chairman of the special conference on state defense for the Ural Region[16]

---

8 Alena Eskridge-Kosmach, "The Boxer Rebellion and the Standpoint of the Russian Press," *The Journal of Slavic Military Studies* 3 (2013): 414–38; Guzei, "Kategoriia 'zheltye' v kontekste rasovogo diskursa v Rossiiskoi imperii v kontse XIX–nachale XX v."; Tat'iana Kudriavtseva, "'Kitai-tsar': kitaitsi v vospriiatii russkogo naroda v period 'bokserskogo vosstaniia' (po materialam russkoi pechati)," *Klio* 8 (2014), 82–85; Aleksandr Popov, "'Bokserskoe vosstanie' v Kitae v vospriiatii sibirskogo prostonarod'ia (po materialam tomskikh i irkutskikh gazet)," *Genesis: istoricheskie issledovaniia* 6 (2016): 1–8.

9 Guzei, "Kategoriia 'zheltye' v kontekste rasovogo diskursa v Rossiiskoi imperii v kontse XIX–nachale XX v.," 174.

10 Moritz Mikhel'son, *Russkaia mysl' i rech'. Svoe i chuzhoe. Opyt russkoi frazeologii: sbornik obraznykh slov i inoskazanii.* (St. Petersburg: Tipografiia Akademii nauk, 1902), 1:225.

11 Gosudarstvennyi arkhiv Permskogo kraiia (State Archive of the Perm Territory), f. 65 (hereafter cited as GAPK).

12 Gosudarstvennyi arkhiv Sverdlovskoi oblasti (State Archive of the Sverdlovsk Oblast), f. 24 (hereafter cited as GASO).

13 GASO, f. 45

14 GASO, f. 643

15 GASO, f. 181

16 GASO, f. 73

contain information about laborers' everyday life, living conditions, sanitary conditions, health, and other aspects of life. The fond of the Supervisor of Migrant Management[17] contains some valuable information about the transport of labor (hygiene, equipment, dispatch of the sick, and so on).

The "Yellow Peril" and the Formation of the Image of "Others"

The term "yellow peril" denotes a collection of notions, ideologemes, and prejudices spread in Europe, the United States, and elsewhere in the second half of the nineteenth and first third of the twentieth centuries. At its base is a racist notion of potential danger emanating from Japan, China, and the East in general. Wilhelm II of Germany introduced the image to the public discourse in 1895 when he presented Nicholas II with the famous painting *Völker Europas, wahrt eure heiligsten Güter* ("Peoples of Europe, guard your dearest goods").

Active recruitment of cheap labor from north-eastern China for the exploitation of the Russian Far East began in the 1870s and 1880s.[18] The census of 1897 recorded fifty-seven thousand Chinese people living in the Russian Empire, of whom forty-one thousand were in the Far East. At the same time, the real number of Chinese people was apparently somewhat higher, as the statistics did not record the considerable numbers of illegal migrants. Japanese (2,600) and Koreans (twenty-six thousand) also formed a notable group included in the category "yellow."[19]

The large numbers of the Chinese and the proximity of China to Russia led to most fears and worries about a "yellow peril" being focused on them. Imperial civil servants identified three basic categories of Chinese people: settled (merchants, traders, artisans, long-term tenants, farmers); seasonal workers; and itinerants ("predators" in the mines, hunters, ginseng gatherers, alcohol deliverers,[20] *honghuzi* [bandits], and so on).[21] Most migration from

---

17 Ob'edinennii gosudarstvennii arkhiv Cheliabinskoi oblasti (Consolidated State Archive of Cheliabinsk Oblast), *fond* I–13 (hereafter cited as OGACHO).

18 Elena Starovoitova and Denis Ianchenko, "Kolonizatsia, migratsii i porto-franko na Dal'nem vostoke Rossii v kontse XIX–nachale XX vv.," *Bylye gody* 1 (2020): 207, 211.

19 "Pervaia vseobshchaia perepis' naseleniia Rossiiskoi Imperii 1897 g. Raspredelenie naseleniia po rodnomu iazku, guberniiam i oblastiam," *Demoskop Weekly*, accessed June 20, 2022, http://www.demoscope.ru/weekly/ssp/rus_lan_97.php

20 Chinese people who illegally trafficked alcohol into Russia.

21 Elena Li, "'Zheltaia ugroza' ili 'zheltyi vopros' v trudakh amurskoi ekspeditsii 1910 g," *Oikumen* 3 (2010): 31.

China consisted of seasonal migrants. They formed the overwhelming majority in trade, services, many crafts, municipal services, construction, and the gold-mining industry. Experts evaluate the total numbers of Chinese migrants at more than a hundred thousand at certain stages.[22]

Koreans migrated to Russia with their entire families, fleeing land shortages and the oppressive Japanese administration. They were firmly motivated to remain for good. They succeeded in becoming Russian subjects, converted to Orthodoxy en masse, and aimed to educate their children and teach them Russian. The Russian powers quickly and highly appreciated the Koreans' loyalty, their ability to farm efficiently in the local conditions, and their immense industriousness. There were no more than a few thousand Japanese immigrants, but they found their niche in the local economy, taking up professions that required a modern education and higher qualifications than those held by the Chinese and the Koreans.

Chinese migrants experienced regular oppression by the local authorities and everyday xenophobia from their very arrival. For the Chinese, insults and unfounded and inflated fines were commonplace, and physical violence was regular.[23] Such incidents often failed to be investigated or censured. In the best case, informal condemnation of such abuse was possible, but on the whole institutional and everyday practices of exclusion of and discrimination against the Chinese were approved de facto.

The wide use of the term "yellow" in official documents shows that it was perceived as completely legitimate by the people of the time. However, this does not provide proof of dominant racist opinions among the ruling elite as such. The term "yellow" was, rather, used as a collective adjective without explicitly negative connotations. The use of racial terminology looked instrumental: it allowed civil servants to group migrants from different Asian countries into a single semantic category. The terminology of racial theory was ideally suited to such description. The members of at least three different ethnic groups formed a single concept, the "yellow" race, by default for many Russian authors. We may observe a lack of a clear concept of its differentiation increasingly distinctly from the second half of the nineteenth century.[24]

The body played an important role in forming the social opposition of "ours" and "other" regarding the Chinese. Physical parameters, such as skin color,

22 Aleksandr Larin, *Kitaiskie migranty v Rossii. Istoriia i sovremennost'* (Moscow: Vostochnaia kniga, 2009), 20–21.

23 John Stephan, *The Russian Far East* (Palo Alto: Stanford University Press, 1994), 74.

24 Guzei, "Kategoriia 'zheltye' v kontekste rasovogo diskursa v Rossiiskoi imperii v kontse XIX nachale XX v.," 172.

eye shape, and build, became the most important criteria for establishing the exotic nature of the Far Eastern peoples. Use of physical parameters allowed the categorization of Far Eastern Asians as a particularly yellow-faced group and confirmed their otherness regarding everything European, that is, civilized. Russian authors named shortness and physical weakness as the main anthropological traits of the "yellow" race. The failure of "yellow-faced" people to match the traditional Russian social vision of "masculinity" was one of the reasons for Russians' contemptuous attitude toward the Far Eastern peoples. The Chinese practice of wearing a skirt and pigtails confused Russians, as they distinguished men from women with difficulty.[25] One book intended for mass-market readership presented the idea that if Asians "enlisted in military service in Russia, they would be rejected for their short height."[26]

In addition to the body, religion inevitably became a marker of the boundary between "yellow" and "white" people. Religion was the most important parameter that defined the structure of the Empire's population; it was also a criterion for dividing the Russian vision of the world into East and West. Russia's place in the Christian West played a significant role in forming its feeling of moral superiority of European culture over the backward, wild East.

In tsarist Russia, being Orthodox was even more decisive for subjecthood than speaking Russian. "Yellow" peoples were seen not just as "other" or non-European but as pagans, lacking any generally accepted religious outlooks. The Asians' lack of knowledge about Christianity gave them a certain aura of complete otherness and of incomprehensible beings beyond the habitual continuum of the time. Periodicals and everyday conversations often called the Chinese *nekhristi* ("non-Christians," "unbelievers"). These notions were the basis for various prejudices about "Chinese people eating the Orthodox," Chinese people's lack of human nature, "steam" instead of a soul,[27] Chinese people's shocking, from a European perspective, violence, and others.[28]

The myth of the "yellow peril" proved widely necessary for the managerial and intellectual elites' social mobilization. The "threat from the East" gained firm purchase in the mass consciousness. Russians were not interested in all

---

25 Kudriavtseva, "'Kitai-tsar': kitaitsi v vospriiatii russkogo naroda v period 'bokserskogo vosstaniia,'" 83.

26 n.a., *O Iaponii i iapontsakh i o tom, otchego i kak nachalas' russko-iaponskaia voina: Knizhka dlia naroda* (St. Petersburg, 1904), 7.

27 Guzei, "Kategoriia 'zheltye' v kontekste rasovogo diskursa v Rossiiskoi imperii v kontse XIX–nachale XX v.," 173. Kudriavtseva, "'Kitai-tsar': kitaitsi v vospriiatii russkogo naroda v period 'bokserskogo vosstaniia,'" 83–84.

28 Leonid Slominskii, "Zheltaia opasnost,'" *Vestnik Evropy* 5 (1904): 308–21.

subject lines and political platforms of the discussions on the "yellow peril,"
but rather only problems connected with the presence of migrant laborers from
China in the Russian Empire.

Chinese Migrants and "Yellow Labor" in Tsarist Russia before the First World War

Many problems related to Chinese and Korean immigration were discussed
using the categories of "yellow labor." China's ability to fill the labor markets
with abundant cheap labor made any competition from local "white" workers
extremely difficult. The unpretentious and rather disciplined Chinese migrant
workers were quickly able to adapt to new occupations. On the other hand,
the Chinese formed communities that were closed, impenetrable, and, most
importantly, not subject to the control of the Russian authorities. Many
publications of the time clearly demonstrate the level of worry that abounded.

Contemporaries undoubtedly realized that the "yellow" labor force was
vitally important for building the economic and military infrastructure in the
newly conquered and sparsely populated Far East.[29] However, the large numbers
of "yellow" migrant laborers both created serious obstacles for populating the
region with Russians and led to its gradual Sinicization. All these views, ranging
from disdain of the Chinese to a humiliating sense of dependence on their
labor, composed a rather complex and contradictory spectrum of perception of
"yellow labor."

The first personal traits of the Chinese to be highlighted were linked to
their alleged flexibility and enterprising nature. They were characterized as
"skilled and shrewd traders."[30] The prominent social figure and Far Eastern
entrepreneur S. D. Merkulov stressed the large numbers of the Chinese and
their great ability to compete with Russian settlers. He considered the migrants'
mass repatriation of their wages a threat to the local economy.[31] The records of
frequent confrontations between Russian and Chinese workers are evidence of

---

29 Mikhail Khodiakov, "Popytki rabochei kolonizatsii vostochnykh okrain imperii v nachale XX
    v. Po dokumentam Rossiiskogo gosudarstvennogo istoricheskogo arkhiva Dal'nego Vostoka,"
    Vestnik arkhivista 4 (2019): 999.

30 Aleksandr Michi, *Puteshestvie po Amuru i Vostochnoi Sibiri* (St. Petersburg, Moscow:
    Izdatel'stvo Knigoproduktsii M. O. Vol'f, 1868).

31 Diatlov, "Migratsiia kitaitsev i diskussiia o 'zheltoi opasnosti' v dorevoliutsionnoi Rossii," 75.

a tangible social tension caused by the presence of the migrant laborers.[32] The Chinese migrants played a significant role in the illegal, large-scale extraction of natural resources in Russian territorial waters and the Ussuri taiga.[33]

Merkulov's opponents saw Chinese migration not as a spontaneous flow but as a temporary commercial resource that could be managed by economic levers without the threat of long-term Chinese settlement in the Russian Empire.[34] P. F. Unterberger, military governor of the Primorskaia Oblast (1888–1897) and governor-general of Amur (1905–1910), played a prominent role in communicating ideas of the "yellow peril" to the central government and in securing the taking of corresponding measures. He stressed that it was "more important to rid ourselves of the Koreans. The Chinese will leave by themselves."[35]

The problem of "yellow labor" was for Russian social democrats an inalienable part of the labor question. They thought that the agitated controversy about labor migration only concealed the danger to the "white" bourgeoisie and modern capitalism. They suggested that the "yellow" proletariat would soon merge with the "white" proletariat and form a united whole.[36] That provided weighty foundations for the confluence of two great xenophobias of late imperial Russia: antisemitism and Sinophobia.[37] Representatives of the right-wing camp claimed that the Jews were consciously sabotaging the struggle with the advancing "yellow peril" with the aim of destabilizing the sociopolitical situation in the country.[38] The idea of one "mortal" enemy using the power of another to achieve its own aims thus gained legitimacy.

The most important characteristic of the Chinese in the Russian pre-revolutionary tradition was their "mass nature." We understand this term to mean the perception of the Chinese exclusively as a mass group or collective, which inevitably dissolved individuality. It was no happenstance that texts referred to

32 Andrei Komov, "O kitaitsakh i koreitsakh v Priamurskom krae," *Sibirskie voprosy* 27 (1909): 18–27; Aleksandr Panov, "Bor'ba za rabochii rynok v Priamur'e," *Voprosy kolonizatsii* 11 (1912): 241–82.

33 Andrei Ivanov, "Inostrannoe khishchnichestvo i okhrana promyslovykh resursov na Dal'nem Vostoke Rossii (konets XIX–nachalo XX v.)," *Nauchnyi dialog* 2 (2019): 221–36.

34 Maksim Kovalevskii, "Porto-franko vo Vladivostoke," *Vestnik Evropy* 255 (1909): 423–37; Aleksandr Panov, "Zheltyi vopros v Priamur'e," *Voprosy kolonizatsii* 7 (1910), 53–116.

35 Vladimir Grave, *Kitaitsy, koreitsy i iapontsy v Priamur'e. Trudy Amurskoi ekspeditsii. Issue XI* (St. Petersburg: Tipografiia V. F. Kirshbauma, 1912), 136.

36 Diatlov, "Migratsia kitaitsev i diskussiia o 'zheltoi opasnosti' v dorevoliutsionnoi Rossii," 64.

37 Viktor Diatlov, "Velikie ksenofobii: vzaimovliianie i vzaimodeistvie (opyt Rossii)," *Idei i idealy* 2 (2010), 51–63.

38 P. Ukhtubuzhskii (Nikolai Obleukhov), *Russkii narod v Azii* (St. Petersburg: Svet, 1913), 87–99.

the Chinese as a "crowd," "ants," "locusts," and "insects." The Russian press in the 1880s primarily depicted the Chinese as "a dead ocean of people doomed to eternal immobility and lifelessness."[39] Then, in the early twentieth century, that "ocean" unexpectedly started to move threateningly. Ideas of a "Chinese crowd pouring over the Russian borders"[2] spread widely in society and left a notable trace on most observers' views. An example of the visualization of the large numbers of Chinese is an illustration from a statistical almanac in which the drawing of a Chinese man (representing China) hovers about the others.[40]

The studied texts also show how the image of the Chinese people was dehumanized. The texts described the Chinese in a haughty, disdainful tone and did not place a high value on Chinese lives. The following passage about the attitude to the Chinese in the Far Eastern borderlands is characteristic: "Robbing or killing a Chinese person was considered a mere trifle, completely harmless, and any consequences for doing so seemed utter nonsense."[41] In its coverage of the Boxer Rebellion and the plague outbreak in Manchuria, the Russian satirical press ridiculed the "natural cowardice" of the Chinese, traditional Chinese medicine, and how the Chinese looked and lived.[42]

Chinese people who brought their national vices to the Russian Empire were subjected to baseless accusations. Many texts contain detailed descriptions of haunts, gambling houses, and other dens of vice as inalienable features of the "Chinese slums."[43] The large-scale and untaxed import of *hanshin*[44] caused concern. This not only deprived the Russian exchequer of funds; it damaged the moral and physical health of the few Russian settlers.[45] An observer in *Sibirskie voprosy* noted: "We drowned the Chinese in the waves of the River Amur,[46] and

---

39 Alena Eskridge-Kosmach, "China and Policy of Russia in Respect to China Before 1894 in the Russian Press," *The Journal of Slavic Military Studies* 3 (2011): 486.

40 Nikolai Rubakin, *Rossiia v tsifrakh: Strana. Narod. Sosloviia. Klassy* (St. Petersburg: Vestnik znaniia, 1912).

41 Aleksandr Vereshchagin, "Po Manchzhurii. 1900–1901 gg. Vospominaniia i rasskazy," *Vestnik Evropy* 1 (1902): 116–18; Nikolai Matveev, "Kitaitsi na Kariiskih promyslakh," *Russkoe bogatstvo* 12 (1911): 30.

42 Elena Starovoitova, "Moi bol'shoi kulak eshche pri mne!: bokserskoe vosstanie v Kitae v rossiiskikh satiricheskikh izdaniiakh nachala XX veka," *Noveishaia istoriia Rossii* 2 (2017): 89; Pavel Ratmanov, "Man'chzhurskaia chuma 1910–1911 gg. v gazetnykh karikaturakh (chast' 1)," *Istoriia meditsiny* 2 (2017): 163–64.

43 David Shreider, *Nash Dal'nii Vostok* (St. Petersburg: Izdatel'stvo A. F. Devriena, 1897).

44 Strong alcoholic drink, a Chinese vodka.

45 Eva-Maria Stolberg, "The Siberian Frontier between 'White Mission' and 'Yellow Peril', 1890s–1920s," *Nationalities Papers* 1 (2004): 168.

46 This refers to the Chinese pogrom in Blagoveshchensk in July 1900. For a more detailed account, see Diatlov, Guzei and Sorokina, *Kitaiskii pogrom. Blagoveshchenskaia 'Utopiia' 1900 goda v otsenke sovremennikov i potomkov.*

they are drowning us in bushels of vodka. This peculiar war not only demands no financial input from China; it is quite profitable for them."[47]

Almost all mentions of the special traits of the Chinese migrants' daily lives contained testimony of woefully insanitary conditions. The words "destitution" and "dirt" were frequently used to describe the Chinese migrant laborers in Russia.[48] Considering the high cost of renting accommodation and the crowdedness of their lodgings, maintaining good sanitary conditions became difficult. The opinion that hygienic norms were "foreign to the undeveloped Chinese mind" was widespread. These unsanitary conditions led to high levels of illness, mortality, and the constant threat of epidemics.[49]

These attitudes were even characteristic of people who were relatively benevolently disposed toward the Chinese, protested discrimination against them and their humiliation, and proposed real measures to improve their condition. The predominant view of that time consisted exclusively of negative tones ("thousands of Chinese are huddling," "the trade in victuals is entirely in the hands of dirty Chinese traders," and so on).[50] Metaphors such as "bottom," "sewer," "hive," and so on were frequently used to describe Chinese districts. It was thus unsurprising that any news of the first signs of epidemics was accompanied both by accusations against the Chinese of creating a hotbed of disease and by corresponding administrative measures. For example, the threat of the spread of the plague in Siberia was connected with the "incessant circulation of Chinese laborers."[51]

The experience of the first mass contacts showed that the Chinese lived in extreme separation from their host society. They did not mix with the Russians, demonstrating an attitude that was, if not aloof, then wary.[52] Study of the pre-revolutionary discourse shows that the space inhabited by the Chinese was perceived as rejected and impenetrable by the Russian state.[53] The authorities were worried by the disorderly, spontaneous nature of migration and the vast

47 n.a., "Ocherki sibirskoi zhizni," *Sibirskie voprosy* 1 (1911): 40.
48 Matveev, "Kitaitsi na Kariiskih promyslakh."
49 L. Bogoslovskii, "Krepost'-gorod Vladivostok i kitaitsy," *Vestnik Azii* 13 (1913): 20–33.
50 "Chernoe bedstvie," *Sibirskie voprosy* 4 (1911): 18.
51 M. Aronov, "'Sibirskaia zhizn' v zaprosakh III Gosudarstvennoi dumy," *Sibirskie voprosy* 30–1 (1911): 42.
52 Ivan Nadarov, *Ocherk sovremennogo sostoianiia Severno-Ussuriiskogo kraia po rezul'tatam puteshestviia general'nogo shtaba podpolkovnika Nadarova 1882–1883 g.* (Vladivostok: Tipografiia Shtaba Glavnogo komandira portov Vostochnogo okeana, 1884); Ivan Nadarov, "Severno-Ussuriiskii krai," in *Sbornik geograficheskikh, topograficheskikh i statisticheskikh materialov po Azii.* Vyp. XXVII (St. Petersburg: Voennaia tipografiia, 1887).
53 Elena Nesterova, "Atlantida gorodskogo masshtaba: kitaiskie kvartaly v Dal'nevostochnykh gorodakh (konets XIX–nachalo XX v.)," *Etnograficheskoe obozrenie* 4 (2008): 55.

scale of unauthorized Chinese arrivals to the Russian Empire. The Chinese people living in Russia formed a completely impenetrable community that lived by its own informal rules and not Russian law. Contemporaries considered the virtual extraterritoriality of the large and ethnically, racially, and culturally foreign community of subjects of a neighboring empire a real threat to the eastern frontiers of the country.

The key element of the image of the Chinese migrant was thus formed in the early twentieth century: facelessness, unpretentiousness, filth, destitution, flexible or ingratiating behavior, high competitiveness, and an ability to acquire new forms of activity quickly.[54]

Civil servants considered the presence of the Chinese in the empire undesirable, but the authorities found some requests to permit "yellow" labor reasonable. A range of legislative and administrative measures was prepared to protect the Far Eastern economy from cheap Chinese and Korean labor.[55] The First World War caused a sharp labor deficit, and the government recognized the need to attract workers from the "yellow race." Opponents of this move made weighty arguments, ranging from the possibility of infiltration by German spies and the dangerous stranglehold of the "yellow faces" on the labor market to the "import of epidemic diseases."[56] The press published ideas for solving the "yellow question" and simultaneously sating the "hunger for labor" by putting the numerous refugees to work.[57]

The realities of the war won out over the anti-Chinese lobby, however, and in 1915 the Russian authorities started the process of inviting Chinese laborers. A total of 159,972 Chinese people were brought to Russia for work between January 1915 and April 1917.[58] A system of regulating the labor performed by the "yellow race" was established. The area in which they could work was delimited by Lake Baikal in the east and the right bank of the Volga in the west.[59]

---

54 Viktor Diatlov, ed., *Vostok Rossii: migratsii i diaspory v pereselencheskom obshchestve. Rubezhi XIX–XX i XX–XXI vekov* (Irkutsk: Ottisk, 2011), 464.

55 Khodiakov, "Popytki rabochei kolonizatsii vostochnykh okrain imperii v nachale XX v."

56 Mikhail Khodiakov and Chzhitsin Chzhao, "Trudovaia migratsiia kitaitsev v Rossiiu v gody Pervoi mirovoi voiny," *Noveishaia istoriia Rossii* 1 (2017): 8.

57 "Zheltyi trud i bezhentsy," *Birzhevie vedomosti* 16 (September 3, 1915): 3.

58 Larin, *Kitaiskie migranty v Rossii. Istoriia i sovremennost'*, 28.

59 Rossiiskii gosudarstvennyi istoricheskii arkhiv (Russian State Historical Archive), f. 37, op. 73a, d. 301, ll. 142–44 (hereafter cited as RGIA).

Images of Chinese Labor Migrants in the Urals

In this section, I shift my focus to territories far from the Russian-Chinese border. The Ural Mountains, with their large industrial base for military manufacturing, had an acute demand for labor and therefore became a significant site of "yellow labor" during the First World War. To allow us to compile an image of the Chinese migrant laborers, I will focus on only the most prevalent characteristics of the time. It should be stressed that this image was primarily constructed by the authorities: there were no broad interactions between the local population and the Chinese. This image consequently bears a certain stamp of the official discourse which spread in late imperial Russia.

Documents from factories in the Urals from before the start of the war demonstrate a concern about labor migration from China. The factories attempted to receive permits to attract Chinese workers. The Bogoslovskii factory was refused permission in 1913 for the import of workers from Manchuria. The reason given was nonconformity with the policy of limiting the influx of the "yellow race." In May 1914, the director of the Mining Department wrote to the district engineer of the Perm Mining District about special agents' journeys to China to recruit workers. The letter stressed the necessity of creating obstacles for Chinese labor migration; otherwise, it would be "colossal."[60]

The mobilization of workers in the Perm Guberniia into the army caused an acute labor deficit. In 1915, 81,800 of the 135,600 workers in the Urals left for the war, which had a negative impact on production.[61] In the early days of the war, the shortage was remedied with the help of women, children, and prisoners of war. Factory owners soon started to explore the possibility of importing labor from China. The manager of the Abamelek-Lazarev factories in the Perm Guberniia stated in 1915 that their obligations for the supply of coal could only be met with the help of Chinese workers.[62]

The experience of large-scale labor migration during war and political instability provoked the rapid formation and reproduction of stereotypes about the Chinese. The example of the Urals, a region far from the epicenter of "yellow labor," convincingly proves the speed and depth of the spread of ethnic stereotypes in the conditions of late imperial Russia. Moreover, far from all widespread clichés about "yellow labor" had any basis in fact.

---

60 GASO, f. 24, op. 32, d. 4512.
61 Aleksandr Taniaev, *Rabochee dvizhenie v gody voiny* (Sverdlovsk: Uralprofprosvet, 1927), 26–27.
62 GAPK, f. 65, op. 3, d. 595, l. 6.

In late 1915, the governor of the Perm Guberniia summarized the first conclusions regarding the labor of the Chinese in the Urals. His report stressed the low cost of the labor and the speed with which it could be brought to the region, in contrast with the slower and more expensive recruitment of laborers from the central Russian regions. He wrote, "In neighboring China vast numbers of penniless peasants were unemployed and starving [...]. They arrived without families and were unfussy about working and living conditions and their choice of work [...]. What is more, the cost of the Chinese newcomers was lower than that of Russian workers."[63] This first experience was noted a failure, however. The main reason for this was, in the opinion of civil servants, the rush by the industrial owners to hire as many cheap workers as necessary while ignoring the workers' lack of suitability for many types of work.[64]

Ideas of the Chinese people's mass nature were reinforced by the weakness of administrative reporting and control and the perception of "all the yellow people looking alike." The Russian authorities did not manage to organize a systematic count of Chinese workers on either the nationwide or the regional level in these conditions.[65] Paradoxically, no one had exact information on the numbers of Chinese migrant laborers, which established the image of the Chinese as a practically uncontrollable and uncountable group. Archive documents allow for an estimate of between eight and ten thousand Chinese workers in the Urals during the First World War.

The authorities experienced problems with registering the first groups of workers as soon as they arrived. Establishing the Chinese people's identities did not seem possible. During transit, workers were replaced, ill and invalid workers boarded the transports, and some workers fled. Many arrived without documents or with dubious documents. Passport photographs were often absent or clearly did not match the holder.[66]

The board of directors of the Beloretsk factory reported that many Chinese workers arrived with no documents at all. The Chinese usually discarded the personal numbers assigned to them during recruitment, which made counting almost impossible.[67] The governor was even forced to order a complete check

---

63 GAPK, f. 65, op. 1, d. 2, l. 7.
64 Ibid.
65 Gregor Benton, *Chinese Migrants and Internationalism: Forgotten Histories, 1917–1945* (London: Routledge, 2007), 21; Kamenskikh, *Kitaitsi na Srednem Urale v kontse XIX–nachale XXI v.*, 50.
66 GAPK, f. 65, op. 5, d. 152, l. 35.
67 Ibid., d. 167, l. 9.

and facial comparison of all Chinese mining workers' passports.[68] The memoirs of Chinese people who fought on the Red side of the Civil War are testimony to how ubiquitously the Chinese migrant laborers consciously declined to become "legalized." Here is a characteristic example: one veteran wrote of how he bought an old passport for three taels and used it to travel for work.[69]

The documents contain frequent explicit or implicit references to the Chinese "all looking alike."[70] This mode of perceiving the Chinese was most strongly exhibited during investigations of riots. The literal impossibility of distinguishing one Chinese person from another made identification difficult and led to the loss of important information, such as the time and place of arrest. After a workers' revolt in the region of Alapaevsk in 1916, it was only possible to identify thirty-one participants out of the 238 arrested.[71]

The Chinese people's outward appearance, in this case both their anthropological type and their dress, confused observers. The Chinese migrants' workplaces always contained a stall where they could buy familiar fare, clothing, and various everyday items. In spite of the ability of the Chinese to buy everything they needed, one of the sources contains a rather exotic depiction of Chinese workers making their way to work "in bast shoes and holding parasols."[72]

Despite the entrenched stereotype of the strong Chinese work ethic and the Chinese workers' ability to master new areas of activity, the material from the Urals often shows us the opposite picture. The poorly prepared system for the mass recruitment of migrant laborers in the Ural factories produced many faults, which helped build the negative image of the "yellow people." The clear lack of mutual understanding between employers and workers resulted in mass breaches of labor discipline, absenteeism, low productivity, and "laziness." The workers often played cards, meddled in the factory management's decisions, and tried to assign themselves days off. The factory owners consequently breached the Chinese workers' rights, which led to serious clashes.[73]

The initial method of paying wages by the day was not highly motivational for productive work. The workers allegedly used all available means to avoid

---

68 Ibid., d. 595, l. 31.
69 *V boiakh i pokhodakh: vospominaniia uchastnikov Grazhdanskoi voiny na Uralev* (Sverdlovsk: Sverdlovskoe knizhnoe izdatel'stvo, 1959), 508.
70 GAPK, f. 65, op. 5, d. 159, l. 26.
71 Ibid., fol. 33.
72 GASO, f. 643, op. 1, d. 333, l. 28.
73 Mikhail Kamenskikh, "O prichinakh volnenii kitaiskikh rabochikh na Urale v period Pervoi mirovoi voiny," *Vestnik Permskogo universiteta. Istoriia* 1 (2009): 109–13; Alexeeva, "Experiencing War: Chinese Workers in Russia During the First World War."

working.[74] Contemporary observers wrote that for most of the time the Chinese workers "simply sat idly at the coalface," did not observe safety procedures, and worked in "shifts" rather than continuously. All attempts by the factory management to introduce order were perceived as oppression.[75] In November 1916, the office of the Kizel factories wrote that the results of the work of an average Chinese worker were rather modest. Their productivity was assessed at between 40 and 50% of that of a freely hired worker, which was "practically the lowest indicator among other categories of worker."[76]

Governor M. A. Lozina-Lozinskii noted that there "were stories of refusal by the Chinese to work simply because on that day they had already earned the twenty kopecks each needed to sustain himself, and they no longer wanted to work."[77] Industry could naturally not fulfil government tenders on time in such conditions, and the factory owners started paying the Chinese workers in accordance with work done.[78]

According to the documents, Chinese and Korean workers primarily "loitered" in the area in their free time. Card games for money were especially popular, particularly in the Nadezhdinsk factory. Such pastimes, as the documents show, exhausted the workers' strength, and "the Chinese and Koreans went to work tired and did not work hard enough."[79]

One of the reasons the Chinese often breached workplace discipline and simply walked away from the job was that they considered the punishment acceptable. Detention under guard had no effect on the workers. By contrast, the conditions in the factory prisons satisfied the Chinese fully, and there were cases of conscious commitment of infractions with the aim of ending up in a cell.[80] The documents show that they liked the conditions: free food, cleanliness, warmth, and the lack of work.[81] There was even one case in which prisoners sent other workers a note in which they described all the positive aspects of imprisonment and recommended that they take advantage of the opportunity.[82] There were frequent cases of self-harm and imitation of illness by the Chinese workers with the aim of not working and spending some time off sick. The

74 GAPK, f. 65, op. 5, d. 154, ll. 14–15.
75 GASO, f. 73, op. 1, d. 395, l. 76.
76 Ibid., d. 388, ll. 35ob., 42–43.
77 GAPK, f. 65, op. 1, d. 2, l. 7; op. 3, d. 595, l. 36.
78 GASO, f. 643, op. 1, d. 333, ll. 28–29.
79 Ibid., d. 301, ll. 114–15.
80 GAPK, f. 65, op. 1. d. 2, l. 42.
81 GAPK, f. 65, op. 5, d. 154, l. 13.
82 GASO, f. 73, op. 1, d. 395, l. 76.

Chinese used various ruses to achieve this: they poured substances such as soap and ashes into their eyes.[83]

Soon after the arrival of the Chinese workers, the management of the Beloretsk factory admitted that the Chinese were not only undisciplined; they were insufficiently qualified. The factory workshops reported that the Chinese workers were at most 50% as productive as necessary.[84] The Ekaterinburg district chief police officer called most of the migrant Chinese laborers rabble that had no understanding of the assigned work. It is no secret that unscrupulous contractors, often in pursuit of profit, recruited workers who lacked the required professional skills. A striking example was woodcutters who had no clue how to use a saw. Many categorically refused to do the earthworks or woodcutting assigned to them.[85]

The industrialists realized, despite their dissatisfaction, their dependence on "yellow labor." They therefore perforce invited more and more laborers until the middle of 1917. The increased volume of cheap labor was intended to mitigate its generally low quality. The Chinese recruits showed interest in working in Russia even if their rights were breached, as they did not see any other options for themselves. We know of cases in which desperate individuals traveled from China to the factories in the Urals independently with the aim of finding work.[86]

It is known that fights between Russian and Chinese workers were common in the Russian Far East. There was also social tension far from the border, but in these cases, the conflicts occurred both inside the migrant laborer communities and with factory management. The sources show a high level of conflict and clear problems with maintaining control over the situation. As soon as the first groups of workers arrived, they acquired informal leaders who prevented hundreds of Chinese workers from going to work, presented numerous demands to the factory owners, and foisted their influence on others.[87] The conflicts were resolved after negotiations, as well as force and isolation of the leaders in some places, but that did not remove the wall of incomprehension dividing both sides. The "other" as represented by the Chinese did not acquire clear, distinct features; rather, the contrary.

The most striking example of the lack of communication was linked to the distribution of candles. Under the agreement between the factory and the workers, the cost of candles for underground work was deducted from the

---

83 Ibid., d. 388, ll. 39–40, 100.
84 GAPK, f. 65, op. 5, d. 167, l. 9.
85 GAPK, f. 65, op. 3, d. 595, ll. 35, 42.
86 Ibid., d. 64.
87 GAPK, f. 65, op. 3, d. 595, l. 12; op. 5, d. 152, ll. 12, 15.

workers' wages. The Chinese did not initially understand this and entertained themselves with "light shows" in their barracks.[88] The candles distributed to the workers very quickly ran out and had to be bought on credit, which became one of the causes of the large revolt in the Polovinnoe mines in 1915.

Let us examine some characteristic examples of these conflicts. In the Verkhnegubakha mines in September 1915, six Chinese workers organized around six hundred of their countrymen and demanded the return of the five rubles each had paid when signing the employment contract. The crowd beat the Chinese foremen and damaged the factory office buildings. The instigators were arrested and repatriated.[89] A conflict occurred in the copper mine of the Verkh-Isetsk factory in October 1915, this time between Chinese workers. After a knife fight and the arrest of the instigators, a crowd of three hundred workers armed with spades and stones tried to reclaim the detainees from the administration. The riot was suppressed with great difficulty. Some workers were injured.[90]

As relations between the factory management and the migrant laborers became more strained, the problem of the Chinese fleeing became ever more apparent. This hardened stereotypes of the lackadaisical Chinese attitude to work and the migrants' unmanageability, reinforcing their perception as a security threat. By the end of 1916, a few hundred workers had fled.[91]

The correspondence of the authorities responsible for overseeing labor migration to companies in the Urals contains evidence of the flight of dozens of workers, orders to create additional posts, searches, and enhanced surveillance of all the Chinese.[92] Chinese people were often employed as guards in the mines and on timber-felling sites; the local authorities and factory management did not, therefore, trust them greatly. One document reads, "The practice of monitoring the Chinese with guards, what is more, with Chinese guards, is naturally insufficient."[93] The document stressed that the Chinese and Korean workers' unauthorized absences contained "the risk of information gathering for enemy intelligence."[94]

The Chinese people who ran away from the works engaged in minor trade, played cards, and distilled moonshine.[95] The Chinese traders worried the

88 GAPK, f. 65, op. 5, d. 152, l. 11.
89 Ibid., l. 48.
90 GAPK, f. 65, op. 3, d. 595, l. 12.
91 GAPK, f. 65, op. 5, d. 151, ll. 44, 93, 96–97 ob.; GASO, f. 621, op. 1, d. 301, l. 75.
92 GAPK, f. 214, op. 1, d. 16, ll. 46–47.
93 GAPK, f. 65, op. 5, d. 151, l. 92.
94 GASO, f. 621, op. 1, d. 292, ll, 6–6ob.
95 GAPK, f. 167, op. 1, d. 12, l. 432.

residents of Perm with their insistent peddling. They surreptitiously sneaked into properties, which became a cause of serious concern for the populace. The local traders were unhappy with the increased competition. It created undesirable incidents that would become disorder.[96]

We know that discussions about banning the import of labor from China made medical and sanitary questions a priority. The governor-general of Amur, L. N. Gondatti, insisted that the Chinese were a "hotbed of all possible illnesses."[97] Special medical control points were established in Harbin and at the station in Manzhouli for the medical inspection of Chinese workers. Further along the way, in Chelyabinsk and Irkutsk, the Chinese migrants were examined, washed in bathhouses, and given the necessary vaccines, and sick workers were sent home.[98] Special trains passed through Chelyabinsk in the opposite direction, with ill Chinese workers being returned from the works. The workers were given hot food and clothing, and workers who had fallen behind their groups were helped.[99]

These serious measures notwithstanding, many workers arrived for work ill, carrying syphilis, various skin diseases, and others.[100] The key words used to describe the Chinese migrants were as a rule repetitive: "overcrowding" and "filth."[101] Furthermore, the workers often neglected basic hygiene standards, which significantly worsened their condition and lowered their already low capacity for work. This was at the same time as the conditions for medical assistance were being created in the mines: the necessary medical personnel, beds, medicines, and so on.[102]

The workers themselves were, however, unwilling to seek medical help and preferred to cure themselves. Even minor health problems therefore led to disability or fatalities. A special commission charged with investigating the workers' living conditions in 1916 discovered a practically blind Chinese man in one of the barracks. He reported having only visited the doctor once and having used "home" remedies, although such cures usually led to complete blindness.[103]

---

96 GAPK, f. 36, op. 2, d. 8, l. 205.
97 GARF, f. 102, op. 71, d. 56, l. 2.
98 Ibid., op. 75, d. 10, ch. 26, l. 133.
99 OGACHO, f. I–13, op. 1, d. 1093, l. 2; d. 1095.
100 GASO, f. 73, op. 1, d. 388, l. 50; f. 643, op. 1, d. 333, ll. 28–29ob.; f. 53, op. 1, d. 109, l. 260.
101 GASO. f. 73, op. 1, d. 388, ll. 46–50, 59, 79.
102 Ibid., ll. 46–50ob.
103 Ibid., l. 39.

The Chinese were sicker more often (19%) than other categories of workers (13%).[104] There are several explanations for this. Most Chinese workers took a long time to get used to working in the difficult climate. Contemporaries frequently gave examples of Chinese workers grossly neglecting safety procedures, failing to dress for winter weather, and blithely ignoring instructions to wear layers of outer clothing in sub-zero temperatures. The most frequent causes of illness in the Kizel mines in 1916 were contusions and fractures (135 of more than five hundred patients).[105]

Rapid change in diet played its part in the migrant workers' unsatisfactory physical condition. The workers suffered from a lack of familiar foodstuffs and, as the documents state, lack of discernment in food (consumption of raw mushrooms and herbs). This often resulted in prolonged digestive disorders. Combined with failure to observe some hygiene standards, intestinal illnesses and parasites incapacitated dozens of workers for long periods. Besides, the Chinese workers' lack of cleanliness and use of dubious remedies (such as sprinkling open wounds with flour) significantly complicated even small wounds, calluses, and abscesses. Some workers consequently died of blood infections.[106]

The short stay of the migrant workers in the Ural factories exhibited particular relationships among the Chinese. They preferred social isolation and solved all internal conflicts in their own way. They elected middlemen to communicate with the factory administration. The archive contains materials on the murder of a workers' representative who supported the administration: "the workers decided to have done with him."[107] Such cases were in all probability not isolated, but their detection and investigation proved extremely difficult.

The local authorities were concerned with the "fraternal communities" of the Chinese, as there were certain grounds to suspect them of criminal activity. The governor wrote to the police commanders and district chief police officers: "the Chinese of Ekaterinburg County are organizing a band to commit murders and robberies when the spring comes. Those who join the gang receive a special oath from the organizers."[108] Such groupings were exposed, and their members arrested. The authorities did not manage to investigate reliably the type of "fraternal oath" that bound the Chinese.

---

104   Ibid., l. 100ob.
105   Ibid., l. 49.
106   GASO, f. 73, op. 1, d. 388, ll. 40, 100; GAPK, f. 65, op. 5, d. 159, l. 4.
107   GASO, f. 181, op. 1, d. 5, l. 3ob.
108   Ibid., d. 1, l. 224.

Conclusion

The sudden enhancement of the instrumental function of the image of threat or enemy, in the form of the Chinese, in the late nineteenth and early twentieth centuries is evidence of the high demand for such a construction. The layers of late imperial society needed a new image of extreme external threat to conform with the domestic and foreign policy agenda. The experience of interaction between late imperial society and Chinese migrant laborers showed that Russians were highly interested not in the Chinese or Chinese migrants but in the collective fears, prejudices, and emotions they embodied, which were reflected in the "yellow peril."

The mass, state-organized, and rapid import of cheap labor to the interior of the country formed the Chinese into "the other" in areas where they had not before been seen. Whereas coexistence with the Chinese and dependence on their labor was a fact of life for the Far East, for the industrialists in the Ural Mountains, the rapid recruitment and organization of "yellow" workers was a sudden, imperative measure. The factory owners recognized the drawbacks and shortcomings of the new employees but at the same time realized the main advantage of the Chinese laborers: their cheapness, unpretentiousness, and large numbers.

Civil servants, factory managers, and people on the street were not interested in who the Chinese migrants were. They were interested in their numbers and in answering a grievous question: whether they were a threat to "us," and if so, of what nature, how "mortal" it was, and how to respond to it. Comparative study of the Russian press coverage of the "yellow peril" and documents from the Ural archives about the Chinese workers have revealed a perception of the Chinese as a mass, a large, ungovernable group of people that required strict oversight and control. Contemporaries believed that any leniency in such control would immediately lead to grave consequences: riots, inability to fulfil government defense contracts, runaways, and "laziness." It was precisely "mass" that concerned all levels of government, from the capital to the border. Quantitative notions formed the basis for the ideologemes of "demographic expansion," "the yellow peril," and offensive comparisons of the Chinese with insects.

The events of February 1917 meant a cardinal change in industry, and the October Revolution led to its collapse. The volume of industrial production fell in 1917 by 43% and in 1918 by 21% compared to 1913.[109] The import of labor from China ceased. The Provisional Government made efforts to repatriate the remaining workers. Nevertheless, according to A. A. Anikst, there were still around sixty-seven Chinese workers working in Russian factories as of September 1, 1917.[110] The chronic disruptions to rail transport and harsh travel conditions complicated evacuation efforts. Special trains carrying Chinese people were often delayed for long periods near Irkutsk or Omsk.[111] The institutional government crisis and economic collapse placed migrant laborers in a catastrophic situation: their relationship with the host society was complicated in the extreme.

Chinese people were soon caught up in violent confrontation on the fronts of the Civil War.[112] The ideas of the "yellow peril" and "yellow labor" were exploited by the belligerents' propaganda,[113] only to be, with time, forgotten or relegated to the periphery of historical memory. Only after the collapse of the Soviet Union and the large-scale influx of Chinese migrants were the prerevolutionary stereotypes and myths reimagined and rationalized into new ideologemes of the "Chinese threat" and demographic expansion.[114]

109 Boris Mironov, "Dostizheniia i provaly rossiiskoi ekonomiki v gody Pervoi mirovoi voiny," *Vestnik Sankt-Peterburgskogo universiteta: Istoriia* 3 (2017): 3, 466.

110 Abram Anikst, *Organizatsiia raspredeleniia rabochei silu v 1920 godu* (Moscow: RSFSR, Narodnyi Komissariat truda, 1920), 42.

111 Larin, *Kitaiskie migranty v Rossii. Istoriia i sovremennost'*, 70.

112 Dmitrii Ispovednikov, "Uchastie Kitaia v Grazhdanskoi voine v Sibiri," *Novyi istoricheskii Vestnik* 3 (2010): 74–81; Mark O'Neill, *From the Tsar's Railway to the Red Army: The Experience of Chinese Labourers in Russia during the First World War and Bolshevik Revolution* (London: Penguin Random House Australia, 2014); Iusin' Chzhan and Ruslan Gagkuev, "Kitaiskie dobrovol'tsy v grazhdanskoi voine v Rossii: mezhdu krasnymi i belymi," *Rossiiskaia istoriia* 1 (2019): 60–71.

113 Stolberg, "'The Siberian frontier between 'White Mission' and 'Yellow Peril', 1890s–1920s," 1, 165–81; Sergei Ippolitov and Valerii Minaev, "'Ot etogo zavisit vsia sud'ba Rossii': k izucheniu demograficheskoi i ekonomicheskoi ekspansii Kitai i Iaponii na Vostoke Rossii vo vremia vtoroi russkoi smuty," *Novyi istoricheskii Vestnik* 3 (2013): 27–45; Yuexin Lin, "Among Ghosts and Tigers: The Chinese in the White Terror," *Revolutionary Russia* 28, no. 2 (2015): 140–66.

114 Viktor Diatlov, "Kitaiskie migranty i dinamika kitaefobii v Rossii," in *Transnatsional'nye migratsii i sovremennye gosudarstva v usloviiakh ekonomicheskoi turbulentnosti*, ed. Vladimir Malakhov (Moscow: Izdatel'skii dom "Delo" RANKHiGS), 246.

Works Cited

Archival Sources

Gosudarstvennyi arkhiv Permskogo kraia (GAPK). Fond 36. Permskoe gubernskoe pravlenie Ministerstva vnutrennikh del (g. Perm').

———. Fond 65. Kantseliariia Permskogo gubernatora (g. Perm').

———. Fond 167. Permskii gubernskii komissar Vremennogo pravitel'stva (g. Perm').

———. Fond 214. Osoboupolnomochennyi po okhrane Ekaterinburskogo i Verkhoturskogo uezdov Ministerstva vnutrennikh del (g. Ekaterinburg Permskoi gubernii).

Gosudarstvennyi arkhiv Rossiiskoi Federatsii (GARF). Fond 102. Departament politsii Ministerstva vnutrennikh del Rossiiskoi imperii (g. Sankt–Peterburg).

Gosudarstvennyi arkhiv Sverdlovskoi oblasti (GASO). Fond 24. Ural'skoe gornoe upravlenie (g. Ekaterinburg Permskoi gubernii).

———. Fond 73. Upolnomochennyi po Ural'skomu raionu predsedatelia osobogo soveshchaniia po oborone gosudarstva i predsedatel' zavodskogo soveshchaniia (g. Ekaterinburg Permskoi gubernii).

———. Fond 181. Osobo upolnomochennyi po Ekaterinburgskomu i Verkhoturskomu uezdam (g. Ekaterinburg Permskoi gubernii).

———. Fond 621. Verkhoturskoe politseiskoe upravlenie (g. Verkhotur'e Permskoi gubernii).

———. Fond 643. Aktsionernoe obshchestvo Nizhnetagil'skikh i Lun'evskikh zavodov naslednikov P. P. Demidova (g. Nizhnii Tagil Permskoi gubernii).

Ob'edinennyi gosudarstvennyi arkhiv Cheliabinskoi oblasti (OCHAGO). Fond I–13. Zaveduiushchii peredvizheniem pereselentsev (g. Cheliabinsk Orenburgskoi gubernii).

Rossiiskii gosudarstvennyi istoricheskii arkhiv (RGIA). Fond 37. Gornyi department (g. Moskva).

Printed Sources and Literature

Alexeeva, Olga. "Experiencing War: Chinese Workers in Russia During the First World War." *The Chinese Historical Review* 1 (2018): 46–66.

Anikst, Abram. *Organizatsiia raspredeleniia rabochei sily v 1920 godu.* Moscow: RSFSR, Narodnyi Komissariat truda, 1920.

Aronov, M. "'Sibirskaia zhizn'' v zaprosakh III Gosudarstvennoy dumy." *Sibirskie voprosy* 30–1 (1911): 38–46.

Arsen'ev, Vladimir. *Kitaitsy v Ussuriiskom krae. Ocherk istoriko-etnograficheskii.* Khabarovsk: Tipografiia kantseliarii Priamurskogo general-gubernatora, 1914.

Benton, Gregor. *Chinese Migrants and Internationalism: Forgotten Histories, 1917–1945.* London: Routledge, 2007.

Bogoslovskii, L. "Krepost'-gorod Vladivostok i kitaitsy." *Vestnik Azii* 13 (1913): 20–33.

"Chernoe bedstvie." *Sibirskie voprosy* 4 (1911): 18–20.

Chzhan, Iusin' and Ruslan Gagkuev. "Kitaiskie dobrovol'tsy v grazhdanskoi voine v Rossii: mezhdu krasnymi i belymi." *Rossiiskaia istoriia* 1 (2019): 60–71.

Datsyshen, Vladimir. "Kitaiskaia trudovaia migratsiia v Rossii. Maloizvestnye stranitsy istorii." *Problemy Dal'nego Vostoka* 5 (2008): 99–104.

Diatlov, Viktor. "Migratsiia kitaitsev i diskussiia o 'zheltoi opasnosti' v dorevoliutsionnoi Rossii." *Vestnik Evrazii* 1 (2000): 63–89.

———. "Velikie ksenofobii: vzaimovliianie i vzaimodeistvie (opyt Rossii)." *Idei i idealy* 2 (2010): 51–63.

———. "Ekzotizatsia i 'obraz vraga': sindrom 'zheltoi opastnosti' v dorevoliutsionnoi Rossii." *Idei i idealy* 2 (2014): 23–41.

———. "Kitaiskie migranty i dinamika kitaefobii v Rossii." In *Transnational'nye migratsii i sovremennye gosudarstva v usloviiakh ekonomicheskoi turbulentnosti.* Edited by Vladimir Malakhov, 230–48. Moscow: Izdatel'skii dom "Delo" RANKHiGS, 2016.

Diatlov, Viktor, ed. *Vostok Rossii: migratsii i diaspory v pereselencheskom obshchestve. Rubezhi XIX–XX i XX–XXI vekov.* Irkutsk: Ottisk, 2011.

Diatlov, Viktor, Iana Guzei and Tat'iana Sorokina. *Kitaiskii pogrom. Blagoveshchesnkaia "Utopiia" 1900 goda v otsenke sovremennikov i potomkov.* St. Petersburg: Nestor-Istoriia, 2020.

Eskridge-Kosmach, Alena. "China and Policy of Russia in Respect to China Before 1894 in the Russian Press." *The Journal of Slavic Military Studies* 3 (2011): 481–528.

———. "The Boxer Rebellion and the Standpoint of the Russian Press." *The Journal of Slavic Military Studies* 3 (2013): 414–38.

———. "Russian Press and the Ideas of Russia's 'Special Mission in the East' and 'Yellow Peril.'" *Journal of Slavic Military Studies* 4 (2014): 661–75.

Grave, Vladimir. *Kitaitsy, koreitsy i iapontsy v Priamur'e. Trudy Amurskoi ekspeditsii.* Issue 11. St. Petersburg: Tipografiia V. F. Kirshbauma, 1912.

Gudkov, Lev. "Ideologema 'vraga': 'Vragi' kak massovyi sindrom i mekhanizm sotsial'noi integratsii." In *Obraz vraga: sbornik.* Edited by Lev Gudkov, 7–80. Moscow: OGI, 2005.

Guzei, Iana. "Kategoriia 'zheltye' v kontekste rasovogo diskursa v Rossiiskoi imperii v kontse XIX–nachale XX v." *Izvestiia Irkutskogo gosudarstvennogo universiteta. Seriia Politologia: Religiovedenie* 2 (2013): 167–78.

Ippolitov, Sergei and Valerii Minaev. "'Ot etogo zavisit vsia sud'ba Rossii': k izucheniu demograficheskoi i ekonomicheskoi ekspansii Kitai i Iaponii na Vostoke Rossii vo vremia vtoroi russkoi smuty." *Novyi istoricheskii Vestnik* 3 (2013): 27–45.

Ispovednikov, Dmitrii. "Uchastie Kitaia v Grazhdanskoi voine v Sibiri." *Novyi istoricheskii Vestnik* 3 (2010): 74–81.

Ivanov, Andrei. "Inostrannoe khishchnichestvo i okhrana promyslovykh resursov na Dal'nem Vostoke Rossii (konets XIX–nachalo XX v.)." *Nauchnyi dialog* (2019): 221–36.

Kamenskikh, Mikhail. "O prichinakh volnenii kitaiskikh rabochikh na Urale v period Pervoi mirovoi voiny." *Vestnik Permskogo universiteta. Istoriia* 1 (2009): 109–13.

———. *Kitaitsi na Srednem Urale v kontse XIX–nachale XXI v.* St. Petersburg: Izdatel'stvo Mamatov, 2011.

Khasanova, Zifa. "Kitaiskie rabochie v gody Pervoi mirovoi voiny na Iuzhnom Urale." *Voprosy istorii* 2 (2019): 133–39.

Khodiakov, Mikhail. "Zheltorossiia kontsa XIX–XX veka v geopoliticheskikh planakh russkoi voennoi elity." *Noveishaia istoriia Rossii* 4 (2018): 880–97.

———. "Popytki rabochei kolonizatsii vostochnykh okrain imperii v nachale XX v. Po dokumentam Rossiiskogo gosudarstvennogo istoricheskogo arkhiva Dal'nego Vostoka." *Vestnik arkhivista* 4 (2019): 995–1006.

———. "Rossiiskoe zakonodatel'stvo nachala XX veka ob ispol'zovanii zheltogo truda v ekonomike Dal'nego Vostoka." *Vestnik Tomskogo gosudarstvennogo universiteta. Istoriia* 60 (2019): 78–83.

Khodiakov, Mikhail, and Chzhitsin Chzhao. "Trudovaia migratsiia kitaitsev v Rossiiu v gody Pervoi mirovoi voiny." *Noveishaia istoriia Rossii* 1 (2017): 7–30.

Kireev, Anton. "Yellow Peril and the Development of the Russian Far East in the 1850s–1900s." *Sotsial'nye i gumanitarnye nauki na Dal'nem Vostoke* 1 (2010): 182–88.

Kolstø, Pål. "Competing with Entrepreneurial Diasporians: Origins of Anti-Semitism in Nineteenth-Century Russia." *Nationalities Papers* 42, no. 4 (2014): 691–707.

Komov, Andrei. "O kitaitsakh i koreitsakh v Priamurskom krae." *Sibirskie voprosy* 27 (1909): 18–27.

Kovalevskii, Maksim. "Porto-franko vo Vladivostoke." *Vestnik Evropy* 1, no. 1 (1909): 423–37.

Kudriavtseva, Tat'iana. "'Kitai-tsar': kitaitsi v vospriiatii russkogo naroda v period 'bokserskogo vosstaniia' (po materialam russkoi pechati)." *Klio* 8 (2014): 82–85.

Larin, Aleksandr. *Kitaiskie migranty v Rossii. Istoriia i sovremennost'*. Moscow: Vostochnaia kniga, 2009.

Li, Elena. "'Zheltaia ugroza' ili 'zheltyi vopros' v trudakh amurskoi ekspeditsii 1910 g." *Oikumen* 3 (2010): 29–40.

Lin, Yuexin. "Among Ghosts and Tigers: The Chinese in the White Terror." *Revolutionary Russia* 28, no. 2 (2015): 140–66.

Matveev, Nikolai. "Kitaitsi na Kariiskih promyslakh." *Russkoe bogatstvo* 12 (1911): 28–43.

Michi, Aleksandr. *Puteshestvie po Amuru i Vostochnoi Sibiri*. St. Petersburg: Izdatel'stvo Knigoproduktsii M. O. Vol'f, 1868.

Mironov, Boris. "Dostizheniia i provaly rossiiskoi ekonomiki v gody Pervoi mirovoi voiny." *Vestnik Sankt-Peterburgskogo universiteta: Istoriia* 3 (2017): 463–80.

Mikhel'son, Moritz. *Russkaia mysl' i rech'. Svoe i chuzhoe. Opyt russkoi frazeologii: sbornik obraznykh slov i inoskazanii*. Vol. 1. St. Petersburg: Tipografiia Akademii nauk, 1902.

Nadarov, Ivan. *Ocherk sovremennogo sostoianiia Severno-Ussuriiskogo kraia po rezul'tatam puteshestviia general'nogo shtaba podpolkovnika Nadarova 1882–1883 g*. Vladivostok: Tipografiia Shtaba Glavnogo komandira portov Vostochnogo okeana, 1884.

———. "Severno-Ussuriiskii krai." *Sbornik geograficheskikh, topograficheskikh i statisticheskikh materialov po Azii*. Vyp. XXVII. St. Petersburg: Voennaia tipografiia, 1887.

Nesterova, Elena. "Atlantida gorodskogo masshtaba: kitaiskie kvartaly v Dal'nevostochnykh gorodakh (konets XIX–nachalo XX v.)." *Ethnograficheskoe obozrenie* 4 (2008): 44–58.

"Ocherki sibirskoi zhizni." *Sibirskie voprosy* 1 (1911): 38–44.

O Iaponii i iapontsakh i o tom, otchego i kak nachalas' russko-iaponskaia voina: Knizhka dlia naroda. St. Petersburg: n.p., 1904.

O'Neill, Mark. *From the Tsar's Railway to the Red Army: The Experience of Chinese Labourers in Russia during the First World War and Bolshevik Revolution.* London: Penguin Random House Australia, 2014.

Panov, Aleksandr. "Zheltyi vopros v Priamur'e." *Voprosy kolonizatsii* 7 (1910): 53–116.

———. "Bor'ba za rabochii rynok v Priamur'e." *Voprosy kolonizatsii* 11 (1912): 241–82.

"Pervaia vseobshchaia perepis' naseleniia Rossiiskoi Imperii 1897 g. Raspredelenie naseleniia po rodnomu iazku, guberniiam i obla022. http://www.demoscope.ru/weekly/ssp/rus_lan_97.php.

Petukhova, Alla. "'Skazhi mne, kto tvoi vrag': antifinliandskii diskurs v prostranstve obshchestvenno-politicheskoi kommunikatsii Rossiiskoi imperii kontsa XIX–nachala XX vv." *Ab Imperio* 3 (2010): 195–227.

Popov, Aleksandr. "'Bokserskoe vosstanie' v Kitae v vospriiatii sibirskogo prostonarod'ia (po materialam tomskikh i irkutskikh gazet)." *Genesis: istoricheskie issledovaniia* 6 (2016): 1–8.

Ratmanov, Pavel. "Man'chzhurskaia chuma 1910–1911 gg. v gazetnykh karikaturakh (chast' 1)." *Istoriia meditsiny* 2 (2017): 161–73.

Rubakin, Nikolai. *Rossiia v tsifrakh: Strana. Narod. Sosloviia. Klassy.* St Petersburg: Vestnik znaniia, 1912.

Shreider, David. *Nash Dal'nii Vostok.* St. Petersburg: Izdatel'stvo A. F. Devriena, 1897.

Siegelbaum, Lewis. "Another 'Yellow Peril': Chinese Migrants in the Russian Far East and the Russian Reaction before 1917." *Modern Asian Studies* 2 (1978): 307–30.

Slominskii, Leonid. "Zheltaia opasnost'." *Vestnik Evropy* 5 (1904): 308–21.

Starovoitova, Elena. "Moi bol'shoi kulak eshche pri mne!: bokserskoe vosstanie v Kitae v rossiiskikh satiricheskikh izdaniiakh nachala XX veka." *Noveishaia istoriia Rossii* 2 (2017): 81–97.

Starovoitova, Elena, and Denis Ianchenko. "Kolonizatsia, migratsiia i porto-franko na Dal'nem vostoke Rossii v kontse XIX–nachale XX vv." *Bylye gody* 55, no. 6 (2020): 206–14.

Stephan, John. *The Russian Far East: A History*. Palo Alto: Stanford University Press, 1994.

Stolberg, Eva-Maria. "The Siberian Frontier between 'White Mission' and 'Yellow Peril,' 1890s–1920s." *Nationalities Papers* 1 (2004): 165–81.

Taniaev, Aleksandr. *Rabochee dvizhenie v gody voiny*. Sverdlovsk: Uralprofprosvet, 1927.

Ukhtubuzhskii, P. (Nikolai Obleukhov). *Russkii narod v Azii*. St. Petersburg: Svet, 1913.

Verezhnikov, A. "Kitaiskaia tolpa." *Sovremennik* 4 (1911): 124–34.

Vereshchagin, Aleksandr. "Po Manchzhurii. 1900–1901 gg. Vospominaniia i rasskazy." *Vestnik Evropy* 1 (1902): 116–18.

V boiakh i pokhodakh: vospominaniia uchastnikov Grazhdanskoi voiny na Urale. Sverdlovsk: Sverdlovskoe knizhnoe izdatel'stvo, 1959.

Yin Hsu, Chia. "A Tale of Two Railroads: 'Yellow Labor', Agrarian Colonization, and the Making of Russianness at the Far Eastern Frontier, 1890s–1910s." *Ab Imperio* 3 (2006): 217–53.

"Zheltyi trud i bezhentsy." *Birzhevye vedomosti* 16 (September 1915): 3.

15

"Own" and "Other": Soldiers, Officers, and the Fatal Zigzags of the Russian Revolution in the Last Year of the Life of General L. G. Kornilov (1870–1918)

Il'ia Rat'kovskii

Abstract

This chapter examines the mutual perception of officers by soldiers and soldiers by officers in 1917, the year of the so-called Great October Revolution. I describe the emerging struggle over the system of elections and undivided authority and explore these two groups' different perceptions of the death penalty and other phenomena and mutual conflicts during the war. I reveal the split and confrontation between them, their reasons, changes in mutual perceptions, and the actions that followed them. I also explore the confrontation between these groups and some of the attempts to reconcile them in 1917, as well as the causes of their failure. The primary sources for the study include personal memoirs and archival material.

The Beginning of the Formation of the Heroic Image of General L. G. Kornilov

The life of General Lavr Georgievich Kornilov (1870–1918) has been the subject of many academic studies. Ushakov and Fediuk argue that "General Kornilov has been written about by many people in many ways. He has been deified and cursed, accused, and mythologized. But, as a rule, all agreed on one thing: Lavr Georgievich Kornilov was a personality, and an extraordinary, manifold personality at that."[1] One can agree with this. His life has been interpreted into the image of Kornilov as "our own," "other," and "outsider," depending on the author's conception. The diametrically opposed assessments of General Kornilov are tied to the multifaceted nature of his life, which has been variously interpreted by his contemporaries and subsequent generations.

The son of a Cossack family that served in the Siberian Cossack Host, Kornilov would often appeal to his ordinary origin. His fellow soldiers would use that fact in a similar way as they drew the image of a people's general. This was undoubtedly connected with the goal of forming the image of "our own" political actor among contemporaries. This image would be particularly in demand during the Russian Revolution of 1917 and the subsequent Civil War.

The image of "our own" is placed in opposition to that of "outsider" and "other"; meanwhile, "our own" is an area of self-identification and positive assessment. Social proximity is an important aspect of the positive image of "our own." In this regard, Kornilov's unprivileged, common origin would become one of the most important building blocks of this image. Many contemporaries thus identified with Kornilov, contrasting his image of "one of our own" with other political activists of the revolutionary period who were, in their opinion, foreign and "outsiders."

This image of "our own" was not, of course, formed immediately but only when it became necessary, when Kornilov was seen not just as one of the many Russian generals of the First World War, but already as a figure of political standing who stood out from the other military ranks. The start of this process was Kornilov's escape from German captivity in June 1916. The Russian army's unsuccessful military campaign required compensation to shore up belief in its moral superiority over the enemy. A Russian general and prisoner of war's escape from German captivity shaped the image of a Russian hero, "our man" in opposition to "the other," the German.

This was the beginning, when two origins and definitions of Kornilov as one of Russia's "own," a man of common origin and his patriotic anti-German escape. Other generals might be defeated by the German army, but Kornilov had secured a personal victory by escaping captivity. The Kornilov who refused to capitulate became a symbol of an approaching victory over Germany. His escape soon received official recognition: he was received at the general headquarters by Nicholas II, supreme commander of the Russian army, who decorated him

---

1   A. I. Ushakov and V. P. Fediuk, *Lavr Kornilov* (Moscow: Molodaia gvardiia, 2012), 5.

with the Order of St. George. All this, as well as General Kornilov's biography, was widely publicized in the Russian press in 1916. "The newspapers and magazines print the general's portrait, articles about him, and interviews with him," Ushakov and Fediuk write "In Petrograd the cadets of the Mikhailovskoe Artillery School pay tributes to him. Sil'vestr, the bishop of Omsk, sends him a telegram. His fellow Cossacks of the stanitsa of Karkaraly send him a cross and an icon pendant."[2] General Kornilov's political biography begins here: his image is presented as necessary for the realities of a Russia at war.

From that moment, Kornilov, who had received a new assignment as commander of the Twenty-Fifth Army Corps of the Special Army of V. I. Gurko on the southwestern front, was already a public figure. The First World War, the Revolution of 1917, the establishment of the Volunteer Army and the Ice March (First Kuban Campaign)—all of these were now inalienably connected with his military and political career. The numerous studies of his life present these events in detail.

Alongside these events, there are several episodes from Kornilov's military and political life that require close study and elaboration. I consider these to include the circumstances of his death and the subsequent events (Kornilov's burial and corpse). These are not merely a chain of events; rather, they demonstrate the attitude to Kornilov, showing him to be both "our own" and an "outsider" to his contemporaries. Both representations of Kornilov were developed in great detail.

Descriptions of the events referred to above primarily rely on White sources, above all White memoirs, which then easily found their way into contemporary Russian historical research.[3] The most important publication of this type on the given topic is the historical material presented by the director of a department of the Federal Archive Agency (Rosarkhiv), N. A. Myshov, in his "Recollections of Staff-Captain A. Tiurin on the Death of General Kornilov."[4] This work contains the most reliable and extensive circumstances of Kornilov's death and

---

2　Ibid., 74.
3　R. M. Abiniakin, *Ofitserskii korpus Dobrovol'cheskoi armii: Sotsial'nyi sostav, mirovozzrenie. 1917–1920 gg.* (Orel: Izdatel' A. Vorobev, 2005); R. G. Gagkuev, *Beloe dvizhenie na Iuge Rossii: Voennoe stroitels'stvo, istochniki komplektovaniia, sotsialn'yi sostav, 1917–1920 gg.* (Moscow: Sodruzhestvo "Posev," 2012); I. N. Grebenkin, *Dobrovol'tsy i Dobrovol'cheskaia armiia: na Donu i v 'Ledianom' pokhode* (Riazan: Riazan State Pedagogical University named after S. A. Yesenin, 2005); A. S. Puchenkov, *Antibol'shevistskoe dvizhenie na Iuge i Iugo-Zapade Rossii (noiabr' 1917–ianvar' 1919 gg.): ideologiia, politika, osnovy rezhima vlasti Spetsial'nost.* (PhD diss., St. Petersburg Institute of History of the Russian Academy of Sciences, 2014).
4　N. A. Myshov, "'Serdtse ne vyderzhalo . . .' (vospominaniia shtabs-kapitana A. Tiurina o smerti generala Kornilova)," *Otechestvennye arkhivy* 4 (2002): 76–83.

subsequent events from a White officer's perspective. The document describes the death of the White side's "own" leader and the subsequent mockery of the symbol of the White movement by "others" and "outsiders." The very circumstances of the description of this action underscore the foreign nature of the opposing side. A. Tiurin's recollections establish many important details; however, I argue that these recollections serve as an interpretation of events of a supporter of the White movement, which establishes, above all, the inhumane nature of the treatment of Kornilov's corpse, without explaining the reasons for it.

Meanwhile, the sources from the other side that describe these events—the Reds—have been virtually absent as research sources, despite their distinct value and the light they can shed on a series of previously unknown circumstances of these events, primarily in the paradigm of the opposition of "our own" versus "other." Some such recollections have been deposited in the Central State Archive of Historical and Political Documents in St. Petersburg (TsGA IPD SPB), primarily in fond R.–4000: Leningrad Institute of Historical and Political Research, Smolnyi District, Leningrad-St. Petersburg.

One of the targets that the present publication sets itself is to bring such sources, which are important in this context, into scholarly circulation. I also consider it important to study the reasons for the events mentioned above, the clearly recorded brutal attitude of the soldiers toward General Kornilov and the subsequent public humiliation of his corpse.

The legendary image of General Kornilov in his supporters' apologist studies from the White movement is also legendary in Red memoirs. While their view of Kornilov is opposed to that of the Whites, they share the sacralization of his image and characterization of him as an intellectual leader among our own or others. All that changes is the color scale of his political and social reception. Whereas for the Whites, Kornilov illuminates and liberates himself from the Bolsheviks (in a sharply defined image of "our own" for participants of the White movement), in the opposite, Red, camp, this figure is of no lesser scale but merely with a minus sign, bearing death and blood to soldiers and the people (an equally sharply defined image of "the other"). From this perspective, Kornilov is a characteristic image of the "other" for the representatives of numerous groups of people: from workers to soldiers and sailors. Kornilov was characterized as the quintessence of the origin of the counterrevolution in 1917 and 1918. Soviet historiography inherited this image of the "other."

Like the first, the second, negative image of the "other" and "outsider" General Kornilov began to be formed during the First World War, particularly during its closing phase, during the revolutionary year of 1917. However, this did not occur at once: Kornilov was initially drafted to Petrograd as a prominent personality and a military leader who was incontrovertibly well regarded in social circles.

The Revolutionary Year 1917 and General L. G. Kornilov

The revolutionary events of February in Petrograd demanded the appearance of a figure who could be widely perceived as suitable. In this sense, the telegram from one of the leaders of the February Revolution, chairman of the Provisional Committee of the State Duma M. V. Rodzianko, on March 2, 1917, to General M. V. Alekseev, director of the Staff of the General Headquarters, is representative:

> For the establishment of full order and rescue of the capital from anarchy, a valorous war general, whose name would be popular and authoritative among the population, must be recruited here to the post of chief commander of the Petrograd Military District [...]. The Committee of the State Duma recognizes the valorous hero, known to all Russia, and commander of the Twenty-Fifth Army Corps, lieutenant-General Kornilov.[5]

The following telegram is also representative. Here, Alekseev addresses Nicholas II: "the popular name of Kornilov will restrain the troops from repeating their mutiny."[6] These telegrams clearly record the established perception of the general as a popular and decisive military leader who could prove useful in the new political environment. Kornilov would become the last holder of senior military rank to be appointed by the emperor. However, although Kornilov was appointed by Nicholas II, he continued to discharge his duties after the abdication, in the new political reality. Formally, he was appointed on March 5.

General Kornilov was initially received as a Russian general who had accepted the February Revolution. This was sustained by his participation in March in the arrest of the royal family and the procedure of the exhumation and burning of Grigorii Rasputin's corpse. Kornilov visited Tsarskoe Selo twice, on the fifth and eighth of March: the first time at night, with A. I. Guchkov, and then three days later with Colonel E. S. Kobylinskii (the future director of

---

5   Ushakov and Fediuk, *Lavr Kornilov*, 76–77.
6   Ibid.

the Tsarskoe Selo Garrison) to conduct the arrest. During these days, Kornilov clearly positions himself as a supporter of a republic. This is confirmed by the following statement of his, recorded by his orderly V. S. Zavoiko: "the road to the throne for any Romanov lay over his, General Kornilov's, dead body."[7]

Kornilov's widely visible actions in March strengthened his image as one of "our own" for the supporters of the new regime. Having stood up against the symbols of the old regime (the imperial family, Rasputin), Kornilov became one of "our own" for the new authorities. As fate would have it, in little more than a year a similar procedure would be carried out, but regarding General Kornilov's corpse itself. Like Rasputin's remains, Kornilov's corpse would be symbolically burned in Ekaterinodar (modern-day Krasnodar).

The first signs of Kornilov's divergence from the image of a revolutionary general also appeared in March 1917. On March 7, Kornilov announced that deploying several units of the Petrograd Garrison to the front was necessary.[8] This was the first conflict with the troops, albeit for now only those of a rear-guard garrison. Such actions did not arouse objections from soldiers on the front. At this time, Kornilov clearly strove, as all officers did, to pursue reinforcement of the army through enhanced discipline. This decision was for him a part of military policy, but for the soldiers who had carried out the February mutiny it was a political action. The soldiers of the Petrograd Garrison considered themselves part of the revolutionary process; moreover, they had then already enjoyed representation in the Petrograd Soviet, one of the key organs of the period, which contained a soldiers' section.

> Order Number 1 of the Petrograd Soviet of Workers and Soldiers Deputies must be considered one of the most important defining acts of the vector of the army's political struggle. The Order proclaimed the soldiers' civil rights, announced elections for committees in army units and their representatives in the Soviets. The document ordered the army units to obey the instructions of the War Commission of the State Duma only if they did not contradict the decisions of the Soviets. The Soviet thus established political control over the military formations and command operations.[9]

---

7   *Delo generala L. G. Kornilov* (Moscow: Rosspen, 2003), 2:81.
8   G. Z. Ioffe, *Semnadtsatyi god. Lenin. Kerenskii. Kornilov* (Moscow: Nauka, 1995), 43.
9   I. N. Grebenkin, "Razlozhenie rossiiskoi armii v 1917 g.: faktory i aktory," *Noveishaia istoriia Rossii* 3 (2014): 148–49.

The soldiers of the garrison therefore viewed Kornilov's announcement as an attack on their rights.

The soldiers viewed the deployment to the front not only as a measure directed against them personally but as one aimed at continuing the war. The soldiers at large had long since considered the generals and officers a force that stood for continuing military operations. Professor Grebenkin writes: "Given the unfavorable development of the course of the war and the growth of fatigue and anti-war feelings among the soldiers, the troops saw each officer as the main figure interested in continuing the war."[10] The February Revolution of 1917 embedded that widely held opinion among the soldiers. Professor Grebenkin concludes: "A significant factor in the soldiers' revolutionary mindset was their conviction that a political revolution would immediately end the war, one of the origins of the formerly unjust social order."[11]

Now, after the Revolution, it seemed to the soldiers that an equally clear message was being sent by the supposedly "revolutionary" General Kornilov. While this message was clearly not a turning point in the formation of the image of Kornilov as "other" for the soldiers, it was nevertheless a harbinger of this very process.

Meanwhile, Kornilov's deployment suggestion in March strongly diverged from the opinion of the liberal circles, who at that time were preparing to introduce a range of democratic measures, including abolition of the death penalty in Russia. The abolition of the death penalty served as a guarantee of the peaceful character of the development of the Russian Revolution, particularly following the sailors' and soldiers' vigilantism in February and March. A. F. Kerenskii said the following on the matter two months later at the military congress in Odessa: "You remember the French Revolution: it was merciless to all who stood in its way on all sides. We do not wish to repeat the bloody horrors and have abolished the death penalty. We do not wish for our great aims to be defiled by violence and blood."[12] This motive was underscored in one of the first biographies of Kerenskii: "The twelfth of March is a bright date in the history of Russian justice. On that day, Kerenskii signed the decree abolishing the death penalty. The nightmare that had plagued Russia for centuries ended. The people did not want more blood, not even the blood of its most evil enemies."[13]

---

10 Ibid., 147.
11 Ibid., 153.
12 A. F. Kerenskii, *Ob armii i voine* (Petrograd: Narodnaia Volia, 1917), 9.
13 E. Vladimirovich, *A. F. Kerenskii narodnyi ministr* (Petrograd: "Vlast' naroda," 1917), 19.

The opinion of the soldiers, the working masses, and the left-wing parties, which then held considerable control in Petrograd, was also important. The toughening of the system of punishments for various infractions was a key moment during the First World War. It affected the soldiers at large. We may look at acts dated March 6, 1915 and January 12, 1916, which specified in greater detail the punishments for desertion and absence without leave. Also significant was an act on August 11, 1915, which expanded the list of breaches of military subordination and sentry duty.[14] It was precisely the common soldiers who were primarily punished with the death penalty, and that is why the abolition of the death penalty was one of their main requirements. The death penalty was abolished in Russia following a resolution of the Provisional Government of March 12, 1917. Crimes formerly punishable by death were now punishable by imprisonment, including of unlimited duration. The document was signed by Prime Minister G. E. L'vov and other ministers.[15]

Liberal circles received news of the decision jubilantly, as confirmation of the arrival of a new era. K. K. Arsen'ev's article "Na temy dnia" (On the topics of the day) in the March issue of Vestnik Evropy was characteristic of this mood. He wrote, "the death penalty has been torn out of the old law wholly and without leaving a trace."[16] G. A. Kniazev made a similar assessment in his diary: "The death penalty has been abolished. This is a noble development. And how can one not believe in the Russian people?"[17]

The generals and most of the officers viewed the abolition of the death penalty negatively. Initially, however, in the light of the events of February and March, they did not object to the abolition, possibly preferring to remain "ours" for the new government and not wishing to be "others" to the common soldiers, particularly after the excesses of March. Naturally, Kornilov, who held his own opinion on these actions, did not voice them publicly. The attitude to Kornilov was changing, however. General V. I. Selivachev wrote in his diary on March 28, 1917, "The deputies ate here. Over lunch they told us about the horrible chaos that reigned in Petrograd. Prince Shakhovskoi said that General Kornilov's situation is extremely difficult: rumors have been put out that he was released

---

14 E. L. Potseluev, "Ulogovno-pravovaia praktika Vremennogo pravitel'stva Rossii v 1917 godu," Vestnik SPbGU 9, no. 1 (2018): 8.

15 Sbornik prikazov i postanovlenii Vremennego pravitel'stva (1917). Vyp. 1. 27 fevralia–5 maia 1917 g. (Petrograd, 1917), 37.

16 V. L. Agalov, "'Krushenie starogo gosudarstvennogo i obshchestvennogo stroia': 1917 god v liberal'nom zerkale 'Vestnika Evropy,'" Novyi istoricheskii vestnik, no. 39 (2014): 40.

17 G. A. Kniazev, "Iz zapisnoi knizhki russkogo intelligenta za vremia voiny i revoliutsii 1915–1922 gg." Russkoe proshloe. Istoriko-dokumental'nyi al'manakh, Issue 2 (1991): 151.

from captivity on purpose so he could seize power."[18] The opinion of General Kornilov was changing in a certain direction. It is also clear that he had become a center of political gravity.

Soon, in April 1917, Kornilov became one of the proponents of force as a political solution to the April crisis. He was ready to oppose the Petrograd Soviet in arms, mobilizing the few units of the Petrograd Garrison loyal to him, primarily from the military academies. We may make a partial assessment of the "Kornilov program" based on documents issued by him during these days. On April 23, 1917, the chief commander of the Petrograd Military District, Lieutenant-General L. G. Kornilov, issued a formal appeal. It spoke "of the danger threatening Petrograd" due to the concentration of Germans in the Baltic Sea ports who were "ready to sail toward our shores as soon as the sea is free of ice." The appeal ended with a call "to be ready for the fight to defend freedom." Two days after the issue of the appeal, the staff of the Petrograd Military District issued an order on the reformation of the reserve battalions into reserve regiments.[19] Kornilov would reuse the argument of the German threat later. The second order allowed for the old idea of the reformation of the Petrograd Garrison. Kornilov's short "revolutionary" period, if it had ever existed, was over. The reimagining of his image began at the same time.

His removal from the post of commander of the Petrograd Garrison and deployment to the southwestern front was natural. The figure of Kornilov became minor again until the June 1917 offensive. He was merely one of many against the background of the ongoing war. General M. V. Alekseev was the mediator between the military and the government in May, and in June the new war minister A. F. Kerenskii tried his hand at the role.

The subsequent events of the revolutionary year of 1917 led to a change in attitude toward Kornilov among the opposing political forces. To an even greater degree, he became "our own" for one side and "other" for the other. The promotion of Kornilov as a "strong hand" simultaneously alienated him further from the opponents of a military dictatorship. The soldiers at large rejected Kornilov particularly quickly, as it was with them that he proposed beginning the introduction of order.

The most important moment in this process was Kornilov's role in the restoration of the death penalty on the front in the summer of 1917, following its

---

18 "Dnevnik gen. V. I. Selivacheva," *Krasnyi arkhiv* 2, no. 9 (1925): 128.
19 Konstantin Tarasov, *Soldatskii bol'shevism. Voennaia organizatsiia bol'shevikov i levoradikal'noe dvizhenie v Petrogradskom garnizone (fevral' 1917–mart 1918 g.)* (St. Petersburg: Izdatel'stvo Evropeiskogo universiteta v Sankt-Peterburge, 2017), 187.

abolition on March 12 that year. The Russian army's long-planned June Offensive was a failure. The hopes of a revolutionary consciousness and acceptance by the troops of the slogans of a revolutionary war against Germany proved empty. The war, and the men agitating for its continuation, seemed increasingly "foreign" to the soldiers.

The attempts to create storm troops from the likes of officers and holders of the Order of St. George also failed. These troops were intended to serve as an example to the other units of military service of the fatherland. However, despite the positive military results of the creation of storm troops, the initiative was a political failure. In this case, we may speak of a deepening schism of "ours" and "others" in the army. The members of the storm troops were seen as betraying the soldiers' unity. V. K. Manakin, one of the organizers of the storm troopers, reported the following to the war minister: "The storm battalions had no particular use in the sense of psychological effect on the neighboring units. On the contrary, they aroused aggression from the units, which refused to serve or which retreated in disorder."[20]

In these conditions, the opinion that the most radical measures were necessary for the strengthening of troop discipline in the army won out. The secret June report by the commissars of the Eleventh Army, I. I. Kirienko and A. M. Chekotilo, stated, "The lack among many soldiers of a sense of personal duty and a conviction of complete impunity for any breach of discipline created extremely fertile ground for influences that disorganize the army."[21] The report noted multiple cases of insubordination in the Eleventh Army before and during the June Offensive of 1917. The failure of the June Offensive and the subsequent chaotic retreat of the Russian army led first to summary executions at gunpoint and then to the restoration of the death penalty on June 12. These latter executions were specifically called "Kornilov executions." This was not without cause.

The initiative for the new execution practice did, indeed, originate directly with General Kornilov and his military and commissar circle.[22] As early as July 8, Kornilov, the commander of the southwestern front, immediately after his appointment to the post, required his subordinates to use machine guns and

---

20 Grebenkin, "Razlozhenie rossiiskoi armii v 1917 g.: faktory i aktory," 155.

21 "Sekretnyi ochet komissarov XI armii I. Kirienko i A. Chekotilo," *Belyi arkhiv. Sbornik materialov po istorii i literature voiny, revoliutsii, bol'shevizma, belogo dvizheniia i t. p* 1 (1926): 14.

22 I. S. Rat'kovskii, "Vosstanovlenie v Rossii smertnoi kazni letom 1917 g," *Noveishaia istoriia Rossii* 1 (2014): 48–58.

artillery against retreating units.[23] The political leadership of the front also helped him advance the idea of a harsher execution practice:

> Individual cavalry units and vehicular armored detachments that were less decomposed formed obstacle detachments and tried, under the leadership of Savinkov, Gobechiia, Filonenko, and some other members of the Iskomitiuz (executive committee of the southwestern front), to stop the avalanche of soldiers and force it to offer resistance to the Austro-Germans advancing on their heels.[24]

Soldiers were executed at gunpoint during this period, and looters and deserters were hanged. This started before the official restoration of the death penalty on the front by the Provisional Government on June 12, 1917. Once Kornilov sent the commander in chief, General A. A. Brusilov, and the Provisional Government his request for the accelerated reintroduction of the death penalty on the ninth of June,[25] he began expanding the application of the death penalty on the front, without waiting for an official response. The first executions at gunpoint are recorded on that very day, before the authorities in Petrograd had officially responded. Kornilov thus implemented his punitive practice without consideration for the decision of the Provisional Government, which took three days to issue a decree. Kornilov initiated such "disciplinary measures," and the majority of the population soon came to see and understand his role in this process.

Kornilov himself issued a backdated order justifying his actions.[26] This document, which preceded the official reintroduction of the death penalty, was intended only for the troops of the southwestern front but became public knowledge and was published in the newspapers. This irked both Kornilov and General Brusilov, who had previously approved of his subordinate's actions. Brusilov, on the initiative of Kerenskii, would later publicly call for the trial of M. Lembich, correspondent on the *Russkoe slovo* newspaper, for publication of Kornilov's order. Brusilov demanded of the general-quartermaster of the southwestern front that Lembich be forced to reveal his informants so they

---

23 E. N. Giatsintov, "Tragediia russkoi armii v 1917 g. Predislovie, podgotovka teksta i kommentarii V. G. Bortnevskogo," *Russkoe proshloe*, no. 1 (1991): 110.

24 B. Leonidov, "Oktiabr' v staroi armii (iz vospominanii o Iugo-Zapadnom fronte)," *Grazhdanskaia voina: materialy po istorii Krasnoi armii* 2 (1923): 131.

25 *Russkoe slovo* (July 11, 1917).

26 Giatsintov, "Tragediia russkoi armii v 1917 g.," 110–11.

could be put on trial with him.[27] Kornilov's immediate military commanders thus did not see any infractions in his order; rather, they wished for less publicity of the matter.

The reintroduction of the death penalty on July 12 retroactively legalized previous similar actions taken by Kornilov. However, this entire story formed a distinct image of Kornilov not only as a proponent of mass executions of soldiers but also as their initiator. Kornilov and his circle were still attempting to combine the practice of executions with revolutionary emotionalism. Academic studies often interpret these measures as purely military actions with no political underpinning, let alone the practice of terror of any kind. At the same time, some initiators of the restoration of the death penalty on the southwestern front often utilized the language of terror. A characteristic example was the fact that B. V. Savinkov, one of the initiators of the new measures, who had been appointed alongside Kornilov to the southwestern front as a front commissar (assistant to M. M. Filonenko and I. P. Gobechiia), spoke at a meeting of the *oblast* committee of Socialist Revolutionaries in Kamenets-Podol'sk. He spoke directly of a return to terror as an old tried method for saving the fatherland and the revolution. Savinkov obviously appealed not only to the Socialist Revolutionary experience but also to the outcome of the French Revolution. Filonenko and Gobechiia, who were present at the meeting, supported Savinkov, indicating his personal experience in this area.[28] For Savinkov, the matter at hand was thus terror, even if it was directed against deserters, robbers, and, in his paranoid opinion, their German Bolshevik agent masters. These twists of Savinkov's, with the aim of justifying a new repressive policy in the army, were not supported by the soldiers at large. Savinkov and Kornilov thus became symbols of an anti-soldier policy and stood as an image of the "other" for most soldiers.

Exactly four months separated the abolition of the death penalty in March and its restoration in July 1917. Contemporaries considered the role of Kornilov, Savinkov, and Kerenskii to be obvious in the reintroduction of the death penalty. G. A. Kniazev of St. Petersburg wrote in his notebook:

> They have brought back the death penalty. What else could you expect? Kornilov and Savinkov demanded it [. . .]. Two stages [. . .] "The death penalty is being abolished forever"—the first days of March. Exultant, victorious sounds, the bright dawn of the Russian Revolution and "The death penalty is being

---

27 *Rech'* (July 20, 1917), 3; *Russkoe slovo* (July 20 and 22, 1917).
28 Leonidov, "Oktiabr' v staroi armii (iz vospominanii o Yugo-Zapadnom fronte)," 133.

applied"—the first days of July [. . .]. Cursed July 1917. Both acts bear the same signature, Kerenskii's [. . .] "*Sic transit gloria mundi.*"[29]

The war conference in Mogilev, which opened on July 16, 1918, gave an indubitable impulse to the wider application of the death penalty on the front. Almost all the delegates supported the reintroduction of the death penalty and furthermore demanded it be applied to the rear units. Kornilov's message to the conference, sent by telegram due to his absence, is characteristic:

> The act on the death penalty and revolutionary field courts re-enacted in the theater of war must be extended to the interior districts with regard to soldiers as penalty for crimes set out in the act. If this measure is not extended to the interior districts, the armies will not receive new recruits that enhance its military readiness but bands of uncontrolled, untrained soldiers capable of decomposing even the strongest units.[30]

The proceedings of the conference were published and further strengthened the new impression of Kornilov as a man implementing new trends in the practice of introducing order to the army. He ever more strongly became "ours" for the officers and more "other" for the soldiers.

Once officially reintroduced, the death penalty was applied in several new cases on the front. This was accentuated by the Provisional Government's replacement, on July 19, of Brusilov with Kornilov as commander-in-chief. Having barely been appointed to his new role, General Kornilov demanded that he be made responsible "only before his own conscience and the whole people," thus establishing, as A. I. Denikin noted with caustic irony, an "original state-legal form of sovereignty of the supreme command right up to the Constituent Assembly."[31]

The ordinary soldiers viewed this practice of military and political repressions very negatively. They objected not only to tougher punishments but also to the aim of the crackdown: the continuation of the war. Warrant officer D. P. Os'kin

---

29 Kniazev, "Iz zapisnoi knizhki russkogo intelligenta za vremia voiny i revoliutsii 1915–1922 gg.," 158.

30 V. D. Polikarpov, *Voennaia kontrrevoliutsiia v Rossii* (Moscow: Nauka, 1990), 212–13.

31 S. S. Voitikov, *Armiia i vlast'. Kornilov, Vatsetis, Tukhachevskii. 1905–1937* (Moscow: Tsentrpoligraf, 2016), 166.

recorded the following conversation with Tsvetkov-Kulikov, an assistant of the commissar of the Eleventh Army: "As for the death penalty," Tsetkov said:

> I won't say anything. Everyone is outraged by it, but I think you'll understand that it's dictated by the government's desire to maintain a battle-ready army, especially after the unfortunate Tarnopol' desertion. The soldier must be presented with a dilemma: he either has a chance of surviving when he attacks, or he will be without a doubt executed if he deserts. Given such a dilemma, a soldier will naturally fulfil his commanding officers' order to attack. If there's no death penalty, why on earth would a soldier attack? The soldier is only afraid for his own skin.

"So, to my mind," Tsvetkov concluded, "the death penalty on the front is a perfectly natural phenomenon, and you are outraged in vain."[32] These actions further deepened the chasm between the soldiers and the officers. The sides became ever more "other" to each other. There were cases in which soldiers directly hindered the application of death sentences. When three soldiers of the Sixteenth Corps were sentenced to death, soldiers of the 637th Kagyzmanskii, 638th Ol'tinskii, 640th Chorokhskii and Sixteenth Engineers' Regiment of the 160th Division immediately revolted. The commandant company who ordered to carry out the sentence refused to fire. Ten soldiers' delegates would later bring a resolution of protest to Petrograd against the introduction of the death penalty in the army.[33]

Tellingly, after the suspension of the death penalty on September 28, 1917 by the Provisional Government (with the words "until further notice"), Tsvetkov-Kulikov himself became a victim of the common soldiers' heightened radicalism. According to a dispatch on October 4, 1917 from A. M. Chekotilo, commissar of the Eleventh Army on the southwestern front, to War Minister Major-General A. I. Verkhovskii, the soldiers of the Fifteenth Shlisselburg Regiment of the Fourth Division attacked Verkhovskii's assistant Tsvetkov-Kulikov and stoned him to death.[34] This may have been the soldiers' natural reaction to his earlier views and attempts to bring them to fruition. After his participation in the punitive practice, he was indubitably "other," not "ours," for the soldiers.

32 D. P. Os'kin, *Zapiski praporshchika* (Moscow: Federatsiia, 1931), 234–35.
33 M. I. Sekachev, *Kursom na revoliutsiiu/Oktiabr' na fronte. Vospominaniia* (Moscow: Voenizdat, 1967), 214–16.
34 *Istoricheskii arkhiv* no. 6 (1957): 48–49.

If the soldiers treated Tsvetkov-Kulikov in this way, what then can be said of the ordinary soldiers' attitude to General Kornilov, the initiator of the executions? Clearly, the level of hatred was much higher, and as 1917 moved further on its sharp collision course, this degree of hatred only intensified. Under the circumstances, was the shooting of Kornilov's train near Kiev, as recorded by General V. I. Selivachev in his diary on July 27, 1917 and in which a second-class carriage was damaged, a chance event? For Kornilov not only facilitated the reintroduction of the death penalty on the front; he also tried after his appointment as commander-in-chief to extend its application to the rear units. This was one of Kornilov's demands at the Moscow State Conference and later.

Kornilov's speech in late August 1917 merely reinforced his personalized image as an opponent of the common soldiers. Kornilov tried to appeal to his common origin in his August speech as he had before, and to place a wager on patriotic rhetoric:

> All in whose breast beats a Russian heart, all who believe in God: go to church, pray to the Lord God for a great miracle, the miracle of salvation of our native land. I, General Kornilov, the son of a Cossack and a peasant, announce to one and all that I personally need nothing but the preservation of Great Russia, and I swear that I will lead the people by the path of victory to the Constituent Assembly, at which the people will decide for itself its own fate and choose the shape of its new life as a state. I am unable to commit Russia into the hands of its primordial enemy, the German tribe, and to make the Russian people the Germans' slaves, and would rather die on the field of honor and battle to avoid seeing the Russian land humiliated and disgraced. O Russian people! The life of your Fatherland is in your hands![35]

The general's address was of little consequence, and Kornilov was unable to restore his authority among the ordinary soldiers after his orders in the summer. It is characteristic that Kornilov's opponents used the image of an "executioner" against him. Flyers with epithets of that kind were scattered from large numbers of trucks.

---

35 A. I. Denikin, *Ocherki russkoi smuty. Krushenie vlasti i armii. Fevral–sentiabr 1917 g.* (Moscow: Nauka, 1991), 470.

Kornilov's personification as a leader of the military opposition and proponent of the breakup of the soldiers' committees and workers' soviets was firmly and finally established. For his opponents, Kornilov was now not only "other" but the very symbol of the "other." Indeed, isolated defenses of Kornilov by soldiers at this time were thoroughly investigated, and some arrests were even made. Some soldiers' speeches in defense of Kornilov were viewed extremely negatively and later meticulously scrutinized.[36] "Kornilovshchina" (the time [rule] of Kornilov) crept into the Russian lexicon and became one of the most famous unflattering terms in the language. The August speeches made by the soldiers, their behavior, and the offices' behaviors were also. K. Tarasov cites many such examples in his monograph.[37] The officer ranks were labeled "Kornilovites" and subjected to numerous investigations.

The many articles in the Russian press that autumn helped to finally cement Kornilov's image as "other." Subsequently, "his name reminded soldiers of the anti-Kornilov hysteria spread by the press in the autumn of 1917. They remembered his demands for the introduction of the death penalty for the kinds of military infraction any one of them could have committed."[38] Following his arrest after the August speech, General Kornilov therefore needed to be held under double guard. This was a measure against lynching, not escape, as there was a real threat of an attempt on Kornilov's life.

Later events in Mogilev confirmed the ordinary soldiers' hatred of Kornilov. After the victory of the Bolsheviks in Petrograd, convoys of soldiers and sailors traveled to take over the High Command and exact justice upon General Kornilov, only for them to discover that he had fled with the help of General N. N. Dukhonin. As a result, he became a fatal sacrificial substitute for Kornilov. A crowd of soldiers and sailors literally tore Dukhonin to pieces on November 20 in revenge for orchestrating Kornilov's escape.

Kornilov merely reinforced his image as an enemy by fleeing. The official Bolshevik press wrote directly at the end of November: "Down with the Kadets [Constitutional Democrats], Kornilovites, Kaledinites, the enemies of the people."[39]

---

36 Some of the relevant materials were archived in fond 504 of the State Archive of the Russian Federation (Gosudarstvennyi arkhiv Rossiiskoi Federatsii): f. 504, op. 1, d. 565 (hereafter cited as GARF).

37 Tarasov, *Soldatskii bol'shevism*, 209–10.

38 O. M. Morozova, *General Ivan Georgievich Erdeli. Stranitsy istorii* (Moscow: Tsentrpoligraf, 2017), 129.

39 *Rabochii i soldat* (November 28, 1917).

1918 and the Reinforcement of General L. G. Kornilov's Image

Meanwhile, Kornilov, having escaped vengeance at the hands of the soldiers, became one of the organizers of the Volunteer Army in the Don basin. He joined forces with General Alekseev and considerably sped up this process. He once more became the symbol of the opposition between low and high army ranks: between "officers-Kadets" and "soldiers-peasants." Albeit the son of a very modest family, he was perceived by many as a defender of the old order and old principles. His opponents saw him as the quintessence of everything that was anti-revolutionary and foreign to the revolutionary process.

Constant new rumors and information from the Don basin reinforced the legend of Kornilov's "bloodthirstiness." Additionally, Kornilov's actions in the Don period were indeed characterized by a series of harsh instructions and orders. The most famous of these was his order to "Take no prisoners!" issued in the Don basin before the Volunteer army's Ice March (First Kuban Campaign) from Rostov-on-Don to Ekaterinoslav. Hundreds of Red prisoners of war were killed because of this order. General Kornilov considered terror in any form an effective and efficient weapon, and he said that it was indispensable in the struggle against the Bolsheviks.[40] Other men fighting alongside Kornilov recorded similar utterances by him.[41] The result was the use of execution at gunpoint as a virtually obligatory measure. As the famous Russian historian V. P. Buldakov wrote, "small wonder that there were volunteer officers who thought that to root out Bolshevism, all workers aged over sixteen ought to be exterminated."[42]

The death sentences of the summer and autumn of 1917 were complemented by the mass "Kornilov executions" of 1918. In both cases, Kornilov initiated a crackdown in the execution policy; moreover, his role was not concealed. For the units of soldiers, primarily in the Red Guards and Red Army, Kornilov's image as an "other," as discussed above, was shaped once and for all. Kornilov became

---

40 R. B. Khadzhiev Khan, *Velikii boiar* (Belgrade: Knizhnoe izdatel'stvo M. A. Surovina, 1929), 349.

41 I. S. Rat'kovskii, "Karatel'no-repressivnaia praktika Dobrovol'cheskoi armii v nachal'nyi period ee sushchestvovaniia," *Vestnik Riazanskogo Gosudarstvennogo universiteta im. S. A. Esenina*, 3 (2019): 77–88; I. S. Rat'kovskii, *Khronika belogo terrora. Repressii i samosudy (1917–1920 gg.)* (Moscow: Algoritm, 2018), 32–50.

42 V. P. Buldakov, *Krasnaia smuta. Priroda i posledstviia revoliutsionnogo nasiliia* (Moscow: Rosspen, 1997), 235.

for them the incarnation of the practice of the death penalty, of reactionary force, and the counterrevolution.

The Volunteer army's First Kuban Campaign reinforced Kornilov's punitive policy, thus further convincing his contemporaries that he stood for merciless vengeance against those who resisted the advance of his army and those who were foreign to the White movement's idea of Russia. For the Whites, on the other hand, Kornilov was "ours." Kornilov's arrival was always anticipated: some with hope, others with fear, as the vengeance exacted by him was well known. For many, Kornilov was a symbol of merciless evil that simply needed to be destroyed and Kornilov's anticipated death became the symbol of freedom from tyranny.

Many contemporaries noted the cruelty of the actions of Kornilov's men. P. A. Filatov wrote in his memoirs about the Volunteer army's advance, "along the way communists, Red Guards, and ordinary Soviet workers were mercilessly killed."[43]

The Volunter Army approached Ekaterinodar under General Kornilov's command in April 1918. The city was expected to be taken by storm. White detachments made several attempts to take the city on April 10. The capture of Ekaterinodar was a key aim for Kornilov; retreating was not an option. Both sides continued to fight ferociously. The Whites saw the taking of the city as a solution to their problems. Their previous victories strengthened their confidence in this goal.

When the first storm of Ekaterinodar began, the nervous tension in the city reached its peak. No one in the city, including wounded Red Army soldiers, expected mercy from the volunteers. The 1927 recollection of a worker from Petrograd, Malysheva, who was being treated for injury in a military hospital in Ekaterinodar, is typical:

> Some comrades were sent to Novorossiisk, but I was not. After a day or two the patients and the injured started to worry and said, "Kornilov will be here soon and will chop us to pieces." We began to worry and started asking the orderlies for medicine because we said we would not surrender alive. Some threw themselves out of the window of the second floor and were smashed into smithereens, but we did not. After some time, about twelve

43 Tsentral'nyi gosudarstvennyi arkhiv Istoriko-politicheskikh dokumentov Sankt-Peterburga (Central State Archive of Historical and Political Documents in St. Petersburg), f. R–4000, op. 5, d. 539, l. 101 (hereafter cited as TsGA IPD SPB).

hours or so, we heard that Kornilov had been killed. We were overjoyed.[44]

The death of Kornilov became a symbol of emancipation from the fear of inevitable death for many people in Ekaterinodar. This was the reason for the rejoicing at his death, which Malysheva recorded in her memoirs. Many residents of Ekaterinodar wanted to verify and assure themselves that Kornilov had indeed been killed. It is not by chance that Kornilov's death was reflected in both White and Red memoirs, and in the latter in rather violent detail.

These recollections are often of little value and are even of a fantastical nature. The Red Army soldier Antonov, for example (seventeen-years-old at the time of the events), recalled in 1926, "Thanks to the backup that arrived from the center, we were able to defeat Kornilov, and I saw him and his whole staff executed at gunpoint with my own eyes."[45] Some memoirs clearly replaced reality with wishful thinking. Such memoirs contain another important element: participation in events, which underscores the significance of the image of Kornilov as "other," as the embodiment of the enemy. The memoir writer believes that events truly happened that way, that he or she participated in the event and is obliged to tell the story. However, neither Kornilov nor his staff were executed at gunpoint.

There are, however, more valuable recollections, which establish the circumstances of Kornilov's death and subsequent events. V. A. Sergeev wrote:

> The night before April 13, a little boy who called himself Grisha Mal'ko ran up to D. P. Zhloba's staff and said that he had seen a lot of generals "on the other side" and even "the most important one, the one who looks like a Kalmyk and shouts at everyone."
>
> "And did you remember, Grisha, what house that little shouting general was in?" asked Zhloba.
>
> "That one over there," the boy indicated, standing on tiptoe.
>
> "That's probably Kornilov himself," Dmitrii Petrovich said to me.
>
> After summoning the battery commander D. I. Rogachevskii, Zhloba ordered him to be ready to open fire by dawn. In the morning the artillery men fired several volleys at the house.

44 TsGA IPD SPB, f. R–4000, op. 6, d. 74, l. 50.
45 TsGA IPD SPB, f. R–4000, op. 5–1, d. 2312, l. 1.

After the attack, we learnt that Kornilov had been killed. Denikin assumed command of the Volunteer Army.[46]

The former second lieutenant and Red Guard V. A. Kipreev gave his assessment of the situation:

> Kornilov's staff was three kilometres from Ekaterinodar and the stanitsa of Elizavetinskaia, and our artillery subjected Elizavetinskaia to constant assault. On April 13, General Kornilov was killed in his staff headquarters by a fragment of an exploding shell, and his detachments quickly retreated. The locals did not know where he was buried, and only the priest who had sung his funeral service showed our spies the grave. Kornilov's corpse was exhumed and brought to Ekaterinodar, where it was placed on Cathedral Square, after which it was burnt near the abattoir and the ashes scattered.[47]

The choice of location for the burning of Kornilov's body is significant. The abattoir underlined Kornilov's otherness and his antihuman essence to justify the actions of those who destroyed his corpse. The public procedure itself was intended to demonstrate his final annihilation. Kornilov was not a usurper like the False Dmitrii in the Time of Troubles in the seventeenth century, whose body was burned, but the citizens and powers of Ekaterinodar saw the public rejection of an "other" reflected in the mutilation of his corpse. Both the False Dmitrii's and Kornilov's corpses were publicly and conclusively burned and the remains destroyed.

The worker Malysheva, cited above, recalled the fate of Kornilov's grave. The final section of her memoirs contains particularly interesting recollections of Kornilov. I present the entire extract, which is relevant to this event, here. It both repeats various rumors about Kornilov and bears personal witness.

> We heard that he had been buried under the New Cathedral in the stanitsa of Elizavetinskaia. But this was deception: they had buried a general who was very similar to him on the site of Kornilov's death, making it look as if they had buried Kornilov there. Rumors were all we had to go on. Then, when the

46 V. A. Sergeev, *V bogatyrskom stroiu/Protiv Denikina* (Moscow: Voenizdat, 1969), 82.
47 TsGA IPD SPB, f. R–4000, op. 12, d. 230, l. 4.

Elizavetinskaia stanitsa[48] was taken, our men arrived and asked who was buried there. "Kornilov," people replied to them. But when they dug the ground up and took a look, it turned out it was not Kornilov. The old soldiers knew what he looked like. They said that one of his arms was shriveled and that he was pugnosed. They took a good look at the body and said no, Kornilov did not look like that, his look was different, it's not Kornilov, and the old soldiers were even able to name the general who'd been buried there instead of Kornilov. Then the parents of the local Red Army soldiers, town folk, as they're called, said that painfully fine music had been played near the New Cathedral, and that someone had been buried with great solemnity, some big shot, only they had not been allowed anywhere near the funeral. They started questioning the priest: "Who's buried here?" He said, "No one's been buried here." They would not leave off: "Tell us where Kornilov is buried. Did you bury him?" No, he said, I did not bury him. Then they grilled the watchman. He said, "This is where Kornilov is buried, right here in this spot. He was buried on such-and-such a date." The Red Army soldiers then started digging the spot up. When they opened the grave, they recognized the body as Kornilov's. They got ready to bring him to Krasnodar. Somebody shouted, "Put some hay under him, it's 15 versts to Krasnodar," but someone else shouted, "Forget about it, a scum's death for scum." They brought him to Krasnodar at six in the evening. All the wounded who could walk came to look. Kornilov was all anyone could talk about; people talked about the kind of man he had been. We came to the Cossack military church. They brought him there and hung him up on an acacia so everyone could see it really was Kornilov. A lot of people recognized him. Some bourgeois types wept, many of the intelligentsia could not even come out, they couldn't look, and a lot of people were very sad and wept. A lot of people were arrested on the spot. I went there on crutches to look at Kornilov, and I saw his face. Then they took him off to the abattoir. They chopped him right up beyond recognition. They tossed some hay on top and set the lot on fire. He burned.

---

48 The name of the locality.

He burned real well. It smelled great. Sometime later I got better again.[49]

The violent dispatch of the dead general's body was not just vengeance: it was repayment for the fear he had instilled. His ashes were destroyed like the ashes of a legendary monster, which is evidently how many of his contemporaries viewed him. It was virtually the ritual destruction of an "other."

Kornilov's death led to the Volunteer army's temporary withdrawal from Ekaterinodar. However, this retreat, accompanied by fresh reprisals, was not the end of the Kornilov case. His burial near Ekaterinodar predetermined a fresh return to that area. Kornilov's supporters interpreted his death as a sacrifice for the White movement and the treatment of his corpse as confirmation of the necessity for reprisals against the enemy. The general had died, but the practice of Kornilov-style reprisals remained and even grew stronger.

The image of Kornilov once and for all became a symbol of the Volunter Army and White movement for supporters and enemies alike. In addition, the demonization of the "image" of Kornilov became an enduring foundation of postrevolutionary Soviet historiography. Kornilov was interpreted as a typical representative of the antipopular movement, foreign to everything related to the people and the revolution. However, precisely this reading provoked a reciprocal self-identification with Kornilov by those who considered the Soviet system foreign. He was foreign to the Soviet system, so he was close to them.

The image of General L. G. Kornilov defined and continues to define to a significant degree the "otherness" of political and historical sympathies. Moreover, the image itself, as the present chapter has shown, was a derivative of the political events in Russia between 1916 and 1918.

Works Cited

Archival Sources

Tsentral'nyi gosudarstevennyi arkhiv Istoriko-politicheskikh dokumentov Sankt-Peterburga (TsGA IPD SPB). F. R–4000, op. 5, d. 539, l. 101.

Tsentral'nyi gosudarstevennyi arkhiv Istoriko-politicheskikh dokumentov Sankt-Peterburga (TsGA IPD SPB). F. R–4000, op. 5–1, d. 2312, l. 1.

---

49 TsGA IPD SPB, f. R–4000, op. 6, d. 74, ll. 51–53.

Tsentral'nyi gosudarstevennyi arkhiv Istoriko-politicheskikh dokumentov Sankt-Peterburga (TsGA IPD SPB). F. R–4000, op. 6, d. 74, l. 50.

Tsentral'nyi gosudarstevennyi arkhiv Istoriko-politicheskikh dokumentov Sankt-Peterburga (TsGA IPD SPB). F. R–4000, op. 6, d. 74, ll. 51–53.

Tsentral'nyi gosudarstevennyi arkhiv Istoriko-politicheskikh dokumentov Sankt-Peterburga (TsGA IPD SPB). F. R–4000, op. 12, d. 230, l. 4.

Gosudarstvennyi Arkhiv Rossiiskoi Federatsii (GARF). F. 504, op. 1, d. 565. Delo Komissii o riadovom 235-go Belebeevskogo polka Ermoshine Semene Stepanoviche, zaderzhannom za agitatsiiu protiv Vremennogo pravitel'stva v pol'zu Kornilova.

Printed Sources and Literature

Abiniakin, R. M. *Ofitserskii korpus Dobrovol'cheskoi armii: Sotsial'nyi sostav, mirovozzrenie. 1917–1920 gg.* Orel: Izdatel' A. Vorobev, 2005.

Agalov, V. L. "'Krushenie starogo gosudarstvennogo i obshchestvennogo stroia': 1917 god v liberal'nom zerkale 'Vestnika Evropy.'" *Novyi istoricheskii vestnik*, no. 39 (2014): 35–48.

Bondarenko, V. V. *Lavr Kornilov*. Moscow: Molodaia gvardiia, 2016.

Buldakov, V. P. *Krasnaia smuta. Priroda i posledstviia revoliutsionnogo nasiliia*. Moscow: Rosspen, 1997.

Delo generala L. G. Kornilov. Vol. 2. Moscow: Rosspen, 2003.

Istoricheskii arkhiv (1957), no. 6.

Denikin, A. I. *Ocherki russkoi smuty. Krushenie vlasti i armii. Fevral–sentiabr 1917 g.* Moscow: Nauka, 1991.

"Dnevnik gen. V. I. Selivacheva." *Krasnyi arkhiv* 9, no. 2 (1925): 104–32.

Gagkuev, R. G. *Beloe dvizhenie na Iuge Rossii: Voennoe stroitels'stvo, istochniki komplektovaniia, sotsialn'yi sostav, 1917–1920 gg.* Moscow: Sodruzhestvo "Posev," 2012.

Giatsintov, E. N. "Tragediia russkoi armii v 1917 g. Predislovie, podgotovka teksta i kommentarii V. G. Bortnevskogo." *Russkoe proshloe* 1 (1991): 73–114.

Grebenkin, I. N. *Dobrovol'tsy i Dobrovol'cheskaia armiia: na Donu i v 'Ledianom' pokhode*. Ryazan: Ryazan State Pedagogical University named after S. A. Yesenin, 2005.

———. "Razlozhenie rossiiskoi armii v 1917 g.: faktory i aktory." *Noveishaia istoriia Rossii* 3 (2014): 145–61.

Ioffe, G. Z. *Semnadtsatyi god. Lenin. Kerenskii. Kornilov.* Moscow: Nauka, 1995.

Kerenskii, A. F. *Ob armii i voine.* Petrograd: Narodnaia Volia, 1917.

Khadzhiev Khan, R. B. *Velikii boiar.* Belgrade: Knizhnoe izdatel'stvo M. A. Surovina, 1929.

Kniazev, G. A. "Iz zapisnoi knizhki russkogo intelligenta za vremia voiny i revoliutsii 1915–1922 gg." *Russkoe proshloe. Istoriko-dokumental'nyi al'manakh* 2 (1991): 97–199.

Leonidov, B. "Oktiabr' v staroi armii (iz vospominanii o Iugo-Zapadnom fronte)." *Grazhdanskaia voina: materialy po istorii Krasnoi armii* 2 (1923): 131–64.

Morozova, O. M. *General Ivan Georgievich Erdeli. Stranitsy istorii.* Moscow: Tsentrpoligraf, 2017.

Myshov, N. A. "'Serdtse ne vyderzhalo . . .' (vospominaniia shtabs-kapitana A. Tiurina o smerti generala Kornilova)." *Otechestvennye arkhivy* 4 (2002): 76–83.

Os'kin, D. P. *Zapiski praporshchika.* Moscow: Federatsiia, 1931.

Polikarpov, V. D. *Voennaia kontrrevoliutsiia v Rossii.* Moscow: Nauka, 1990.

Potseluev, E. L. "Ulogovno-pravovaia praktika Vremennogo pravitel'stva Rossii v 1917 gody." *Vestnik SPbGU* 9, no. 1 (2018): 4–22.

Puchenkov, A. S. *Antibol'shevistskoe dvizhenie na Iuge i Iugo-Zapade Rossii (noiabr' 1917—ianvar' 1919 gg.): ideologiia, politika, osnovy rezhima vlasti Spetsial'nost.* PhD diss., St. Petersburg Institute of History of the Russian Academy of Sciences, 2014.

Rabochii i soldat. November 28, 1917.

Rat'kovskii, I. S. "Vosstanovlenie v Rossii smertnoi kazni letom 1917 g." *Noveishaia istoriia Rossii* 1 (2014): 48–58.

———. *Khronika belogo terrora. Repressii i samosudy (1917–1920 gg.).* Moscow: Algoritm, 2018.

———. "Karatel'no-repressivnaia praktika Dobrovol'cheskoi armii v nachal'nyi period ee sushchestvovaniia." *Vestnik Riazanskogo Gosudarstvennogo universiteta im. S. A. Esenina* 3 (2019): 77–88.

Rech'. July 20, 1917.

Russkoe slovo. July 11, 20 and 22, 1917.

Sekachev, M. I. *Kursom na revoliutsiiu/Oktiabr' na fronte. Vospominaniia.* Moscow: Voenizdat, 1967.

Sbornik prikazov i postanovlenii Vremennego pravitel'stva. Vyp. 1. 27 fevralia–5 maia 1917 g. Petrograd, 1917.

"Sekretnyi ochet komissarov XI armii I. Kirienko i A. Chekotilo." *Belyi arkhiv. Sbornik materialov po istorii i literature voiny revoliutsii, bol'shevizma belogo dvizheniia i t. p* 1 (1926): 13–34.

Sergeev, V. A. *V bogatyrskom stroiu/Protiv Denikina*. Moscow: Voenizdat, 1969.

Tarasov, Konstantin. *Soldatskii bol'shevism. Voennaia organizatsiia bol'shevikov i levoradikal'noe dvizhenie v Petrogradskom garnizone (fevral' 1917–mart 1918 g.)*. St. Petersburg: Izdatel'stvo Evropeiskogo universiteta v Sankt-Peterburge, 2017.

Ushakov, A. I. and V. P. Fediuk. *Lavr Kornilov*. Moscow: Molodaia gvardiia, 2012.

Vladimirovich, E. *A. F. Kerenskii narodnyi ministr*. Petrograd: "Vlast' naroda," 1917.

Voitikov, S. S. *Armiia i vlast'. Kornilov Vatsetis, Tukhachevskii. 1905–1937*. Moscow: Tsentrpoligraf, 2016.

Contributors

Kati Parppei is a university lecturer (title of docent) in the Department of Geographical and Historical Studies at the University of Eastern Finland. Her interests include the history of mentalities and ideas, image studies, Russian history, and borderland issues.

Bulat Rakhimzianov is currently a PhD student at University College Dublin. His research interests include the relations between the Tatar khanates and Moscow in the fifteenth and sixteenth centuries, and the uses of Tatar medieval history in contemporary historical writings and politics.

David M. Goldfrank worked as a professor at Georgetown University until retiring. He is an expert in early Russian history and imperial foreign policy.

Charles J. Halperin is an independent scholar residing in Bloomington, Indiana, USA. He is the author of *Ivan the Terrible: Free to Reward and Free to Punish* (2019), *Ivan IV and Muscovy* (2020), and *Ivan the Terrible in Russian Historical Memory since 1991* (2021).

Jaakko Lehtovirta is a graduate of the University of Turku, Finland. His dissertation "Ivan IV as an Emperor: The Imperial Theme in the Establishment of Muscovite Tsardom" explores the applicability of a general, imperial idea of rulership to define Ivan IV's role as the first Russian tsar. Since 2001, Lehtovirta has worked as a diplomat in the Finnish Foreign Service.

Maxim Moiseev is an associate professor at the Moscow Pedagogical State University and the head of the sector exhibition of the work of Museum Association "Museum of Moscow." His research interests cover the eastern policy of the Moscow state of the late fifteenth to early seventeenth centuries, source studies, and the history of the post-Horde states.

Ricarda Vulpius is a professor of East European history at the Westfälische Wilhelms-University of Münster in Germany. She is a historian of the Russian Empire and of Ukraine and author of the book *The Birth of the Russian Empire: Concepts and Practices of Imperial Rule in the 18th Century*" (in German).

Michael Khodarkovsky is a professor of history at Loyola University Chicago. He is a historian of the Russian Empire who specializes in the history of Russia's imperial expansion into the Eurasian borderlands.

Yury Akimov is a leading research fellow at the International Laboratory "Russia's Regions in Historical Perspective" at the National Research University Higher School of Economics in Moscow. He is also a full professor at the School of International Relations at St. Petersburg State University. His fields of interest include comparative history of early modern colonialism, as well as the history of international relations.

Vladimir Puzanov is a professor of history at the State University of Shadrinsk. He specializes in the policies of the Russian state in Siberia in the sixteenth to eighteenth century, relations between Russia and nomadic peoples, and the history of military servants.

Nikita Khrapunov is a leading researcher at the V. I. Vernadsky Crimean Federal University. His research interests include travel writings on Eastern Europe, Black Sea history, archaeology, and historical imagology.

Dominik Gutmeyr-Schnur is currently an FWF-Erwin-Schrödinger-Fellow at the University of California, Los Angeles (Center for Near Eastern Studies, 2021–23). His research encompasses visual cultures in Southeastern Europe and the Russian Empire, with a particular interest in the entangled history of photography in the wider Caucasus region.

Marina Shcherbakova is a PhD candidate at Heidelberg University. The title of her dissertation is "Soviet Jewish Museums within the Framework of the Nationalities Policy of the USSR." She was trained in Yiddish studies and German philology at the universities of St. Petersburg, Trier, and Potsdam. She worked as associate at the Russian Ethnographic Museum and taught in St. Petersburg State University's Department of Jewish Culture.

Stephen M. Norris is the Walter E. Havighurst Professor of Russian History and the director of the Havighurst Center for Russian and Post-Soviet Studies at Miami University in Ohio. His research focuses on modern Russian history with an emphasis on visual culture and propaganda since the nineteenth century.

Alena Rezvukhina is a master of philosophy and a master's student in German studies at the Masaryk University in Brno, and a volunteer research assistant at the Biography Research Centre "AITIA" in St. Petersburg. Her research interests include twentieth-century Russian emigration, issues of cultural memory preservation in emigration in general, and the ethics of responsibility.

Anna Rezvukhina is a master of arts in cultural studies, a master's student in culture management at the Masaryk University in Brno, and a volunteer research assistant at the Biography Research Centre "AITIA" in St. Petersburg. Her research interests include cultural landscapes (especially ruins and ruined landscapes and border areas) and how they function as actors of cultural memory.

Sergey Troitskiy is an associate researcher at the Estonian Literary Museum. His scholarly interests include the history of Russian philosophy, the history and theory of Russian culture, gelology (laughter studies), the theory of cultural exclusion and frontier zones, and the methodology of cultural studies from the perspective Russian philosophy.

Immo Rebitschek is an assistant professor at the Chair for East European History at the Friedrich-Schiller-University in Jena. He has published on the history of Soviet criminal justice and war crime tribunals, as well as on Stalinist and post-Stalinist statehood. His recent research project deals with famine and food policies in late imperial Russia.

Johanna Wassholm, PhD, is an adjunct professor of Russian and Nordic history at Åbo Akademi University, Finland. She is a specialist in Finnish-Russian relations in the nineteenth and early twentieth centuries, and she has published extensively on national and linguistic identification, on the political uses of history, and on ethnified mobile trade. Her current research deals with expulsion practices in Finland from 1809 to the early 1920s.

Oleg Minin is a visiting assistant professor at Bard where he teaches Russian modern art, literature, and language. His fields of specialization include the literature and visual and performing arts of the Russian Silver Age; the Russian avant-garde; the satirical press of the Russian fin de siècle; Habermas's social theory and Bourdieu's theory of cultural production; and language pedagogy.

Andrey Avdashkin, PhD, is an associate professor at South Ural State University. He also works as a senior researcher in the Laboratory of Migration Research. His research interests include migration, interethnic relations, ethnic and demographic processes in the Asian part of Russia in the twentieth and twenty-first centuries, and the image of the "other" in Russian history.

Il'ia Rat'kovskii is an associate professor in the Institute of History at St. Petersburg State University. His research interests include the history of the Russian Revolution and Civil War, and the history of state institutions in Russia and the Soviet Union.

Abbreviations Used
by the Authors

GAPK	Gosudarstvennyi arkhiv Permskogo kraia
GARF	Gosudarstvennyi arkhiv Rossiiskoi Federatsii
GASO	Gosudarstvennyi arkhiv Sverdlovskoi oblasti
LLS	*Litsevoi letopisnyi svod Ivana Groznogo*
MVD	Ministerstvo vnutrennykh del
OGACHO	Ob'edinennii gosudarstvennyi arkhiv Cheliabinskoi oblasti
PSRL	*Polnoe sobranie russkikh letopisei*
PSZRI	*Polnoe sobranie zakonov Rossiiskoi Imperii*
PVL	*Povest' vremennykh let*
RGADA	Rossiiskii gosudarstvennyi arkhiv drevnikh aktov
RGIA	Rossiskii gosudarstvennyi istoricheskii arkhiv
RLI	*Litsevoi letopisnyi svod XVI veka. Russkaia letopisnaia istoriia*
RPC	*Russian Primary Chronicle*
SRIO	*Sbornik russkogo istoricheskogo obshchestva*
TsGA IPD SPB	Tsentral'nyi gosudarstvennyi arkhiv Istoriko-politicheskikh dokumentov Sankt-Peterburga

Index

CPSIA information can be obtained
at www.ICGtesting.com
Printed in the USA
BVHW050327220423
662834BV00002B/4